CULTURAL AND SOCIAL
ANTHROPOLOGY

E. Adamson Hoebel
Regents Professor Emeritus of Anthropology
University of Minnesota

Everett L. Frost
Associate Professor of Anthropology
Eastern New Mexico University

McGraw-Hill Book Company

New York St. Louis San Francisco Auckland Düsseldorf Johannesburg
Kuala Lumpur London Mexico Montreal New Delhi Panama Paris
São Paulo Singapore Sydney Tokyo Toronto

**To Irene
and Janet**

**CULTURAL
AND SOCIAL
ANTHROPOLOGY**

2 3 4 5 6 7 8 9 0 M U M U 7 9 8 7 6

This book was set in Helvetica by Black Dot, Inc.
The editors were Lyle Linder, Janis M. Yates, and David Dunham;
the designer was Jo Jones;
the production supervisor was
Thomas J. LoPinto.
The drawings were done by Eric G. Hieber
Associates Inc.
The Murray Printing Company was printer and binder.

Cover art: Bushman rock painting. The dancers.

Library of Congress Cataloging in Publication Data

Hoebel, Edward Adamson, date
    Cultural and social anthropology.

    A revision of the cultural sections of
E. A. Hoebel's Anthropology: the study
of man, 4th ed.
    Includes index.
    1. Ethnology. I. Frost, Everett Lloyd,
joint author. II. Title.
GN315.H6 1976   301.2   75-17999
ISBN 0-07-029145-4

CONTENTS

PREFACE

When one "introduces" friends, one is bringing people together, usually in the hope that the meeting will be mutually enjoyable and rewarding. So it is with this "introductory" text. We have prepared this volume to introduce inquiring students to a most interesting field of knowledge and so bring the two together. Since both the senior author (E. A. H.) and the junior coauthor (E. L. F.) have found, and continue to find, anthropology a fascinating discipline and an eminently satisfying profession, it is natural that we should wish to impart some of the excitement and sense of discovery which we have experienced in pursuit of our studies.

One of the most intriguing and appealing aspects of anthropology is that it deals with fundamental and universal human concerns. It is instructive to know that the earliest forms of human beings had to deal with many of the same problems we face today: making a living, understanding and dealing with the environment, finding a place in a social order, living in a family, establishing sufficient political harmony to survive, inventing and placating the spirit world. In sum—being born, maturing, mating, working, worshiping, dying—trying to make sense out of the whole enterprise! It is an insensitive and incurious person, indeed, who can study what is known about all these aspects of human beings and their various adaptations and human societies and not be stimulated to a deeper view of oneself, the natural world, and the social order. Further, one's understanding of both other natural sciences (geology, botany, physiology) and the social sciences (geography, history, political science, sociology, psychology) is greatly enhanced by an anthropological perspective. As for the humanities and the arts, it is doubtful if one can attain the fullest appreciation of these fields without understanding something of the ubiquitous creative expressions, exemplified in sculpture, music, dance, graphic arts, and other ornamentation found in all societies however simple.

The foregoing suggests some of the content and potential uses of this volume. Anthropology, however, is an exceedingly complex discipline, one that is at present divided into a number of subfields: physical anthropology, archaeology, cultural anthropology. Linguistics, ethnobotany, ethnomusicology, urban anthropology, and applied anthropology are only a few of the numerous additional specializations.

An earlier forerunner of this text, Hoebel, *Anthropology: The Study of Man* (fourth edition, 1972), comprehensively covers all the major aspects of the discipline, and at least describes the narrower specializations. Many professors prefer to structure their classes around this broad, all-inclusive approach. Other anthropologists, however, prefer to organize introductory anthropology into two, or more, basic courses, separating the subdisciplines of physical anthropology, prehistoric archaeology, and cultural anthropology into more or less discrete units. To serve the need of those who choose the second approach, we have prepared this new volume on cultural anthropology. Essentially it is built on pertinent chapters of Hoebel's *Anthropology* with appropriate updating, reorganization, and newly written sections to maintain continuity and consistency. We have undertaken to balance a good body of descriptive fact with significant theory, organizing the whole as clearly as we are able.

Although the primary focus of the book is cultural anthropology, we have taken care to keep it within the framework of anthropology at large. The unity of the biocultural approach to anthropology has not been neglected. Thus, in Part 1 (Introduction) anthropology is introduced as an entity. Part 2 (The Cultural Response to Ecology) opens with a new chapter which ties together the evolutionary development of the human species and prehistoric cultures as interacting phenomena. The remainder of the book continuously interweaves cultural structures, functions, meanings, and ecological adaptation in a framework of change and development intended to further an understanding of human society as the dynamic product of human intelligence.

Anthropologists have always been sensitively aware of the importance of women in human affairs. In keeping with the emphasis of the times, we have paid attention to the use of gender-free nouns and pronouns, such as "humanity," "human being," and "their," rather than "man," "he," and "his," when referring to the generic category of the species *Homo sapiens*. We have not, however, made a fetish of absolute application of the principle, for we believe our readers are wise enough to understand that in our occasional use of "mankind," "man," and "his" in reference to the species as a whole, these terms do not denote or imply any quality of sex discrimination.

Illustrations have been selected to enhance and supplement the text without distracting attention or extravagantly raising the cost of the book to the student. Section headings have been set up so that the user may readily see the basic structure of each chapter and thus more quickly organize his own knowledge of what is being learned. The Selected Readings at the end of each chapter have been retained and updated, and full footnote references are offered throughout the text for the use of instructors and students who wish to delve in deeper detail or to know the sources of our information. A separate bibliography has not been included, however. Index identification has been arranged to serve this need in an efficient and less costly manner. In addition, to meet the special needs of instructors, the full bibliography of all references cited in this volume is included in the Instructor's Manual which accompanies this text. A comprehensive glossary is also provided. A new feature is a headlining set of Learning Goals to be found on each chapter-opening page. We hope that they will help the reader in fixing the main ideas of the chapter.

Authors are responsible for a book's substance. We are indebted, however, to many colleagues not only for the results of their basic research and thought which have so enriched our field, but also to our contemporaries who have constructively contributed to the steady improvement of this book over the years.

The publisher's editorial and production staff are responsible for a book's format and design. We appreciate the respect for scholarship and the desire for excellent bookmaking shown by the McGraw-Hill staff members involved in this particular academic partnership. Our thanks go especially to Janis Yates, delightful friend as well as helpful senior editor; also to Lyle Linder, anthropology editor, David Dunham, development editor, and Jo Jones, designer, for their parts in the creation of this book.

E. Adamson Hoebel

Everett L. Frost

INTRODUCTION

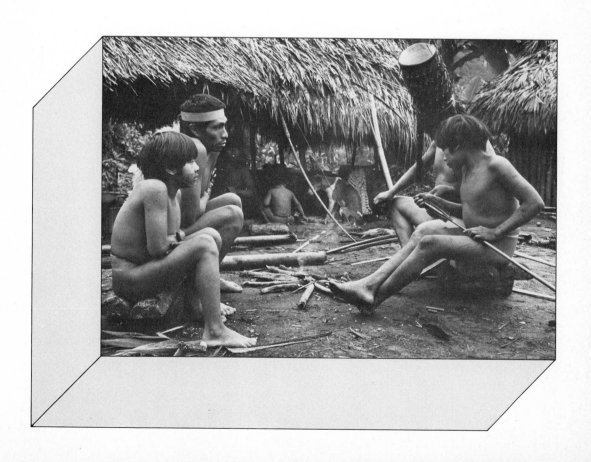

1

ANTHROPOLOGY: THE STUDY OF MANKIND

LEARNING GOALS

Define anthropology and discuss its three distinctive attributes as a field of study and research. ¶ List five major subdivisions of cultural anthropology; explain the distinguishing features of each. ¶ Enumerate some of the uses of anthropology. ¶ Specify the common interests of anthropology and other social sciences, notably history, sociology, and psychology, and indicate in what ways anthropology differs from each of them.

It is a characteristic of being human that people wish to know themselves. Therefore, if for no other reason than to bring satisfaction to our probing curiosity, mankind deserves study for its own sake. Yet, there are further possibilities in the study of humanity. An improved understanding of ourselves, by ourselves, may enhance our ultimate capabilities to direct our futures with greater intelligence concerning where we want to go and how to get there. By knowing mankind we can more effectively understand human problems and how to cope with them.

Anthropology has few final answers, but it sheds the light of fact and reason on many pressing questions.

Are there, for example, any universals in mankind's behavior? Is the family necessary? Are there "better," i.e., happier and more socially satisfying, ways for people to mature and to rear children than those the contemporary nuclear family offers? Is there a better way to use our environment and natural resources than the one we are witnessing toward the end of the twentieth century? Is it wise to promote more efficient agriculture, modern health and sanitation measures, advanced technology, monogamy, family planning, and higher education in areas and societies which have long existed without them? Are there common denominators in human values and systems of social control which make the ideal of a world law possible? Or is there some basic aggressive instinct, "territorial imperative," or other deep-seated factor which makes the achievement of such a goal totally unfeasible? Is violence ubiquitous? Is war inevitable? As human beings start out to colonize new worlds in space, are there any rules or values from the Ice Age past and the chaotic present—the five million years of human experience—they should carry with them? If so, which ones?

Anthropologists have now developed quite definite knowledge of what the earliest human beings looked like; even a good deal about their thought processes, their creations, their "religion," if you will. Is it to be expected that the future will see equally radical changes in human physique, physiognomy, brain power? Or are human beings now biologically "complete," "finished"? Have they "gone about as far as they can go," evolutionally speaking?

Incidentally, what is man? A "naked ape," as a noted zoologist calls him?[1] What sets him apart

---

[1]D. Morris, *The Naked Ape.*

3

from the rest of the animal world? The use of tools? The development of language? A penchant for religion? Or the self-curiosity which we noted in the first sentence of this book?

THE USES OF ANTHROPOLOGY

If it is presumptuous (and it is!) to claim that only anthropologists seek the answers to such questions or that anthropology provides definitive answers to all of them, it is not too much to state that all of these are basic concerns of anthropology, and further, that it is impossible to reach any satisfactory answers without some understanding of anthropological findings.

The helpfulness and relevance of anthropology to the broad quest for deeper knowledge about human nature and behavior may be seen in the rapid growth of anthropology as an academic discipline. Prior to World War II, only a handful of universities and colleges had anthropology departments, and a small number of others offered merely a course or two. In 1975 there were more than 250 recognized departments giving anthropology degrees, and courses dealing with anthropology are increasingly being offered in junior colleges, adult education programs, high schools, and even grade schools.

Further, both the methods and the concepts of anthropology have had a noticeable impact on natural and physical sciences, social sciences, businesses, and government. Such terms as "primitive culture," "cultural relativity," "comparative method," and "culture shock" are no longer the special property of anthropologists. It is perhaps not widely known that Ruth Benedict's wartime study of Japanese culture and character unquestionably influenced, with beneficial results, the successful policy of United States relations to Japan at the end of World War II.[2] Better known is the more recent Peace Corps emphasis on steeping its volunteers in the basic cultures of the peoples they seek to aid. With the emergence of independent, developing countries from the erstwhile empire holdings in Asia and Africa, the practitioners of law, political science, and economics have become actively interested in the indigenous cultures of the Third World.

Technical-assistance programs and schemes for economic development, agricultural projects, educational missions, even missionary activities—all, it is now recognized, can be successful only insofar as they relate meaningfully to the fundamental cultures of the peoples involved. Planners, administrators, and business men or women, either within the separate new nations or acting as consultants or entrepreneurs from other countries, give increasing attention to this basic premise.

The expansion of public health programs to all parts of the world has had a like effect in stimulating close cooperation between anthropology and the practice of medicine. Cultural anthropology is now widely accepted as indispensable to the training of public health professionals and has recently been recognized by the United States National Institutes of Health as a basic, medically related science.[3] To change a society's food-raising methods, its eating habits, its sanitation practices, and the size of its ideal family are not projects to be undertaken lightly, even for such lofty goals as increased longevity, better health, and less physical suffering. Such changes are not easily accomplished, either! Anthropology offers clues as to why.

But anthropology has other roles, functions, and pleasures than furnishing guidelines for those who would change the world. Basically, its goal is to explore the nature of man as an evolving, culture-bound creature, living in organized societies—each different from every other and yet similar in many ways. Anthropology tells us what the known limits to the range of human experience to date are and what the common denominator of being human is—what is shared by all mankind. The primary task of this book is to set forth the underlying facts and essential theories of cultural anthropology as they now stand.

THE DISTINCTIVE QUALITIES OF ANTHROPOLOGY

Mankind is a part of nature—of the universe with all its phenomena. The study of mankind, called *anthropology* (Gr. *anthropos*, man + *logia*, study),

---

[2]R. F. Benedict, *The Chrysanthemum and the Sword.*

[3]B. D. Paul, "Teaching Anthropology in Schools of Public Health," in D. G. Mandelbaum, G. W. Lasker, and E. M. Albert (eds.), *The Teaching of Anthropology*, p. 503.

when followed in accordance with the principles and methods of science, is consequently a natural science. One of its branches is concerned with the evolutionary origin, the physical structure, and the physiological processes of mankind. This branch is traditionally known as *physical anthropology*, or sometimes as *human biology*. But anthropology involves a good deal more than just the study of the natural history of man's physical nature, for the human being is also a culture-producing animal. Therefore, anthropology is the *science of mankind and culture*. As such it is a major social and behavioral science, and more, for in its concern with the arts and in the anthropologist's efforts to sense and communicate the total life-ways of specific peoples, it is also a *humanistic discipline*.

Anthropologists study human beings wherever they find them—in arctic snows or desert wastes; in temperate prairies and woodlands; and in verdant jungles. They search out their remains in prehistoric sites, and they carry on living field studies in primitive villages and in the urban settings of modern civilizations. Anthropology is concerned both with fossil man and living peoples. It, in the words of Clyde Kluckhohn, "holds up a great mirror to man and lets him look at himself in his infinite variety."[4] For many years the thrill in anthropology for the Western mind was the discovery of new and undreamed-of (by Western standards) customs and societies. Anthropologists were busy gathering the worldwide inventory of human social and cultural invention—filling in the image of the human being that would be reflected in the mirror. That task is now nearly done. There are but a few remaining societies to be discovered and reported on. The record is nearly in, although many problems wait to be solved.

The frontiers of anthropology are shifting from survey reports to in-depth analysis of what lies behind the image, to questions of human evolution, motivation, social structure, and function. Descriptions of the variations of life styles which have been observed in one society after another are basic grist to the anthropological mill, and students of anthropology will find much of descriptive interest as they progress in their study.

But they will also find that description serves to provide the facts for explanation of human social behavior, which has become the major concern of anthropology today.

However, many other sciences and disciplines are also concerned with one aspect or another of man or his works. What, then, is so special about anthropology that it should be named "*the* science of mankind"?

The Study of Mankind as a Whole

First of all, anthropology sets as its goal the study of mankind as a whole. Political science studies man's governments; economics studies his production and distribution of goods; neurophysiology, his nervous system; architecture, his housing and building; musicology, his music; and sociology, his society. But none of these, nor any of the other specialized disciplines one might name, such as geography or history, professes systematically to research all the manifestations of the human being and of human activity in a unified way.

The human being is a culture-creating and culture-bound animal. As evolving creatures, hominids (see pages 76–81) reached a level of development of the nervous system which enabled them to invent many new ways of behaving which were not preset in their genetic codes. This began to be manifest some five million or more years ago. Since that time all human behavior has been simultaneously biological *and* cultural. The basic premise flowing from this fact has been well put by the anthropologically oriented geneticist Theodosius Dobzhansky: "Human evolution can be understood only as a product of interaction of these two developments."[5] Herein lies the biological and social unity of mankind. A fundamental proposition of anthropology is that no part can be fully, or even accurately, understood apart from the whole. And conversely, the whole cannot be accurately perceived without acute and specialized knowledge of the parts. To understand any aspect of human sexual behavior, for example, one must examine it in terms of genetics, physiology, climatic features, the value system, and the

---

[4]C. Kluckhohn, *Mirror for Man*, p. 11.

[5]T. Dobzhansky, "Evolution: Organic and Superorganic" (*The Rockefeller Institute Review*, vol. 1, no. 2, 1963), p. 1.

technical, economic, kinship, religious, and political structures of each human society. Anthropology touches upon, draws from, and feeds into virtually any field of knowledge one might care to name. The skills of the anthropologist must be highly diversified, but the unity of the discipline is maintained by concentration on the holistic character of man and culture.

The Concept of Culture

A second distinguishing feature of anthropology is its development of the concept of culture and the importance of this concept in anthropological thought. *(Culture is the integrated system of learned behavior patterns which are characteristic of the members of a society and which are not the result of biological inheritance).* Culture is not genetically predetermined; it is noninstinctive. It is the result of social invention and is transmitted and maintained solely through communication and learning.

These are the essential components of the concept of culture as the term is currently used by most anthropologists. Other phrasings are, of course, possible. Thus, Kroeber and Kluckhohn, after review and evaluation of some five hundred phrasings and uses of the concept, gave the following definition:

Culture consists of patterns, explicit and implicit, of and for behavior acquired and transmitted by symbols, constituting the distinctive achievements of human groups, including their embodiments in artifacts; the essential core of culture consists of traditional (i.e., historically derived and selected) ideas and especially their attached values; culture systems may, on the one hand, be considered as products of action, and on the other as conditioning elements of further action.[6]

Every separate society has its distinctive culture. The consequent effect is that the characteristic behaviors of the members of one society are in some respects significantly different from the characteristic behaviors of the members of all other societies. Anthropology has demonstrated that the distinctive behavior of different human populations is overwhelmingly the product of cultural experience rather than the consequence of genetic inheritance. The importance of the cultural concept in anthropology is so great that most of the remainder of this book is devoted to a consideration of its nature and its manifestations in human behavior.

The Use of the Comparative Method

A third hallmark of anthropology is its deep-rooted and long-standing commitment to the use of the *comparative* method.[7] The anthropologist is not like the careless thinker who pronounced that all Indians walk single file, and when challenged for evidence, declared, "Well, the one I saw did!" Anthropologists refuse to accept any generalization about human nature that emerges from their experience with their own societies alone, or even with two or three other societies, especially if these are a part of the same cultural tradition in which they have been brought up. If one is going to talk about human beings and human nature, one needs to know what the whole range of human biology, human behavior, and human social forms actually is. To acquire this knowledge, the physical anthropologist studies and compares the widest possible range of human populations, ancient and modern, to determine the common and the unique biological qualities of mankind. The cultural anthropologist studies and compares the widest possible range of human societies, primitive and civilized, in all parts of the world, to determine the common and the unique social and cultural features of humanity's behavior. The general anthropologist tries to relate the physical and cultural manifestations in all their variety.

The importance of comparative cross-cultural testing for another behavioral science has recently been stated by an eminent psychologist:

---

[6]A. L. Kroeber and C. Kluckhohn, *Culture: A Critical Review of Concepts and Definitions* By permission of Papers of the Peabody Museum of American Archaeology and Ethnology, Harvard University, vol. 47, 1952, p. 181.

[7]One of the very earliest anthropological studies, written by the French missionary Joseph François Lafitau, compared Iroquois and Huron Indian cultures with those of Greece and Rome. It was based upon Lafitau's fieldwork as a Jesuit missionary in western New York between 1712 and 1717 and was called *Moeurs des sauvages Ameriquains, comparées aux moeurs des premiers temps* (Customs of American Savages, compared with Customs of Early Times).

. . . [A]nthropological evidence has been, and can continue to be, of invaluable service as a crucible in which to put to more rigorous test psychology's tentative theories, enabling one to edit them and select among alternatives in ways which laboratory experiments and correlational studies within our own culture might never make possible.[8]

Fieldwork as an Equivalent to the Experimental Laboratory

A fourth distinctive feature of anthropology is its long-standing emphasis upon fieldwork for obtaining its data and testing its hypotheses. When scientists such as chemists are confronted with a problem, they work out an experiment designed to test the validity of the hypotheses about which they are concerned. The method of laboratory experimentation is to manipulate and thereby control the quantity and action of certain known factors in order to determine how they influence one another or an unknown x factor. This fundamental tool of the physical sciences is ordinarily not available to the social sciences, which must to a great extent limit themselves to observation of existing situations rather than of those which may be experimentally designed to suit their needs. Anthropologists, however, have found a highly useful substitute in the combination of field studies with the comparative method. Faced with a problem to be solved, modern anthropologists seek a society or a series of societies that already contain the combination of factors necessary for a testing of the theory or hypothesis in question. They may search for the data in preexisting field reports in anthropological libraries, or they may plan a fieldwork expedition to study an appropriate tribe or society.

Margaret Mead's study of adolescence in Samoa

Margaret Mead's famous study of adolescence in Samoa is a classic example of this procedure. What adults consider teen-agers' turbulent emotional state and propensity to rebellion has long concerned psychologists and educators. In the United States during the 1920s, the storm and stress of adolescence were generally accepted as natural parts of the process of growing up. This view had the scientific imprint of the authoritative work of the psychologist G. Stanley Hall.[9] Dr. Mead had her doubts, entertaining an alternative hypothesis that the emotional disturbance suffered by adolescents in American and Western European society is a psychological reaction to specific stresses built into American and European cultures. If a society could be found in which these stress conditions were absent (and in which no hidden variables were present that could also produce the emotional upset), that society should reveal an absence of adolescent disturbance and the presence of an easy transition from childhood to adult life. Such a conclusion, then, would point to the cultural determination of adolescent behavior. Familiar with the ethnographies of the South Seas (Polynesia), Dr. Mead believed that the culture and social organization of Samoa, which was also reasonably accessible, probably would provide the requisite "controlled" conditions. She therefore chose Samoa as her first laboratory. Her field observations, as reported in *Coming of Age in Samoa* in 1928, fulfilled the expectancy, or prediction, and demonstrated the invalidity of Hall's theory.

THE SUBDIVISIONS OF ANTHROPOLOGY

Anthropology is so diversified that in order to achieve precision, its practitioners must of necessity specialize. The two major aspects of the subject are the biological and the cultural; the two main subdivisions are therefore (1) physical anthropology and (2) cultural anthropology. Each, in turn, has a number of specialized subdivisions of its own. This structure is illustrated in Fig. 1-1.

Physical Anthropology

The human being is first of all a biological organism and only secondarily a social animal. The study of the nature of the human organism

---

[8]D. T. Campbell, "The Mutual Methodological Relevance of Anthropology and Psychology," in F. L. K. Hsu (ed.), *Psychological Anthropology*, p. 334. By permission of Schenkman Publishing Co., Inc.

[9]G. S. Hall, *Adolescence.*

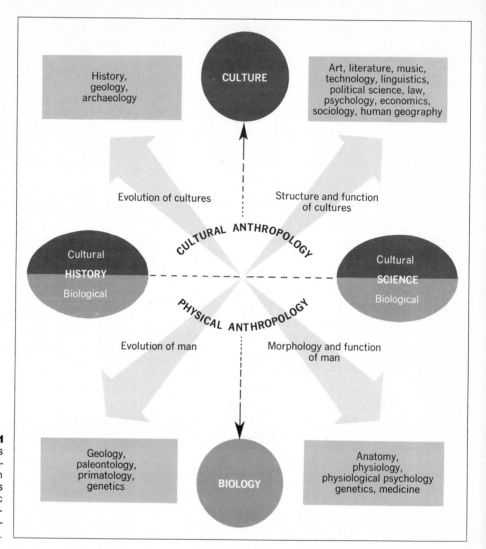

FIG. 1-1
Anthropology: its subdivisions and related sciences in terms of its historical-scientific and biological-cultural orientations.

through physical anthropology is therefore basic to understanding the nature of the human being. The aim of physical anthropology is to develop an exact body of knowledge concerning the biological characteristics of human populations, ancient and modern. It is, of course, only through the study of living or recently deceased people that physical anthropologists can learn about the structure, growth, and physiology of the human body in any very detailed way. They have developed ingenious instruments and special tech-

niques for precisely measuring innumerable ratios of size, composition of the body, dental patterns, hair form and color, skin color, blood pressure, blood groups, basal metabolism, and so forth. Because physical anthropologists are interested in the characteristics of populations, they customarily deal with large masses of measurements which are statistically processed. Their field is also closest to physiology, anatomy, and zoology among the collateral sciences.

Human evolution is also the special concern of

physical anthropology. Evolution raises two questions: "What happened?" and "How did it happen?" The first is answered largely through the comparative study of fossils, including those of the monkeys, apes, and human beings, known as *paleontology* (Gr. *palaios*, old + *onta*, living things + *logia*, study). The answer to the query "How?" is derived largely from human genetics and the study of biological adaptation to environment—both the province of the physical anthropologist.

A "new" physical anthropology has developed since World War II. Its major quality is a shift of emphasis from measurement and classification of human types toward a much greater concern with the influence of genetics on stability and variation in human populations. Experimental and field studies are carried out on adaptation to climatic extremes. Physical anthropologists have also, since 1960, become increasingly involved in field studies of primate behavior (especially of baboons, chimpanzees, and gorillas) in an effort to obtain insight into protohuman social behavior as an aspect of evolution.

Cultural Anthropology

That branch of anthropology which deals with learned behavior characteristics in past, present, and future human societies is known as *cultural anthropology*. It, in turn, has many subdivisions, of which *archaeology*, *ethnography*, *ethnology*, *social anthropology*, and *linguistics* are the most prominent.

Archaeology

Civilization began subsequent to the domestication of plants and animals and the rise of cities some nine thousand years ago (see Chapter 5). History started with the invention of writing, after the dawn of civilization. Civilization, which means the culture of cities, is a degree of complexity of culture. Civilized cultures are more complex than are primitive cultures, but they are not necessarily "better" or more "moral." By "primitive," anthropologists mean those peoples, cultures, or societies which have not acquired writing; hence, they are preliterate in an evolutionary sense, or nonlit-

erate. All cultures that existed before the invention of writing were preliterate and prehistoric. As will be seen later, the spread of literacy and its accompanying urban mode of life has been steady and inexorable, but nonetheless slow. Only five hundred years ago, the vast majority of all human cultures were without writing, and therefore primitive. Until the moment of discovery by travelers and explorers from Oriental and Western civilizations, they remained nonliterate and prehistoric.

Cultural anthropologists, traders, missionaries, and government administrators who have written about still nonliterate peoples brought the latter within the ken of history, although it may have taken them somewhat more time before they learned and adapted a written language to their own uses.

What has all this to do with archaeology? Archaeology (Gr. *archaios*, ancient, + *logia*, study) is concerned with filling out the human record by stripping the mantle of the earth from the buried remains of ancient cultures and the skeletal remnants of human beings and their associated plant and animal life (See Fig. 1-2). It tells us all we know of prehistoric peoples and cultures. The importance of prehistoric archaeology to anthropology is manifest in the fact that most of the data known about the evolutionary development of humanity and culture are derived from the work of prehistoric archaeologists.

CLASSICAL ARCHAEOLOGY Archaeologists who concentrate on the excavation and reconstruction of classical civilizations, such as those of Sumer, Egypt, Greece, India, and China, are more commonly thought of as classicists than as anthropologists. This is an expression of the fact that classical studies were central to European universities long before anthropology and its interests were established. Classical archaeology, dealing as it does with literate civilizations, serves to fill out the early historical record and it is less closely tied to prehistory than anthropological archaeology is. Nonetheless, the goals and functions of both prehistoric and classical archaeology are the same—to provide hard and tangible evidence of humanity and its past.

Although field archaeologists have their own

FIG. 1-2 Archaeology recovers the material evidence of early peoples and past cultures. Archaeologists of the Middle Missouri Salvage Program race a reservoir's rising waters in the excavation of a prehistoric village site. (U.S. Department of the Interior, National Park Service.)

meticulous and refined techniques of excavation,[10] in their larger intellectual tasks of giving meaning to what they have found, they are no different from other anthropologists who are concerned with cultural history and developmental processes. The job is one of relating the facts to general principles that adequately explain what was taking place. A student of prehistory must understand cultures and cultural processes to breathe life and meaning into the dead bones and silent stones of the long-lost past.

Not only must modern prehistoric archaeologists have full command of general anthropology, but they must also be well versed in geology and paleontology, in addition to possessing the special skills of archaeological techniques. Archaeol-

ogy is an exacting specialization to meet the canons of modern science, but the archaeologist is first of all an anthropologist. It is significant that although a number of American universities give training in archaeology, none gives a degree in this discipline.

Ethnography
The foundation of cultural anthropology is ethnography (Gr. *ethnos*, race, peoples + *graphein*, to write). Literally, the word "ethnography" means to write about peoples. As we use the term, it refers to the descriptive study of human societies. Early ethnographies were almost wholly derived from the reports of explorers, missionaries, traders, and soldiers. It was only toward the end of the nineteenth century that trained observers such as Franz Boas entered the field to study human societies directly. Now, most ethnograph-

---

[10]See B. M. Fagan, *Corridors in Time: Introductory Readings in Archaeology*; and F. Hole and R. F. Heizer, *An Introduction to Prehistoric Archaeology*.

ic work is done by trained anthropologists who have carefully learned participant-observer techniques calling for objective and penetrating observation and interviewing, empathic rapport with a people, and accurate reporting. Modern cultural anthropologists are expected to earn their spurs in ethnographic fieldwork before they are fully qualified as anthropologists.

All ethnographic monographs have some theoretical framework implicit in their organization, but they do not deal explicitly with theoretical problems. They are, we may repeat, descriptive reports of data and are little concerned with comparison per se, hypothesis, or theory. Ethnography provides the building blocks for cultural anthropology, but it is necessary to look elsewhere for the grand design.

Ethnology

Ethnology is the "science of peoples, their cultures, and life histories as groups."[11] It differs from ethnography in that as a science it seeks interrelationships between peoples and their environments, between human beings as organisms and their cultures, between different cultures, and between the differing aspects of cultures. As a science, ethnology strives to derive explanations that go beyond description, emphasizing analysis and comparison. Since each culture is clearly a changing continuum through time, ethnology is much concerned with the historical background of cultures. This aspect of ethnology is sometimes called *cultural history*. When its concern is with general principles of cultural development, it expresses itself as *cultural evolutionism*.

Ethnology, in turn, breaks down into a number of subdivisions in accordance with degree of specialization. Thus there are specialists in, and specialized studies on, primitive kinship and family life, economic activities, law and government, religion; material culture and technology; language, the arts of painting, sculpture, music, and dance; folklore and mythology—almost any major aspect of human cultural manifestations that one might think of.

Social anthropology

Ethnologists who concentrate on social relations, such as family and kinship, age groups, political organization, law and economic activities—in short, what is called *social structure*—prefer to be called *social anthropologists*. English anthropologists who accepted the position of A. R. Radcliffe-Brown deny the usefulness of historical studies in anthropology and wish to divorce cultural anthropology from history. They have established a separate subdivision of cultural anthropology under the rubric *social anthropology*, which they also at times call *comparative sociology*. Social anthropology is nonhistorical, in their view, while ethnology is historical.

Linguistics

Linguistics is the science of language. Many linguists look upon their discipline as a completely autonomous science in its own right, and there is a growing trend in American universities to establish independent departments of linguistics. However, languages are aspects of cultures, intimately interacting with all the other manifestations of culture, and are therefore best understood in the cultural context. Consequently, among the social sciences, the scientific study of languages is widely held to be a branch of cultural anthropology. In the United States, at least, all the larger departments of anthropology include linguistic analysis as a part of their programs. However, traditional language studies in archaic (Sanskrit, Greek, and Latin, for example) and modern Indo-European languages have been part of university activities in areas outside anthropology for centuries.

Anthropologists, once they had begun to base their studies on objective fieldwork, were forced to learn many primitive languages from scratch, with never a book of grammar to guide them. This proved to be a good thing. A universal system of phonetic writing had to be developed so that records could be kept of what native informants were saying in tongues for which no system of writing existed. This soon led to a realization that some cultures organize speech in accordance with grammatical principles very different from those which govern the old, familiar Indo-

---

[11]A. L. Kroeber, *Anthropology* (2d ed.), p. 5.

European languages. Some anthropologists, fascinated by their new discoveries, began to concentrate their efforts on recording and analyzing primitive languages, and linguistics as a specialized branch of anthropology developed in a way that revolutionized all language study (see Chapter 22).

Other subspecialties of cultural anthropology

Every major field of human endeavor is cultivated as a special subfield of anthropological study. The adaptation of human beings to their total environment is the concern of the *ethnoecologist*.

Material culture is the province of the specialist in primitive technology. There are the fields of primitive dance, *ethnomusicology*, and primitive art. Since the time of Sir Edward Burnett Tylor (1832–1917), primitive religion has been central to the interests of anthropologists, while specialists in social organization have focused on family and kinship. Political anthropology (the study of primitive and colonial political systems) has come into its own since 1950. Legal anthropology and primitive economics are burgeoning. Folklorists deal with oral traditions, and symbolic anthropologists try to fathom the social meaning and cultural functions which are indirectly expressed in the imagery of myth, art, and ritual.

There are medical anthropologists who try to interpret nonoccidental systems of medical thought and practice to Western medicine men, and there are a few *ethnobotanists* who specialize in primitive herbalism and vegetable stuffs. Although some anthropologists have studied ethnic populations in urban settings since the beginning of this century, it was out of the ashes of the summer riots and burnings in United States cities in 1967 that there has sprouted a new breed of specialists, called *urban anthropologists*. They strive to bring the unique attributes of anthropology to the study of subcultures in contemporary cities. Then there are the *applied anthropologists* who work as advisors to government, industries, and human relations organizations in the effort to put anthropology to work, today. Practically every chapter in Parts 2 through 5 of this book is an expression of the thought and findings of a special subfield of anthropology.

Area Specialization

Finally, all anthropologists specialize by geographic areas. One can be a North American archaeologist or cultural anthropologist, or a South American, African, Oceanian, South or East Asian, or Middle East specialist, as the case may be.

Anthropologists are expected to know about peoples in all parts of the world, but as area specialists, they concentrate their fieldwork in one or two selected areas and they will undoubtedly know the published literature on that area in greater depth.

THE RELATION OF ANTHROPOLOGY TO THE SOCIAL SCIENCES

Anthropology is usually organized as a social science in American universities, although it is clear from all that has been said thus far that anthropology is a good deal more than that. Nonetheless, its dominant identity among the social sciences is due to the fact that the bulk of anthropological work is focused upon culture and, within culture, upon social organization. We have discussed the features of anthropology that distinguish it as a discipline. Each of these bears on the question of the relation of anthropology to the sister sciences, and yet the often-asked question: "How does anthropology tie in to history, sociology, and psychology?" deserves a more specific answer.

History

Early in this century, the English anthropologist R. R. Marrett (1866–1943) declared that anthropology is history, or it is nothing. He did not mean that it is history in the formal sense; he was emphasizing that time is a basic dimension in all human experience. The stream of life is a continuous flow. All anthropologists grant this fact, but they differ over how much value there is to anthropology in history and historical research. Archaeologists are of course staunchly committed to the value of the historical component. Many social anthropologists, on the other hand, are apt to hold that it is sufficient to concentrate on the search for understanding of societies that currently exist, the "now" anthropology of today. Prehistoric and historic data, they aver, can never be obtained in sufficient detail or with sufficient validity to serve adequately the demands of science.

A balanced view of the relation of anthropology to history would hold that a comparison of directly observable societies does indeed put the study of mankind on a firmer scientific footing in terms of verifiable and validated results. Yet it would also agree that it is scientifically important to study the processes of the growth and change of cultures. Culture and society are not momentary things. They come out of the past, exist in the present, and continue into the future. What they *are* is the product of what they *have been*, worked upon by presently impinging conditions and influences. What they *will be* is the product of what they *have been* and *are*, worked upon by the conditions and influences that engage them today and will engage them in the future. Neither the present nor the future can be wholly understood without a knowledge, however faulty, of the past.

There are, of course, historians and historians, histories and histories. Historians are social scientists when they undertake to derive general laws of social change or to explain specific events by noting repeated regularities observed through time. Or they may be philosophers of history if they strive to explain what took place at particular times in history in terms of an a priori scheme of interpretation. Or, if their interest is no more than the "scholarly pursuit of special knowledge of particular fact," they are neither social scientists nor philosophers; they are simply historians *sui generis*. Their emphasis is then on the uniqueness of the situation. "History never repeats itself," they say. The time and the place and what happened then and there—stated exactly, accurately, and specifically—are what is important to historians as chroniclers.

In science, as opposed to history, a fact is not itself of central interest. The object of science is to relate a multitude of facts to one another so as to make valid, general propositions about the nature of things. Anthropologists' ways of organizing their knowledge are different from those of historians, and their methods of operation are basically different also (see Fig. 1-3). The "field" for historians is the library. Their working unit is a document. Their joy is the discovery of a long-lost packet of letters or reports. For anthropologists, the "field" is a remote tribal group, a central-city population, or an archaeological site. Their working unit is the person and a people. Their joy is the discovery of a new type of social relation, fossil, or set of artifacts. A student of contemporary Africa puts it succinctly: "Africa has two kinds of history: the conventional kind to be studied through European accounts of exploration, settlement, and colonial rule, and an unconventional kind to be studied through anthropological accounts of indigenous economic and social organization."[12]

Sociology

Sociology and anthropology are the closest kin among the social sciences. It is for this reason that they are frequently to be found in the same department in American universities. Their similarity is in their interest in social organization and behavior. In these fields, the basic theoretical approaches have much in common; indeed, in many respects they are indistinguishable. But the specific interests of the sociologist and the anthropologist and their ways of going about their work may be very different. Sociologists do not usually receive the biological, archaeological, and linguistic training that is so important to anthropologists. Anthropologists work as participant-observers in small societies, supplemented by intensive, day-after-day, person-to-person discourse on cultural practices. Their emphasis is on people-in-culture. Sociologists usually work with larger samples of more limited aspects of society; hence their heavy emphasis on statistical data and procedures. The questionnaire and the cen-

---

[12]G. Dalton, "Traditional Production in Primitive African Economies" (*The Quarterly Journal of Economics*, August, 1962), p. 378.

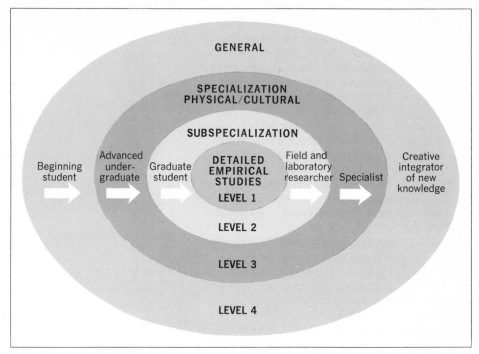

FIG. 1-3 Students beginning to study anthropology as a science first approach the subject through the mastery of general principles. As they move on to more specialized courses, they enter an area in which generalizations become narrower and the empirical data loom larger. As graduate students, they master the technique of empirical observation and research in the field and laboratory. As professional anthropologists, they move on to the formulation of specialized hypothesis and theory. Finally, they may formulate new and encompassing generalizations that are aimed at synthesizing all the empirical findings of the subspecializations of physical and cultural anthropology.

sus reports are likely to be the sociologist's major factual resource. Also, American sociology devotes a great deal of attention to problems of social pathology and social work: delinquency, crime, poverty, mental illness, and broken homes, as they occur in society. This has been a commitment of sociology in the United States from the very beginning. Anthropology has only lately turned its conscious attention to social problems and administration.

Psychology

Anthropology and psychology are both concerned with behavior and hence have much in common. But whereas anthropology is interested primarily in group organization of behavior, and the cultural patterning of behavior, psychology is more concerned with the behavior of the individual organism and how it responds to specific stimuli. Psychologists are much more oriented to the use of laboratory experiments, tests, and measurements and to statistical expression of their findings in an effort to achieve scientific precision in their field. The behavioral situations studied by experimental psychologists tend to be simplified and neat, that is, controlled experiments that are designed to eliminate extraneous variables. Anthropologists undertake to relate the simple but verified findings of psychology to the complexities of the real-life situations which they confront in going societies, where their findings are indeed less rigorously verified. Anthropologists study anthropoids almost exclusively. Experimental psychologists are more than likely to forsake the human animal, with all its complexities, to study the more manageable mouse, rat, guinea pig, monkey, or pigeon.

While contemporary social psychologists also incline strongly toward laboratory experimentation, clinical psychologists and psychoanalysts are forced by the nature of their tasks to treat whole persons in the context of their total social settings. The deep probing of psychoanalysis into the hidden psychic processes has engendered a number of insightful concepts that have proved very useful to anthropologists in the interpretation of cultural systems and their relations to tribal personality types. The field of culture and personality (see Chapter 4) was one of the most active and productive areas of anthropology in the decades of 1930 to 1960.

Learning theory as developed in psychology is of course of great importance to anthropology; culture is acquired only through learning. Psychology probes the processes of how all animals learn and how they learn to learn. Anthropology, in turn, teaches us what is learned in various societies, how it is taught, and what the rewards and punishments provided by each society for proper learning or failure to learn are. "Culture," as viewed by Miller and Dollard, ". . . is a statement of the design of the human maze, of the type of reward involved, and of what responses are to be rewarded. In this sense it is a recipe for learning."[13] Because cultures vary so widely, the conditions of human learning and human behavior vary widely. Anthropology offers psychology a wider factual base against which to test its theories and assumptions. This is recognized by the psychologist Donald Campbell in these terms:

Implicitly, the laboratory psychologist still assumes that his college sophomores provide an adequate base for a general psychology of man. . . . For social psychology these tendencies have been very substantively curbed through confrontation with the anthropological litera-

ture. Continued confrontation, however, will be required to prevent relapse. For the general psychologist, most of the lesson is yet to be learned.[14]

Law, Political Science, Economics, and Public Health

Law is an aspect of any society's culture, and it is exceedingly important as a shaper of cultures, since it is explicitly devoted to discouraging certain forms of behavior while supporting others. Because legal anthropology places so much emphasis on the functions of law in total social systems, it has proved particularly fruitful in illuminating by comparison the foundations of our own law system. "Law," according to Bohannan, "is one of the best-studied subdisciplines of anthropology; the literature is small but of high quality."[15]

Only since World War II and the consequent emergence of independent, developing countries from the erstwhile empire holdings in Asia and Africa have economics and political science in the United States become actively interested in the indigenous cultures of these parts of the world. But now the economics and government of these areas have taken on extreme importance.

The expansion of public health programs to all parts of the world has had a like effect in stimulating close cooperation between anthropology and the practice of medicine.

It should be clear by now that anthropology in many of its aspects participates vitally in the dynamic complex of the social sciences. If we can refer to anthropology as the study of dead bones and live issues, we can also say that this subject gets livelier by the year.

SELECTED READINGS

Beattie, J., *Understanding an African Kingdom: Bunyoro* (1965). A straightforward, short account of the tech-

---

[13]N. Miller and J. Dollard, *Social Learning and Imitation*, p. 5.

[14]D. T. Campbell, "The Mutual Methodological Relevance of Anthropology and Psychology," In F. L. K. Hsu (ed.), *Psychological Anthropology*, p. 334. By permission of Schenkman Publishing Co., Inc.

[15]P. J. Bohannan, *Social Anthropology*, p. 284.

nique and methods used in the field study of a given society.

Casagrande, J. B. (ed.), *In the Company of Man* (1960). Twenty distinguished anthropologists each offer a profile of the one key informant who has been central to his or her own anthropological fieldwork. In so doing, they convey the human aspect of teamwork between the scientist and his "subjects" in a way that is highly empathic.

Gillin, J. P., *For a Science of Social Man: Convergences in Anthropology, Psychology and Sociology* (1954). Seven leading American social scientists examine the interrelations of their various fields.

Golde, P. (ed.), *Women in the Field* (1970). Twelve North American women-anthropologists write about their personal field experience in all parts of the world.

Hammel, E. A., and W. A. Simmons (eds.), *Man Makes Sense* (1970). A reader in cultural anthropology in which part I, "The Personality of Anthropology," with articles by Arensberg, Maybury-Lewis, Lévi-Strauss, Kroeber, and Geertz, provides an extended introduction to the nature of anthropology.

Henry, J., *Culture against Man* (1964). A hypercritical look at American culture and society which should be read for an appreciation of the way in which the author combines the technique of the participant-observer with the use of anthropological theory to shed a flood of new light on aspects of American family life, schooling, mental illness, and treatment of the aged.

Honigmann, J. J. (ed.), *Handbook of Social and Cultural Anthropology* (1973). A collection of twenty-eight essays by modern anthropologists on the current "state of the art" in several subdisciplines of anthropology. Each essay gives a broad perspective on its topic directing the reader to other sources that offer detailed substantive and theoretical contributions to the area.

Mandelbaum, D. G., G. W. Lasker, and E. M. Albert (eds.), *The Teaching of Anthropology* (1963). Written by a number of anthropologists, primarily for teachers of anthropology, it covers all the subdivisions of anthropology and all the relations of anthropology to other subjects. Inquisitive students should find it interesting to see how their teachers go about deciding what to teach them.

Powdermaker, H., *Stranger and Friend* (1966). The personal growth and fieldwork maturation of a fine and sensitive anthropologist, who describes her early fieldwork in Lesu (Melanesia), a Mississippi town, Hollywood, and Zambia (Africa).

Sills, D. L. (ed.), "Anthropology" (*International Encyclopedia of the Social Sciences*, vol. 1, 1968), pp. 304–344. Six articles by anthropologists summarize the content and recent trends in cultural anthropology.

2
MAN, CULTURE, AND SOCIETY

LEARNING GOALS

Discuss the noninstinctive nature of culture. ¶ Explain the significance of fundamental cultural postulates. ¶ Comment on the idea of cultural relativity. ¶ Discuss behavioral norms as culture elements, complexes, and institutions. ¶ Explain why anthropologists distinguish such ideas as ideal culture, real culture, and culture construct. ¶ Give five criteria of a human society. ¶ Specify the six functional prerequisites of the survival of any human society. ¶ Show how anthropologists arrive at a scientific definition of race and what they have to say on the question of race and culture.

Once there was neither humanity nor culture. Today mankind threatens to crowd all other animals from the face of the earth, save only those which serve its purposes. Human beings have invented culture, and by means of culture they have domesticated themselves and numerous plants, animals, and natural forces. They promise to "domesticate" the entire world before long. By means of its cultural achievements, mankind has begun to probe outer space, has left its footprints on the moon, and has junked the first auto driven on lunar soil. In the near future human beings may be capable of interplanetary travel.

THE CULTURE-CREATING CAPACITY

How did man, the animal, become man, the human being, *Homo sapiens*? The process has been a prolonged and unceasing response to environmental situations in which the biological processes of natural selection, working upon genetic variations in living organisms, have produced biological, or organic, evolution. Five million or more years ago, the hominids had become sufficiently differentiated from the other animals so that we can now look back on them as representing a new form of life. A feature of this differentiation was the elaboration of their nervous system, the brain in particular, to the point where they could not only see, smell, and act but also symbolically represent a wide range of experience. They acquired the capacity to think and to speak. They could experience things and situations vicariously, not in the instant act but "dramatized" within the nervous system. They learned how to communicate experience to themselves and to others through those symbolic representations we call "concepts," or "thoughts," expressed in gesture, word, dance, and art. The "animal" became contemplative. And, in thinking, a process of self-organization began. Human beings started to "see" the universe about them not only in terms of the immediately confronted stimulus but also in terms of what they "remembered;" not just through conditioned habit but also through word representations of past experience. They acquired the capacity to project past experience into the future by thinking of what might be. Mankind learned to create experience which had not yet happened and which might never take place at all. They began to shape a world of experience according to images of their own creation. They became imaginative.[1]

Along with the development of a thinking brain, these creatures also were broadening the range of their physiological processes and physical activity. But the great innovation lay in the degree to which they could organize a relatively small number of movements into large and various combinations. They acquired the capacity to invent new behavior.

As a result of biological evolution, humanity acquired the capacity to produce culture on the grand scale and in turn to become the product of its cultures. Culture, like life, began very simply and humbly. Like life, it has gradually grown and assumed a greater and greater variety of forms in an unbroken continuity from preexistent forms.

The Noninstinctive Nature of Culture

In the first chapter, culture was defined as the integrated system of learned behavior patterns that are characteristic of the members of a society and that are not the result of biological inheritance. It is the essence of the concept of culture that instincts, innate reflexes, and any other biologically predetermined forms of behavior are ruled out. Culture is therefore acquired behavior. But it is as much a part of the natural universe as the stars in the heavens, for it is a natural product of human activities, and the human being is part of nature.

Learned behavior

That cultural behavior is learned behavior may be demonstrated by answering the question: "What would happen if a group of babies were cut off from all adult care, training, and supervision?" The answer is, of course: "They would die." Therefore, we must modify our question and put it in this form: "What would happen if a group of babies could be fed and protected without adult supervision or training and without any form of contact with adults? Would they manifest any of

the special traits of behavior that were characteristic of their parents?"

Our answer cannot be based upon direct empirical observation; legend, mythology, and the testimony of honorable individuals notwithstanding, wolves, jailers, or scientific experimenters have not set up such a situation under conditions of control or observation that meet the elementary canons of scientific acceptability. But enough is known of infant physiology, learning, and psychology to justify an answer in unequivocal terms. Assuming the survival of the infants, they would eat, drink, defecate, urinate, and gurgle and cry. These would be direct responses to basic biological drives. But what they would eat, when they would eat, and how they would eat would not be according to the tastes and palates of any group of people we now know. It is quite unlikely that they would cook their food. Presumably they would sooner or later get up on their hind legs, and even before adolescence they would experiment in mating without benefit of incest tabus or any preferred approaches of courtship. They would communicate emotional states through gesture and sounds. But they would be devoid of language, utensils, fire, arts, religion, government, and all the other features of life that distinguish humanity from other animals. They would develop few of the traits which we characterize as "human."

In spite of their shortcomings, however, these hapless children would enjoy a kind of social life. They would constitute not only an animal aggregation but also an animal society. It is quite probable, however, because they are human beings, that they would very quickly begin the accumulation of incipient culture.

Instinctive behavior

Many animals in addition to human beings have a social life and even social organization. Ant society has long been recognized for its well-delineated division of labor among drones, workers, fighters, males, females, and queen. The organization of the colony, with its living quarters and storage rooms for eggs, presents the picture of a well-ordered society. The ants interact with

---

[1] William Golding treats this process in a simple and empathic way in his novel *The Inheritors*, a fictionalized account of the last of the Neandertals.

one another in an integrated, sustained set of relationships. These relationships are preset in the genetic organization of the ants. So far as is known, little if any of their behavior is learned from adult ants. If eggs are hatched without any adult ants being present, a host of new ants is produced, which, when they attain maturity, apparently reenact every single aspect of all the forms of social life that have characterized their species for untold generations.

THE DANCE OF THE BEES   The behavior of certain other insects is also highly social and involves the communication of information within the society. Honeybees have been studied with great care and with fascinating results in a series of experimental observations by Karl von Frisch, of Munich. Female "scout" bees search out the location of sweet, pollen-bearing plants. When she has found a good source, the scout determines the location, takes a fix on the sun, and returns immediately to the hive. She then executes a dance in which she moves along a straight line pointing toward the source. She circles back to the starting point, alternately to the left and right. The speed at which she makes her straight runs indicates approximately how far away the source of supply is. The smell of the pollen indicates the sweetness, or potential honey content. The workers fall in behind her in the dance, and when they have received the message, they take off unerringly to the right spot. Different species do different dances, but the basic pattern is the same.

This fascinating dance of the bees emphasizes the importance of communication in group living, but it does not represent cultural behavior. As von Frisch himself has written:

The brain of the bee is the size of a grass seed and is not made for thinking. The actions of a bee are mainly governed by instinct. Therefore, the student of even so complicated and purposeful activity as the communication dance must remember that he is dealing with innate patterns, impressed on the nervous system of the insects over the immense reaches of time of their phylogenetic development.[2]

---

[2]From K. von Frisch, "Dialects in the Language of the Bees," p. 79. Copyright © (1962) by Scientific American, Inc. All rights reserved.

Protoculture among Apes and Monkeys

On the other hand, we would be taking undue credit unto ourselves if we denied *all* culture-creating capacity to *all* subhuman creatures.

Monkeys and apes have been shown to be quite capable of solving a number of problems posed for them by experimenters. Chimpanzees show considerable intelligence and inventiveness. What is more, they are quite definitely capable of learning from one another through direct imitation. Apes ape each other.

Thus, when one of a group of experimental apes accidentally jabbed the end of a pole into the ground and found to his immense delight that he could hoist himself skyward, all the other members of the colony were soon searching for sticks; pole vaulting was the rage. Another discovered that by scattering bread outside the bars of his cage, he could lure unwary chickens in close, while he lurked with a stick in his hand with which to jab them. Annoying the chickens then became the current sport of the group. The alarmed squawks of the hens provided rich simian diversion. These and other tricks were discovered by the apes without help from psychologists. When they had spread among the group, they had for the time being all the qualities of customs. But, alas, when interest wore off and enthusiasm waned, as it always did after a few days or weeks, each practice was forgotten, never to be performed again. Their destiny was that of fads; they did not endure to become customs.

However, the semiwild Japanese monkeys which are being carefully studied in their seminatural habitats by Japanese scientists clearly show that elemental discoveries are communicated within the group and do become established as cultural features. Direct observation of colonies of Japanese monkeys *(Macaca fuscata)* reveals, for example, that each troop has its own characteristic food prejudices. This, surely, is the most elemental of cultural universals.

According to Syuno Kawamura: "The monkeys of the Minno Ravine know how to remove the earth of the slope by scratching with their hands to get the roots of Boehmeria nivea, and also probably of Lilium spp. and Dioscorea spp., while those of Takasakiyama entirely lack such knowledge."[3]

Food habits are established among unweaned infant monkeys who, sitting by their mother, pick up the food she drops from her mouth. Without their mother's example, experimental infants of the same species find it hard to learn to take any food but milk.[4]

New foods have been experimentally introduced to troops of wild monkeys by the Japanese scientists with very illuminating results. When candy is introduced, the two- or three-year-olds are the first to take it up as a food. Later the mothers learn from their children to eat it. And once a mother has acquired a taste for candy, that taste is "handed down to her baby without exception." The adult males who supervise the young monkeys also soon learn to eat candy, but the young males who have little to do with juveniles take it up last of all. New culture traits spread differentially within the troop.

In another troop, the new habit of eating wheat was introduced by an adult male. His example was followed by the "chief" of the troop and from him was passed on to the "chief female," who in turn transmitted it to her offspring. Within four hours, wheat had been tried and accepted by the entire troop. Only half of another troop ever accepted the candy eating that had been introduced by a child, however.[5]

Incipient culture building is clearly within the province of primates other than human beings. Yet they evidently lack the capacity to express experience symbolically. David Kaplan has put it well in stating, "Some scholars would question whether the ability to symbolize is unique to man, but all would agree, I think, with [Morton] Fried . . . that 'only man, on this planet, engages in massive, systematic and continuous symboling.'"[6]

---

[3]S. Kawamura, "The Process of Sub-culture Propagation among Japanese Macaques," in C. H. Southwick (ed.), *Primate Social Behavior*, pp. 83–84.
[4]*Ibid.*
[5]*Ibid.*, pp. 85–88.
[6]D. Kaplan, "The Superorganic: Science or Metaphysics?" (*American Anthropologist*, vol. 67, 1965), p. 961.

SYMBOLISM AND CULTURE

Many of the elemental behavior patterns that make up a culture may be learned directly, without reliance on symbolic content. This may be seen in the behavior of deaf children who learn to master simple manual skills without the use of language and without the usual means of assimilating many of the more complex ideas which other children get at an early age. It is equally obvious just how much of their society's culture is shut off from such children. Without skillful remedial education, available only in the most advanced cultures and societies, congenitally deaf children can rarely share the thoughts, beliefs, or attitudes or acquire the reasoning skills of their people except on the crudest level. They will know only a little of their people's gods, music, folktales and legends, star lore, or magic. They will be barred from more than elementary comprehension of their people's kinship system, law, politics, and rules of inheritance and trade. They may learn to paint through imitation, but they will know little of the meanings of the designs they copy or the significance of the colors they use. All these manifestations of culture, and more, will be beyond them, for their infirmity denies them the one truly distinctive attribute of mankind—language, the "purely human and non-instinctive method of communicating ideas, emotions, and desires by means of a system of voluntarily produced symbols."[7]

The clue to understanding the nature of language, that cultural product without which culture is limited, is to realize that language is the major device for *symbolizing*. A sound may be no more than a noise, a disturbance of the air that stimulates no discernible response in man or beast. A sound may also be a *signal* that evokes a response, such as the whistle that calls a dog to the master's side. On a higher level a sound may be a *symbol*, which is a signal or sign that stands for something. It has *meaning*. Languages are arbitrary systems of vocal symbolism, to which civilized cultures have also added visual symbols: writing. Symbols may also be tactile, such as the piece of sandpaper that is conventionally put on a

---

[7]E. Sapir, *Language*, p. 7.

bottle which contains poison so that it may be felt in the dark.

It is not necessarily a matter of conscious recognition among all peoples, but some, such as the Caduveo of Brazil, understand quite clearly the symbolic functions of their visible, artistic facial paintings. As reported by Claude Lévi-Strauss, "The Indians have replied for us. The face-paintings confer upon the individual his dignity as a human being: they help him to cross the frontier from Nature to culture, and from the 'mindless' animal to the civilized Man."[8] Mythology and religion, with its ritual drama, exist as elaborated symbol systems, impressing and sustaining the cultural system of a people (see Chapter 20).

So it is that almost all aspects of culture come to be symbolically transmitted to the members of a society. So it is that the very way in which the members of a society see and understand the world in which they live is shaped by the symbol system that makes up their culture.

THE INTEGRATION OF CULTURE

The members of a society never exhibit *all* the behaviors of which we now know human beings are capable. This is one of the great lessons that modern anthropology has taught us. Many people around the world think that what they were brought up to do is *ipso facto* an expression of human nature. Little do they realize that other human beings have found quite different ways of doing the same thing. Or perhaps they do not do it at all. In the succeeding chapters of this book, the main varieties of known culture patterns are examined. The range of variability is surprisingly wide.

The Imperative of Selection

As each society builds its culture through the ages, it ignores or rejects many of the potential behavior patterns of which men are capable. Of course, this is partly due to the fact that the majority of these potential patterns remained undiscovered by most of the isolated societies of the

past and hence were not available for inclusion in their cultures. Yet even if they had been available, many of them would necessarily have been excluded. Social behavior must be predictable within a range of limited leeways. Expectancies must be realized, if individuals are to gauge their actions in terms of experience. Individuals in society are individuals interacting. If everyone were to go off behaving in any one of the multitudes of ways in which human beings are capable, the result would be bedlam and disaster. Society is possible only in terms of a limiting order.

Limitation of ways of behaving is not only a social necessity but also an individual necessity. Experimental animal psychology, as well as psychiatry, has demonstrated that habit formation and habitual rewarding of psychological responses are necessary for individual mental health.[9] Behavior must be integrated to a high degree for effective functioning of personality.

Further, many behavior patterns are mutually contradictory and inherently incompatible. A people cannot enjoy free sexual license and at the same time practice celibacy; no one has yet discovered how to eat his cake and have it too. This principle applies to thousands of other aspects of culture and is the basis of the *imperative of selection*, as summed up by Ruth Benedict:

The culture pattern of any civilization makes use of a certain segment of the great arc of potential human purposes and motivations. . . . The great arc along which all the possible human behaviours are distributed is far too immense and too full of contradictions for any one culture to utilize even any considerable portion of it. Selection is the first requirement.[10]

Fundamental Cultural Postulates

The selection of the customs that go to make up a culture is never wholly random and haphazard. Selection is made with reference to a set of deep-lying assumptions, or postulates, about the nature of the external world and the nature of man

---

[8]C. Lévi-Strauss, *Tristes Tropiques*, p. 176.

[9]S. J. H. Masserman, *Principles of Dynamic Psychiatry*, pp. 126–129.

[10]R. F. Benedict, *Patterns of Culture*, p. 237. By permission of Houghton Mifflin Co.

himself. These assumptions as to the nature of existence are called *existential postulates*. There are also deep-lying assumptions about whether things or acts are good and to be sought after, or bad and to be rejected. These are called *normative postulates* or *values*.

For a brief example of what is meant here, consider the following Trobriand Island existential postulate, first noting that the Trobrianders, who live in the South Pacific, are socially organized in matrilineal clans. At the foundation of Trobriand life is the following self-evident (to the Trobriander) proposition:

Pregnancy results from the entry by a spirit *(balomà)* of a dead matrilineal clan ancestor into the body of a woman.

From this flow two corollaries: (1) the father is not genetically related to the child; and (2) a person belongs only to the clan of his or her mother. Any Trobriander knows this "as a matter of course." This is elemental Trobriand truth. Many Trobriand specifics of social life and feeling are understandable only in these terms.

Both existential and normative postulates are the reference points which color a people's view of things, giving them their orientation toward the world around them and toward one another.[11]

The basic assumptions of a culture are generally consistent among themselves, although there are usually some exceptions. If a society is to survive, the gears of its culture must mesh, even though they may growl and grind.

In selecting its customs for day-to-day living, even in little things, the society chooses those ways which accord with its thinking and predilections—ways that fit its basic postulates concerning the nature of things and what is desirable and what is not. If these ways are consistent with the basic postulates, and if these in turn are consistent with one another, integration is achieved. The culture is then a harmonious working whole.

To recapitulate:

1. Every culture represents a limited selection of behavior patterns from the total of human potentialities, individual and collective.

2. The selection tends to be made in accordance with certain postulates (dominant assumptions and values) basic to culture.

3. It follows that every culture exemplifies a more or less complete and coherent pattern, structure, or system of actions and relationships.

"The quality of a society," observes Otis Lee, "will vary with the quality of its basic values . . . with their suitability to its needs and circumstances, and with the consistency and thoroughness with which they are worked out."[12]

Some of the basic postulates of a culture may be explicitly stated by the people who hold them. Others are not explicitly stated, either because they are so taken for granted or because the people are so unused to reflecting about their beliefs that they are not themselves able to state them. In anthropology, when social scientists are thoroughly familiar with the observed behavior of a society in all its aspects, they may generalize as to the principles that underlie the behavior; thus they identify the postulates for the society,[13] like the linguist who analyzes a primitive language and formulates the rules and principles of grammar. The people who speak the tongue know only that one form is right and another is not, without being able to express the principles in so many words. There are striking parallels between general cultural and linguistic processes which are discussed in Chapter 22.

Configurations of Culture

Although a culture is built up of elements and traits, the significance lies less in its inventory of traits than in the manner of their integration. For this reason we have phrased the definition of culture in terms of the "integrated system of learned behavior."

Benedict, who introduced the configurational

---

[11]For fuller exposition of several systems of fundamental cultural postulates, see Chapter 19 on culture and world view.

[12]O. Lee, "Social Values and the Philosophy of Law" (*Virginia Law Review*, vol. 32, 1946), pp. 811–812; reprinted in O. Lee, *Freedom and Culture*, pp. 89ff.

[13]A detailed description of how basic cultural postulates are expressed in Cheyenne culture may be found in E. A. Hoebel, *The Cheyennes: Indians of the Great Plains*. Other examples may be found in J. A. Hostetler, *Amish Society*, and, for traditional (pre-Communist) China, in F. L. K. Hsu, *The Study of Literate Civilizations*, pp. 61–71.

idea into modern anthropological thought, has written of culture: "The whole, as modern science is insisting in many fields, is not merely the sum of all its parts, but the result of a unique arrangement and interrelation of the parts that has brought about a new entity."[14]

This is a sound principle for the understanding of the nature of cultures and the uniqueness of divergent societies, for it is theoretically possible for two societies to possess identical inventories of culture elements and yet so arrange the relationships of the elements to one another as to produce two quite unlike societies. By simple analogy, two masons may take two identical piles of bricks and equal quantities of mortar. Yet, with these materials, one may build a fireplace while the other builds a garden wall, depending on the way they integrate the bricks. The configuration of a culture is its distinctive and characteristic form that derives from the special relationship of its parts to one another. It presumes internal integration established by the process of custom selection carried out in accordance with some basic and dominant principles or value systems underlying the whole scheme. Thus, Pueblo culture is characterized by collectivistic, ritual emphasis under priestly direction, while the nomadic Plains Indian cultures emphasize individual self-realization through aggressive fighting against outsiders and hallucinatory vision experiences. (See pages 326–329.)

Cultural Relativity

All cultures differ in their basic postulates at some points. Each has general features in common with all others, but in specifics every culture is different from every other in some respects. Some are very different. "Mankind is one. Civilizations are many," the great anthropologist Franz Boas used to say. The anthropological realization of this fact has led to the establishment of the *concept of cultural relativity*, which is closely related to the intensive anthropological use of the comparative method.

The concept of cultural relativity states that standards of rightness and wrongness (values)

and of usage and effectiveness (customs) are relative to the given culture of which they are a part. In its most extreme form, it holds that every custom is valid in terms of its own cultural setting. In practical terms, it means that anthropologists learn to suspend judgment, to strive to understand what goes on from the point of view of the people being studied, that is, to achieve empathy, for the sake of humanistic perception and scientific accuracy. Anthropologists undertake to assume the role of detached observers rather than those of apologists, condemners, or converters. They learn to laugh with people, not at them. They must have a real respect for human beings, whoever they may be. Students who lack this trait—who cannot put aside all chauvinist ethnocentrism, that is, the habit of uncritically judging other peoples' behavior according to the standards set in their own culture—can never become first-rate cultural anthropologists.

THE FUNCTIONAL NATURE OF CULTURE

The fact that each culture is made up of a multitude of selected traits integrated into a total system means that all parts have a special relationship to the whole. Each part may have its specific *form* as, for example, a bow, a canoe, a pot, a marital arrangement, or a legal process. No one of these elements of culture exists in a vacuum, however, or stands as an isolated unit. It plays its part in contributing to a total life-way. The way it and all the other parts relate to one another and influence or affect one another forms the *structure* of the culture. The contribution that each part makes to the total cultural system is its *function*, in contrast to its form.

Thus the bow, whose form may be expressed in measurements and pictures, may function in meeting the needs of food getting and defense, in ritual symbolism in the religious and governmental systems, in fire making, and in musical activities. To understand all the functions of the bow in any culture, it is absolutely necessary for anthropologists to follow through all its relationships to every other related aspect of the culture. They must do this for each unit of culture, to see finally how all units work to maintain the total life-way of the people they are studying.

---

[14]Benedict, *op cit.*, p. 47.

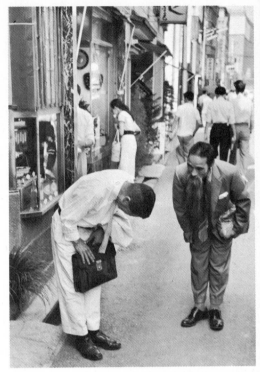

(a)

FIG. 2-1 Culture patterns situations, but patterns vary by cultures. Greetings symbolize social relations: (*a*) a Japanese student keeps physical distance and bows deeply to his professor (Marc Riboud, Magnum.); (*b*) two Arabs rub noses (Courtesy of the American Museum of Natural History); (*c*) the Latin American abrazzo emphasizes emotional expressiveness (photo by Reni Burri, Magnum).

A strange custom may seem meaningless and incomprehensible, or tantalizingly exotic, at first acquaintance. Within its cultural setting, and in relation to the basic postulates of those who practice it, and in terms of its functions within the system of which it is a part, the significance of the custom becomes scientifically meaningful. It is no longer a queer custom, but a socially significant act—always with reference to the system or structure of which it is a part. (See Fig. 2-1.)

Functionalism emphasizes the dynamics operating within a culture. It is concerned with a good deal more than the mere description of habits and customs.

A. R. Radcliffe-Brown (1881–1955), who was one of the early exponents of functionalism and who contributed a good deal to its development, has used a biological analogy to make its meaning clearer. In his words:

An animal organism is an agglomeration of cells and interstitial fluids arranged in relation to one another not as an aggregate but as an integrated whole. For the biochemist, it is a complexly integrated system of complex molecules. The system of relations by which these units are related is the organic structure. . . . [T]he organism *is not* itself the structure; it is a collection of units (cells or molecules) arranged in a structure, i.e., in a set of relations; the organism *has* a structure. Two mature animals of the same species and sex consist of similar units combined in a similar structure. The structure is thus to be defined as a set of relations between the entities. . . . As long as it lives the organism preserves a certain continuity of structure although it does not preserve the complete identity of its constituent parts. . . . Over a period its constituent cells do not remain the same. But the structural arrangement of the constituent units does remain similar. . . . [T]he life of an organism is conceived as the *functioning* of its structure . . . a cell or an organ has an *activity* and that activity has a *function*.[15]

The functions of each part are found in the

[15]A. R. Radcliffe-Brown, "On the Concept of Function in Social Science" (By permission of *American Anthropologist*, vol. 37, 1935), pp. 394–395; reprinted in A. R. Radcliffe-Brown, *Structure and Function in Primitive Society*, pp. 178–187. See also B. Malinowski, "Culture" (*Encyclopaedia of the Social Sciences*, vol. 4, 1931), pp. 621–646.

(b)

(c)

contributions the part makes to maintenance of the life process of the whole organism. So it is with culture. The functions of each custom and of each institution are found in the special contributions they make to the maintenance of the life-way that is the total culture.

Malinowski emphasized that the interrelatedness of all parts of a culture means that the modification of any single part will inevitably produce secondary changes in other parts. Missionaries and officials of governmental technical-aid-and-development programs have often overlooked this simple principle, with the result that their efforts have had many an unforeseen and unwished-for consequence. But even with the most intelligent awareness it is exceedingly difficult to foresee the ultimate social consequences of any act of induced cultural change.

The Components of Culture

Cultures are built up of *behavioral norms*, or *customs*. They are sometimes identified as *culture*

elements, which may be combined as *culture complexes*. Complexes may in turn constitute *institutions*. Norms may be classified according to the scope of applicability to the members of a societal population, namely, as *universals*, *alternatives*, and *specialties*. All these concepts are useful in the analysis of culture.

Behavioral norms and patterning

Cultural behavior is organized and patterned. This means that it is ordinarily not random but repetitive and fairly consistent. It is customary. For analytical reasons social scientists prefer to think in terms of *norms* rather than *custom*, for "custom" has too many popular meanings. A norm is the average or modal behavior of a given type that is manifested by a social group. Statistically, it means either the average or the greatest frequency of a variable. If variation is observed in a certain type of behavior on the part of a population, a count may be made of the number of times each variation occurs in a given sample. The

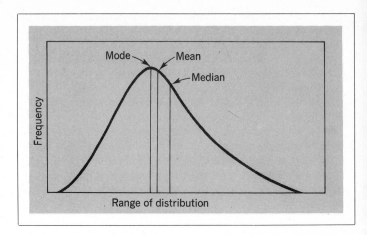

FIG. 2-2 Three kinds of norms in a skewed frequency distribution curve.

variations may be ranged in a continuous series in accordance with their degrees of likeness, with the most unlike forms at the two ends, or poles, of

FIG. 2-3 Model of a J curve. Hypothetical frequency distribution of homicides per male in an Eskimo community.

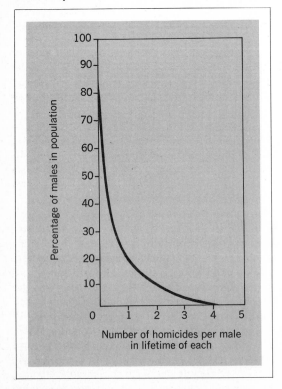

the scale. This gives the *range* of variability in the behavior. Next, the number of times each class of behavior occurs is plotted along the range of variability. This gives the *frequency distribution*. The frequency distributions may then be transferred to a graph which has the range of distribution as its base line and the frequency incidence for each class produces a *frequency-distribution curve* (Fig. 2-2).

In most situations, the curve shows a high point with a slope away on either side. This is a *bell curve*. In some situations, variation away from the high point will be in one direction only. This is a *J curve* (Fig. 2-3). A norm is a statistical expression of the most common class, called the *mode*; the average class, called the *mean*; or the middle class, called the *median*, in the total frequency distribution.

Customs are social norms statistically identified. They are that which is normal. When feasible, analyses of social behavior should be statistically based. Anthropological experience has shown, however, that it is not usually feasible to make rigorous statistical studies of all kinds of behavior. Consequently, when anthropologists describe a custom, they are usually stating what appears to be the modal behavior. Only in extremely rare cases do they make an actual statistical count of all behavior over a given period of time to determine an arithmetically accurate distribution. Such precision may be ideally desirable but under the given situation either impossible or impractical.

Modern canons of anthropology do insist on observation of the behavior described whenever possible. Yet sometimes it is not possible to observe what is recorded, since the behavior may have died out or may be secret, or the field worker may not be around at the particular time the event occurs. Therefore, to find out whether a given habit is modal or not, we frequently must take a people's word for it. They say this is what they always do, usually do, or would do if they did it at all (the hypothetical ideal).

Culture elements, complexes, and institutions

A *culture element* is a pattern of behavior (or the material product of such behavior) that may be treated as the smallest unit of its order.

Anthropologists often speak of *culture complexes*. A complex is a network of closely related patterns. For example, the activities of a dance taken together form a dance complex; the activities of the hunt form a hunting complex; the activities of child training form a child-care complex.

The complexes that are woven together in relation to the basic interests of social living are called *institutions*. For example, those concerned with subsistence activities and the production and distribution of goods are called *economic institutions*; those concerned with sex, reproduction, and kinship are called *kinship institutions*. (See Chapter 8.)

Universals, alternatives, and specialties

Norms that apply to every member of a society, such as an incest tabu (see pp. 171–178), are called *universals*. Although certain kinds of behavior may be required of everyone in a society, most cultures allow some degree of choice between norms for specific situations. These are known as *alternatives*. A Cheyenne warrior, for example, could make a personal choice between a bow and arrow, a spear, or a club wherewith to smite the Crow. Each is a norm, but one does not exclude the other within the culture as a whole.

The traits that are restricted to a particular subgroup, such as the common tabus of medicine men or the hairdos of married women, are *specialties*.

The specialties of one group may be known to the other members of the society and yet not used by them, because they are not patterns for their behavior. Many American adult men know the Boy Scout salute, having once been scouts, but they do not use it as a form of greeting after they have left scouting behind. In a complex society, however, most specialties remain unknown to most of the people. This may be because the specialties require unique aptitudes or a rigorous course of training which is undertaken by only a few, or it may be that the specialties are the secret and hidden knowledge of a few, kept within their closed circle for the benefits that may be derived from secretiveness. The result is that no individual can ever acquire or personally manifest all the elements of his or her society's culture. It means also that no anthropologist, even the most assiduous, can ever make note of, to say nothing of record, all the aspects of any culture, even the simplest known to humanity.

This, then, provides one answer to the question, often asked: "How can one speak of American culture when there is such a difference between the culture of New Yorkers and that of Kentucky mountaineers?—between the Italians of Lower Manhattan and the Scandinavians of Minnesota? —between the Yankees of Vermont and the *paisanos* of Monterey?" The universals shared by all Americans are the common binding and integrating elements of American culture and society. The specialties of the different regional groups and socioeconomic classes are internally differentiating elements which, when taken together, are referred to as subcultures.

The cohesive strength of a society is in part a product of the relative proportion of *universals* to *specialties*. In any analysis of a society and its culture, it is absolutely essential, in the interests of clarity and accuracy, never to generalize from the norms of a subgroup to make statements about the society as a whole, unless it has been observed that the norms of the subgroup are also characteristic of the whole. Americans who live west of the Hudson River and north of the Long Island Sound can appreciate the meaning of this injunction if they will reflect on their feelings about European authors who write about America after a visit to New York City.[16]

CULTURE AS CONSTRUCT OR REALITY

Do cultures really exist, or do they exist only in the imagination of the social scientist? This is a question of epistemology, or the nature of knowing. The culture whole, or *the* culture of a society, is an abstraction of a high order. When we speak of a culture, we talk as though it were a neatly taped-off entity, when in point of fact each culture is woven into other cultures at many points of intersocietal contact.

The Culture Construct

Cultures are constantly changing and modifying. Yet in anthropology we investigate a society on a field trip of greater or less duration, after which we write up a monograph describing its culture. In so doing, we fix for the moment those main lines of characteristic behavior that have been perceived and noted as though they were all taking place at any given moment. It is as though a fast-moving action had been stopped with a high-speed camera shutter to obtain an instantaneous picture. We get the main contours of the action frozen for an instant in what Linton called the *culture construct*.[17] It is a statement that lumps together descriptions of modal behavior, in which each mode typifies or represents what is actually a variable range of behavior produced in the members of a society by a given stimulus.

The Real Culture

It should be realized, then, that what we deal with in anthropology is the *culture construct* rather than the *real culture* itself. The culture construct presents the real culture as accurately as scientific methodology permits.

The real culture is what all the members of a society do and think in all their activities in their total round of living, except for truly idiosyncratic behavior. The real culture, however, is never sensed by anyone in its entirety. It can be only partially perceived as it is ordered and translated into understandable terms by the anthropologist, the philosopher, or the novelist. This is why such radically different accounts of the same society and culture can be formulated by different reporters. Reality is never known raw, for it is always processed through one's instruments of knowing. A scientific knowledge of culture can never give us the real culture; it professes only to bring the culture construct as close to the real as the most advanced and reliable methods of anthropological research make possible.

The Ideal Culture

Ideal culture consists of a people's verbally expressed standards for behavior, which may or may not be translated into normal behavior. Ideal norms are generally selected and phrased in terms of group well-being, and they are often violated when individual self-interest induces another course of action or even when hidden, or covert, values stimulate contradictory behavior.

An outstanding example of the clash between public and private interests is found in Malinowski's account of clan incest among the Trobriand Islanders:

If you were to inquire into the matter among the Trobrianders, you would find that . . . the natives show horror at the idea of violating the rules of exogamy and that they believe that sores, disease and even death might follow clan incest. . . . [But] from the point of view of the native libertine, *suvasova* (the breach of exogamy) is indeed a specially interesting and spicy form of erotic experience. Most of my informants would not only admit but actually did boast about having committed this offense or that of adultery (*kaylasi*); and I have many concrete, well-attested cases on record.[18]

The Trobriand native manages to get away with it, provided he keeps it from becoming a publicly recognized scandal, because the Trobrianders have a system of magic which ensures immunity

---

[16]The analytical concepts of universals, alternatives, and specialties were introduced into anthropology by Ralph Linton (1893–1953). See his *Study of Man*, pp. 272–275.

[17]R. Linton, *The Cultural Background of Personality*, pp. 43–46.

[18]B. Malinowski, *Crime and Custom in Savage Society*, pp. 79 and 84. By permission of Routledge & Kegan Paul, Ltd., and Humanities Press.

from the threatened diseases if a person has the proper charms. One segment of the culture provides the means for making a mockery of the other. Preservation of the clan is a social interest loudly acclaimed. Intercourse with a clan cousin is an individually motivated sport that is a genuine custom.

We need not discuss here the gaps that exist between our own ideals of democracy and our practices that negate them. It is because of such ever-present gaps between the thought and the deed, between the ideal and the action, that the realistic social scientist will not take a people's say-so as valid evidence of the real behavior norm.

THE RELATION OF SOCIETY TO CULTURE

Society and culture are not one. A human society is made up of people; a culture is made up of the behavior of people. We may say that a person belongs to a society, but it would be wrong to say that a person belongs to a culture; the individual manifests a culture.

Society Defined

Although a society is made up of people, it is more than just a human aggregation. It is a population or a group of individuals united by some common principle or principles.

A society occupies an identifiable space, for it is territorially localized even though its boundaries may not be marked by an Iron Curtain or a Great Wall of China. Its members interact in a centripetally oriented network of relationships. Even though they may have numerous contacts with the members of other societies, the majority of their activities are in relation to each other. Further, their relationships are far from random. They are patterned and ordered according to learned norms of conduct and belief which differ in some respects from their counterparts as manifested by other populations. In short, the patterns of relationships in a society are distinctive, culturally defined, and limited. Finally, the members of a society are affectively bonded by common linguistic and symbolic representations. They speak a

common language, even though there may be wide dialectic variations or even two or more distinct languages present. They are emotionally stirred to a consciousness of kind by common life experiences, myths, rituals, and other symbolic identifiers: clothing and ornaments, foods ("as American as apple pie"), totemic and tribal markers. The discovery of how fabulously intricate, imaginative, and effective the systems of symbolic representations can be in so-called primitive cultures continues to delight and interest the best-informed of anthropologists. And in our contemporary days of challenge, the alienated counterculture revolutionary strikes sensitive social nerves by turning societal symbols upside down.

In sum, a human society is: (1) a spacially identifiable population, (2) interacting in a centripetally oriented network of relations, (3) which are culturally patterned and limited, (4) distinctive in some respects from their counterparts in other cultures, and (5) affectively bonded by common linguistic and other forms of symbolic representations.

Culture and Societal Maintenance

Cultures develop as answers to the problems of individual and group living. One imperative of living is to keep alive, and all surviving biological forms are so built that a sufficient number of the species stays alive long enough to reproduce a succeeding generation. Living forms, therefore, have a built-in survival capacity relative to the environments they have experienced in the past. Cultures consist, on the one hand, of set ways of meeting the survival needs of individuals. Because of the prolonged dependency of the human infant, a stable societal and group relationship is a biological prerequisite to continuance of the species. Cultures provide individuals with ways in which to hunt and fish, make fire and tools, defend themselves, relate to other members of their society, cure their illnesses, and assuage their fears and anxieties. Cultures provide the individual with "proved" ways to meet the needs for food, shelter, safety, reproduction (sex), relaxation, and psychic security.

Societies, too, have their needs which must be met by each culture if the societies are to survive.

These have been identified as the "functional prerequisites of societal survival and continuity." The anthropologist John W. Bennett and the sociologist Melvin M. Tumin identify six such prerequisites:

(1) To maintain the biologic functioning of the group members; (2) to reproduce new members for the group; (3) to socialize new members into functioning adults; (4) to produce and distribute goods and services necessary to life; (5) to maintain order within the group, and between itself and outsiders; and (6) to define the "meaning of life" and maintain the motivation to survive and engage in the activities necessary for survival.[19]

Every cultural system therefore includes established ways of providing food, shelter, and health and of organizing sex relations, enculturation of individuals, the economy, technology, trade, government and law, war and defense, and meaningful world and religious views. (Parts 3 and 4 of this book are organized in terms of these institutions.)

It is not enough that a people *know how* to do things, however. It is also imperative that they find satisfaction in doing what they are to do. Individuals must *want* to eat, drink, and mate. Motivation on this level is so elementally physiological that societies have no great difficulty in eliciting such engagement from their members. The rewards of reproduction and enculturation of children are much less direct, however, and require adequate cultural provision. Not to work is easier than to work. To work in order to procure enough food is an automatic animal response to food deprivation. But if people are to be induced to work to satisfy secondary and derived wants in terms of self-gratification and social duty, there must be very special cultural rewards. Each society must learn how to provide the rewards that keep its workers working.

Cultures vary in the quality of the institutional devices they provide for societal survival. Traits that are ineffective or less effective in meeting the demands of the functional prerequisites reduce the efficiency and survival capacity of the society. Although cultural relativity teaches us that each custom or usage is valid in terms of its own cultural context and therefore should not be

judged morally good or bad, the fact remains that one type of trait or another may be more or less effective in serving societal ends. Societies that invent and do not control lethal customs are doomed. Thus, if the notion that sex is evil and incompatible with the pure life were spread to all the members of a society, resulting in the practice of enjoined celibacy, that society would soon be extinguished because the secondary prerequisite, that of reproduction of new members for the group, would not have been met. Today, the great danger which threatens us all is the development through technology of the potentially lethal trait of uncontrolled use of atomic energy in war.

Cultures are humanity's means of improved survival, but cultures are limited by biological and social imperatives. They need not be implicitly successful.

Finally, the most human of all the functions of culture is to define the meaning of life and to maintain the motivation to keep going. The humanities are called "the humanities" because they search for the humane in an individual's work—that which provides the psychological commitment to life and society on the part of the animal being who has reached the state of development wherein he or she can demand to know: "What is it all about?"

THE RELATION OF RACE TO CULTURE

All the living members of the human family (the hominids) form one genus and one species, named *Homo sapiens*. Within this single species there are no two individuals (except for identical twins) who are exactly alike in genetic make-up. Attend any gathering of human beings and it is easy to observe that there is much variability within the general similarity of those present. Beyond the variability of a local group, any world traveler can observe different clusters of physical traits in different populations. Such populations are what are commonly referred to as the races of mankind, or, in taxonomic terms, as subspecies within the species *Homo sapiens*.

Frequently it can be observed that human subspecies not only look alike physically but also behave similarly or have a common culture and form a discrete society. This pattern of correlation

---

[19]J. W. Bennett and M. M. Tumin, *Social Life*, pp. 45–59. By permission of Alfred A. Knopf, Inc., copyright © 1945.

between physically similar groups of human beings and clusters of similar cultural behavior raises the question:."Do physically similar clusters of people behave similarly because of their common racial or genetic make-up?" A more specific question frequently asked is: "Does racial variation cause differences in cultural behavior and intelligence?" The anthropologist's response to both of these queries is: "No!" The scientific basis for this negative response resides in both: (1) the results of the physical anthropological study of the causes of human variation and its correlation with cultural behavior and (2) the anthropological knowledge (discussed at the beginning of this chapter) that culture is learned, noninstinctive, nongenetically determined behavior. Anthropologists know that physically similar clusters of people may share similar behavior patterns, but their research demonstrates that this sharing of culture is due to common culture learning (enculturation), common adaptation to similar environments, and intercommunication, and that it is not due to a common genetic background.

The study of human race falls within the anthropological subdiscipline of physical anthropology and ideally requires a background knowledge of biological taxonomy, evolution, and population genetics. Cultural anthropologists must also be familiar with the nature of human physical variability so that they may separate the biological aspects of race from the cultural. Only then can the two aspects of race (physiology and behavior) be rationally analyzed and sensibly controlled.

Closed and Open Genetic Systems: Species and Subspecies Defined

Biologists define a Mendelian population (the population unit within which genetic stability and change is measured) as a localized grouping of members of a species who interbreed mostly among themselves but occasionally with members of sister populations within the species. A species is defined as one or more populations whose members are capable of intrabreeding among themselves, while at the same time they are incapable of interbreeding with members of other species, or they do not habitually do so. Put

in other words, this involves: (1) community of inheritance among the members, (2) capacity of the genes to spread throughout the group, and (3) inhibition of genes spreading to other groups.[20] Each species is therefore genetically isolated from all other species. It is a *closed genetic system*. Members of the species *Homo sapiens* are incapable of interbreeding with any other animals; therefore, they constitute a closed genetic system.

Within a species, however, populations may be found which possess gene pools in which certain genes occur in frequencies different from their frequencies in other populations. These populations may be distinguished as *subspecies* or *races*. They have somewhat differing inheritances, or gene pools. However, the members of the several populations are not incapable of interbreeding and exchanging genes. They are *open genetic systems* (Fig. 2-4). Within a species, genetic systems by their very nature can be readily altered by genetic inputs from other populations; they can also initiate their own genetic changes which are not merely the result of mutations.

If the changes within a gene pool of a subspecies population accumulate to the point where exchanges of genetic materials can no longer take place with other subspecies populations, then the two populations have become, by definition, separate and distinct species. There is no evidence that any such genetically isolated subgroups of *Homo sapiens* have existed since Middle Pleistocene times, and this is why we can say there is only one species of human beings, *Homo sapiens*.

The kind of population commonly meant when people talk about race is an aggregation of people who have inhabited in the past, and who still do inhabit to a great extent, a given continent or a large section of a continent. Such populations tend to be sufficiently isolated from the inhabitants of other continents so that they have more common ancestors among themselves than they share with other populations on other continents. These populations are open genetic systems that tend to interbreed but can breed out with other continental or subcontinental aggregates.

---

[20] I. M. Lerner, *Heredity, Evolution, and Society*, p. 16.

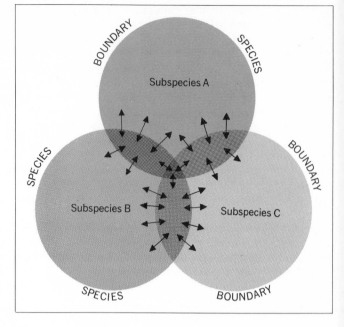

FIG. 2-4 A species is a closed genetic system. Its members are incapable of interbreeding with those of other species; therefore, it receives no genes from any other species. On the other hand, the Mendelian populations which constitute subspecies, or races, are open genetic systems. Although the members of a subspecies usually intrabreed, they are capable of interbreeding within the species; hence, some genes are transmitted from one subspecies to another.

In current anthropological usage, such races are called *geographic* races. A geographic race is a human population that has inhabited a continental land mass or an island chain sufficiently long enough to have developed its own distinctive genetic composition, as compared with that of other continental populations.

Within a continent, there may be barriers to easy intermixture of the continental population. Thus, the people of the North Baltic area of Europe interbreed among themselves to a much greater extent than they do with the people of the Mediterranean belt of southern Europe. They can be distinguished as subpopulations, localized over broad areas *within* a continent or island chain. This produces a lower-level classification of races called *local* races, such as the European subgeographic groups of the Nordic, Alpine, and Mediterranean regions.[21] These local races are also open genetic systems. There is no evidence at present that any known geographic or local

races of *Homo sapiens* are sufficiently different genetically to prevent successful interbreeding with other geographic or local races. Clearly, the genetic similarities between all subspecific groups of human beings are physiologically more significant than the differences; the differences are not severe enough to prevent subgroup interfertility.

Race and Cultural Capacity

In 1777, when the American Colonies were struggling to win their war of independence, William Robertson, the clearest thinker of the eighteenth century in terms of modern anthropology, wrote in Scotland:

A human being as he comes originally from the hand of nature, is everywhere the same. At his first appearance in the state of infancy, whether it be among the rudest savages, or in the most civilized nations, we can discern no quality which marks any distinction or superiority. The capacity of improvement seems to be the same and the talents he may afterwards acquire, as well as the virtues he may be rendered capable of exercising, depend, in a great measure, upon the state of society in

·¹S. M. Garn and C. S. Coon, ''On the Number of Races of Mankind'' (*American Anthropologist*, vol. 57, 1955), pp. 996–1001. See also S. M. Garn, *Human Races*, chap. 2; and C. S. Coon, S. M. Garn, and J. B. Birdsell, *Races: A Study of Race Formation in Man*.

which he is placed. To this state his mind naturally accommodates itself, and from it receives discipline and culture. . . . It is only by attending to this great principle, that we can discover what is the character of man in every different period of his progress.[22]

Time has not altered, nor the doctrines of racism impaired, the clarity of this simple truth.

In this century, there have been numerous efforts, beginning with the first intelligence tests administered to American soldiers in World War I, to test the validity of the proposition that there are (or are not) significant differences in the behavioral potentials of different races. After fifty years of ingenious, and also ingenuous, efforts in psychological measurements, the evidence from psychology is largely inconclusive.[23] It does, however, demonstrate several points: (1) So-called intelligence tests measure innate skill plus cultural experience. No test has yet been evolved that can eliminate the cultural factor, and differential ratings of the various races in intelligence tests must be critically evaluated. (2) Aptitude tests do reveal racial differentials in visual, motor, and vocal skills, but these too are subject to cultural influences that have not been eliminated in tests and measurements. (3) Many skills of intelligence and aptitude definitely change when the cultural environment changes.

The whole result of scientific race psychology has been to throw the explanation of significant behavior differences among people of different races over into the field of cultural experience. The findings of psychology harmonize with those of anthropology and history, which we treat simultaneously in the next section.

Race and Culture History

It is the judgment of anthropologists that all races are equally capable of cultural development and that culture operates independently of racial heredity. How, then, it is often asked, can it be that some races are culturally more advanced than others? How does one account for the fact that the Africans did not attain civilization until it was brought to them by Europeans? Is it not true that the highest modern civilizations have been developed by the European whites?

Three principles must be grasped in formulating the answers to these questions: (1) Although all cultures are fundamentally similar in their nuclear cores, the range of cultural variability as manifested by human societies is truly remarkable. Limits to the range of culture are imposed by the physical nature of human beings. These limits are so basic and so generalized, however, that they are common to all races of mankind. The forms of variation are the result of the processes of culture growth, not of racial predisposition. (2) The behavior and cultural ingenuity of different peoples within any given race are so variable that obviously the racial factor can be of little importance. (3) The same people may exhibit astounding cultural energy at one period of their history and be almost wholly devoid of it at another. Peoples who have been culturally quiescent for centuries suddenly burst into a veritable fury of cultural development without any determinable change in racial composition. The Japanese are the most spectacular example in modern times.

It is easy for North Europeans and their descendants to forget how late they came to the forefront of civilization and cultural development. The centers of cultural invention did not shift to northern Europe until the Renaissance, only 500 years ago. During the Dark Ages, the Maya Indians of Central America showed greater cultural accomplishments than the European whites.

The history of the Uto-Aztecans is also pertinent. The Aztecs, Comanches, and Shoshones are all Indians who speak similar languages indicative of a common historical background. They are racially quite similar, and 700 years ago they stood as lowly hunters and gatherers at the bottom of the cultural scale, living in the western deserts of North America and possessing a meager cultural inventory. Historical events radically altered their basic characters and cultural development.

The Aztecs wandered southward until they settled in what is now Central Mexico among several long-established high cultures. In A.D. 1325, they

---

[22]W. Robertson, *History of America*, vol. 1, pp. 368–369.
[23]See especially the comprehensive article by the geneticists W. F. Bodmer and L. L. Cavalli-Sforza, "Intelligence and Race" (*Scientific American*, vol. 223, 1970), pp. 19–29, who conclude (p. 29): ". . . currently available data are inadequate to resolve this question in either direction."

founded Tenochtitlán (the present Mexico City), and 175 years later they were overlords of the land: maize growers, road builders, astronomers, artists, and possessors of a city with public buildings of cut stone so magnificent that Cortez cried out that in all Andalusia there was nothing to compare with the glory of this city.

The Comanches wandered into the southwestern plains at a somewhat later date. There they acquired Spanish horses and guns and came into contact with the warlike tradition of the Plains tribes. They became truculent, nomadic robbers and fighters, so violent that to this day the plainsman's saying, "as wild as a Comanche," is still heard in the West.

The Shoshones, who retained the attitudes and culture once shared with the Comanches, obtained neither guns nor horses. They were regularly mauled by the Blackfeet, who had guns and horses, so they timidly hid out in the desert—peaceable, because they dared not make war. They developed a strong inferiority complex, and they are the only Indians the senior author of this book has ever worked with who welcomed the coming of the whites. "If the white man had not come, there would be no Indians left," they said. By Indians, they meant themselves.

As circumstances found them, the Aztecs and Comanches had become definitely achieving people, and the Shoshones miserable by any man's count. But race was a constant element. The accidents of culture history had frowned upon the Shoshones.

What causes cultural spurts is a complex and difficult question that must be analyzed in terms of cultural process. Outstanding among the multitude of factors is cross-fertilization of cultures, the stimulation of new ideas and new ways of coping with the environment. Isolated peoples always stagnate, whether they are Asian, African, or European. But the bent of the culture is important too—a backward-looking, ancestor-worshipping culture is not readily amenable to change and further development. The physical environment is also influential. All these can be shown to be active factors. But since it cannot be shown that races differ in the possession of hereditary mentality and capacities, because the performance of different groups within a single

race ranges from high to low, and because the performance of a single racial group varies so markedly through time, it becomes evident that race per se is of small moment in cultural achievement. Culture, not race, is the molder of human societies.

The UNESCO Statement on Race

In summarizing the evidence about the influence of racial differences on cultural behavior, we can do no better than cite the closing paragraphs of the *Statement on Race*, formulated in 1950 by an expert panel of physical anthropologists and geneticists convened in Paris by the United Nations Educational, Scientific, and Cultural Organization. It reads as follows:

We have thought it worth while to set out in a formal manner what is at present scientifically established concerning individual and group differences.

(*a*) In matters of race, the only characteristics which anthropologists have so far been able to use effectively as a basis for classification are physical (anatomical and physiolgoical).

(*b*) Available scientific knowledge provides no basis for believing that the groups of mankind differ in their innate capacity for intellectual and emotional development.

(*c*) Some biological differences between human beings within a single race may be as great as or greater than the same biological differences between races.

(*d*) Vast social changes have occurred that have not been connected in any way with changes in racial type. Historical and sociological studies thus support the view that genetic differences are of little significance in determining the social and cultural differences between different groups of men.

(*e*) There is no evidence that race mixture produces disadvantageous results from a biological point of view. The social results of race mixture, whether for good or ill, can generally be traced to social factors.[24]

The anthropological study of race does not end with this accumulation of facts and theory which indicate that genetic differences between subgroups of human beings do not cause cultural differences. Instead, the focus of the study of race

---

[24]For the entire statement, see H. L. Shapiro, "Revised Version of UNESCO Statement on Race" (*American Journal of Physical Anthropology*, vol. 10, 1952), pp. 363–368. By permission of Wistar Press.

and culture shifts to the investigation of how physical differences between populations are perceived by different cultures and how these perceptions influence human behavior. The analysis of this topic often falls within the anthropological study of social organization. Research concerning the patterns of how people mark and treat social differences between subgroups of people has revealed the use of physical differences to signal and rationalize social differentiation. This subject is studied as an aspect of the analysis of social classes and castes (see Chapter 16).

SELECTED READINGS

Benedict, R., *Patterns of Culture* (1934). The classic formulation of the idea of cultural configuration in relation to ideal personality types. Persuasively written in fine literary style, it should not be taken as a reliable ethnography of the cultures discussed, although its major theme is acceptable.

Klass, M., and H. Hellman, *The Kinds of Mankind: An Introduction to Race and Racism* (1971). An exploration of the biological differences between human beings and the possible causes of this variation. The authors also discuss the relation between human variation and intelligence and suggest why there is so much confusion and controversy about human variation.

Kroeber, A. L., and C. Kluckhohn, *Culture: A Critical Review of Concepts and Definitions* (Papers of the Peabody Museum of American Archaeology and Ethnology, Harvard University, vol. 47, 1952). An encyclopedic survey and analysis of the concept of culture. Possibly not of much interest to the beginner, but a very useful guide nonetheless. Now available in a paperback edition (1964).

Langness, L. L., *The Study of Culture* (1974). A brief critical historical summary of the major theoretical trends in anthropology that have developed as dominant perspectives in the study of culture.

Levy, M. J., Jr., *Modernization and the Structure of Societies* (1966). A detailed two-volume presentation of the structures and functions of society that differentiate relatively modern from nonmodern groups.

Montagu, M. F. A. (ed.), *The Concept of Race* (1964). Eleven essays by ten anthropologists, biologists, and zoologists challenging the traditional social and biological concepts of race. These readings especially focus on the question of whether it is valid to conclude that human races exist.

Singer, M., "Culture: The Concept of Culture" (International Encyclopedia of the Social Sciences, vol. 3, 1968), pp. 527–543. Summarizes and compares the competing theories of culture and social structure in anthropology.

Social Science Quarterly (vol. 53, no. 2, 1972), *The Idea of Culture in the Social Sciences*. Nine papers by authorities representing several social science disciplines and illustrating how the concept of culture is applied to an understanding of human behavior.

Spuhler, J. N., *The Evolution of Man's Capacity for Culture* (1959). A symposium discussing factors relating to the development of the capacity to create and maintain culture.

UNESCO, *The Race Concept* (1952). A balanced evaluation of the idea of race: what it is and what it is not.

3

CULTURE CHANGE

LEARNING GOALS

List some of the factors which bring about change in human cultures. ¶ Discriminate between invention and a discovery, and discuss the role of accidental juxtaposition. ¶ Note the nature of diffusion, and give some examples of cross-cultural borrowing in both the material and the nonutilitarian realms. ¶ Cite the factors which determine whether a given culture trait will be borrowed or rejected. ¶ Define acculturation, and discuss the effect of force versus volition in producing culture change. ¶ Characterize culture crisis, reactive movements, and identify the contexts in which they may develop.

As we plunge into the Atomic Space Age, technological change and social transformations are the order of the day. Both are the products of the most far-reaching cultural revolution that humanity will have experienced in the five million years of its existence up to A.D. 2000. We have seen that culture is a system of learned behaviors. Although human behaviors can become standardized as habits or social usage, behavior is always variable, even when it is habit-bound. Because of this propensity to variability, it is impossible to fix behavior absolutely so that it never changes. Since culturally patterned behavior is learned and not fixed in the organism, it is modifiable and flexible. Therefore, cultures are changeable. Rates of change vary from place to place and from time to time. Some cultures have grown and changed with great rapidity; others have remained relatively stable for hundreds of thousands of years. Archaeologists have discovered that the changes in Stone Age cultures from generation to generation were minuscule and that it took tens of thousands of years to develop even so simple a thing as a chipped-stone hand ax. Yet the culture of Japan changed from that of a feudal-peasant society to that of a front-rank industrial society in less than one hundred years.

The problem of differential rates of culture growth intrigues and puzzles the lay person and the scientist alike. Truly satisfactory answers cannot yet be given, but certainly a start can be made. At this point let us consider the mechanisms of culture change and growth.

Culture changes by accretion of inventions and the modification or replacement of old ways. An individual culture changes and grows by acceptance of inventions devised by members of its own society or by acceptance of new ways invented elsewhere and brought to the attention of its members through diffusion and borrowing of ideas and behaviors. Acceptance and rejection of changes is not random, but as with culture building (see The Integration of Culture in Chapter 2, pp. 21–23) fundamental cultural postulates operate to provide guidelines for change; unless of course it is the fundamental cultural postulates themselves that are changing. Therefore, the analysis of culture change must include not only a consideration of what is available that is new to a culture but also how the potential change will integrate with or be modified by the ideology and structure of the culture.

INVENTION AND DISCOVERY

What is an invention? Does it differ in any way from a discovery? These questions are not merely of theoretical importance for analytical purposes. They are of tremendous practical significance in the operation of modern patent law, under which an invention is patentable while a discovery is not.

In the view of a United States District Court of Appeals, for example, a valuable patent on the process of irradiation of foodstuffs by exposure to ultraviolet light was invalid because it merely utilized a physicochemical process that has existed since life began. A distinction is drawn between the invention of a lamp for artificially producing ultraviolet light and the discovery that exposure to ultraviolet rays increases the vitamin content of the exposed organic materials. The one is patentable—that is, subject to certain legal limitations; the other is not.[1]

A discovery is the act of becoming aware of something which has been in existence but which has not been previously perceived. Vitamins and sunspots were discovered, not invented.

An invention is an alteration in, or a synthesis of, preexistent materials, conditions, or practices so as to produce a new form of material or action. We must, therefore, deal with new patterns of action that are translated into concrete form (material inventions), and also with inventions that remain in the realm of nonmaterial action patterns solely. The latter are sometimes called *social inventions* or, by philosophers, *moral inventions*.

To illustrate the distinction between discovery and invention more fully, it might be noted that the first ninety-two elements, from hydrogen to uranium, were *discovered* by means of scientific perception. But the new transuranium elements, such as neptunium and plutonium, which have come into being since 1940, are truly *invented* elements. They were not found to exist in nature; they were produced as a result of human ingenuity in the development of techniques for separating neutrons from their elemental nucleus and causing them to enter another elemental nucleus without producing fission. New combinations of

protons, neutrons, and electrons were produced—hence, the new elements.

However, to invent or discover something (we are not here speaking of discovering a new continent or a mountain) involves a mental act, one which requires that two or more existing things be conceptually broken into parts and that one, or some, of the parts be modified or replaced or recombined so that a new structure exists. Homer Barnett, the anthropologist who has devoted more thinking and research to the problem of cultural innovation than any other in our time, uses the invention of producer gas as one example of this process:

Innumerable people have known that vapors emitted from crevices in certain parts of the earth are inflammable. About 1684, John Clayton verified reports of this phenomenon in Lancashire and then proceeded to produce such a gas himself. Conjecturing that there was a relationship between the gas, the earth's heat, and the coal deposits in nearby mines, he applied heat to coal placed in a retort . . . as a substitute for the earth. . . . Then, in a second step, he caught the released gas . . . in a bladder . . . formerly used for many . . . [other purposes], instead of letting it escape into the atmosphere. . . . He punctured the bladder with a pin, brought a candle flame near the vent, and so produced the precursor of gas lights and burners.[2]

Clayton *discovered* that a volatile, flammable gas is locked in a solid state in coal; he *invented* an artificial technique for releasing and capturing it. In each act, however, there is a common element. Invention creates a new material combination by synthesizing a new idea from previously disconnected ideas. Discovery involves a new perception of something that has been present but unnoticed because preexisting ideas were not equipped to deal with it. Until such time as someone performs the mental act of separating and isolating the unnoticed event from its natural context and then recombining it with other things in a new way, it has no recognized significance; it remains undiscovered. This was the case, for instance, when ultraviolet rays were isolated from

---

[1] *Vitamin Technologists v. Wisconsin Alumni Research Foundation* (*Federal Reports*, 2d series, vol. 146, 1945), pp. 941ff.

[2] H. G. Barnett, "The Innovative Process" (*Kroeber Anthropological Society Papers*, no. 25, 1961), p. 32. By permission of Kroeber Anthropological Society.

sunlight, artifically produced, and applied to cereals and milk.

Volitional invention of this order is a rational process of imaginative substitutions and recombinations. It represents the most sophisticated level of cultural modification. Such a process is characteristic only of highly complicated societies with a cultural bent toward dynamic change. Even among advanced civilized nations, relatively few include within their populations a great number of active, willful inventors.

Because invention is highly valued and richly rewarded in our culture, many aspiring minds struggle to find new relations as solutions to set problems. In the process of volitional invention, the inventor recognizes a need or thinks that there is an insufficiency in some form or function. The inventor sets a problem for solution on the basis of this recognized need and proceeds from this point to attempt a rational solution in the form of a practicable invention.

Accidental Juxtaposition and Invention

In the primitive world, volitional inventiveness is truly a rare occurrence. Conscious tinkering with the social structure or with gadgetary improvement is not the order of the day. Most primitive inventions are nonvolitional. They result from what Greenman has called *accidental juxtaposition*.[3]

The operation of the principle of accidental juxtaposition on the crudest level may be illustrated by the activities of Sultan, one of Köhler's famous apes. Sultan was presented with a problem—how to get a banana. He was also presented with two hollow bamboo sticks, neither long enough in itself to reach the banana. They were so fashioned, however, that one could be snugly fitted within the other to make a stick long enough to meet the need. An invention was called for, and the means were at hand. Sultan strained his simian brain for a solution, but the best he could work out was to push one stick toward the banana with the other. This failed to capture the banana. At length, like many another disgusted inventor, he gave up. His efforts at volitional invention were

a flat failure. He dropped the sticks and turned his attention to less frustrating activities.

As he roamed around his cage looking for amusement, his attention was once more directed to the sticks. He picked them up and began to play with them in a casual manner and entirely without interest in the elusive banana. Suddenly he found himself holding the two sticks end to end. He pushed the one into the other. Lo, he had it! Accidental juxtaposition had resulted in a new set of relationships, a synthesized combination that constituted an invention. At this critical point, his intelligence was equal to the occasion. He could recognize a useful relationship when he saw it. Immediately he went to the bars, used his tool, and swallowed the banana.[4]

We actually know very little of the precise steps by which most primitive inventions came into being. Long archaeological sequences such as those established for Old World and Southwest prehistory reveal the external form of the gradual steps by which many artifacts have been developed over generations of time. A less empirical method, of which earlier anthropologists were quite fond, was to reconstruct the inventive steps by mesological inference. This is a most intriguing pastime, but too often the result is more "just so" story than objective substantiated analysis worthy of scientific attention.

The Cheyenne Indian account of the invention of the tipi is of this order. Grinnell recorded that:

The first lodge of modern shape is said to have been suggested by a man who was handling a large poplar leaf, and quite by accident bent it into the shape of a cone—that is to say, of a lodge, such as are used today. As he looked at the leaf it flashed into his mind that a shelter like it would be better than those they then had. He showed it to the people, and they made lodges in the shape of this leaf, and have used them ever since.[5]

Although it is extremely unlikely that any Cheyenne Indian invented the conical lodge in this manner,[6] the story illustrates quite perfectly the operation of the principle of juxtaposition. Sul-

---

[3]E. F. Greenman, "Material Culture and the Organism" (*American Anthropologist*, vol. 47, 1945), pp. 212ff.

[4]W. Köhler, *The Mentality of Apes*, pp. 130–133.
[5]G. B. Grinnell, *The Cheyenne Indians*, vol. 1, p. 50. By permission of Yale University Press.
[6]The Cheyennes did not acquire the conical skin tipi until well into the nineteenth century. Other Plains and Woodlands tribes had it before them, so it is quite certain that the Cheyennes borrowed the idea.

tan's invention was the result of the close juxtaposition of two objects, the sticks; the supposed invention of the Cheyenne tipi was the result of the juxtaposition of two mental images, the cone formed by the leaf and the potential house. The two accomplishments together exemplify Greenman's final definition of juxtaposition:

The creation of a new implement as the sequel to the establishment of a close spatial relationship between two or more objects, or of a close temporal relationship between the mental images of two or more objects, by natural or artificial means without foreknowledge of the result.[7]

In the technical field, therefore, the creation of a new type of artifact as a result of juxtaposition is a mental reaction to a stimulus in the environment. For the most part, "the progressive evolution of technical forms had to wait upon such accidental juxtapositions."[8]

Of course, accidental juxtaposition can lead to inventive errors as well as to beneficial creativeness. The heavy freight of shibboleths, nonsense tabus, and false dogma carried through the ages by mankind results from erroneous association of images in juxtaposition.

Furthermore, mere juxtaposition does not in itself automatically generate an invention. The use, meaning, and function of particular artifacts or social forms may be such as to block acceptance of new forms, uses, meanings, and functions that are proposed in conjunction with the new inventive ideas. Resistance to new inventions is proverbial, and inventors are by no means always heroes.

Any new idea or new form must find its first creation somewhere, and at a specific time. Therefore it would be the height of foolishness to deny all inventiveness to primitive men. Were they not inventive, cultures would never have changed. There would be none of the rich diversity in cultures which anthropology has discovered for us, nor would there have been any evolution of culture whatsoever through the ages. But the protracted span of the Old Stone Age—nearly five million years of hunting and gathering technology before the domestication of plants and animals—testifies to the rarity of innovation before the dawn of civilization.

The vast majority of human societies can claim relatively few inventions to their credit. Abundant evidence proves that most trait accretions occur through borrowing, and this leads us to a consideration of diffusion.

DIFFUSION OF CULTURE TRAITS

When we find a particular trait or trait complex spread over a wide area and practiced by a number of different tribes, we are confronted with several theoretical possibilities. Each tribe may have invented the same trait independently; one tribe may have invented it, after which it spread to the others by borrowing; or several may have invented it separately, after which it spread over the area.

We can safely say that the first hypothesis is an impossibility. Historical observation establishes that all peoples are always borrowing from others. We know, for instance, that Indians did not invent the domestication of the horse, nor the art of riding, nor halters, bits, reins, saddles, or any of the other accouterments of riding. They were all adopted from the Spaniards, first by the tribes of the Southwest frontier, who passed them on to the north and east.[9] An interesting fact to note is that the Western saddle, horn-pommeled and deep-backed, was copied from the Spanish saddle, as was the Indian's. But the Eastern riding saddle is copied from the English type that made its first appearance in the New World on the Atlantic Coast. The McClelland army saddle is a fusion of the two types.

Even such simple matters as hide dressing are acquired by borrowing. According to Grinnell:

When the Cheyennes first found the buffalo, they had no knowledge as to how to dress hides. Later, the Sioux on the east side of the Missouri showed them how to cut hides in two, dress them, and sew them together again. These they used as robes. After they reached the Black

---

[7]Greenman, *op. cit.*, p. 215. By permission of *American Anthropologist*.

[8]*Ibid.*, p. 218.

[9]C. Wissler, "The Influence of the Horse in the Development of Plains Culture." (*American Anthropologist*, vol. 16, 1914), pp. 1–25; F. Haines, "Where Did the Plains Indians Get Their Horses?" (*American Anthropologist*, vol. 40, 1938), pp. 112–117; also "The Northward Spread of Horses among the Plains Indians" (*American Anthropologist*, vol. 40, 1938), pp. 429–437.

Hills the Kiowas and Comanches taught the Cheyennes how to dress buffalo-hides in one piece, and also showed them the use of a mixture for softening the hide.[10]

The Diffusion of Material Culture

Material culture and mechanical processes of technology are much more readily borrowed than ideas and abstract concepts.

No one has expressed this more impressively than the two missionaries to the Shipibo of the Upper Amazon, Fathers Girbal and Marques, who in 1792 wrote to their headquarters:

To reap it wholly and to bring to God all these heathens certain things are necessary, of which we are in need and of which we shall be in need. Send them to us; God and our most blessed father San Francois will know how to acknowledge it. . . . You will find added to our letter a note of these requisitions. . . . 400 axes, 600 cutlasses, 2000 straight knives, 1000 curved knives, 4 quintos of iron, 50 pounds of steel, 12 books of small fish-hooks, 8000 needles, one case of false pearls, 500 flints and steels, 4 gross of scissors, 2 gross of rings, 3000 brass crosses, 1000 varas of calico to cover the skin of those who are naked, an assortment of colours to paint our church, a very immaculate Virgin and some ornaments. We also want two skins of wine, both for the celebration of the holy sacrifice and to stop diarrhoea and bloody flux among the infidels.[11]

Fathers Girbal and Marques sensed that if metal were first accepted, *then* these Stone Age gardeners might be ready to consider a new religion, the assumption being that a superior technology is the product of a more powerful mastery of the supernatural.

It does not take long to perceive the value of iron implements. Captain Cook, who was deified by the native Hawaiians in 1779, was later killed by them when he tried to recover one of his ship's longboats which had been stolen so it could be stripped of its metal parts. It was thirty years later that Hawaiians decided to abandon their old ideational order and social system for the culture presented by sailors and missionaries; they realized that the material and ideational aspects of that culture went together, and they wanted both—plus the fact that certain members of the Hawaiian royal family (especially the women) found the tabu and social class system increasingly onerous and repugnant.[12]

The Tiwi of Australia, according to Hart and Pilling,

. . . were first drawn out of their hostile insularity by curiosity and the desire for iron, the same factors which had attracted them toward the Portuguese a century earlier. Iron looted from shipwrecks, channel markers, and the camps of casual visitors to the islands was not sufficient; the Tiwi desired a permanent avenue by which they could obtain the metal. The oldest Tiwi in the early 1950's stated that during the 1890's the Tiwi began to feel that opportunity was passing them by as they noted ship after ship sail in and out of Darwin; the islanders therefore came to the conclusion that they wanted a permanent European settlement in their midst, like the earlier Fort Dundas, for only in this way could they be guaranteed an uninterrupted source of iron.[13]

It is much easier to establish a steel mill in a newly developing country than it is to diffuse the ideology and processes of Western democratic political culture—a simple fact, belatedly recognized by many who hoped for too much, too rapidly, from American foreign-aid programs.

The Diffusion of Nonutilitarian Culture

Complex nonutilitarian culture structures also spread through borrowing. In reconstructing histories of cultures, a number of similar traits are frequently found to have existed in two or more cultures. It is a canon of anthropological analysis that such similarities are the probable result of diffusion rather than of independent invention, especially if the group of traits has no inherent reason for existing as a complex.

Tylor was the first to formulate and apply this principle in a study of the diffusion of the ancient East Indian game of pachisi into prehistoric Amer-

---

[10]Grinnell, *op. cit.*, p. 52. By permission of Yale University Press.

[11]Quoted in H. Hoffman, "Money, Ecology, and Acculturation among the Shipibo of Peru," in W. H. Goodenough (ed.), *Explorations in Cultural Anthropology*, p. 266. By permission of McGraw-Hill Book Co.

[12]W. Davenport, "The 'Hawaiian Cultural Revolution': Some Political and Economic Considerations" (*American Anthropologist*, vol. 71, 1969), pp. 1–20.

[13]C. W. M. Hart and A. R. Pilling, *The Tiwi of North Australia*, p. 100. By permission of Holt, Rinehart and Winston, Inc.

ica, where it appeared among the Aztecs as *patolli* and in various other forms among other Indians.[14] Tylor undertook to prove the historical connection between the Asiatic and American forms of these games by "analysing such phenomena into constituent elements showing so little connection with one another that they may reasonably be treated as independent. The more numerous such elements, the more improbable the recurrence of the combination."[15]

Myths

The technique may be applied to any aspect of culture,[16] but there is a remarkable stability in myth complexes the world over.

Frazer's *Folklore in the Old Testament* is a fascinating study of comparative distributions of Old World myth complexes and is challenging reading. For our demonstration of the application of the principle of diffusion analysis by means of internal congruity of traits, we shall use the "Tale of the Wandering Animals."

This story is familiar to all readers of Grimm's *Fairy Tales* as the "Musicians of Bremen." The old donkey, the worn-out hound, the abused cat, the rooster destined for the pot, and other rejected, decrepit animals all joined forces to go to the fair port of Bremen to become *Stadtmusikantern*. Night closed in on them as they found themselves deep in the woods. Frightening a band of robbers out of a forest hut, they made themselves at home, each in his favorite spot—the cat on the hearth, the rooster in the rafters, the dog on the doorstep, the donkey on the dungheap. The robbers sent back a spy in the darkness. But when he lighted the fire, the cat flew in his face; the dog chewed

his leg as he fled through the door; the donkey planted a kick; and the rooster crowed his doom. The weak and despised creatures frightened away the robbers, who are symbolic of those who normally rule and dominate "the little man," and lived prosperously ever after in the nice snug little hut in the woods.

In Southeast Asia and Japan an ancient story is told, which in its simplest outline runs as follows.

An egg, a scorpion, a needle, a piece of feces, and a rice mortar (or any hard, heavy object) came together upon a journey. They entered the house of an old woman during her absence, and in order to do her harm, they disposed themselves in different places. The egg lay on the hearth, the scorpion in the water basin, the needle on the floor, the feces in the doorway, and the mortar over the door. When the old woman came home in the evening, she went to the hearth to light the fire, but the egg sprang up and smeared her face. When she went to the basin to wash, she was stung by the scorpion. Seized by terror, she rushed from the house, but the needle stuck in her foot; she slipped on the feces and was upset, and the mortar fell on her head, killing her.[17]

Here is the "Musicians of Bremen" all over again. Aarne justifiably concluded: "The concurrences between the tales are so significant that in my opinion we must conclude that the stories stand in an interdependent relationship in their origin."[18] He traced the story through India, into South Russia, up through Central Europe, and into Germany, where it arrived in the late Middle Ages.

Now let us shift our attention to the Northwest Coast of North America. A favored story of the Northwest Coast Indians has now a familiar ring. It is "Raven's War on the South Wind."[19] Raven is the mythological culture hero of this area, and the South Wind often brings too much rain from the ocean.

The South Wind, so the story runs, was blowing so incessantly that all the creatures had to stay in their huts. They could not hunt, and they were

---

[14]E. B. Tylor, "On the Game of Patolli in Ancient Mexico, and Its Probable Asiatic Origin" (*Journal of the Royal Anthropological Institute of Great Britain and Ireland*, vol. 8, 1879), pp. 116–129.

[15]E. B. Tylor, "American Lot Games as Evidence of Asiatic Intercourse before the Time of Columbus" (*Internationales Archiv fur Ethnographie*, vol. 9, supplement, 1896), p. 66. For a critical evaluation of Tylor's method, see C. J. Erasmus, "Patolli, Pachisi, and the Limitation of Possibilities" (*Southwestern Journal of Anthropology*, vol. 6, 1950), pp. 369–387.

[16]F. Boas, *Tsimshian Mythology* (Bureau of American Ethnology, Annual Report 31, 1916), pp. 393–558. This is the classic study of the reflection of a people's material culture and social organization in their mythology.

[17]A. Aarne, *Die Tiere auf der Wanderschaft* (Folklore Fellows Communications, no. 11, 1913), p. 100.

[18]*Ibid.*, p. 162.

[19]Eleven versions are recorded in Boas, *op. cit.*, pp. 79–81, 658–660.

hungry. The smoke blew back down their smoke vents and made their eyes sore. At last Raven called a council of war to propose an attack on the Master of the South Wind. A special canoe was procured, and the war party made the journey to the home of the South Wind. They had trouble landing because the gale caused by the flatulence of the Master of the South Wind was so strong that they were nearly overcome.

But once ashore, Halibut and Flounder or Skate (all flat, slippery fish) arranged themselves according to Raven's orders just outside the South Wind's doorstep. Red Cod or the Wren went in and started a smudge (in another version, Mouse went in and bit the South Wind's nose). As the Master of the South Wind staggered from the house, he slipped on the fish and slithered down the beach, where the waiting animals tried to beat his brains out with clubs—which are as hard as a rice mortar or a donkey's hoof. The South Wind made a successful deal for his life—four days of good weather to alternate with four days of bad.[20]

Here, then, is a basic plot in which pusillanimous animals overcome masterful human beings in their very houses by combining their own little natural aptitudes to undo mankind. No matter that human beings were the authors of the tale. It is the story of the little person triumphing over the big people who order their lives. Its appeal as a vicarious release of suppressed resentments is clear. The ludicrousness of the event provides an elemental sort of gusty humor. The story is too good to keep. It has a broad appeal because it meets a common need. From Asia it spread westward into Europe and northeastward into the northwest corner of North America. This, however, is not the end of its history. In post-Columbian times, variants of the "Musicians of Bremen" form of the tale were brought to the eastern American Indians by early trappers, and on the Plains and in the Woodlands these variants were adapted into a charming story known as "Big Turtle's War Party."

Thus, by word of mouth, crossing language barrier after language barrier, the "Tale of the Wandering Animals" has girdled the globe; penetrating North America from the west and from the east, it met itself along the rocky spine of the Western mountain area. Either by reliance upon historical data or by inferential reconstruction from distributional analysis, trait after trait may be followed through the course of its diffusion.

Dynamics of Diffusion: Selective Factors

Diffusion is no simple, straight-line process in which a people put an idea on wheels, figuratively speaking, and give it a shove to send it on its way around the world.

Every spreading trait or complex, as it moves from one society to another, must face the test of its acceptability in the culture of the receivers; and if it is accepted, it is invariably reworked in form, use, meaning, or function. No people take an alien trait without altering it to some degree.

The sun dance

The fate of the Plains Indian sun dance illustrates this clearly. The sun dance is a fairly complex ritual shared by a score of tribes in the western part of the Plains area. The ceremony is most elaborated and developed among the Arapaho and Cheyenne. From these tribes, according to Spier's classic analysis, the complex spread out among the other nomadic tribes.[21] In its core, the sun dance shows remarkable stability wherever it occurs. The fundamental form of the dance is universal within the area of its distribution. Nevertheless, considerable variation in content occurs from tribe to tribe. As Spier observed, strong systematic selection was exercised.

Selection often works in subtle ways that we cannot determine *ex post facto*. Some of the more obvious determinants, however, may be quite clear. Thus, two features of the Arapaho sun dance are the use of medicine bundles and the special roles played by the military fraternity of the man who sponsors the dance. Among the Wind River and Idaho Shoshones, neither of these

---

[20]An analysis in full detail is given in E. A. Hoebel, "The Asiatic Origin of a Myth of the Northwest Coast" (*Journal of American Folklore*, vol. 54, 1941), pp. 1–12.

[21]L. Spier, *The Sun Dance of the Plains Indians* (American Museum of Natural History, Anthropological Papers, vol. 16, part 7, 1921).

occurs in connection with the dance. The reason is simply that the limited culture of the Shoshones has no military societies within its social structure and no priesthood of bundle owners. The Shoshones stripped the complex ritual down to the structure of their meager social framework. As they adapted it, the sun dance became primarily a purification and curing ceremony, designed to bring general well-being to the entire tribe. For the closely related Utes, the function and meaning were quite similar, although details, such as an increased emphasis on dreaming, varied.[22]

The Crows used the sun dance to generate war power against specific enemies. Revenge was the motif; a scalp, the object; a war party, the follow-up.

The Cheyenne sun dance was, and still is, a world-renewal ceremony. In the Cheyenne world view, the energy of the universe is being continuously used up and must be annually recharged mimetically through the ceremonies. Although the dance is pledged by one individual, the entire renewal effort is directed toward the welfare of all members of the tribe.

There is one recorded instance where the dance was "borrowed" by a tribe, tried once, and forever dropped. Urged on by their "messiah" and in need of "war medicine," the Comanches presented one sun dance that was to endow them with immunity to bullets. Soon after, they were thoroughly defeated in battle. The ritual had failed in its desired function, and it is improbable that it ever developed any meaning for them.[23]

Thus, the function and meaning of the sun dance varied as it was worked into one tribal culture after another. For the buffalo hunters in the mid-nineteenth century, its chief function was that of tribal integration. The scattered bands that eked out the winter separately were brought together in early summer for a grand socializing prior to the communal buffalo hunt. For individuals, the dance functioned to relieve anxiety. It also expressed a subconscious submissiveness to the supernatural through self-imposed hunger and thirsting and bloody immolation of the self to

gratify the spirit forces. It functioned to make more probable the acquisition of power through visions by means of heightened social suggestion.

As the sun dances are performed on the reservations today, they function mostly as reinforcers of tribal integrity in the face of all the surrounding forces of disintegration.

The selective effect of ideology, or meaning, on cultural diffusion and reinterpretation may be seen if we look at the celebration of the Fourth of July by the Crows and Cheyennes in the 1960s. On the Crow reservation, a large crowd gathers at a racetrack. The betting is as spirited as the horses, the latter ridden by Crow Indians splendid in colorful jockey costumes. The shouting is loud. The fireworks are deafening. There is no sun dance. For the Crows, the old sun dance is dead, and although a new form of the dance was borrowed from the Wind River Shoshones after 1941, it has not become a tribal ceremony of major significance.

At the Cheyenne reservation, a few miles away, an essentially traditional sun dance comes to its four-day climax. The dancers move through the ceremonial forms with somewhat weary dignity. The audience watches quietly. A neatly lettered sign reads: "Quiet. No Fireworks Allowed."

Why such a difference between two tribes of Plains Indians, whose acquaintance stretches back over many years and who currently live boundary to boundary?

It is obvious that both groups are celebrating the Fourth of July and that as citizens of the United States, they recognize this date as a symbol of American identity. However, each group has recombined certain elements of the national rite in such a way as to produce two very different kinds of celebration. The Cheyennes, with their age-old emphasis on world renewal and group solidarity, seem not so much to be celebrating the birth of the nation as seeking to revivify it through their tribal efforts. The basic meaning of the dance has changed little, although its form has worn a bit thin. The time of the dance has been changed from early June to July 4, signifying tribal integration into a new and larger society. School vacations and work schedules make this a convenient and natural date. Perhaps, too, the

---

[22]M. K. Opler, "The Integration of the Sun Dance in Ute Religion" (*American Anthropologist*, vol. 43, 1941), pp. 550–572.
[23]E. Wallace and E. A. Hoebel, *The Comanches*, pp. 319–326.

selection of the national holiday indicates that they are sufficiently identified with the larger society to wish to proclaim their membership in it and help keep it strong and vital.

The original function of the Crows' sun dance, to bring success in scalp-hunting, has long vanished. The meaning of the dance was too specialized to permit adaptation to contemporary conditions. But gambling and horse racing, with their attendant noisy clamor, are ancient pastimes. It was natural for the Crows to seize on the festive aspect of July Fourth and to make of it a noisy carnival as they, too, proclaim their identity with the United States.

The importance of meaning

This fundamental anthropological fact—in cultural transference a trait or complex will be evaluated and rejected, or accepted or modified, in terms of the meaning it has for the receiving people—is one of the most difficult for professional civilizers to perceive and apply. This applies to teachers, Peace Corps volunteers, economic-development programmers, public health workers, and missionaries, whose numbers are steadily increasing. When this principle is ignored, the consequent mischief worked is often monumental.

Over one hundred years ago, a wise and not too doctrinaire Episcopalian missionary demonstrated his full recognition of this aspect of intercultural transference. Sensing the likelihood of misinterpretation of the Christian rite of communion by the Tsimshian Indians, among whom he was working, he was induced to omit the ritual from his services. Cannibalism among the Northwest Coast Indians, although quite different in meaning for the Indians, was too similar to communion in form and function. Not only in this but in other points as well did Duncan, the missionary in question, deliberately and as a matter of policy eliminate "many of the potential danger spots in Christian metaphysics for a native whose only basis for interpreting new belief was in terms of the old."[24]

Even with foresight, one cannot anticipate some consequences of interpretation of new phenomena in terms of old meanings. For example, the Dani tribesmen of the Balim Valley in western New Guinea (Irian) are active cannibals. American missionaries who entered the area in the 1950s discouraged the practice in their efforts to promote civilization and Christianization. As the Dani became familiar with eating canned goods, they quickly comprehended that a tin bearing a picture of beans on its label contained beans, that one picturing pears contained pears, and so forth. When one of the mission wives gave birth and cans of Gerber's baby food with pictures of healthy babies on the labels were flown in, the Danis' idea of the eating habits of American missionaries need not be guessed.[25]

Commonly, in diffusion and culture growth, the form of a trait or complex will remain the same, at least initially. But the meaning is almost certain to be altered, and, possibly, the use and functions also. Thus, a highly technical artifact, such as a film spool or a light bulb when it has fulfilled its originally intended function, may be adopted for entirely different use, meaning, and function within another cultural context. The delight of the New Guinea girl pictured in Fig. 3-1 is not at all unusual, as, confident of her beauty, she has converted burnt-out light bulbs into aesthetic objects of artistic ornament. The form of each bulb is unaltered but its use is as costume; its meaning is aesthetic and perhaps also magical; and its function, that of prestige enhancement and ego gratification in a ceremonial context. The bulb is thus culturally acceptable because it readily fits into the context of the native culture in a positive way.

THE SELECTIVE CONSEQUENCES OF NEGATIVE MEANINGS Traits that have positive meaning in one culture may be blocked in diffusion because their forms are associated with negatively colored uses, meanings, or functions in the existing cultures of potential receivers.

At a Northern Cheyenne peyote meeting, the senior author once became interested in a decorative staff used in the ritual. It seemed to be

---

[24]H. G. Barnett, "Applied Anthropology in 1860" (*Applied Anthropology*, vol. 1, 1942), p. 24.

[25]Personal communication from a member of the mission organization, 1962.

FIG. 3-1 Cultural significance of use, meaning, and function. A New Guinea girl converts burnt-out light bulbs into aesthetic objects of ceremonial costumery. (Courtesy of the American Museum of Natural History.)

carved with figures of bison quite similar to those of Franco-Cantabrian cave art. The thought was intriguing. Upon closer examination, however, the carved scenes proved to be of toreadors and charging bulls. There was also the Mexican eagle sitting on his cactus, but the snake in his claws had been scraped out with a knife. Black Wolf, the peyote leader, explained that the staff had come from Mexico, and he pointed out that the eagle is good medicine. The toreador confronting the bull suggested the vision-seeking Indian confronted by a bison. However, he said, "Those people down there worship snakes, but we don't. So we took the snakes out. We can't have any snakes in our ceremony." The Cheyennes, in point of fact, are not simply neutral with respect to snakes. In their mythology, the Horned Snake (or the Plumed Serpent) is a creature much to be feared and avoided.

Barnett has detailed a number of such rejections by several northern California tribes. When the bobbing of women's hair came into vogue, it met heavy resistance because that hair style was believed to cause death. Corsets and hairpins

were rejected at first because they resembled the warrior's rod armor and the bone pins that he used in his hair.[26]

On a larger scale, the efforts of the Belgian administration in the Congo to make the Pygmies of the forest more economically self-sufficient by inducing them to take up gardening were rejected outright. A few Pygmies made the try on "model" plantations, and although they demonstrated the ability to cultivate, "they degenerated socially and physically at an alarming rate, losing all sense of individual or family responsibility and dying from sunstroke and stomach disorders."[27] These were merely symptoms; they were dying because they had accepted a new way of life utterly devoid of meaning. Other Mbuti "clearly see and state that once they abandon their nomadic forest existence they will cease to be Mbuti."[28]

These examples demonstrate that the preexisting biases of the members of a receiving society facilitate or block the accepting or borrowing of any new cultural possibility. The compatibility of a new way with the basic postulates and derived corollaries underlying the receiving culture is of vital importance (Fig. 3-2). On the other hand, the acceptance of materials of apparently neutral significance but of demonstrated technical efficiency, such as iron or tractors, may ultimately lead to value and postulational disruptions that were never anticipated. The successful development of lunar and interplanetary rockets, for example, obviously holds undreamed-of cultural consequences in store. Yet we seem quite willing to take our chances on what the penetration of space will mean for the future.

THE SELECTIVE CONSEQUENCES OF CULTURAL INDIFFERENCE The selection of culture traits in accordance with their compatibility with a specific set of cultural postulates and related cultural values leads not only to negative rejection. It may also result in the neutral nonacceptance of alien possibilities because of indifference. A thing or an idea may be seen or encountered and yet not be

[26]Barnett, "Applied Anthropology in 1860," *op. cit.*, pp. 31–32.
[27]C. M. Turnbull, "The Mbuti Pygmies of the Congo," in J. L. Gibbs, Jr. (ed.), *Peoples of Africa*, p. 313.
[28]*Ibid.*

FIG. 3-2 Diffusion of a culture trait. The memorial epitaph of European culture is adapted to a traditional type of Kwakiutl Indian grave post. In this carving, a frock-coated chief holds a representation of a valuable copper shield upon which is painted the English sentiment. (Courtesy of Robert Gardner.)

borrowed, adapted, or even desired. It meets no felt need of a people; or its usefulness is not perceived by them; it rings no bell. Their interest is in other things or ideas. Loren Eiseley astutely comments of the Maya, who were capable of inventing such an abstraction as the concept of the zero, plus a hieroglyphic symbol to represent it:

These men who could predict eclipses never learned to weigh or use the wheel for transportation, though wheeled toys were in use among their neighbors. No better example could be utilized to reveal that a given society has just so much energy and interest at its disposal, and that its intellectual achievements will move in the path of its deepest motivations. The Mayan intellect centered upon a divine mathematics that con-

trolled the human world, just as different cultures, including our own, have pursued reality in other shapes and guises.[29]

IDEOLOGY AND STRUCTURE IN CULTURAL CHANGE

We have been discussing the acceptability and rejection of innovations in terms of their compatibility to preexisting cultural standards (ideal norms). Usually, however, this is not a clear and simple matter. Every innovation begins with the act of somebody. Who that somebody is and how he or she manages the strategy of introducing the new idea in relation to existing patterns can make a great difference—as can, of course, the temper of the times.

The Role of the Individual

Values are never absolutely consistent and tensions engendered by alternative choices are always present. In no phase of human life is this more evident than in the area of conflict between the urges of individual sexuality and the standardized channeling of sex in social structure.

To take a Cheyenne case in illustration: Cheyennes (as we shall see on pages 329–331) viewed the energy quotient of the universe as limited, and they extended this view to sexual relations. Unlike their neighbors the Comanches, they did not allow for sexual competition among the males. The Comanches frequently stole one another's wives; the Cheyennes did not. But then a wily Cheyenne who wanted another man's wife schemed to alter the Cheyenne pattern. Here is how it went, as told by Blackwolf in 1935.

A war party was organizing. Walking Rabbit approached the leader with a question. "Is it true that you have declared we must all go afoot? If so, I would like to be able to lead a horse to pack my moccasins and possibles." The leader gave him an answer. "There is a reason for my ruling. I want no horses, that it may be easier for us to conceal our movements. However, you may bring one horse." Then Walking Rabbit asked for instructions concerning the location of the first and

[29]L. Eiseley, "In the Beginning Was the Artifact" (By permission of *Saturday Review*, Dec. 7, 1963), p. 52.

second nights' camps, for he would start late and overtake the party.

Walking Rabbit's sweetheart had been married only recently to another. "My husband is not the man I thought he was," she told her former suitor. So Walking Rabbit took her to join the war party. [The Cheyennes have a phrase describing the single man who marries a one-time married woman—"putting on the old moccasin."] In this way, it turned out that the "moccasin" he was packing was a big woman.

When they saw this woman there, the warriors got excited. The party turned into the hills and stopped. The leader opened his pipe. The leader's pipe was always filled before they left the camp, but it was not smoked until the enemy was seen or their tracks reported. Now the leader spoke. "When we take a woman with us it is usually known in the camp. Here is a man who has sneaked off with another's wife. Now what is going to happen?" That is what they were talking about.

The leader declared, "The only thing this man can do is return and make a settlement with the husband. Then he may follow us up."

One warrior was for aiding Walking Rabbit. "Why can't we let him stay?" was his proposal. "If we take any horses, we can give them to her husband." That was rejected.

The decision was that he had to go back. "If you had told us you wanted her so badly, we might have waited for you to settle for her. Then we could have taken her the right way. If you really want to go to war with us, you will be able to overtake us. We are afoot."

Then three or four warriors spoke up, each promising Walking Rabbit a horse to send to the husband. Everyone gave one or two arrows to be sent as well.

In the meantime Walking Rabbit's father had fixed it up with the aggrieved husband. Since he and his wife were incompatible, he was willing to release her. When Walking Rabbit came in and told his father the story of the soldiers' action, the father said, "Just let that stand. The thing is fixed. When those fighters come back they may want to give to the girl's parents. You go back after your party." But Walking Rabbit preferred to stay at home.

When Walking Rabbit did not go out, his closest relatives raised a big tipi. When they heard of the approach of the returning war party, everything was in readiness.

The warriors came charging in, shooting; they had taken many horses. The first coup-counters were in the van. Walking Rabbit's father had a right to harangue; he was a crier. "Don't go to your homes! Don't go to your own lodges! Come here to the lodge of Walking Rabbit, your friend!"

When they were all in this lodge the old man entered and told them his story. "I had this thing all settled before my son returned. You have sent arrows and promised horses. Now I have kept this girl here pending your return. I shall send her back to her parents with presents. I have waited to see what you are going to do."

The leader replied for his followers. "Yes, we will help you. We promised to help your son. When you send her back, we'll send presents with her." The men who had promised horses went out to get them. Others gave captured horses.

Sending her back with these presents was giving wedding gifts. Her relatives got them all. They gathered up their goods to send back. The war party was called together once more; to them this stuff was given. It was a great thing for the people to talk about. It was the first and last time a woman was sent home on enemy horses the day they came in.[30]

In this instance, which took place about 1820, an innovation was rejected and, with ceremony and gift-giving, was made so memorable that the people could never forget it. What is more, the reinforced norm against wife-stealing stuck: from then until the end of the raiding days (1878), there were no more attempts by lovers to abscond with war parties. Walking Rabbit failed as an innovator. Cheyenne moral ideology was reaffirmed and reinforced.

Successful innovation

On the other hand, a Kapauku schemer, who was wholly successful in abrogating the incest rules of his society, illustrates in fine detail some of the specific factors of motivation and action involved in cultural ideology and change of social structure. The case is reported in full, and analyzed, by Professor Leo Pospisil.[31]

The Kapauku are patrilineal gardeners living in western New Guinea. Awiitigaaj is a Big Man (*tonowi*), a village headman, and a leader of a political confederacy that links a pair of lineages and their several villages. Up to 1935, the penalty for incest within the lineage was death. Like Walking Rabbit, Awiitigaaj took a fancy to a for-

---

[30]K. N. Llewellyn and E. A. Hoebel, *The Cheyenne Way*, pp. 13–15. By permission of University of Oklahoma Press, © 1941.

[31]L. Pospisil, *Anthropology of Law*, pp. 214–232; also "Structural Change and Primitive Law: Consequences of a Papuan Legal Case," in L. Nader (ed.), *Law in Culture and Society*, pp. 208–229.

bidden woman and wanted to marry her. "I liked her; she was beautiful." So he ran off with her, the traditional death penalty notwithstanding. The formal reaction was right and proper. "The infuriated relatives of the couple pursued the lovers, and the girl's father, Ugataga, who was a coheadman of the Ijaaj-Jamaina sublineage . . . ruled that both his daughter and her lover must be executed by arrow according to Kapauku customary law. His decision was upheld by the head of the Ijaaj-Pigome Confederacy."[32]

Awiitigaaj knew, however, that when the girl's father's anger had cooled, he would realize that the execution would deprive him of a very large progeny price and an important son-in-law—a serious conflict of public and private interests. So the couple hid out in the jungle, aided and abetted by Awiitigaaj's mother's brothers and other maternal kin, who were custom-bound to protect him regardless of his offense. Eventually, the upholders of law and traditional morality tired of beating about the bush. The outraged father of the bride continued to put on public temper tantrums and speeches, but under pressure from neutral leaders gradually agreed to settle for a progeny-price payment. In so doing, he accepted the legitimacy of the marriage. Eventually, because the members of the girl's sublineage became impatient over delays in the payment of the progeny price, they attacked Awiitigaaj's lineage mates with sticks. In a counter suit the latter were freed of the need to pay any progeny price whatsoever, whereupon they too publicly agreed to the acceptability of the marriage. The precedent became a new alternative. By 1954, 22 per cent of the marriages within the lineage were with previously forbidden lineage mates.

Neighboring lineages followed suit and a fundamental change in the postulates requiring sib-exogamy was clearly effected. A significant change in the social structure had been brought about by a skillful self-seeker who successfully manipulated a complex situation to achieve a change in ideology, kinship organization, and law. A change effected in the real culture brought about modifications in the ideal culture. In 1954, nearly two-thirds of the adult members of the

village originally involved told Pospisil that they approved of the change.

Stimulus Diffusion

Culture contact generates culture change. Only isolated societies retain prolonged stability. Contact opens up new alternatives and unthought-of possibilities. In the two case studies just cited, the Cheyenne had the Comanche example to give him his idea, and Awiitigaaj knew of the existence of lineage endogamy among another population in a nearby region. In these instances the process is one which is known in anthropology as *stimulus diffusion*.

Stimulus diffusion occurs when the general idea of a culture trait or complex is transferred from one people to another without a transmission of the actual detailed content. The content of the pattern is more or less invented by the borrowers of the idea. Sequoya, the Cherokee inventor of the syllabary used by the Cherokees for writing their tongue, got the idea of writing from contact with whites, but he did not learn to write the English language. He took some alphabetic symbols directly from English, modified some, and invented others. His English symbols, however, bear no relation to the English phonetic system. He made them stand for Cherokee syllables. He took the idea, but not the form, of writing.

Stimulus diffusion as a process stands midway between independent invention and genuine diffusion. Awareness of a need or an inventive possibility is stimulated by contact with a trait or a complex from an alien source. The stimulated people, who lack the trait, attempt independently to invent an equivalent of it.

ACCULTURATION

Acculturation occurs when a society undergoes drastic culture change under the influence of a more dominant culture and society with which it has come in contact.[33] The acculturating society

---

[32]L. Pospisil, *Anthropology of Law*, p. 216.

[33]A standard definition of acculturation emphasizes "changes in the culture patterns of either or both groups"; R. Redfield, R. Linton, and M. J. Herskovits, "Memorandum for the Study of Acculturation" (*American Anthropologist*, vol. 38, 1936), p. 149. However, the concept as it is most frequently used applies to the process as we have defined it here.

alters its culture in the direction of adjustment and (greater or lesser) conformity to cultural ideology and patterns of the dominant society. However, the acculturating society, although significantly modified in its life-way, retains its discrete identity.

Acculturation is thus to be seen as a special form of culture change. The rapid spread of tobacco from the American Indians all around the world is a prime example of diffusion of a culture trait, but it would hardly be correct to say that tobacco-smoking Chinese became acculturated to the American Indians. To carry the point further, European Americans, as they built up the culture of the United States, borrowed many new traits from the American Indian: cultivation of maize, beans, and squash in hills; maple syrup and sugar production; snowshoes, toboggans, and canoes, to name only a very few items. The government of the United States built an elaborate legal subculture to accommodate to the presence of the many tribes within the federal legal system. There was indeed a good deal of culture change produced in response to the presence of American Indian tribal societies on the continent. But most white Americans were not acculturating to the Indian way of life. On the other hand, many American Indians were, over the decades, changing their ideologies and cultures in the direction of Westernized modes of life.

Differential Acculturation

Once again it must be emphasized that culture change occurs first in individual behavior. The change appears as a deviation from previous customary norms. It can be hailed with enthusiasm, be overlooked, be mildly disapproved and lightly sanctioned, or be rejected outright and heavily sanctioned. At any rate, it never takes place totally and instantaneously throughout any society.

Menomini Indian acculturation

The most effective demonstration to date of the point of differential acculturation is found in the study of the psychology of Menomini Indians, living in Wisconsin, done in the early 1950s by George and Louise Spindler.[34] By using a schedule of twenty-three sociocultural indices "for placing subjects on an acculturative continuum and defining explicit values associated with the native or American culture," plus autobiographies and intensive personal interviews over a period of seven seasons of fieldwork, the Spindlers arrived at a fivefold classification of the mid-twentieth century Menomini population in terms of degree of acculturation. In summary form, they are stated as follows:

A. *Native-oriented*—all members of the Medicine Lodge and/or Dream Dance group where the patterns of traditional culture survive to the greatest extent.

B. *Peyote Cult*—composed of participating members of the Cult and constitutes a unique variation of culture conflict resoluton with the transitional position.

C. *Transitional*—consisting of persons in cultural transition who have participated in native-oriented religious activities and groups but have moved towards Catholicism and Western culture during their lifetimes, and are at present not clearly identified with either Western or native-oriented groups and values.

D. *Lower status acculturated*—persons who were born Catholic and maintained this identificaton, know little or nothing of native traditions, but who have acculturated to a laboring class standard.

E. *Elite acculturated*—composed of persons who participate regulary in Catholic services, are members of the prestigeful Catholic Mother's and Holy Name Societies, and, if male, occupy managerial or semi-professional positions in the tribal lumber industry or agency.[35]

Figure 3-3 shows the relative positions of the Menomini groups on the continuum of acculturation from native to American, combined with degree of socioeconomic status *within* the larger, regional society of midwestern Wisconsin.

The most valuable and significant feature of the

[34]G. D. Spindler, *Sociocultural and Psychological Processes in Menomini Acculturation* (University of California Publications in Culture and Society, vol. 5, 1955). L. Spindler and G. D. Spindler, "Male and Female Adaptations in Culture Change" (*American Anthropologist*, vol. 60, 1968), pp. 217–233.
[35]L. Spindler and G. D. Spindler, *op. cit.*, pp. 218–219. By permission of American Anthropologist.

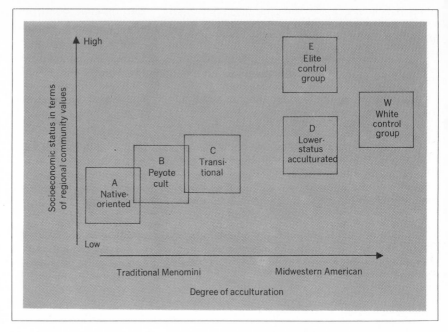

FIG. 3-3 Differential acculturation and socioeconomic status of Menomini Indians in relation to the larger American regional society. [Adapted from G.D. Spindler, "Socio-cultural and Psychological Processes in Menomini Acculturation" (*University of California Publications in Culture and Society*, vol. 5, 1955, p. 118)]

Spindler studies lies not so much in the explicit demonstration of differential acculturation in the external behavior but rather in the revelation of parallel differences in the deeper psychological adjustments which are characteristic of the different Menomini groups. This was achieved through sophisticated use of Rorschach's psychodiagnostic inkblot tests. Rorschach analysis shows that

. . . [T]he native-oriented group operate with deep internal controls over aggression. The people are inward-oriented, not achievement-oriented; they lack overt emotional responsiveness but are sensitive to the nuances of interpersonal relations; they are fatalistic in orientation, and exhibit quiet endurance under stress or deprivation, a pattern Louise Spindler has termed "latescent". . . . There is no marked evidence of anxiety or internal conflict, nor a free-flowing spontaneity.

The Peyotists are a special case. They are highly committed to the ideology and ritual of Peyotism stressing rumination about one's self, sins, and salvation, attainment of power individually and through partaking of Peyote in an acceptant mood. There is significant relaxing of controls over emotions and overt expression of feelings, with public crying during testimonials and rituals and bids for collective expressions of sympathy, which are offered freely.

The ungrouped transitionals are characterized by very uneven adjustments to the vicissitudes of transformational culture change. Some are striving for an orderly way of life, towards goals recognizable in the surrounding non-Indian community; others are withdrawn and mostly just vegetate; others go on destructive rampages, during or between drunks. Beating, murders, illegitimacy, dirt and disorder are a way of life for many in the latter group. The Menomini transitionals are like human populations everywhere who have lost their way; for them neither the goals of the traditional or the new culture are meaningful.

The acculturated, and particularly the elite, are radically different from any of the other groups. The roles they occupy demand punctuality, regular hours of concentrated work, orderly behavior and planning, pride in material possessions and economic status. The psychological data on them shows that they are emotionally open, but not disorganized. They utilize their emotional energy in the attainment of goals—personal success, material acquisition—approved of by middle-class persons in the surrounding communities. They are concerned about production and competition. They react to environmental pressures in a controlled but aggressive manner. They are also more anxious and tense than the native-oriented, but this anxiety is focused, rather than diffuse (as it is among the transitionals).

The acculturated Menomini deny their identity as Indians and specifically disclaim any relationship to "those Indians"—the members of the native-oriented group. Most of them do not speak their own language. The few who do rarely use it. Their homes and possessions are indistinguishable from those of Whites in nearby towns.

It is evident that the radical departure represented by the elite acculturated in the acculturative continuum of the Menomini occurs in both the manifest and psychological phases of adaptation. In order to "make the grade" on the terms of American middle-class culture the elite had to learn to stop being Menomini and learn how to be middle-class, achievement-oriented Americans. This reorganization occurred in depth and was not merely an overt adjustment.[36]

If the Spindlers' study were redone in the 1970s, it would probably be necessary to add a sixth identifiable Menomini group, the "elite, acculturated Militant." Its membership would consist of educated Menominis with urban experience who have a revived desire to nurture Menomini tribal identity.[37]

Finally, not only are the psychological characteristics of the male Menomini different according to degree and kind of acculturation, but Menomini women show much less psychological change than do Menomini men. In their more traditional roles as wives and mothers, less is demanded of them in acculturative adjustments. "They do not find the flux and conflict of rapid change as disturbing as do the males."[38]

To sum up: some Menominis have acculturated so completely that they are assimilated within Midwestern white society—behaviorally and psychologically. Some are in marginal transition. Some have sought a new type of adjustment in a "reactive movement," the Peyote Cult, which is neither white nor old Menomini, and a small handful cling to a residual belief in what is left of old Menomini ways.

Can one say that all the Menomini Indians are acculturated? No. Can one say that most Menomini Indians are significantly acculturated? Yes. Can one say that all Menomini Indians have experienced significant culture change in the past 200 years? Most definitely. With variations in degree and forms, it seems probable that a Menomini-like model will hold good for all Eskimos and Indians who have survived in the Western Hemisphere—from Point Barrow to Tierra del Fuego, and in many other parts of the world.

Forced and Voluntary Culture Change

Throughout human history, trade and alliance have evidently provided the major pipelines of diffusion and cultural change. Traders bring new objects of material culture and news of people who have different life-ways. Traders are almost always welcomed (once the nature of their roles is perceived) and their technically superior or more easily acquired goods are quickly incorporated. This is as true of prehistoric and aboriginal traders as it is of the harbingers of civilization (see pages 262–264, on trade).

Intertribal alliances produce intermarriage and ceremonial visitations in which cultural forms may be copied or transferred. In the early 1930s, religious specialists from Taos pueblo, for instance, were invited to Santa Ana pueblo, in New Mexico, ritually to repair the roof of the mission church. In exchange, the Santa Anas taught them the songs and the steps of a dance, giving them the right to perform it thereafter. Such culture change is obviously voluntary.

In the modern economic context, the desire for money with which to buy today's goods quickly leads to many voluntary shifts in cultural practices and social structure in order to acquire that mystic token of economic value.

Slave taking from alien peoples is something else again. The forcible removal of individuals from their home societies and their injection into an alien one requires anguishing cultural readjustments on their part. Conquest and political subjugation, with or without slavery, has even greater acculturative effects, for the conquered must accommodate to the rule and presence of the conquerors in their own territory, often with little or no choice.

[36]G. D. Spindler, "Psychocultural Adaptation," in E. Norbeck, D. Price-Williams, and W. M. McCord (eds.), *The Study of Personality*, pp. 329–330. (Copyright © Holt, Rinehart and Winston, Inc., 1968. Quoted with permission.)

[37]D. McNickle, *Native American Tribalism: Indian Survivals and Renewals.*

[38]L. Spindler and G. D. Spindler, *op. cit.*, p. 229.

Settlers, missionaries, educators, medical and technological specialists, and even tourists and travelers all play their roles, as do medical and technological specialists. Nor are we speaking only of the European expansion and colonial imperialism of recent centuries. The Indonesian archipelago was Hinduized by conquering Indian princes and priests beginning in the tenth century and continuing until overthrown by Muslim converts in the fifteenth and sixteenth centuries. Centuries before (600 B.C.), Greek traders and settlers Hellenized the Upper Indus Valley, and later, Greek teacher-slaves gave much to the intellect of Rome, while Rome transformed the barbarian world of Europe. For some hundreds of years, Arab slavers, traders, and teachers have pressed their cultural mark on the Africans of the Sudan. Acculturation is the product of response to militantly dominant cultures and/or those which offer more effective adaptive uses of physical environments and responses to the mysteries of life—i.e., the management of meaning and symbolic systems.

CULTURE CRISIS AND REACTIVE MOVEMENTS

When value systems are out of joint because they are too inconsistent with existing realities, a condition of cultural crisis may build up. Culture crisis breeds reactive movements. Such movements are the product of the gap between present circumstance and dreamed-of expectancy. The reactive movement may present a reformed value code or it may propose drastic changes in the environmental condition or in the social system which is contributing to the sense of crisis. Or it may attempt to deal with all these possibilities simultaneously.

If the dominant aim of a movement is to raise up a depressed, pariah group which has long suffered in an inferior social standing and which has its own special subcultural ideology, the movement is called *millenarism*. Prophetic Judaism and early Christianity are examples.

If the movement aims to reconstitute a destroyed but not forgotten way of life, it is called *nativistic* or *revivalistic*. The Plains Indians' ghost dance is an example.

If the movement seeks to speed up the acculturation process in order to share more quickly and fully in the supposed benefits of dominant cultures, it may be called *transitional*.

Finally, if the aim of the movement is directed primarily to the ideological system and the attendant social structure of a cultural system from within, the movement is called *revolutionary*.

Millenarism

Although aspects of millenarism may be found in other parts of the world, it is particularly a Western phenomenon found in the Judaic, Christian, and Islamic cultural traditions. It is a form of religious utopianism based upon a firm conviction that the gap between the ideal in culture and the real in social life can be and will be closed—the Kingdom of God realized on earth. Man and life will be perfected according to the blueprints set forth by the prophets in a form of collective salvation for True Believers.

The Latin term *millenium* and its Greek equivalent, *chilias*, literally mean a period of a thousand years. According to the millenarian tradition, which is based on Jewish apocalyptic literature and the Revelations of St. John, Christ will appear in the guise of a warrior, vanquish the Devil, and hold him prisoner. He will then build the Kingdom of God and reign in person for a thousand years. Those saints who have remained steadfast and who have given their lives for their faith shall be raised from the dead and serve as His royal priesthood. At the end of this period, Satan will be let loose again for a short while and will finally be destroyed. The victory will be followed by the general resurrection of the dead, the last judgment, and final redemption.[39]

Millenarism promises the absolute conquest of evil, symbolized in the person of the Devil, forever. "The new dispensation will bring about not mere improvement but a complete transformation and perfection itself . . . ultimate and irrevocable . . . revolutionary and catastrophic."[40]

Through the centuries, millenial cults have

---

[39]Y. Talmon, "Millenarism" (*International Encyclopedia of the Social Sciences*, vol. 10, 1968), p. 349.
[40]*Ibid.*, p. 351.

risen and fallen, often with a messianic leader as spokesman, often without. The means are always supernatural and mystic. The end is cultural perfection realized—at a stroke.

Nativistic Movements: The Ghost Dance

Wave after wave of crisis movements swept through the American Indian populations in the nineteenth century. Of these, the Ghost Dance Movement of 1890 is the most famous.

The last of the tribes had been subjugated by the United States, the buffalo were gone, measles and smallpox had decimated many tribal populations, most of their lands had been ceded and opened to white settlement, the religious powers on which their security rested had been proven pitifully inadequate. Destructive catastrophe had overwhelmed virtually all the tribes.

Visits to the Land of the Dead and return to the living were not uncommon aboriginal experiences among Indians of the Great Basin. In 1870, a Paiute named Taivo from western Nevada visited the "Great Spirit," who told him a massive earthquake was coming to destroy all whites and Indians; however, after three days all Indians would be resurrected in a state of plenty—with the whites destroyed forever. Later, the prediction was amended to include only "believing" Indians in the resurrection. Belief was attested in a Round Dance.

Twenty years later, a new prophet arose. Wovoka, "The Cutter," was his name. He had learned some Christian theology from the ranch family for whom he worked.

In a delirium of fever, he was lifted up to see God. Heaven was full of happy dead persons who would never grow old and who enjoyed pleasant work and games. Their idyllic life would be brought to all on earth in a grand reunion of dead and living, in a good life that would never end, God said, if living human beings would stop fighting, live in loving goodness, and dance the ceremony God gave to him. An earthquake or flood would wipe out the bad old earth in preparation for the new, but good people need not fear it.

At the news of the messiah, various tribes reacted variously. Since they would soon rejoin the dead, the Arapaho gave up shooting their horses and gashing

their arms in mourning when someone died. To escape the flood, they should go to high mountains, leaving skeptics behind to turn to stone and the whites to be covered. On the new skin of the earth, game would once again abound. The Cheyenne said the Earth was getting old, grass and trees were worn out, and the people getting bad. Besides, the Earth was too small, so God was going to do away with heaven and remodel a bigger Earth for both living and dead. The Shoshone said a deep four-day sleep would come over all believers, and they would awaken on the fifth to a new world. Kiowa thought the new earth would slide from the west over the old one, bearing buffalo and elk upon it, and their sacred dance feathers would lift the faithful up onto the new world. Some Arapaho spoke of a wall of flame that would drive the whites back to their own country; sacred feathers would lift them over the fire and a twelve-day rain would subsequently extinguish it. The Walapai awaited a hurricane, the thunder of which would kill the whites and unbelievers. All these tribes believed the whites would be eliminated through supernatural means, and they bitterly blamed the warlike Sioux for later taking naturalistic means to this same end.[41]

A few Sioux, under Yellow Shirt, turned the Ghost Dance into an active resistance movement. They died at Wounded Knee.[42]

Transition Movements: The Cargo Cult

In the South Seas, crisis cults first began in the 1870s and 1880s as nativistic movements, but by 1914 the emphasis shifted from overturning the white colonialists (so as to revert to "the good old days") to getting direct access to the largesse of European goods. Proper ceremony would bring in the cargo ships loaded with canned food, tobacco, cloth, lamps, axes, knives, and rifles. These were all material objects which the whites did not make (so far as the Melanesians could observe). Nor did most of the whites in the South Pacific know *how* to make them. Asked how to make glass for a window, could you tell a native? How about paper? A gasoline engine? If you want these things, how do you get them? You order

---

[41]W. LaBarre, *The Ghost Dance*, p. 230. (Copyright © 1970 by Western LaBarre. Reprinted by permission of Doubleday & Company, Inc.)

[42]J. Mooney, *The Ghost Dance Religion and Sioux Outbreak of 1890*.

them! The ships, and later, the planes, bring them. That is all there is to it, as any reasonable person can see.

"Ordering" is a form of ritual control over the remotely located, unseen beings who make the goods. Old aboriginal rituals are abandoned, masks destroyed or sold off to Europeans; fields may be abandoned, new ceremonies with new symbols introduced, marching drills abound. Wharfs are built to receive the ships and welcoming miniature air strips are hacked out on jungle mountain ridgetops to receive cargo planes far from the ocean.

A central idea among New Guineans is that their own spirit ancestors actually produce all the material goods, which are intended for them and not for the Europeans. But white people developed a magic (religion) to divert the goods to themselves. The new cargo cult religions will ritually rectify that.

World War II intensified the cargo cult movements in Melanesia. The thousands of American ships and planes which flooded the beaches and bases with seemingly inexhaustible supplies of goods, many carelessly tossed away or generously given to the Melanesians, confirmed the belief that all these things could be theirs—always—if only the proper compelling rituals could be invented. In 1967, the most ambitious cult, which developed among the inhabitants of the Sepik River Valley, proposed to dry up the river, after which a ribbon of concrete would unroll to form a superhighway up the river bed, along which fleets of trucks would flow, bringing cargo to the interior.

Transition cults reach out to the new. They may appear to be irrational and unrealistic when viewed from the outside, but they do have their own logic, in terms of the original world views and the limited knowledge of the total cultures with which the groups are confronted. And be it not forgotten that many Melanesians are learning the basic techniques of road building, truck driving, bookkeeping, malaria control, modern agriculture and marketing—fast.[43]

Revolutionary Movements: Cultural

Max Gluckman has written with much insight on the social function of "rituals of rebellion" designed to "oust the incumbents of offices of power or influence without attempting to alter the nature of those offices or the claims of particular types of persons to be their incumbents."[44] Rebellions "throw the rascals out" and substitute another set, but there is no attempt to alter either the cultural ideology or the form of the social structure. In political revolution, attempts are made to seize the offices of power in order to change social structure, belief systems, and their symbolic representations. Political revolutions are usually turbulent, violent, and not long-lasting. A successful revolution soon moves to reestablish a stable, though changed, social structure; yet, "it has far-reaching political, social, and sometimes economic and cultural consequences."[45] Political revolution as a means of cultural change is largely a matter of recent centuries (the French, American, Russian, Turkish, and Chinese revolutions are outstanding). Certainly, it is not characteristic of either primitive societies or preindustrialized civilizations. For them change has not been engineered through organized political parties.

Cultural revolutions, on the other hand, extend over centuries and decades. They are the cumulative product of culture change which has moved technologies and societies in a given direction which can hardly be discerned while the change is going on. Looking back, however, evolutionary leaps can be seen to have occurred. The quality of human living has been fundamentally and irrevocably altered. In human culture history, we have seen that the first such revolutionary change was the development of Paleolithic culture, when human beings learned toolmaking, controlled the use of fire, and developed speech along with belief and symbolic systems, organizing new patterns of social life. The second such revolutionary change was initiated in the Mesolithic Age when mankind forsook hunting and gathering for intensive foraging. It was established in the Neolithic

---

[43]For an overall view of cargo cults, see P. Worseley, *The Trumpet Shall Sound.*

[44]M. Gluckman, *Politics, Law and Ritual in Tribal Society,* p. 137.

[45]W. Laqueur, "Revolution" (*International Encyclopedia of the Social Sciences,* vol. 13, 1968), p. 505.

urban revolution and the rise of civilization. It is just now being completed as the last of the globe's primitive peoples are being brought within the cultural network of civilization at the very time that civilization itself is completing its course. For civilization, as a phase of cultural evolution, is in the process of being replaced by new forms of culture expressive of the newly born Atomic Space Age.

SELECTED READINGS

Arensberg, C. M., and A. H. Niehoff, *Introducing Social Change* (1964). Intended as a handbook for non-social scientists engaged in overseas programs of technical, medical, and social development, this book provides a readable and interesting introduction to the principles and processes that influence success or failure in projects in effecting culture change and development.

Barnett, H. G., *Anthropology in Administration* (1956). A leading anthropologist dissects the problems of making anthropological expertise effectively available to administrators in United Nations trust territories and in colonial governments.

———, *Innovation: The Basis of Culture Change* (1953). The most intensive effort so far at systematic analysis of the processes of culture growth.

Bee, R. L., *Patterns and Processes: An Introduction to Anthropological Strategies for the Study of Sociocultural Change* (1974). A systematic review of the different theoretical and methodological approaches to the study of change. An excellent starting point for readers seeking a brief but representative survey of the current status of culture change studies.

del Prado, O. N., and W. F. Whyte, *Kuyo Chico: Applied Anthropology in an Indian Community* (1973). A detailed description of the experiences and orientation of an anthropologist directing a program of cultural change in an impoverished Peruvian Indian community.

Foster, G. M., *Applied Anthropology* (1969). What is the basic relationship between theoretical and applied science in general? How does applied anthropology as an agent of culture change fit into the general scheme? The author discusses the relevance of the flexible and adaptive research methods of applied anthropologists at work on specific problems.

Gerlach, L. H., and V. H. Hine, *People Power, Change: Movements of Social Transformation* (1970). Based on field studies of the Black Power and Pentecostal movements of social transformation in contemporary America, this fascinatingly written book spells out the individual and organizational factors at work.

Goodenough, W. H., *Cooperation in Change: An Anthropological Approach to Community Development* (1963). Two-thirds of this excellent book is devoted to a conceptual analysis of culture and culture change. The rest is given over to practical problems in community development.

Hogbin, H. I., *Social Change* (1958). This book discusses change and acculturation in Africa and Melanesia with great acumen. A very worthwhile book.

Lawrence, P., *Road Belong Cargo: A Study of the Cargo Movement in the Southern Madang District, New Guinea* (1964). A truly excellent historical-functional in-depth study of reactive movements in a given area of New Guinea, extending from 1871 to 1950.

Mead, M. (ed.), *Cultural Patterns and Technical Change* (1955). Prepared as a manual by The World Federation for Mental Health, this book lives up to its claim of showing "how modern technological and scientific methods, if carefully related to the group's cultural values, can advance the well-being of . . . communities which have lived for centuries according to ancient hallowed patterns."

Mooney, J., *The Ghost Dance Religion and the Sioux Outbreak of 1890* (1896). The classic, firsthand study of the great nativistic movement among the Plains Indians at the end of the nineteenth century.

Moore, W. E., *Social Change* (1963). A compact introduction to a modern sociological view of social change; theoretical and conceptual.

Niehoff, A. H. (ed.), *A Casebook of Social Change* (1966). Highly recommended for its specific, detailed accounts of nineteen projects of planned community development, land reform, or eradication of disease in South America, Africa, the Middle East, and Asia.

Singer, S., E. J. Holmyard, and A. R. Hall (eds.), *A History of Technology*, 3 vols. (1954). Definitive. The most comprehensive summary of invention and the steps that have occurred in the development of material culture.

Worseley, P., *The Trumpet Shall Sound: A Study of "Cargo" Cults in Melanesia* (1957). A comparative study of reactive movements in the South Pacific.

4
ENCULTURATION AND PERSONALITY

LEARNING GOALS

Identify the cultural processes that produce personalities, including enculturation, child training, and education. ¶ Summarize the relationships between the various factors which determine personality. ¶ Enumerate the varieties of anthropological approaches to the study of personality.

Societies are made up of individuals, and cultures, while manifest through the behavior of individuals, set patterns for individual behavior which exist before a person is born and persist after that person has died. All cultures change through time, but they have an enduring continuity that supersedes the mortal span of a human being. Some anthropologists have held that culture exists *in* personality. Yet, considering how much more than the individual personality culture actually is, this view seems to be too narrow. Culture, with roots in individual behavior, is superindividual. The problem, then, in considering humanity, culture, and society is to see how humanity and culture are interrelated. Thus, we approach the problem as one of personality and culture. An important focus in studying this problem is the analysis of how an individual derives a distinct personality through the process of enculturation.

A personality is the integrated system of behaviors, learned and unlearned, that are characteristic of an individual. A culture is the integrated system of learned behavior patterns that are characteristic of the members of a society. The interrelations of the two have posed three kinds of problems for mutual study by psychologists and anthropologists: (1) How does culture affect personality? (2) How does personality affect culture? (3) How does the personality response to specific cultural experience influence other aspects of the culture? Or in what sense are individual personalities intermediary links in a chain of cause and effect between different parts of cultures? An investigation of these problems must consider two facets of the study of personality. First, from what and by what processes does the individual derive a particular personality? Second, what are the factors that determine the shape and content of this personality?

THE DERIVATION OF PERSONALITY: CHILD TRAINING, ENCULTURATION, AND EDUCATION

"As the twig is bent, so grows the tree." A major factor in the development of the child as a person is the accumulation of innumerable pressures, most of them subtle, others not so subtle, that shape his images and his feel of the surrounding world. He strives to act in accordance with these understandings (Fig. 4-1). The child's feel of the world and his gradually growing perception of what that world will give and what it demands serve as his guides for getting on.

All these perceptions must be explored and tested. At the instant of birth, the world is nothing for the newborn infant. It is sensed only as a rude and sudden change from the all-encompassing perfection of the womb to the coldness of the air that first strikes it. Its first response is a wail and not a laugh.

The world that awaits the child is a world of people who already have a multitude of cultural commitments concerning how to behave—people with culturally colored emotions, expectancies, and anxieties. It is a world of many physical things, some beneficial, even essential to human existence; some inexorably destructive; some now one and then the other. Of these the infant is

blankly ignorant. Of all these the newborn child must in time become knowledgeable.

Investigations of human adults show that much of their behavior consists of patterns derived from processes of conditioning in early childhood. Under ordinary circumstances the child's first experience, and its experience for some time thereafter, is in the primary conjugal family. This is the child's world. Margaret Mead, for one, has shown how this world differentially puts the imprint of its finger on the newborn:

The Arapesh [of New Guinea] treat a baby as a soft, vulnerable, precious little object, to be protected, fed, cherished . . . When the mother walks about she carries the child slung beneath her breast in a bark-cloth sling, or in a soft net bag in which the child still curls as he

FIG. 4-1 Cultural patterning of behavior. New Zealand Maoris threatened enemies with popeyes and thrust-out tongues. (a) The pattern is portrayed in the image of a protective spirit on the panel of a food storehouse; (b) Maori warriors portray it in dance; and (c) Maori small boys practice it. (Courtesy of the American Museum of Natural History.)

(b)

(a)

(c)

curled in the womb. Whenever it is willing to eat . . . it is fed, gently, interestedly.

Among the neighboring latmul headhunters:

From birth the baby is handled as if it were a separate little entity capable of a will of its own. . . . As soon as the latmul child is a few weeks old, the mother no longer carries it everywhere with her . . . but instead places it at some distance on a high bench, where it must cry lustily before it is fed. . . . [T]he sense of the mouth is built up as an assertive, demanding organ, taking what it can from a world that is, however, not unduly unwilling to give it. The child learns an attitude towards the world; that if you fight hard enough, something which will treat you as strong as itself will yield—and that anger and self-assertion will be rewarded.

And again:

The Mundugumor [another New Guinea tribe] women actively dislike child-bearing, and they dislike children. Children are carried in harsh opaque baskets that scratch their skins, later, high on their mother's shoulders, well away from the breast. Mothers nurse their children standing up, pushing them away as soon as they are the least bit satisfied. . . . Here we find a character developing that stresses angry, eager avidity. In later life lovemaking is conducted like the first round of a prizefight, and biting and scratching are important parts of foreplay.[1]

Child training encompasses a good deal more than consciously directed education. As a biological organism, each individual is moved by a mass of impulses or drives. Many of these are innate, that is, inherent in the neurophysiological make-up.

Enculturation

The ways in which these needs may be satisfied are always limited and standardized in every culture. No society permits its members to eat any which way at any time they please. No society permits its members to urinate and defecate whenever or wherever they get the urge. Sphincter control is always demanded. No society permits unlimited expression of the sex drive; on the contrary, all societies exert considerable social control in this matter.

Each person must learn what kinds of responses to drive pressures lead to goal achievement and need satisfaction. Antisocial responses—that is, culturally prohibited behavior—are punished through social efforts to extinguish them. The individual must learn to inhibit the impulse to act in prohibited ways and to habituate one's behavior to culturally indicated ways.

The total process is called *enculturation*, which is defined as conscious or unconscious conditioning occurring within that process whereby the individual, as child and adult, achieves competence in a particular culture. A well-adjusted personality is one that successfully gratifies the personal urges within the allowable expectancies of the social environment. In social psychology and sociology, the term of long-standing use that is synonymous with enculturation is *socialization*.

Human life is lived in a state of continuous tensions that may only be minimized, never permanently eliminated. The battle between inner urge and the challenged limitations allowed by culture is unending. "Inner psychic conflict would seem to be of the very essence of man."[2] Maturity in personality represents an acceptance of the terms according to which life can and must be lived in any given society. When growing children have adjusted their behavior to the patterns of their culture, when its pertinent values, beliefs, and modes of action have become a normal part of their thinking and behavior, they have *internalized* their culture and have become thoroughly enculturated. Their personalities have thus matured.

Along the way they will have acquired many drives and attendant goals that were not in them at birth. These drives are not *basic* but are, rather, *acquired* or *secondary*. They are extensions of a more elemental need for warm social response. The goals are culturally symbolized in the social rewards that go with prestige status. Most individuals in most societies struggle to achieve and shape their personalities in accord with the demands of such acquired drives with as much intensity of action as the basic drives evoke.

---

[1]M. Mead, *Male and Female*, pp. 65 and 68–69. By permission from William Morrow and Company. Copyright 1949 M. Mead.

[2]A. I. Hallowell, "Psychological Leads for Ethnological Field Workers," in D. Haring (ed.), *Personal Character and Cultural Milieu*, p. 296.

FIG. 4-2 The Amahuaca boy of the Peruvian rainforest learns to fashion arrows in direct association with his father (Cornell Capa, Magnum.)

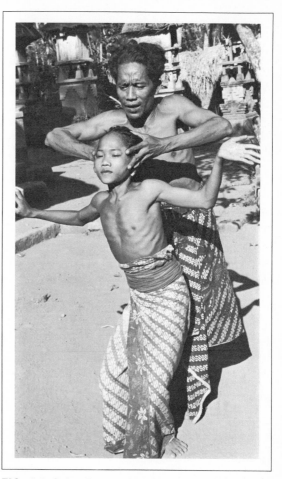

FIG. 4-3 Cultural patterning of behavior. Learning to dance in Bali. The Balinese does not learn by watching but through kinesthetic experience firmly guided by the adult master. (Henri Cartier-Bresson.)

Primitive education

Education, as opposed to child training, implies the more formal efforts of adults to mold the personalities of the young, but among primitive peoples the gap is nowhere as great as it is in American society, for example. Primitives never make an issue over "education for life," as our school people do. In a tribal group, education *is* life. Fathers do not work in factories or offices the children never see. Children are not shut up in a school away from the home for hours and days on end. In the simple camp or village, children are around and underfoot while all the fundamental activities of adult life take place. They can play with a bow and arrow until they are old enough to tag along on the hunt and learn by precept in action just how to handle it expertly (Fig. 4-2). They can play around the older boys who are watching the herds until they are ready to herd themselves. They can see and imitate the dancers until they themselves are admitted to the dance (Fig. 4-3). They can listen to the tales of tribal lore and myth until they know them by heart (Fig. 4-4). Most knowledge comes as a by-product of living, with one or another of the family members as a natural, nonprofessional instructor. And much is

FIG. 4-4 Enculturation. Young Bushman boys, with youths, learn the band's traditions from an elder as they sit around the campfire. (From Jens Bjere, *Kalahari*, Hill and Wang New York.)

learned from play with other children who are just a bit older.

Formal learning is usually limited to the more esoteric or specialized aspects of religion and magic. Where tribal initiations are held, they almost invariably involve formal instruction in these affairs.

C. W. M. Hart has pointed out that in most primitive societies, the education of children before puberty is left to the informal ministrations of parents and other relatives. In many societies, however, the boys are hauled off to a "bush school" at puberty to be put through a severe course of discipline and training in esoteric knowledge covering the "value system of the culture, its myths, its religion, its philosophy, its justification for its own entity as a culture."[3] Hart continues: "The initiation schools are directed at imparting instruction that cannot be given in the home, under conditions as unlike home conditions as possible, by teachers who are the antithesis of the home teachers the boy has hitherto had."[4]

INITIATION EDUCATION AMONG THE TSWANA   An example of the scope of such initiation education,

[3]See C. W. M. Hart, "Contrasts between Prepubertal and Postpubertal Education," in G. D. Spindler (ed.), *Education and Anthropology*, p. 141.

[4]*Ibid.*, p. 140.

from the Tswana, is provided in the following paragraph by Professor Schapera:

All the eligible boys were initiated simultaneously in groups, kept secluded in one or more special "camps" (*mephatô*) away from all the villages for three months or so. The details of the ceremony were kept a profound secret from women and all other non-initiates, who were forbidden under penalty of severe assault and even death to approach too near to the camp. At the camp the boys were first circumcised in order of tribal precedence. They were then systematically taught a number of secret formulae and songs, admonishing them to honour, obey, and support the Chief; to be ready to endure hardships and even death for the sake of the tribe; to be united as a regiment and help one another; to value cattle as the principal source of livelihood, and so herd them carefully; to attend the *kgotla* regularly, as this was the place for men, and to look after its fire; to honour and ungrudgingly obey old people; and to abandon all boyish practices. Much of this instruction dealt also with the important topic of sex, the boys being taught the physiology of sex relations, the duty of procreation and other rules of conduct in married life, and the dangers of promiscuous intercourse with ritually "unclean" women. They were further taught tribal traditions and religious beliefs, and the tribal songs of war and self-glorification, and were made to participate in symbolic dances of many kinds. They were, moreover, subjected to starvation and blows, discomfort and actual torture, and rigorous and irksome taboos of many kinds, and were made to participate in strenuous hunting expeditions, all with the object of hardening them.[5]

The rituals of priests, and often of shamans, must ordinarily be taught on an apprenticeship basis, for these are frequently so complex, as well as secret, that they can be imparted only under isolated conditions which encourage students' strict attention and rigorous study.

On the whole, it is safe to say that primitive children find their education less irksome than ours do. It demands less of them, and they can readily see the utility of what they learn because it is evident all about them in everyday living. They use their knowledge as they acquire it; they do not have to learn in a vacuum things that they will not have a chance to put to use for some years to come—or, perhaps, never.

---

[5]I. Schapera, *A Handbook of Tswana Law and Custom*, p. 106. By permission from Oxford University Press, London, and the International African Institute.

THE DETERMINANTS OF PERSONALITY

A given personality is the product of many interacting factors, which may be classified under four main categories: (1) the constitutional characteristics of the individual (biology, neurophysiology, endocrine system, body type, etc.); (2) the nature of the physical environment in which the individual lives; (3) the culture in accordance with which the individual lives; and (4) the unique, or idiosyncratic, biological-psychological-social experience or history of the individual. These components are fused in the creation of each personality. (See Table 4-1.)

Constitutional Characteristics

The most obvious, although not necessarily the most important, factors in the determination of personality are the physical and mental capacities with which the individual is endowed at birth. These are the traits which are frequently termed

TABLE 4-1   THE COMPONENTS OF PERSONALITY*

Determinants based on level of natural order		*Determinants based on degree of universality among human beings*			
		Universal	Communal	Role	Idiosyncratic
	Cultural	Incest tabu, kinship systems, property, magic, religion, housing, time reckoning, etc.	Special forms of kinship, property, magical and religious beliefs, etc.	Special roles culturally differentiated for status groups within each society	
	Social	Group life, child care	Size, distribution, density of population, etc.	Play groups, congeniality groups, cliques, etc.	Fortuitous experiences in social relations
	Biological	Birth, death, hunger, thirst, metabolic action, skeletal-muscular structure, basic drives, etc.	"Racial" variations of universal traits, health conditions of society at large, etc.	Age and sex differences, racially based class and caste	Individual peculiarities of stature, physiognomy, glandular functions, etc.
	Physical environmental	Atmospheric pressure, gravity, earth, sun, moon, stars, clouds, water, wind, precipitation, etc.	Local climate, topography, wild plant and animal life, other natural resources, etc.	Differential access to material goods by different status groups	Unique relations to flood, storm, lightning, and other physical phenomena

*Modified from C. Kluckhohn and O. H. Mowrer, "Culture and Personality" (*American Anthropologist*, vol. 46, 1944), pp. 1–29.

"inherited" or "innate," although these labels are in themselves misleading and open to a variety of interpretations. Included are such factors as body build, intelligence, neurological make-up, presence or absence of deformities, and the like.

Morphological factors which can be readily seen as having a direct influence on personality are stature, weight, and physical appearance. The personality of a dwarf cannot be that of a giant. We must keep in mind, however, that the social meaning of a physical characteristic is culturally determined. In Western culture, big men are expected to be dominant in ascendant-submissive relations. Differing cultures attach individual and often widely differing meanings to such physical attributes as larger-than-average size.

To illustrate this point, we may contrast American behavior with that of the Trobriand Islanders with respect to identification of physiognomy among kinsmen. In American society a newborn baby is carefully evaluated by relatives and friends to see whether it looks like the mother or the father, or this uncle or that aunt, or this grandfather or that grandmother. Americans have a real obsession to find points of resemblance to kinsmen. Maternal kinsmen project maternal identities upon the infant. Paternal kinsmen project their counterparts. If the physical traits are definitely identifiable with those of one line or the other, the stimulus value is quite marked, and the role behavior may be influenced one way or the other.

In the Trobriands, on the other hand, the dogma of the culture is that children do not and cannot resemble the mother or her kin in spite of the Trobrianders' theory of procreation. To hint as much is offensively bad taste. Yet resemblance to the father is always assumed and affirmed. Physical aspects of the father as well as aspects of his personality, but not those of the mother, are thus imputed to the children.

A queerer quirk in Trobriand culture is the dogma that brothers never look alike. Malinowski once suggested, apropos of some Trobriand Islanders' remarks about how much a group of brothers looked like their father, that it followed from this that the brothers must look like one another. The natives made it plain that they thought he had very crude manners to make such a gauche remark.[6] Syllogistic reasoning could not stand in the face of culturally controlled perception. From the Trobriand point of view, any fool can see that brothers just never do look alike.

Physical Environment

Anthropogeographers of the nineteenth century attempted to explain national character in terms of physical environment. Mountain dwellers are ruggedly individualistic, it was suggested. Enjoyers of temperate climates are creative and vigorous. Dwellers in the tropics are indolent and sexually precocious, and so on through a long list of stereotypes. Most early anthropogeographic work was so facile and superficial that it was tossed out, along with the concept of race as a determinant of psychological and behavioral characteristics, by twentieth-century anthropologists. Nonetheless, the mineral content of diet can and does affect the endocrine system of whole populations. Whether a people must adapt to an arctic, desert, or rain-forest environment is a factor of significant influence. Differences in the altitudes at which people live and the characteristic barometric pressures to which they must adjust are not without personality effects. Such matters are therefore not to be overlooked, and the imaginativeness of Professor John Whiting in seeking a causal relation between male initiation practices, multiple marriages, and climate is a good example of taking the environmental factor into account (see pages 69–70).

Cultural Determinants

Cultural determinants set the patterns and limits for normal behavior within any society. In Miller and Dollard's phraseology, culture is ". . . a statement of the design of the human maze, of the type of reward involved, and of what responses are to be rewarded."[7] The operation of these determinants, together with the feedback effect of per-

---

[6]B. Malinowski, *The Father in Primitive Psychology*, pp. 87–92.
[7]N. Miller and J. Dollard, *Social Learning and Initiation*, p. 5.

sonality responses to them, constitutes the subject of the rest of this chapter.

Idiosyncratic Features of Individual Experience

Every individual has a unique personal history. Not all aspects of the society's culture are open to all persons, and differences in status mean differences in social opportunity and experience. These mean differences in status roles and personalities. Even more important, however, is the fact that persons of identical status nevertheless do not have the same experiences. The mother prefers one child over the other. One child burns its finger; another does not. One person has an automobile accident; another does not. One infant falls in the river; another does not. No two persons ever have the same social experience, not even identical twins. From psychoanalysis we have learned how important the fortuity of history can be in shaping the direction of personality development.

Culture tends to standardize personalities by channeling the experience of all individuals along the same broad stream. But life is made up of so many instances, so many situations, such rich variety of experience, that absolute standardization can never be realized.

A Comprehensive Classification of Personality Determinants

Personality is therefore to be understood as a behavioral synthesis of an individual's physical (including neural and glandular) constitution, the physicochemical character of the environment, the patterns of the culture, and the individual's internalization of, and reactions to, his total life history in relation to people and things. These four categories are drawn on the basis of *levels within the natural order* and the nature of the individual's experience.

A hint of the immense complexity of interacting factors that should ideally be understood may be obtained from trying to imagine all the steps which would be involved in getting all the data for just one person—to say nothing of a representative sample of a society. The model that accounts for this classifies determinants in terms of the criterion of *degree of universality among human beings*. The four categories based upon this principle are (1) the *universal*—those determinants which are relatively constant for all mankind, whatever the environment, culture, or race; (2) the *communal*—those determinants which are relatively constant and unique for all the members of a given society as opposed to the members of other societies; (3) the *role*—those determinants which are linked to different statuses within a society; and (4) the *idiosyncratic*—those determinants which are uniquely individual, in either constitution or life history. Combining these with the four determinants based upon the level of natural order gives fifteen major components of personality (Table 4-1).

This framework points the way for sifting out "group personalities." Thus the universal determinants, which apply to all mankind, produce what there is of "human nature" the world over. The communal traits lead to national or societal character types. The role determinants shape the distinctive personalities of persons belonging to various age, sex, occupational, class, and caste groupings within societies. The idiosyncratic determinants guarantee the uniqueness of every individual as long as human beings endure.

Clyde Kluckhohn and Henry A. Murray expressed the foregoing epigrammatically in their well-known quotation:

Every man is in certain respects
   a. like all other men,
   b. like some other men,
   c. like no other man.[8]

ANTHROPOLOGICAL STUDIES OF CULTURE AND PERSONALITY

The first anthropological research reports on personality and culture were Malinowski's *Sex and Repression in Savage Society* and Margaret Mead's *Coming of Age in Samoa*. Malinowski

---

[8]C. Kluckhohn and H. A. Murray, "Personality Formation: The Determinants," in C. Kluckhohn and H. A. Murray (eds.), *Personality in Nature, Society, and Culture* (1949), p. 35.

tested Freud's theory of the Oedipus complex against the facts of Trobriand society. In the matrilineal system of social structure of the Trobriand Islanders, authority over children is exercised by the maternal uncle (mother's brother), rather than the father. Malinowski asked the question: "In this type of social setting does a boy have incestuous desires for his mother and 'hate' his father as an authority figure and rival for the affections of the mother?" After analyzing Trobriand behavior and Trobriand mythology, Malinowski concluded that the answer is "No." It is the uncle who is resented and the sister (particularly the clan sister) who is the object of intrafamilial sexual interest. Therefore, the basic principle of the Oedipus complex exists, but its manifestation alters with the cultural complex.[9]

Mead's work in *Coming of Age in Samoa* was discussed in the first chapter as an example of the use of the comparative method in anthropology as a substitute for laboratory-controlled experimentation to test hypotheses. It will be remembered that Mead's conclusion was that Samoan adolescents do not go through the period of psychological stress that characterizes American adolescence because Samoan culture is free of certain stress-producing features.

Neither Malinowski nor Mead expressed an explicit theory of culture and personality at that time (1926 and 1928, respectively). In 1934, however, Ruth Benedict (1887–1948) published her famous *Patterns of Culture*, which became the theoretical prototype for a number of later "configurational studies." Subsequently, Abram Kardiner, a psychoanalyst, with the cooperation of Ruth Benedict, Cora DuBois, Ralph Linton, and other anthropologists, developed and published a "theory of basic personality structure" for handling questions of the effect of culture upon personality and vice versa. This, too, became the model for a number of studies. All these theoretical systems rest on intensive psychocultural analysis of one or a few tribes. John Whiting, a former colleague of G. P. Murdock in the initiation of the statistical method of cross-cultural studies, entered the lists in 1953 with the publication of a broader theory of culture and personality, in which specific hypotheses are put to correlational tests that are statistically devised.

Each of these theories will now be considered.

The Configuration of Culture and the Ideal Personality Type

The central thesis of Ruth Benedict's approach to this problem was that the ideological contours of a tribal culture are impressed upon individuals in terms of an ideal personality type. Each society has a more or less clear idea of what constitutes the "good man" and the "good woman," the kind of person an individual ought to be.

In Benedict's analysis, the precepts, maxims, rewards, and punishments are all directed toward molding all individuals in the image of the ideal. One who approximates the ideal is an object of social cynosure. The character of this ideal personality is equated with an abstracted tribal character structure.

In *Patterns of Culture*, Benedict purported to demonstrate the empirical validity of the theory by detailed descriptions of what she called the "Dionysian configuration," represented by the Kwakiutl Indians of the Northwest Coast of North America, and the "Apollonian configuration," exemplified by the Zuñi Indians of New Mexico.

Dionysian-Apollonian configurations

The Dionysian and Apollonian concepts were phrased as follows:

The basic contrast between the Pueblos and the other cultures of North America is the contrast that is named and described by Nietzsche in his studies of Greek tragedy. He discusses two diametrically opposed ways of arriving at the values of existence. The Dionysian pursues them through "the annihilation of the ordinary bounds and limits of existence"; he seeks to attain in his most valued moments escape from the boundaries imposed upon him by his five senses, to break through into another order of experience. The desire of the Dionysian, in personal experience or in ritual, is to press through it toward a certain psychological state, to achieve excess. The closest analogy to the emotions he seeks is drunkenness, and he values the illuminations of frenzy. With Blake, he believes "the path of excess leads to the palace of wisdom." The Apollonian distrusts all this, and has often little idea of the nature of such

---

[9]B. Malinowski, *Sex and Repression in Savage Society*; also *The Father in Primitive Psychology*.

experiences. He finds means to outlaw them from his conscious life. He "knows but one law, measure in the Hellenic sense." He keeps the middle of the road, stays within the known map, does not meddle with disruptive psychological states.[10]

The factual validity of Benedict's characterizations of Kwakiutl and Pueblo society is open to serious challenge.[11] She drew her configurations with the artistic license of a poet, rather than with the exactitude of a scientist. Nonetheless, her beautifully written exposition of her configurational theory has exerted great influence on anthropology, education, and public thinking from 1934 to the present. It is the most popular book on anthropology written thus far in the twentieth century.

A much clearer, if less lyric, presentation of ideal personality types may be found in Aztec literature, and may aid in understanding Benedict's hypothesis.

Aztec ideal personality types

Not every society formulates these ideals explicitly, but the Aztecs did in terms that seem simultaneously familiar and quaint. As stated in the Florentine Codex, the ideals for father and son are as follows:

One's father [is] the source of lineage, the beginning of lineage. [He is] the sincere one. One's father [is] diligent, solicitous, compassionate, sympathetic; a careful administrator [of his household]. He rears, he teaches people; he rears, he teaches others. He advises, he admonishes one. He is exemplary; he leads a model life. He stores up for himself; he stores up for others. He cares for his assets; he saves for others. He is thrifty—he saves for the future, teaches thrift, looks to the future. He regulates, distributes with care, establishes order.

One's bad father [is] lazy, incompassionate, negligent, unreliable. He is unfeeling, neglectful of duty, untrustworthy; a shirker, a loafer, a sullen worker.

One's good son [is] obedient, humble, gracious, grateful, reverent. [He is] one who shows reverence, who obeys, humbles himself, is thankful, shows appreciation, resembles [father or mother] in body and character, [and] in way of life.

One's bad son [is] perverse, wicked, rebellious; a vile brute—mad, deranged, disobedient; one who ignores commands; a fool, lewd, gaudy, vain, untrained; a dunce who accepts not, who receives not the counsel of mother [and] father. Training, teaching, reprimands, corrections go in one ear and out the other. He belittles; he is disrespectful, bold, defiant, agitated, impetuous, rash, fitful.[12]

Guidelines for mother and daughter as well as for a host of other persons, are spelled out with the same specificity.

Like culture, the ideal personality type is a construct. While it suffers from dangers of over-simplification, it nonetheless offers a fundamentally useful approach. For example, when we speak of the "national character" of a people we are really speaking of a collective ideal personality type. The French national character is different from the British, and the British is in turn different from the German. Plains Indians' personalities are typically strikingly unlike those of Pueblo Indians. The Benedict approach has pointed up and driven home the theory that the personalities of the majority in any society are largely reflections of the ideal personality presented by that society's culture.

The collective actions of a nation are to a certain degree the reactions of the ideal personality type to given stimulus situations. Accurate analyses of national character can aid in understanding national conduct. The problem from the point of view of social science is to see that such characterizations are validated by adequate empirical data and critical checking.[13]

Basic Personality Structure and Cultural Projection

Although the concept of basic personality structure developed by Abram Kardiner originated in the concept of the ideal personality type, it devel-

---

[10]R. F. Benedict, *Patterns of Culture*, pp. 78–79. By permission from Houghton Mifflin Company, New York.

[11]See V. Barnouw, *Culture and Personality*, pp. 41–48, for a bill of particulars.

[12]C. E. Dibble and A. J. O. Anderson, *Florentine Codex*: Book 10, *The People*, pp. 1–2. By permission of School of American Research and University of Utah Press.

[13]The March, 1967, issue of the *Annals of the American Academy of Political and Social Sciences* is devoted to "National Character in the Perspective of the Social Sciences." It provides a good, up-to-date overview of the subject.

oped from the latter and is not identical with it.[14]

Whereas the use of the concept of ideal personality type demonstrates the close interrelation between culture and personality, it presents a characterization that is essentially descriptive and nongenetic. It describes a type of personality without attempting to probe deeply into questions of how it got that way.

Kardiner, a psychoanalyst by training and in practice, focused interest on the psychodynamics of personality and culture. The unique aspect of his approach is the way he undertakes to determine the effect of social institutions upon personality and of personality upon institutions.

Out of the interaction of this generalized psychoanalytic proposition that social institutions and personality do affect each other, and from the anthropological materials on cultural determinism have emerged these constructs: (1) Certain culturally established techniques of child treatment, called *primary institutions*, shape basic attitudes toward parents; these attitudes exist throughout the life of the individual. (2) The "group of nuclear constellations" of attitudes and behavior formed by the culturally standardized patterns of child treatment in any society, and persisting among the adults, is the *basic personality structure* that is characteristic of that society. (3) By means of the mechanisms of projection, the nuclear constellations derived from primary institutions are subsequently reflected in the development of other institutions such as religion, government, and mythology. Institutions derived as a result of projective systems are called *secondary institutions*.

The Kardinerian system is a limited system that attempts to establish two things: (1) the identification of the basic personality structure and the process of its formation as a reaction to child-care customs; and (2) the carry-over effect of the basic personality patterns into certain of the larger institutional structures of the society.[15] In other words, Kardiner is striving to show how one phase of culture shapes personality and how the resultant personality in turn shapes other phases of the culture. He is really probing the interrelation between culture and personality, not just the influence of culture on personality.

The method in its present stage of development is avowedly self-limited. It does not attempt to discover how the primary institutions, the child-care complexes, came into being. "The primary institution is treated as the taking-off point for the individual, not for the culture."[16] Furthermore, it assumes that various elemental aspects of culture, such as certain technologies (for example, basket making), may have no direct bearing on the basic personality structure. And yet further, it acknowledges that in many cultures certain institutions lie outside and are independent of the projective system.

On the positive side, a precept of psychodynamics which is essential to the whole scheme, and which we have not yet mentioned, is that the individual is not wholly the passive receptor of a particular cultural system. Culture is transmitted through learning, but the individual works emotionally upon what has been experienced and what has been taught.

The point is that [direct] learning processes do not account for the integrative character of the human mind in so far as the emotional relationships of the individual to his environment are concerned. . . . In addition to direct learning processes, the individual builds up a highly complicated series of integrative systems which are not a result of direct learning.[17]

In a dynamic situation of cultural change, such as the present, a new "youth culture" which is not the result of parental enculturation may result. The effect is a generation gap.

---

[14]A. Kardiner, *The Individual and His Society*; and A. Kardiner et al., *The Psychological Frontiers of Society*. A concise summary of the historical development of the concept may be found in Kardiner's article, "The Concept of Basic Personality Structure as an Operational Tool in the Social Sciences," in R. Linton (ed.), *The Science of Man in the World Crisis*, pp. 107–122.

[15]Note that Kardiner's secondary institutions are institutions in the ordinary sociological sense. However, his primary institutions are what anthropologists usually call *trait complexes*. In a strict sense they are not institutions at all. This leads Kardiner in his later work to amend the concept of primary institution to read: "primary institution or related practices, whether institutionalized or not." (*The Psychological Frontiers of Society*, p. 25.)

[16]*Ibid.*

[17]A. Kardiner, "The Concept of Basic Personality Structure as an Operational Tool in the Social Sciences," *op. cit.*, pp. 109–110. By permission of Columbia University Press.

Alorese culture and basic personality structure

It is quite impossible to convey the meaning of an operational application of the basic personality structure with anything like reasonable adequacy here. Yet a skeletal sketch will portray the idea better than none at all. We have selected Alor for the purpose, since it is the only one of the primitive cultures on which Kardiner has published results of psychodynamic analysis based upon adequate data.[18] All his other analyses of primitive cultures (Marquesan, Tanala, Comanche) must be recognized as experimental probing; the conclusions drawn from such probing must be treated as wholly provisional and indicative of potential results rather than final fact.

The Alorese, who live on the island of Timor in eastern Indonesia, are gardeners; their environment is that of the tropical forest. For women, the main cultural activity is gardening; for men, it is an endless round of wealth exchanges, the making and collecting of loans. Money, which in Alor consists of pigs, Javanese bronze vessels (*moko*), and gongs, is lent out at interest with tight bonds of obligation that bind the debtor to his creditor. Marriage and death, among other occasions, call for extravagant consumption of pork along with tremendous exchanges of *moko* and gongs. The heavy burdens of these occasions force the principals deep into debt.

Capitalism in Alor is primarily a vehicle for egotistical dominance over one's associates. In the family, the internal tensions and hostilities of the Alorese household fail to gratify the security needs of the infant child. Alorese culture is integrated about the basic insecurity of the individual. Dominance through credit control is an attempt at compensatory adjustment.

In like manner, Alorese wars in the past rested not upon any military interest.[19] War was only a means of getting even, a sort of irritable gesture expressed not in any art of warfare but in a series of long-drawn-out feuds marked by cowardly assaults carried out by trickery and stealth. Women, as well as men, were the victims.

[18]C. DuBois, *The People of Alor.*
[19]War among the Alorese was suppressed by the Dutch administration of the Netherlands Indies, now Indonesia.

The Alorese child is neglected. The child is wanted, not rejected, but is neglected. The mother works, and works hard, in her scattered fields. After the fourteenth day following childbirth, she has little time for her child. The father is away from home much of the time. The hunger pangs of the infant are irregularly and inconsistently met. The mother does not take the child to the fields with her; someone else around the house must tend the newborn—the grandmother, an older child, or the father, if he is home. Several women may nurse the child now and then; the infant is given gruel and premasticated bananas almost from the outset. Hunger cravings are physiologically met, but no consistent image of any person upon whom the child can depend for relief of hunger tensions is developed. Premasticated food may be given by anyone who wants to stop the infant's incessant bawling, but rejection and spitting out of such food, which is often observed, indicate that food thus given does not relieve the emotional tensions of the child. Hunger is more than an empty stomach.

Although the child is not left alone and is usually lugged around half-sitting in a shawl, parents do not relieve the child's tensions through fondling or caressing. The mother or elder brother or sister, or whoever else is paying any attention masturbates the infant for purposes of placation. This is merely a distraction and does not help to build the child's ego, for it is no more than an absentminded gesture.

In the primary institutions of Alor child feeding, there is no possibility of production of a parental image as a reliever of tensions. The intermittent appearance of the mother makes of her a tantalizing object who gives but inadequately the satisfactions so desperately needed.

Early childhood illnesses are indifferently treated and are aggravated by rough handling and irritating medication. The child learns to walk without assistance or encouragement. Again no one is available to enter into a relationship eliciting trust and dependence in response to receiving security and abetment. Defecation and urination are not brought under any particular coercive control. In this respect, Alorese child neglect is of a slight psychological benefit to the growing child. No anal eroticism is produced.

When weaning comes, the rejection of the child by its mother and mother substitutes, while not abrupt, is damaging. The breast-seeking child is pushed away or slapped. Then jealousy and rage are deliberately evoked by taking another child to the breast. Food is promised but not given. The adults think this is very funny.

These are the main lines of the primary institutions. What is the basic personality structure?

As children the Alorese are shy and reserved—they do not expect favorable response—but they readily fly into tantrums and become vituperative. Because they cannot obtain their desires or rewards in a direct way, they steal and forage as a regular thing. Aggression becomes canalized and predatory. The child, in turn, may reject his family by running away from home to live with some more remote relative.

This is the most extreme gesture of defiance and independence that the child is permitted and offers both a safety valve for pent-up aggressions and an opportunity to sustain the hope that the child may find in one of its other relatives the long-sought-for kind parent.[20]

None of the childhood patterns builds toward emotional solidarity within the family.

The ego development and social conscience of the adult are very weak. There is little self-confidence or sense of responsibility to others or to society. The adult male's relations to women are a projection of his almost complete defeat, as a child, in his relations to his mother. Husband-to-wife relations are bitter and nonintimate. Woman is the economic provider, and the male is dependent upon her. He cannot really dominate her. Compensation is found in the elaborate activity of loans and exchanges, the functions of which are essentially to gratify the psychological rather than the production-consumption needs of the economy.

Warfare and religious institutions in Alor bear quite clearly the impress of the projective system. War is disorganized, fitful, and vengeful. Religion falls within the category of ancestor worship, as is characteristic of the cultures of this part of the world. But the ancestors are neither exalted nor revered. Their powers for good are not exaggerated, and the Alorese feel no desire to assuage them by suffering or renunciation in their names. Because there is no interest in, possibility of, or benefit to be derived from getting back in their good graces, there is no restitution by penance. One expects no more from the ancestral gods than one expects from parents.

Ancestors, however, want to be fed. Their descendants' failure to feed the gods makes them angry—failure to feed the child was the supreme frustration. Angry gods punish their descendants. With great reluctance and only under the duress of misfortune, the Alorese make sacrificial food offerings to the ancestral spirits.

Religious art is careless and slipshod. Gods are projected "fathers" and "mothers." With no idealization of parents in the culture, there is no idealization of the gods. Representative carvings of ancestral deities are carelessly made, perfunctorily used, and quickly discarded. The dead are projections of the powerful and insistent creditors who bedevil adult life. In short:

The basic personality in Alor is anxious, suspicious, mistrustful, lacking in confidence, with no interest in the outer world. There is no capacity to idealize the parental image or deity. The personality is devoid of enterprise, is filled with repressed hatred and free floating aggression over which constant vigilance must be exercised. The personality is devoid of high aspirations and has no basis for the internalization of discipline. Individuals so constituted must spend most of their energy protecting themselves against each other's hostility. Cooperation must be at a low level and a tenuous social cohesion can be achieved only by dominance-submission attitudes, not by affection and mutual trust.[21]

Alor is a society with an old culture. It has survived for quite some time. This means that it has made the necessary minimal adjustments to the physical and biological imperatives. Yet that it is a precarious adjustment cannot be doubted; the continuance of the society must hang on a very thin thread. One of its strengths has been that the protection of island isolation has sealed it off from too much external competition.

[20]A. Kardiner, et al., *The Psychological Frontiers of Society*, p. 156. By permission of Columbia University Press.

[21]*Ibid.*, p. 170. By permission of Columbia University Press.

As an object lesson in the interaction of culture upon personality and of personality upon culture, however, it is superb.[22]

The Whiting-Child Theory and Correlational Method

J. W. M. Whiting, Harvard anthropologist, and I. L. Child, Yale psychologist, have combined Kardinerian-Freudian theory; the learning theory of Dollard and Miller, Skinner, Hull, and others; and the cross-cultural statistical techniques of G. P. Murdock to produce a different and an intriguing approach in *Child Training and Personality*. Although many hypotheses derived from psychoanalytic thought are used in this theory, the emphasis of the approach is on hypothesis testing—something in which psychoanalysis has been weak. The data for testing the hypotheses are drawn from the Human Relations Area Files.

Essentially, Whiting and Child set the following propositions:

1. Child training is universal: "In all societies the helpless infant . . . must be changed into a responsible adult obeying the rules of his society."[23]

2. Societies differ in their rules and in their methods of teaching conformity to the rules. These differences have differential personality effects.

3. Specific qualities of personality effects are projected on adult institutions and influence their content.

[So far, this is no different from Kardinerian theory. Now behavioral theory comes in.]

4. Adults reward responses that correspond to culturally established patterns of behavior. Positive sanctioning (positive reinforcement) increases the tendency to repeat the approved response. Responses that do not correspond to culturally established patterns of behavior are not rewarded and may be punished. Negative sanctioning (negative reinforcement) decreases the tendency to repeat the unapproved response.

5. The intensity of negative sanctions and the ages at which they are applied contribute to socialization anxiety. Approved responses bring drive reduction or satisfaction. Because they are rewarded, each successful repetition intensifies the satisfaction potential of the behavior.

6. Excessive frustration or excessive gratification in socialization results in negative or positive fixation. Fixation means that events of a certain kind have greater or lesser psychological importance for someone who has had the fixating experience than for someone who has not.

7. Illness is anxiety-producing. Explanations of illness, or causes to which illness is usually attributed, are fantasy-colored by projection of fixations customarily established in the members of a given society by child-training experience.

For example, oral fixations will produce such "causes" of illness as eating and drinking (especially "poisonous" foods) or curses and other magical spells. Anal fixations will generate explanations of illness in terms of failure to hide one's feces or other personal waste.

A number of special hypotheses were refined for testing. The method consisted in giving numerical values on a scale of rating for degree of severity of socialization of oral, anal, sexual, dependent, and aggressive behaviors. This was done wherever possible for fifty selected societies. (Interestingly enough, middle-class practices in Chicago, which represented the United States in the sample, rated very high in severity and low in indulgence in virtually every measure of early child training. Americans, it seems, are severe with, and demanding of, their children.) Each society was also classed, if the data warranted it, as *having* or *not having* oral, anal, sexual, dependent, or aggressive explanations for illness. Correlations were statistically derived between negative and positive fixations on the one hand and type of "disease theory" on the other.

The study established high correlations for the effect of severe, or negative, sanctions in producing illness projections. Positive fixations were not

---

[22]In this context, the analysis of the Mandan Indian Okipa ceremony, given in Chap. 20, is relevant.

[23]J. W. M. Whiting and I. L. Child, *Child Training and Personality*, p. 63.

shown to be effective in influencing adult theory of disease causation.

Additional social and cultural correlates of child-training practices

Extensions and modification of the Whiting-Child theory and method have subsequently been worked upon by Whiting and his associates, as well as by independent investigators.

GAMES   John M. Roberts and Brian Sutton-Smith have studied the occurrence of types of games relative to quality of child-training practices in a cross-cultural sample of fifty-six societies. Tribal societies possessing *games of strategy* (in which the outcome is the product of rational choice among several courses of action) are societies which emphasize and reward obedience, while punishing disobedience on the part of children. Such societies are relatively more complex in culture and social organization. Societies with a cultural emphasis on *games requiring physical performance skills* pay less attention to obedience in child training while rewarding achievement. Societies in which preadolescent children are shouldered with the responsibility of tending their younger siblings show a cultural preference for *games of chance.*

Games provide models for cultural participation. Strategy games prepare one for finding one's way in a complex cultural setting, while the associated child training conditions one to role conformity. Games of physical skill prepare one for individual initiative and extroverted activity and are indicated as linked to hunting types of societies. Games of chance take control of life out of the hands of the player, whose role is passive.

The studies also show that, across the board, "[T]here are consistent differences cross-culturally in the training of boys and girls. Boys, for example, are given higher achievement training, while girls are given more consistent obedience and responsibility training."[24]

PARENTAL REJECTION AND ADULT PERSONALITY TRAITS   A recent cross-cultural statistical study by R. P. Rohner indicates that parental rejection of children, as manifest in an absence of doing things to please the child, enjoying it, playing, singing, plus other failures to exhibit warmth and affection, generates children who are "anxious, hostile, insecure, and who devaluate their feelings of self-worth." Further, "adults who were rejected as children tend to devaluate their feelings of self-esteem and self-adequacy (low self-evaluation) . . . to be dependent, emotionally unresponsive and to evaluate the world negatively, . . . lacking in generosity."[25] Whether children are deprived of food, or fed generously, is indicated not to be a major correlate of the type of personality syndrome indicated above.

Evaluation of the Whiting-Child method

This method stands or falls on the true randomness of the ethnographic sample on which any particular study rests and on the validity of the value-rating judgments (coding) made by the evaluators of the descriptive ethnographic reports. The evaluations are usually subjective and often rest on inadequate ethnographic data. Yet the judgments are processed as though they were "hard" quantitative units. Those who feel that a science must have numbers applaud the effort. Those who are skeptical of the value of the results are apt to think of it as "the method of putative precision." It does, however, produce a provocative new look at the materials.

SELECTED READINGS

Aberle, D. F., *The Psychological Analysis of a Hopi Life-history* (Comparative Psychological Monographs, vol. 211, no. 107, 1951). A systematic interpretation in terms of general personality and culture theory of what took place in the life history of Sun Chief, the Hopi Indian whose autobiography was edited by L. Simmons (see below). Aberle's contribution is highly suggestive of illuminating examples. It should be read in connection with *Sun Chief.*

Barnouw, V., *Culture and Personality* (rev. ed., 1973). Useful as a general introduction to what has been

---

[24]J. M. Roberts and B. Sutton-Smith, "Child Training and Game Involvement" (*Ethnology*, vol. 1, 1962), p. 176.

[25]R. P. Rohner, "Parental Rejection, Food Deprivation, and Personality: Tests of Alternative Hypotheses" (*Ethnology*, vol. 9, 1970), p. 421.

done in the field and the methods that are used in relation to theory.

Haring, D. (ed.), *Personal Character and Cultural Milieu* (2d ed., 1956). A well-balanced anthology of technical papers written by professionals for professional reading. It will be hard going for the beginning student, but it is rewarding for those who want to go further into the subject.

Kardiner, A., et al., *The Psychological Frontiers of Society* (1945). Contains a general statement of the Kardinerian theory, with description and analysis of the Comanche, Alorese, and a midwestern United States community.

Mead, M., *Male and Female* (1949). Dr. Mead's provocative summing up of the interplay of culture and individual psychology in the shaping of men and women in seven primitive societies and the United States.

———, and M. Wolfenstein (eds.), *Childhood in Contemporary Cultures* (1955). Applies culture and personality theory to growing up in a number of contemporary societies. Includes a number of interesting chapters.

Middleton, J. (ed.), *From Child to Adult* (1970). Contains selected articles on enculturation and education in a variety of societies, mostly primitive.

Opler, M. K., *Culture, Psychiatry and Human Values* (1956). Mental illness and culture expertly interrelated.

Simmons, L., *Sun Chief: The Autobiography of a Hopi Indian* (1942). A fascinatingly rich and revealing document of personal experience. Not only does it give the inside view of what it means to grow up as a Hopi, but it also lays bare the severe personal conflicts caused by the need to integrate a single personality while living under two incompatible cultures.

Whiting, J. W. M., and I. L. Child, *Child Training and Personality* (1953). Spells out the theory, method, data, and results of their application of the correlational technique and use of cross-cultural data.

THE CULTURAL RESPONSE
TO ECOLOGY

5

STAGES IN THE BIOCULTURAL DEVELOPMENT OF MANKIND

LEARNING GOALS

List the procedures for classifying the development of mankind. ¶ Cite the major characteristics of the australopithecines and their biocultural developments. ¶ Describe *Homo erectus* and the early spread and proliferation of culture. ¶ Identify the distinguishing traits of *Homo sapiens* and their cultural developments. ¶ Enumerate the characteristics of intensive foraging and the development of agriculture. ¶ List the characteristics of civilization and its development in the Old and New Worlds. ¶ Summarize the general trends and significant developments in material culture and food-getting styles since the beginning of culture.

To understand human culture one must know the steps by which mankind has transformed itself from an instinct-dominated anthropoid into a culturally adaptive human being. Since the time of the earliest origins of culture, all human development has been both biological *and* cultural. No attempt to study mankind can ignore this fact. Therefore, as a background to all the chapters which follow, a brief overview of the prehistoric development of human culture is very much to the point.

The physical transformation and evolution of prehistoric human beings over the span of more than five million years is read from the paleontological record of hominid fossils. The basic materials for the study of culture change over the same span of time are found in the discoveries of prehistoric archaeology, which provide the outlines of temporal sequence in human cultural evolution. Together, primate paleontology and prehistoric archaeology weave the story of mankind's continuous biocultural evolution as the many-faceted product of intimate interaction with a wide variety of environmental settings. Only the major features of evolving fossil hominids are limned out in the discussion to follow; we concentrate mostly on the interrelations of these changes with mankind's ever-increasing and diversifying cultural achievements.

THE DEVELOPMENTAL CLASSIFICATION OF MANKIND

It is not difficult to identify mankind as to kingdom, phylum, and class. Each primate is clearly a member of the animal kingdom and not of the vegetable kingdom. Because of a spinal cord and nervous system, mankind belongs to the *phylum* of chordates. A spinal column of bony segments and the associated skeletal structure put us in the *subphylum* of vertebrates. The practice of nourishing the young on nutrient fluids generated by the female mammary glands gives us membership in the *class* of mammals. Because the unborn young are developed in the maternal womb, the human being qualifies for membership in the *subclass* of eutheria, within which it is identified as belonging to the *infraclass* of placentals, since the fetus is nourished directly from the bloodstream of the mother through the placenta.

Within the *order* of primates, taxonomists identify two *suborders*: (1) the anthropoid, which includes all apes, monkeys, and mankind, and (2) the prosimian, which includes the tarsier, lemur, and tree shrew—the most primitive in development of the primates.

Within the suborder of anthropoids there are two *infraorders*: (1) the catarrhines (Gr. *kata*, downward + *rhis*, *rhinos*, nose), the Old World anthropoids, whose nostrils are usually narrow and closely spaced, and (2) the platyrrhines (Gr. *platys*, broad + *rhis*, *rhinos*, nose), the New World monkeys, whose nostrils are usually flat and widely spaced. Mankind is clearly a catarrhine. The catarrhines in turn subdivide into two *superfamilies*: (1) the hominoids (mankind and the apes) and (2) the cercopithecoids (Gr. *kerkos*, tailed + *pithekos*, ape), which include baboons, macaques, vervets, and langurs.

The hominoids group into three *families*: (1) hominid, mankind; (2) pongid, the great apes; and (3) hylobatid, within which fall the gibbons and siamangs. The hominid family today has but one surviving *genus*, *Homo*. It also produced at least one other identified *genus*, *Australopithecus*, long since extinct. There are two living *genera* of pongids: (1) *Pan* and (2) *Pongo*. *Pan* is made up of at least two *species*: (1) the chimpanzees and (2) the gorillas. *Pongo* exists today only in the form of the orangutan, in Sumatra and Borneo. And finally, there is but one surviving *species* of mankind, *sapiens*, and but one surviving *variety*, also called *sapiens*. For mankind, then, the taxonomic identity is:

```
kingdom—animal
  phylum—chordate
    subphylum—vertebrate
      class—mammal
        subclass—eutheria
          infraclass—placental
            order—primate
              suborder—anthropoid
                infraorder—catarrhine
                  superfamily—hominoid
                    family—hominid
                      genus—homo
                        species—sapiens
                          variety—sapiens
```

For fun, one may say (and be quite correct) that the human being is a hominid, hominoid, catarrhine, anthropoid, primate, placental, eutherian, mammalian, vertebrate, chordate animal.

GEOLOGIC ERAS AND PERIODS

Stratigraphy is the analysis of geological deposits in terms of discernible layers. Time sequences are inferred from the relative positions of the strata, for the underlying strata are older than those overlying them—barring serious disturbances of the earth. In any local site, the relative ages of major geological strata are ordinarily clear. But in no single locality is one likely to find the entire sequence of major strata for all geologic periods. The master key is then built up by matching overlapping sequences. Once the key is established, the relative position of an isolated geological stratum can be determined by matching it to the homologous stratum in the key. Stratigraphy thus makes it possible to tell the relative ages of rocks and the fossils and archaeological materials that may be contained within them. This in turn makes it possible to place the sequences of the evolutionary development of life forms in time by means of hard facts.

The time that elapsed from the beginning of our universe to the birth of the earth is *cosmic time*. *Geologic time* began with the laying down of the first sediments four to six billion years ago, and extends to the present. Major blocks of geologic time are called *eras*. Eras are brought to a close by drastic changes in earth conditions, called *revolutions*.

Minor changes in earth conditions, called *disturbances*, take place within eras, producing the subdivisions of eras, called *epochs* and *periods*. The evolution of the primates occurred entirely within the final geologic era, the *Cenozoic*. Within this era are seven epochs: the *Paleocene*, the *Eocene*, the *Oligocene*, the *Miocene*, the *Pliocene*, the *Pleistocene*, and *Recent* (see Fig. 5-1). The Miocene, Pliocene, and Pleistocene epochs are of critical importance for humanity's immediate antecedents, and Pleistocene geology is crucial for the study of mankind, for this is the period in which the hominids finally evolved.

THE ORIGINS OF MANKIND

Human beings are, as H. L. Mencken used to write, superapes on a petty planet. Humanity's ancestry is anthropoid, and its marks are still with us. And yet, humanity has transcended its ancestry.

We have been transformed from mere anthropoids to hominids—human beings, the most complicated and, up to this point in the history of living things, the most generally successful adaptive product of all organic evolution.

Although the fossil history of Miocene apes and the changes in living habits which led to new adaptations in the direction of mankind makes a fascinating story in its own right, and although the observation and study of the natural habits of monkeys and apes sheds intriguing, though indirect, light on basic aspects of human behavior, we shall bypass that in this volume and begin with the appearance of "well-certified" human precursors—the first of the man apes who were on the road leading to the final emergence of mankind. This transformation took place at the close of the Pliocene epoch, some two or three million years ago. The Pliocene had been a time of protracted and catastrophic heat and aridity, when most of Africa and South Asia had become a searing desert. Some apes came out of the trees and migrated to open grasslands at high and moister altitudes. The other alternative, of course, was extinction. Most Miocene apes, of which there had been a number of genera and species, suffered the latter fate. A few survived to become the progenitors of the living great apes—the gorilla, chimpanzee, and orangutan. One genus had produced two species of two-footed ground dwellers. These were the australopithecines, the immediate primate precursors to *Homo*.

AUSTRALOPITHECUS AND THE TRANSITION TO MANKIND

The "Austral" in *Australopithecus* refers not to Australia but to the South. *Australopithecus* is the southern ape. Although the several discoverers of the various australopithecine fossils at first enthusiastically named four or five different genera from their finds, in addition to several species, the consensus of scientific opinion now recognizes but one genus, *Australopithecus*, and two species, *Australopithecus africanus* and *Australopithecus robustus*.[1]

----

[1]Consensus does not mean unanimity. Differences of opinion, interpretation, and naming continue to exist among some specialists.

Differences in Adaptation

Australopithecus robustus is pictured as a somewhat slow, plodding primate who went poking about with a digging stick or with bare hands, prizing out roots and eating berries, seeds, and fruit in a rather pleasant, if slightly dampish, stream and lake environment. *Robustus* lived from Late Pliocene to Middle Pleistocene times (5,500,000–700,000 B.P.), as did *Australopithecus africanus*. *Africanus* was habituated to somewhat drier environments and probably had little love for groves and vines. *Robustus* was not averse to a bit of meat, but the fossils associated with this form show that *robustus* took the easy pickings and was not a great hunter. Essentially, the life of *robustus* was that of the graminivorous gatherer. *Africanus's* life-way, on the other hand, was that of the small-game hunter *and* seed and vegetable gatherer.

Clearly, these two species represent divergent branches of some common ancestral stock which had probed the open areas between the forests for living space in Miocene times. *Africanus* is more advanced phylogenetically than *robustus*. *Robustus* was still largely a vegetarian but had achieved uprightness. *Africanus* shared the upright trait, but, in addition to being a seed eater, had become a carnivore with hominid dental and cranial features. He was evolving rapidly in the direction taken by mankind. *Africanus* had also become a bone-tool user and a maker of stone tools. Definitely, *Africanus* had acquired culture. Both *robustus* and *africanus* had made the critical evolutionary adaptation of bipedalism. They had fully freed their hands for potential tool using. But only *africanus*, through more varied responses to the potentialities of savanna life, made the shift to include fairly extensive meat eating in its diet.

It is possible that if *africanus* had strong and prominent canine and incisor teeth, the adaptation to direct hunting like a lion could have been made. But during the earlier natural selection for a graminivorous diet by *africanus's* predecessors, these teeth had become reduced in size and the dental possibilities for a hunting adaptation were eliminated. Further, *africanus* was adapted to upright locomotion and most likely had the primate order's typical propensity to social and cooperative group behavior patterns; both of which would have facilitated a social hunting adaptation

10,000 years

200,000 years

1,000,000 years

3,000,000 years

12,000,000 years

25,000,000 years

RECENT

Upper

PLEISTOCENE
Middle

Lower

PLIOCENE

MIOCENE

Homo sapiens sapiens

Homo sapiens neandertalen

Homo sapiens steinheimensis

Homo erectus pekinensis

Homo erectus erectus

Australopithecus robustus

Australopithecus africanus

Ramapithecus punjabicus

Economies	Technologies
	Metal
Food production	Neolithic cultures with pottery
Intensive foraging and hunting	Mesolithic culture with microblades and milling stones
Specialized hunting and gathering	Upper Paleolithic cultures with flake and blade tool technology and art
	Mousterian culture with the prepared-core technology and bone tools
Big game hunters	Acheulean tradition and chopper-chopping tool tradition and fire
Hunters and gatherers	Oldowan "pebble" culture and bone tools
Small object and seed eater	

FIG. 5-1 The known types of mankind and economies and technologies. (Skull drawings adapted from S. L. Washburn, "Tools and Human Evolution," *Scientific American*, with permission of publisher, and C. L. Brace, H. Nelson, and N. Korn, *Atlas of Fossil Man*, 1971.)

that could involve and reinforce tool use and communication.

If Raymond Dart's interpretation of the animal bones and jaws found with the South African *africanus* fossils is correct (and the case he has made is impressive), *africanus* had killing and cutting tools in profusion. Whether *africanus* "made" them or simply used them is beside the point. If they served the purpose well, they were an effective *cultural* adaptation sufficient for survival at that time and place. What is to the point is that *henceforth all hominid evolution became simultaneously biological and cultural.* "Human evolution," to repeat Dobzhansky's dictum, "can be understood only as a product of interaction of these two developments."[2]

Thus, the emphasis on meat eating in the diet of *africanus* placed a greater premium on social hunting. Social hunting, with its needs for cooperation, communication, and tool using, is enhanced by superior intelligence, and a selective factor in favor of those with greater brainpower was probably operative on the australopithecine populations.

The social consequences of the new dietary adaptation of *africanus* held tremendous implications for the future evolution of hominid temperament and relationships. Although present-day foraging monkeys and apes move about their territories in groups, each individual is independent in the plucking of fruits and shoots to feed itself. The operation is collectively organized largely in terms of mutual protection against outside aggressors. With their unweaned infants clinging tightly to their furry bodies, females forage exactly as do the males, who feed only themselves. Hominid hunters and foragers must, however, act differently. Their hands have been freed to fashion and use tools and weapons, and hunting has elicited a further bisexual differentiation in food getting. The role of females in hunting is functionally limited. The mother (with her young) gathers seeds and vegetables near a home base. The active male brings home his kills to share with his mate and offspring. The freeing of the female's hands for tool using has been accompanied by the prolongation of infant dependency, which is

related to the prolonged postnatal growth of the increasingly complex hominid brain. At the same time, the human species was losing its body hair. Eventually, there was nothing much for babies to cling to as the mother moved from place to place, and infants lost their instinctive ability to cling. In the transitional stages of cultural development, the mother had to carry her young in her arms. Later cultural adaptations have provided net, woven, and fur slings, or even more specialized cradleboards, but still women do not actively hunt.

So it is that, even as among predators, the mothering female became interdependent with the male for sustenance, and the male evolved in the direction of external predation. *Australopithecus africanus* made the big break which opened the path in this direction for mankind.

Life and Culture of Australopithecus africanus

Prehistoric cultures, especially those of Pleistocene hunters, may be reconstructed in only their thinnest outlines. So much rests on inference from limited facts that enthusiastic opinion and intellectual prejudice frequently run far beyond the reasonable limits of the evidence. This leads to a surprising amount of argument over the tool habits of the australopithecines.[3]

The most substantially defined and described cultural remains thought to be associated with *Australopithecus africanus* are those found at the famous Olduvai Gorge, Tanzania, in East Africa by the well-known Leakey family.[4] In 1960, L. S. B. Leakey and Mary Leakey discovered fragments of

---

[2]T. Dobzhansky, "Evolution: Organic and Superorganic" (*Rockefeller Institute Review*, vol. 1, no. 2, 1963), p. 1.

[3]The conflict is well summarized by D. L. Wolberg, "The Hypothesized Osteodontokeratic Culture of the Australopithecinae: A Look at the Evidence and the Opinions" (*Current Anthropology*, vol. 11, 1970), pp. 23–38. Also see R. A. Dart, "Predatory Implemental Technique of the Australopithecines" (*American Journal of Physical Anthropology*, vol. 7, 1949), pp. 1–16; "The Predatory Transition from Ape to Man" (*International Anthropological and Linguistic Review*, vol. 1, 1953). The argument for *Australopithecus africanus* as killer is given in great detail and with no little vehemence by Robert Ardrey in *African Genesis*, especially chaps. 7, 9, and 10. Per contra, see S. L. Washburn, "Australopithecines: The Hunters or the Hunted?" (*American Anthropologist*, vol. 59, 1957), pp. 612–614; and Elaine Morgan, *The Descent of Woman*, pp. 159–190.

[4]There is a controversy as to whether the fossil hominids found in Bed I at Olduvai are *Australopithecus africanus* or *Homo habilis*. See P. V. Tobias, "Early Man in East Africa" (*Science*, vol. 149, 1965), p. 27. See also S. Tax (ed.), "The Origin of Man" (*Current Anthropology*, vol. 6, no. 4, 1965), pp. 342–438.

a child on a living surface that also contained crudely chipped stone tools of quartz rocks. This is the famous Oldowan pebble (or chopper) culture, which extends all the way through Bed I and into Bed II at the Olduvai site, and which is also widespread elsewhere in Africa and Asia. There is not much to describe in this oldest of known lithic (stone) industries. In Leakey's summing up:

The Oldowan culture has from time to time been referred to as a "pebble culture," and this description is to some extent correct, for the vast majority of the implements of this culture are in fact made from water-worn pebbles. It must, however, be clearly understood that other forms of raw material were also used by the makers of this culture. Specimens occur which have been made from nodules of chert, and others from rough irregular lumps of quartz and quartzite, and there seems to be little doubt that sites containing assemblages of this culture might be found where tools made of actual water-worn pebbles were entirely absent.

The commonest tool type of the Oldowan culture is a crude chopper, varying in size from about the dimensions of a ping-pong ball to that of a croquet ball. The chopping edge is made by removal of flakes in two directions along one side of the pebble or other lump of stone which has been chosen, the intersection of the flake scars resulting in an irregular jagged cutting edge.[5]

The most important feature of the tools is that they are, indeed, intentionally constructed. There is a plan and a purpose, an idea and its execution, in these simple worked stones. A hominid was coordinating mind and hand to improve the means of achieving goals. If one definition of man is *a primate who is capable of the manufacture of definite tools*, then there were indeed manlike creatures at Olduvai when Bed I was being deposited. The pebble tool was a kind of hacking knife—a chopper of sorts—used in all likelihood to cut up meat, which was eaten raw. (There is no evidence of the use of fire in the Bed I deposits.)

HOMO ERECTUS AND THE LOWER PALEOLITHIC AGE

The evolutionary development of the earliest, large-brained, fully upright-walking primate, *Homo erectus* (upright man), was accomplished

in the Old World by the first interglacial times— some two-thirds of a million years ago. *Homo erectus* stands midway between the australopithecines and modern man, *Homo sapiens*, in the sequential order of hominid development. Although the opinion is still provisional, the dominant view among human paleontologists is that *Homo erectus* evolved rather rapidly out of the *Australopithecus africanus* gene pool. For a long while, australopithecine populations that had become noticeably *Homo*-like would exist simultaneously (but in different areas) with those which remained conservatively australopithecine. Thus, fossil remains of *Homo erectus* and *Australopithecus* are found in geological deposits of the same geological age. In Java and Africa, fossil australopithecines and the earliest representatives of the genus *Homo* are both found in Lower or Early Middle Pleistocene beds. By the end of the Middle Pleistocene both *Australopithecus africanus* and *Australopithecus robustus* were no more. They had become extinct; they were replaced by *Homo erectus* who was now their successor, for their roles in the drama of evolution had been played out.

Fossil remains of *Homo erectus* have been found in Asia, Africa, and Europe, and are classified into six subspecies. *Homo erectus erectus* (Java man) was located in central Java in a geological context that did not contain any associated cultural materials. The homesite of the second Asian form, *Homo erectus pekinensis* (Pekin man), was found near the capital of mainland China in the caves of Choukoutien. A third possible subspecies of *Homo erectus* would be the Vértesszöllös cranium discovered in northern Hungary. It is often grouped with the two Asian types because all three are associated with a similar stone artifact tradition called chopper-chopping tools.

The second cultural cluster of *Homo erectus* subspecies includes two African finds: *Homo erectus mauritanicus*, discovered at Ternifine, Algeria, and fossils from Bed II of Olduvai Gorge, *Homo erectus leakeyi*. A fossil removed from Lower Pleistocene sands near Heidelberg, Germany, *Homo erectus heidelbergensis*, forms the third subspecies of the western *Homo erectus* cultural cluster associated with artifactual materials that have been named Acheulean.

---

[5]L. S. B. Leakey, *Olduvai Gorge*, p. 34. By permission of Cambridge University Press.

The Life and Industries of Homo erectus in the East

Of the cultural developments associated with the three eastern subspecies of *Homo erectus*, most is known about those of Pekin man. Because he lived at least in part at the caves at Choukoutien, there is good preservation of a wide range of material that would normally not survive in open sites, giving us a rich picture of aspects of Pekin man's behavior. There is no way of knowing whether Pekin man habitually made the Choukoutien caves his home base or whether he just periodically visited them, but that he camped out in the caves again and again is clear. Deliberately broken and split bones of animals are found by the thousands throughout the deposits; ashes and scorched bones give testimony of the first-known hearths of mankind. The quantities of worked choppers show the continuation of the australopithecine tool tradition.

Pekin man dined mostly on venison. Other game that graced his menu included sheep, antelope, roebuck, small horses, and camels. But *Homo erectus pekinensis* was clearly a more wily and ferocious hunter than this inventory alone would indicate. Making up another sizable part of the solid remains of his garbage are the bones of elephants, rhinoceroses, bison, and water buffalo. Pekin man could have killed these huge beasts by means of fire drives, stampeding them over cliffs in wild panic before deliberately set grass fires or lines of men, women, and children waving flaming brands. He might also have trapped them individually in pitfalls, or, like the Congo Pygmy, he might even have brought down the great elephant by hiding near the game trails and leaping up under the belly of the lumbering beast, thrusting fiercely into the soft underbelly with a fire-hardened wooden spear. Or, again like the Pygmies, he might have collected the carcasses of the big game which had stumbled to their death through disease or old age.

As for the monster cave bears, saber-toothed tigers, leopards, and giant hyenas, whose fossil bones—also burned and sometimes split—are mingled throughout the debris, it is hard to believe that he fought them face to face, although he might have.

Lithic industry

The chopper tools of Pekin man did not reach the level of technical excellence attained by *Homo erectus* at the same time in Africa and Europe, where the Chellean-Acheulean tradition was well under way. The Pekin, or Choukoutien, industry, as described by Kenneth Oakley,

... consists principally of roughly broken pieces of quartz, with a few crudely flaked pebbles of greenstone, quartzite and cherty rocks. ... only a small percentage of the pieces are recognizable as tools, but these include chopper-like cores and flakes trimmed as points and scrapers. The industry proved to be practically uniform throughout the thickness of the . . . deposits. ... Most of the raw material was evidently collected from the bed of a nearby stream, but crystals of quartz with well-formed facets were found among the tools, and these must have been sought by Pekin Man in the granite hills some miles away to the north-east or south of the Choukoutien caves.[6]

Cannibalism

An interesting aspect of Pekin man's cultural adaptation was cannibalism. There is no way of knowing why Pekin man indulged in cannibalism, but that he ate human brains and the marrow of the long bones of fellow human beings seems quite evident. First, the recovered bones of *Homo erectus* in the Choukoutien caverns were found scattered helter-skelter throughout the deposits, just as were most of the animal bones; both kinds of bones are fractured and split. This might have been done to produce tools, but most of the bones are unworked and unused. Nor are these river-terrace deposits, in which the bones could have been scattered by running water. The bodies of human beings and animals had been dismembered, and the bones smashed and tossed aside by those who crouched and cooked about the campfires.

More significant is the fact that in all five of the skulls of Pekin man, the foramen magnum at the base of the brain case had been artifically enlarged so that it would admit a fist. Presumably,

---

[6]K. P. Oakley, *Man the Tool-maker*, p. 113. By permission of the British Museum, © 1949, Trustees, British Museum.

this was done to facilitate removal of the brain for consumption.

The Life and Industries of Homo erectus in the West

We know that *Homo erectus* had established itself throughout much of the Eastern Hemisphere in Middle Pleistocene times (CA. 700,000 to 100,000 B.P.)[7] Its fossil remains have been found in North and East Africa, southwestern Europe, and Southeast and East Asia. These people were clearly wanderers who pushed to the outer limits of the available land areas of the Eurasiatic heartland. Northern Europe and Asia were evidently climatically too intemperate for most of these warmth-loving creatures. With greater adaptability than the australopithecines, they pressed their range of occupation somewhat further north than had their hominid predecessor. In their living habits, *Homo erectus* had continued the first thrust of *Australopithecus africanus's* biocultural innovations. They mastered walking, specialized toolmaking, and hunting. To these were added the controlled use of fire, thus passing well beyond the limits of ordinary animal life.

Tools of the Middle Pleistocene hunters

In the West, including North Africa, and as far east as the Indus Valley in Pakistan, the basic tool tradition of *Homo erectus* is known as the Acheulean, after the type station (original site) at St. Acheul, in France.

THE HAND AX   The Acheulean is a lithic tradition focused upon the hand ax or *coup de poing*, in the terminology established by French archaeologists in the last century. Although the hand ax is the dominant diagnostic artifact of the Acheulean, varieties of flake tools such as scrapers and knives were also important parts of *Homo erectus's* tool kit.

The hand ax is an almond- or pear-shaped tool with a broad butt end which fits comfortably into the fist. Projecting below the grip is the pointed

working edge of the artifact. As a weapon, it was serviceable as a skull crusher in hunting or in fighting. As a tool, it served for hacking limbs from trees, butchering large game, and cracking bones for marrow. In view of the tens of thousands of Middle Paleolithic hand axes recovered in the past hundred and fifty years, it must have been that no early man or woman was ever without one—except by accident.

The perfection of the learned skills of flint knapping as applied to the hand ax continued steadily from its earliest manifestations to develop the beautifully shaped and finished hand axes of the Upper Acheulean types. The evolution of technological skills of tool production, extending from the Chellean through the Acheulean, spanned 500,000 years and more than 20,000 generations! Early human beings could pattern and retain the mental blueprint of their learned behavior. They could communicate and transmit their slowly won mastery of new achievements to other members of the group and from group to group, so that the tool traditions became part of an intercontinental cultural pool. But the rate of technical growth and diffusion over half a million years was minuscule. Compare, in contrast, the technical and social innovations which have been added to the cultural inventory of man since James Watt first invented the steam engine eight generations ago.

FLAKE TOOLS   The Acheulean inventory included, in addition to the hand ax, nicely retouched and especially shaped stone flakes for cutting, planing, and scraping the flesh off hides to be made into leather, and awls to punch holes for sewing.

The use of fire

Important discoveries made in the early 1960s by F. Clark Howell in the Ambrona valley northeast of Madrid, Spain, show that Early Ice Age Man had taught himself how to master the use of fire.[8] The valley served as a passageway for herds of the

---

[7]B.P. means Before Present.

[8]See F. C. Howell, *Early Man,* pp. 83–84. Also for the use of fire and its ecological consequences, see O. C. Stewart, "Fire as the First Great Force Employed by Man," in W. L. Thomas (ed.), *Man's Role in Changing the Face of the Earth*, pp. 115–133.

great straight-tusked elephant (*Elephas antiquus*), deer, aurochs, horses, and many lesser beasts. There, individuals armed with Acheulean weapons awaited them. But they were also armed with the controlled use of fire, as evidenced by the random appearance of charred pieces of wood and charcoal throughout and around the great kill sites. The sites themselves, as soil and pollen analyses indicate, were bottomland bogs into which the herds were stampeded, quite possibly by setting fire to the dry, late summer grasses. The racing flames would then drive the animals deep into the muck from which there was no escape. Armed with heavy hand axes and wooden spears, wary and courageous *Homo erectus* males could then move in for the kill—after the beasts had worn themselves out in fruitless struggles against the sucking embrace of the deadly swamp. The vast numbers of helter-skelter skeletons, well-preserved (but few complete), reveal that they were butchered on the spot, with such parts as could be carried away to the campsites stripped and hacked off. The skeletal bulk remained where the beast had died.

One can imagine the gluttonous gorging that followed such a kill. Like Eskimos who, after a big whale kill, can and do eat as much as 10 pounds of meat each at one sitting, so the Torralba hunters may have similarly indulged themselves a half million years ago.

Consumption of game in such quantities also meant that human beings had learned the rudiments of cookery. Knowledge of the art of outdoor barbecuing is surely among the most ancient marks of being human. Our long ancestry of primate vegetarianism did not equip us with the correct hormonal digestive input to handle large amounts of uncooked meat. Cooking effects the chemical and physical transformations necessary to give the digestive process a prestart before ingestion.

It may be too much to attribute the success of *Homo erectus* to the mastery of fire, but there is good reason to believe that this was a key factor in his ecological adaptation. The Greeks well knew the importance of fire to mankind. Prometheus dared as *Homo erectus* dared. According to the myth, fire was the cherished possession of the gods and was not meant for mankind. When

Prometheus stole it from the lightning of Zeus and gave it to man, the gods could not take the gift away, but they condemned Prometheus, the firebringer, to the torture of the damned, chaining him hand and foot to a rock, belly exposed to the tearing beak of a vulture. The Greeks were not alone in seeing fire as a divine possession that an individual could steal through intelligence alone; the myth is one of the primeval basic conceptions of all mankind. The story of the theft of fire is told in one form or another in virtually all societies, primitive and civilized.[9]

Pekin man, like *Homo erectus* in the West, was probably a "fire stealer" rather than a fire maker. At any rate, no fire-producing instruments have come from his caves. Lignite and coal beds, which lie close to the surface and could have been subject to spontaneous combustion, lie near to Choukoutien. And, of course, lightning sets fire to trees. The precious tending of the "eternal ember" of the household fire was surely a matter of great concern and could well have been the focus of simple basic, ritual anxiety.

Settlement pattern and housing

A picture of the settlement patterns and preferences of *Homo erectus* in the western Old World is emerging from the evidence analyzed during the recent increase in archaeological excavations in Africa and Europe. Rich Middle Pleistocene sites with deep stratigraphy covering tens of thousands of years have been exposed all over Africa except for heavy rain-forest areas of the Congo Basin.

Seasonal migration and housing at Terra Amata

Some bands of Middle Paleolithic human beings did indeed live in caves, but others roved the forests, tundra, and open plains, building themselves not only temporary shelters but, in some instances, real houses.[10] This knowledge comes

---

[9]See "Sun Snarer" in M. Leach (ed.), *Standard Dictionary of Folklore, Mythology, and Legend*, vol. 2, p. 1089.

[10]H. deLumley, "A Paleolithic Camp at Nice" (*Scientific American*, vol. 220, 1969), pp. 42–50.

as the result of the great discovery made in the very heart of the fashionable city of Nice, France, in the Fall of 1965, of a Paleolithic campsite known as Terra Amata. Three hundred volunteer excavators helped in a crash archaeological salvage enterprise to unearth more than 35,000 cultural objects which were associated with twenty-one house sites.

No human fossils were discovered at Terra Amata but the diagnostic artifacts at the location represent the Acheulean cultural tradition which is associated with *Homo erectus* fossils throughout the western Old World. Thus it is inferred that populations of *Homo erectus* were the house builders at Nice.

Postholes in the compacted sands show the oval outlines of the houses. Circles of boulders around the postholes lay in place as sometime reinforcements. A line of large postholes down the center of the elongated floor marks the location of the uprights which supported the ridgepole. Each house faced the sea, where the southern sun shone through the doorway. Inside the doorway, where ventilation would be best, lay a small, scooped-out hearth. And on the northwest side of each house was a loose wall of stones to shield the fire from the drafts that blew along the floor. Evidently, the walls were not too windproof. The floor on the east side of each dwelling shows a clear area surrounded by myriads of flint chips. Here squatted the master toolmaker of the household, preparing and repairing the hand axes and flake tools for the band of hunters and food processors.

Human feces found in the same sand strata as the floors of the cabins (but always outside them) contain undigested pollen such as is shed by plants in the late springtime. It could be that these early nomadic hunters came down to the warm coast mainly to eat their fill of fresh greens after a long winter of heavy meat protein and carbohydrate diet. While on the coast, they also dined on fish and shellfish. Yet this alone could not have been their reason for the seasonal visits to the coast, because seafood is available the year around, and the coprolites indicate the migrants stayed only as long as the spring plants were fresh.

It is clear, however, that these meat eaters did not go wholly vegetarian in the spring. Fossil remains of *Elephas meridionalis* (southern elephant), Merk's rhinoceros, stag, ibex, ox, and wild boar show that the house builders were true Paleolithic big-game hunters who yearned for a little variety in their diets.

Finally, it is evident that they were an industrious people given to activity. They stayed at Terra Amata for only a few weeks in the spring. Yet on arrival they built themselves noteworthy houses, both for comfort and, one might surmise, as functional expressions of their band unity and their humanness. They were clearly conscious of being different from mere animals.

The pattern of the domicile is very likely that of a joint family household. The family was probably bilateral (see pages 212–213), since there was little inheritable property to stimulate the development of unilateral descent. Most likely, these people practiced the incest tabu, which forced a male to seek his mate from outside the family and household (see pages 171–178). Because subsistence was predominantly by hunting, it may be inferred that residence was with the band of the husband rather than with that of the wife (see pages 198–200). This means that the composition of the band would have consisted of an older male or two, one of whom would be the household headman, their wives, their sons and the sons' wives, plus children. The whole group could number, say, from ten to thirty people living in one house. Related households might have formed a hamlet, made up of a somewhat larger composite band, but probably not numbering more than 100 persons.

HOMO SAPIENS AND THE MIDDLE AND UPPER PALEOLITHIC

The evolutionary progression that resulted in *Homo sapiens* was slow but accelerating. The associated development of culture proceeded at a similar pace. Nearly two and one-half million years elapsed from the time of the first pebble tools to the threshold of the Upper Paleolithic Age. The process had been started by the australopithecines and was consolidated in Africa, Asia, and southern Europe by *Homo erectus*. In the Middle Paleolithic it was carried forward by *Homo sapiens*.

As in earlier times, hunting and gathering were still the source of human sustenance, but the techniques were slowly changing, and mankind's mentality was changing even more rapidly. Upright posture was no longer the predominant feature. The human brain caught up with, and surpassed, morphological development. The human being was becoming more and more the toolmaker and the thinker.

By the middle of the long second interglacial period, the development of mankind had expanded to the point where, for the first time, present-day paleontologists are willing to classify its fossil remains as those of *Homo sapiens* (Gr. *homo*, man + L. *sapiens*, intelligent). In this group are the Steinheim, Swanscombe, and Neandertal forms of early *Homo sapiens*. They are initially associated with late Acheulean cultural material, a continuation of the traditions maintained by *Homo erectus*, but more prominently, they are seen as the developers of the Mousterian tradition (see Fig. 5-1). The Middle and Upper Paleolithic technological developments are primarily refinements of tools and techniques developed in previous traditions. What is new during these periods is the development of art and the appearance of fresh adaptations, reflecting mankind's new subsistence and shelter needs as the northern continental areas, such as the European plains, are invaded and occupied.

The Mousterian Culture of Homo sapiens neandertalensis

The basic subsistence of Neandertal *Homo sapiens* was not appreciably different from that of the pre-Mousterian big-game hunters of the *Homo erectus* type. The Neandertal time span ran from the end of the third interglacial through the first half of the fourth glacial, when it came to an abrupt end. The Mousterian complex began approximately 100,000 years ago and ended around 35,000 B.P.

The Mousterian complex

The distribution of tool assemblages of the Mousterian complex is vast—Europe, Africa, and all South and East Asia. But variety in the local assemblages is also considerable, for human beings were now becoming able to recognize and put into effect more and more alternative possibilities in their basic technologies. In the main, it may be said that Neandertal man's Mousterian stone technology continued the evolutionary trend which had been slowly developing through all the Lower and Middle Paleolithic. However, a definite shift from the production and use of hand axes to more and more emphasis on varieties of flakes marks the general trend.

BONE-TOOL INVENTORY   Neandertal man made extensive use of bone implements. It has always seemed reasonable to suppose that early man surely made as much use of wood and bones for tools and weapons as he did of stone. Rare fragments of worked wood are proof of wood use, but the loss of most pieces through decay gives little idea of what the relative importance of wooden artifacts may have been. The situation with respect to bone is different. Bone fossilizes better than wood and many more fragments have been preserved in and about human living sites.

In 1969, an English archaeologist, James Kitching, concentrated on the analysis of an osteodontokeratic (bone, tooth, and horn) assemblage from Mousterian deposits in the English site known as Pinhole Cave. Only seventy-three Mousterian stone tools were found, but hundreds of used bone flakes were discovered. The teeth of rabbits were used as sharp punches.

Half jaws of carnivores, with their projecting canines, were used as ripping tools. Antlers, shoulder blades, jawbones of reindeer, and leg bones of rhinoceros were used as splitting wedges and hammers. Split and trimmed ribs of reindeer and bison, and spirally broken splints of leg bones served as knives. Shoulder blades of rhinoceros and reindeer were trimmed and used as spades for digging. Rounded bone flakes from large leg bones, the hip blade (ilium) of rhinoceros, the shoulder blades of reindeer, bison, and horses were all used as skinning tools. Other bones were put to use as hide scrapers. A really nice adaptation was the use of the large hip socket of the rhinoceros as a pounding bowl or mortar. And for pestles with which to grind and pound, what could be better than the foot bones (carpal and tarsal) of rhinoceros? The brain case of reindeer made a cup or scoop, as did the hip socket of the rhinoceros. Kitching also thinks that the hollow humerus (shinbone) of the rhinoceros, with the marrow removed, served as a prepottery tankard.[11] The hardware of a Neandertal household was plentiful.

HOUSING   Most known Mousterian homesites have been found in caves. In the more extreme fluctuations of cold in the fourth glaciation, caves were clearly appealing to the Neandertaler for the shelter they offered. So also were overhanging rock cliffs, especially those which formed rock shelters on the north side of a river valley. The noonday sun provided welcome reflected solar heat which continued to radiate into the cold night. Yet no more than the pre-Neandertal *Homo sapiens* predecessors was the Neandertaler exclusively a cave being.

One example of Mousterian open-plains housing comes from Molodova, in western Russia. A ring of huge mammoth bones, lying close together, surrounds a floor which is clear of bones and 18 feet in diameter (Fig. 5-2). Within the floor are the remains of fifteen hearths. This Mousterian home was probably made of supple tree trunks inserted at the base into hollow tubes of mammoth leg bones, which were found buried upright in the ground. Animal skins would have covered the frame. The piles of bones around the circle are believed to have served as weights to help hold the structure in place and especially to keep the skins tight against the ground so as to shut out wintry blasts along the floor. Outside a break in the bone ring, to the northwest, is an accumulation of mammoth bones left from butchering operations. The large number of hearths within the tent space could indicate that the basic materials were left "on location," so to speak, for seasonal use by a wandering band that returned for the hunt from time to time.

RITUAL AND DANCE   If "hearth and home" had come to have emotional meaning for the Neandertaler, so too, the evidence tells us, had living and dying. Of the prerequisites for the maintenance of human society suggested in Chapter 2 (page 30), the most uniquely human is a definition of "the meaning of life" which maintains the motivation to survive and engage in the activities necessary to survival. This concept is expressed in symbolic representations of feelings and ideas.

To date, there is little evidence of material art produced by the Neandertalers. On the other hand, two expressions of human feeling do stand out: burial of the dead and a ritualized bear cult. A good many of the recovered fossil skeletons of Neandertal man have been found carefully bedded in shallow pits and accompanied by flint tools and occasional bones. One Neandertal was buried in Shanidar Cave, Iran, on a bed of pine boughs and flowers, according to the pollen concentrated in the earth surrounding his skeleton. Whatever this might or might not lead us to infer about belief in immortality and a continued spiritual existence apart from the body, it does show concern for the individual as a person. Even newborn infants were buried in the cavern of La Ferrassie in France.

The evidence of a bear cult among different groups of Neandertal man is ample. Bear burials have recently been discovered in the Cavern of Regourdon, in southern France, confirming the importance of the bear-skull cache from the Dragon's Lair (the Drachenloch) in Switzerland, where a stone-lined pit, or cist, held a collection of packed bear skulls, including the lower jaws. The hole was closed with a large stone slab. The Drachenloch has yielded a bear skull without a lower jaw but with the right thighbone of another bear pushed between the cheekbone (malar) and the brain case (calvarium) on the right side. This device was found placed upon two shinbones (femurs) from still two other bears.

Variations in cults are so tremendous that it would be foolhardy to try to reconstruct even by speculation what the Neandertal cave dwellers were up to. However, the possibilities may be sensed in the Bear Dance, and its accompanying mythology, as it is still performed every spring among the Ute Indians of Colorado and Utah. It commemorates the emergence of the bear from his long hibernation and his confrontation by a legendary Indian who learned the dance from a

---

[11]J. W. Kitching, *Bone, Tooth and Horn Tools of "Paleolithic Man."*

FIG. 5-2 Ground plan of the site of a Mousterian dwelling on the open plains of western Russia at Molodova. The small dark dots represent mammoth teeth; the larger dark areas are hearths within the original hut and indicate repeated occupation. (After F. Bordes, *The Old Stone Age*, p. 143.)

0   1m

bear. When the Utes perform "his dance," they are sure that the friendship of the bear for human beings is secured. They are confident that it makes hunting safer.[12]

Upper Paleolithic Cultures

The Upper Paleolithic age and *Homo sapiens sapiens* made their first appearances together, in Southwest Asia and Europe, around 35,000 B.C. The earliest known manifestations of the Upper Paleolithic are found in Iraq (Shanidar Cave),

---

[12]J. H. Steward, "A Uintah Ute Bear Dance, March 1931" (*American Anthropologist*, vol. 34, 1932), p. 265. See also A. I. Hallowell, "Bear Ceremonialism in the Northern Hemisphere" (*American Anthropologist*, vol. 28, 1926), pp. 1–175.

Afghanistan (Kara Kamar), Israel (Mt. Carmel), and Cyrenaica, North Africa (Haua Fteah). The earliest C[14]-dated Upper Paleolithic sites in western Europe fall about 2,000 years later, at Arcy-sur-Cure in the Yonne department of France. Some prehistorians suggest that this implies an origin of the Upper Paleolithic culture complex in Asia Minor, followed by rapid diffusion westward via migrating *Homo sapiens sapiens*. More reliable dates are needed before jumping to such a conclusion, however.

Yet one thing is certain. The Upper Paleolithic lasted from 35,000 B.C. to 8000 B.C., when the first great cultural revolution of human history began. Upper Paleolithic human beings were still living in the tradition of the meat-eating predators. The hand ax had almost wholly disappeared from their working kits but flake and blade tools directly traceable to earlier forms abounded. In the latter phases of the Upper Paleolithic, as reindeer became relatively more numerous than the rhinoceros and elephant, harpoons carved from antlers became the chief weapon. This was a new invention, but it was still only a refinement of what had existed for several hundred thousand years—the stone-pointed spear. The spear thrower (called *atlatl* after the Aztec name for the tool) was introduced early in the Upper Paleolithic.

What modern human beings, the Paleolithic hunters, did do was to bring the Stone Age hunting tradition to a climax. To an improved material technology they added a fabulously imaginative intellectual culture. With sympathetic magic they enhanced their faith in their own likelihood of success and survival. Because they were now human beings, they were capable of worry and fear of things and events which had not yet come to pass. In short, they developed imagination. Out of this was generated their remarkable cave art of multicolored wall paintings and low-relief murals, plus etchings and engravings on bone, and very "modernistic" sculpture.

Upper Paleolithic traditions in Europe

The subdivision of the European Upper Paleolithic into separate traditions is based primarily on variations in the relative frequencies of different flake-tool types, etc., forming local manifestations out of a generally similar tradition. These period and local differences, often of a rather technical nature, reflect adjustments to different European climates and habitats, and to the ongoing change in climate, as well as to technological variations. Five subdivisions are commonly defined for the period of 32,000–8000 B.C. The Early Upper Paleolithic consists of the Châtelperronian (also called Lower Périgordian), Aurignacian, and Gravettian (also called Upper Périgordian) traditions. A brief, somewhat alien, interlude, the Solutrean, constitutes the Middle Upper Paleolithic. It was followed by the Magdalenian tradition of the Late Upper Paleolithic.

PALEOLITHIC ART   One focus of anthropological studies of the Upper Paleolithic has been on the intriguing sequence of artistic development. Painting, engraving, sculpture, and modeling were familiar media of expression, and Upper Paleolithic individuals (except the Solutreans) were skilled in all these fields. Their art began in experimental crudeness and developed steadily to the sure technique of masters.

Although they represent different techniques, engraving and painting were closely integrated by the Gravettian-Magdalenian artists. They developed hand in hand to produce closely similar forms of expression. It appears that when an engraving was made first, its incised lines were always painted in afterward. Sometimes a wall surface was given a paint wash, after which the engraving was incised. The effect was to set out the engraving in fresh contrast to the painted background.

Early Gravettian engravings and paintings were no more than crude, stiff outlines. Later Gravettian pictures became more accurate representations, and in the Lower and Middle Magdalenian, skill in composition, contour, and the use of polychrome were achieved. Some comparative examples of Gravettian-Magdalenian art are given in Fig. 5-3.

Sculpture does not show such a progressive trend, since most of the known examples reveal reasonably good technique, whatever the phase. Mural sculpture was wall engraving developed to produce medallion types of low and high relief. The best work, however, was done in sculpturing in the round on bone, antler, and ivory, and in shaping such articles as dagger grips and dart throwers in animal and bird forms. The most famous example of plastic modeling is a family group of a bison bull, cow, and calf from the cavern of Tuc d'Audubert.

Much light is shed on the beliefs and mentality of Upper Paleolithic individuals by the art that they produced. If ever an art reflected the spirit of its culture, it was this. There have been argumentative exchanges of opinion between utilitarian-minded anthropologists and those who insist that art be evaluated as an end in itself. Aesthetes have held that it manifests the essential artistic and creative genius of its makers. Anthropologists have insisted on the symbolic utilitarianism of the

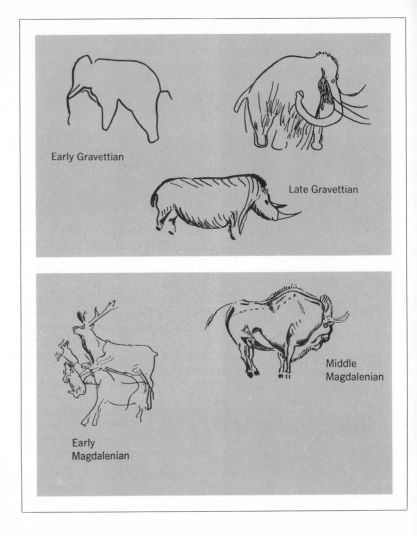

Early Gravettian

Late Gravettian

Middle Magdalenian

Early Magdalenian

FIG. 5-3 Four phases of Upper Paleolithic art: from simple silhouette to polychrome contouring.

art, for they see the cultural functions of art as more significant than the aesthetic aspects alone.

Upper Paleolithic art had the gross purposes of filling human beings' stomachs and of maintaining the population by serving as a magical aid in hunting and procreation. It also gave expression to a deep feeling of identity between humanity and its universe. But besides being a means to these ends, it was also an end in itself. Upper Paleolithic artists produced not merely images, but beautiful images. They not only strove to produce magically efficacious representations of the goals of their desires but also developed

artistic skill for the intrinsic pleasure it gave. In regard to sculpture, the Upper Paleolithic artist deserves to be called "the Paleolithic Greek," and because of the paintings of this tradition, it is not hyperbole to call the cavern of Lascaux "the Sistine Chapel of the Ice Age."[13]

It is likely, however, that magical purposes never left the minds of Paleolithic artists. This is

[13]In 1956, the senior author visited Lascaux at Christmastime and had an hour alone in the cave with its discoverer, Henri Ravidat. A week later he visited the Sistine Chapel. His feeling is that it would not be amiss to call the Sistine Chapel "The Lascaux of the Renaissance."

especially evident in the case of their mural art, which is rarely found where it may easily be seen. Upper Paleolithic artists did not adorn the walls of their homes or the entrance to a cavern. On the contrary, their works of art are found deep in the earth's bowels, in the dark, mysterious caverns where the artist worked by the fitful smoky flare of a stone lamp. There Upper Paleolithic artists drew their animals: the woolly mammoth, bison, reindeer, wild cow, bear, woolly rhinoceros, horse, and ibex—most of them now long since extinct in Europe. Again and again they painted red gashes on the animals' bodies, gashes dripping with blood. They often showed projectile points piercing animal flesh, and in some instances streams of red blood are painted flowing from nostrils and mouth. Diagrammatic scenes of log-covered pits into which mammoths are crashing have been found in such sites as the cavern of Font de Gaume. All these expressions of realism are acts of wish fulfillment through compulsive, mimetic magic (see also pages 351–352).

Some magic may be wholly beneficient. This is particularly true of fertility magic. The Gravettians were especially fond of statuettes of pregnant women of whom the Venus of Willendorf (Fig. 5-5) is the most famous. The parts of her torso which swell with pregnancy are given lavish exaggeration and virtually every line is a segment of a perfect circle: the apotheosis of the feminine curve. The face, arms, legs, and feet are ignored. The artist has composed her with selective interest. The detail of her coiffure shows that the hairdo had its social, and probably cult, significance 20,000 years ago and that the hairdresser existed as an artisan long before our era.

Whether the charming statuettes, which stand only 2 to 6 inches high, were talismans to be carried by the woman who wished for a child, or whether they were worshipped by men and women alike as mother-goddess idols, cannot be known. It seems possible that they represent a cult of this goddess, for in the Mesolithic and Neolithic ages to follow, there is no question of

FIG. 5-4 (left) "The Sorcerer," an Upper Paleolithic cave painting of a masked deer dancer in the Caverne les Trois Frères, Ariege, France. (After the tracing and restoration by H. Breuil.) (right) A modern San Ildefonso Pueblo deer dancer as painted by Alfredo Montoya in 1908–1909. (Courtesy of the School of American Research, Santa Fe, New Mexico.)

FIG. 5-5 The Venus of Willendorf, Gravettian goddess of fertility. She represents the idealization of a reproducing mother in which nearly every curve on the statuette is a segment of a perfect circle. (Courtesy of the American Museum of Natural History.)

culture complex as an entirety must have brought about an efficient environmental adjustment. Aurignacian complexes are found throughout the Middle East, in the Crimea, and into Siberia, where they are associated with remains of semi-subterranean houses (Fig. 5-6). Eastward, these complexes extend into India to the boundary of the old Acheulan and East Asian chopper- and flake-tool complex. Aurignacian and Gravettian traditions also occur in East Africa and the Mediterranean coastal areas as the Capsian tradition.

In Africa, the Middle Paleolithic Acheulean traditions went through a number of local developments, but a general Upper Paleolithic complex, called the *Sangoan*, which spread over East Africa and the Congo basin, is representative. As a forest tradition, the Sangoan could not do away with the hand ax, which became elongated to take on the form of a pick, or broadened along the cutting edge and narrowed at the butt to become very similar in form to a modern steel ax. The Sangoan also included tanged and shouldered points resembling those found in the Solutrean tradition. In other words, the Upper Paleolithic traditions of most of Africa evolved in much the same directions as those of Europe and Asia Minor, while at the same time developing certain distinctions.[14]

As for East and Southeast Asia, Movius's concise summary may still be sufficient:

Uninfluenced by contemporary innovations in Africa, Europe, and western Asia, the archaic and very primitive tradition of making implements of the chopper and chopping-tool varieties either on pebbles or roughly tabular blocks persisted in the Far East as long as the practice of making stone tools survived.[15]

Upper Paleolithic men from South Asia were pushing down into what is now the Indonesian archipelago and into Australia. They may have needed rafts at points, but they reached Australia around 33,000 B.C.[16] The absence of big game and good flaking stone reduced their technology to crude choppers and flakes, with reliance on wood

the importance of worship of the mother goddess in the Middle East.

We may conclude by saying that the Upper Paleolithic art of Europe and North Africa was a vividly representational art—an art of flesh, blood, and hope—a functional art which aided in survival, an art which was eagerly used by a hunting people in a glacial age as a symbolic expression of their major interests.

The Paleolithic age in Africa and Asia

The distribution of the archaeological remains of the Paleolithic tradition reveals that the basic

[14]For details, consult S. Cole, *The Prehistory of East Africa*, pp. 183–199, or J. D. Clark, *The Prehistory of Africa*.

[15]H. L. Movius, Jr., "Old World Prehistory: Paleolithic," in A. L. Kroeber (ed.), *Anthropology Today*, p. 181. By permission of University of Chicago Press. Copyright © 1953.

[16]J. P. White, "New Guinea: The First Phase in Oceanic Settlement," in R. C. Green and M. Kelly (eds.), *Studies in Oceanic Culture History*, vol. 2, pp. 45–52.

spears, dibbles, and simple utensils. A way of life developed which remained little changed for millennia after the rising postglacial seas cut the prehistoric Australians off from Asia.

Ancient Human Beings in the New World

Toward the end of the fourth glacial period, men out of Asia following the big-game trails through the grasslands, pressed eastward across the land bridge connecting Siberia to North America. The indications are, however, that the availability of open land routes between the extremes of the Canadian ice mass and those of the mountain glaciers varied from time to time. J. D. Jennings, whose contributions to our knowledge of early American prehistory are outstanding, accepts as most probable the thesis that 18,000 to 10,000 B.C. "would seem to bracket man's entry into the New World . . . with some certainty."[17]

It is not possible to specify the first peopling of the New World with fine detail for the period before 15,000 B.C. But that the first arrivals came sometime between 30,000 and 10,000 B.C. is highly probable.

The chopper-tool complex of early man in America

Many enthusiastic searchers for early man in North America have recovered thousands of chopper tools and scrapers from sand blowouts and exposed high beaches and terraces in desert areas of the western United States where glacial lakes and rivers once lapped. On the basis of these artifacts, it is held by some that the earliest migrants brought the Asiatic chopper tradition with them and that this tradition is antecedent to all else. The trouble is that *all* the chopper implements have been surface finds. They could be simply heat-cracked rocks or even unfinished artifacts which had been roughed out at a quarry and carried to the spots where they are found. There is no stratigraphic identification for any of them. Their true age is, therefore, wholly a matter of guesswork and an expression of faith. Tough-minded archaeologists insist that until such a day as a chopper assemblage is found in a strati-

(a)

(b)

FIG. 5-6 (*a*) Ground plan of an Upper Paleolithic (Pushkari I) joint family homesite on the open Russian plains. The three hearths down the middle of the long tent, each surrounded with a cluster of debris of mammoth tusks, teeth, and bones, could have been the foci for individual conjugal families within the joint family establishment. (From A. Mongait, *Archaeology of the USSR*, p. 79.) (*b*) An ethnographic reconstruction of the dwelling. (By V. D. Zaporozhaskaya, in A. Mongait, *Archaeology of the USSR*, p. 80.)

graphic setting indubitably ascribable to the earlier phases of the fourth (Wisconsin) glacial epoch, the chopper-tool phase remains problematic, and little can be said about the cultures of the very first Americans.

The lithic—or "big-game projectile"—traditions

After 15,000 B.C. it is a different story. Since 1925, a number of sites yielding the fossil skeletons of mammoths and bison in direct association with

[17]J. D. Jennings, *Prehistory of North America* (2d ed.), p. 52.

skillfully made projectile points have been found in the High Plains and the Plains, while assemblages of similar projectiles without the fauna have been found all the way to the East Coast. These big-game hunting patterns have been divided into three traditions according to differences in climate, the animals hunted, and styles of lithic artifacts. The first of the three is the *Llano tradition*, characterized by the distinctive fluted Clovis projectile point. The tradition lasted from about 12,000 to 10,500 B.C., a period with a cool, moist climate in the North American heartland beyond the reaches of the Pleistocene ice sheets. Here, there were vast expanses of grass and lightly forested parklands. Lakes and marshes, the products of rain and glacial runoff, abounded. Here, teeming herds of mammoths, great-horned bison, elk, giant beavers, antelope, horses, wolves, and many lesser mammals fed and watered. It was a paradise for meat-eating peoples.

The second tradition, named *Folsom*, with its distinctive Folsom fluted projectile point, lasted from 11,000 to 9000 B.C. The mammoths of the previous tradition had become extinct, and the long-horned bison, camels, and other Pleistocene mammals that have since become extinct were the focus of the hunting.

The disappearance of the Pleistocene fauna was followed by the localization of stylistic differences and more diversified hunting patterns. This was the period of the third big-game hunting tradition, called the *Plano*, lasting from 10,000 to 5000 B.C. The distinctive fluted projectile points of the earlier two traditions had disappeared, and the warming and drying climate left herds of bison and antelope as the primary hunting resources.

THE DAWN OF CIVILIZATION

Homo erectus had lived as a predator and simple toolmaker. The predatory way of Stone Age life was raised to a high level by *Homo sapiens sapiens* in the Late Pleistocene period of Europe, Siberia, Africa, and North America. Then, with the waning of the glaciers, human beings became gatherers of small foodstuffs, fish, shellfish, and game, rather than roving big-game hunters. Around 9000 B.C., in the Middle East and in parts of the New World, they shifted from hunting and

food gathering to intensive foraging and hunting, in which a band focused upon seed and vegetable collecting supplemented by hunting and fishing. Vegetation became a primary source of sustenance once again in human affairs. People settled down in more or less permanent locations and developed the *Mesolithic Era of Intensive Foraging* as their form of adaptation to new environmental situations.

Intensive foraging led to the domestication of plants and animals and to the establishment of settled farming communities. In their early phases (*ca.* 7500 to 4800 B.C., in the Middle East), these developments produced the *Early Neolithic Era of Incipient Agriculture*. As the complex was expanded and refined through time, it became the *Full Neolithic Era of Developed Agriculture* (4800 to 3800 B.C., in the Middle East). In time, ceremonial and market centers became towns and cities. Bronze was accidentally invented, and the first metallic tools and weapons were produced. Writing evolved from pictographic notations (see pages 396–399), while specialized artisans made diverse quantities of goods. Priests and kings organized religion and government. The urban revolution was on, the world of primitive human beings was being transformed, and the first civilizations were taking shape. In due course, organized states struggled for dominance and survival. South Asia and Middle America were following parallel courses at roughly the same time, but whether they did so independently or in interaction is a much-investigated and often-debated question.

The Mesolithic Era of Intensive Foraging

In Africa, Europe, Asia Minor, and Asia, the lithic hallmark of Mesolithic technology is the microblade. Microblades were minute to small flakes of more or less geometric form that were set in a row along a piece of wood or bone to give a durable cutting edge to harpoons, swords, and above all, sickles. Equally important to the complex was the introduction of milling stones for grinding seeds.

Mesolithic populations, like their Paleolithic predecessors, were still hunters and food gatherers, but they lived by stalking and trapping deer, wild boars, and many lesser animals while relying heavily upon wild seeds, berries, nuts, and roots, and in special places upon fish and shellfish. Their subsistence base became much more diversified than that of the Paleolithic big-game hunters. It was a mode of life more conducive to experimentation and elaboration of culture. The result was wide local and regional diversity leading to a degree of cultural and social change far beyond any previously experienced in human history.

The Mesolithic in North America
While Late Upper Paleolithic big-game hunters were still searching out their prey in Europe and parts of Asia, seed-gathering foragers were already at work in North America laying the foundations for their horticultural revolution.

The Mesolithic foraging complex of the New World developed quite independently of that of the Old World, so far as one can tell. The situation seems to have been one of parallel development. Small bands of men were settled in favorable locales near good sources of water and were squeezing their land for all it was worth in terms of plants and readily accessible fish and small game. As Emil Haury has written, "The long and intimate experience of a wide range of plant life undoubtedly saved them during adverse climatic shifts, for changing the dependency from desirable to less-desirable, and perhaps hardier, plants was made relatively easy."[18]

In the Middle East, in Mexico, and perhaps in Southeast Asia, such intimate environmental knowledge led to the domestication of plants and animals: the phase of cultural development known as *Incipient Agriculture*, which occurred during the Early Neolithic Age and is the immediate prelude to the dawn of civilization.

The Early Neolithic Era of Incipient Agriculture
The domestication of both plants and animals was a gradual process that took place in a number of

different parts of the world along independent lines. Domestication consists merely in controlled cultivation and husbandry. A domesticated plant is one that is useful to human beings and is cultivated by them.

Domestication began when seeds, roots, or shoots were deliberately planted or stored from one season to the next for later planting. Not only did this call for foresightedness and self-restraint (you cannot eat your seed and plant it, too), but it also required dry storage to prevent mildew and rot and to ensure security from rats and mice (a good reason for domesticating cats). There was also the very difficult task of preparing the soil and selecting those particular plants which would yield the largest or the most easily harvested and processed seeds. The idea of plant domestication was hard to come by, but once established, the concept quickly caught on, and it spread over all continents and the isles of the Pacific in a matter of 8,000 years. Even before the Age of Exploration, during which European traits were disseminated around the world, the bulk of mankind's societies had already become preagricultural gardeners.

Lightly forested upland grass areas may strike the reader as strange places for the origins of primitive gardening, but new evidence does not support the old theory that gardening first began in irrigation oases of the arid river valleys of the Old and New Worlds. Irrigation comes later, and it is where the grasses grew naturally but not too densely that the process of plant domestication began. Primitive wild wheat and barley grow in a natural state at elevations of 2,000 to 4,300 feet above sea level in the Anatolian highlands of modern Turkey and on the hilly flanks of the Fertile Crescent, which swings from the Nile along the eastern edge of the Mediterranean and down the Tigris and Euphrates Rivers. In Mexico, at the site of the earliest known manifestation of plant domestication, pollen analysis indicates a semidry climate supporting mesquite and grassland.

Çatal Hüyük
Hüyük is Turkish for a mound built up by generations of village or town life on a given spot, such

[18]E. W. Haury, "The Greater American Southwest," in R. J. Braidwood and G. R. Willey (eds.), *Courses toward Urban Life*, p. 112.

as the one Schliemann found at Troy. Ever since excavations were begun at one such *hüyük* in southern Turkey in 1961, under the direction of James Mellaart, the picture of Early Neolithic culture has been undergoing rapid change. The first three years of work (1961 to 1963) were sufficient to establish that barley, wheat, lentils, and peas were thoroughly domesticated and were producing surplus yields in Anatolia by 6385 B.C. ± 101 years. Sheep were domesticated and sheared for wool, which was woven into fine cloth. Cattle were domesticated by 5800 B.C. ± 92 years. An amazingly rich inventory of specialized handicrafts included beautifully worked wooden bowls and boxes; baskets; obsidian and flint daggers, spearheads, lance heads, arrowheads, knives, scrapers, awls, and sickle blades; jewelry of bone, shell, and copper; obsidian mirrors; and bone awls, punches, knives, ladles, spoons, clay bowls, spatulas, bodkins, belt hooks, toggles, and pins. This was a creative and well-off people.[19]

The town itself (for that is what existed at Çatal Hüyük) was a solid community structure of adjoining rooms not dissimilar to the Indian pueblos of the southwestern United States. Like the pueblos, the rooms had to be entered through an entrance in the roof, which also served as a smoke vent for the fires in the hearth and oven on the floor beneath. This structure made a defensive citadel of the community house, and the doorless and windowless walls of mud brick gave added protection from flooding by the river on whose banks the prehistoric town stood.

Numerous shrines are scattered throughout the complex, with full-sized clay cattle heads protruding from the walls, some with statuettes of a fertile mother goddess, as well as of a bearded consort god seated on a bull. Layer after layer of religious murals, painted on the walls and then plastered over to make way for the next painting, bespeak a vital and highly developed cult and religious-belief system, much concerned with the mystery of life and death. Life-associated scenes, done in symbolic red paint, are on the west walls of the shrine rooms. Death scenes created in black paint are on the east side (Fig. 5-7).

Mellaart's view that the city's wealth depended on its control of a well-organized trade carries conviction. The heart of the trade appears to have been the obsidian that came from the volcanoes some fifty miles away—obsidian that found its way to Jericho (in Jordan) and Jarmo (in Iraq), and to Cyprus in the Mediterranean. Clearly, the social, political, and theological structure of Çatal Hüyük and the environs over which it held sway was strong. It would seem that the people of the town were too specialized in trade, politics, and religion to have spent much time in farming. They hunted for sport and for game food; bones of wild animals are profuse in the refuse dumps, and excavations in 1965 and 1966 uncovered wall paintings of hunts containing hundreds of human and animal figures. But compact as it is, it hardly seems likely that a town which covered only one-twentieth of a square mile (32 acres) could have housed so diversified a productive system within its confines.

The town at Çatal was burned out and rebuilt a number of times between its Early Neolithic founding *ca.* 6500 B.C. and its final abandonment in the Hittite period *ca.* 1900 B.C.

One cannot help being impressed, on the basis of what is now known from the excavations at Çatal Hüyük, at how rapidly the transition from Paleolithic hunting bands to regionally organized communities occurred, once the domestication of plants and animals—the food revolution—had taken place in the Middle East. The swiftness with which the cultural explosion occurred indicates how much more fully *Homo sapiens* were utilizing their intelligence potential than was the case in Late Paleolithic times. Once human beings had evolved a nervous system capable of producing language and culture on anything more than the most rudimentary level—and this was achieved in the *Homo sapiens* of third interglacial times—cultural adaptation was henceforth the product of cumulative experience, limited mostly by the productive potential in food and energy control that could be marshaled. This has been true for at least the last 100,000 years of human experience. There is little indication, which can only be indirect, of genetic change in human beings' nervous equipment during all the time that cultural development has moved on apace.

---

[19]J. Mellaart, "A Neolithic City in Turkey" (*Scientific American*, vol. 210, no. 4, 1964), p. 99.

FIG. 5-7 A mortuary ceremony at Çatal Hüyük performed by priestesses of the vulture cult. The large bull heads, wall paintings, room shape, and human remains are just as excavated. The vulture priestesses are artistic reconstructions. (From Mellaart, *Earliest Civilizations of the Near East*, with permission of Thames and Hudson, London.)

The domestication of wheat and barley

Charred kernels of wheat and barley and impressions of kernels in clay are the proof of domestication of plants at Çatal and Jarmo. The wheats at Jarmo are wild einkorn (*Triticum aegilopoides*), which has a single seed per spikelet, and domesticated einkorn (*Triticum monococcum*). Wild einkorn is still a common grass in many parts of Asia Minor, and domesticated einkorn is still cultivated in hilly regions with thin soils in the Middle East, although it is much inferior to the free-threshing strains of hybrid wheat which have been found at Çatal and which were introduced into Europe from Anatolia during the sixth millennium B.C.[20]

Two-row barley (*Hordeum spontaneum*) is present in quantity at Jarmo. Six-row barley, a less primitive form, occurs further south and also at Çatal Hüyük. It is found that barley is associated with wheat throughout the Old World Neolithic and in the later phases of culture. Wheat, however, is the foundation crop and the "staff of life" for all the Middle East and European village-farming communities and civilizations. Barley is an adjunct. Carbonized field peas, lentils, and vetchling at Çatal and Jarmo reveal that these early horticulturalists also had the wherewithal for making basic vegetable soup, and the remains of their pottery show that they had the vessels in which to cook it.

[20]J. Mellaart, *op. cit.*, p. 97.

The domestication of animals

The animal remains at Jarmo include the skeletons of wild goats, sheep, cattle, pigs, horses, and asses, all of which originally inhabited the highland in a wild state. Dogs had already been domesticated elsewhere during the Mesolithic, but there is no certain evidence that they were at Jarmo, although pottery models of doglike figures with upturned tails could indicate the canine presence.

Early Neolithic manifestations in East and Southeast Asia

The dim outlines of the Neolithic transformation in the Far East are only just beginning to take shape as new archaeological findings are newly reported. The discovery of pottery with carbon 14 dating of 8000 B.C. from the Jomon culture of Japan indicates an early start on some of the technical aspects of post-Pleistocene development in that part of the world. But even more important is the discovery, by the University of Hawaii archaeological expedition to Thailand in 1967 and 1968, of nuts, oil seed, spices, water chestnuts, cucumbers, beans, and peas in strata dating (C^{14}) from 10,000 to 6000 B.C. This would indicate that when the facts are finally in and evaluated, it may be proven that the Asians had made the transition from hunting to gardening before the Middle Easterners.[21]

Parallel developments in the New World

While the hillmen of the Near East were taming wheat and barley, and subsequently chick peas, beans, lentils, rye, flax, and sundry vegetables, and so laying the foundations for the first civilizations of Mesopotamia and the Nile, the American Indians of the highlands of southern Mexico were engaged in the same process at almost the same time.

In 1960, minuscule corncobs, bearing kernels that were best studied under a magnifying glass, were found in a habitation site in a cave in Puebla,

Mexico. They were the product of wild corn. Their carbon 14 date goes back to 5000 B.C. This was not cultivated corn, but the Mesolithic foragers of Mexico were definitely harvesting the parent of modern corn 7,000 years ago.

In South America, the domesticated potato became the staple for Andean peoples, while in the Amazonian rain forests, techniques for growing and processing manioc were developed to meet special environmental conditions (pages 114–115), much as the Southeast Asians developed rice culture in lieu of wheat and barley as their special adaptation of agriculture to the requirements of their physical environment.

New World cultures did not build extensively upon domesticated animals until the Spanish introduced horses, sheep, and cattle. Andean tribes domesticated the llama and alpaca—whose wild ancestors were native American camels—and the guanaco and vicuña. The llama was bred and used largely as a beast of burden, and the alpaca largely for its wool. Guinea pigs, those gentle little beasties, were domesticated for food in the Andes. The earliest known American domesticated dog was unearthed from an Archaic site near Eldred, Illinois, in the summer of 1970. It had been deliberately buried and is dated at approximately 7000 B.C.

The independent domestication of cotton in the semitropical parts of Asia and the Americas produced a new source of fiber for weaving. Cotton was substituted for the flax that was domesticated earlier in the Middle East as a source of thread for weaving, in addition to the fleece of goats and sheep.

The Full Neolithic Era of Developed Agriculture

The Full Neolithic—the phase of cultural evolution in which mankind depended mainly on gardening and the exploitation of domesticated animals for food and sustenance—came out of the simple beginnings of the previous era as prehistoric human beings experimented with selective breeding and domestication of more plants and animals. Communal life focused in the village or town, and although it may have been necessary to move the villages periodically as fields became

[21]See K. C. Chang, "The Beginnings of Agriculture in the Far East" (*Antiquity*, vol. 44, 1969), pp. 175–182, and W. G. Solheim, II, "Reworking South Asian Prehistory" (*Paideuma*, vol. 15, 1969), pp. 125–139.

exhausted, except for full pastoralists and marginal hunters, the nomadic way of life was gone.

Domesticated plants and animals

Wheat and barley, plus the goat, sheep, and dog, as already indicated, had been domesticated by the end of the Era of Incipient Agriculture. During the Era of Developed Agriculture, the remaining basic cereals, rye, flax, and millet, were added to the list of domesticated plants of Asia Minor, western Asia, Africa, and Europe. Wheat, however, remained the fundamental foodstuff.

In Southeast Asia, the cultivation of rice was developed as the staple food source for Neolithic societies located in the rain forests of the Eastern Hemisphere, where wheat and barley will not grow. Yams and taro were also added.

Wild Late Pleistocene cattle (*Bos primigenius*) provided the stock from which, by 3500 B.C., the humped domestic cattle of India and Mesopotamia were derived. The cult of the sacred cow, already established at Çatal by 5500 B.C., spread with domesticated cattle in a great arc from eastern Africa through Egypt and Mesopotamia and into India.

The pig did not fare so well, and it was not domesticated at Çatal. It was hunted in Mesolithic times and has continued to be sought throughout historic ages. But the pig is nonmigratory, and can be herded only by thoroughly settled farmers. As Zeuner writes: "It is indeed difficult to imagine how a nomadic community, and even tribes that changed their habitations twice annually according to the season, could cope with the art of pig-driving, since the animal is notoriously unaccommodating in this respect."[22] Neolithic farmers achieved domestication of the succulent pig at the same time that they domesticated the cow, however.

Although wild horses were of much interest to Upper Paleolithic artists, no horses were domesticated in Mesolithic times. Horses are free-spirited and skittish. There is nothing timid about them, and taming a wild horse is no gentle operation. Possibly the first domestication of the horse occurred in the steppe country of southwestern

Russia and Asia, where gardeners saw their lands becoming desiccated and therefore combined sporadic gardening with horse nomadism. This took place around 2500 B.C. As a way of life, it swept across the steppes and spawned the later Mongol hordes of historic times.

Other domesticates of the Neolithic Old World are the buffalo and yak, elephant, camel, ass and mule, cat, ferret, mongoose, rabbit, and dormouse. It is not likely that birds were domesticated in Neolithic times.

Artifacts

In contrast to Paleolithic hand axes, Neolithic adzes and axes were generally hafted to a handle. Wooden drills and wet sand were commonly used to drill holes through stone axheads into which the handle could be fitted.

War clubs and maces became differentiated from industrial axes. In the Middle East, they were pear- or ball-shaped. In North Africa and the Danube region, disk-shaped club heads were more prevalent. This type spread to the north in Middle Neolithic times.

A prevalence of flint arrowheads throughout all Neolithic deposits, except for those of the Lower Neolithic in the Balkans and parts of the Near East, attests to the wide use of the bow and arrow for both hunting and war. In the area where the bow was little used, baked-clay sling pellets show that the weapon with which David felled Goliath was not just a Hebraic device, by any means. Daggers of flint and bone, as well as the familiar scrapers and blade sickles, continue well into the Bronze Age.

Perhaps most significant of all is the manifold development of pottery, which fits in with the making of gruel, so important to the diet of Neolithic man. Early Neolithic pottery is usually plain and undecorated, and the forms are simple and clean-lined. The body color of the clay varied from area to area, according to the nature of the natural clay and the additives put into it. Although plain ware continued to be used for kitchen purposes, painted and decorated pots were usually developed quite rapidly. The possibilities for distinctive variations led to numerous local types.

---

[22]F. E. Zeuner, *A History of Domesticated Animals*, p. 260.

The urban revolution

More important than pottery or artifacts were the new gardening techniques that were developed in the Full Neolithic in the great river valleys of Mesopotamia (the Euphrates and Tigris), Egypt (the Nile), and western Pakistan (the Indus). In the fertile floodwater lowlands, it was possible to carry on intensive gardening to the extent that continuous settlements could develop along the Nile, while in Mesopotamia and Pakistan, full cities emerged. The development of towns into cities changed the whole scheme of life for more and more of humanity from that time onward. Civilization means "city making." Where civilization took over, the member of a primitive tribe moved into town and became an urbanite (of whom the most sophisticated were "urbane"), or remained on the land as a satellite peasant villager. Of the first towns and cities, the essential characteristic described by Henri Frankfort is worth noting:

Now one may say that the birth of Mesopotamian civilization, like its subsequent growth, occurred under the sign of the city. To understand the importance of the city as a factor in the shaping of society, one must not think of it as a mere conglomeration of people. Most modern cities have lost the peculiar characteristic of individuality which we can observe in cities of Renaissance Italy, or Medieval Europe, of Greece, and of Mesopotamia. In these countries the physical existence of the city is but an outward sign of close communal affinities which dominate the life of every dweller within the walls. The city sets its citizens apart from the other inhabitants of the land. It determines their relations with the outside world. It produces an intensified self-consciousness in its burghers, to whom the collective achievements are a source of pride. The communal life of prehistoric times became civil life.[23]

Although in America the Maya built a civilization without cities, and although Egypt, too, achieved a civilized level before it developed cities, it is reasonable to hold with the great English prehistorian V. Gordon Childe that the food-producing revolution of the Mesolithic and Early Neolithic ages laid the basis for the urban revolution of the Late Neolithic age and the Bronze age.

Characteristics of early civilization

The urban revolution fostered the aspects of civilization that have been of enduring significance for humanity. As identified by Childe,[24] they are:

1. The great enlargement of an organized population means a much wider level of social integration (organized social interaction) than ever occurred in any prehistoric tribal society of food gatherers and hunters.

2. Social means for collections of "surplus" production of farmers and artisans are devised to produce a central accumulation of goods for "managed" use.

3. Specialization of production among workers is instituted, along with systems of redistribution and exchange of goods.

4. Specialization and exchange are expanded beyond the city in the development of far-reaching trade.

5. Monumental public works in the form of temples, palaces, storehouses, and irrigation systems are constructed and maintained through the centrally organized use of surplus productive time not devoted to food production or basic manufactures.

6. Highly developed art forms give expression to symbolic identification and aesthetic enjoyment.

7. The art of writing is developed to facilitate the process of organization and management. It is later expanded to other uses, especially theological and protoscientific.

8. Arithmetic, geometry, and astronomy are developed as rational thinking techniques. This constitutes the initiation of exact, predictive science.

9. Well-structured political organization comes about in which membership based on residence replaces political identification based on kinship.

10. A privileged ruling class of religious, political, and military functionaries organizes and directs the whole system.

All this took place in what Julian Steward identified as a regular phase of civilizational develop-

---

[23]H. Frankfort, *The Birth of Civilization in the Near East*, p. 48. By permission of Ernest Benn, Ltd.

[24]V. G. Childe, *The Dawn of European Civilization; What Happened in History; Man Makes Himself*.

ment in early times, and labeled *the era of regional development and florescence.*[25] It is a time in which the first magnificent realization of the human potential is seen, the first era of cultural creativeness on the grand scale.

SELECTED READINGS

Adams, R. M., *The Evolution of Urban Society: Early Mesopotamia and Prehistoric Mexico* (1966). Parallels and deviations in evolutionary patterns in the urban revolutions of the Old and New Worlds.

Brace, C. L., "The Fate of the 'Classic' Neanderthals: A Consideration of Hominid Catastrophism" (*Current Anthropology*, vol. 5, no. 1, 1964), pp. 3–46. A strongly colored, but highly informative, coverage of the question: What were the Neandertals and what happened to them?

Braidwood, R. J., *Prehistoric Men* (8th ed., 1975). This book has long provided students with a basic discussion of the cultural development of mankind. Of particular interest is the information on the beginnings of food production and settled villages, and the development and spread of civilization in the Near East and Europe.

Bronowski, J., *The Ascent of Man* (1973). A respected mathematician, biologist, and humanist writes of the significant cultural developments of mankind from the time of the first hominids to the present. This essay inspects the changing image that people have of themselves and their habitat as cultural developments change their ability to influence and control their destiny.

Buettner-Janusch, J. (ed.), *Yearbook of Physical Anthropology, 1973* (Yearbook Series, vol. 17, American Association of Physical Anthropologists, 1974). This collection of essays shows some of the areas of interest to the modern physical anthropologist. It contains valuable information of recent discoveries and reinterpretations presented in a symposium on hominoid development.

Chard, C. S., *Man in Prehistory* (2d ed., 1975), pp. 107–130. Emphasizes ecological factors in Middle Pleistocene developments.

Fagan, B. M., *Corridors in Time* (1974). This book is a collection of articles showing the variety of approaches taken by archaeologists in studying the prehistory of mankind. Some of the articles are "classic" contributions to the development of the archaeological discipline, and others show the range of interests of twentieth century archaeologists.

Hockett, C. F., and R. Ascher, "The Human Revolution"

(*Current Anthropology*, vol. 5, 1964), pp. 135–168; reprinted with critical evaluations by a number of specialists in M. F. A. Montagu (ed.), *Culture: Man's Adaptive Dimension* (1968). A highly stimulating presentation and discussion of possibilities in the biocultural adaptations, including speech, that could have effected the transition to man.

Hole, F., and R. F. Heizer, *An Introduction to Prehistoric Archaeology* (3d ed., 1973). A guide to archaeological methods, prepared for the nonprofessional, that includes excellent sections on stratigraphy and dating.

Jennings, J. D., *Prehistory of North America* (2d ed., 1974), pp. 47–125. The best comprehensive introduction to the question of Early Man and Upper Pleistocene cultures of the New World.

Kummer, H., *Primate Societies: Group Techniques of Ecological Adaptation* (1971). A distinguished zoologist analyzes primate social behavior, focusing on how patterns of behavior form adaptive modifications affecting the ecological and social survival of *Homo sapiens'* close primate relatives. This brief, interesting, and very readable work broadens the anthropological perspective on the difference between biological versus cultural behavior.

Lamberg-Karlovsky, C. C., and J. A. Sabloff (eds.), *The Rise and Fall of Civilizations* (1974). A collection of papers designed to provide a survey of ancient civilizations in the New World and the Old World. The articles deal with how and why civilizations "rise" and "fall," and they portray to the reader a variety of methodologies and theories that have been used to study these questions.

Poirier, F. E., *Fossil Man: An Evolutionary Journey* (1973). A student-oriented, up-to-date review of hominid evolution treating fossil man and his life-ways. The coverage begins with primate evolution, continues through the trends and theories of early hominid development, and inspects in detail the various stages or grades in hominid evolution.

Ribiero, D., *The Civilizational Process* (1968). A new and sweeping formulation of trends and types of civilizations in an evolutionary synthesis from the first agricultural revolution to the Atomic Space Age. A modernization of V. Gordon Childe's book.

Simpson, G. G., *Principles of Animal Taxonomy* (1961). An expert coverage of the subject.

Stein, P. L., and B. M. Rowe, *Physical Anthropology* (1974). This book is a well-written introduction to, and survey of, the discipline of physical anthropology. The text reveals both what physical anthropologists have been concerned with in the past and the information and conclusions they have accumulated, as well as demonstrating how the study is a relevant contribution to our attempts at survival.

---

[25]J. H. Steward, *Theory of Culture Change*, p. 195.

6
FOOD GETTING

LEARNING GOALS
Formulate the sequences of development of the major food-getting techniques. Enumerate the modern distribution of these techniques among the different areas of the world. ¶ What are the major food-getting techniques and tools used by hunting peoples? Identify the general features of ritual and social organization that characterize their life-ways. ¶ Note the changes that take place in the cultures of intensive foragers and in the development of incipient agriculture. ¶ Explain the further cultural transformations that accompany reliance by a people on intensive agriculture. ¶ Explain the anthropological interest in Melanesian pig culture.

Human beings eat to live. The cravings of hunger are sensory stimuli which provoke the organism into food-getting activities. Ingestion of food is an absolute necessity to the maintenance and functioning of every living organism. Food as fuel to be released as energy is necessary to bodily action. Food as repair material to replace the continuous loss of substance from the body is necessary to bodily maintenance. True foods are either energy yielders or nonenergy yielders which supply inorganic materials for body replacement. Human beings must get an adequate intake of both. In addition, they must take in indigestible materials, called roughage, to assist the passage of true food and its residues through the alimentary canal.

Food getting is a physical imperative; subsistence, a fundamental interest; and hunger, a diffuse primary drive.

Any society which fails to develop at least minimal subsistence techniques is doomed. The ghost of Malthus haunts all mankind. In the ghastly light of the twentieth-century population explosion, the ghost becomes ever more restless.

The subsistence resources available to a people depend upon three factors: natural environment, population, and culture. People who subsist by gathering roots, berries, seeds, and insects are for the most part directly dependent upon what the natural environment offers for the taking. People who have acquired the techniques of planting, cultivating, and harvesting crops, or of the husbandry of animals, and who have mastered methods of cooking or otherwise changing the chemicophysical substance of natural products so as to make them useful or more desirable as foods, are less directly dependent upon the natural offerings of their physical environment. As human beings learn to expand their food-producing resources through cultural techniques and devices, they push back the specter of starvation and lay the base for the expansion of society, but only insofar as food production can keep ahead of population increase.

THE DEVELOPMENTAL SEQUENCE OF SUBSISTENCE TECHNIQUES

In Chapter 5, as we followed the evolutionary development of humanity and culture, we saw how the australopithecines and Early Man lived by hunting and gathering for five million years of Paleolithic existence throughout the Ice Age. Then, shortly after the end of the Pleistocene, when *Homo sapiens sapiens* was fully established, humanity quickly shifted to intensive foraging as a new way of life in the Mesolithic Era. Out of the new preoccupation with seeds and symbiotic animals, the Neolithic Era of Incipient Agriculture, with its domesticated plants and animals, quickly followed. The urban revolution was generated and social organization was transformed from primitive to civilized. Subsistence was on a new base. In the following Bronze and Iron Ages, draft animals were linked to the newly developed plow. At this time, intensive agriculture supplanted incipient agriculture (hoe culture or gardening).

In areas not readily adaptable to gardening, some peoples intensified their reliance upon domesticated animals as a source of food energy, thus inventing pastoralism as a way of life. As a subsistence base, pastoralism is neither earlier nor later than incipient agriculture in evolutionary emergence. Evidence of this is found at Tepe Sarab, a goat herders' campsite, 100 miles southeast of and contemporary with Jarmo. Pastoralism is an alternative form of ecological adaptation designed for a specialized environment.

Each successive food-producing system has, in the main, increased the food energy available per capita in inverse ratio to the amount of work energy expended in producing it. This means that increasing surpluses of energy are made available for other social uses. Whether these surpluses will be utilized, and how, will depend upon the values and goals which come to characterize a people's culture. But, in general, stepping up the ladder of subsistence technologies does result in increased levels of social complexity and heterogeneous integration, and in diversity of specialized functions, functionaries, and organization. The simpler societies are often classified as more primitive in that the subsistence techniques on which they rely were the first to be developed in prehistoric times. They are also evaluated as more primitive in their relative lack of social complexity and internal differentiation. These, in turn, are functions of the size of the population supportable by existing subsistence resources.

The kinds of subsistence techniques, arranged from bottom to top in the order of their evolutionary priority *and* increasing complexity of cultural integration, can be summarized as follows:

4. Intensive agriculture (plow culture)
3. Incipient agriculture (gardening/hoe culture) and pastoralism
2. Intensive foraging
1. Hunting and gathering

Modern Distribution of Subsistence Technologies

In 10,000 B.C. all human populations were hunters and/or gatherers.

By 7000 B.C. intensive foraging had taken hold in North Africa, Asia Minor, and South Asia, in the Old World; and in the Desert and Archaic Cultures of the New World.

By 3000 B.C. civilizations based upon incipient agriculture were well underway in the Mediterranean and the South and East Asiatic belts of the Old World; and in Nuclear America (the area of high cultures which extended from central Mexico to the southern Andes).

After A.D. 1500, when Columbus had opened all the world to European exploration, Murdock estimates, perhaps only 15 per cent of the earth's surface was still occupied by hunters and gatherers.[1] There were no hunting and gathering *or* foraging peoples left in Europe or the Mediterranean areas. On the edges of Greenland, Eskimos clung to their precarious hunting existence. The Lapps had become intensive reindeer pastoralists. Across the north of Siberia, the Yukaghir, Samoyed, and Tungus continued as hunters who also herded reindeer.

Africa was given over wholly to pastoralists and food-growing peoples, except for the Bushmen, Congo Pygmies, and a few other scattered groups. All Indonesians, except for a few small groups, were gardeners or agriculturalists.

Agriculture in the Old World attained a continuous distribution from Europe, around the Mediterranean and well into Africa, and across India and South Asia.

In North America, although hunting and gather-

---

[1]G. P. Murdock, "The Current Status of the World's Hunting and Gathering Peoples," in R. B. Lee and I. de Vore (eds.), *Man the Hunter*, p. 13.

ing predominated, all the prairie and eastern woodland tribes south of the Great Lakes and the St. Lawrence River raised some maize, beans, and squashes. The Indians of the Southwest were intensive gardeners and growers of maize.

Even in the Great Plains, settled villagers gardened in the river bottoms, and there were few hunting tribes on the far reaches of the Plains themselves. Hunting and foraging were characteristic of California, the Great Basin desert, the woodlands of Canada, and the arctic wastes inhabited by the Eskimos. Texas and northern Mexico were still mostly exploited by food foragers, but most of Central and South America was given over to horticulture.

Throughout the Pacific the islanders were gardeners and fishers, except for natives in Australia and Tasmania and small enclaves of Pygmies. Only in Australia did hunting and gathering survive as the dominant form of food getting. However idyllic the "natural existence" of the primitive hunter and gatherer may seem to the city-bound romantic, human beings have readily abandoned it for more reliable food sources whenever the cultural opportunity has been offered.

By the nineteenth century, Neolithic and Iron Age gardening and agricultural techniques had so diffused around the world that, of the 863 selected cultures in Murdock's *Ethnographic Atlas*, analyzed by Bourguignon and Greenbaum,[2] only a residual 26 per cent were "heavily dependent" on hunting, fishing, and gathering as a combined subsistence base. In contrast, nearly 72 per cent were gardeners or agriculturalists who used these modes of production for 25 per cent or more of their subsistence. Even more important, two-thirds of all the cultures of the world had become dependent on horticulture or agriculture for more than half their subsistence requirements. We emphasize this because Americans are apt to be misled by their image of American Indians as representative of non-European peoples in the world at large. Nine out of ten North American cultures were still those of hunters and gatherers, while this was true of seven out of ten South American cultures. In spite of the high cultures

based on intensive agriculture in Middle America and the Andes, the New World was clearly lagging far behind the Old in the development and spread of advanced subsistence techniques.

Animal husbandry definitely shows up as a secondary, rather than a primary, food source. A mere 2 per cent of the 863 cultures were pastoral to the degree that they relied on herds of domesticated animals for three-fourths or more of their food. All but one of these cultures were concentrated in the Mediterranean and Asiatic areas. On the other hand, virtually every African culture included the care and use of some domesticated animals for food. In Oceania, the care of domestic animals in the form of pigs and water buffalo (in Indonesia) was ancillary to fishing or gardening in more than three-fourths of the subsistence economies. In the New World, in post-Spanish times, horses came to be herded by a quarter of the North American tribes, but by very few in the continent to the south.

None of the categories of subsistence techniques, it must be emphasized, is absolutely exclusive. All food economies are mixed, to a greater or lesser degree. Gardeners still hunt and fish. Pastoralists raid or exchange meat for flour. Even an atomic, industrialized society such as ours includes agriculture, pastoralism, fishing, and hunting within its activities. When we identify a subsistence economy as agricultural or pastoral, it means only that this is the predominant food source. A hunting and gathering economy is just that, however.

HUNTING

We have distinguished hunters from foragers in that the former are predominantly predatory carnivores in their subsistence habits. Human beings are omnivorous by nature. This more than any other single trait distinguishes them from their vegetarian hominoid relatives. The revolutionary meat-eating habit first took hold in the evolutionary development of the australopithecines. Yet hunters always rely to some extent upon berries, nuts, and roots to round out their diet. The Cheyenne Indians, for example, were great meat eaters, like other nomadic Plains Indian tribes. Nonetheless, it was the women's task to gather roots,

---

[2]E. Bourguignon and L. Greenbaum, *Diversity and Homogeneity*, tables 1 to 9, pp. 23–31.

seeds, and berries to cook with the meat. Some sixteen varieties of wild fruit, a dozen or more kinds of vegetable stalks and buds, plus eight to ten varieties of roots, were regularly included in their diet.

Weapons

It is difficult for human beings to down their animal victims without the aid of tools. In almost all hunting situations, they rely upon some inventive device to assist them in bringing down their quarry. Thus they use clubs, spears, darts, arrows, deadfalls, pitfalls, snares, nets, weirs, hooks, axes, knives, and poisons to accomplish their ends. They may enlist the aid of a dog, or mount a horse or camel. They may fashion boats to carry them. Whatever device they may use, their hunting techniques are those of assault (shooting, spearing, clubbing, axing, stabbing), trapping and snaring, the pitfall, and poisoning. Shooting, while the most commonly preferred technique among recent primitives, was probably the last of these methods to appear in human prehistory. The bow was not invented until late Paleolithic or early Mesolithic times. Paleolithic man had clubs, spears, and hand axes. While there is no direct evidence that traps and snares or pitfalls were utilized, it is likely that Paleolithic man had invented simple devices of this order. We know that he used fire drives in Middle Pleistocene times, half a million years ago (pages 83–84). There is no way of knowing whether Paleolithic man wittingly used poisons or not.

Because it is so efficient a weapon, the bow had attained almost worldwide distribution by the seventeenth century. The skill of most primitive hunters in tracking game to bring it within bowshot is so well known as not to bear repeating here. Devices of disguise are cleverly used in some tribes. Bushmen artists have depicted disguised bowmen stalking the unwary ostrich. Western Indians were wont to wear antelope skins to approach that fleet and shy beast. To down eagles on the wing, Cheyennes hid under grass in a pit from which they slowly rotated a stick with a bit of cloth on the end. This aroused the curiosity of the king of birds, who warily soared lower and lower until the patient hunter could spring from his blind for a shot. Cheyennes also caught eagles barehandedly by luring the eagle to land on a pit blind, where it could be seized by the legs.

In the jungles of Malaysia and South America and in the woodlands of the southeastern United States, the blowgun with dart has often been preferred for the hunting of small game and birds. The blowgun is a hollowed-out tube of bamboo or wood (sometimes 8 or 10 feet long), used exactly like a beanshooter. The heavy jungle growth inhibits any long-distance shooting, and in such a setting darts are often more effective than arrows, especially in South America and Indonesia, where they are poison-tipped.

Communal Hunts

Most primitive hunting involves sustained, organized group effort by bands of men, although it may engage the participation of all able-bodied women and children as well. Among Plains Indians individual hunting of bison and antelope was permitted during the fall and winter seasons, when game was hard to come by and people were widely scattered in small camps. In the late spring and summer, however, the bands came together for the great tribal ceremonies, such as the sun dance. Then they moved en masse to seek out the huge herds of buffalo. Scouts went ahead to find the herds, and the whole line of march was policed by the members of a military society. When a herd was discovered, all the hunters approached in a line from down wind, with the soldiers keeping them in order. At last, upon signal from the hunt chief they would ride out to surround the herd in an enveloping circle. If the circle was successfully closed, the bison could be run down and shot between the ribs from the right side by a bowman shooting to the left from across the neck of his rushing steed.

The Ritual of the Hunt

The hunting of large animals is not usually a matter of technique pure and simple. Ritual and magic are evoked to reinforce the hunter, whose anxiety for personal safety and fear of failure are overriding. Much of the cave art left by Cro-Magnon man is eloquent, if mute, evidence of this.

The Cheyenne antelope hunt

Although the secular, soldier-policed hunt sufficed for the buffalo surround on the plains, the skittish antelope required different methods. For killing it a magic technique was used.[3] A shaman who had received his power from antelopes in vision experiences directed the hunt. Guns and bows and arrows were forbidden; only clubs could be used. After an all-night ceremony to activate his power, the shaman led the people to the open prairie. Two highly esteemed virgins were given sacred wands; they then set out in the direction of the antelope along each arm of a V path. The shaman used his power to draw the antelope into the V. After a while, two young men on fast horses rode forth on the paths of the virgins. As they overtook the girls, they received the antelope wands, like relay runners. Behind the leaders a line of hunters on their fastest horses followed along the routes to post themselves at intervals on the sides of the V.

As soon as the horsemen were on their way, the women and children formed a circle at the foot of the V, with the shaman in the center. After several miles, the lead riders would have reached the herd; they crisscrossed behind it and rode back outside the lines of hunters. Other riders drove the antelope down the V and into the waiting circle of women and children. While the medicine man directed the movements of the animals caught within the circle, the women and children waved blankets and branches to keep them from breaking through. As panic and exhaustion immobilized the befuddled creatures, the hunters moved in with clubs to kill them. One such hunt, observed by the frontier trader George Bent in 1858, produced a kill of over 600 antelope at one time.[4]

The Alaskan Eskimo Whale Cult

Whaling among the Eskimos and certain Northwest Coast Indians is assuredly one of the bravest and most technically skillful hunting-by-assault accomplishments of any primitive people. However, in order to reinforce hunting skills, to give social recognition to the outstanding hunter, and merely in consequence of the belief in the spirit nature of whales and all the denizens of the animal world, the Alaskan made of whale hunting not only a hunt activity but also a cult of magical and religious observances.

Lantis's analysis of the Alaskan Whale Cult[5] has revealed it as a complex of technological, economic, sociopolitical, magicoreligious elaborations. The Whale Cult is only one example among the many that come to our attention when we observe actual subsistence activities by means of fieldwork.

Whale hunting, then, in addition to the actual chase, which involves skilled use of boats, paddles, harpoons, lines, and floats to locate, trail, attack, destroy, and land the great sea monster (Fig. 6-1), is worked into a web of behavior and beliefs that includes the following chief elements:

1. The headman of a whaling crew is a headman of the local group. Whaling leadership is integrated with social leadership.

2. Distribution of the parts of the whale is regulated by customary usage in accordance with which the boat owner, harpooner, and others hold particular rights.

3. Initiation into the Whale Cult is through a long, arduous period of instruction in which the young whaler learns the rituals and songs and seeks a vision.

4. Special amulets to ensure good luck are used in the whale hunt and are hidden away in a secret cave between seasons. Knowledge of such caves and of the use of the amulet is passed from father to son.

5. Whaling songs are sung. They are private incorporeal property (see pages 254–255).

6. The season of whaling is a special ceremonial and tabu season. The whalers are isolated from the main village. They are unclean, must sleep in the open, and (in northern Alaska) must not eat raw meat.

7. Whalers must be sexually continent before and during the whaling activities.

---

[3]The magic surround was widespread throughout the Plains, the Great Basin, and the Southwest of North America. See R. Underhill, *Ceremonial Patterns in the Greater Southwest*, pp. 28–34.

[4]G. B. Grinnell, *The Cheyenne Indians*, vol. 1, p. 288.

[5]M. Lantis, "The Alaskan Whale Cult and Its Affinities" (*American Anthropologist*, vol. 40, 1938), pp. 438–464.

(a)

(b)

(c)

FIG. 6-1 The whale hunt. Point Hope (*a*) (Alaska) Eskimos attack with hand harpoon; the detachable head is lashed to a line which leads to an inflated seal-bladder float. (*b*) The flukes of a harpooned bowhead whale show as it sounds for the depths; the line float in the water marks the position of the submerged mammal. (*c*) The exhausted 34- to 40-foot-long prey is dispatched with a spear thrust to its vitals. The highly maneuverable, but fragile, skin *umiak* is used for this hazardous operation. (Courtesy of the American Museum of Natural History.)

8. All those left in the village during the actual hunt must neither sleep nor work.

9. The wife of the chief whaler must remain quietly at home without eating, "in order to draw the whale to her."

10. Corpses or parts of the bodies of deceased whalers are used in ceremonial preparation for the hunt or are carried in the whale boat.

11. All gear must be repaired and cleansed before the onset of the whaling season; otherwise the whale will be offended.

12. When the whale is hauled ashore, it is given a symbolic drink of water by the whaler's wife.

13. As the whale is cut up, certain parts of its body are ceremonially handled, and very special rituals are performed to return the whale's spirit to the sea unangered. It is given food, and no disturbing noises are permitted.

14. The length of the ritual period following a whale killing is the same as for a human death (three to five days).

This is only a brief sketch of the Whale Cult complex, but it indicates how much more there is to hunting than tracking and killing.

INTENSIVE FORAGING

Foraging differs from gathering in the intensity of the dependence upon wild seeds, fruits, and roots. Instead of using wild plant life to supplement a predominantly meat diet, foragers rely upon hunting to supplement a predominantly vegetarian diet, but they have not yet domesticated plants.

To illustrate the subsistence techniques of a group of hunters and foragers, we might describe the activities of one or another Australian tribe (Fig. 6-2) or the Tasmanians, Semangs, Andaman Islanders, African Pygmies, or African Bushmen. Any of numerous California tribes would do equally well, as would one of the three main tribes of Tierra del Fuego. However, we take the Great Basin Shoshones as our exemplars.

The Shoshones of the Great Basin

The Shoshoneans (speakers of Shoshone, a linguistic family within the Uto-Aztecan stock) lived in small local groups thinly distributed throughout the Great Basin. They are carriers of the Desert tradition of North American Mesolithic foragers. Each band was named for the food with which it was most intimately associated.

Bands were bilateral and very loosely organized. There were no chiefs, but each had a headman, called tɛgwoni, "good talk thrown out to the people." The headman knew fully the ecology of the area, directing camp movements to where the ripened seeds and roots were to be found at appropriate times. Every morning he ritually warned his people not to waste food and not to forget that hard times and food shortages were surely ahead.

In 1860, Abbé Domenech noted of the Great Basin Shoshones: "According to the season, they emigrate from one place to another to seek miserable roots, which form their only nourishment; even animals are seldom to be found there."[6] It is because of their root-grubbing activities that the Shoshonean food gatherers are known throughout the Western states as *Diggers*. Julian Steward lists over 100 species of seeds, roots, and nuts known to have been eaten by the Shoshones.[7] Roots were extracted with a simple, pointed digging stick, or dibble. Seeds were collected with the aid of a woven basket and a fanlike beater with which to knock the grass seeds into the basket. Of all the delectable seeds offered by the desert, those of the sunflower were the most prized. Roasted lightly and ground on a stone metate, they were reduced to an oily paste which tasted, according to the Shoshones, "just like peanut butter." In ethnological fieldwork among the older members of the Hɛkandika (Seed Eater) Shoshones, who live on Bannock Creek in Idaho, gallon jars of peanut butter made most acceptable presents, apparently stimulating memories of olden days. Pine nuts also played a great part in the social economy of the various Shoshones—with results that we shall look into when discussing settlement patterns in Chapter 7.

Not only was the environment exploited for

---

[6]E. Domenech, *Seven Years' Residence in the Great Deserts of North America*, vol. 1, p. 242.

[7]J. H. Steward, *Basin Plateau Aboriginal Socio-political Groups* (Bureau of American Ethnology, Bulletin 120, 1938), pp. 21–32.

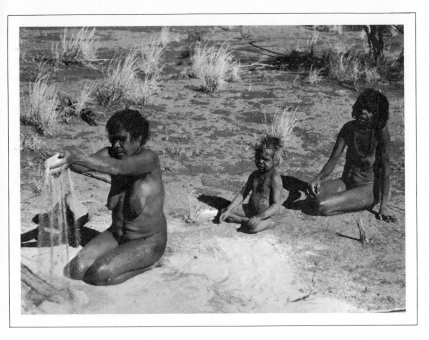

FIG. 6-2 Central Australian intensive foragers winnowing dried root meal. (Courtesy of the American Museum of Natural History.)

roots, berries, and nuts, but insects were looked upon as an epicurean delight. Regular communal grasshopper drives were organized. A sizable pit, 3 or 4 feet deep and 30 to 40 feet across, was laboriously prepared. Then men, women, and children formed a large circle, which converged slowly on the pit as they drove the grasshoppers before them with brush beaters. A good drive netted countless grasshoppers, which could then be roasted to provide a feast of plenty.

Ants were a more favored delicacy because of their pungent flavor when properly prepared. In March, when the ants had left the larva stage but were not yet up and around, a woman would scoop up an entire ant nest in her large, scallop-shaped winnowing basket. With dextrous and wonderful manipulation, she shook the basket so that the ants gathered in its heel, while the sand and dirt bounced off the outer edge. When only ants remained, she scooped up hot coals with the basket. Rapidly jouncing them in the air, she kept the coals and ants turning together and the basket from burning up. When at last the legs were burned from the ants and their bodies properly toasted, her motions were deftly altered; the

ashes bounced off the edge of the basket, while the ants once again foregathered in its heel. They were then dumped upon a grinding stone, rolled out, and reduced to a delectable paste—from the Shoshone point of view.

Small rodents were trapped by means of simple deadfalls. Rabbit hunting took the form of a great communal hunt under the direction of a hunt chief.[8] Nets were set up, and beaters drove the quarry into the waiting meshes. Soft robes were plaited from thin strips of rabbit fur for winter use. Antelope were occasionally hunted in much the same way, but with the addition of magical lures and antelope disguises worn by the hunters. A fence of brush supplanted the nets of the rabbit hunt.

Deer, mountain sheep, and mountain goats were sometimes pursued alone by the most energetic hunters. A hunter with much endurance would chase a deer or sheep for two whole days until exhaustion of the quarry made it possible to get close enough for a shot. Should this seem like

[8]Communal rabbit hunts extend down through the Southwest into the pueblos, where participation is not only a lark but also a religious duty, and into the various groups of the Gila River area.

incredible exertion, perhaps the motivation can better be appreciated if we quote Lewis and Clark on the meat hunger of the Shoshones. One of the expedition's hunters had killed a deer on Friday morning, August 16, 1805. The Shoshones accompanying Captain Lewis, after a pell-mell race to the spot where Lewis's man had dressed the deer,

. . . all dismounted in confusion and ran tumbling over each other like famished dogs; each tore away whatever part he could, and instantly began to eat it; some had the liver, some the kidneys, in short no part on which we are accustomed to look with disgust escaped them; one of them who had seized about nine feet of the entrails was chewing at one end, while with his hands he was diligently clearing his way by discharging the contents at the other.[9]

This method of eating "sausage" was still remembered by the senior author's Shoshone informants in 1934.

Shoshone deer hunting was much like that of the Tarahumara Indians of Mexico, of whom Bennett and Zingg reported:

Hunting deer consists of chasing the deer for two days—never less than one day. The Tarahumara keeps the deer constantly on the move. Only occasionally does he get a glimpse of his quarry, but he follows it unerringly through his own uncanny ability to read the tracks. The Indian chases the deer until it falls of exhaustion, often with its hoofs completely worn away.[10]

Fear of starvation constantly haunted the Shoshones. Like the Eskimos, they sometimes took a desperate last resort in cannibalism. But cannibals were feared and hated, and occasionally lynched.[11]

It would be an error to conclude from the above remarks that the Shoshones were devoid of all fastidiousness. They would and will eat neither dogs nor coyotes, for Coyote is a supernatural culture hero—a lovable rapscallion who figures in many a myth as an Indian equivalent of Tyll

Eulenspiegel. He is the younger brother of Wolf, whom some Shoshones look upon as the Supreme Deity.[12] To kill a coyote or his cousin the dog is unthinkable; to eat them, impossible. Modern Shoshones, in 1934, were even loath to eat the surplus Navaho sheep sent them by the government. Skinned sheep look too much like flayed dogs.

Bands of food gatherers are necessarily seminomadic. They must cover wide areas to skim off sufficient provender to keep them alive. But a given band tends to stay within its own familiar territory because (1) any animal may secure food and water more efficiently if it knows the land; (2) all human groups practice some storage of food; (3) they may also practice conservation of food resources; (4) their movements are hindered to a certain extent by their possession of material goods; and (5) property concepts are universal among mankind; tacit agreement allocates to each group its landed property unless the equilibrium is upset by war and migration.[13]

INCIPIENT AGRICULTURE: HOE CULTURE OR GARDENING

Rainfall and the seasons control the basic patterns of primitive agriculture outside the tropical rain forests. There are four major crop complexes that have been developed by mankind. Two are basically adapted to dry uplands and seasonal variation in climate; two are adapted to tropical rain forests. One of each type is found in the Old World and the New. Thus, a suitable agricultural combination exists for all environments except those which are too extremely cold or too sere and dry to support intensive plant life.

The Old World upland-seasonal complex is the old Neolithic one of Asia Minor centered on wheat, barley, flax, rye, and millet. These crops are fall-sown, make a large part of their growth of stalk and leaf in cool weather, and complete their maturity during the long summer days of warmest

---

[9]M. Lewis and W. Clark, *History of the Expedition of Captains Lewis and Clark, 1804–05–06*, vol. 1, p. 401.

[10]W. C. Bennett and R. M. Zingg, *The Tarahumara*, p. 113. By permission of University of Chicago Press.

[11]E. A. Hoebel, *The Political Organization and Law-ways of the Comanche Indians* (American Anthropological Association, Memoir 54, Contributions from the Laboratory of Anthropology, 4, 1940), p. 141.

[12]R. H. Lowie, *The Northern Shoshone* (American Museum of Natural History, Anthropological Papers, vol. 11, part 2, 1909), pp. 233ff.

[13]J. H. Steward, "The Economic and Social Basis of Primitive Bands," in *Essays in Anthropology in Honor of Alfred Louis Kroeber*, p. 332.

weather. These climatic adaptations made easy the diffusion of such plants into northwestern Europe. In the European lands, there was still the same condition of a cool, moist starting period, although the start was shifted to spring, and maturity still took place during the long days of midsummer.[14] Old World cereals are sown broadcast. New World plants are individually planted in hills.[15] Threshing may still be a primitive process among certain peoples.

The Old World wetland complex centers around rice cultivation or the growing of such tubers as yams or taro. The New World dryland-seasonal plants are the maize-beans-squash complex and in the Andean region, also the potato. The New World tropical-wetland complex centers on the cultivation and processing of manioc.

Forest Horticulture

Lightly forested highlands may strike the reader as strange places for the origins of gardening. Clearing forests is hard work, and it would seem at first careless thought that open country would be more suitable. However, two factors militate against horticultural origins in open lands. Deserts are deficient in water, even if the soil is friable. Archaeological evidence does not support the thesis that gardening first began in "irrigation oases" of the arid river valleys in the Old and New Worlds. Grasslands are impenetrable to planting by peoples who do not have heavy plows. Even our own pioneers avoided the heavily sodded prairies, until special sod-breaking plows were developed (which was not so long ago). Although the best grain-producing lands in the world are the American and Russian prairies, they have become so only under modern conditions. Tropical rain forests could have been made to support gardens by primitive men, but the environment was not conducive to the first efforts at plant domestication. Archaeological evidence and botanical facts do not indicate great antiquity for domesticated jungle plants.

Slash and burn clearing

Clearing the forest for planting requires energetic labor; it is not for lazy individuals. But for people who are not rushed for time, it can be effectively done with primitive tools by the "slash and burn method." Each tree is girdled by cutting a ring through the bark and cambium layer. Death follows. The dead trees may then be burned out or left standing. Their leafless branches no longer shade the ground. The weedless floor of the virginal forest is a light rich humus, and the gardeners simply plant among and around the dead stumps. Stumps are a serious nuisance only to the farmer with a plow.

Dry-rice cultivation in the Old World: Borneo

As practiced by the Siang Dyaks of central Borneo, whose methods are typical of dry-rice cultivation, each man selects a sloping plot for clearing and planting. If it is a new one, he cuts partially through the trees on the lower side of the slope. Large key trees at the top of the plot are then felled so as to smash down the lower trees. All are trimmed, left to dry, and, after several weeks, burned. In all this he is usually helped by neighbors, whom he must help in turn. Work parties often get drunk on rice wine at lunchtime, when the party phase washes out the work aspect of the joint undertaking.

Planting is done by poking holes in the ground with a pointed stick, after which a couple of grains of rice are dropped in (Fig. 6-3). Weeding is done occasionally, but it is so disheartening a task that most gardeners prefer to clear a new field every two or three years. In Borneo, where culture is primitive and communities are small, there is still more than enough land to support this method of land use.[16]

Maize cultivation among the Maya

High cultures that support large populations may enjoy no such margin of safety. The *milpa* system, as it is known among the Mayas, was (and still

---

[14]C. Sauer, "American Agricultural Origins," in *Essays in Anthropology in Honor of Alfred Louis Kroeber*, p. 285.

[15]The modern use of long rows, or drills, is a modified improvement on this practice.

[16]J. H. Provinse, "Cooperative Ricefield Cultivation among the Siang Dyaks of Central Borneo" (*American Anthropologist*, vol. 39, 1937), pp. 77–102.

FIG. 6-3 Slash and burn horticulture in Borneo. The jungle has been felled and burned to open a gardening space. A cooperative work group of Dyaks, planting dry rice, is using dibbles to make holes for the seed rice among the fallen logs and remaining stumps. (Courtesy of William W. Conley.)

is)[17] basically similar to the *ku*, *kaingin*, or *jhum* system, as it is known in Borneo. In J. E. S. Thompson's account in *The Civilization of the Mayas*, we read that:

The Maya system of agriculture was primitive. Land suitable for agriculture was prepared by burning off trees and undergrowth. After the first rains, the sower, with a bag of seed and a sharp-pointed stick, crossed and recrossed the field, making a hole with his stick in the ground at every pace, and throwing a few grains of maize into the pit. . . . At the end of the season the field was abandoned, and next year the Maya farmer marked out a new piece of land to be cleared and sown. In the course of time and with the large increase of population that undoubtedly occurred, the Mayas must have been driven farther and farther afield in search of virgin soil. The exhausted soils nearer home must have been re-sown after shorter and shorter periods of recuperation. In time the yield of the district would have fallen below the level of consumption, and faced with evacuation or starvation, the people chose the former.[18]

In this we have one of the theories to account for the decline and abandonment of the great centers of the Old Empire of the Mayas (A.D. 320 to 890). Morley has advanced the theory that intensive slash and burn gardening by the ancient Mayas resulted in the invasion of grasses that converted the tropical forest of southern Yucatán to tough sod savanna. With their primitive dibbles, they were unable to pierce the sod, he thinks, and so by the natural consequences of their own efforts, they were driven from their cities.[19] Thompson's view, however, relies on less direct factors than the effect of *milpa* farming on the soil or vegetation. Old Maya cities were not urban centers of population concentration. They were religious and court centers supported by small farms more or less evenly distributed for miles around, not clustered like European peasants' homes beneath the walls of citadels. Such a pattern requires a pacifistic society. It is quite possible that the upset of the delicate social balance by the introduction

---

[17]See R. Redfield, *The Folk Culture of Yucatan*, pp. 115ff.

[18]J. E. S. Thompson, *The Civilization of the Mayas*, Field Museum of Natural History, Anthropology Leaflet 25, 4th ed., 1942, p. 15. By permission of Field Museum of Natural History.

[19]S. G. Morley, *The Ancient Maya*, pp. 71–72.

of war forced the abandonment of Mayan centers in southern Yucatán around A.D. 900.[20]

Yam cultivation in the Old World
Throughout all the tropical rain forests of Africa, Melanesia, and New Guinea, the yam is the staff of life. Clearings in the rain forest provide growing space for the yam tubers and their vines. Giant yams can grow to 20 pounds, while their vines lace across the ground or climb stakes and trees. In both Africa and Melanesia, yam growing, processing, and eating evoke intense cultural passion and provide a focal point for numerous socio-magico-religious rites.

THE TROBRIAND ISLANDS   For no people has this been more explicitly and meticulously documented than for the Trobriand Islanders by Bronislaw Malinowski in his classic two-volume study, *Coral Gardens and Their Magic*. A few of Malinowski's observations are quoted to convey the meaning of gardening in this one people's lives:

> The gardens are, in a way, a work of art. . . . A considerable amount of energy is spent on purely aesthetic effects, to make the garden look clean, showy and dainty [page 80].

> As to the varieties of yam, taro and taytu, they have literally hundreds of names for each of them [page 76].

> It may be said that among the forces and beliefs which bear upon and regulate gardening, magic is the most important, apart, of course, from the practical work [page 62].

> Garden magic . . . is in the Trobriands a public and official service. It is performed by the garden magician . . . for the benefit of the community [*idem*.].

> To each village community this magic . . . is a very precious possession and a symbol of its social integrity as well as of its standing in the tribal hierarchy [page 68].

Food is displayed on all occasions—at death and at dancing, at marriage and at mourning feasts [page 82].

> Accumulated food is to them a good thing—its absence is not only something to be dreaded, but something to be ashamed of [*idem*.].

> The crops harvested each year . . . are . . . the economic foundation of public and private life, of most institutions and pursuits in the Trobriands [page 83].[21]

The richness of practice and belief, of which these statements are but the driest essence, is truly an expression of the human capacity to invest mundane survival activities with meaning and purpose.

Wet-rice cultivation in the Old World
Wet-rice irrigation was probably developed in India some 3,000 or more years ago, whence it spread into China, Southeast Asia, and western Indonesia. Prior to its penetration of Indonesia, yams, taro, and millet were the staple crops of this part of the world. In the central islands of Indonesia (the eastern Lesser Sundas and the southern Moluccas), American maize, introduced in post-Columbian times, has won out over rice as the staple crop; but in the extreme east, where Indonesia merges into Melanesia, sago prevails. Rice cultivation belongs to the Asiatic, not the Oceanic, province.

Wet-rice culture requires extensive water control and irrigation systems (Fig. 6-4), which sustain and require heavy population density combined with societies that are confined to specific localities because of the work required to build and maintain the systems. Some of the most populous areas of the world are those of wet-rice-growing societies in the Orient.

The economic organization of irrigation cultures is too complex for us to attempt to analyze here. Barton has given us a useful study of the Philippine Ifugaos,[22] to which the reader may refer, and Linton also published some illuminat-

---

[20]J. E. S. Thompson, "A Survey of the Northern Maya Area" (*American Antiquity*, vol. 2, 1945), pp. 2–24. The whole problem of the possible causes of the decline of the Mayan society of the Old Empire is being subjected to restudy by prehistorians and ecologists. It has also been convincingly demonstrated in the fieldwork of Dennis Puleston that the protein-rich nut of the ramon tree was the subsistence resource for the peasant Maya gardeners. Maize was the highly valued ritual food of the managerial priestly classes.

[21]B. Malinowski, *Coral Gardens and Their Magic* (vol. 1, 1935). By permission of American Book Company.

[22]R. F. Barton, *Ifugao Economics* (University of California Publications in American Archaeology and Ethnology, vol. 15, no. 5, 1922).

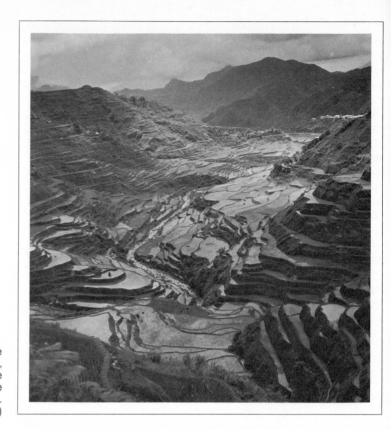

FIG. 6-4 Ifugao rice terraces in the valley below Benaue, a modern town, in the Northern Province, Luzon, the Philippines. Neolithic-type wet-rice culture in its most intensive form. (Courtesy of Fred Eggan.)

ing materials on the social adjustments that were forced when a primitive dry-rice culture changed over to wet-rice techniques in Madagascar.[23]

Manioc cultivation in the New World

Manioc, also called cassava, is a New World plant whose tuberous roots are rich in carbohydrates. It is the source of tapioca. The use of manioc as a basic foodstuff by Amazonian Indians reveals a genuine ingenuity. Sweet manioc, which grows wild, gives relatively small yields. The domesticated forms with large yields contain poisonous prussic acid. This necessitates a leaching process of some complexity before the manioc tubers can be converted to edible cassava. The roots, after

being dug, must be sliced and fermented to free some of the poisons. Next they are pulped on hand graters and then wrung dry of liquids. The dried pulp must then be ground to a flour or meal and heated to free the remaining volatile poisons. Only then is it safe for use.

The Kuikuru of central Brazil grow eleven varieties of manioc, all of which are poisonous. Yet manioc makes up 80 or 85 per cent of their diet, according to the estimates of Robert Carneiro, who has given us a thoughtful analysis of their system.[24] The heavy rain forest is opened for gardens exactly as we have described. Before 1900, stone axes and the jaws of the sharp-

[23]R. Linton, "The Tanala," in A. Kardiner, *The Individual and His Society*; also *The Tanala: A Hill Tribe of Madagascar* (Field Museum of Natural History, Anthropological Series, vol. 22, 1933).

[24]R. L. Carneiro, "Slash and Burn Cultivation among the Kuikuru and Its Implications for Cultural Development in the Amazon Basin," in *The Evolution of Horticultural Systems in Native South America: Causes and Consequences—A Symposium, Anthropologica Supplement No. 2, Caracas, 1961.*, pp. 47–67.

toothed piranha, a voracious predatory fish, were used to girdle the trees. Now trade axes, machetes, and brush hooks are used. Plants are allowed to grow for one and one-half years to get a maximum starch output, although they could be harvested in half a year. From their fixed village, the Kuikuru cultivate about 95 acres from among the 13,500 acres of rain forest that are available to them. Men do the gardening and have to put in only two hours at agricultural labor and an hour and a half at fishing, daily. The remaining ten to twelve waking hours are spent in dancing, wrestling, loafing, or other informal means of recreation. They could grow much more food as surplus with the available time and land. But the jungle has not favored extensive trade, so no more is raised than is required to eat well. There is no population pressure or other immediate reason to dig in harder. Carneiro emphasizes that the mere possibility of food surplus is not enough to engender the work that produces a surplus and a concomitant elaboration of other parts of the culture and an expansion of its scope and complexity.

INTENSIVE AGRICULTURE: PLOW CULTURE

The development of plow culture combined the two basic inventions of the Neolithic Age—domestication of plants and domestication of animals—into a synthesized productive unit. The hand hoe was enlarged and changed from a hacking tool to a scarifier dragged through the earth by one or two harnessed draft animals yoked to the service of man. The most common animals used were oxen in the West and water buffalo in the East; horses and camels have done field service, too. Plow culture enhanced the limited energy input of the primitive hoe wielder with the greater energy input of the grain- and grass-eating draft animal. The result was basic to the urban revolution and the support of city artisans and cadres of priestly and military managers and landowners.

Origin and Spread of the Plow

Whether the plow was first developed in the Middle East or in Asia, or in both areas more or less simultaneously, is not yet established. In any event, it came late in human history. The oldest extant evidence of the plow goes back to Mesopotamian cylinder seals and Egyptian paintings, both from their respective early Dynastic periods in the fourth millennium B.C.—a good 3,000 years after the first development of horticulture in the Old World. After 3000 B.C. the plow was known in Cyprus, Greece, and India. Fifteen hundred years later, plows were in use in Bronze Age northwestern Europe. At the other end of Eurasia, China did not receive the plow until 300 B.C.

In Africa, the Sahara desert and the tough grasslands of the Sudan were evidently barriers to the southward diffusion of the plow. No native cultures of Africa south of the Sahara were, in modern times, based upon plow agriculture, even though 82 of 116 African societies in Murdock's *World Ethnographic Sample* were horticultural. In contrast, forty-nine of seventy-eight Mediterranean societies included in that sample practiced plow agriculture.

In Asia, fifty-four of eighty-five societies in Murdock's sample used the plow and a mere five were still gardeners.

The spread of plow agriculture in 5,000 years is phenomenal testimony to its productive efficiency, especially when combined with fertilizing.

Yet in all that time, no American Indian ever invented the plow, nor did it diffuse to the New World. No culture, however high in other arts, ever rose above the gardening level in North or South America.

PASTORALISM

Pastoralism, the term applied to cultures whose major subsistence technique centers around the herding and husbandry of domesticated animals, is, as we have seen, a specialized adjustment to specific ecological factors. Primitive dwellers in heavy grasslands or deserts cannot readily become gardeners, and as the original peoples in these areas moved from hunting and foraging to higher levels of economic development, they became herders, relying primarily upon their animals for food and trade with which to sustain their societies. Historically, this occurred in the Neolithic Age, at the same time that incipient agriculture was developing in regions more suitable to the raising of crops.

Pastoralism is preeminently an Asian-African economic complex. In Africa it covers the whole Sahara, where it centers on the camel and the horse, as it also does in eastern Arabia. In the northern Sudan and most of East Africa, it combines with hoe culture, and in the extreme south, the Hottentots and Hereros live on their cattle. The great Asian steppes, from the east shores of the Caspian to the boundaries of China and from the Himalayas to the arctic wastes, support such eminently pastoral peoples as the Kazaks, Tartars, Altai, Kalmucks, and Mongols with their herds of horses, sheep, and cattle.

It should be mentioned that the possession of animals is not the exclusive prerogative of pastoralists; all gardeners keep some domesticated animals—pigs, goats, and dogs being the most common. Such animals may or may not be eaten. Many are not. Indeed, so frequent is the abjuration of the flesh of domesticated animals among their primitive masters that Lowie concluded that "the original reasons for keeping animals were not practical ones."[25] Domesticated animals are seemingly kept as pets, for emotional reasons, or as objects of religious sacrifice as often as for food.

It should also be noted that pigs, goats, and dogs, even when not eaten, are not as economically useless as is often imagined. Hambly notes that goats, for instance, are ubiquitous and neglected in Africa; they are neither milked nor used extensively as a meat supply. But "goats pick their own food supply, and since they are almost omnivorous in their selection of vegetable food, there is no cost of maintenance."[26] What Hambly failed to note is that in their omnivorousness, goats are good garbage disposers. So are pigs and dogs, a fact that has led Ashley Montagu to suggest this as the original reason for the domestication of dogs in Neolithic times.[27]

The known practical uses to which domestic animals can be put are, according to Forde, (1) consumption of their meat and blood; (2) use of their hides; (3) use of their hair or wool for weaving or felting; (4) milking and dairying; (5) load carrying or pulling; and (6) riding.[28] To these should be added the use of their dried dung for household fuel, especially in India, and their value as media of exchange and reciprocity.

Yet most primitive peoples ignore or fail to take advantage of one or several of these practical uses. In East Africa south of Abyssinia, the art of riding was totally unknown to the native people. In Africa beef is eaten only occasionally. Women may toil under heavy loads, but cattle must not be burdened or set to pulling loads. So, although the cult of the cow is the dominant theme of most East African cultures, the use of this animal falls far short of full realization of all its potentialities, and in India the religious tabus which surround it severely limit its utility.

Of course, we, in our use of horses, reverse the situation. We ride them, make them haul burdens, and pet them. But we neither milk nor eat them. The mayor of New York City in 1943 insisted that the eating of horse flesh is "immoral and uncivilized," and upon these lofty if ethnocentric principles he forbade the sale of horsemeat as a wartime measure to relieve an acute meat shortage.

The failure of most pastoralists to make maximum use of their chief economic resource, their animals, has baffled many observers and scientists in addition to Lowie. The rejection of most dairy products by both the Chinese and the East Africans has presented one such puzzle. It has long been known that Chinese pastoralists do not milk their cattle, nor do they eat cheese or other dairy products (although they are not averse to beef as food). Similarly, most East Africans drink little sweet milk, although they draw cattle blood to drink and make a cult of sour milk. For all their familiarity with sour milk, few Africans have developed the art of cheese making, and butter is less often eaten than used in dressing the hair or applied as a cosmetic for lending the body a glossy sheen.

Until 1966, the Chinese aversion to all dairy

---

[25]R. H. Lowie, *An Introduction to Cultural Anthropology*, p. 52.

[26]W. D. Hambly, "Source Book for African Anthropology" (*Field Museum of Natural History, Anthropological Series*, vol. 26, part 2, 1937), p. 596.

[27]M. F. A. Montagu, "On the Origin of the Domestication of the Dog" (*Science*, vol. 96, 1942), pp. 111–112.

[28]C. D. Forde, *Habitat, Economy, and Society*, p. 401.

products, and that of Africans to sweet milk, seemed to be a deep-seated cultural fixation. New medical research now suggests that it has a genetic base. Lactase, an enzyme produced in the small intestine, is necessary to the digestion of milk sugar, or lactose. Medical studies now indicate that most adult Chinese, Asiatics, and American Indians, and 70 per cent of Afro-Americans and West African Negroes, are unable to digest milk. Most, but not all, whites have no difficulty. The symptoms of lactase deficiency are abdominal bloating, cramps, and diarrhea after drinking more than a glass of milk. By implication, European populations have developed genes for lactase production. Most Asians and Africans have not. It appears that, except for infants not "everybody needs milk." Not everybody can stand it. After all, the possibility for human access to dairy products is not more than 8,000 years old.[29]

Pastoralism in Africa

It is well known that in India the cow is considered sacred, but in East Africa, it is the heart and core of life. "First, last, and always the role of cattle in Karamojong life is to transform the energy stored in the grasses, herbs, and shrubs of the tribal area into a form easily available to the people."[30] The cattle do not represent wealth; they *are* wealth. As Elizabeth Marshall Thomas has written of the pastoral Dodoth of East Africa, among whom the women are millet growers:

For the Dodoth, cattle are the warp of life. They are the only wealth, the foundation of economic and social stability, the origin of all human ties. . . . Cows give milk. This is drunk daily, and churned into butter, and curdled with cow's urine into a salty cheese. Oxen give their blood. . . . People drink the blood raw after squeezing it with their fingers to break the clots, or they cook it with green millet flour into a delicate delicious pudding, as airy as a soufflé. Cowhides make sleeping mats and clothing. Cow dung makes flooring. Fresh cow urine, in its sterile stream, washes dirty hands or cleans

utensils or softens leather or curdles milk for clabber or speeds the making of ghee. The first morsel a baby eats in his life is a drop of butter. From then on, he will be involved with cattle; every day and night of his life his nostrils will be filled with their sweet odor, his ears with their vibrant voices; and when he dies, if he dies at home, his body may be wrapped in the hide of one of his oxen and buried in the soft earth of their pen.[31]

This passage conveys a small touch of the significance of cattle for African pastoralists, but the intensity of emotional identification of a man with his cattle, although it may be written about, cannot really be sensed by an outsider. An indication of the complexity of exchange of cattle at marriage may be found in the example concerning the Nuer tribe on pages 258–259.

In the New World, only the Navahos became predominantly pastoralists—and then only in modern times with sheep acquired from the Spanish. In the southern Plains, such tribes as the Comanche became herders, but not pastoralists, in the mid-nineteenth century. Their horse herds numbered in the thousands, but horses were eaten only occasionally, were never milked, and were used mostly for riding in war and hunting. As mounted cavalry, the Comanches overwhelmed the sedentary horticultural Apaches of the South Plains and drove them out of Texas. Horses were also useful in trade and as prestige tokens akin to the war bonnet. A man identified so completely with his favorite horse that the killing of such an animal was treated as murder. It required a revenge killing of the horse killer, even as a man would avenge the death of his brother.

Transhumance

Transhumance is pastoralism linked to sedentary agriculturalism. Basic subsistence is derived from cultivation, but is rounded out by the work of shepherds who take the sheep, goats, and cattle to upland summer ranges for grazing.

The Jie of Uganda

The Jie of northeastern Uganda, as reported by Phillip Gulliver, are an excellent example of this

[29]Shi-Shung Huang and T. S. Bayless, "Milk and Lactose Intolerance in Healthy Orientals" (*Science*, vol. 160, 1966), pp. 83–84.

[30]R. and N. Dyson-Hudson, "Subsistence Herding in Uganda" (*Scientific American*, vol. 220, 1969), p. 78. Copyright © 1969 by Scientific American, Inc. All rights reserved. Quoted with permission.

[31]E. M. Thomas, "The Herdsmen" (*The New Yorker*, May 1, 1965), p. 52. By permission from *The New Yorker* and Alfred A. Knopf, Inc., New York.

mode of subsistence. In Gulliver's summary statement:

The life of the Jie is based on a mixed economy; but although agriculture provides the bulk of the staple food—sorghum for porridge—the Jie themselves give major importance to the care and value of their livestock, particularly cattle. . . . Unlike agriculture, livestock have a significance beyond food production. They have a notable aesthetic value, and they are essential to the rich complex of rituals that would be thought ineffective without the slaughter of oxen [page 159].

Permanent settlement is limited to a small area in the middle of the country. . . . Here in fixed homesteads [see Fig. 7-7, page 135] arranged in stable communities live some four fifths of the population—women, children, and most of the men. . . . The bulk of the herds are kept in separate mobile camps in the pasture lands and are tended by youths and young men subsisting directly off the livestock [pages 161–162].

The pastoral cycle is briefly as follows: by about the middle of the rainy season the stock camps are all located in the eastern region, where, by that time, new grass has grown sufficiently and surface water collects in pools and stream beds. Camps are scattered throughout the region. Dairy herds are at their largest in the homesteads, and milk supply is at its peak. As the dry season sets in, both grass and water quickly become exhausted and camps must shift westward. There is an irregular migration of the camps, for it is entirely the responsibility of each herd owner to determine the timing and direction of movement as he assesses the situation. At first in the western region water supplies are sufficient to allow a widespread scatter of camps, but as the time of the last rains recedes, surface water dries up and camps are compelled to converge on one or another of the half-dozen permanent watering places for the remainder of the season. The choice of watering place is a matter for each herd owner to decide, although usually he tends to put his camp near the same one each year. Nevertheless, some readjustment of locations does occur each dry season when some places tend to become overcrowded or when men decide to shift for personal reasons. With the onset of the next rainy season it again becomes possible for camps to scatter through the western region as fresh grass and water are available. Then there is a shift back to the east, where the rains come a little later [page 162].[32]

Transhumance is essentially an Old World phenomenon.

PIG CULTURE IN MELANESIA

Throughout the southwest Pacific the raising of pigs on a share-crop basis is a focus of motivational energy in striving for prestige by men in most societies. Gardening provides the yams that are the staple food, but pigs are wealth, and a big man is the one who can put a "call" on hundreds of pigs for slaughter and distribution when he wishes to dedicate a new men's meeting house, settle a dispute, or appease his ancestors. When pigs are slaughtered, cooked, and distributed among the guests, it may be that only a minute portion is actually eaten. The slabs of pork may pass through a number of hands, like worn currency, in payment of debts or as gifts, imposing new obligations on others, until at last, in rancid decay, their usefulness is over.[33]

SELECTED READINGS

Barth, F., *Nomads of South Persia* (1961). Middle East pastoralism, based on sheep, described and analyzed by an outstanding social anthropologist.

Coursey, D. G., *Yams* (1969). The ethnobotany of yam culture in Africa presented with detail and imagination. Includes an account of the modern production of yams in Mexico and China, for their yield of steroids from which are synthesized the hormones of "the Pill."

de Schlippe, P., *Shifting Cultivation in Africa: The Zande System of Agriculture* (1956). A modern study based on anthropology and agronomy, with very enlightening results.

Ekvall, R. B., *Fields on the Hoof* (1968). A culture case study of the pastoral complex of a remarkable people, the nomads of Tibet, who have adopted yak culture (with subsidiary animals) to the maintenance of human society at altitudes of 16,000 feet. The culture is being subjected to doctrinaire destruction by modern China as incompatible with the teachings of Mao.

Forde, C. D., *Habitat, Economy, and Society* (1937). Contains condensed descriptions of the subsistence activities of a number of tribes and the relation of their

---

[32]P. H. Gulliver, "The Jie of Uganda," in J. L. Gibbs, Jr. (ed.), *The Peoples of Africa.* Copyright © 1965 by Holt, Rinehart and Winston, Inc. Used by permission.

[33]See Chap. 15, "Economic Organization," pp. 257–258, for a more detailed description of the pig-exchange networks.

social structures to such activities. Also presents a general comparative summary of the subject.

Klima, G. J., *The Barabaig: East African Cattle Herders* (1970). A culture case study of a pastoral tribe.

Nelson, R. K., *Hunters of the Northern Ice* (1969). A systematic study of traditional and modern techniques of hunting on sea ice and of the life of the Eskimos of the Arctic coasts of Alaska.

Netting, R. M., *Hill Farmers of Nigeria* (1968). A modern ecological-social anthropological study (1960 to 1962) of a contemporary intensive-gardening society in Northern Nigeria, West Africa.

Richards, A. I., *Land, Labour, and Diet in Northern Rhodesia* (1939). How the Bemba tribe makes its living.

Steward, J. H., *Basin Plateau Aboriginal Socio-political Groups* (1938). The ecology and livelihood of the peoples of the Great Basin desert.

7
SETTLEMENT PATTERNS

LEARNING GOALS

Identify five major types of human settlement patterns, and state the relative frequency of each. ¶ Describe the predominant characteristics of land tenure among food gatherers and hunters, pastoralists, and gardeners. ¶ Show how house forms relate to types of settlement patterns and the physical environment. ¶ Explain and illustrate Morgan's and Malinowski's theories on the relation between kinship organization and house types. ¶ Trace the evolution of Anasazi pueblo settlement patterns and house types.

The impact of the environment on a culture can often be primarily perceived through an inspection of where and how the members of a social group locate, arrange, and shelter themselves. *The spatial arrangement of the subgroups of a society in relation to each other, to their environmental resources, and to other societies* is called the *settlement pattern*. No single factor ever determines where and how a given group of people will settle. In the previous chapter it was made clear that one variable affecting the location of a society is the kinds of food resources its members seek and the skills they have to make use of them. Evolutionary experience is another important settlement factor, as shown in Chapter 5. The developmental complexity of food-getting procedures and the general area of habitation of a society depend in part on its previous adaptations, developmental changes, cultural contacts, migrations, and locations. No society exists in a vacuum apart from other groups of mankind; thus another factor in settlement is the relations between societies sharing a geographical area.

TYPES OF SETTLEMENT PATTERNS

Anthropologists have found it useful to classify societies into a few general settlement pattern categories based on the relative permanence with which the social group locates itself and the comparative symmetry and spacing of the territorial arrangement.[1] The world distribution of these categories for a sample of 863 cultures, as reported in Murdock's *Ethnographic Atlas*, has been grouped by Bourguignon and Greenbaum into five types of settlement patterns according to their occurrence in the six geographic areas (see Fig. 7-1).[2] Societies that make frequent or occasional changes in location (including *migratory bands*) make up 7 per cent of the sample; *seminomadic or semisedentary communities* consist of 24 per cent of the sample; and *compact, impermanent villages shifting locations every few years* form 2 per cent of the sample. In contrast, societies more permanently located in the pattern of *scattered neighborhoods* total 20 per cent of the

[1] R. K. Beardsley, P. Holder, A. D. Krieger, B. J. Meggers, J. B. Rinaldo, and P. Kutsche, "Functional and Evolutionary Implications of Community Patterning," in *Seminars in Archaeology: 1955* (Memoirs of the Society for American Archaeology, no. 11, 1956); and G. P. Murdock, *Ethnographic Atlas*, column 30.

[2] E. Bourguignon and L. Greenbaum, *Diversity and Homogeneity*, p. 40.

sample, while those groups having *compact, permanent towns or villages, or complex towns with outlying settlements*, form nearly half (47 per cent) of the sample.

An important factor determining the relative permanence versus mobility in a society's settlement pattern is its food-getting procedures. Practices such as hunting and gathering and intensive foraging often require the social group to move frequently from location to location, seeking out plants when they are ready for harvest and animals where they naturally inhabit. Similarly, pastoralism may require mobility of settlements so that herders can reside with their animals as they seek plentiful grazing areas. In contrast, agricultural practices both allow and may demand that people reside in one location while the land is prepared and planted and the crops weeded, watered, and harvested. Many semisedentary societies are those which practice hoe or garden agriculture in one location for several years until soil fertility is exhausted. Then, these societies must seek out virgin lands for new planting or otherwise return to lands which have been lying fallow.

The internal arrangements within settlements are influenced by many variables, especially including such factors of social organization as kinship groupings, class and caste differences, and varying roles in the division of labor. The relative compactness of a settlement may be determined by defensive needs, land hunger, population size, or topography of the location.

LAND TENURE

A human settlement consists of more than just the land on which a people reside and the shelters they have constructed. Settlements also include the outlying land from which natural resources for production are obtained. In the process of adapting to their environment, human groups take natural resources from their habitat and convert them to cultural resources through the economic processes of production, distribution, and consumption. The social recognition of the raw material of the environment as a cultural resource changes the environmental raw materials into *property*.

The concept of property as such is defined and examined in Chapter 15 (Economic Organization). In this chapter, the study of land as a cultural resource is focused specifically on *land tenure* as a concept of property related to subsistence technologies. By land tenure is meant the interrelated network of rights, duties, privileges, and immunities (see pages 249–250) which individuals and groups within a society observe in relation to land resources. Such practices include more than simple ownership, for custom and law may allow a "non-owner" limited privileges of access or use. Such privilege-right to use property without possessing an actual title of ownership is commonly called *usufruct*. As will be seen in the following descriptions, rights of usufruct in land are frequently allotted to individuals and kinship groups with the traditionally recognized understanding that the rights may be rescinded when the plot of land is no longer actively used, or if the user defaults in other duties to the owner, kinship group, or community holding title to the land.

Land Tenure among Food Gatherers and Hunters

Most human societies claim property rights in land as communities. The Australians, African Bushmen, the Veddas of Ceylon, and the Tasmanians recognize clearly discernible natural boundaries as marking off local group territories. Each resents uninvited or surreptitious incursions—usually reacting with recourse to war or to regulated expiatory combat. Recognition of communal possession as a true communal property right is seen in the Australian practice whereby one band sends an emissary to another to ask permission to collect certain foods on the lands of the second community. It is up to the band elders to consider and grant or reject the request.

In addition to the obvious economic reasons for exclusiveness in the use of their land, some Australian tribes have a vital, mystic relation to the land. The land is tied up with their dead ancestors; they cannot migrate from it because that would break an immutable tie to the ancestors, and neither do they wish to have upsetting strangers poking around their sacred territory.

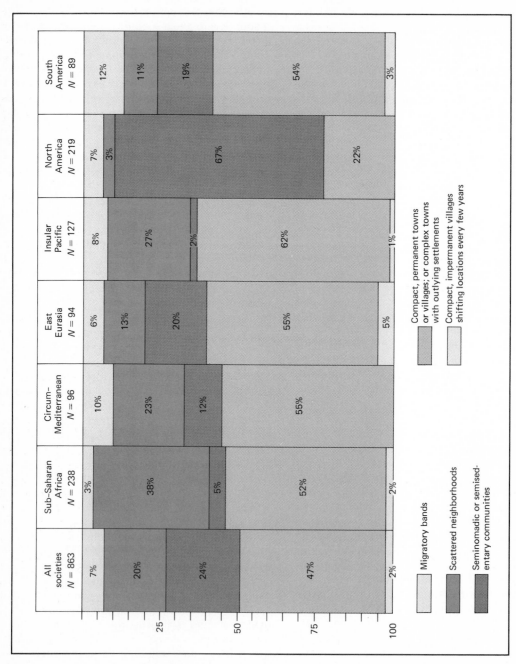

FIG. 7-1 Relative frequency of settlement patterns according to geographic area. (Data adapted from E. Bourguignon and L. Greenbaum, *Diversity and Homogeneity*, table 17, p. 39.)

Special sharing of resources

Although Shoshone Indians of the Great Basin identified local groups with their home territories, they freely moved into one another's domains under certain conditions.

Steward has given an admirable explanation of the situation in terms of ecological factors. The uncertainty and variability of the pine-nut and wild-seed crops are so great that territories exploited by different groups shifted widely from year to year. When there were good crops in any locality, they ripened so fast and fell to the ground so quickly that the people who ordinarily lived in the area could not possibly gather them all. When a good harvest was promised, they therefore spread the news abroad so that other Shoshones whose crops had failed could come to share their harvest with them. "Under such conditions," asserts Steward, "ownership of vegetable food resources would have been a disadvantage to everyone."[3] Nonetheless, the Shoshones held a country they called their own—they owned it and shared it among themselves.

An almost identical practice existed in Australia. There, certain tribes were dependent upon a fruit known as *bunya-bunya*, which, like pine nuts, is uneven in its yield. A territorial group which anticipated a large yield in a given season might send out messengers carrying invitation sticks to other groups, sometimes as far as 100 miles away, or they might raise smoke signals. The visitors were under no circumstances permitted to hunt in the hosts' territory, but they could harvest to their hearts' content for about a month and a half. One observer counted more than twenty tribes, speaking different languages, amicably gathered at a single *bunya-bunya* harvest.[4]

Among the Eskimos, land is not considered property in any sense, nor is local group sovereignty applied to territory. All persons, whatever their local group, may hunt where they please; the idea of restricting the pursuit of food is repugnant to all Eskimos (except for some groups in western Alaska, who were influenced by the very property-minded Indians of the Northwest Coast).

Eskimo interest is in game per se. Land is ignored and not conceptualized as property, in spite of the fact that each local group is identified by the territory in which it lives.

Such exceptions as these indicate that territorial exclusiveness is by no means universal. However, it is perfectly correct to say that the vast majority of food-gathering and hunting tribes do hold their land in common. Any member of the tribe may hunt where he will; as Neighbors once wrote of the Comanches: "No dispute ever arises between the tribes [bands] with regard to their hunting ground, the whole being held in common."[5]

Land as joint or individual property

On the other hand, a few hunting peoples have developed practices of joint, and even individual, ownership of hunting and fishing areas. Notable among these are the Algonkian (formerly spelled "Algonquian") tribes of Canada and certain Indians of California and the Northwest Coast.

The Kwakiutls of British Columbia partitioned coastal areas of water as private property for fishing purposes. All intruders were driven off. In a similar vein, the California Yuroks exhibited a partial private proprietary right to ocean areas. Kroeber told of a Yurok family that "owned" a portion of the sea off the beach extending about four miles in either direction from their house site. Other people could fish there, but they had to surrender the flippers of all sea lions taken within the area.[6] Dentalium beds beneath the ocean were also owned by families. No others could harvest them.

Land Tenure among Pastoralists

Among pastoral herders, there is a notorious "carelessness as to land." The Comanches, for instance, who were horse herders and hunters of

---

[3]J. H. Steward, *Basin Plateau Aboriginal Socio-political Groups* (Bureau of American Ethnology, Bulletin 120, 1938), p. 254.

[4]J. Dawson, *Australian Aborigines*, p. 22.

[5]R. S. Neighbors, *History of the Indian Tribes of the United States*, vol. 2, p. 131.

[6]A. L. Kroeber, lecture, "Seminar in Psychological Approaches to Culture" (University of California, Spring, 1941). An interesting legal case arising from failure to surrender the flippers is analyzed in E. A. Hoebel, *The Law of Primitive Man*, pp. 54–55.

game, had no concept of land. "Land was a matter of unconcern for them, being held neither individually, jointly nor communally."[7] Buffalo herds could be found anywhere, and pasturage for their horses was unlimited.

Even among people whose grazing resources are limited, the tendency is to treat the pasturage as public domain. Notable exceptions have, nevertheless, been reported for the Tungus reindeer herders of Siberia and the Kazaks (or Kirghiz, as the Russians call them to avoid confusion with the Cossacks) of Central Asia east of the Caspian Sea.

Although the Chukchi and Samoyed, neighbors of the Tungus, do not subdivide their pastures within the tribe, the Tungus treat the pastures as the common property of a group of cooperating and intermarrying clans, from which they exclude other groups and their herds by force, if necessary. In some instances, a territory is divided among clans as such. In recent times, individual families have utilized customary grazing grounds somewhat exclusively and irrespective of clan ties.[8]

Kazak practices are even more distinctive. These excellent horsemen subsist on large flocks of sheep and a few goats and camels. As is so often the case in primitive economy, they vary their life and social organization according to the seasons. It is their custom to summer in the lowlands, where they graze their herds at will in the tribal territory. In April, each household sneaks out of the winter village in an attempt to get to good pasturage before the others. In midsummer, drought so parches the land that constant movement from one grass spot to another is necessary. The families and clans do not lay claims to any piece of the country at this season, for the richness of the herbage varies greatly from year to year. Winter camps are fixed settlements conveniently located near a well-protected pasturage amid the trees in a deep river valley. Each lineage or family group has its winter grazing sites established with natural boundaries or rock piles and stakes.

Land Tenure among Gardeners

Land as property is seen in quite a different light in societies based on gardening and agriculture than in those we have previously discussed. Since full-fledged gardeners and farmers are more or less intimately bound to the soil, it is hardly surprising that they show greater interest in it.

For the most part, primitive gardeners work their lands individually, by lineages or by clans, and occasionally by clubs, but the ultimate title to the land commonly rests in the community. This makes it necessary to draw a clear distinction between proprietary title and *rights of use*. The basic principles of land ownership and use in Indonesia clearly exemplify the distinction.

Land tenure in Indonesia

In Indonesia, among the indigenous rice growers, we find the relationship between communal ownership and individual holding clearly delineated. In the autonomous villages of the independent tribes, all land belongs to the village, which is made up of a core of related clansmen. The solidarity of the group is strong and mystically symbolized in the possession of a common temple and sacred relics. The deceased village ancestors are buried in the soil, which contributes to the group's feeling of sacred intimacy with its land. Any member of the community may reclaim and cultivate from the unused communal land as much ground as can be handled, provided that the member first informs the headman, obtains his consent, and makes a ritual sacrifice. Then that member alone is entitled to cultivate that land as long as he works it and keeps it clear. He has continuing rights of use. Among some Indonesians, however, if he neglects to prepare the field at the start of any season, he may be confronted by someone else who wants to take it up. Then he must set to work or let the field go. Generally, however, if he abandons a field, he retains his rights of use until the jungle has reclaimed it. Then it reverts wholly to the community domain. If he has built dikes, it may be that his hold remains unimpeded until all traces of the dikes have disappeared.

He may borrow goods or money on such lands as he holds by pledging the land as security. But he may never "sell" the land, nor can a creditor ever obtain a complete foreclosure. There is no

[7]E. A. Hoebel, *The Political Organization and Law-ways of the Comanche Indians* (American Anthropological Association, Memoir 54: Contributions from the Laboratory of Anthropology, 4, 1940), p. 118.

[8]C. D. Forde, *Habitat, Economy, and Society*, p. 361.

possibility of alienation. Land belongs forever to the community.

Outsiders may acquire use of land from the community domain by arranging for payments to the local headman. The contract is in theory for one year only and must be renewed annually. The importance of inalienability to survival of native life was recognized by the Dutch in the last century when they forbade the selling of Indonesian land to nonnatives and limited the duration of leaseholds by Europeans and other aliens.

Among the inhabitants of a village, the rights of use are inheritable within the family line, but if a line dies out, the land reverts directly to the community domain for redistribution by the headman.

An interesting aspect of the close social bond between the community and its land is seen in the event of a secret murder of an outsider on community land. If the murderer cannot be found, the community owning the land must indemnify the victim's kinsmen. After all, the individual died on their common property, so it is assumed that he was killed by someone in that group.[9]

IFUGAO LAND TENURE In the Philippines, the Ifugaos reveal a pattern basically similar to the one just generalized for Indonesia at large. The Ifugaos are extreme individualists, however, and have no organized villages. Terraced rice fields belong to families, with rights of use inherited by both males and females as a part of their marriage portions. *Camote*, or sweet potato, fields are hewn from the public domain in the mountainside forests by man and wife together and are owned by them jointly as long as they are cultivated. Soil depletion in *camote* fields is so rapid, however, that they are abandoned after several years. Still, the title remains with the clearers of the fields until the second growth of underbrush has reached the thickness that prevailed before clearing.

Abandoned rice fields may be taken up without permission by a person other than the owner for a period equal to the exact number of years they have lain unused. After that, the title of the original owner becomes active once again. This certainly seems to be a sensible safeguard against

withdrawal of needed land from production by overlanded gentry.[10]

The rule that a person must work lands recently acquired from the public domain in order to retain title is a general and basic one among primitive gardeners the world over. It effectively guards against one of humanity's besetting social evils—land hoarding by a wealthy few and the closing of the doors of opportunity to the land-hungry.

Pueblo Indian land tenure

How fundamental and widespread the Indonesian land-use principles are in the primitive gardening complex can be seen from Titiev's comment on the Hopi pueblo of Oraibi in Arizona:

The village chief is the theoretical owner of all his town's lands; these lands are divided among the clans residing in his pueblo; and each individual farms a specified portion of his clan's holdings. In addition, there is a large piece of unassigned land, part of which may be used by any villager with his chief's consent. Under such a system land is never bartered or sold, and only rarely exchanged. Ownership is restricted to the privilege of use, but this right is so carefully recognized that if a man decides to allow some of his fields to lie fallow, no other farmer may use them without the specific permission of the owner.[11]

Grazing land for sheep, goats, cattle, and horses is communally shared. The Hopi practice is characteristic of all the pueblos of New Mexico and Arizona.

The rights of use in pueblo land are, however, contingent upon the fulfillment of obligatory duties toward the maintenance of the well-being of the pueblo as a whole. These duties are many, including participation in ceremonial dances. For failure to fulfill these duties the members of a Sia Pueblo family, who had been converted to the Pentecostal faith, were exiled from the peublo and their rights of use in the land, which had been inherited by the family for generations, were revoked. They received no compensation for their

---

[9]B. ter Haar, *Adat Law in Indonesia*, pp. 81–127.

[10]R. F. Barton, *Ifugao Law* (University of California Publications in American Archaeology and Ethnology, vol. 15, no. 1, 1919), pp. 40–44.

[11]M. Titiev, *Old Oraibi* (Papers of the Peabody Museum of American Archaeology and Ethnology, Harvard University, vol. 22, no. 1, 1944), p. 181. By permission of Harvard University Press.

houses, for these were made of the earth and stone belonging to Utset, the Mother Creator, and through her assigned to the pueblo forever.[12] Persons and families receive their rights of use contingently from the pueblo.

Land tenure in African tribal states

On a higher level of political development, as seen in a number of West African tribal states such as that of the Ashanti of Ghana, all land belonged to the paramount chief, or king. He assigned it to various chiefs; they allocated it to clans, whose headmen assigned individual plots to each gardener. In return, the land-working populace owed fealty to the chiefs and above all to the king. They had to do public work, pay taxes, and perform military service. As long as they were loyal and faithful in their duties and as long as they did not get involved in serious crime, they could not be ousted from their lands. The privilege of use passed down through the family. However, an individual could not transfer or sell a plot outside the family without approval of the clan elders. Often the family would pawn or sell a member into slavery in order to avoid alienation of its hold on the land. Since the services which were called for from landholders were general public duties, they were actually services to the king only in theory. The king's ownership of all land was therefore largely ideological. The kingship served as the symbol of community unity, and landed property was phrased in terms to fit the ideal.

The symbolic and emotional overtones of the relation of individuals to their lands are nicely expressed in the words of Max Gluckman:

The secular value of the earth lies in the way it provides for the private interests of individuals and groups within the larger society. They make their living off particular gardens, pastures, and fishing-pools; they build their homes, make their fires, and eat their meals on their own plots of ground; they beget and rear their children on the earth. Their ancestors are buried in the earth. Men and groups dispute over particular pieces of earth to serve these varied ends. But men live, work, dance, breed, die, on the earth in the company of other men.

They obtain their rights to earth by virtue of membership of groups, and they can only maintain themselves by virtue of this membership. To live on the earth they require friendship with other men over a certain area. The earth; undivided, as the basis of society, thus comes to symbolize not individual prosperity, fertility, and good fortune; but the general prosperity, fertility, and good fortune on which individual life depends. Rain does not fall on one plot, but on an area; locust swarms and blights and famine and epidemics bring communal disaster, and not individual disaster alone. With this general prosperity are associated peace and the recognition of a moral order over a range of land. In West Africa men worship the Earth, and in this worship groups who are otherwise in hostile relations annually unite in celebration. In Central and South Africa kings, who symbolize the political unity of tribes, are identified with the earth: the Barotse word for king means 'earth.' And in some African tribes there is a dogma that the king must be killed when his physical powers decline, lest the powers of the earth decline simultaneously. Among the Nuer, the ritual expert who is connected with the earth, in its general fertility, and who therefore symbolizes the communal need for peace and the recognition of moral rights in the community of men, acts as mediator between warring sections.[13]

HOUSING

All cultures contain patterns for the physical establishment of a home. House types are variable in structure, depending upon the nature of the local climate and materials, the kind of subsistence economy indulged in, and the nature of the social organization of the society and the kinds of aggressive threats it must face from enemies. A strange conservatism marks the entire development of housing. Certainly individuals have not concentrated interest or attention on the problem of providing functionally sound housing with anything like the degree of assidity with which problems of myth making, religion, art, song, and dance have been treated. (Fig. 7-2.)

Despite a wide variety of housing forms around the world and across time, we find again and again that human beings have modified their dwellings not at all or only with the most perverse obstinacy, even when opportunities for "improvements" were well known or close at

---

[12]The case is described in full in E. A. Hoebel, "Keresan Pueblo Law," in L. Nader (ed.), *Law in Culture and Society*, pp. 112–116.

[13]M. Gluckman, *Custom and Conflict in Africa*, pp. 16–17. By permission of Barnes and Noble, Books.

hand. Navahos have lived in their crude wood and dirt hogans for hundreds of years, in close proximity to the sophisticated stone or adobe apartment houses of the Pueblos, without manifesting the slightest revision of their own house style. Obviously, the materials and the know-how for sturdier, better-insulated shelter have long been readily available, yet consistently rejected until quite recently. Since World War II, a minority of Navahos have moved into simple Western-type ranch houses. More is at stake than a change in house forms. If the Navahos were to give up their widely scattered and separated hogans for the consolidated, communal dwellings of the pueblo, they would have to reorganize their lives and stop being Navahos as they now know themselves. They could not continue their present amorphous system of social organization or nurture their individualistic separateness.

Thus, whether people build and live in scattered single-family dwellings, joint-family households, or communal structures will closely tie in to social structure and even model personality types.

CAVES AS HOMESITES

We have seen that caves and rock shelters have served as homes for some human beings since the earliest Pleistocene times. If not too damp, they function as comfortable refuges from beasts, weather, and prowling enemies. Archaeologists always probe cave sites when looking for remains of ancient man because the chances of finding some human refuse in a cave are always good. Not that there is the least evidence that primitive men suffered from agoraphobia—the morbid fear of being in an open space. Nor is there much empirical evidence to support the psychoanalytic notion that our earliest ancestors preferred caves because, in the snug, enveloping darkness of the cavern, these unsophisticated people subconsciously recaptured an ineffable sense of security once enjoyed in the prenatal state—even as an English author, contemplating the atomic bomb, has declared, "In these parlous times, what I want is a womb with a view!"

Although caves have served human beings well as homes (and the time may again come when any number of us will be grateful for a good, secure

FIG. 7-2 Details of decorated front of a 50-foot high men's club house (Haus Tamberan), Maprik District, Sepik River, New Guinea. The elaborate magico-religious paintings are in yellow, orange, brown, black, and white. (Photo by E. A. Hoebel.)

cave), caves are few and individuals are many. There never were enough to go around. More than that, caves have a number of serious disadvantages as homesteads. They may not be well situated with respect to water and game. They cannot be moved around, and in consequence they inhibit the nomadic tendencies which are characteristic of hunters and gatherers. They are always unhealthy spots. Garbage accumulations are bothersome. If dampness is present, arthritis threatens, as well as rheumatic fever.

No, even Old Stone Age man preferred an open campsite, climate permitting, and by and large, mankind has favored building shelters and houses to curling up in nature's holes in the ground. After all, even our primate relatives do not patronize dens. Every one of them sleeps above ground. There never really was an Era of the Cave Man. Most people live in houses, however humble. To this we now turn our attention.

ENVIRONMENT AND HOUSE TYPES

The walls and roofing of primitive houses are variously made of snow, thatch, bark, mats, hides, felt, mud, planks, or stones. In the arctic, the Eskimos use snow blocks for their well-known igloos. What is used depends partly on availability of materials, the exigencies of climate, and on culture-bound predilections.

Taking the world as a whole, the most readily available building material is, of course, wood and vegetable fiber. Poles have formed the framework for houses since Lower Paleolithic times. In the arctic, however, where wood is scarce, the ribs of whales served prehistoric peoples in the construction of their summer houses.

Forest peoples, contending with frequent rain, roof their houses with thatch or slabs of bark. Thatch is also effective in providing numerous pockets of dead air to serve as insulation against the heat of the overhead sun. In the rain forests of Southeast Asia, the Pacific, and South America, the raising of the house floor on stilts (the pile dwelling) provides dryness and improved circulation of air for better health and comfort. In the coastal areas of the Melanesian Islands, pile dwellings are commonly built over the waters of lagoons (Fig. 7-3), just as the Neolithic lake dwellers of Switzerland built their homes on the shores of the sub-Alpine waters.

Heavy mud or baked-clay roofs provide maximum heat insulation for the searing temperatures of desert dwellers. The same holds true for the walls of homes. But earth cannot be used for home construction in areas where rain is heavy and frequent.

Stone houses were built only by extremely sophisticated primitives—Mayas, Aztecs, Incas, and other groups in Central and South America; Pueblo Indians in the Southwest; and the early predecessors of Mediterranean civilization.

SUBSISTENCE AND HOUSE TYPES

If environment influences the choice and availability of materials suitable for housing, the food-

FIG. 7-3 Pile dwellings in the new village of Peri, Manus Island, New Guinea. (Above) The old people's houses stand over the waters of the lagoon, as they did before World War II. (Below) The relocated modern settlement with street and village square located on the island itself. Peri is the village made famous by Margaret Mead in *Growing up in New Guinea* (1930) and *New Lives for Old* (1953). (Photo by E. A. Hoebel.)

getting activities of peoples constitute a second important factor. Nomads and hunters on the move can be readily seen to have different housing demands from those of more settled farmers—just as the contemporary camper may recall settling for makeshift accommodations for one night, while building more elaborate arrangements if a lengthy stay is planned.

One interesting generalization that may be made is that the houses of wanderers are likely to take the form of a *circle*, while those of permanent settlers are usually *square* or *oblong*. This difference is not a matter of mere happenstance. Living habits and geometry combine to produce the following results.

Marginal Foragers: The Windscreen

Contemporary foragers live in marginal environments. The productive grasslands which first gave rise to foraging in Mesolithic times have long since been given over to agriculture and pastoralism. What remained in recent centuries for the small and dwindling handful of humanity that clung to foraging as a way of life were deserts and deep jungles—places where technologically more advanced people did not press in.

The shelter of such people is usually the simple windscreen. Such dwellings are little more than temporary nests. Murdock describes the usual Tasmanian shelter as "a simple windbreak, constructed of interlaced boughs or strips of bark in the form of a crescent and open on the leeward side."[14] This is the exact counterpart of the Shoshones' windbreak used in summer wanderings. The natives of Patagonia huddled before similar shelters made of skins. For more permanent settlements, beehive-shaped grass houses, called *wickiup*, were the Shoshones' highest attainment in housing.

The Arunta *wurley* is no more than a lean-to constructed of leafy branches laid against a horizontal pole, which in turn is supported in the crotches of two upright sticks set into the ground 6 to 8 feet apart. In the jungles of the Malay Peninsula, Negrito Pygmies build lean-tos of palm leaves on a frame very much akin to the *wurley*. The hut of the African Bushman is simply a dome of light sticks not more than 5 feet high and thatched with straw or leafy branches.

All these people wandered in search of food. None of them had domesticated animals capable of carrying house materials from campsite to campsite. Therefore, they built no more than was minimally necessary, something that could be abandoned with little loss of labor expended.

Hunters and Herdsmen: The Tent

Hunters who have dogs or horses, such as the Plains Indians, and hunters whose food supply is sufficiently adequate that they need move only seasonally, have developed something better than the windscreen. They rely on the tent as their form of dwelling. The same is true of nomadic herdsmen. (Fig. 7-4). Although modern technology makes rectangular, roofed tents feasible, primitive tents are rarely of this type. They are either dome- or cone-shaped: the floor plan is round or elliptical. The tent is indeed a "structurally brilliant invention . . . light in weight, composed of small members and easily erected, dismantled . . . [which] if we judge it by the modern structural criterion of 'the most work from the least material' (like all tension structures), ranks as a very advanced form of construction."[15] Compared with other structures, the tent offers maximum resistance to strong winds, exposes the least surface area against wind, heat, and cold, and requires the least structural support for the volume of enclosed space. And it is portable. Yet few people live in tents if they can help it.

Gardening and Agriculture: Fixed Dwellings

Recent examination of housing patterns and subsistence activities results in an interesting correlation between ground plans of housing and food-getting practices. As summed up by Michael Robbins,[16] cross-cultural statistical tests demonstrate that circular ground plans tend to be associated with relatively impermanent settlements, occupied by small populations who hunt or practice only incipient (hoe) gardening. Rectangular ground plans tend to be found in relatively sed-

---

[14]G. P. Murdock, *Our Primitive Contemporaries*, p. 5.

[15]J. M. Fitch and D. P. Branch, "Primitive Architecture and Climate" (*Scientific American*, vol. 207, 1960), p. 136. Copyright © 1960 by Scientific American, Inc. All rights reserved. Quoted with permission.

[16]M. C. Robbins, "House Types and Settlement Patterns: An Application of Ethnology to Archaeological Interpretation" (*The Minnesota Archaeologist*, vol. 28, 1966), pp. 1–25.

FIG. 7-4 The nomadic Rendille of Kenya transport the framework and covering of their beehive-shaped tents by packing the parts on the backs of donkeys in a traditionally standardized way. (East Africa Tourist Agency.)

entary settlements with larger populations and the practice of intensive gardening or plow agriculture. Since less than 20 per cent of recent societies subsisted by hunting while only 13 per cent were pastoralists, we may deduce that the vast majority of humanity houses itself in square or rectangular dwellings.

Oblong, gabled structures are formed by joining two lean-tos at the ridge. The gabled structure is almost always raised on walls. By such simple means, the internal cubage, or volume of usable living space (especially head room), is greatly increased. Not only is more space made available, but a tighter roof and stronger walls can also be produced. These improvements are bought, however, at the price of firmly embedded house posts and an elaborate superstructure of tie-beams and trusses. A great deal of additional work is required—work which will not be expended unless the house is going to stay in place for at least some time. People with cultivated fields are those most likely to be stable in their residence; therefore, it is not surprising to find the more costly (in time and energy) rectangular houses associated with agriculture economies.

From the Neolithic Age onward, this pattern has been true of most of humanity. More space means more work, and only settled peoples find it worth the effort.

SOCIAL ORGANIZATION AND DOMICILE
In recent years, there has been some concern expressed about the physical isolation of the American family in its private home or apartment unit, and the ways that this affects relations between children, their aunts and uncles, and their lonely elderly grandparents (see pages 230–232). Yet, the intimate and subtle relations between house forms and the functional manifestations of individual, familial, and kinship behavior and the more general aspects of social and economic institutions have been largely neglected in both anthropological and sociological literature.

Morgan's Theory
Almost a full century ago, Lewis Henry Morgan attempted a pioneer study in the relation between house form and social living.[17] His keen mind perceived the possibility of close interrelations, but his study was vitiated by his preconceptions. The pertinent presuppositions were: (1) The gens (clan) was universally "the unit of social organization and government, the fundamental basis of ancient society."[18] (2) Since food and house hospitality was universal among American Indians, it

[17]L. H. Morgan, *Houses and House Life of the American Aborigines* (Contributions to American Ethnology, vol. 4, 1881).
[18]*Ibid.*, p. 2.

follows that the law of hospitality implies common stores and communistic living in large households.[19] (3) "These and other facts of their social condition embodied themselves in their architecture."[20] From these premises, Morgan attempted to demonstrate that the housing of the Iroquois, the Pueblo Indians, and the Northwest Coast tribes were manifestations of primitive communism. The individualistic Ojibwas in their one-family huts gave him a momentary pause. They certainly were not practicing communal living in the nineteenth century, but he thought they must have done so in ancient times.

In all this, Morgan grappled with some truth and a large amount of error. Social organization and type of dwelling *are* interrelated. Emphasis upon kinship tends to gather relatives under a common roof. This, however, is not necessarily a communistic unit. It may be merely a joint-family household. And the clan, as we shall see in Chapter 12, is not characteristic of the more primitive levels of human society.

Family Attitudes and Living Patterns

It is difficult to make valid general statements about the many nuances of the relation between household structure, attitudes, and living patterns. Malinowski, however, provided a good capsule summary in the following terms:

The isolated homestead distant from all others makes for a strongly knit, self-contained, economically as well as morally independent family. Self-contained houses collected into village communities allow of a much closer texture in derived kinship and greater extent of local cooperation. Houses compounded into joint households, especially when they are united under one owner, are the necessary basis of a joint family or *Grossfamilie*. Large communal houses where only a separate hearth or partition distinguishes the various component families make for a yet more closely knit system of kinship. Finally, the existence of special clubhouses, where the men, the bachelors or the unmarried girls of a community sleep, eat or cook together, is obviously correlated to the general structure of a community when kinship is complicated by age grades, secret societies and other male or female associations

and is usually also correlated to the presence or absence of sexual laxity.[21]

Within the dwelling, the place of the hearth and attitudes surrounding it are of great importance. "Hearth and home" were once inseparable.

In the Trobriand Islands, for instance, the hearth has to be placed in the center, lest sorcery, which is mainly effective through the medium of smoke, should be carried in from outside. The hearth is the special property of women. Cooking is to a certain extent tabu to men and its proximity pollutes uncooked vegetable food. Hence there is a division between storehouses and cooking houses in the villages. All this makes the simple material arrangements of a house a social, moral, legal and religious reality.[22]

The positioning of sleeping places relates to sexuality and parenthood, to incest tabus, and to sexual segregation based upon notions of pollution of male virility.

Separation of Men and Women

In some parts of the world, sexual segregation produces individual "family" houses for each woman, her unmarried daughters, and her prepubescent sons. The adult males, however, live together in jointly owned clubhouses. This basic pattern is widespread in Melanesia, especially.

The Enga

Among the Enga-speaking peoples of the Central Highlands of New Guinea, for example, the men's house is a meeting and sleeping center only. It holds no ritual activities. By the time a boy is six years old, he is expected to have left his mother's house to take up life in a men's house whose members belong to his own patrilineage. In a demographic survey done by M. J. Meggitt in the 1950s, 309 men and boys were found to live in 57 men's houses. Associated with these were 155 women's houses for 235 women and 266 girls (under fifteen years of age) and little boys—plus 9 men who "were elderly or poor, and their behav-

---

[19]*Ibid.*, p. 61.
[20]*Ibid.*, p. 105.

[21]B. Malinowski, "Culture" (*Encyclopaedia of the Social Sciences*, vol. 4, 1930), p. 632. Copyright © 1934 by the Macmillan Company. Quoted with permission.
[22]*Idem.*

ior was thought to be eccentric."[23] Linked to this separateness is a pervading belief among men that women are dangerous to their powers and that their polluting effect must be reduced through minimal contacts.

In Africa generally, partial residential segregation of adolescent boys is usually practiced. However, the total segregation of adolescent boys of warrior age into settlements of their own is marked among such tribes as the Masai and Kipsigi of East Africa, and the Nyakusa further south.

Joint-family Households

In contrast to the dispersed settlement pattern just described for the Enga, the notorious head-shrinking Jivaros of eastern Ecuador reveal sexual segregation within a communal joint-family household.

The Jivaro Indians

The unit of Jivaro social organization is the patrilineal family group living under a single roof. "Such a household is quite independent and self-sufficient, being subservient to no one."[24] The typical Jivaro house (jivaria) is about 75 feet long and some 40 feet wide, elliptical, with parallel sides and rounded ends. The walls are made of 10-foot laths of palm or bamboo lashed vertically to the frame. The roof is thatched. At each end of the house is a door of heavy planks, which must be lifted and set aside to gain entrance. These doors are barred from the inside. An interesting sexual dichotomy reserves one door for men only and the other for women. In like manner, one-half of the interior is for men, and the other half for women. Each man has his private sleeping platform against the wall on his side; each woman has her platform on the women's side. Women's platforms are enclosed with mat walls but the men seek no such privacy. Thus, within the *jivaria*

separation is based upon sex. Although several conjugal families may be living in a single house, they are not spatially separated on a family basis. Lamentably, we know little about interpersonal relations within the household group or about how the Jivaros manage their sex lives.

In Jivaro society there are no clans, villages, or other forms of social organization beyond the isolated household, except a loose and amorphous federation of five or six households under a common war leader.

The Iroquois long house

In the long house of the Iroquois Indians we find an internal organization more typical of joint-family households. The structure of an Iroquois long house was something like that of a Quonset hut. A roof consisting of slabs of dried bark was laid on vertical walls. The house could be enlarged or shortened merely by adding or removing sections at either end. Doors were at the ends, with an open passage down the entire house, which in one instance was 110 yards long—more than the length of a football field (Fig. 7-5). On either side of the passage were cubicles about 12 feet wide and 6 feet deep, closed on the sides but wide open to the passageway, like the long corridor of bedrooms in the Palace of Versailles. Down the center of the passage were spaced the fireplaces (Fig. 7-6). As was observed by Lafitau in the eighteenth century:

Along the fires there extends on each side a platform of twelve to thirteen feet in length by five or six in width and nearly as high. These platforms, shut in on all sides except that towards the fire, serve as beds and as chairs to sit down upon; on the bark which forms the floor of the platform they spread rush mats and furs. On this bed, which is hardly a fit support for the effeminate or lazy, they stretch themselves without ceremony, wrapped in the same clothes that they wear during the day. . . .

The base of the platform, on which they sleep, is elevated at most one foot from the ground; it is given this elevation to avoid the dampness, and it is not greater, on the other hand, to avoid the inconvenience of the smoke which is insupportable in the cabins when standing erect, or even a little raised.

The bark which covers the platforms above and which forms the ceiling of the bed, serves them as a closet and

[23]M. J. Meggitt, "Male-Female Relationships in the Highlands of Australian New Guinea" (*American Anthropologist*, vol. 66, no. 4, part 2; Special Publication, 1964), p. 207.

[24]M. W. Stirling, *Historical and Ethnographical Materials on the Jivaro Indians* (Bureau of American Ethnology, Bulletin 117, 1938), p. 38.

FIG. 7-5 Recent excavations have revealed the vast dimensions attained by Iroquois long houses at the height of their development. The length of this joint-family dwelling exceeds that of a football field by 30 feet. The stakes, set by the archaeologists, mark the location of postholes. The small round house on the right probably housed a sublineage. A second long house was located behind the round house. (Courtesy of J. A. Tuck.)

larder, where they place, in the view of every one, their dishes and all the little utensils of their household. Between the platforms are placed large chests of bark, in the form of tuns, and five or six feet high, where they put the corn when shelled. . . .

While it is possible to walk back and forth in the cabins on either side of the fires between the hearths and the mats, it is nevertheless not a comfortable place for a promenade; moreover, the savage, wherever he is,

unless he is actually traveling, is always either seated or lying down, and never walks.[25]

Who lived in this big building, and what were

[25]Translation from the French by M. L. LeBrun in L. H. Morgan (H. B. Lloyd's ed.), *League of the Ho-dé-no-sau-nee or Iroquois*, vol. 2, appendix B, pp. 290–291. By permission of Burt Franklin Publishers.

FIG. 7-6 The ground plan of a "five-fire" Iroquois long house, according to LaFitau's description. (From L. H. Morgan, *League of the Ho-de-no-sau-nee or Iroqouois*.)

E Entrance lobby
S Storeroom
B Bed
C Child's bunk

Ө Bark barrels
P Posts
X Fire
V Exterior vestibule

their arrangements? Each long house "belonged" to a lineage of related women. At the head of the long house was an influential older woman. The household certainly included all her daughters and their husbands and children. It usually also included her sisters and their families, as well as the families of her married granddaughters. All the women of the long house, in theory at least, belonged to the same clan. The long house bore the name and clan insignia of its dominant matrilineal family (except in the case of the Seneca tribe). Married men were supposed to move into the long house of the wife, but the son of an influential mother married to a girl from a family of less account might choose to stay in his mother's home. And since the Iroquois were given to adoption of captive enemies as replacements for dead relatives, there were always some of these in the household.

The women could throw their husbands out at any time. For the dispossessed divorcé, there was nothing to do but pick up his gear and leave. He had no legal claim on children or home.

The social organization of the Iroquois long house was that of a joint matriarchate (see the discussion of the composite unilineal family, pages 205–207). Segregation within the long house was not, as among the Jivaro, by sexes but rather by conjugal families. Each woman had her cubicle, which was shared by her husband and children. Eating was partly a joint-family, partly a separate-family, affair. Each conjugal family shared a cooking fire with the occupants of the opposite compartment. Down the center of the passageway lay a hearth for each pair of families.

An Iroquois village consisted of several to many long houses within a protective palisade. A number of villages together made up a tribe. The six original Iroquois tribes made up the Iroquois nation. Loyalties reached out far beyond the lineage group in the long house. Further, the Iroquois were militant expansionists. They could release their internal tensions in outward aggression.

As the cultural environment of the Iroquois changed under the impact of white colonization of their country, the long-house organization began to break down, giving way to log houses of

smaller dimensions, until by 1800, the long house as a dwelling form was no more.[26]

In Southeast Asia, where long houses are common, they tend to be associated with clans.[27] Where the village unit is formed on territorial rather than kinship bonds, as in Java and the Philippines, each family has its own separate house. The lineage and joint family do appear to go together. Morgan had a certain amount of truth to back him up. But lineages and clans do not by any means always live in long houses, while some clanless people do. The relationship is not absolute.

The Compound Homestead of African Pastoralists

The joint households previously described are those of gardeners who live in wooded areas where long timbers are available and where the main problem is protection of human, not animal, life. African pastoralists give a different form to the joint-family homestead. In their ecological setting, materials for large buildings are frequently rare, and a major need is to protect both people and stock from raiders. The homestead of the Jie, whose seasonal cycle was described in a previous chapter, may be taken as generally typical (Fig. 7-7).

A Jie homestead ordinarily contains the families of from six to eight men, all descendants of one grandfather. The social base of the household is therefore the patrilineage (see pages 215–216). Families are polygynous (see pages 200–202). All the wives, their children, and the married sons with their wives and children live within the compound—thirty to forty people in all. The compound is a palisaded pole brush fence in which the only openings are small apertures 3 feet square. Anyone entering must crawl on his hands

[26]W. N. Fenton, "Locality as a Basic Factor in the Development of Iroquois Social Structure," *Symposium on Local Diversity in Iroquois Culture* (Bureau of American Ethnology, Bulletin 149, 1951), pp. 35–54.

[27]E. M. Loeb and J. O. M. Broek, "Social Organization and the Long House in Southeast Asia" (*American Anthropologist*, vol. 49, 1947), pp. 414–425. See also the discussion in Chap. 11, pages 205–207.

and knees, presenting his head for a death blow in case he is not welcome.

Ringing the inner side of the wall is a series of fenced yards—one for each married woman. Here she has a small thatched hut with no windows, which is used only for sleeping in rainy weather. Otherwise, sleeping, cooking, and eating are done in the open yard, although some wives build themselves a kitchen hut with open sides. Every woman's yard also contains a small house for young cattle, and this is used as an emergency kitchen if there is no regular one. Each yard also has at least two large plastered baskets on stilts for storage of grain. The yard of each wife is her own domain. Although the yards of the co-wives of a common husband are adjacent to each other, no door leads directly from one to another. It is necessary to go out into the cattle pens to achieve passage to any other yard. The cattle and goat pens (kraals) take up about half the interior courtyard of the homestead. Here the livestock are herded at night, except in the rainy season, when they are kept in outside kraals.

The homestead is the base of a corporate lineage which inherits and owns all the cattle in common. The unity of the lineage as against all the rest of the world is clearly symbolized and reinforced by the very nature of the homestead.[28]

FIG. 7-7 The ground plan of a Jie household. The yards lettered A belong to the wives of one man. The B's are the yards of a brother of the first man, the C's are the yards of the wives of a second brother, and so forth. The entire homestead is physically and socially a tight unit, discrete among all the other homesteads of the tribe. (From P. H. Gulliver, *The Family Herds,* Routledge & Kegan Paul, Ltd., London, 1955. By permission.)

Pueblos: From Pit House to Communal Apartment House

From the pit house to the great five-storied apartment buildings of the Pueblos of the Southwest United States is a great distance to travel in the span of a prehistoric millennium.

Three main archaeological patterns of prehistoric culture have been found in the Southwest. The first is the Anasazi, of which the contemporary living Pueblos are a part. Because of its geographic localization on the high plateaus of northern Arizona, New Mexico, southern Utah, and Colorado around the Four Corners,[29] it is sometimes referred to as the *Plateau Culture*. It

must not be confused with the ethnologist's Plateau Culture area, which is located on the Columbia River Plateau. The second cultural pattern is the Hohokam, also called the *Desert Culture* because of its location in the central and southern Arizona deserts. The third is the Mogollon-Mimbres, also known as the *Mountain Culture* because of its association with the mountainous area of southeastern Arizona and southwestern New Mexico. In their earliest known phases

---

[28]For more detail, see P. H. Gulliver, *The Family Herds*.
[29]The only place in the United States where four states touch one another.

(about 2,000 years ago), each of these cultures included pit houses as the dwelling type.

The pit house

The technique of sinking the floor of the house into the ground before raising the superstructure above it represents a distinctly different line of development in house forms. This technique is adapted to the conditions of temperate climates with cold winters. For obvious reasons, it never occurs in the tropical areas where the ground is too wet. The semisubterranean house has two advantages: (1) it is easier to keep warm, and (2) it can be made roomy without raising high side walls. The first reason is the functionally effective one, since many primitive people have solved the problem of getting sufficient inside height when building above ground.

Among recent primitives, the pit house has found greatest favor with numerous peoples of western North America and North Asia. The description of the pit houses seen by Lewis and Clark just below the Dalles of the Columbia River could very well have applied to the Campignian house types of 14,000 years ago:

They are sunk about eight feet deep, and covered with strong timbers, and several feet of earth in a conical form. On descending by means of a ladder through a hole at the top, which answers the double purpose of a door and a chimney, we found that the house consisted of a single room, nearly circular and about sixteen feet in diameter.[30]

Almost identical words describe a traveler's view of the pit dwellings of the Samoyed tribes of Siberia: "They lived in little, half underground lodges, with circular upper parts and without windows. In the middle of the latter there is a hole, through which smoke and people pass."[31]

Here we have the parallel occurrence of two similar culture traits on separate continents. In this case, they do not represent independent inventions, however, for the combination of facts covering their archaeological distribution and details of structure indicates clearly that this mode

of dwelling, which was in frequent use in Late Pleistocene Siberia and survived into the present century among the sedentary fishing cultures of that land, was carried into western North America by early migrants from the Asian mainland.[32]

The Anasazi tradition

The evolution of the Anasazi begins with what is known as the *Basket Maker period* (A.D. 100 to 500). Basket Maker houses were constructed of inclined posts, poles, and twigs laid horizontally to form a dome around and above a saucerlike pit 10 to 20 feet in diameter. The frame was plastered over with mud. Individual houses were built in small groups, either within shallow caves or in the open.

In the succeeding *Modified Basket Maker period* (A.D. 500 to 700), pit houses still prevailed. They now consisted of a framework of four or five uprights supporting a flat roof. Entrance was gained either through the smoke hole over the fire pit or through a projecting passageway on the south side of the house. A low ridge of mud separated the south from the north half of the house. A new feature that marked this period, however, was the long, flat-roofed structure of poles and mud that contained two rows of contiguous rooms. Some of these buildings were in the shape of crescents. Two lines of architectural development had emerged.

In the period of the Modified Basket Maker, the pit houses were used for ceremonial and dwelling purposes. The multiroomed surface houses were apparently used mostly for storage. Later, in the Pueblo periods, the pit house evolved into the underground ceremonial chamber, or *kiva*. The aboveground storage rooms became the multiple apartment houses for which the Pueblo Indians are justly famous. The climax was reached between A.D. 1000 and 1300 in the *Pueblo III period*. To this period belong the famous cities in the caves, including Cliff Palace in Mesa Verde National Park (Fig. 7-8). Of the open sites of this period, Pueblo Bonito in Chaco Canyon, New Mexico, is the best known. These buildings con-

[30]M. Lewis and W. Clark, *History of the Expedition of Captains Lewis and Clark, 1804–05–06*, vol. 2, pp. 253–254.

[31]Olearius, *The Description of a Journey in Moscovia*, pp. 167–168.

[32]See W. Jochelson, "Past and Present Subterranean Dwellings of the Tribes of North Eastern Asia and North Western America" (*Proceedings of the 15th International Congress of Americanists*, 1907).

FIG. 7-8 Cliff Palace at Mesa Verde, in southwestern Colorado, was constructed nearly a millenium ago. The many round ceremonial chambers, called *Kivas*, are indicative of the complexity of religious organization in this multiple dwelling that housed an entire village. (Courtesy of the American Museum of Natural History).

tained hundreds of rooms built of coursed masonry walls rising often to four stories. The modern pueblos are merely shrunken survivals of the *Great Period*.

The configuration of Pueblo culture

There is a close nexus between the communal houses of the Pueblos and the general configuration of Pueblo culture. The pueblos of the Great Period were defensive citadels as well as domiciles. The outer ground-level walls of the open-site pueblos were blank surfaces with no doors or windows. To enter a house, one had to climb to the roof and go down the smoke hole, as in the pit house. To the hostile outer world the pueblo turned its back. It faced inward upon the court, in which the public dances of its rich ceremonialism occurred. The great building formed a compact, architecturally integrated, in-turned whole. The members of the pueblo were forced to live in

the closest intimacy with one another; not just the members of one household, each of which had its own apartment of one or several rooms, but all families, all clans were piled together in a great heap. The cooperative emphasis of Pueblo life was required by the nature of their housing, if nothing else. And, of course, their housing could not have come into being had they not simultaneously been developing cooperative values.

We would agree with the conclusion of Steward in speaking of the Basket Maker and Pueblo I cultures: "It is difficult to reconcile the division of the early villages into small house clusters with any other social unit than the unilateral lineage or band."[33] Steward and Titiev[34] both suggest that a movement of consolidation of independent clans

[33]J. H. Steward, "Ecological Aspects of Southwestern Society" (*Anthropos*, vol. 32, 1937), p. 99.

[34]M. Titiev, *Old Oraibi* (Papers of the Peabody Museum of American Archaeology and Ethnology, Harvard University, vol. 22, no. 1, 1944), pp. 96–99.

or bands in Pueblo II times resulted in the building of communal houses. "The formerly separated small groups are amalgamated, but do not lose their social and ceremonial integrity.[35] And because these formerly discrete groups did not lose their integrity when compressed into the larger pueblo units, plus the irritability engendered by too close living, vindictive factionalism is an inherent aspect of Pueblo life. The crowded intimacy of Pueblo living seems also to have left its impress in the form of excessive touchiness, quarreling, backbiting, and fear of witchcraft—centrifugal forces which led again and again to the breakup of pueblos and the establishment of new settlements. The hundreds of ruined pueblos which make the Southwest an archaeologist's paradise are rich testimony to the long Pueblo struggle to adjust their house forms to their social conservatism.

Well-integrated religio-ceremonial structures have to a great degree counteracted the tendency toward breakup in Pueblo society. In the political sphere, however, the Pueblos have failed in the development of governmental mechanisms which combine reasonably centralized authority with flexibility in the handling of divergent interests. This is, of course, the eternal problem of healthy government. In the case of the Pueblos, their compact form of housing contributed to an intensification of the imperative need for political skill.

Earlier in this chapter we remarked that the Navahos could not adopt the Pueblo house form and remain Navahos in spirit and action. We have seen something of the difficulty the Pueblo Indians themselves have had to reckon with in the solution of their housing problem. Those who have wondered how it is possible for the Navahos after centuries of contact with the Pueblos—centuries in which they have absorbed much of Pueblo ritual, imagery, and arts—to live even yet in wretched log and mud hogans, when they have for so long had the exemplar of Pueblo masonry houses before them, may find the answer in the Navaho's devotion to his form of social organization. Present-day Navaho social forms are un-

doubtedly much closer to those of the society that was enjoyed by the Basket Maker and Pueblo I peoples than are the modern social forms of the Pueblo Indians. The scattered Navaho communities of individual hogans are not greatly different from the ancient open-site pit-house villages of the Anasazi.

SELECTED READINGS

Beals, R., P. Carrasco, and T. McCorkle, *Houses and House Use of the Sierra Tarascans* (1944). A study of the relationship between architectural and social forms in highland Mexico.

Fortes, M., *The Web of Kinship among the Tallensi* (1949), chap. 3, "The Homestead and the Joint Family." A model study of the functional interrelation of home and family.

Gluckman, M., *The Ideas in Barotse Jurisprudence* (1965), chaps. 3, 4, and 5. Presents and analyzes the concepts and uses of a South African tribe with respect to status and rights in land, immovable property, and chattels. A thorough and sophisticated piece of work.

Loeb, E. M., and J. O. M. Broek, "Social Organization and the Long House in Southeast Asia" (*American Anthropologist*, vol. 49, 1947), pp. 414–425. A useful analysis of the relation between lineage and homestead.

Murdock, G. P., *Our Primitive Contemporaries* (1934). Sections in each chapter devoted to the ethnography of a tribe describe a variety of house types.

Roberts, J. M., *Three Navaho Households* (Papers of the Peabody Museum of American Archaeology and Ethnology, Harvard University, vol. 40, no. 3, 1951). An intensive study of the membership, possessions, and household activities of the occupants of three representative Navaho hogans.

Steward, J. H., *Theory of Culture Change* (1955), chapter entitled "Ecological Aspects of Southwest Society." Includes a highly suggestive historical treatment of the relation of dwelling patterns to social organization.

ter Haar, B., *Adat Law in Indonesia* (1948), chaps. 2 and 10, "Land Rights" and "Inheritance." A comprehensive survey of adat law among the many tribes in this area of Southeast Asia.

Waln, N., *The House of Exile* (1933). A beautifully written novel giving the inside view of life in a traditional Chinese compound household.

---

[35]Steward, *op. cit.*, p. 96.

SOCIAL ORGANIZATION

8

STATUS AND ROLE

LEARNING GOALS

Identify the concepts of social organization, institutions, and personnel as aspects of culture. ¶ Describe ascribed and achieved status in relation to social rank. ¶ Discuss cultural determination of status and role in relation to sex, age, technical skill, wealth, kinship, and marriage. ¶ Explain the nature and function of transition rites. ¶ What universal features in status and role are found in all cultures? ¶ To what extent do status and role differences appear to be culturally determined?

In the previous chapters we have been concerned with identifying the discipline and subdisciplines of anthropology, the basic concepts of cultural anthropology (including culture, society, and personality), and the processes by which cultures change. Also we have briefly reviewed the relationship between humanity and its environment through time and in traditional patterns of food getting, land use, housing, and settlements. We turn now to the organization of society and to that part of anthropology known as *social anthropology*, the study of social organization and relationships.

SOCIAL ORGANIZATION

By *social organization* (also called *social structure*) we mean the patterned ways in which groups and individuals are organized and related to one another in the functioning entity that is society. The culture of every society includes a figurative "manual" that lays out the major tasks to be performed, the job definitions of key personnel, and specific directions for carrying out the assigned functions. The tasks to be performed (as values) constitute what Malinowski called the *charter of social institutions*. The job definitions and the assignment of specified persons to carry them out may be called *social statuses*. The directives for accomplishing various tasks may be called *roles*.

Social Institutions

An institution is a network of procedures centered upon certain focal interests. Economic institutions, for example, comprise the characteristic behaviors that center upon the production, the allocation and distribution, and the use and consumption of goods. Economic institutions include behavioral networks of food production and the manufacture of artifacts; gift exchange, trade, sale, preemption, and inheritance; utilization, hoarding, and consumption; and ownership, possession, and rights of use—everything which focuses upon production and utilization of goods and services. Marital institutions focus upon organization of intersexual relations, particularly the stabilization of mating, the nurture and enculturation of the young, household economic activities, the establishment and maintenance of mutual aid between kinship groups, and the legalizing of inheritance. Religious institutions focus upon the conceptualization of the supernatural, the formulation of effective ritual for dealing with the supernatural, and symbolic representation of the social entirety. All institutions within a society overlap and interweave. That is why we have emphasized "focused upon" in stating the central interests or goals of given types of institutions. Institutions are far from being mutually exclusive.

The charters of institutions

The charter of an institution consists of "statements" explaining why the institution exists and for what purpose. Myths, legends, beliefs, and judgments give sanctity and authority to the choices and commitments a society has made; they state why things are as they are and why they must be as they are, and they state why individuals must commit themselves to the goals as the goals are given.

Institutional charters, social statuses, and social roles may or may not be explicitly spelled out in any given culture. Most of them are not; they are implicit in customary, or normalized, action.

Symbolic art, music, ritual, and dance express and reinforce with emotional overtones the structural relationships between persons and groups which constitute the institutions.

The personnel of institutions

All institutions have personnel. Institutions represent stability and order established by the traditional past; yet they exist only in present action—in the behavior of functioning persons. The groups of people who carry out the roles of any institution constitute its personnel. Institutionally organized groups in preliterate societies are recognized as *kinship groups* (family, extended family, ramage, lineage, clan, phratry, and moiety) or *associations* (age sets, clubs and fraternities, cults, corporations, work groups, guilds, and the state). The personnel of an association consists of *members* and *specialists* (functionaries or officials).

THE NATURE OF STATUS

An individual's status is his or her social position with reference to the other members of the society as determined by a cluster of attributes or the generalized summation of all his attributes. Thus, every person has a number of statuses simultaneously. Each individual has, in the most specific and narrow sense, as many statuses as there are recognized characteristics of the individual in the culture. Such characteristics are age, sex, bodily traits, and specific social experiences and affiliations. On the next level of abstraction, the individual has the more commonly recognized statuses that derive from the possession of certain combinations of traits, for example, the wisdom, courage, kindness, generosity, and even temper that characterized the Plains Indian peace chief. Finally, each person may have the generalized sort of status that is referred to as "social" status. This last sort of status identification calls for gross stereotyping of individuals. It seizes upon a small number of obvious criteria for lumping individual personalities into an undifferentiated class. The first sort of status identification, in contrast, calls for knowledge of numerous attributes of the individual and thus leads to a greater concern with the uniqueness of his personality.

Therefore, it should be kept in mind that status can be either specific or generalized and that there are varying degrees of generalization.

Ascribed and Achieved Status

The statuses that an individual holds are attained in various ways. They may be sought through striving and competitive mastery of the roles linked to the various statuses. Such statuses in the terminology suggested by Linton are called *achieved*.[1] MacIver calls them *functional determinants* of social position.[2] Other statuses devolve upon the individual by virtue of innate biological characteristics such as sex, age, and race or by virtue of preexisting social affinities, such as the statuses of parents and kinsmen and the involuntary associations into which the individual is born. These statuses are *ascribed* to the individual by the social system, and there is little that can be done to escape them or to alter them.

It is important to note that achieved statuses are attained only by first mastering the roles. As

[1]R. Linton, *The Study of Man*, pp. 113–114.
[2]R. M. MacIver, *Society*, pp. 78–79.

Barton has observed of the Kalinga in northern Luzon: "Elevation to rank and power in the community is a gradual process of emergence in which power is attained before the rank is acknowledged by the people."[3] When the role is finally mastered, the status flows from this fact. A master hunter must first master hunting.

In the case of ascribed statuses, on the other hand, the status comes first, and the roles are mastered subsequently. It is even possible to inherit ascribed status without mastery of the roles. There are betimes unkingly kings, ignoble nobles, unladylike ladies.

Ascribed status distinctions based on age, sex, the premarital state, childbearing, and kinship are the universal foundations of human social structure.

Achieved status criteria that are ubiquitous to all societies are those based on technological skill or artisanship (all peoples make tools), supernaturalism (all peoples have magico-religious specialists), the marital state, fecundity, and political leadership.

Nonuniversal ascribed statuses include caste-determined occupations, inherited supernatural-

ism, inherited possession of wealth, inherited possession of various religious and social perquisites and paraphernalia, and inherited political position (i.e., royalty) (Fig. 8-1).

Nonuniversal achieved statuses include those based upon hunting skills, skill in games and dances, bravery and skill in war, skill in head-hunting, storytelling ability, possession or distribution of wealth, bodily mutilation, and membership in various specialized associations. (This list is not exhaustive.)

The functional importance of all these different statuses rests in the fact that they limit and influence the degree and direction of cultural participation and the manner and amount of interaction for individuals and groups. No one person ever manifests all the behavior characteristic of a particular culture because, for one reason, no one person ever inculcates all the statuses existent in the culture.

The greater the number of achievable statuses in a culture, the greater the opportunity for full participation (potentially, at least) by all members. The more extensive and rigid the ascribed statuses, the more constrained are the individuals in their culturally prescribed roles.

Cultures that emphasize achievable status are

[3]R. F. Barton, *The Kalinga*, p. 148.

FIG. 8-1 A Dahomean chief and retinue protrayed in cast bronze. The royal chief, wearing a hat and robes of state, rides at ease in a hammock, smoking his pipe, while surrounded by the carriers of his royal paraphernalia. (Smithsonian Institution.)

marked by internal social mobility, social striving, and (on the whole) competitiveness and individualism. Emphasis is placed upon "fulfillment of self" and assertiveness, as in contemporary American society. The social gain is ideally a greater ultimate efficiency because capable persons are not barred from effective performance in those capacities for which they have adequate aptitudes. Conversely, caste and rigid class systems are socially wasteful because they ascribe roles to people who are not necessarily well suited to their performance, while at the same time they bar potential adepts.

On the other hand, the advantages of social systems that emphasize ascribed statuses lie in reduced strain and anxiety for the participating members of the society. Competitive insecurity is presumably reduced. Frustration born of failure to achieve a sought-after status is avoided.

When ascribed status systems begin to lose their authority, however, and persons in statuses of marked social disability begin to aspire to achievable statuses, their frustration and the anxiety of those in the threatened ascribed positions become acute and difficult to tolerate, in the way that marks interracial relations and social class in many parts of the world today.

Status Hierarchy: Rank

The status system of every society involves also a certain amount of ranking. But, it should be noted, status and rank are not the same. "Status" is a neutral term, which refers only to position. "Rank" refers to hierarchical status—higher or lower with reference to other statuses. The rank order of a society is its system of status gradations. A high status is one that carries prestige; i.e., the attitudes associated with it are those of deference, reverence, submission, and subordination on the part of those of lower status. Prestige translated into action means power—the capacity to influence or direct the behavior of others. A low status carries little prestige; there is little power capacity associated with it.

The range embraced in a rank order will be wide or narrow depending upon the disparities in power structures formed by the culture. In simple democratic hunting and gathering societies, such

as that of the Eskimos, the range is narrow. In complex, class-organized societies, such as that of the Yoruba, the range between slave and king is great.

THE NATURE OF ROLE

Role is the customary complex of behavior associated with a particular status. Every individual is to some degree a poseur. All are actors, for life in society is a playing of roles.

The command, "Just be your natural self," does not mean what it says. It really means, "Suppress your conscious awareness of the roles you must enact." Human behavior is "natural," is free of posing, only when individuals have become so habituated to all their roles that they do not register awareness of them while performing them. Newborn infants in their first hours have no acquired roles as complements to their statuses. No one expects much of them, either.

Because every person has multiple statuses, one also manifests many different roles. A married professor behaves differently with his family (the husband and father roles) from the way he does in the classroom (the professor role). And if he is a volunteer fire fighter, he behaves quite differently when engaged in "firemanic" activities of either a fire-fighting or a social nature. At different times, therefore, different roles come to the fore. Several roles may be operative simultaneously, but the intensity of their effectiveness is variable.

At times, various roles may be held in abeyance or inactivated. A Pueblo Indian, while cultivating his fields, holds his dancing roles as a member of a religious secret society in abeyance. A person's roles could be likened to a wardrobe, from which the costume suitable for each occasion is selected with many quick changes called for. Roles are therefore *latent*, except when they are being activated or made *manifest*.

SEXUAL STATUSES AND ROLES

Sex dichotomy is a biological fact upon which culturally determined statuses are built. But what is biological and what is cultural in sex differences are not established with certainty for all types of activity. True, certain physiological functions are sex-linked. Females produce ova, while males produce sperm. Females have specialized sex organs for the nurture and incubation of fertilized ova; males do not. Females are capable of parturition; males are not. *Homo sapiens* is a bisexual animal in which the basic reproductive roles are biologically fixed. So long as babies are born of women, differential statuses of male and female will be recognized and culturally reflected. The real social revolution will come when perfected biogenetic techniques make possible the fertilization and incubation of the human ovum outside the womb.

But even this impressive possibility will evidently be bypassed in favor of *cloning*. In this process a whole new organism will be grown from a single body cell of an already existing organism. The new individual will be an exact genetic replication of the genitor, for every normal body cell contains the genetic code for the entire organism within its nucleus. Human reproduction will then be accomplished without the medium of sex. There will no longer be a biological need for males and females. Sex will be obsolete, and so, in all probability, will be status differences between men and women. Responsible biologists, such as J. B. S. Haldane and Lord Rothschild see cloning as a reality in the very near future.[4] In the meantime, however, every society assigns different roles to males and females, as in the following instances.

San Ildefonso Pueblo

In San Ildefonso there is a sharp line between men's work and women's work, and in the respective attitudes of the sexes towards their work. Men's work on the whole tends to be cooperative. The ditches are dug by the male community in the spring; the fields are tended as a group enterprise. . . . Among women, on the contrary, work has tended to become competitive; women seldom carry on any of their activities as a group. . . . Theoretically, at least, women play comparatively minor roles. San Ildefonso men do work which elsewhere is frequently the task of women. Their special province is called "outside work." Traditionally they hunt, dress the skins of the animals they kill, cut and sew moccasins for themselves and for the women, weave baskets, and

weave and create their own dance costumes. . . . Men till the fields and the gardens, plant and reap, cut and haul firewood. Within the village itself they build the houses, care for the kivas, and clean the plaza before fiestas and dances. . . . Women's work is "inside." They care for the household, grind the grain, cook, and tend their children. They make and fire the pottery, and if there is no man in the family who can decorate it, the women may decorate their own.[5]

Lesu, New Ireland

Of Lesu, a gardening, fishing, and pig-raising society in Melanesia, Powdermaker wrote: "It is the sexual division of labour adhered to so rigidly that first strikes the ethnological observer. Men have one kind of work and women another, and a third kind may be done by either one of them or jointly."[6] The division of labor is set forth in Table 8-1.

Sexual Division of Work Roles

Although each society divides men's work and women's, what is distinctly men's work in one society may, however, be women's work in another. As obvious examples we may note that the weaving of Navaho blankets is women's work, while among the neighboring Hopi, both spinning and weaving are confined to men. In nineteenth-century America, boys were supposed to be able to swim, and girls were not; yet among the Yahgan of Tierra del Fuego, women are the swimmers. Among the Pueblo Indians, most garden work is done by men; among the Iroquois, hunting and fighting were for men, but tilling was for women only. Among the Maricopa Indians of southern Arizona, pottery making was "wholly a woman's occupation and a year-round task."[7] Weaving was properly men's work. Women harvested and ginned the cotton, which was grown exclusively by the men, and both sexes spun the yarn.

Because of such facts, anthropologists have learned to reject all generalizations such as that

[4]See G. R. Taylor, *The Biological Time Bomb*, pp. 22–30. See also pp. 416–417.

[5]W. Whitman, *The Pueblo Indians of San Ildefonso*, pp. 99–100. By permission of Columbia University Press.
[6]H. Powdermaker, *Life in Lesu*, p. 161.
[7]L. Spier, *Yuman Tribes of the Gila River*, p. 104.

TABLE 8-1   THE DIVISION OF LABOR IN LESU, MELANESIA

Masculine	Feminine	Joint
Clearing ground for new garden and building garden fence	Planting taro and yams; weeding; gathering crops and carrying them home	
Planting trees		
Getting sago		
Fishing	Catching crabs on the reef	Catching the sea worm, *beta*
Hunting wild pig and phalanger	Feeding domestic pigs	
Cutting firewood; making the *liga;* bringing the leaves for cooking	Drawing water	
Preparing pigs, fish, and sago to be cooked	Preparing taro and yams to be cooked	
Burying bananas in the sand		
Housebuilding and repairing	Sweeping the house and keeping it in order	
Making of masks, canoes, *malanggans,* fishing-nets, spears, ornaments	Carrying heavy burdens with the exception of fish and pigs	Making baskets and mats. Taking care of children. Medicine and magic. Making "paint" for the hair

SOURCE: After H. Powdermaker.

women are "naturally" housekeepers or that they are more "peaceful" or more "religious" than men. But anthropology has also established that throughout the world, certain kinds of work activities are quite consistently assigned to men and other kinds to women. In three-fourths of all societies, the tasks of food and fuel gathering, grinding seeds and grain, preparing foodstuffs for preservation, weaving, and manufacturing pottery, baskets, and mats are assigned to women. These are all jobs that, except for the gathering of foodstuffs, can be carried on in the immediate vicinity of the hearth and infant.

World distribution of division of labor by sexes
Hunting, on the other hand, is exclusively men's work in all societies covered in Murdock's *Ethnographic Atlas*, except in Siam (now Thailand).

Fishing is largely, but not exclusively, a male activity (in 84 per cent of the 717 societies in which fishing contributes to subsistence). Cattle herding in the Old World is almost exclusively limited to men, but no clear division of labor by sex is discernible with respect to other kinds of domesticated animals in other parts of the world.

Participation of men and women in gardening and agriculture varies from region to region. Women predominate in sub-Saharan gardening in Africa. Around the Mediterranean, men carry on most plow agriculture. In Asia men and women gardeners work side by side, while in the South Seas, gardening responsibilities are held by women in one-third, by men in one-fifth, and by both sexes in nearly half of the societies.[8]

[8]E. Bourguignon and L. Greenbaum, *Diversity and Homogeneity*, p. 12.

In sum, the anthropological position is that certain sex-linked behaviors are biologically based, although subject to cultural modifications within limits. The roles in any society must be empirically observed and objectively recorded.

AGE STATUSES AND ROLES

From a gross biological point of view, life may be reduced to a simple formula: to be born, to mature, to reproduce, and to die. However, even the biologist will acknowledge that at least a few other events of significance occur along the way. Humanity embroiders upon the fundamental pattern.

Age statuses are recognized in all societies. The universal minimum includes at least three categories: child, adult, and old person, or, respectively, those not yet ripe for full social participation, those who perform the major maintenance activities of the society, and those who are beyond the stage of active participation and responsibility. Generally, recognized age statuses are more numerous. Thus, the Comanches recognized five ages: baby, preadolescent, unmarried "brave" or girl, grown person, and old man or woman. Each age has its separate, specific appellation. Young children may be highly valued as objects of desire, but they never have prestige merely by virtue of their status as infants. In the exceptional instances in which infants do enjoy high status and prestige, it is always as a consequence of some special factor other than age, as in the case of a princeling by birth or a twin with imputed supernatural qualities (as among the Dahomeans).[9]

Youths and persons of middle age rarely enjoy favored status by virtue of their age, as such, although prowess and wealth may bring prestige status to them.

Adulthood means full participation in the responsibilities and privileges of the society. It means marriage and parenthood and political, religious, economic, and club life, all to be spelled out in detail in the remaining chapters.

As for the aged, they have almost always enjoyed statuses of respect, reverence, and privilege because of the attributes that are ascribed to them by virtue of their being old.[10] It is not just being old that brings prestige; it is the accumulated wisdom and lore of the oldsters—the association of ancient custom with ancient people. As has been said of the Haida Indians of Queen Charlotte Island on the Northwest Coast: "They had great respect for the aged, whose advice in most matters has great weight."[11]

In the primitive world, the oldsters are "elders" in politics and government, magicians and priests in supernaturalism, and owners of property in some systems of economic organization. These are sources of power. Since such sources are more available to men than to women, old men usually have higher status than old women.[12] The positions of the aged are more secure in the settled horticultural tribes than among hunting and collecting peoples, especially those who live in the arctic and its fringes, where old people are unable to participate in primary productive activities to any extent.

The support of the aged is a luxury which many marginal societies find themselves unable to sustain in times of stress. Senilicide used to be general among the Eskimos. Old people might be blocked up in a snow hut to be abandoned to cold and starvation, or they might be killed by more violent means when they themselves requested it.[13] However, of the seventy-one societies tabulated by Simmons, only two (both Eskimo) violently remove the aged; seven abandon or expose them to natural elements to hasten their deaths.[14] This does not mean that in these seven societies, all old people are destroyed when their powers wane. It depends upon individuals and circumstances.

Almost all observers remark that old people are respected in the tribes they have visited. Only the Bushmen of South Africa and the Witotos of South America are said definitely to withhold respect from aged men. Eight of the seventy-one

---

[9]M. J. Herskovits, *Dahomey*, vol. 1, pp. 263, 270–272.

[10]L. Simmons, *The Role of the Aged in Primitive Society*, p. 79.

[11]A. P. Niblack, *The Coast Indians of Southern Alaska and Northern British Columbia* (Board of Regents of the Smithsonian Institution, Annual Report, 1890), p. 240.

[12]Simmons, *op. cit.*, pp. 47–49.

[13]E. A. Hoebel, *The Law of Primitive Man*, pp. 76–79.

[14]Simmons, *op. cit.*, table 6.

tribes studied by Simmons deny deference to old women.

The Andaman Islands provide anthropologists with a favorite example of age as a status determinant. Kinship, which is so important in most primitive societies, is here somewhat muted. Rather:

The duties that one person owes to another are determined much less by their relation to one another by consanguinity and marriage, than by their respective ages and social status. . . . There is very little of any special customs relating to conduct towards different kinds of relatives. Corresponding to this we find very few terms to denote relationships and a considerable development of terms which denote age and social status.[15]

Older persons had many food privileges denied to the young. Gradually, and with elaborate ritual, the food tabus were removed for the growing youth, until at full maturity he could enjoy all the delicacies permitted for his sex. Younger persons had to defer to the older ones in all matters.

In Australia, where, as in the Andaman Islands, lived some of our most primitive peoples, seniority reached its greatest significance—so much so that Australian social organization is dubbed *gerontocracy*, "the rule of elders." The preeminent domination of the Australian local group by old, grizzled men gave birth and impetus to the nineteenth-century notion that the primeval condition of man was that of browbeaten youth frustrated by the hoary patriarch. Australia, however, represents a special elaboration of age status in a way not universally characteristic of the hunters and gatherers (in contrast are the African Bushmen and American Shoshones).

In stable societies, accumulated experience is valuable. Elders really do know more than youngsters, and what they know holds good. But in rapidly changing cultures, such as now prevail everywhere, accumulated knowledge often becomes quickly shopworn. What was valid in the youth of the aged is no longer so. Wisdom based on outdated knowledge is, alas, of little use to one who clutches it as a source of prestige.

---

[15]A. R. Radcliffe-Brown, *The Andaman Islanders*, p. 81. By permission of Cambridge University Press.

Changing Statuses: Transition Rites

Early in this century, Arnold van Gennep (1873–1957) published the classic work known in English as *The Rites of Passage*.[16] Van Gennep demonstrated that changes of status are frequently apprehended as crisis situations. In the transition from one basic status to another, as a person moves through the developmental stages of life, he must be detached from his previous status and incorporated into the new one. In the "in between" (liminal) phase the transient is viewed, and looks upon himself, with anxiety. The transient is leaving familiar roles and has not yet acquired new ones. He is unpredictable, dangerous—a threat to himself and his associates. Hence he is, in many societies, isolated and quarantined—sometimes even ritually "killed." At the climax of the transition rites he is then reborn (a neophyte)[17] as a new and more mature person, well-schooled in the new roles, ready to be reincorporated into community life.

To take an example from Western society, when old-time Army sergeants bullied and insulted rookies, they were not being merely sadistic, nor were they necessarily working off personal frustrations. Although sergeants may not be aware of any principles of functional anthropology, they do know that recruits have to be made over and put through a quick transition rite. A first act is the destruction of civilian ways and civilian thoughts: "You're in the Army now." Induction means death of the civilian, and the "top kick" is the executioner. Completion of basic training means resurrection in a new status—General Issue.[18]

Torture in the puberty rites of Australian and many African tribes rises to heights of sheer cruelty. Yet beneath it can usually be found a functional rationalization. In Australia, circumcision and subincision, painful and dangerous surgical operations when crudely performed with

---

[16]Written in French, the original title was *Les Rites de Passage* (1909). The English version appeared in 1960.

[17]Note that the very word means "produce anew" (Gr. *neos*, new + *phytos*, grown).

[18]It will be highly instructive to see what happens to the United States Army following its "humanization" of the indoctrination program for new recruits and the implementation of its 1971 slogan, "The Army wants to join you!" The slogan itself failed as a recruiting device and was dropped before the year was out.

stone knives (Fig. 9-2), are but symbolic acts signifying the sexual and social completeness of the males in a type of society that rejects and culturally suppresses the significance of women.

In all cases, transition is the main theme—transition from the limited and undeveloped state of childhood to that of the adult endowed with the wisdom and privileges of a mature person. Thus, death and resurrection and recurrent themes of stepped-up puberty rites: death means the destruction of the childhood personality, and resurrection means that the person is restored to the community in a new status with new roles. The boy who retires to the hidden initiatory school in the bush, secreted from the eyes of all females and preadolescent boys, is "dead." When he returns to the camp of the band, circumcised, subincised, and cicatrized, with a few teeth knocked out and with new knowledge of totemic mythology, he is a new man.

In like manner, Gerlach and Hine, in their studies of contemporary movements of social change, such as the Black Power and the Pentecostal, note that one basic feature is, "*Personal commitment* generated by an act or experience which separates the convert in some significant way from the established order (or his previous place in it), identifies him with a new set of values, and commits him to changed patterns of behavior."[19] Transition rites are not things of the past.

Functions of transition rites

Crisis periods are times of critical uncertainty when the fate of the individual or the group seems to hang in the balance. At such times individuals are not inclined to leave the outcome to chance or unbridled circumstance. Natural and supernatural forces may be controlled in fact and in belief. Therefore, positive techniques of rational assistance are employed, along with magic and ritual ceremonialism, to frustrate destructive and disruptive supernatural powers or to encourage and invoke positive and helpful forces. Through ritual and ceremony, a bridge is thrown across the yawning chasms of fear and doubt that carries the individual over transitional states to a safe arrival and a firm footing in the new status awaiting them on the other side. Their very enactment also serves another purpose. For those who participate and those who watch, the scene and the ceremony provide reassurance that, like the neophyte, life and society shall be reborn through unending cycles of regeneration.

The next chapter, on the life cycle, deals in more detail with the transition rites encountered in birth, puberty, marriage, and death.

APTITUDES AND STATUS

Not all statuses, by any means, are linked to the biological phases of the life cycle. The division of labor and functions worked out in each culture is always reflected in the status system of social relations.

If skill is a joy to any person, it should also be true that skill in any function valued by a society brings prestige and high status to the expert. By and large, anthropological data support this supposition. Proficiency in craftsmanship usually brings moderately high status among primitive people, but it tends to rank below military prowess, supernaturalism, political leadership, and wealth manipulation as a prestige generator. Polynesians, among all recorded primitives, gave the most conscious and organized recognition to craftsmanship. The *Tuhunga*, or "great adept," of the Tonga tribe in Polynesia was highly revered whether he was a master of oratory, tribal lore, house building, or canoe manufacture. Only by virtue of much mana (see page 350) was it possible for an individual to excel in anything. And all Polynesians were impressed by mana.

At the other extreme, occupations linked to inferior castes in Africa, India, and Japan bring no kudos to their practitioners, no matter how skilled the craftsman. A Masai blacksmith is doomed for life to subordination, for that is the status his culture ascribes to blacksmiths. Among Japanese, the *Eta* form a polluted caste of hereditary butchers, or in some instances fishermen, whose pariah pollution is unmodified by the importance of their work or their skill in performing it.[20]

---

[19]L. P. Gerlach and V. H. Hine, *People, Power, Change*, p. xvii; see also pp. 110–158.

[20]E. Norbeck, *Takashima*, pp. 113–114.

WEALTH AND STATUS

There are definite limits to the amount of goods that roving collectors of food are able to carry around with them. It is not possible for such people to accumulate wealth; there are no rich individuals. The possession of wealth is not, for the simpler primitives, a status determinant of great significance.

The giving away of food and goods is another matter, however. Food claims are communal in nature in almost all hunting societies. Prestige and leadership go to hunters who have food to dispense, hides to bestow, arrows to give, and (among Plains Indians) horses to lavish upon favored friends, wayfaring visitors, and indigent neighbors. Plains Indians recognized as families of good standing those whose tipis were well kept and decorated and whose industrious men and women kept their lodges well supplied with victuals, fine robes, and handsome clothes; but above all, they respected those who gave freely of what they possessed. Fluid wealth brought high status in its train. Hoarded wealth brought only contempt. This is what settlers on the Indian frontier could not understand when silent Indians appeared at the cabin door expecting a ready handout.

Reciprocal-exchange systems are not likely to generate wealth distinctions: they tend toward reciprocal equality in goods. Yet, the organization of wealth as carried out by the "Big Men" in Melanesia (pages 257–258) links economic and political activities in status determination (Fig. 8-2). To rise through the various degrees of the all-important men's club of the Banks Islanders calls for the payment of heavy initiation fees. Only the richest can afford to purchase the higher degrees. Indeed, as Lowie has summarized the data:

It is only the man of wealth who can reach the highest degrees and thus acquire prestige. Yet the aboriginal conception is not that of avariciously hoarding wealth but rather of displaying one's greatness by exhibiting contempt for property. So a man of the loftiest status in the club may still promote his renown by providing the lavish entertainment associated with certain festivals; nay, a suggestion of niggardliness on these occasions would go far to destroy his influence.[21]

[21]R. H. Lowie, *Primitive Society*, p. 277. By permission of Liveright Publishing Company.

The Potlatch of the Northwest Coast Indians of North America

Among the tribes of the Northwest Coast, elaborate honorific status distinctions were ascribed through family and clan inheritance. At the same time, they had to be validated and kept up through ostentatious display and manipulation of wealth in the most conspicuously ostentatious manner possible. This was done in part by means of showy totem poles and the potlatch—an elaborate institution of feasting accompanied by the lavish distribution of presents by the host and his kinsmen to guests of another lineage or tribe. Its primary function was to serve as a demonstration of the family and individual statuses of the hosts. The guests were witnesses to the hosts' claims to certain statuses. Although accumulations of wealth were necessary for potlatching, it was not the wealth that gave status; it was the legitimate possession of honorific prerogatives, which were linked with specific names and titles, which were inheritable, but which could not be used until publicly assumed at a potlatch given for the purpose. To use a name not publicly notarized at a potlatch was a shameful presumption, and to address a person by a name he had inherited but not yet validated was an insult to his standing.[22]

Record of a Tsimshian potlatch that took place around 1930 illustrates the old principle with some modern touches. It is the story of the chief of the Gitlan tribe and a member of the Wolf clan. When Gusgai'in, chief of the Gitlan, died, his nephew announced that he would take up his uncle's name at some later date. Before this could be done, he and a Wolf clansman jammed their motorboat between the piles of a bridge. They were hung up when the tide flowed out from beneath them. This would be enough to cause any good boatman chagrin, but when they were badgered with the remark, "We saw a Wolf hanging up under the bridge," the status of all Wolves was impaired.

A potlatch was necessary to rehabilitate their position, and so they undertook to give a traditional ceremony, the family Feast of the Early Snow, commemorating the exploit of the ances-

[22]See P. Drucker, "Rank, Wealth, and Kinship in Northwest Coast Society" (*American Anthropologist*, vol. 41, 1939), pp. 55–65. Occasional potlatches are still given.

FIG. 8-2 A Melanesian "Big Man" and his associates. Two Chimbu men of wealth and power. Central Highlands, New Guinea. (Photo by E. A. Hoebel.)

tral chief, Gusgai'in, whose name was now to be assumed by his descendant. This ancestor had passed beneath a glacier in his flight from enemy captors, so with poetic flavor the *pièce de résistance* of the commemorative banquet was to be a native sherbet made of snow mixed with olachen grease, berries, and crabapples. In keeping with the times, however, ice cream was served instead at this potlatch. A heaping dish of ice cream, more than he could possibly eat, was placed before each person who had taunted the Wolves.

Gorging a guest and then making fun of him was a favorite form of ridicule and provided much amusement for the guests. . . . When the feast and hilarity were over, the chief arose and explained the mythological background for the feast they were giving. He thanked the guests for coming and announced that, in so far as he was able, he would fill the position of his late uncle. Then La'is, the senior Wolf of the Gilustsa'u tribe, arose as the chief's spokesman and said that, as the chief had been publicly addressed as Gusgai'in, the latter was hereby acknowledging the name and assuming the position. . . . Spokesmen for each guest chief affirmed

FIG. 8-3 A Northwest Coast Indian potlatch around 1910. (left) Ready for the display and distribution of food and blankets (in the trunks). (right) A chief orates before the pile of Hudson Bay blankets which he is bestowing upon his rival. (Courtesy of the American Museum of Natural History.)

Gusgai'in's right to the name and welcomed the new chief as a brother. They also acknowledged that the bridge incident and other slurs would be forgotten. Much of tribal history was narrated during the speeches and many compliments were paid the host and his lineage.

Gifts of food and handkerchiefs were then distributed among the guests. Dancing ended the potlatch.[23]

The potlatch serves to affirm the status of the host; and the protocol of seating, serving of food, and distribution of gifts does the same for the guests. Invariably the giving is in order of rank. The person with the highest rank is called upon to come up first to receive his allotted share, and so on down the line. The position of each person with respect to every other is rigidly determined by the nature of the validated titular prerogatives he holds. The mere giving of a potlatch does not validate a person's claim to status. The real validation comes when he is called forth to receive his gifts when he is a guest at other potlatches. Only if his hosts call him forward at the moment warranted by the position he has claimed is his claim validated.

Be it noted, too, that the recitations of tribal history reaffirm and perpetuate the institutional charters of Tsimshian society.

KINSHIP AND MARITAL STATUSES AND ROLES

Marriage is a universal phenomenon at all levels of cultural development. Premarital, marital, and postmarital statuses are therefore ubiquitous. The roles of husband and wife are of such extreme importance in any society that marriage and the family are subjects requiring special treatment in separate chapters (Chapters 10 and 11).

Kinship, which consists of networks of reciprocating statuses and roles, is also of such fundamental significance in all societies that it too will require special chapters (Chapters 12 and 13) for exposition and analysis.

[23]V. E. Garfield, *Tsimshian Clan and Society* (University of Washington Publications in Anthropology, vol. 7, no. 3, 1939), pp. 205–206. By permission of University of Washington Press.

SELECTED READINGS

Drucker, P., and R. F. Heizer, *To Make My Name Good* (1967). A contemporary reexamination of the potlatch as practiced by the Kwakiutl Indians.

Giffen, N. M., *The Roles of Men and Women in Eskimo Culture* (1930). Treats the division of labor by sexes in a simple culture.

Goodenough, W. H., "Rethinking 'Status' and 'Role': Toward a General Model of the Cultural Organization of Social Relationships," in M. Banton (ed.), *The Relevance of Models for Social Anthropology* (1965), pp. 1–22. Presents a somewhat different conceptualization of the terms "status" and "role," and demonstrates their application to the analysis of kin behavior among the Truk Islanders of Micronesia.

Kuper, H., *An African Aristocracy: Rank among the Swazi* (1947). Royalty and commoners in a South African tribe.

Mead, M., *Male and Female* (1949). An insightful and informative cross-cultural study of sexual roles in a changing world.

9

THE LIFE CYCLE

Birth, maturity, reproduction, and death are the four basic and universal crises in the completed life cycle. In the earthly span of the human organism, all individuals who fulfill their biological destiny must pass through each of these peaks in the cycle of life. Therefore, in no human culture are these critical periods wholly ignored. They may, however, be approached and surmounted with varying degrees of intensity. Some peoples are habituated to treat one or another of the life crises in a matter-of-fact manner. Others exhibit much anxiety. In the latter situation, there is considerable cultural emphasis on the crisis situation.

CONCEPTION

The life cycle begins with conception. Yet no primitive peoples have a scientifically accurate knowledge of the nature of conception. This ignorance is not too surprising, if we keep in mind that even civilized human beings have acquired a sophisticated knowledge of genetics only in the last hundred years, and there is still a good deal of talk about storks in our society.

However, most primitive peoples can recognize causal sequences with sufficient astuteness to be able to associate the act of sexual intercourse with conception. Some are acute enough to recognize that the male semen plays a role in the generation of life. Yet the naive notion that the male plants a seed, which the female nurtures, is the closest primitive human beings can come to reality.

Explicit notions of miraculous conception abound in the primitive world. In its most common form, the belief is expressed that a child is the reincarnation of an ancestral spirit who has slipped into the womb of the mother to be regenerated.[1] In Australia, this belief was raised to the status of a dogma so strong that the natives denied any relation between the sex act and conception other than to admit that the womb must first be opened so that ancestral spirits might enter.

The Physiology of Paternity

Earlier anthropologists took the Australoid denial of the physiology of paternity at face value. Mod-

---

[1]See, for example, B. Malinowski, "Baloma; The Spirits of the Dead in the Trobriand Islands," in *Magic, Science and Religion and Other Essays*, pp. 125–227.

ern anthropologists see it as a cultural suppression of recognizable fact, the purpose of which is to sustain the shibboleths of the social system.[2] Ancestor worship and totemism are important themes in aboriginal Australian culture. The continuity of the totemic group is sustained by means of the doctrine of spiritual reincarnation. To give expression to the fact of physiological paternity would be a subversive undermining of the sacred institutions of Australian social life—it would be definitely un-Australian.

The matrilineal (see page 215) Trobriand Islanders say that the male plays no role in conception. Rather, the spirit of a dead clan ancestor (called *baloma*) enters the womb when a woman is wading in the lagoon. It grows and becomes a child. The nearby Dobu, who believe that semen is voided coconut milk, which, when it enters a woman, causes the blood within her womb to coagulate and form a fetus, say bluntly that the Trobriand Islanders lie. The point is a sore one. So many angry words have been exchanged over this moot issue in the past that nowadays when Dobus and Trobriand Islanders meet, they tacitly avoid the touchy subject. Fortune's Dobu companions scolded him for broaching the subject on a visit to the Trobriand Islands.[3] Not without reason is anthropology sometimes called the "study of rude cultures by rude people."

The Dobu notion that babies are formed by the coagulation of blood is shared by many primitives sporadically distributed about the globe. They reason from the observed fact of cessation of menstruation during gestation. By inversion, they say that the clotting of the blood to form the baby stops the regular flow.

Pregnancy

Life begins with conception, and conception produces pregnancy. No matter how they may envision conception, all peoples recognize pregnancy in empirical physiological terms. There are a number of externally observable biological alterations that occur in mothers of all races. More notable among them are enlargement of the breasts and nipples, exudation of colostrum, cessation of menstruation, abdominal enlargement, and frequently, nausea.

From the little that has been written on this subject by anthropologists, most peoples seem to focus on one or two of the symptoms as signs of coming events, although it is probable that they make note of all of them. Cessation of menstruation is the one universally recognized sign. A fair percentage of the tribes even calculate the expected birth at ten lunar months after the last menstrual period.

Various Oceanic and African tribes make note of breast changes; the Arunta of Australia, the Pukapuka of Polynesia, and others have been put on record as noting "morning sickness." Others have told field workers that a significant clue is diminution of appetite and a tendency to become lazy.[4]

Prenatal tabus

Pregnancy is the foreshadowing of birth. It is, therefore, in itself a crisis condition, or a preliminary phase of the critical event of giving birth. Most peoples seize upon the gestation period as calling for a cultural relief of their anxieties. Chief among these anxieties are fear that (1) the child will not develop ideally, (2) the fetus will miscarry, and (3) the birth will be difficult. Pregnancy tabus and injunctions are supposed to bring freedom from these fears.

Thus Ray reports for the Sanpoil Indians of Washington that a childbearing woman and her husband could not eat trout, lest the child shake like that lively fish. They could not eat rabbit, lest the child get weak legs. They could not eat "fool hen," lest the child be a moron. More than this, the mother-to-be had to rise before sunrise, stay awake through the day, swim in cold water, walk and run, and ride horseback to strengthen her for the ordeal to come.[5]

It may reassure some contemporary mothers,

[2]See M. F. A. Montagu, *Coming into Being among the Australian Aborigines.*

[3]R. F. Fortune, *Sorcerers of Dobu*, pp. 238–239.

[4]C. L. Ford, *A Comparative Study of Human Reproduction* (Yale University Publications in Anthropology, No. 32, 1945), p. 44.

[5]V. F. Ray, *The Sanpoil and Nespelem* (University of Washington Publications in Anthropology, vol. 5, 1932), p. 124.

and induce some husbands to more indulgent understanding, to know that queer food preferences in pregnancy are not silly whims. Quite a number of peoples recognize that the pregnant woman has a craving for peculiar foods. Ford notes, however, that there do not seem to be any particular kinds of foods that are craved. The desire is for *variety*. What the basis of this desire may be we do not know.[6]

CHILDBIRTH

It is strange, perhaps, that most of the anxiety over the crisis of childbirth comes before the event, not during it. Magic, ritual, and tabu dominate the prenatal period; yet when the moment of birth is reached, the obstetrical problems are, in normal cases, handled with matter-of-fact effectiveness, free of mumbo jumbo. For the most part, birth is strictly a woman's affair. However, a few tribes permit or require the husband to assist or to be present. Generally, however, the expectant mother retires into the house with one or two older female relatives to assist her. Midwife specialists are called upon among some peoples.

A widely accepted falsehood is that childbirth is easy for primitive women. It has even been anthropologically maintained that just as domestication increases birth difficulties for animals, so increasing domestication through civilization makes birth progressively more difficult for the civilized mother. There is little evidence for this idea. On the contrary, there is much empirical evidence in the record to prove that primitive women often suffer much agony and difficulty in childbirth; the multifarious magical provisions designed to assure an easy birth are surely ample evidence of the primitive's fear of hard delivery.

Practically all peoples have special emergency medical practices to call into play when birth is unusually difficult. In easy cases, there is little use of magic at the time of birth, but in drawn-out labor, medicine men and women are hastily invoked. The Cheyennes sent for a medicine man who had derived power from the otter. Otters make a delightful sport of sliding down mudbanks. This is the way the baby should behave

and an otter medicine man could bring it about— so they say.

The Couvade

A truly quaint custom is the *couvade*. On the birth of the child, the mother gets up and goes about her affairs, while the father goes to bed, apparently to recover from the effects of childbirth. During the period of his confinement, he is subjected to many tabus. This may be variously interpreted as a demand for attention on the part of the male, as a symbolic assertion of the father's identification with the child, or as a form of magical assistance in the establishment of the child in the everyday world. But it is hardly, as some young fathers might think, a consequence of sheer exhaustion. That it is the symbolic assertion of identification of father and child seems to be the likeliest possibility.

As a matter of fact, not many cultures have produced the couvade. The Caribs and various of their South American neighbors are the outstanding couvadists. The Ainus of Japan and also the Chinese of Marco Polo's time should be included, as well as certain tribes of South India. In the northern mountains of the Iberian peninsula, the couvade was practiced until very recent times.

According to Seed Eater Shoshone informants, they also practiced a real couvade in the old days.[7] When the expectant mother retired to her birth hut, the father went into a retirement hut of his own made for him by his mother. There he stayed isolated for five days, until the umbilical cord dropped from the newborn babe.[8] He observed all the tabus that normally applied to a menstruating woman. No meat or soup could be eaten, only cereals. On the day of birth, his mother came to him, and he rubbed himself with sage. If

---

[7]E. A. Hoebel, *Shoshone Field Notes* (unpublished, 1934); also R. H. Lowie, *Notes on Shoshonean Ethnography* (American Museum of Natural History, Anthropological Papers, vol. 20, part 3, 1924), pp. 265–270.

[8]"A striking instance of numerical imposition is the frequent relationship between the sacred number of a group and the day on which the umbilical cord 'falls off': in Bali, where the mother is in a special state for the first three days after birth, the cord falls off in three days; in Iatmul, where the magic number is five, it falls off in five." M. Mead, "On the Implications for Anthropology of the Gesell-Ilg Approach to Maturation" (*American Anthropologist*, vol. 49, 1947), p. 74.

she said, "You have a boy," he took a long walk in the mountains—where the game abide—but he did not hunt. If she said, "You have a daughter," he walked down into the valleys, where the wild seeds grow. Thus he symbolically associated his child with its future occupation. When the five days were up he bathed, and then, when he killed his first game, he gave it away to the people.

The four widely scattered centers of the couvade (East Asia, the Pyrenees, northeastern South America, and the Plateau area of North America) indicate independent development and elaboration of the father's role in the birth crisis in these areas.

Naming and Presentation of the Child

The mere fact of birth does not necessarily complete the transition of the child from the status of fetus to that of a member of the community. Many people feel that there must be a formal presentation to the people and the spirits. Many people feel that until this act is completed, mother and child must remain in isolation. The mother is contaminated by her blood and by the dangerous forces of the birth crisis. This is the putative rationalization. Practically, of course, it is a good thing for the mother to have a chance to rest.

Postnatal isolation

The Hopi child and mother, although visited by relatives on the day of birth traditionally remain isolated for twenty days. On the twentieth day, mother, father, and child are bathed many times over. Relatives of every clan give the infant at least one name associated with their individual clan. Then as the sun rises, the infant is carried out to be held before the Sun God, who is told all the names of the child.[9]

The Seed Eater Shoshone mother and child were isolated even longer—forty days. The birth hut was built by the woman's mother a long way from the camp. When the baby's umbilical cord dropped off after five days, the hut was moved closer to the camp. All menstrual tabus were observed, but, in addition, the maternal grandmother prepared each day a bed of grass over hot coals for the mother to lie upon. (Today a hot-water bottle is used.) Throughout the day, the mother worked busily at weaving and other small tasks. Few friends came to visit her. After six weeks, she and the child rejoined the village.

Naming ceremonies

The Omaha Indian child was touchingly introduced to the entire cosmos in a traditional ritual always performed by a priest of a given subclan. On the eighth day after birth, the priest was sent for. When he arrived, he took his place at the door of the lodge in which the child was born. His right hand raised, palm up to the sky, he intoned this beautiful invocation in a loud, ringing voice for all the world to hear:

Ho! Ye Sun, Moon, Stars, all ye that move in the heavens,
I bid you hear me!
Into your midst has come a new life.
Consent ye, I implore!
Make its path smooth, that it may reach the brow of the first hill!

Ho! Ye Winds, Clouds, Rain, Mist, all ye that move in the air,
I bid you hear me!
Into your midst has come a new life.
Consent ye, I implore!
Make its path smooth, that it may reach the brow of the second hill!

Ho! Ye Hills, Valleys, Rivers, Lakes, Trees, Grasses, all ye of the earth,
I bid you hear me!
Into your midst has come a new life.
Consent ye, I implore!
Make its path smooth, that it may reach the brow of the third hill!

Ho! Ye Birds, great and small, that fly in the air,
Ho! Ye Animals, great and small, that dwell in the forest,
Ho! Ye Insects that creep among the grasses and burrow in the ground.
I bid you hear me!
Into your midst has come a new life.
Consent ye, I implore!
Make its path smooth, that it may reach the brow of the fourth hill!

---

[9]A fascinating autobiographical description of the entire birth ritual may be found in L. Simmons (ed.), *Sun Chief*, chap. 1.

Ho! All ye of the Heavens, all ye of the Air, all ye of the
    Earth,
    I bid you all to hear me!
Into your midst has come a new life.
Consent ye, consent ye all, I implore!
Make its path smooth—then shall it travel beyond the
    four hills.[10]

Yet even this ritual did not make the child a real member of the tribe, for a baby did not complete its transition until it could walk. Then it went through a "turning of the child ritual," wherein it discarded its baby name and got new moccasins. Baby moccasins always had a hole cut in the sole so that if a messenger from the spirit world came to claim the infant, the child could answer, "I cannot go on a journey—my moccasins are worn out!" New moccasins without holes were an assurance that the child was prepared for the journey of life and that its journey would be a long one.

Presentation: Becoming a tribal member

In Africa, the Ashanti entertained similar notions. The child was not ceremonially named and publicly presented until eight days had passed. Then it became a genuine human being. Should it die before that time, its little corpse would be casually thrown on the garbage heap, for it was believed to have been but the husk of a ghost child whose mother in the spirit world had pawned it off on a living mother for a short period while she went off on some jaunt or other. On returning from her undertaking, she recalled her little spirit baby.

Further to the south in Africa, a Swazi baby, until the third month of life, is described as a "thing." It has no name, it cannot be handled by the men, and if it dies, it may not be publicly mourned. It is recognized as being very weak and vulnerable (infant mortality is tragically high), and the parents perform various rituals to protect it against dangers emanating from animals, humans, and nature herself. In the third month, the infant is shown to the moon and symbolically introduced to the world of nature. It is entered into the category of persons and is given a name, which may be sung to it in its first lullaby.[11]

Not all societies undertake a formal presentation, but most of them, including Western Christianity with its christenings and baptisms (Fig. 9-1), seem to do so. Virtually all societies do isolate mother and child for periods of time varying from a few days to several months.

Naming, incidentally, is a universal human practice. Shakespeare to the contrary, there is much in a name. It symbolizes the individual's personality and often indicates some aspects of his social status. The name is usually bestowed at the end of the seclusion period. If the name is ceremonially bestowed, this is usually done by a near relative; otherwise, the most common practice is for the mother to decide what her child is to be called. Names that are associated with good luck or great deeds tend generally to be preferred. Thus the Menominee discarded their original names if they were chronically sick, in the hope that a new name would bring a healthier state of being.

Change of names or acquisition of additional ones often occurs in the course of the individual's lifespan in many societies, as new names are assumed to indicate new statuses.

CHILDHOOD

Producing, rearing, and educating children to take their role in the full life of the community are prime motivations in all societies. We have already seen in Chapter 4 (pages 56–61) that a wide variance exists in attitudes toward and handling of children. The momentarily popular myth that all primitive peoples treat their children gently, with a maximum of bodily contact and a tender indulgence of all behaviors, is, alas, only a myth. Some do, some don't. Primitive peoples are primarily concerned with the eventual readiness of their children to assume their proper place and responsibility in their particular social order. Grandparents and other relatives frequently assume major parenting responsibilities. In some parts of Polynesia adoption is frequent and casu-

---

[10] A. C. Fletcher and F. LaFlesche, *The Omaha Tribe* (Bureau of American Ethnology, Annual Report 27, 1911), pp. 115–116.

[11] H. Kuper, *The Swazi*, p. 50.

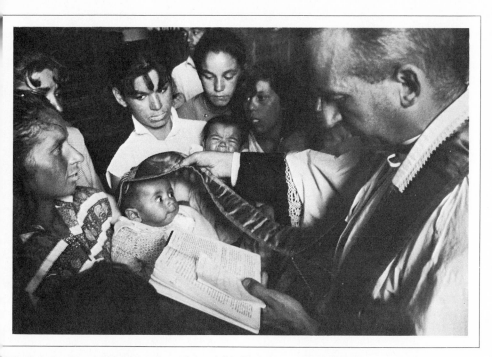

FIG. 9-1 Naming and presentation of the child. Romany gypsies offer their infants for baptism and blessing. (Photo by Sabine Weiss, Rapho Guilumette.)

al, and parenting is diffused among older siblings and numerous members of the extended family.

It is probably safe to say that no primitive society is marked by the "child-centered family" as it is known in the contemporary United States. Children are valued primarily for their potential roles as members of the lineage or clan. They spend their childhood learning these future roles. While not participants in most adult activities, they are free to watch much of what occurs. Imitative play is a major medium of all children's learning. In some societies boys are removed from their mothers' homes at about six years of age, and their education is more formally structured after the habits of men. In most instances, however, all children remain with their parents and with no particular sex segregation of siblings until puberty. Helping with tasks begins relatively early and progresses gradually as strength and skill permit.

PUBERTY

The second crisis in the life cycle is adolescence or puberty. Puberty, like birth, is a manifestation of a basic alteration of the biological state of the individual. It is the time of maturation of the secondary sexual characteristics and the final growth to functional capacity of the sex organs. Puberty marks the twilight of youth and the dawn of adulthood.

Puberty Rites and Transition of Status

In both boys and girls, puberty is not an abrupt transition, but an accelerated development extending from about the eleventh to the sixteenth year. Body hair does not sprout overnight on boys; the lengthening of the vocal cords, with embarrassing sound effects, is not instantaneous; and the relative broadening of the shoulders is a process of adolescent growth as much as the activation of the testicles and the production of fully formed seminal fluid are.

In the female, the majority of puberty changes, including emergence of body hair, broadening of the hips, increase of subcutaneous adipose tissue (especially on the hips and breasts), and development of the sex organs, all occur over a period of months. One function alone, however, first manifests itself at a particular moment. The onset of menstruation quite definitely signals the attainment of puberty for the female.

The Cultural Definition of Puberty

The transition from adolescence to adulthood is fundamentally a biological phenomenon. Yet for human beings it represents also a sociological transition. Because social status is culturally defined, adolescence is for most peoples more a cultural than a biological problem. The first fact to note is that some cultures handle adolescence most casually.[12] The second is that some ritualize it for one sex or the other or for both, with most cultures placing heaviest emphasis on adolescence rites for boys. The third factor is that puberty rites do not necessarily synchronize with biological pubescence. They occur when, sociologically, childhood is left behind and adulthood is entered.

Incision of the foreskin (supercision) to mark the attainment of manhood was practiced by some of the Polynesian societies, but by no means all. Among the Marquesan Islanders the operation was performed after a man had reached twenty-five years of age, and it might be postponed even until fifty. It had nothing whatsoever to do with puberty. And then again, among the Tongans, although boys were usually supercised between the ages of twelve and sixteen, it could be done as early as six. Adolescence was not important, but the status symbol of manhood was. As Gifford has written:

Supercision was regarded as a sign of manhood and

---

any youth who declined to be operated upon would be forbidden to eat with the other members of the household, could not touch another's food, and would be spurned by the girls. An uncircumcised person is called *kou* or *taetefe*.[13]

Among the warrior tribes of the Plains and eastern North America, there were no puberty rites per se. But at adolescence young men set out on vision quests to obtain the supernatural power that was believed so essential to a successful life. However, vision vigils were carried on by adults too, so it cannot be said that any great emphasis was placed upon puberty by these people. In the same manner, they treated the adolescence of girls casually. Although all the tribes isolated the menstruating woman, nothing much was made of the first menses, except that the Cheyenne father proudly stood in the door of his tipi shouting the good news to the whole camp and celebrated his daughter's womanhood by a giveaway of a fine horse to some poor oldster.

But the Northern Shoshones and other peoples of the Columbian Plateau made a real crisis of the event for the girl. The pubescent Shoshone girl was isolated just for the period of her flow, but she had to be very busy so that she would not become a lazy woman. "Whatever she does then lasts for life." She could eat no meat and could not scratch herself except with a special stick. At the end of her first isolation, she was brought new clothes by her mother—women's clothes.

In such societies as those of Africa and aboriginal Australia, both peoples who place much emphasis on age grading (see Chapter 14), adolescence rites become genuine "tribal initiations" (see Fig. 9-2). This is especially true where men's secret societies are of great importance. Consequently, boys' initiations are also striking in many parts of eastern Melanesia.

Andaman Island rites

As an example of the more dramatic forms of puberty rites, we may quote from Radcliffe-Brown's account of the Negrito Andaman Island-

---

[12]For example, in Samoa, "Adolescence represented no period of crisis or stress, but was instead an orderly development of slowly maturing interests and activities. The girls' minds were perplexed by no conflicts, troubled by no philosophical queries, beset by no remote ambitions." M. Mead, *Coming of Age in Samoa*, p. 157.

[13]E. W. Gifford, *Tongan Society* (Bernice P. Bishop Museum Bulletin 61, 1929), p. 187. By permission of Bishop Museum Press.

(a)

(b)

FIG. 9-2 Puberty rites of Australian aborigines. (*a*) Initiates lying upon their ceremonial sponsors undergo circumcision. (Photo by Fritz Goro, *Life*, © Time, Inc.) (*b*) After further instruction in totemic mythology and religious symbolism, the continuity of totemic membership is symbolized in the act of letting blood run from the arm of the sponsor to flow over the initiate's body. (From Jens Bjerre, *The Last Cannibals*, William Morrow, New York.)

ers. These pygmy people had no secret societies or other associations, but they did place great emphasis upon age status. To be marked and accepted as an adult, each boy and girl had to go through specific ceremonies. Beginning early in childhood, both sexes were gradually scarred over their entire bodies with small incisions "to help them grow strong," but the culmination was reached at puberty in the following manner. At the first sign of her menses, the girl was wept over by her mother and other female relatives. Such weeping did not express sorrow but rather marked an occasion of importance. The lass then plunged into the ocean for a two-hour bath—an act of ritual cleansing—after which she was tastefully decorated with pandanus leaves and clay.

Thus covered with leaves the girl must sit in the hut allotted to her, with her legs doubled up beneath her and her arms folded. . . . The girl sits thus for three days. Early every morning she leaves the hut to bathe for an hour in the sea. At the end of the three days she resumes her life in the village. For a month following she must bathe in the sea every morning at dawn.[14]

When the friends and relatives of a boy decided that he was old enough to have the incisions made on his back, a dance was held throughout the night and the next morning.

The boy kneels down and bends forward until his elbows rest on the ground in front. One of the older men takes a pig-arrow and with the sharpened blade makes a series of cuts on the boy's back. Each cut is horizontal, and they are arranged in three vertical rows, each row consisting of from 20 to 30 cuts. When the cutting is finished the boy sits up, with a fire at his back, until the bleeding stops. During the operation and a few hours following it the boy must remain silent.[15]

Immediately upon completion of the puberty rites, a number of food tabus were imposed upon both sexes. These were gradually removed in a series of formal ceremonies over a period of several years. Neither a boy nor a girl became a full-fledged adult until all the tabus had been removed.

If the whole ritual cycle is viewed as an entity, we see again that adolescence rites do not represent a fixed biological phenomenon so much as a social event roughly correlated to the biological.

West African rites

West African initiatory rites are frequently extremely elaborate and impressive. Of the Kpelle of Liberia, where initiation is into the tribal secret fraternity, the Poro, James Gibbs writes:

While a boy is in the Poro bush, he is instructed in tribal lore: farming, house building, crafts, the use of medicines, dancing, warfare, history, the treatment of women, and deportment before chiefs and elders. Physical ordeals, hazing, and the meting out of harsh punishment not only ensure that he learns well but that he acquires a deeply ingrained willingness to submit to authority because it is authority.

When a Poro initiate enters the bush it is said that he is "eaten" by ŋamu. By the time he comes out, he has acquired a lɔi laa or "bush name," by which he is known thereafter. The uninitiated person has died, and a new person has been born in his place. His new status and rebirth are also evident in the cicatrices on his back and chest, said to be the teeth marks of the Great Masked Figure imprinted in the process of disgorging the initiate at his rebirth. Circumcision is usually arranged individually before the boy becomes an initiate.[16]

Relation of Puberty Rites to Other Factors

Becoming a man or a woman means finding one's adult place in the social system. It means accepting ascribed statuses and winning those which may appropriately be achieved. Psychologically, it means internalization of a self-identity that is adequately related to the social system in which one must function. It means anchoring of the self primarily within the kinship group or, alternatively, to social units outside the kinship group. In either case, since every society is larger than the nuclear family (see page 212), it becomes universally necessary to detach the individual to some degree from his family of birth.

---

[14]A. R. Radcliffe-Brown, *The Andaman Islanders*, p. 93. By permission of Cambridge University Press.

[15]*Ibid.*, p. 95.

[16]J. L. Gibbs, Jr., "The Kpelle of Liberia," in J. L. Gibbs, Jr. (ed.), *Peoples of Africa*, p. 222. Copyright © by Holt, Rinehart and Winston, Inc., publishers. Used by permission.

The factor of social independence

Yehudi Cohen classifies two types of societies: (1) those which train for social independence, i.e., those in which anchorage and identification are in the nuclear family, and (2) those in which children are brought up for sociological interdependence, i.e., anchorage of the individual in wider kinship groups such as lineages and clans (see Chapter 12). Statistical correlations based on data from sixty-five societies show that type-2 societies overwhelmingly (36 to 1) use initiation ceremonies as a part of the socialization process. Among the type-1 societies in Cohen's sample, the ratio is only ten with initiations to eighteen without.[17] Societies that train for family identification use other means than initiatory techniques.

Circumcision and personal identity in relation to other culture traits

In pre-Columbian times circumcision was exclusively an Old World culture trait of which the American Indians knew nothing. Not one single Indian tribe was found to practice it. In the Old World, it has been predominantly a feature of the Mediterranean area—an expression of Semitic and Arab cultural symbolism. Thus, 68 per cent of the Mediterranean societies in the *Ethnographic Atlas* are found regularly to practice circumcision or some other surgical modification of the male genitals. Among the Negroes south of the Sahara, slightly more than half (56 per cent) of the societies circumcise or subincise their boys. In Asia, only a handful of peoples (17 per cent) mutilate male genitals, while in Oceania the proportion is somewhat higher (one-fourth).[18]

Whiting and his associates have engaged in an intensive search for the whys and wherefores of circumcision as a part of transition rites. They discovered that the circumcision of boys, particularly when it occurs as a part of initiation rites, is strongly associated with three other cultural phenomena: (1) the custom of having a mother and baby sleep together, while the father sleeps

separately; (2) a tabu of a year or longer on resumption of sexual relations between parents after the birth of a child, the so-called postpartum tabu; and (3) virilocal residence, in which a married couple resides with the husband's kin. The first two customs result in strong mother-son identification, and the third intensifies the ultimate claim of the father's kinsmen to the boy's social allegiance or identification. Hence, the severe hazing at puberty serves to break the mother-son tie and to transfer the boy into the world of men (Fig. 9-3).[19]

Female puberty rites

In a representative ethnographic sample of sixty societies drawn from Murdock's *World Ethnographic Sample*, Judith Brown found that approximately one-half observed mandatory puberty rites for girls between the ages of eight and twenty. Cross-cultural correlations shed some light on which types of societies initiate girls and which do not. In sum, if girls bring their husbands to live with them in their mothers' homes (uxorilocal residence), the chances are greater that the culture will include female puberty rites. By implication, removal of a girl from her parental home to her husband's sufficiently signals the status change from unmarried to married. If the girl remains at home, a ceremonial "booster shot" is helpful in effecting the personal identity transfer from mother (and her family) to the husband (and his). Brown also found that most female initiation rites are not painful. The relatively few societies (30 per cent of those which initiate girls, or 15 per cent of the total sample) which do inflict pain, such as in clitoridectomy (the female analog to circumcision), tend to be societies in which little girls sleep after birth with their mothers to the exclusion of their fathers. They first identify

---

[17]The correlations read: $X^2 = 26.44$, $T = .64$, $p < .001$. Y. Cohen, *The Transition from Childhood to Adolescence*, p. 114.

[18]E. Bourguignon and L. Greenbaum, *Diversity and Homogeneity*, table 35, p. 57.

[19]J. W. M. Whiting, R. Kluckhohn, and A. Anthony, "The Function of Male Initiation Ceremonies at Puberty," in E. E. Maccoby, T. M. Newcomb, and E. L. Hartley (eds.), *Readings in Social Psychology*, pp. 359–370. (It should be mentioned that by no means all anthropologists accept the validity of these data on the grounds that the sample of tribes used in the study is not adequately representative.) See also the discussion of Professor Hart's thesis concerning prepubertal and postpubertal education on p. 59.

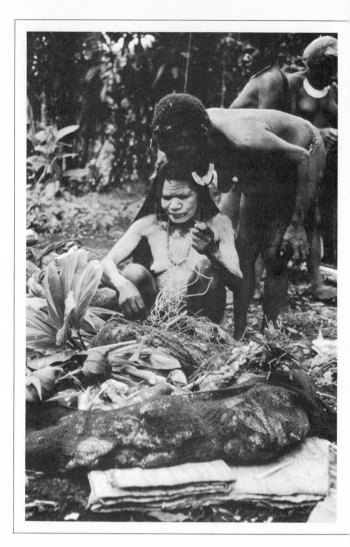

FIG. 9-3 Old age and mourning in the jungle market of the Gururumba of the Eastern Highlands of New Guinea. An elderly widow, wearing the white clay paint of mourning, displays her net bag of garden produce for sale or exchange. (Photo courtesy of the American Museum of Natural History.)

with the mother; later, they must move into a male-dominated domestic unit. Painful initiation imprints the status transfer. Finally, the greater the woman's contribution to subsistence activities, the more likely her society will be to emphasize her passage from the child's to the woman's statuses and roles. What is important in life tends to be signalized.[20]

There are a number of ancillary functions tied

up with puberty ceremonialism. Cicatrization and the filing or knocking out of front teeth serve as both decorative elements and status identifications and also as tests of the neophyte's ability to endure physical pain.[21] Strict discipline imposed during the rites works to fix the authority of elders. The instruction in etiquette, mythology, and magic that usually accompanies puberty initi-

---

[20]J. Brown, ''A Cross Cultural Study of Female Initiation Rites'' (*American Anthropologist*, vol. 65, 1963), pp. 837–853.

[21]When Elizabeth M. Thomas acknowledged to a Dodoth of Kenya that Americans do not pierce the lower lip so as to be able to wear a labret, he said, ''That is cowardly.''

ations embraces education and training in a practical sense and enhances ties or individual loyalty to the institutions of the tribal society. Yet under and through it all is the basic fact of transition—a transition that is fundamentally biological but often elaborately cultural—the transition to maturity.

MATURITY

Adulthood in every society means full participation in the responsibilities and privileges of that society. It means marriage and parenthood, as well as economic, political, religious, and club life. As new roles are acquired in each of these areas, various transition rites are again observed to note the passing into new life phases and new behaviors. Maturity is what most of the remainder of this book is about as we spell out marriage and family, kinship, club life, law, politics, religion, and art. The management and the maintenance of a society are in the hands of those who have proven themselves in age and skills.

DEATH

For the individual, death is the last of the life crises. Every person lives with awareness of his or her own death, and every society has evolved some method for coping with the death of its individual members. "Death, like birth or marriage, is universally regarded as a socially significant event, set off by ritual and supported by institutions. It is the final *rite de passage*."[22] Death has no absolute finality for any primitive people. All of them believe in the immortality of the soul.[23]

Yet all individuals well know that death marks the end of corporeal existence. Belief in the transition from the carnal to a wholly spiritual existence at death comes through faith and imagination, a projection of life from a tangible and material state to an ethereal illusory condition sustained in the dogma of culture. Because the dead are no longer constantly among the living but appear, or make their influence felt, only

indirectly, they are almost always relegated to another state of being in human cosmogony. Hence, one societal task associated with death is that of assigning new relationships between the deceased and the survivors. The new status of the deceased (spirit) may be viewed as hostile or benign, and the new behavior of the living may range from excessive fear, with attempts to placate, to idolatrous worship. In any event, the need for transition rites is clear, and such rites are usually highly circumscribed.

In Middle Paleolithic times, Neandertal man was the earliest human being to have left tangible evidence of concern over death. He deliberately buried his deceased fellow tribesmen—a boon to archaeologists and an indication that he had developed imaginative intelligence to the point where the soul concept had become possible. All later human beings have consistently worked into their cultures some form of disposal of the corpse. A great variety of methods has been recorded. A partial listing by Kroeber includes: "burial, cremation, water burial, setting away in vaults or canoes or houses, scaffold burial, exposure or simple abandonment, cremation with eating or drinking of the ashes by the relatives, temporary inhumation with either reburial or preservation of the bones—not to mention previous mummification, dismemberment, and other related practices."[24] As we have seen from archaeological evidence in Chapter 5, even burials were handled in a wide variety of ways, with bodies stretched out, curled up, richly adorned, undecorated, etc. Regardless of how the deceased body is disposed of, similar variations in preparation occur, and all are accompanied by a greater or lesser development of transitional funerary rites.

Death Rites: Funerals and Mourning

Death is ritualized in two directions. The first deals with the deceased, the separation of the spirit from the body, and the disposal of the corpse: the funeral. The second focuses on the bereavement of the survivors (Fig. 9-3), the transfer of property rights and other statuses from

---

[22]J. W. Riley, Jr., "Death and Bereavement" (*International Encyclopedia of the Social Sciences*, vol. 4, 1968), p. 19.
[23]See Chapter 21 for a discussion of the soul concept.

[24]A. L. Kroeber, *Anthropology* (2d ed.), p. 402.

the dead to the quick, and the reincorporation of the bereaved into the ongoing community: mourning.

Death practices of the Siuai

In societies where social structure is complex, we expect the probability that funeral rites and mourning will be quite elaborate.[25] Certainly this holds true for many societies, such as the Lo Dagaa peoples of West Africa, for whom we have the most thorough study of death and its societal consequences.[26] It holds true, also, of such Melanesian peoples as the Solomon Islanders studied by Douglas Oliver, whose results we briefly summarize.

The Siuai of Bougainville are sharers of the Melanesian cultural tradition of "Big Men," reciprocal pig exchange, and shell money. They are horticulturalists. Status ranking is of great significance. "The death of a child or young person occasions smaller funerals, and an infant's dying is usually a matter for near relatives alone. On the other hand, the death of a high-ranking leader gives rise to a more elaborate train of events and the funeral may be attended by hundreds of persons."[27]

If a leader dies in the prime of life, it is assumed a sorcerer had a hand in his death. Few primitive societies have a conception of death due to natural causes; most assume supernatural or magical reasons. (See Chapter 19.) At the moment of death, his nearest kin crowd around his corpse and wail loudly. The largest slit gong in the men's house to which he belonged is sounded. The news is out! After an hour of keening, the men withdraw to make plans, and more female relatives crowd into the house to carry on the crying.

After consulting with the widow, a son gives valuable shell money to his paternal uncle and mother's brother's son (matrilateral cross-

cousin). An even larger amount of shell money is then distributed among other relatives and friends to pay them for the pigs they must contribute to the funeral. Enough pigs are required to feed all who will be invited to attend from other villages. The bigger the man, the more villages to be invited. Relatives keep arriving throughout the day to join the wailing.

During the next day a funeral pyre is built and delegations continue to arrive between sunset and midnight. There is much ritualistic weeping.

Before dawn the corpse is prepared and placed on the pyre, which is then lighted. The bereaved members of the family cling close to the burning heap as long as they can stand the heat, loath to let the moment of separation come. By dawn, most of the hundreds of visitors have drifted away. The widow and son gather up unburnt bits of bone, dispose of them, and purify their hands in a final act of separation. The funeral is over, but the period of mourning goes on. For some days, no work is done by the kin. Little is eaten. No one washes, for this would remove the mourning clay. It used to be (before Australian administration suppressed revenge expeditions) that an ally and his henchmen symbolically killed the supposed sorcerer during this phase. After a week or two, the kin resume normal activity. Phase 1 of mourning is ended.

Phase 2 ends several weeks later when every relative who has received shell money brings in his reciprocating pigs. The pigs are butchered and strips of pork are carried to all the villages whose members had attended the funeral.

Seclusion and separation continue for months for the widow—and many widowers undertake this voluntarily, in honor of their wives—until some relative or friend presents a "bringing-out" gift of a pig or shell money. Thus, the last of the mourners is incorporated once again into normal social life.

Yet a form of symbolic exclusion, or separation, may linger for years in the gardens, forest, or parts of rivers which are "set-aside"—tabued in memory of the deceased. For a child, it might be only a corner of a garden. Reincorporation of a "set-aside" area requires a feast and a formal release of the ghost of the dead from its guardianship of the space.

---

[25]This proposition has not, in fact, been subjected to extensive cross-cultural testing and no satisfactory general theory has been developed to account for the wide range of variation in form and intensity of death rites. A generation or two ago, death and mourning in the United States, for example, were more seriously observed than they are today. Does this relate to a qualitative change in American social structure?

[26]J. Goody, *Death, Property and the Ancestors*.

[27]D. L. Oliver, *A Solomon Island Society*, pp. 214–215.

Functions of Mortuary Rites

Thus it may be seen that as transition ceremonies, funeral rites serve five basic functions. (1) Participation in mortuary ceremonies, by habitual dramatization of the faith in immortality, prepares the living for the death that awaits them. "The belief in immortality," wrote Malinowski, "lived through ritually . . . makes him cherish more firmly the belief in his own future life. . . . Thus the ritual before death confirms the emotional outlook which a dying man has come to need in his supreme conflict."[28] (2) Funeral rites serve magically to assure the separation of the soul from its body, to guide the deceased through the supreme transition safely and properly. (3) The rites serve to readjust the community after the loss of a member and to regularize the emotional disturbances resulting from the upset of affective habits in connection with the deceased. Death usually evokes grief. (4) Where feasting and property giveaways are involved, mortuary rites effect a redistribution of wealth and statuses. (5) Finally, the rites lend color, richness, and depth to life through the drama of their performance. They are often somewhat theatrical, and may be seen as having a certain entertainment function.

---

[28]B. Malinowski, "Culture" (*Encyclopedia of the Social Sciences*, vol. 4, 1931), p. 641.

SELECTED READINGS

Cohen, Y. A., *The Transition from Childhood to Adolescence* (1964). Undertakes to distinguish prepubertal and postpubertal rites of separation of the child from its family and to correlate each type with specific social orientations.

Erikson, E. H., "Life Cycle" (*International Encyclopedia of the Social Sciences*, vol. 9, 1968), pp. 286–292. A very compact and useful statement of the attributes of the major (eight) psychosocial crises in the individual developmental cycle.

Ford, C. S., *A Comparative Study of Human Reproduction* (Yale University Publications in Anthropology, no. 32, 1945). Summarizes primitive natal attitudes and birth practices.

Goody, J., *Death, Property and the Ancestors* (1962). The most comprehensive analysis available of the death practices and their functional significance in a primitive culture.

Jocano, F. L., *Growing Up in a Philippine Barrio* (1969). Written by a native of the Philippines, this book details the ways in which infants become adult members of a society, fulfilling their roles as bearers of their village culture.

Read, M., *Children of Their Fathers* (1968). The life cycle among the Ngomi tribe of Malawi, East Africa.

Simmons, L., *The Role of the Aged in Primitive Society* (1945). A general survey of the status of old people.

Van Gennep, A., *The Rites of Passage* (1960). First published in French in 1909, this is the classic foundation for all anthropological research in puberty rites.

10
MATING AND MARRIAGE

The prolonged dependence of the human individual on adult nurture, character shaping, and culture transmission, tied in with the peculiarities of relations within the conjugal-natal family, which is a nearly universal form in all human societies, makes untrammeled expression of sexuality socially impossible. Thus, all societies impose rigorous limitations on sexual activities and undertake to steer such sexual activity as is allowed in certain clearly defined directions. There is no such thing as a promiscuous human society. To be human is, in the nature of things, to be subject to sexual inhibition. The amount of inhibition and the forms it takes vary, as does everything else, from culture to culture. Anthropological examination of the cross-cultural record shows that American society imposes and engenders a greater degree of inhibition than is usual, although in recent times it has been moving away from this distinctive position as reproduction becomes less and less an urgent social need, as education is more and more of a public function, and as access to economic resources is increasingly managed by the welfare state.

Murdock's comprehensive survey of kinship institutions among the representative sample of 250 societies in the Yale University Cross Cultural Survey led him to estimate: "From available evidence . . . it seems unlikely that a general prohibition of sexual relations outside of marriage occurs in as many as five percent of the peoples of the earth."[1] From this it can be seen that the American position has been highly atypical. Nevertheless, it still remains true that all societies impose a number of limitations on sexual activity and attempt to regulate reproduction and mating.

MATING

Mating is *the pairing off of individuals of opposite sex under the influence of the sex drive*. It is preponderantly a psychophysical phenomenon, basically instinctive in nature. But among human beings it is definitely influenced by various culture patterns that control the forms of its expression. The purpose of this chapter is to describe the nature of the cultural channeling of mating and to explain it as far as is possible.

Mating implies more than mere sexual intercourse; a degree of permanence is involved in the association of the mated pair. However, mating is

---

[1]G. P. Murdock, *Social Structure*, p. 264.

not to be confused with marriage; intimately related though the two may be, they are not inseparable. As in the case of nonhuman animals, mating can occur on a purely biological plane, without benefit of marriage. Conversely, marriages can occur without mating.

Marriage is a social institution determined by culture. Marriage is *the complex of social norms that define and control the relations of a cojoined pair to each other, their kinsmen, their offspring, and society at large.* It defines all the institutional demand rights, duties, privileges, and immunities of the pair as husband and wife. It shapes the form and activities of the association known as the *family*.

Premarital Mating

Taking human societies as a whole, the majority accept premarital sexual experimentation without serious disapproval. Of the 863 societies in Murdock's *Ethnographic Atlas*, 67 per cent impose little restriction on premarital sexual behavior. The greatest proportion (75 per cent) of permissive societies is found in the Pacific area, thus supporting the romantic image of the South Seas brought back by nineteenth-century sailors. The most restrictive area of the world is the Circum-Mediterranean, the home of the Semites and Muslims. Here only 41 per cent of the societies are found to be tolerant of premarital sexual behavior.[2]

Malinowski's description of the Trobriand Islanders exemplifies, perhaps in a somewhat extreme fashion, the pattern. In his words:

Chastity is an unknown virtue among the natives. At an incredibly early age they become initiated into sexual life, and many of the innocent looking plays of childhood are not so innocuous as they appear. As they grow up, they live in promiscuous free-love, which gradually develops into more permanent attachments, one of which ends in marriage.[3]

In the absence of the severe guilt feelings that traditionally color premarital sex activity among our youthful population, premarital activity may function among primitives to prepare young people for marriage. It can provide an intimate test of the compatibility of mating pairs before they actually enter into marriage, with all its social and economic responsibilities. This is Malinowski's principle of the *social function of premarital sexual activity*.[4] There is little doubt that the purpose to which Malinowski calls attention may so be served in some societies, but it seems more likely that societies are apt to permit the free play of the biological drives, outside the limits of the incest tabu, before marriage because of indifference to the effects of such activity.

This set of attitudes is well exemplified by the Kadara of the Nigerian plateau, a gardening and hunting people who practice infant betrothal. The young groom, after his fiancée has become three or more years of age, labors in his betrothed father's gardens for a set number of days each year until, after ten years, he may claim his wife. Marriages, however, are very brittle and are expected to last only through the births of the first three offspring. These children belong to the husband and his kinship group. What is valued are the children per se, not the family or the chastity of the bride. "It is fairly common," writes M. G. Smith, "for unmarried girls to be impregnated or to give birth to children by youths other than their betrothed. Offspring of such premarital pregnancies are members of the patrilineage of the girl's betrothed and are welcomed as proofs of the bride's fertility."[5]

Restrictions on premarital mating

At any rate, not much emphasis can be placed upon the function of premarital experience as a factor in mate selection in the vast number of primitive societies in which the boy and girl have very little to say about whom they marry. It will be shown later to how small a degree marriage in primitive society is concerned with sexual gratification and personal compatibility on the basis of

[2]E. Bourguignon and L. Greenbaum, *Diversity and Homogeneity*, p. 54.

[3]B. Malinowski, *The Argonauts of the Western Pacific*, p. 53. By permission of E. P. Dutton and Co., Inc.

[4]B. Malinowski, "Culture" (*Encyclopaedia of the Social Sciences*, vol. 4, 1931), p. 630.

[5]M. G. Smith, "Secondary Marriage among Kadara and Kagoro," in P. Bohannan and J. Middleton (eds.), *Marriage, Family, and Residence*, p. 113.

romantic love. Primitive societies are much more concerned with (1) the biological perpetuation of the group, (2) the perpetuation of the culture and social existence of the group through proper nurture and training of the oncoming generation, and (3), last but not least, the furthering of immediate special interests in prestige, property, and prerogatives of the *extended families* of the pair to be joined in marriage; i.e., the transmission of social status.

This last point is well illustrated in the practices of the Philippine Ifugaos, who permit free premarital sexual activity only for members of those classes in which there is not much at stake in property and prestige. Each night, adolescent boys of the lower and middle classes must seek the congenial comfort of the house of a widow, which also serves the regular purpose of a dormitory for unmarried adolescent girls, who, by custom, are not permitted to sleep under the family roof. In the deep of the night, the boys try their luck at lovemaking. Much experimentation in different dormitories ultimately leads to a permanent attachment to some one girl—a form of companionate marriage that may eventually blossom into a fully accredited marriage, after numerous exchange gifts have been made and family rituals of marriage have been observed.

Upper-class Ifugaos, however, behave in quite a different manner, since the parents do not care to run the risk of permitting their children to mate in accordance with mere amatory whim. The society of the Ifugaos rests on a subsistence base of wet-rice culture in paddies that have been carved in rugged mountainsides (see Fig. 6-4, page 114) through the prodigious efforts of untold generations of labor. Possession of rice fields is a precious heritage: a necessary means to wealth, prestige, and upper-class status—the cherished goal of the Ifugao. Because family status rests heavily on property, marriage is a useful instrument for augmenting the status of the next generation by combining the resources of two families of property. To have a scion find a compatible but propertyless bride in the damsels' dormitory is, for the upper-class Ifugao, an economic calamity. To avert such an eventuality, rich children of the Ifugaos are betrothed in infancy, or even before birth. Fig. 10-1 shows such a contract marriage. A

contract marriage is arranged by the parents, who guarantee the amount of land and other goods to be conveyed to the bride and groom. Throughout childhood, the boy and girl take turns living in each other's parents' homes until they establish a home of their own on marriage, shortly after adolescence.[6]

The illustrations cited above indicate that economic factors can influence the imposition of checks on free premarital sexual activity. This must have played an increasingly important role in the unfolding of human history as societies built up more and more property. Mating became more than a simple expression of biological drives. Controlled by marriage, it tied reproduction to allocation of property and its transference from one generation to another.

While economic determinism has a sturdy finger in the pie, other factors must also be recognized. Religious belief is pervasive. In the area of sex control, its power cannot be overestimated. Inca maidens dedicated to serve the sun in the nunneries of Cuzco were required to remain virgins until they were married off to a worthy dignitary, who was the recipient of royal favor from the demigod, the Great Sun, the ruling Inca. Rome had her vestal virgins. And the military societies of the Cheyenne Indians each had four honorary virgins to perform ritual services in the society ceremonies. An active sexual life is often incompatible with religious specializations.

Shamans are generally devoted to this principle. Unless they are engaged in fertility rites to bring on a crop of babies or corn, they almost universally submit themselves to temporary celibacy when they are about to invoke their mystic powers. The belief is that the female physiology is itself charged with a mystic power of great potency. In this man-dominated world, the unique female power is interpreted as evil and dangerous, dangerous especially to the mystic powers of men. Contamination of a male's supernatural power by the negative power of the female is believed to result from sexual association. When this attitude is exaggerated, it leads to the sexual

---

[6]R. F. Barton, *Philippine Pagans*; also *Ifugao Law* (The University of California Publications in American Archaeology and Ethnology, vol. 15, 1919), pp. 15–22.

FIG. 10-1 A married Ifugao boy and girl at their elevation to the rank of kadangyang—the highest social class. The boy, who stands in the center, wears a headdress and has a white chicken hanging from his belt. His contracted wife stands next to him, with a chicken in her left hand. (Photo courtesy of Lowie Museum of Anthropology, University of California, Berkeley.)

asceticism of some of the Late Classical cults and early Christianity, an asceticism that survives in the celibacy of the Catholic clergy and the Puritan distrust of sex still embedded in much of our culture. Such intense elaboration of sex asceticism is only another example of the principle of skewed elaboration of culture. Sociology can adduce few good functional reasons for its existence. Psychiatry and psychology can adduce manifold instances of malfunctioning as a result of it—the psychotic and neurotic quirks of the repressed personality.

Various combinations of one or more of the considerations just mentioned have led a slight majority of contemporary primitive societies to inhibit, or at least to try to check, premarital sexual activity among their young. The Trobriand Island instance represents a minority situation. The primitive societies that do impose a check on adolescent premarital sex experience do so for the most part not because they view such activity as inherently evil, but rather because economic and other social interests have priority over sex. Ubiquitously, however, *every society prohibits sexuality between brother and sister at all ages.* This is the consequence of the universal prohibition of incest.

THE PROHIBITION OF INCEST

Mating with any person who is *culturally defined* as a member of one's kinship group is commonly forbidden. Any such prohibited mating is incestuous. The prohibition of sex relations between culturally identified relatives is therefore known as the *incest tabu*. It automatically follows that marriage between persons subject to this rule is also forbidden.

Incest tabus are universal among all peoples. The universality of incest prohibition and the fact that it is concerned with a basic biological act have led to the common view that it is instinctive. Universality, however, is not in itself any evidence of instinct. We might as well say that fire making is an instinct, since all peoples practice it. The weight of the evidence is on the other side. Incest prohibition is not instinctive; rather, it is rooted in a social, not a biological, basis.

Exceptions to the Incest Tabu

Let us observe how this works. *The tabu on the mating of brother and sister occurs everywhere, as does the tabu on mating between parent and child*. The exceptions that bar absolute universality are few and far between, nor do they in any case apply to the entire population of any society. The exceptions to the brother-sister rule are the famous cases of the royalty of Egypt, Hawaii, and the Incas. In these instances, marriage between brother and sister of royal lineage was required in the belief that the supreme royalty was divine and that marriage with mortals was a corruption of the divinity. But alas for ideals! Cleopatra, although she married her twelve-year-old brother, saw to his murder while she mated with Julius Caesar and Mark Antony. Whether because of the example of the Ptolemies or as a result of other historical causes, brother-sister marriage as a means of keeping property within the family was evidently not uncommon in Egypt during the period of Roman rule following the death of Cleopatra.[7]

Another special and very peculiar exception to the brother-sister tabu exists among the Balinese, who suppose that boy and girl twins have been too intimate in their mother's womb. The penalties for incest are severe in Bali, but in the case of baby twins, temporary banishment of the parents and the "erring" twins, followed by a ceremony of purification and atonement, negates the sin. This makes it permissible for the mating in the womb to be completed as a true marriage in later life.[8]

Ordinary brother-sister marriages are said to have been permissible among the aboriginal Ainus of Japan, but the evidence for this is merely mythological, and myth is not good historical evidence. It has also been reported that the Lamet tribe of Southeast Asia countenances brother-sister marriage if the pair have been raised in separate households, i.e., are not sociologically members of the same family.[9]

Edmund Leach has recently reported another tribe of Southeast Asia who permit half brothers and sisters to marry under certain circumstances. In calling attention to the Lakher, he writes:

They consider that the child of a properly married man is exclusively his and that his divorced wife has absolutely no rights in the child whatsoever. It follows that if a woman has a son and a daughter by two different husbands the children are deemed unrelated to one another. Therefore they may marry without restraint. In contrast, the son and daughter of one man by two different mothers stand in an incestuous relationship to one another.[10]

In ancient Hawaii, title to chieftainship rested on high-ranking descent and inherited supernatural power, called *mana* (see pages 339–345). Incestuous marriage in the royal lines (called *pi'o*) intensified the inherited *mana* and the accompanying sacredness of the royal heir beyond that held by either of his or her parents. Such marriages occurred not only between brother and sister but also between uncles and nieces, aunts and nephews.[11]

The Penalties for Incest

The punishments, or negative sanctions, for the violation of the incest tabus vary greatly from one society to another, but a definite regional distribution of characteristic reactions is discernible. In

---

[7]R. Middleton, "Brother-Sister and Father-Daughter Marriage in Ancient Greece" (*American Sociological Review*, vol. 27, 1962), pp. 603–611.

[8]J. Belo, "A Study of a Balinese Family" (*American Anthropologist*, vol. 38, 1936), p. 30.

[9]K. G. Izikowitz, *Lamet, Hill Peasants in French Indochina*, pp. 134–135.

[10]E. R. Leach, *Rethinking Anthropology*, p. 14. By permission of Humanities Press, Inc.

[11]W. Davenport, "The Hawaiian Cultural Revolution: Some Political and Economic Considerations" (*American Anthropologist*, vol. 71, 1969), p. 7.

Australia, where kinship is a subject of intense interest, most tribes punished incest with death. Plains Indians, on the other hand, did not consider incest either a crime or a sin. They simply looked upon it as impossible behavior, so inconceivable that only insane persons indulge in it. Yet the punishment was mild in the few rare cases that have been recorded. A Dakota father of an incestuous brother and sister proclaimed, "Now I am the father of dogs!" Comanche informants could not remember a single actual case of incest among their people, nor could they stretch their imaginations sufficiently to give a specific statement of what the public reaction would have been had such a case occurred, except to say that the people would have shunned them and called them *keshuant* (crazy).

In ancient Bali, the punishment was symbolic and devastating. The hapless couple were adorned with yokes customarily worn by pigs. They were then made to crawl on all fours to drink from the swill trough of the hogs. After this humiliation, they were banished forever from the village, and their lands were confiscated. No other village would take them in for fear of ill luck and disaster. They were doomed to a fearsome existence alone in the jungle.[12]

The forensic Ashanti of the West African Sudan give vivid reasons for the imposition of the death penalty for incest. According to them, if the sinful crime were to have gone unpunished, ". . . hunters would have ceased to kill the animals in the forest, the crops would have refused to bear fruit, children would have ceased to be born, the 'Samanfo (spirits of dead ancestors) would have been infuriated, gods would have been angered, *abusua* (clans) would have ceased to exist, and all would have been chaos *(basa basa)* in the world."[13]

Biological Explanations of the Incest Tabu

It has been argued by Westermarck[14] and Morgan,[15] among earlier anthropologists, that primi-

tive human beings became cognizant of genetic deterioration resulting from close inbreeding. They averred that on this basis, humanity preserved its genetic health by preventing close inbreeding through the establishment of incest prohibitions. This is the popular belief of most people in the United States. The fact is, however, that inbreeding does not necessarily produce physical deterioration. Inbreeding does no more than intensify the phenotypic traits that the inbreeding population possessed at the outset. Recessive traits have a better chance of obtaining somatic realization where inbreeding is marked. If undesirable recessives are in the stock, they may well come to the fore, and deterioration may then result. Nevertheless, it is equally true that inbreeding intensifies the influence of dominant traits. A stock with desirable dominants becomes stronger. The end result may be good or bad; it all depends on the distribution of traits with respect to dominance and desirability. Cleopatra, the last of the Ptolemies and the product of twelve generations of brother-sister marriages, was hardly a specimen of physical degeneration.

In the long run, however, modern population genetics makes it quite certain that the effect of gene mutations in such a slow-breeding animal as a human being would be powerfully negative. This comes about because deleterious and lethal mutations are many times more frequent than are those which are adaptively advantageous. In small tribal populations there would be small margin to allow for selective culling out without extinction of the whole group. The danger would be intensified by the fact that the closer the inbreeding, the greater the relative frequency of homozygous inheritance: hence, the greater probability of destructive mutations wreaking their effect and endangering survival. The incest tabu, whatever its specific cultural content, inhibits close inbreeding. We can now feel certain, on sound scientific grounds, that its effects are genetically beneficial for mankind.

Westermarck's instinct theory
Westermarck also stated that human beings raised in the intimacy of the same family circle have an instinctive aversion to sexual relations among themselves. He held that the social rules

---

[12]J. Belo, "A Study of a Balinese Family," *op. cit*, p. 29.

[13]R. S. Rattray, *Ashanti Law and Constitution*, p. 304.

[14]E. Westermarck, *The History of Human Marriage*, vol. 2, pp. 218–241.

[15]L. H. Morgan, *Ancient Society*, p. 424.

prohibiting incest lend cultural expression to a biologically natural repugnance.[16] Most anthropologists of today have wholly rejected this hypothesis on the ground that there is too much evidence of an actual proclivity for sexual relations with those who are conveniently at hand; it is to suppress this tendency in favor of structural solidarity of the basic kinship groups that the strong anti-incest rules exist, they maintain. Indeed, they ask, if an instinctive aversion exists, why the heavily sanctioned social rules to prohibit an act that would not occur anyway?

ADOPTED SISTER MARRIAGES IN TAIWAN Nonetheless, support for Westermarck's position has recently been revived by Arthur Wolf through his study of two forms of marriage among Chinese settlers in Taiwan. The prestigious form of marriage is the "grand" or "major" marriage, called *ta-hun*. It binds an alliance between two extended families, establishing important interfamily obligations, along with payment of dowry and progeny price (pages 184–186). Such marriages, which were common before 1930, were arranged by the elders, and the bride and groom did not see each other until their wedding day.

The "minor" marriage was also common (40 per cent of all marriages from 1900 to 1925). This type, however, was "socially despised." The minor marriage pattern, used only by disadvantaged families, worked in the following way: poor parents adopted a baby girl to raise as a future wife for a son, thus obviating the need to pay out the progeny price which would have been due for the bride if she had come as a mature member of another kinship group. And by giving away their own baby daughters to other families, they also eliminated the raising of dowries for them when their time came to marry.[17] In other words, by accepting the idea that minor marriages were despised, they acknowledged the claim of the propertied classes to the social prestige and power derived from property manipulation in conjunction with marital alliances. Possessing little property, they dropped out of the social game and

arranged marriages without property exchanges. Yet they seemed to think that the stigma of propertyless marriages could be reduced by effecting the betrothal through infant adoption years before the marriage would occur. How does this affect the Westermarck argument?

Professor Wolf proposes that if Westermarck's hypothesis is right, then couples who were raised together would find that sexual aversion persisted after marriage and would permanently mar their marital relations; they "should be less intimate and more prone to marital discord." With data that are unusually good, he shows that "minor" marriages resulted in 33 per cent fewer children than did the "major" variety, along with a relative frequency of divorce and/or adultery of $4\frac{1}{2}$ to 1.[18] Wolf believes his data establish that there is "some aspect of childhood association sufficient to preclude or inhibit sexual desire" in the "minor" marriages. There is no question but that such marriages produced fewer children and were less enduring than the ideal "grand" marriages.

But the question still remains: are these facts the indices of lesser sexuality in "adopted sister-brother" marriages in Taiwan? Or do they indicate only that in the old Chinese society there was less at stake socially in the prestigeless and disdained "minor" marriages, and that there was less commitment to the structural form of marriage when there was less to win or lose by maintaining such marriages? For reasons that will unfold as our discussion of marriage and kinship develops in the succeeding pages, we believe the answer will still be found in sociopsychological rather than purely psychological causes.

The Relation of Social Structure to the Incest Tabu

Although the incest tabu may well serve eugenic ends, there is much about the specific manifestation of the principle of incest prohibition that can be explained only in sociocultural terms. The fact is that although parent-child and sibling sex relations are almost universally prohibited, the incest

---

[16]E. Westermarck, *op. cit.*, p. 192.

[17]A. P. Wolf, "Adopt a Daughter-in-law, Marry a Sister: A Chinese Solution to the Problem of the Incest Taboo" (*American Anthropologist*, vol. 72, 1970), pp. 864–874.

[18]A. P. Wolf, "Childhood Association and Sexual Attraction: A Further Test of the Westermarck Hypothesis" (*American Anthropologist*, vol. 72, 1970), p. 506.

tabu is often extended far beyond the membership of the conjugal-natal family. No Chinese, for example, may marry another who bears the same surname, even though they come from far-separated parts of China with no family contact whatsoever. The assumption is that they have a common clan ancestry, and between clan members there may be no marriage.

Marriage with known cousins is tabued in two out of every three cultures.[19] In a notable number of social systems, however, sex relations with cousins who fall outside a person's kinship group are allowed, and marriage with these particular cousins may even be socially encouraged or prescribed.

Cross-cultural anthropological research amply demonstrates that the degree of genealogical closeness is irrelevant to the application of the incest tabu. Rather, the specific identification of the individuals who are brought within the scope of the incest tabu is a function of the forms of kinship organization that prevail within a given society.

The effect of kinship terminology on the scope of the incest tabu

Modes of addressing relatives reflect the structure of the kinship groups in any society (see Chapter 13). American Indians, when talking to whites, may speak of "my sister" and "my Indian sister." What is the distinction? In standard American terminology, a sister is a girl born of the same parents as oneself. However, Catholics do stretch the term to include nuns, and members of a sorority extend the term to include one another. When the Indian of today makes the distinction between "sister" and "Indian sister," he is trying to make clear that the Indian concept of "sister" is somewhat different from the standard American concept. If the speaker is a Seed Eater Shoshone from Idaho, the term "sister" in its native sense means not only "daughter of my own mother" but also all female cousins through both father and mother. Relationship terms may be taken quite literally; therefore, a girl called "sister" *is* a sister and must be treated as such in all respects. Sex

relations and marriage with all "sisters" are therefore automatically tabued.

This broadening of relationship categories has been aptly called *lumping*.[20] It is the usual characteristic of relationship systems that are identified as *classificatory*. Because most primitive systems are classificatory, many individuals are embraced within the incest prohibitions by the simple fiat of a social system that dubs them "father," "mother," "brother," or "sister," when in biological fact, they are not actually such. (See pages 225–226 for a more detailed discussion of this phenomenon.)

The terminological distinction in types of cousins

The Shoshones and the Hawaiians, for example, lump all cousins in a single sibling (brother and sister) category. Many other peoples indulge in a form of discrimination that intensifies the impression of arbitrary disregard of biological reality. A certain type of cousin is classified as brother or sister, but another type of cousin is regarded as not being a kinsman at all. The first type of cousin we call *parallel-cousins* because the parents through whom they are related are of like sex. The other type of cousin we call *cross-cousins*, not because of temperamental peculiarities, but because the parents through whom they are related are of opposite sex; there is a crossing over from one sex to the other in the genealogy of relationship (Fig. 10-2). In any tribe in which cross-cousins are distinguished from parallel-cousins, cross-cousins are never reckoned as belonging to the same kinship group. In the dogma of the social system, they are not kinsmen. The logic of such a premise produces a biological absurdity, but the biologist protests in vain. To marry a parallel-cousin may be incest, and to marry a parallel-cousin who is a member of one's own clan *is* incest. However, to marry a cross-cousin may be the accepted thing to do; it may even be the required thing to do. Thus, one is forbidden to marry a first cousin of parallel relationship, whereas it is good form to marry a first cousin of

[19]Bourguignon and Greenbaum, *op. cit.*, p. 53.

[20]R. H. Lowie, "Kinship" (*Encyclopaedia of the Social Sciences*, vol. 3, 1931), pp. 568–572.

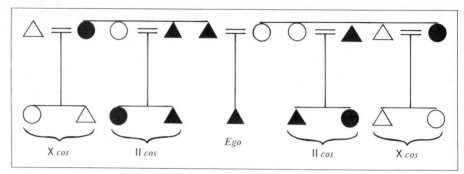

FIG. 10-2 Genealogical separation of cross- and parallel-cousins.

cross relationship. Both are equally close in genetic kinship, but the second is no relative at all in *culturally determined* kinship.

Functional-Structural Explanations of the Incest Tabu

There are two types of functional-structural theories in explanation of the incest tabu. One rests primarily on psychological principles and emphasizes the potentially disruptive effect of sexual competition within the kinship group. The fullest statement of this theory comes from Malinowski. The other emphasizes principles of social structure and the importance of marital alliances as a means of broadening the scope of social integration. Sir Edward Tylor, Leslie White, and Claude Lévi-Strauss are major proponents of this view.

Both schools of thought, however, were anticipated by Lord Bolingbroke (1678–1751), who rejected the idea that incest aversion is the expression of an innate moral sense, as was argued by eighteenth-century Scottish moral philosophers. Bolingbroke baldly stated that far from being instinctive or innate, "the abhorrence of incest, as well as other forms of sexual modesty, is wholly artificial." Rather, he argued, exogamy works "to improve sociability among men, and to extend it as wide as possible, in opposition to that insociability which is so apt to grow up between distinct families and states." Lord Bolingbroke anticipated Malinowski's psychological-functional theory of incest prohibition by holding that an additional effect of the incest tabu and exogamy was to prevent the destruction of the foundations of society. Children who marry their parents, he reasoned, will have less respect for them as the chief magistrates of the family; and what weakens the family weakens the greater commonwealth.[21]

The psychological theory

Malinowski posited the proposition that sexual affection is anteceded in the development of the individual by strongly conditioned parental and fraternal affection, based on intimate family associations, which occurs before the maturation of the sex drives. These are the affective emotions that cement the bonds of family and kin and give solidarity to the foundation group of any society—the group of immediate kinsmen. The family is founded in part upon the sexual association of spouses, between whom the sex drive may have legitimate play. But sex is a dangerous element. From its drives arise powerful emotional disturbances of great disruptive potentiality. In preadolescence, the sex drives are unmatured; they are not yet dangerous. On maturation under unrestricted conditions, however, gratification of the sex drives would frequently be sought with those nearest at hand, toward whom one already has affection—the members of one's own household. This would naturally lead to mating between siblings and parents and offspring. The violent emotions engendered by sexual affection would blast and disrupt family unity built upon the earlier established filial-fraternal affections.

[21]For further details, see A. O. Aldridge, "The Meaning of Incest from Hutcheson to Gibbon" (*Ethics*, vol. 61, 1951), pp. 309–313.

A house divided against itself cannot stand; it will become all one thing, or all the other. Overt sexual rivalry within the functioning kinship group cannot be permitted. The solidarity of the foundation unit of society is protected against its disruptive effects through the universal incest prohibition and its variant extensions.[22] Promiscuity and the family cannot exist side by side; sex relations, except for those of the father and mother, must be barred within it. Thus the preservation of the kinship group, the foundation unit of society, is maintained.

The alliance theory

In its very simplest form, the alliance theory holds that by marrying out of the kinship group primitive human beings avoided conflict and widened their chances for survival and prosperity. It was put simply by Sir Edward B. Tylor: "Again and again in the world's history, savage tribes must have had plainly before their minds the simple practical alternative between marrying-out and being killed-out."[23]

The earliest extant ethnographic account of this principle in action is found in the Bible, Genesis 34 (King James version). Jacob had migrated with his flocks and his followers to new territory. There his daughter, Dinah, had been seduced by the son of the prince of the city of Shechem. Her brothers were spoiling for blood. Hamor, the ruling prince of the town, however, sued for Dinah's hand in marriage to his son and proposed a general marital alliance: "And ye make marriages with us, and give your daughters to us, and take our daughters unto you. And ye shall dwell with us: and the land shall be before you; dwell and trade ye therein [Gen. 34:9–10]." The advantages in the alliance through marriage were clear-cut, but the outcome of the event drives home the lethal alternative. Jacob's sons feigned acceptance of the offer with the proviso that all the men of the city must be circumcised like themselves. This

was done, and while they were convalescing, Simeon and Levi killed them all, recovered their sister, took the surviving women and children as captives, plundered the city, and made off with the flocks [Gen. 34:14–29]. Indeed, the alternative to being killed out cannot be based upon misplaced trust.

The Demographic Theory of the Incest Tabu

Anthropologist Mariam Slater has proposed a demographic theory of the incest tabu which argues simply that in the earliest hominid groups incestuous matings were unlikely or not possible because no sexual mates were available in the primary family.[24] Men in these early societies were forced to breed out of the family, and this pattern motivated the organization of kinship structures and rules by which nonprimary mates and their families could be organized and selected for mating. This led to the structuring of society around social practices that were based on outbreeding. As humanity's demographic situation changed through time, especially following the development of agriculture as a significant food-getting pattern, then interfamilial mating became possible; but by then it was too late! Society was already structured on rules that assumed outbreeding and that could not be changed without affecting a wide variety of basic kinship patterns. Although no longer demographically limited, the proscription of interfamilial mating was maintained because it was a rule basic to other ongoing patterns of kinship organization.

A basic premise of the demographic theory is that an explanation of the origin of the incest tabu might be different from an explanation of its persistence. The tabu's origin is hypothetically postulated from the demographic limits on mating among early hominid populations by anthropologist Robin Fox:

Life would have been short (a maximum expectation of say 35 years), and puberty late—say 15 or later. The infant mortality rate would have been high—at least 50 per cent. Man tends to produce infants singly rather

[22]B. Malinowski, "Culture" (*Encyclopaedia of the Social Sciences*, vol. 4, 1931), p. 630.

[23]E. B. Tylor, "On a Method of Investigating the Development of Institutions Applied to the Laws of Marriage and Descent" (*Journal of the Royal Anthropological Institute of Great Britain and Ireland*, vol. 18, 1888), p. 267.

[24]M. K. Slater, "Ecological Factors in the Origin of Incest" (*American Anthropologist*, vol. 61, 1959), pp. 1042–1059.

than in litters, and hence there is spacing of births. This spacing can be increased by the death of a child, and by such population-control measures as infanticide, abortion and abstinence, all of which are known to have been practised in very primitive conditions. There is also a possibility that long suckling in relatively undernourished mothers inhibits ovulation. As most children under primitive conditions suckle for a number of years, this too would limit births and increase spacing. All these factors would place severe limits on the possibilities of inbreeding. By the time a young boy reached puberty, his mother would probably be past breeding age or dead. Similarly with siblings, although the chances would be better for brothers and sisters, they would still be slender, especially if, as the theory assumes, a sexual division of labor was necessary for survival and men wanted mates for this purpose as well as simply for sex. A boy's elder sister would in all probability be 'taken' by the time he reached puberty, and he himself would be mated by the time his younger sister came of age. A run of same-sex children in the family would of course increase the chances of outbreeding.

Thus, the theory claims, the earliest hominids were perhaps unable to commit incest very often even if they wanted to. In the simplest ecologies (and similar ones exist today) most of the people most of the time mate out, not because of the problem of inbreeding and competition, but in order to mate at all.[25]

According to Fox the persistence of the incest tabu has a different explanation. As culture evolved the demographic conditions of hominid families changed with the increased production of improving food-getting patterns. These changes allow the closer spacing of children, an earlier and longer period of sexual fertility, and a greater possibility for interfamilial mating.

. . . because since earliest times men have bred out, they have erected a whole lot of institutions at the kinship level that assume outbreeding—that are predicated on it. Now, as technological sophistication increased, life lengthened and infant mortality and all the other barriers to incest progressively disappeared. In many societies today, therefore, it would be quite possible for most people to commit incest if they wished, i.e. there would be a partner available. But it is in a sense too late. We have already built up our societies on the premise that people will breed out of the family, and we cannot easily reverse this. The improvements we have

mentioned are, in evolutionary terms, very recent. So the taboo persists.[26]

EXOGAMY

Exogamy (Gr. *ex*, outside + *gamos*, marriage) is defined as *the social rule that requires an individual to marry outside of a culturally defined group of which he is a member.* The conjugal-natal family is, with the few exceptions already noted, always exogamous. Whether other kinship groups are exogamous, and in what manner, is a reflection of the particular social organization that prevails in the society.

Simple Exogamy

When the prohibition against marrying a kinsman is applied without discrimination to all known genetic relatives, exogamy is simple or undifferentiated. Two-thirds of the societies in the *Ethnographic Atlas* practice simple exogamy, as indicated by the existence of a tabu on marriage to any kind of cousin whatsoever.[27] Generally speaking, simple exogamy occurs in societies in which kinship is organized bilaterally; i.e., without the presence of lineages or clans. Hence, the occurrence of simple exogamy is unevenly distributed around the world. It was highest in North America (83 per cent), where 65 per cent of the Indian tribes were bilaterally organized. It was (and still is) lowest in the Mediterranean area (34 per cent), where only 31 per cent of the societies are bilaterally organized.

Restricted Exogamy

Restricted exogamy is selective. It is the residual consequence of the cultural development of the alliance principle when applied to lineages and clans within a society. In this form, marriage is forbidden with certain categories of kinsmen, while at the same time it is preferred or required, as the case may be, with other categories of genealogic relatives who are not culturally de-

[25]R. Fox, *Kinship and Marriage*, pp. 66–67. By permission of Penguin Books Ltd.

[26]*Ibid*, p. 68.
[27]Bourguignon and Greenbaum, *op cit.*, pp. 51, 53.

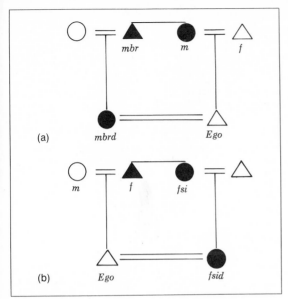

(a)

(b)

FIG. 10-3 (a) Matrilateral cross-cousin marriage in a patrilineal society. A male ego marries his mother's brother's daughter (*mbrd*), who does not belong to his patrilineage. (b) Patrilateral cross-cousin marriage in a matrilineal society. A male ego marries his father's sister's daughter (*fsid*), who does not belong to his matrilineage.

fined as being kinsmen. These persons are almost always one kind or another of cross-cousin. This calls for marriage to a mother's brother's child *or* a father's sister's child (Fig. 10-3) among first cousins, or to their equivalents if the preference applies to second or third cousins or beyond. Such cross-cousin marriages are *symmetrical*.

In the *Ethnographic Atlas*, 20 per cent of the societies forbid marriage to parallel-cousins but make it permissible with either kind of cross-cousin (defined as *duolateral cross-cousin marriage*). A mere 4 per cent (32 out of 762) require marriage of a male to a mother's brother's daughter *(matrilateral cross-cousin marriage)*, and less than 1 per cent (4 in 762) require marriage to a father's sister's daughter *(patrilateral cross-cousin marriage)*.[28] Such cross-cousin marriages are *asymmetrical*.

Lévi-Strauss's Theory of Matrilateral Marital Exchange

Why should cousin marriage, especially cross-cousin marriage, be so frequently preferred? And why should so many peoples prefer the symmetrical to the asymmetrical form of cross-cousin marriage? Why are matrilateral cross-cousins preferred as wives three times as often as patrilateral cross-cousins? The distinguished French anthropologist Claude Lévi-Strauss argues that cross-cousin marriage exists because it promotes social integration through regularization of group interdependence in the exchange of women.[29] He builds on the theory of his predecessor, Émile Durkheim (1858–1917), to the effect that the expansion of human society involves specialization and division of labor; such specialization requires stabilization of interdependence, if the society is not to come apart at the seams. The basic function of exchange and trade is to promote interdependence and social solidarity. Women, holds Lévi-Strauss, are the most highly valued scarce commodity because it is through them that children, the continuers of the group's survival, are born. Therefore, exchange of women is of prime importance in ordering interdependence. In duolateral, or symmetrical, cross-cousin marriage, woman swapping is practiced in all directions; it may tie closely related groups more tightly to one another, but it does not produce a strong integrating principle. Lévi-Strauss demonstrates that matrilateral cross-cousin marriage in a society with matrilineal descent groups results in group A's giving its women to group B, which gives its women to group C, which gives its women to group A. The three groups, which constitute a society, are thus bound to one another in a closed circle (Fig. 10-4).[30] This presupposes that matrilateral cross-cousin marriage is prescriptive, or required, rather than merely preferential. Lévi-Strauss argues that matrilateral cross-cousin marriage in matrilineal societies is a "best" way of producing social solidarity. (See Chapter 11, pages 205–207, for a detailed description of a

---

[28]*Idem.*

[29]C. Lévi-Strauss, *Les structures élémentaires de la parenté (The Elementary Structures of Kinship).*

[30]Of course there may be more than three kinship groups in the system.

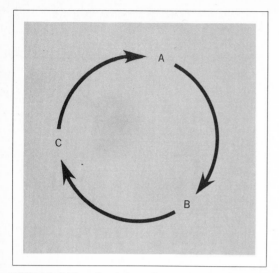

FIG. 10-4 The circulation of women through prescribed matrilateral cross-cousin marriage creates a closed circle of interdependence. Group A gives women to B and receives them from C; B gives to C and receives from A; C gives to A and receives from B. Progeny price, dowry, and gift giving are means of more direct, complementary equivalence; so, B receives women from A and gives other items of value to A in exchange.

matrilateral cross-cousin marriage system in Karo-Batak society.)

Lévi-Strauss's theory is built on the proposition that the needs of social solidarity produce asymmetrical cross-cousin marriage (a structural argument). However, the empirical fact that so few societies have incorporated matrilateral cousin marriage as a preferred form indicates that although the system logically leads to social solidarity, it obviously is not a necessary condition for societal maintenance. Most societies survive quite well without it, and there is no empirical evidence that societies with circulating matrilateral cross-cousin marriage are in fact more solidly bound than others.

ENDOGAMY

Endogamy (Gr. *endo*, within + *gamos*, marriage) is the converse of exogamy. It is *the social rule that requires a person to marry within a culturally defined group of which he or she is a member.*

Endogamy is much less common than exogamy. Unlike exogamy, there is no particular universal type of social group to which the endogamous rule applies, although in the entire Middle East and North Africa close in-family endogamy (outside the first-degree relatives) is the most favored marriage preference. In many societies some degree of endogamy is found, although the rule is not always explicit and verbalized. It frequently expresses itself as a tendency, without actually being a requirement. It may also apply to any kind of social group. Rules of exogamy and endogamy are contradictory and cannot apply simultaneously to the same social group.

The world's most famous system of endogamy is the caste organization of India, with its two thousand or so castes and subcastes, between which marriage was formally prohibited on the ground that contact with lower castes is ritually polluting for members of upper castes. The new constitution of India attempts to apply Mahatma Gandhi's principles of democratic equality and brotherhood through the legal abolition of castes and caste rules of endogamy, but, as with racial integration in the United States, India still has a long way to go to achieve Gandhi's ideal.[31]

Slightly less than 10 per cent of the world's societies are organized in *demes*, or village communities which tend to be endogamous. The highest proportion of such units of community organization are found in the rain-forest areas of South America. In North America, intravillage endogamy is almost an absolute must among the Pueblo Indians.

While castes are explicitly endogamous, social classes are prone to exhibit similar tendencies without recourse to explicitly prescribed rules. We are all familiar with many subtle manifestations of this. Its roots are in the desire to retain the exclusive and distinctive qualities of self-regarding in-groups. Intermarriage is a leveler and universalizer of culture and race. In-groups who implicitly feel that their values are too dear to leave open to competition raise the barricade of endogamy. Orthodox Jews may not marry Gentiles on pain of banishment from synagogue and

[31]M. Gallanter, "Law and Caste in Modern India" (Asian Survey, 1963), pp. 544–559.

family, followed by the performance of mourning rituals for the dead. Stumbling blocks are put in the path of marriage between Catholic and non-Catholic.

Parallel-Cousin Marriage

The marriage of a man to his father's brother's daughter is a unique exception to the usual rule of lineage and clan exogamy. It originated among the biblical Semites, who were patrilineal pastoralists; it became firmly fixed among the Muslim Arabs (followers of Islam, the religion founded by Muhammed in the seventh century) and later converts to Islam, such as the Muslims of India and Pakistan. As a preferential, and sometimes prescribed, form of marriage, it requires selection of a wife from within the kinship group. Thus in the King James version of the Old Testament (Num. 36:8–9), it is stated: "And every daughter that possesseth an inheritance in any tribe of the children of Israel, shall be wife unto one of the family [patrilineage] of the tribe of her father, that the children of Israel may enjoy every man of the inheritance of his fathers. Neither shall the inheritance remove from one tribe to another tribe."

And so it was that Jacob, when he followed the orders of Isaac, his father, that he not take a wife from among the daughters of Canaan (where his sons later slaughtered the newly circumcized menfolk of Shechem), but rather marry a daughter of his mother's brother, was marrying within his own patrilineage. The fact that Leah and Rachel were his cross-cousins (mother's brother's daughters) was incidental and irrelevant. The significant fact can be readily seen if Jacob's and his wives' ancestries are traced back to Terah and his sons, Abraham and Nahor. Abraham is Jacob's father's father, through Isaac. Jacob's wives, Leah and Rachel, are direct patrilineal descendants of Terah through Nahor, Bethuel, and Laban (Fig. 10-5). Jacob married his father's father's brother's son's son's daughters—all members of the same patrilineage derived from Terah (Gen. 12–30).

Among some Middle Eastern peoples, a man has a right to marry his father's brother's daughter; a girl must marry her father's brother's son unless he explicitly waives his preferential rights in favor of another. For this waiver of his right to

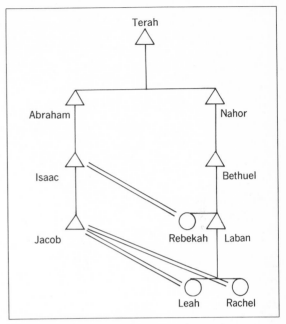

FIG. 10-5 Patrilateral parallel-cousin marriage among the pastoral Hebrews of the Old Testament. The patrilineage of Terah, showing the prescribed marriage of Isaac to his patrilateral cousin (*fbrsd*) Rebekah, and of their son Jacob to his parallel-cousins (*ffbrssd*) Leah and Rachel. (This diagram is limited to the male offspring through whom the line of descent devolved.)

his parallel-cousin, he can demand and receive a good payment. What is more, if a girl marries another man without her cousin's permission, he may undertake to kill her or her father, his uncle, if the uncle is the one who arranged her illegal marriage.[32] In Pakistan, refusal to assent to such a marriage frequently produces intense conflict between brothers. Leach is quite right in suggesting that the Islamic legal specification of large rights of inheritance for a daughter runs counter to the patrilineal principle and that parallel-cousin marriage serves to keep her share of the property within the lineage.[33] R. F. Spencer, and Murphy and Kasdan, suggest that parallel-cousin marriage is a consequence of a low level of political

---

[32]R. Patai, *Golden River to Golden Road: Society, Culture, and Change in the Middle East*, pp. 135–176.
[33]E. R. Leach, *Rethinking Anthropology*, p. 110.

organization among fighting, pastoral predators, who in the absence of a centralized tribal authority need all their manpower and herds to counter the assaults of competitive local lineages. By marrying within, they intensify the solidarity of the fighting male cadres.[34]

Barth demonstrates that among those Kurds who have developed a feudalistic political structure in addition to the lineage one, parallel-cousin marriage is statistically much less frequent. Where moderately adequate politico-economic institutions of a different type supplement the Arabic lineage structure, parallel-cousin marriage becomes functionally less significant and, in fact, much less frequent in occurrence.[35] Patai's report shows that modernized city Arabs, for whom the lineage increasingly loses its significance, are rapidly reducing the practice of cousin-right to a vestigial custom, as its functional reasons for existence dissolve.

The powerful insistence on parallel-cousin marriage among the Muslims reinforces the principle that the incest tabu is largely nonbiological in nature. When there are impelling reasons for marriage within the culturally defined kinship group, they may even negate the normal exogamic tendencies.

AFFINAL, SUBSTITUTION, OR CONTINUATION MARRIAGE

Much more pervasive than the general rules of endogamy are the rules of preferential marriage that bring about exogamous marriages between in-laws, hence called *affinal marriages*, or marriages to relatives through marriage. To identify such marriages as affinal, as is the usual practice of American and English anthropologists, is to emphasize the form of the marriage. The Dutch anthropologists, who have given more weight to the functional aspects of such marriages, call them *substitution* or *continuation marriages*, for

their function is to continue the relationship between the two kinship groups of the original marriage partners and to hold the children of the original marriage within the extended family.

The Levirate

Marriage of a woman to her brother-in-law, known as the *levirate* (L. *levir*, brother-in-law), is the most popular affinal marriage form among the peoples of the world. Under the simple levirate, the marriage occurs only after the death of the husband, when the widow is inherited by the dead man's brother. In the case of the *junior levirate*, only a younger brother may be the inheritor. This practice occurs in all parts of the world among peoples of the most diverse levels of cultural development. The Stone Age Australians made it a rule; the Bible, codifying old popular custom [as reflected in Gen. 38:8, and the Book of Ruth], made it a legal requirement in case the deceased husband had no offspring [Deut. 25:5–6]; the civilized Incas provided for the inheritance of all a man's secondary wives by his younger brother or perhaps by his sons. An Inca first wife never remarried. She was supported by the state, if necessary, with a widow's pension proffered by an effective social security system.

Whether the young man who finds himself with his brother's widow on his hands likes it or not depends partly on personalities but also on cultural determinants. The Comanche inheritor of a widow was apt to look on this inheritance as a right and a privilege, especially since the widow might not marry another man without that person's obtaining a quitclaim from the heir. And that required a consideration—a horse or two, or perhaps some blankets. In other cases there is no element of choice for the collateral heir. The woman is his, willy-nilly. Her family has a claim on him as much as he has a claim on her. His family also has a voice, as in the case of a Shoshone Indian who in 1933 was forced to divorce the wife of his own choice in order to marry his dead brother's wife. His people wanted to keep the girl in the family, and the laws of Idaho do not permit a man to have two wives.

The purpose of the levirate is not hard to discern. It effects a continuation of the link be-

[34]R. F. Spencer, "The Arabian Matriarchate: An Old Controversy" (*Southwestern Journal of Anthropology*, vol. 8, 1952), pp. 481–490; R. F. Murphy and L. Kasdan, "The Structure of Parallel Cousin Marriage" (*American Anthropologist*, vol. 61, 1959), pp. 17–29.

[35]F. Barth, "Father's Brother's Daughter Marriage in Kurdistan" (*Southwestern Journal of Anthropology*, vol. 10, 1954), pp. 164–171.

tween the two kinship groups that was established through the original marriage. It is a manifestation of the intergroup character of marriage in that the defunct husband's kin have the privilege and right to prevent the widow from leaving their group. Her obligation is not only to the man she married but also to his kin. Of equal importance, in view of the fact that in primitive society the children usually follow the mother when a home is broken, the children are not lost to the father's group. On the other hand, the claims of the widow's kin upon the group of the defunct husband are maintained in the substitution of a brother. The situation is one of balanced reciprocity.

The Sororate

As in the levirate, where a living brother takes the place of the dead father in a bereaved household, so in the sororate a sister is substituted for the mother. Therefore, in the sororate a bereaved husband marries his deceased wife's sister. From the woman's angle, a girl marries her dead sister's husband.

The sororate goes hand in hand with the levirate; each is the complement of the other. It is observed by virtually every tribe of North America outside of the Pueblo area and is widely distributed throughout the world.

The common mistake of confusing the sororate with *sororal polygyny* should be avoided. Under the true sororate, a man is married to only one sister at a time. Under sororal polygyny, he does not wait for the death of his wife to marry her younger sister; he takes her when she becomes of age.

Extended Affinal Marriages

In a few societies, if a sibling is not directly available within the immediate conjugal-natal family for substitution for a husband or wife and if there is not an available cousin who stands in the brother or sister category, a substitute from an older or younger generation may be taken. This results in such practices as (1) marriage of a man to his wife's brother's daughter, (2) marriage of a woman to her father's sister's husband, and (3) marriage of a woman to her husband's sister's son (see Fig. 10-6). Wife's-brother's-daughter marriage is an extension of the sororate principle to another generation. Such extensions are limited to societies in which the unilineal principle of descent is strong, and each type of marriage is closely related to the kind of unilinealism that prevails.

Thus, in a patrilineal system, a girl automatically belongs to the same clan as her father's sister (her paternal aunt). She has the same clan identity as her aunt, and her individuality is submerged in the corporate identity. She steps up to represent her unilineal group in the continuation of the marital alliance.

On the other hand, in a matrilineal system, a boy automatically belongs to the same clan as his mother's brother (his maternal uncle). He has the same clan identity as his maternal uncle, and his individuality is submerged in the corporate identity of the maternal kinship group. He steps forward to represent his unilineal group in the continuation of the marital alliance (see Crow Kinship System, page 230).

Marriage with extended affinal relatives is not common; only a small minority of societies find it worth bothering with or necessary to fall back

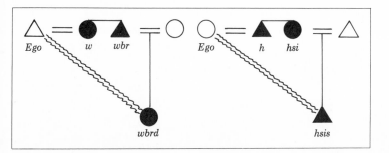

FIG. 10-6 (Left) Marriage of the wife's brother's daughter in a patrilineal system represents the secondary affinal marriage. Wife and wife's brother's daughter belong to the same lineage. (Right) Marriage of the husband's sister's son in a matrilineal system. Husband and husband's sister's son belong to the same lineage.

FIG. 10-7 A Kana courtship, Waghi Valley, Central Highlands of New Guinea (Laurence Le Guay.)

upon. But in a strong unilineal system inclined to generalize the principle of clan identity, such marriages follow logically enough.[36]

MODES OF MARRIAGE

We have thus far been concerned with the matter of whom one may or may not marry. The next question is: "How does a man get a wife, or a woman, a husband?" Very few societies leave it to individuals who are to be married to decide for themselves. The near-anarchy of American practice in this respect is most exceptional, although it represents a discernibly increasing trend in many parts of the world as the acids of "modernity"

corrode the old kinship bonds. Most marriages either are still arranged by the families concerned or involve family consent and participation. For this reason, to understand marriage at all, and primitive marriage especially, it is necessary to grasp this basic principle: *marriage constitutes an alliance between two kinship groups in which the couple concerned is merely the most conspicuous link.* Every man learns, sooner or later, that when he marries the "one and only," he marries not only her but her relatives as well. Brides, of course, have the same experience.

In spite of what aspirant youth may feel about it, marriage is not a concern of the marrying pair alone. Society at large has its stake in the affair and what ensues from it. The families of the principals to a marriage have their very direct interests in its many ramifications.

Thus, of the seven formalized modes of acquiring a wife, only two (marriage by capture and marriage by elopement) do not heavily involve the active participation of the kinship groups of the bride and groom. The seven modes are (1) by progeny price, or bride wealth; (2) by suitor service; (3) by gift exchange; (4) by capture; (5) by inheritance; (6) by elopement; and (7) by adoption.

Progeny Price

In the primitive world, the formal exchange of goods of value for the offspring a woman is expected to produce is the normal, or most usual, method of getting a wife. *Progeny price* has been found to prevail in virtually all tribes of Negro Africa, where 214 of 238 (90 per cent) of those listed in the *Ethnographic Atlas* practice it, usually in the form of payment of cattle, called *lobola*, a Bantu term. Taking the world as a whole, well over half (58 per cent) of all societies in the *Atlas* expect progeny price to be paid to the family of the bride by the kin of the groom.

It must not be assumed that the payment of progeny price for a woman means that women are degraded slaves to be sold from the auction block of a marriage mart—a sordid commercial commodity.[37] A commercial element necessarily col-

---

[36]See L. A. White, "A Problem in Kinship Terminology" (*American Anthropologist*, vol. 41, 1939), pp. 569–570.

[37]The Native Administration Act of 1927, Union of South Africa, in recognition of the importance of progeny price in native society, expressly forbade any court from setting aside

ors the institution, for, after all, a family with five daughters and one son for whom a bride must be acquired is economically better off than the family with one daughter and five sons to be provided for. But women are not fluid goods in a free market.

Nor does the occurrence of progeny price mean that the position of woman in terms of prestige, privilege, power, and labor is necessarily high or low. It does mean, however, that women as progenitors have value as members of the kinship group. The value of a woman in terms of progeny price is determined by a compound of the social and economic status of the groom's family balanced against that of the bride's family. In some instances, the personal qualities of the bride and groom may also be factors.

The social prestige of a married woman is directly influenced by the amount of the progeny price that has been paid on her account. A twenty-cow wife in East Africa has a definite advantage in any argument with a woman on whose account only ten cows have been given. Among the Yuroks of California, this was so fixed that the social status and wergild of a man were determined absolutely by the progeny price paid for his mother.

Progeny price may be in part compensation for the loss of the girl by her kinship group, but it is much more an act of compensation to that group for its loss of a legal claim to the children that she will bear. Two facts make this clear. The transference of progeny price is closely correlated with patrilineal-descent systems and residence of the married couple with the groom's kin. Again referring to Murdock's comparative data, we learn that of 217 societies demanding progeny price, all but 18 are virilocal. Of the 18 nonvirilocal societies, only 6 are uxorilocal.[38] Clearly, the loss of the woman's children from the residential seat of her kin is a factor that must be balanced by reciprocal payment of other items of value. But beyond this, there is the circumstance that virilocal residence

tends strongly to generate patrilineality. Although the wife does not become a member of her husband's unilineal group, her children do. In patrilineal societies, therefore, each marriage of a woman means that her lineage suffers a loss of all the progeny that may be born through her. For this sacrifice, it expects and receives redress. Patrilineal kinship groups and progeny price show a high phi correlation at 0.412, while matrilineal kinship groups and progeny price show a negative correlation of −0.112.

That it is in exchange for a quitclaim, so to speak, on posterity rather than for the bride herself that the progeny price is demanded may be seen more clearly in the fact that an implicit warranty of the fertility of the bride is part of the transaction. It is therefore a common expectancy among Africans that the bride's family must substitute a younger sister without charge if no children are forthcoming from the first daughter for whom they have received progeny price. As an alternative, the sum of the progeny price must be refunded. This is often difficult, however, because the capital received in payment for the daughter may already have been invested in the acquisition of a wife for a son. Thus, it has been reported (for the Thonga, for instance) that the family may be required to surrender their son's wife to their son-in-law in lieu of their barren daughter. These same requirements hold if the married daughter deserts her husband, who has paid for her.

Establishment of jural rights

Linton's report on the Vezo Sakalava of Madagascar shows to what extent progeny price is actually the establishment of a jural, or a legally effective, right to children among these people. In the case of divorce, neither a refund of the cattle paid nor the substitution of another woman is socially permissible. The divorced wife may remarry, but only with her former husband's permission. This will be forthcoming upon agreement by the wife and her new husband-to-be that the first children born to them (up to the limit of three) will be deeded over to the first husband, who is the one who paid the progeny price to her family. The woman nurses and keeps the children until weaning, whereupon they are turned over to her first

---

lobola or *bogadi* as "repugnant to natural law." J. Lewin, *Studies in African Native Law*, p. 57.

[38]A. D. Coult and R. W. Habenstein, *Cross Tabulations of Murdock's World Ethnographic Sample*, p. 378. The phi for progeny price/virilocality is 0.391; for progeny price/uxorilocality, it is 0.192, and for avunculocality, 0.055.

husband and become his legal heirs without the formality of adoption.[39] All this illustrates another basic principle to be referred to in more detail later on: *among primitives, jural fatherhood is generally of more significance than biological fatherhood.* A nice Sakalava refinement is that although legally a divorced husband may demand a refund, good form does not countenance it. That would be putting material values above human values. Such a man would put cattle above children.

Finally, among the Bavenda of South Africa and other tribes, if the progeny price is paid in installments, the children do not pass to the husband's kinship group until the sum is paid in full.

An interesting twist to progeny price as a means of obtaining offspring is found among the Dahomeans of West Africa. Here a married woman may arrange for a second wife for her husband as a means of providing him with children. These children call their sire's first wife "father" because she, after all, is the one who paid for them.[40] This may seem to be carrying the principle of sociological fatherhood a bit far, but who can deny that it is logical? In one form or another, this practice is not uncommon among the patrilineal tribes of Africa.

Progeny price as a social institution cannot be comprehended unless it is viewed also in terms of its functional effects in cementing the links in the web of kinship that makes possible the expansion of the scope of society. Social groups are often in opposition to one another, disputing, quarreling, even feuding and fighting. Intermarriage imposes a check on the disruptive tendencies of intergroup conflict. Marriage alone tends to exert a tranquilizing effect in this direction, but it takes more than marriage in and of itself adequately to achieve cohesion. Progeny price involves a number of kinsmen in a network of economic obligations and expectancies. Many more than just the husband, on the one side, and the bride's parents, on the other, are drawn into the activity. The distribution of marriage cattle among the Nuer, to be discussed under "Economic Organization" (Chapter 15), is a concrete example of the broad. network of persons involved. Figure 15-3 shows the range of relatives concerned with the progeny price (see page 259).

Suitor Service

A cheap, but not easy, way to obtain a wife and rights to her children is to work for them. Jacob put in seven years of labor to win the hand of Rachel, plus seven for Leah, who was not part of his bargain. Among the Siberian Chukchi, Koryak, and Yukaghir tribes, service for the bride is the regular practice; it seems to have replaced progeny price, which was the earlier form for acquisition of a wife.

Scattered tribes in all parts of the world have been found to require service in the bride's household as the price the groom must pay (77 out of 565 cultures).[41] Many of these tribes allow no alternative, but in others, suitor service is simply a substitute for payment of the progeny price, similar to the arrangement by which a vagrant washes dishes to pay for his meal.

The obligation of a son-in-law to work for his wife's parents may be an enduring responsibility. Although the Comanche Indians did not require outright suitor service, a son-in-law was expected to send a good share of the game he slew to the tipi of his mother-in-law. This was why parents wanted their daughter to marry a good hunter. A son-in-law did not have to do this, but he was a good son-in-law if he did and a poor one if he did not. His reward was a younger daughter as his second wife. But no meat, no second daughter.

Gift Exchange

In cultures in which descent is not exclusively vested in any particular line of kinsman (i.e., bilateral descent), there is little likelihood of payment of progeny price (phi = −0.349). Equivalent exchanges of gifts between the families are an alternative possibility.

[39]R. Linton, *The Tanala* (Field Museum of Natural History, Anthropological Series, vol. 22, 1933). For numerous like examples from Africa, see M. D. W. Jeffreys, "Lobola Is Child-price" (*African Studies*, vol. 10, 1951), pp. 145–184.

[40]M. J. Herskovits, "A Note on 'Woman Marriage' in Dahomey" (*Africa*, vol. 10, 1937), pp. 335–341. The term "father," incidentally, in its more exact meaning, should be understood as "person who paid the progeny price."

[41]Coult and Habenstein, *op. cit.*, p. 424.

FIG. 10-8 Marriage is an incorporation rite among the Karamojong, Uganda, in East Africa. The groom presents at least one animal—a cow, sheep, goat, or donkey—to each of the bride's close relatives. In return, he receives their pledge of future support for himself and the family he is about to found. After the bartering, the bride is dragged with mock protestations from the hut where she has been hiding (top left). At the groom's village, the co-wives and sisters-in-law of the bride each present a neckwire to the bride, then smear her with milk fat (top right). The bride is hazed by the women, including the girls of her husband's group (bottom left). She carries a ridiculously small pot which she must steady on her head as if she were a clumsy novice who cannot carry a pot as a proper wife should. To emphasize her low status as the newest female member of her affinal group, the pot is repeatedly knocked from her head with sticks. A mock attack with switches upon the bride and her attendants by the boys of the groom's village completes the ritualistic pattern (bottom right). (Photos by Rada and Neville Dyson-Hudson, *Natural History*.)

When gift exchanges are customarily equal, no one comes out ahead. This is the case with the Cheyenne Indians. A boy who had set his heart on a particular girl talked it over with his family. If they saw the choice as a good one, after taking into consideration not only the qualities of the girl but also the character of her family, they mustered their nicest transferable possessions to place at the disposal of the young swain. These were carefully loaded on a fine horse. They then called upon a respected old woman to lead the horse to the tipi of the girl's elder brother. There she staked it out for all the camp to see, while she entered the lodge to press the suit of her protégé. The elder brother called in his cousins for a family conclave. If they decided that the proposal was acceptable, they unloaded the horse and distributed the gifts among themselves, the brother taking the horse. All then dispersed to their separate lodges to rustle up what each would offer as a return gift. Each was expected to bring back in the next day or two something equal in value to what he had received. In the meantime, the bride was made beautiful, and when all was ready, she was mounted on a good horse, the presents loaded on another, and the old woman was called upon to lead the bride and the gift horse back to the groom's tipi. There she was received by all his family, and her accompanying gifts were distributed among them in accordance with what they gave. So far as economic value goes, they were then exactly where they were before.

Perhaps we can understand the social function of such activity better if we reemphasize the elaborate American gift exchanges at Christmas. The amount of energy, trouble, and effort that goes into acquiring and distributing suitable gifts is immense, and the results are frequently discouraging. As often as not, we end up with a collection of items we would just as soon do without. Nevertheless, in the exchange we reaffirm and bind anew the friendships and relationships we value or find desirable.

It may come as a shock to those who enter into the elaborate wedding gift giving institutionalized in American culture to learn that equivalent exchange of gifts at marriage is actually the rare exception, not the rule. Only 82 out of 860 cultures provide for it.[42] The fact that it is negatively correlated with patrilineal (phi = −0.014) and matrilineal (phi = −0.007) societies reinforces the point that progeny price is compensation for loss of jural rights over the children who are to be forthcoming from a marriage. (Because gift exchange is so infrequent, however, the phi correlations given here have low levels of statistical significance.)

Capture

Novelists and romanticists formerly wrote of the days when the cave man was supposed to beat his beloved into insensibility with a knobby club and then drag her by her flowing hair to his lair, where she forthwith became his loving wife. When anthropology was young, serious consideration was given to this fantasy as the earliest method of getting a wife. Indeed, marriage by capture was the first premise underlying the theory of social evolution put forth by the Scottish anthropologist J. F. McLennan a hundred years ago.[43] Suitors' trials and sham battles at marriage were thought to be symbolic survivals of the scuffles that accompanied the abduction of the feminine prize.

Mock capture is a real and not uncommon practice. When a young Bushman and his bride are to be married, the folk gather from all around to join in the wedding feast. In the midst of the meal, the groom seizes the bride. This is the signal for all her relatives to grab their dibbles and set to beating him. A minor battle royal takes place among the guests while the groom receives his drubbing. If he can keep his hold on the girl, he succeeds in his marriage. If he lets go under the hail of blows, he loses her.[44]

The African Bahima subject the bride to a tug of war between her clan and the groom's, which always wins. When the final pull is given in the groom's favor, the bride is hustled to a cowhide and lifted from the ground by the groom's cohorts, who rush off with her, chased by friends and relatives.[45]

[42]Bourguignon and Greenbaum, *op. cit.*, p. 3.
[43]J. F. McLennan, *Primitive Marriage*.
[44]G. W. Stow, *The Native Races of South Africa*, p. 96.
[45]J. Roscoe, *The Northern Bantu*, vol. 2, p. 256.

Of course, the hilarious horseplay that climaxes our own weddings and the escape of the bride and groom are cut of the same cloth. If this is not a survival of bride capture, what then is it? Modern anthropology prefers a functional to a pseudo-historical explanation. More properly, it is to be understood as a symbolic expression of latent and repressed hostilities of the two marrying families. True, they are to be allied in marriage, but alliance is possible only where differences exist. Alliance always involves a measure of antagonistic cooperation. Common interests must dominate any alliance, or it will not be forged. Yet the antagonisms are felt, unconsciously or otherwise. The bride-giving family resents the successful intrusion of the suitor, and they are given the ritual opportunity of letting him know it in a harmless way. Thereby, the deep emotions of resentment are drawn off. Likewise, any feeling that the swain is considered unworthy of the precious daughter may be dispelled by forcing him to prove his worth.

All this is not to contend that marriage by capture does not exist. It does. But we must realize that it could never have been *the* prevailing technique in any supposed stage of human history. Rather, it is a supplementary way of getting a wife. Its advantage is that it is cheap and adventuresome, if risky. On the other hand, its disadvantages, aside from risk, are heavy. Since marriage is an alliance between kinship groups, capturing a wife brings none of the advantages that are to be derived from such an alliance. There are no wife's relatives to back a man up or contribute their share of property. The man who captures his wives will therefore be at a disadvantage, compared with the man who has gotten his by reciprocal means. His children will not have the advantages and status that his wife's family might bestow, and if his sole wife is from an alien tribe, his children will not be raised in the pure tradition of his own culture.

Plains Indian warriors, like the men of many another primitive tribe, did capture and mate with alien women. Many are the nations who have considered women the legitimate prize of war. However, unless a man is poorly off, he first marries a girl of his own tribe in the regular manner. His captured wives are secondary additions to his household: his concubines and his wife's household drudges. Here, as elsewhere, the position of the captive woman may be closer to that of a slave than of a true wife.

Again and again, we find that the abduction of women is the cause of bitter wars and annihilations. Helen of Troy may be the most famous such *bella causus belli*, but she was neither the first nor the last among her sex.

Inheritance

Inheritance of widows through the operation of the levirate and filial inheritance is of course of extreme importance as a form of marriage. However, nothing further need be added here to what we have already said on this subject except to note that the Palvic and Bura tribes of northern Nigeria allow a man to inherit his grandfather's wives.

Filial inheritance

Attention has already been called to the Inca practice of permitting a brother or a son to inherit the secondary wives of a dead man. Inheritance of the wives of his father, none of whom was his uterine mother, is also known to have been practiced by the Caribs of South America and by a number of African tribes. Filial inheritance is obviously possible only where there is polygamous marriage. It also serves to keep the women in the family.

Elopement

Elopement is a safety valve. It is one of those saving cultural forms whose function is to provide an acceptable byroad for escape from the dictates of formal custom. Marriage, as we have seen, is rarely left open to the untrammeled choice of the marrying individuals. There are incest and exogamic prohibitions; there are the limitations of preferential mating; and there are the personal prejudices of family members to be considered. On the other hand, there is love. Few people are so given to romantic love as Americans, who in individualistic sentimentalism exalt the ideal of marriage based on love—that mysterious psycho-physiological reaction. Although many primitive cultures do not allow very much weight to love in marriage (indeed, many seem to ignore it entirely), the fact is that all primitives have their amorous likes and aversions, too.

From the evidence, it would appear that elopements take place in every known society. When familial or social disapproval blocks a fervently desired marriage, or when a planned marriage with a distasteful partner is about to be forced on the unwilling one, elopement with someone else is a way out. The tribes which require that elders and relatives seek the consent of marriageable youths to the arrangements they plan for them are surely a minority among mankind. This makes a general human necessity of the path of elopement.

Of course, the existence of a formal rule does not mean that it will always be insisted upon. Cheyenne men held the legal right to dispose of their sisters as they wished. But as Calf Woman put it, "Kindhearted brothers always found out how their sisters felt about it before they promised them to any man."

It is difficult to formulate a generalization concerning the status of elopement marriages. Among the Cheyennes, the elopement would ultimately be recognized as a marriage and be validated by gift exchanges only if the pair ran off before the girl had actually been engaged by her brother to another man. It was a different matter if the promise had already been made. In several Cheyenne cases, brothers committed suicide when their sisters eloped after they had been promised to someone else.[46]

In parts of the Pacific area, the tendency to *cultural orthogenesis* resulted in elopement becoming the *regular* way of getting married. This was the situation in a number of Australian tribes. According to the reports of Howitt,[47] elopement became the *reductio ad absurdum* of overdeveloped marriage rules among the Kurnai tribe. Broad rules of exogamy combined with narrow

rules of localized mating (i.e., the mate had to be taken from a specific band) to narrow strictly the field of legitimate choice. Old men dominated the society and had the first choice of young girls. Matters were so carefully controlled that a boy could scarcely find a girl whom he would be permitted to marry. Fortunately for the Kurnai they made "pretend rules" of these principles. Most marriages of young couples were by elopement, and customarily medicine men were expected to help them escape. What then? The righteous citizenry (most of whom married in just this way) were terrible in their anger. A posse of vigilantes set forth to do social justice. The couple fled to a traditional place of asylum. If they were overtaken, they were cruelly wounded and could be killed. Once at the place of asylum, however, they were safe. They stayed there until a baby was born. Then they could return home to face a softer music, for they would merely be given a beating and then be accepted as legitimately married.

Adoption

In Indonesia and modern Japan, a man may obtain a wife by being adopted into her family.[48] It is a device by which a patrilineally organized family may maintain its line when there are no sons. By legal fiction, the son-in-law thus becomes a "son" in his wife's family, and his children belong to her family and not his. A peculiar aspect of this device is that technically the groom's bride becomes his own "sister." It is necessary that the people close their eyes to this bit of logic, for that, of course would be incest. Convenience masters logic, and the husband is a "son" of his father-in-law for purposes of reckoning descent. The adoption of a girl to become a son's wife in Taiwan has already been discussed in detail.

FICTIVE MARRIAGE

Forms of fictive marriage occur occasionally. Among them are the special practices of the Kwakiutl and the Nuer. In the case of the Kwakiutl the inheritance of chiefly prerogatives traditional-

---

[46]K. N. Llewellyn and E. A. Hoebel, *The Cheyenne Way*, chap. 9.
[47]A. W. Howitt, *The Native Tribes of South-east Australia*, pp. 273ff.

[48]B. ter Haar, *Adat Law in Indonesia*, pp. 175–176; and J. F Embree, *The Japanese Nation*, p. 162.

ly passed from a titled man to his grandson through his son-in-law, the grandson's father. It was not possible for the titles to pass to succeeding generations through the chief's sons directly. If there were no daughters, such inheritance could be blocked for lack of a son-in-law. Boas wrote:

In such a case a man who desires to acquire the use of a crest and the other privileges connected with the name performs a sham marriage with the son of the bearer of the name. . . . The ceremony is performed in the same manner as a real marriage. In case the bearer of the name has no children at all, a sham marriage with a part of his body is performed, with his right or left side, a leg or an arm, and the privileges are conveyed in the same manner as in the case of a real marriage.[49]

The son-in-law acquired the titles and then begot children by a second wife. These children were able to inherit from their jural grandfather.

In the Trobriand Islands the leader of a chiefly clan *(guyau)* who wishes to link a commoner clan *(tokay)* to himself may, in the absence of a suitable girl, "marry" a man, who becomes known as a *tokwava* (male wife). Through him the customary *urigubu* payments of yams[50] can be made in redistributive exchange (see pages 255–262).

We have already seen how strong the ties of kinship are among the Nuer, as expressed in progeny-price exchanges. So important is the maintenance of lineage inheritance that the Nuers often rely on what they call *ghost marriage* to give offspring to a male, man or boy, who has died without begetting heirs. For it is necessary to "keep green" the name of a man whose position in the lineage structure is important. In such an instance, one of his "brothers" (from a kinship line that is overstocked or less important) marries a woman on behalf of the dead man or, as they say, "to the name of his brother." This man lives with the woman as in any ordinary conjugal family except that *he* is not married to her. The children that he begets take their place in the lineage as the offspring of their ghost father; they inherit

accordingly and receive and give progeny price and wergild in like manner.[51]

The Nuer also have a form of "wife marriage" that differs from that already noted for the Dahomeans (page 186). Among the Nuer, a woman who is beyond childbearing age may sometimes use the cattle that belonged to her dead husband to set up a marriage between a man and woman in the name of her husband and herself. The children of such a marriage then belong to her deceased husband and herself, and they inherit accordingly.

In another Nuer variant, an old woman whose lineage is about to die out because she has no living paternal relatives may, if she has the requisite cattle for the progeny price, marry a woman to the name of a dead man of her lineage. Then she invites some unrelated male to have intercourse with the "ghost bride," thus legally establishing a line of heirs.

Pushing the use of fiction to its ultimate, the Nuer give a barren woman the status of a male. After all, has she not demonstrated that she is lacking in the essential attribute of the female? In exceptional cases, then, a wife may be married to her name. That is, a marriage between a man and woman is arranged in which the *man* is the legal substitute for the barren woman in question. The children belong to her name, which means, because she is accorded the status of a male, that they take their patrilineal descent from her, so closing a link in the patrilineal lineage.[52]

Professor Paul Bohannan prefers that these arrangements not be viewed as marriages at all, since in some instances no man is joined with a woman.[53] This is true of the Kwakiutl case and of several of the Nuer practices that emphasize the importance of passing jural and property rights from one generation to another through the production of jural offspring. In these situations,

---

[49]F. Boas, *Social Organization and Secret Societies of the Kwakiutl*, p. 359.

[50]H. A. Powell, "Competitive Leadership in Trobriand Political Organization," in R. Cohen and J. Middleton (eds.), *Comparative Political Systems*, p. 177.

[51]Compare the ancient Hebrew practice spelled out in the Old Testament: "If brethen dwell together, and one of them die, and have no son, the wife of the dead shall not be married without [the lineage] unto a stranger: her husband's brother shall go in unto her, and take her to him as a wife, and perform the duty of a husband's brother unto her.

"And it shall be, that the first born which she beareth shall succeed in the name of his brother which is dead, that his name be not put out of Israel" (Deut. 25:5–6).

[52]P. P. Howell, *A Manual of Nuer Law*, pp. 74–75.

[53]See P. J. Bohannan, *Social Anthropology*, p. 77.

however, the arrangement is treated as if it were a marriage, and the social and legal consequences of a regular marriage flow from it even though the marriage be fictive.

DIVORCE AND THE DISSOLUTION OF MARRIAGE

In spite of the desire of kinsmen to retain the marriage link, primitive marriages are brittle things. Romance and individual desire may not play so great a role in determining the choice of a first partner as they do with us, but they are permitted more sway in the shifting of mates after marriage. Only a small proportion of marriages among primitives are for life.

Hobhouse, Wheeler, and Ginsberg found in their study that of 271 tribes, only 4 per cent forbade divorce; 24 per cent allowed it for specific causes; 72 per cent permitted it on the basis of mutual consent based on incompatibility or whim.[54] The sample may not be statistically perfect. Nevertheless, the results just quoted are probably not too far from accurate fact.

Aside from the economic arrangements that may have to be untangled where a high progeny price was paid or a rich dowry given, divorce does not entail such difficulties among the primitives as it does in Western society. The first reason rests in the fact that although religious ritual may enter into the marriage ceremonies, marriage is hardly a religious affair. In addition, the problem of the care and disposition of the children is more easily handled. Ordinarily, they go with the mother. It has already been noted that sociological fatherhood is more significant to primitive man than biological paternity.

There is little evidence on record to indicate that when the primitive mother remarries, the emotional transition for the children is difficult. If the mother does not remarry right away, it is easy for her and her brood to settle among her relatives, for the tribal community is small and she has not been far from her kin at any time. If she is a captive from an alien tribe, she probably remarries without delay. Unmarried adult women are unthinkable to most primitive people.

The prevalence of wife stealing is another important unsettling factor. In societies in which sexual competition among the men is a means of attaining social status, no home is truly safe. Eskimos may cooperate economically, but they engage in violent competition for women. To steal another's wife and get away with it proves the abductor a better man than the loser. The risk is great, however, because the husband, if half a man, will attempt to murder the absconder. A would-be wife taker often anticipates this by killing the husband first and marrying the widow afterward.

In the 1920s, Knud Rasmussen visited a village of Musk Ox Eskimos in Canada. He found that every adult male in the community had been involved in a murder centering about wife stealing.[55]

Special practices, such as the licensed wife stealing of the Crow Indians, may also break up the family. This used to be a phase of competition between two rival military associations, the Foxes and the Knobby Sticks. Each spring one or another of the fraternities was privileged to capture any wife of a member of the other fraternity, provided she had had premarital sexual relations with the captor. The husband could not resist the abduction or take his wife back. The triumph of the kidnaping fraternity was supreme.

Cheyennes and other Plains tribesmen considered it a great feat ceremonially to throw away wives at a special dance. The Cheyenne warrior tossed a stick among the male spectators, and whoever was struck by it had to marry his wife, if only for a day.

Until recently, anthropologists were of the opinion that men were allowed more leeway than women in the matter of divorce. However, a cross-cultural survey by Murdock invalidates this conclusion. Among forty objectively selected cultures from all parts of the world, it was impossible in three-fourths of the sample for Murdock to detect any substantial difference in the rights of men and women to terminate an unsatisfactory marriage. Six cultures, it is true, stack the cards in

[54]L. T. Hobhouse, G. C. Wheeler, and M. Ginsberg, *The Material Culture and Social Institutions of the Simpler Peoples*, p. 164.

[55]K. Rasmussen, *Across Arctic America*, p. 250.

favor of the men. But on the other hand, four cultures allow superior privileges to the women as regards divorce. Insofar as the right to get divorced is concerned, Murdock concludes that "the stereotype of the oppressed aboriginal woman proved to be a complete myth."[56] Matrilineal descent, plus residence in the locality of the wife's kin, strengthens the hand of the woman. Among the highly matrilineal Hopi and Zuñi, where women own the houses, a woman can divorce her husband simply by setting his gear outside the door. Any man who comes home and sees his pile of belongings outside the door knows just what it means. It is time to go home to mother.

The causes of divorce and the grounds for it may be two quite different things. Yet it may be illuminating to close this chapter with a listing of what the Ifugao of Luzon consider grounds for divorce:

1. A bad omen of the bile sac of the sacrificial animal at any one of the four feasts of the marriage ritual
2. A bad omen of the bile sac at any of the three principal rice feasts of either family during the first year after the completion of the marriage rituals
3. Barrenness
4. Death of several offspring
5. Permanent sexual disability
6. Unwillingness to perform the sexual act
7. Neglect in time of sickness; "failure to cherish"
8. Insulting language by an in-law
9. Reduction of the area of fields agreed on in the marriage contract
10. Selling of a rice field for insufficient reason and without consent of the other spouse

11. Continued refusal of a father-in-law to deliver the fields called for in the marriage contract when the couple reaches a reasonable age
12. Incurring of unreasonable debts[57]

SELECTED READINGS

Bohannan, P. J., and J. Middleton (eds.), *Marriage, Family, and Residence* (1968). A book of readings. Part I, pp. 1–46, consists of two very useful papers on the incest question.

Dumont, L., "Marriage Alliance" (*International Encyclopedia of the Social Sciences*, vol. 10, 1968), pp. 19–23. Provides a more detailed but not overly technical view of the theory of marital alliance.

Evans-Pritchard, E. E., *Kinship and Marriage among the Nuer* (1951). An authoritative study based upon detailed knowledge of a tribe of cattle raisers in the African Sudan.

Josselin de Jong, J. P. B., *Lévi-Strauss's Theory of Kinship and Marriage* (1952, 1970). A much more detailed précis of Lévi-Strauss's theory, expressed in reasonably understandable terms.

Marshall, G. A., "Marriage: Comparative Analysis" (*International Encyclopedia of the Social Sciences*, vol. 10, 1968), pp. 8–19. A brief, contemporary statement.

Radcliffe-Brown, A. R., and D. Forde (eds.), *African Systems of Kinship and Marriage* (1950). Synoptic analyses of nine African marriage and kinship systems.

Schapera, I., *Married Life in a South African Tribe* (1950). Old and new ways in the setting of South Africa.

ter Haar, B., *Adat Law in Indonesia* (1948), chap. 9, "Marriage Law." Gives a straightforward exposition of basic marriage forms as they occur in Indonesia.

Westermarck, E., *The History of Human Marriage* (1925). Although the theoretical system of this work has been long outdated, it contains a wealth of very useful descriptive material on marriage practices around the world.

---

[56]G. P. Murdock, "Family Stability in Non-European Cultures" (*The Annals of the American Academy of Political and Social Science*, vol. 272, 1948), pp. 195–201.

---

[57]R. F. Barton, *Ifugao Law*, pp. 23–24.

THE FAMILY

LEARNING GOALS

Note the definition of the family, and list its four basic functions. ¶ List the characteristics and structures of the elemental conjugal-natal families and their relationships to five postmarital residence patterns. ¶ Compare polygyny and polyandry, and account for their occurrence as marriage forms. ¶ Describe the variations and functions of composite unilineal families. ¶ Define and describe the matrilateral group as a social variant differing from the conjugal-natal family. ¶ Write a brief paragraph on the characteristics of communes as family variants.

Marriage establishes the conjugal-natal family, a group consisting of mated spouses and their offspring. Marriage defines sets of statuses and related roles and expectancies governing the relations of the conjugal-natal group as spouses, parents, offspring, and siblings. It defines their statuses and roles in relation to wider groups of kinsmen and to the wider world of nonkinsmen. Marriage, it will be remembered from the previous chapter, is the institution; the family is the group, or body of personnel, whose actions are designed to fulfill the aims of the institution.

FUNCTIONS OF THE FAMILY

M. J. Levy, Jr., and L. A. Fallers suggest that the functions of the family may be grouped in four categories: (1) sexual, (2) reproductive, (3) economic, and (4) educational.[1] More explicitly, the functions of the family may be stated as follows: (1) The institutionalization of mating and the channeling of sexual outlets, thus establishing a legal father for a woman's children and a legal mother for a man's children; each acquires a "monopoly" in the sexuality of the other. (2) The nurture and basic enculturation of the young in an atmosphere of intimacy, preparing them to accept the statuses that will come to them as the jural heirs of their established parents and kinsmen. (3) The organization of a complementary division of labor between spouses, allocating to each certain rights in the labor of the other and in such goods or property as they may acquire through their individual or joint efforts. (4) The linkage of each spouse and the offspring within the wider network of kinsmen: the establishment of relationships of descent and affinity. These functions are universally performed by the family as a social unit. Other social arrangements may also exist wherein these functions are performed, such as the matrilateral group (pages 207–209), in which the mother's brother either displaces the father or takes on some of the functions normally performed by the father in the conjugal-natal family. Matrilateral groups are, however, relatively rare.

The family, in one form or another, is the primary unit of human culture and sociality. In the words of Marion Levy, Jr.:

---

[1]M. J. Levy, Jr., and L. A. Fallers, "The Family: Some Comparative Considerations" (*American Anthropologist*, vol. 61, 1959), pp. 647–651.

1. There is no known case of a society lacking families as subsystems thereof.

2. There is no known society in terms of which initial placement of individuals fails to be in family terms—and almost certainly overwhelmingly, if not exclusively, in family terms.

3. There is no known society in terms of which not only initial but a substantial part of the basic learning—that is, the learning institutionally expected to be shared by all or virtually all the members of a given society—is not learned in a family context for the vast majority of the members of the society.[2]

In many societies, the sex drive may be legitimately satisfied prior to marriage; in such cases, there would be no reason for the individual to take on the responsibilities of marriage if sex gratification alone were a function of the family.

The care of infants and children is the matter of overriding concern. The rather casual interest of primitive societies in the question of actual biological fatherhood has already been sufficiently emphasized. But that some man or group of men must be tagged with the responsibility of performing the adult male activities necessary to keeping the young ones alive, growing, and learning is universally recognized as of the utmost importance. There must be jural fatherhood to regularize transference of statuses from one generation to the next. In meeting the requirements of infant care and child development, the sex differences of male and female are such that a cooperative division of labor makes for greater efficiency and skill in the work that is to be done. Childbearing can still be done only by women, the prospects of asexual reproduction from body cells (cloning) in the laboratories (see Chapter 8, page 148) notwithstanding. Nursing ties women down, while men have greater freedom of movement. Mobility, combined with greater strength, inevitably allows men to become more efficient hunters. Many skills can be performed equally well by either sex, but inasmuch as practice makes perfect, each sex is more likely to develop high skills if it concentrates on certain tasks and relies on the opposite sex to do likewise with certain others; so the spouses and the children all harvest greater benefits from such an arrangement.

The basic functions of the family may be performed with varying degrees of effectiveness from culture to culture, and the details of the ways in which families within different culture systems carry out these functions produce the remarkably different individual personalities of children and adults, as was indicated in Chapter 4. At this juncture, the most relevant fact is that evidently no substitute can serve the functions of child development as well as an intimate kinship group, family or otherwise. Those anthropologists who have paid especial attention to the relations of culture to personality formation by means of direct observation of primitive societies agree that anthropological data give universal significance to the conclusions drawn from recent studies of children in institutions. Margaret Mead sums it up:

It has been . . . effectively demonstrated that children do not thrive, in spite of good physical care, if kept as young infants in impersonal institutions, and that separation from the mother—especially at certain periods—has serious deleterious effects on the child. Retardation, failure to learn to talk, apathy, regression, and death all appear as accompaniments to institutionalization when no mother surrogate is provided.[3]

Substitute, or surrogate, mothers may, if the relationship is personal and within the intimate setting of the family circle, provide that direct emotional response with which the human infant must be provided. Nursing involves more than the imbibing of mother's milk. The surrogates may in many instances be direct substitutes for the biological mother or father, as in the operation of the sororate and the levirate, or they may be collateral surrogates who play the parental roles on a less intensive level. Navaho children may find themselves cared for, and nursed by, a number of clan sisters of their mother, whom they learn to call "mother" under the Navaho system of kinship terminology and who, for their part, call them "son" or "daughter" from the beginning. The

---

[2]M. J. Levy, Jr., "Notes on the Hsu Hypothesis," In F. L. K. Hsu (ed.), *Kinship and Culture*, p. 34. By permission of Aldine Publishing Co.

[3]M. Mead, "Some Theoretical Considerations on the Problem of Mother-Child Separation" (*American Journal of Orthopsychiatry*, vol. 24, 1954), p. 474. Copyright © 1954, the American Orthopsychiatric Association, Inc. Reproduced by permission.

family is not necessarily the small, nuclear family, isolated in its separate dwelling unit; it may be this, but it may also exist as a regular cell-like feature of a larger familial structure.

Thus, although the independent conjugal-natal family of the Euro-American form occurs in all societies, it is the sole form of familial unit in about half of them. In the other half of the world's societies, the nuclear family is encysted within some kind of composite extended family, a larger kinship group that includes more than a single set of spouses and their children.[4]

THE CONJUGAL-NATAL FAMILY

All individuals who are legitimately born and forthwith orphaned, and who ultimately marry, are members of a primary and a secondary conjugal-natal family: that of their parents, into which they are born, and that which they found with their spouses in wedlock. In the first they are offspring; in the second they are progenitors (Fig. 11-1). Viewed from the outside, the two families are alike in terms of form and function. The statuses of the given individual within the two families are very different, however, and the role experiences in each are quite unlike.

The conjugal-natal family is limited both in scope of membership and in duration. It can include no more persons than a mated pair can produce or adopt, and it cannot endure for more than the lifespan of two generations: the lifespan of the founding spouses, and the lifespan of the children who are born into their marriage. The lone surviving founder of an independent conjugal-natal family, in societies such as the American, can face a bleak and lonely old age. Each conjugal-natal family gradually wastes away as death takes its toll, until at last it is no more. This type of family is a discontinuous social unit. Each such family is born and destined to die within the span of a century.

This is a consequence of the universal incest tabu, for if parent could marry child and brother could marry sister, a conjugal-natal family could be continued indefinitely through internal re-

placement as the original members died off. Perpetuity of the conjugal-natal family is forgone, however, in the interests of societal stability. The individual family sacrifices itself as an entity in the interests of maintenance of the stability of the whole society, for this is of more fundamental importance.

However much the independent conjugal-natal family may be cherished as a social unit, it has certain functional disabilities. In the first place, the conjugal-natal family is very unstable. There is the constant possibility of divorce, and where divorce is not countenanced, emotional disturbances arising from the incompatibility of the father and mother can easily destroy the affective solidarity that is so important to good family functioning. If a primary purpose of marriage is to fix the biological father of the children with the economic and social responsibility of providing for them, his ability to perform this essential social function is seriously impaired when he divorces or leaves the mother. True enough, the consequences of a conjugal-natal family breakup are not so serious in societies in which the mother is securely embedded in the protection of her extended family and where remarriage is easier than it is in urbanized Western civilization.

Also, the conjugal-natal family is a temporary association. It begins with the union of the married pair and ends with the dispersal of the children. Furthermore, upon marriage, a person enters a new conjugal-natal family, and his or her loyalties are split. From our own experience, we know the tensions that can result from the pull of loyalty to our husbands or wives as against our fathers and mothers. The instability of the conjugal-natal family and its short lifespan also limit its usefulness as a means of inheritance of property and perquisites.

Nonetheless, R. T. Smith notes that sociologists such as Talcott Parsons maintain, and probably rightly, that

the family system of the urban United States is not a denuded form of a more "normal" or "natural" family system but is itself a highly specialized form that articulates most satisfactorily with a highly differentiated economic and political system and with institutionalized values that stress achievement rather than inheritance. It is argued that the smallness and relative isolation of

---

[4]E. Bourguignon and L. Greenbaum, *Diversity and Homogeneity*, p. 49.

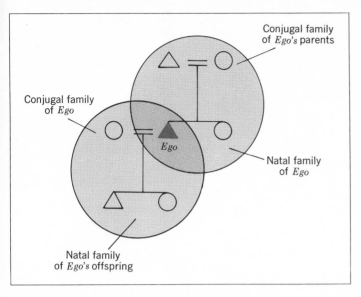

Conjugal family
of *Ego*'s parents

Conjugal family
of *Ego*

Ego

Natal family
of *Ego*

Natal family
of *Ego*'s offspring

FIG. 11-1 The dual nature of the conjugal-natal family. Each family is a conjugal family for the spouses who establish it and a natal family for the offspring who are born into it.

the family from other kinship ties is an adaptation that makes possible the spatial and status mobility of its members[5]

(See, also, the discussion of the American kinship system in Chapter 13, pages 230–232.)

Monogamy and Family Structure

The independent conjugal-natal family is possible only when marriage is monogamous, but monogamy is the sole permitted marital form in only a minority of human societies (in one in six societies).[6]

The normal state of affairs is to allow polygamy, especially among men in positions of power and social leadership. Still, it is important to realize that what is *permitted* in a culture and what *prevails* in fact may be two different things. Thus, it is usual to refer to societies whose cultures permit multiple marriages as *polygamous*; yet it is unlikely that more than a few marriages in any society will actually be polygamous, since a number of factors limit multiple marriages.

First, there is the relative balance of the sex ratio. Approximately equal numbers of males and females are born. Unless some selective factor operates in favor of one sex and against the other, there will be an approximate equality in the numbers of adult males and females available for marriage. If this is the case, whenever one man has two wives, some other man in the tribe has to do without. There is, of course, the possibility that the short-wived men may band together to share one wife among themselves, but such polyandrous arrangements are very rare.

If it is the current practice for a man to settle in the household of his wife, he obviously cannot live with all his wives simultaneously unless they are sisters. Uxorilocal residence[7] discourages the polygynous form of polygamy. Beyond this, the attitudes of his in-laws will discourage marriage with women from other kinship groups, especially if the society is matrilineal and the wife's relationship group is in a strong position. Marriage is a kinship-group alliance, and a son-in-law whose affinal allegiances are multiple is apt to be less desirable than one whose affinity is to one group alone.

---

[5]R. T. Smith, "Family: Comparative Structure" (*International Encyclopedia of the Social Sciences*, vol. 5, 1968), p. 311. Copyright © 1968, Crowell Collier and Macmillan, Inc. Quoted with permission.

[6]Bourguignon and Greenbaum, *op. cit.*, p. 49.

[7]The practice whereby a married couple settles in the locale of the wife's parents.

Few precise statistics are available, but all reports indicate that monogamous marriages actually predominate in most societies that permit polygamy. Contrary to the notions of nineteenth-century anthropologists, monogamy most definitely is not the end product of an evolutionary series narrowing down from primitive promiscuity to civilized monogamy. The very primitive Andaman Islanders and the Semangs of the Malay forests limit themselves to one wife apiece, but the Semangs marry again and again in serial monogamy, Hollywood style. Inca commoners were forbidden to marry more than one wife, but a man might receive a concubine as a gift in reward for faithful service to his overlord. The occurrence of prescribed monogamy among the matrilineal, uxorilocal Iroquois in New York and the equally matrilineal, uxorilocal Hopi and Zuñi suggests that in these instances, monogamy is correlated with female-dominated residence and economy. Monogamy prevails among all the Southwest Pueblos, but among the Eastern Pueblos of New Mexico, where female dominance fades out, it is impossible to tell whether this is due to ancient Pueblo custom or whether it has been brought about by the influence of the Catholic Church. Among the Zuñi and Hopi monogamous marriages are very brittle. Among the Keresan Pueblos, however, the Catholic injunction against divorce is rigidly adhered to. Clandestine relations outside marriage occur among all these people.

Exclusive monogamy is not correlated with any stage of culture. Its absence among pastoral nomads, who are predominantly patrilineal, is nevertheless a notable fact.

Residence Patterns

A conjugal-natal family almost always has a home. Because of the sentiments that suffuse the family relationship, "home" connotes a good deal more than "house." A long-abandoned dwelling is a house, but it was once also a home. We sing fondly of "home, sweet home," but it is unimaginable, for reasons that are clear enough, that we would ever, within the family circle, burst into heart-moving song over "house, sweet house."

The rules of exogamy require that a man and

wife come from separate conjugal-natal families and separate households. Upon marriage, the first question to be settled is: "Where shall we live?" In most societies, this issue is resolved ahead of time and therefore does not call for debate or allow much room for individual preference. The custom of the society may be *virilocal (L. vir*, male + *locus*, place), according to which the newlywed couple settles in the locality of the husband's primary conjugal-natal family. Or it may be *patrilocal* if most of the husband's paternal relatives customarily live in the same camp, neighborhood, village, or district.

On the other hand, the custom of the tribe may be for the couple to settle in the locality of the wife's parents, in which case it is called *uxorilocal* (L. *uxori*, wife + *locus*, place).

Following Murdock, we may call the practice *matrilocal* if the couple settle in the locality of the wife's matrilineal kinship groups.

A few tribes with little fixed property and weak social organization give the couple free choice on whether to settle in the locality of the bride's or the groom's primary conjugal-natal family. This practice is known as *bilocal* or *ambilocal* (L. *ambo*, both + *locus*, place) residence.

A small number of matrilineally oriented societies expect the couple to settle in the locality of the male's mother's brother. In this situation, we have *avunculocal* (L. *avunculus*, mother's brother + *locus*, place) residence.

Finally, some social systems, such as the Euro-American, provide for independent establishment of residence without too much reference to the prior location of the primary conjugal-natal families of the newly married pair. This condition bespeaks *neolocal* (Gr. *neos*, new + L. *locus*, place) residence, which is in effect an absence of restrictive rules of residence, leaving the options open for the newly founded, independent conjugal-natal household.

There are, then, five basic varieties of residence: (1) virilocal (with patrilocal), (2) uxorilocal (with matrilocal), (3) avunculocal, (4) bilocal (or ambilocal), and (5) neolocal. In most societies, one rule alone prevails for the married life of a couple, although some may use combinations of two or more. Thus, among the nomadic Plains Indians, a couple's first tipi was usually set up

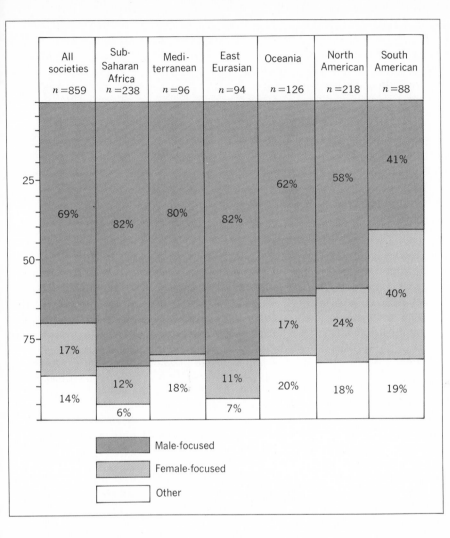

FIG. 11-2 Relative frequency of male- and female-focused residence patterns according to geographic areas. The male-focused pattern represents viripatrilocal; the female-focused one, uxorimatrilocal, plus avunculocal. (Data adapted from E. Bourguignon and L. Greenbaum, *Diversity and Homogeneity*, table 28, page 50.)

beside that of the bride's parents for a year or so. Then, when the new household was well established, the young couple was likely to camp beside the groom's family. Among the Dobuans, a couple alternated residence in each other's village every other year. And in some complex primitive societies, such as the Ashanti in Ghana, where the ideal rule is virilocal, there may actually be a good deal of informal variation from case to case.[8] Furthermore, it is not a simple open-and-

closed matter as to whether a given household represents one kind of residence pattern or another, if it contains a mixture of several conjugal-natal families. It may also remain a moot matter as to how to classify a society as a whole, when two or more residential patterns are found to exist with equal frequency.[9]

A glance at Fig. 11-2 will quickly show that a great majority of human societies are male-

[8]M. Fortes, "Time and Social Structure: An Ashanti Case Study," in M. Fortes (ed.), *Social Structure*, pp. 54–84.

[9]Cf. W. H. Goodenough, "Residence Rules" (*Southwestern Journal of Anthropology*, vol. 12, 1956), pp. 22–37, for a very pertinent exemplification of these problems in the study of the social organization of Truk in the Micronesian Islands.

oriented in residence patterns. The average for the world sample in the *Ethnographic Atlas* is 69 per cent virilocal and patrilocal. But in the continental Old World the ratio rises to over 80 per cent, while in North and South America the figures are 58 and 41 per cent, respectively. Conversely, female-focused marital residence is virtually nonexistent in the Mediterranean area and in Negro Africa, thus reflecting the importance of intensive agriculture and pastoralism as subsistence bases in that part of the world. In the New World, women hold a better power position. Over a third (40 per cent) of the South American societies in the sample are uxorilocal or matrilocal—still not as many as are viri/patrilocal but an impressive figure, nonetheless (Fig. 11-2).

It should be immediately obvious that the nature of residence patterns strongly affects the internal quality of the family unit and its extensions. If residence is uxorilocal, the woman is in constant daily interaction with *her* parents and sisters. The children of sisters grow up together, and the children of brothers do not. Husbands are "aliens" in a new setting. Sisters are grouped in a continuing solidarity. The opportunity for women to exert a solid front is enhanced, and their position in the direction of social affairs is stronger. With virilocal residence, just the opposite occurs.

Another factor that affects the quality of the family is whether marriages are based on village exogamy or endogamy. If the marriages take place within the local group or village, the differentiating effects of residence rules are much reduced. In spite of virilocality, if the home of the bride's parents is only 100 yards away, the continuity of her tie to her primary conjugal-natal family is not so seriously strained as it is when she is transported to another village; concomitantly, the influence of the paternal group cannot be so strong.

THE COMPOSITE CONJUGAL-NATAL FAMILY

Within polygamous marriages, we have been drawing a distinction between polygyny and polyandry. *Polygamy* means multiple marriages; *po-lygyny* means multiple women and *polyandry* means multiple men. Polygyny is therefore that form of family in which a husband has more than one wife at a time. *Bigamy* is the more special form of polygamy in which the husband limits himself to two wives, or a woman to two husbands. In societies where there may be more than one husband or wife in a family at the same time, the conjugal-natal families are not independent but are, rather, segments of a *composite conjugal-natal* family. The latter is therefore a family consisting of two or more conjugal-natal family segments.

Polygyny

In spite of the Judeo-Christian insistence upon monogamy, this practice is a cultural emphasis shared by a relatively small number of societies (16 per cent of the sample in the *Ethnographic Atlas*). Nearly half (44 per cent) of all societies hold the polygynous family to be the norm, while nearly as many permit polygyny but do not attempt to make it the regular thing. Almost all African societies are emphatically polygynous (see Fig. 11-3), enough to readily block a zealous effort to have polygyny declared contrary to fundamental human rights in the United Nations Commission on Human Rights in the early 1950s.

Functions of polygyny

There are a number of social motives underlying polygyny as an institution. If a man has the means to support several wives, he is able to present a richer and better-equipped household to the world. More women can prepare better clothes and food. If women's handicrafts are marketable or suitable for exchange, his household wealth will be increased. When the Blackfoot Indians found a lucrative outlet for tanned hides in the Canadian fur trade, women as tanners became an economic asset, and polygyny grew to an extent unprecedented in the Plains. Progeny price went up, and the age of marriage for girls went down, while the age of marriage for men was set back; well-established Blackfoot entrepreneurs cornered the available women, and it took young

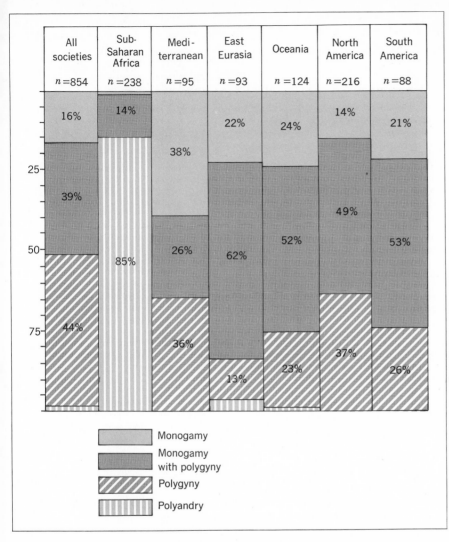

	All societies	Sub-Saharan Africa	Medi-terranean	East Eurasia	Oceania	North America	South America
	n=854	n=238	n=95	n=93	n=124	n=216	n=88

FIG. 11-3 Relative frequency of monogamy, monogamy with polygyny, polygyny, and polyandry as expected marriage forms according to geographic areas. (Data adapted from E. Bourguignon and L. Greenbaum, *Diversity and Homogeneity*, table 26, p. 48.)

men a longer time to acquire enough capital to purchase wives.[10]

Polygyny may also serve as a mechanism for competitive status in the sexual field when to have and to hold several wives against all comers is a dangerous task, as among the Eskimos.[11]

---

[10]O. Lewis, *The Effects of White Contact upon Blackfoot Culture, with Special Reference to the Role of the Fur Trade* (American Ethnological Society, Monograph 6, 1942), pp. 38–40.

[11]E. A. Hoebel, *The Law of Primitive Man*, pp. 75–76.

Strange as it may seem to some, it is repeatedly reported that in many tribes the women do not object to their husbands' taking on additional wives. This is most apt to be true when additional wives are co-workers or "chore wives," as among the Comanches of the Plains. A secondary wife may be desired because she will perform special functions, as with the African Baganda, among whom a second wife is chosen from the husband's paternal grandmother's clan. This wife is charged (among other things) with the responsibility of caring for her husband's hair and nail clippings in order to protect him against sorcery.

On the other hand, instances are on record of primitive women who have shown extreme jealousy when their husbands brought home a new wife. A Cheyenne woman hanged herself because her husband took a Pawnee captive to wife, but her own grandmother remarked, "She was foolish to hang herself over such a little thing."

Most primitives aver that polygyny works out best when a man's several wives are sisters. This is psychologically reasonable, inasmuch as sisters are more used to one another's ways than unrelated women are; they are subject to the influence of emotional loyalty acquired in childhood as members of the same conjugal-natal family. As representatives of the same marriage group, their nonpersonal interests in the marriage are identical, which is not the case with unrelated women. *Sororal polygyny* is in effect an anticipation of sororate privileges. A man does not wait for the death of his wife before he marries her younger sister. Instead, as among the Comanches, he has an expectation that if he performs his son-in-law obligations to his wife's parents, they will reward him with his wife's younger sister when she becomes of age.

Where exchange marriage between two families prevails, the levirate will also work to produce sororal polygyny, for example, when brothers have married sisters and a man inherits his deceased brother's wife.

Various household arrangements are made as adjustments to the requirements of the multiple-wife family. The Angola practice is probably typical of Sudanese African tribes. Hambly tells of an Angola headman with eleven wives, each of whom had a separate hut in his compound. The husband customarily slept with each wife four or seven successive nights, as his personal habit might be.[12] Among the Jie, it will be remembered (pages 134–135), each wife in a polygynous unit within a joint-family household has her own fenced-in yard and sleeping hut. If a Comanche had less than four wives, they usually shared the same tipi.

More than four wives necessitated at least two tipis for the household.

Within composite families, there is usually a firm hierarchical distinction between the wives. The first-married wife is given a No. 1 position of authority, so that even though she may be displaced by a later wife as a sexual favorite, she still has the gratification of priority in formal status. The Comanches, again, definitely made such distinctions, for secondary wives were "chore wives" who had to do household work under the direction of No. 1. No wonder the busy wives of great chieftains were usually quite willing to have their husbands marry extra housekeepers. It helped lighten their load.

Polyandry

The actual marriage of several men to one woman is as rare (occurring in 4 of the 854 cultures in the *Ethnographic Atlas*) as the marriage of several women to one man is common. Tibetans and the Todas and other tribes of India are the most famous polyandrists.[13] The Toda polyandrous union is usually, but not necessarily, fraternal.[14] Some polygynous marriages also occur, and quite a few monogamous ones. Children are ordinarily betrothed in infancy, and the boy makes progeny-price payments twice a year all through his childhood. He also has to provide a buffalo to help pay funeral expenses of members of his betrothed's family. Just before puberty, the girl is deflorated by a man from some clan other than her own. Then she is ready for marriage. Right after puberty, she is given a dowry and taken to the home of her husband. Although she may have been betrothed to just one man, it is understood that she is also the wife of all his brothers. Even a boy yet unborn may become her husband, along with his elder brothers, when he becomes of age.

All the brothers live together and share their wife without friction and supposedly without jealousy. When the wife becomes pregnant, one of the brothers goes through a ritual of "presenting

---

[12]W. D. Hambly, *Source Book for African Anthropology*, pp. 418–419.

[13]See G. D. Berreman, "Pahari Polyandry: A Comparison," in P. J. Bohannan and J. Middleton (eds.), *Marriage, Family, and Residence*, pp. 147–167.

[14]Called "adelphic polyandry" in British social anthropology.

the bow." This makes him the jural father of the ensuing child and the next couple of children to be born. There is no concern over whether he may be the biological sire or not. After he has his share of offspring to sponsor, another brother "presents the bow," thus making himself the father of the next group of children, and so on.

This disregard of biological paternity in favor of ceremonially established sociological fatherhood is also manifest in a way reminiscent of Sakalava progeny-price privileges mentioned previously (page 185). Occasionally, a Toda woman may leave her legitimate husbands to live with another man without official approval, or she may take a concubitant, who pays her husbands for the privilege; in either case, her subsequent children still belong to the man (her husband) who performed the bow-and-arrow ritual.[15]

Polyandry in the Darjeeling district of India is restricted to the younger brothers of the man who performs the wedding rite with the wife. If the elder brother dies and the common wife has no children, she may break the polyandrous bond by first tying a string to a finger of her No. 1 husband's corpse and binding it to one of her own fingers. Then by severing the string, she symbolically destroys the marriage tie.

Tibetan and Eskimo polyandry have been attributed to the practice of female infanticide. While it is quite true that both peoples practice infanticide, census figures do not indicate a surplus of adult men in Tibet, and reliable censuses of the primitive Eskimo indicate that women outnumber men in almost all Eskimo communities, in spite of the common destruction of baby girls.

Although rare, polyandry is more common (at least in a modified form) than was thought to be the case a few decades ago. A form of polyandry has been reported from at least two East African tribes, leading us to expect that there are probably several other unreported instances. Among the Bahima of Ankole, where progeny price is high, a poor man may call on his younger brothers to contribute cattle to his cause.[16] All the brothers who have contributed take turns living with the bride until she becomes pregnant; she then lives with her "husband." Whoever the sire may be, the resultant child is the jural offspring of the elder brother who married the girl.

Property and polyandry

Edmund Leach has proposed that fraternal, or adelphic, polyandry is "intimately associated" with inheritance of land through males only, combined with virilocal residence and dowry. In the South Asian cases, a woman who marries patrilocally may surrender her dowry but receive movable goods from the husband in its stead. Brothers jointly pay the dowry, thus obtaining a joint interest in the sexual prerogatives of the husband.[17]

Extensions of brotherhood

Leach's hypothesis is appropriate to the South Asian data, but it does not fit the facts for North America. While economic factors may be at the bottom of polyandry in some societies, there appear to be other motivations elsewhere. Both the Shoshones and the Eskimos practice polyandry, and yet neither show much concern with property considerations. These are bilateral societies in which a man must depend on his brothers (and cousins) for security and survival. In Shoshone and Comanche kinship terminology, there is no separate word for "brother-in-law" or "sister-in-law." All female sisters and cousins of a wife are addressed by a single term, *kw3h3*. A woman addresses all her husband's brothers and cousins by the term for "husband," *kumaxp*. The polyandrous emphasis is on the mutuality of the bond of brotherhood.

"A man loves his brother; he knows that if his brother dies, no one can replace him; he gives him everything he can," explained That's It. "A brother therefore sends his wife over to him occasionally as a gift. She cannot go of her own free will or meet him secretly, or her husband will be angry." It was also expected that when a man was on the warpath, his brother could sleep with his wife.[18]

[15]W. H. R. Rivers, *The Todas*, pp. 477–480.

[16]J. Roscoe, *The Banyankole*, p. 123; "The Bahima, the Cow Tribe of Enkole in the Uganda Protectorate" (*Journal of the Royal Anthropological Institute of Great Britain and Ireland*, vol. 37, 1907), p. 105.

[17]E. R. Leach, *Rethinking Anthropology*, pp. 104–113.

[18]From *The Comanches* by E. Wallace and E. A. Hoebel, pp. 138–139. Copyright 1952 by the University of Oklahoma Press.

This notion of the sexual equivalence of brothers crops up in the quaint Shoshone and Comanche custom whereby an aggrieved husband courteously addressed an adulterer who had made him a cuckold as "brother." Men who have had sex relations with the same woman are "brothers," even though unrelated and even while the husband prosecuted the adulterer for damages.

Comanche young men frequently entered into a relation of institutionalized friendship with a chosen "chum," called *haints*. They usually married sisters, whom they freely lent to one another as wives. Shoshones and Comanches had to rely on "brothers," real or putative, in war and in law, in love and in play.[19] Their adelphic polyandry expressed the structural-functional significance of "brotherhood" as the keystone of their social life.

That such attitudes are not mere aberrations of the Comanches is fully attested by Murdock's findings to the effect that nearly two-thirds of the 250 societies in the Yale Cross Cultural Survey for which data are available permit postmarital sexual intercourse between a man and his brother's wife (anticipatory levirate) or between a man and his wife's sister (anticipatory sororate).[20]

Eskimo polyandry is of the same order as Shoshone, except that the putative brother with whom an Eskimo normally exchanges wives does not usually live in the same village. A traveling Eskimo needs a woman to dry his fur clothes and chew the hides to keep them soft, among the more necessary amenities of arctic living. Most Eskimo men have at least one regular partner in each village, who will make his wife available on a basis of amicable mutuality. At the same time, he needs someone at home to look after his own wife when he goes off traveling. A good friend will normally agree to take on the task with all its responsibilities and sexual amenities.[21]

WIFE HOSPITALITY   The widespread primitive practice of men sharing their wives with certain other men on specific occasions is closely related to the institution of polyandry. Most commonly, a host deems that proper social form requires him to offer the hospitality of his wife to an overnight guest. An early white trader on the upper Missouri River, Jean Baptiste Trudeau, took note that "So true is this, that husbands, fathers and brothers, are importunate with the white men who visit them, to make free with their wives, daughters and sisters, particularly those who are most youthful and pretty. . . ."[22]

Wife hospitality was practiced because a man who accepted the woman for the duration of his stay in the village became a putative son-in-law or brother of his benefactor. Such arrangements helped to establish a network of trade in the eighteenth and early nineteenth centuries throughout the upper Plains. French, English, and American traders solidified their business interests with various Indian tribes by becoming "kinsmen" through sexual sharing.

Similar concepts of hospitality have been noted in all parts of the primitive world by countless explorers, travelers, and lay observers, as well as by anthropologists.[23] As an institutionalized practice, wife lending is functionally analogous to *blood brotherhood*, "a pact or alliance formed between two persons by ritual act in which each swallows the blood of the other. The pact is one of mutual assistance and is backed by powerful sanctions."[24] The formal exchange of wives is analogous to intimate exchange of "magical" personal essence. At any rate, it should be clear that wife hospitality in societies that emphasize kinship obligations and privileges of brotherhood is not an act of immorality in the context of those societies. It serves as a means of broadening and strengthening social bonds.

Leach's hypothesis and that offered above are not incompatible or contradictory. Each explains special sets of circumstances. Fraternal polyandry in South Asia and that in North America are alike in that a group of brothers share sexual privileges in a wife or wives, while the woman's

[19]*Ibid.*, p. 132.

[20]Murdock, *Social Structure*, p. 268.

[21]For more detail, see R. F. Spencer, "Spouse Exchange among the North Alaskan Eskimo," in P. J. Bohannan and J. Middleton (eds.), *Marriage, Family, and Residence*, pp. 131–144.

[22]G. H. Smith, "J. B. Trudeau's Remarks on the Indians of the Upper Missouri, 1794–95" (*American Anthropologist*, vol. 38, 1940), p. 567.

[23]See E. Westermarck, *The History of Human Marriage*, vol. 1, pp. 224–230, for a more detailed body of references to the custom.

[24]E. E. Evans-Pritchard, "Zande Blood-brotherhood," in *Essays in Social Anthropology*, p. 131.

offspring are jurally the heirs of a specific male. Although the social reasons (structural and functional) for this are quite different in the two cases, the unlike conditions have produced similar results. This is called *convergence*: separate lines of development have led to a single point.

THE COMPOSITE UNILINEAL FAMILY

In following the extensions of polyandry beyond the immediate limits of the patrilateral, composite conjugal-natal family, we were led into considerations of "brotherhood." Let us now return to an examination of some ways in which the concept of the family may be extended to incorporate a group of closely related conjugal-natal families into a single property-holding, residential group. Such units are usually called the *joint family* or the *composite unilineal family*. Half the world's societies in the nineteenth century organized their family residential units in this way.[25]

The essential difference between the composite conjugal-natal family and the composite unilineal family is that the former involves only one spouse with several mates, while the latter involves married kinsmen living together in a single household, each with his or her own distinct spouse and offspring.

The Tanala Joint Family

Linton's description of the patrilineal joint family among the Tanala of Madagascar presents a good example of the smaller version of the composite unilineal family. A Tanala joint family begins with a single conjugal family. When the sons grow up and marry, they build new houses for themselves close to their parental home. The father, as head of the joint family, directs all its activities concerning clearing and cultivating the fields for dry-rice culture, caring for the family cattle, and similar tasks. All earnings of the male members are placed in his hands for investment in cattle and for dispersal for progeny price and such little cash needs as the sons may have. As long as his father lives, a man has little chance to accumulate any wealth in his own right. The joint family is a cooperative work group and a corporate unit in dealing with other members of the society.

As long as the founder lives, his male lineal descendants are bound to the joint family, and it is not uncommon for a patriarch to have a dozen or more able-bodied sons and grandsons under his control. Upon his death, the process of fission starts. Although the family continues to live and work together under the leadership of the eldest son, his brothers do not have to put their earnings into the common holding unless they wish to. When he, in turn, is at last succeeded by his eldest son, the joint family begins to break up. The third-generation leader is younger than most of his uncles, who become restive under his leadership. Moreover, it is likely that the group will have grown too large for its land holdings. Then one or more men split off to found a new joint-family household elsewhere.[26] The functional significance of economics for the joint family is shown by Linton's analysis of the breakdown of the joint family resulting from the introduction of wet-rice culture among the neighboring Betsilio tribe.[27]

The Karo-Batak Joint Family

The Karo-Batak of Sumatra, who have been described by the Dutch anthropologist Geert van den Steenhoven, exemplify both the composite unilineal family and asymmetrical matrilateral cross-cousin marriage. All Karo people belong to one of five exogamous patrilineal clans. These clans are divided into smaller units (subclans) and are further divided into lineages named after the villages they originated in (though they may have lineage members living in other villages). Villages are ruled by the lineage formed from the direct male descendants of the village founder.

The desired partner in marriage is a man's mother's brother's daughter in the pattern called asymmetrical matrilateral cross-cousin marriage (see Chapter 10, page 179), although van den Steenhoven notes that this ideal pattern is followed infrequently. Because the clans are exogamous even when the ideal matrilateral cross-

---

[25]Bourguignon and Greenbaum, *op cit.*, p. 49.

[26]R. Linton, "The Tanalas of Madagascar," in A. Kardiner, *The Individual and His Society*, pp. 189–192.
[27]*Ibid.*, pp. 282–290.

cousin is not selected, the wife will be taken from one of the five clans other than that of the potential groom. This places each clan in the role of being a "wife-taker" from one or more other clans and a "wife-giver" to one or more other clans. Through time each clan has come to identify one other clan as its traditional wife-taking clan and another as its traditional wife-giving clan, although in practice, because the ideal is not adhered to, all of the five clans have played both roles with each other at some time.

Each Karo man can place all other Karo men into one of three categories in reference to these lineage marriage-partner exchange practices. Individuals who belong to the same patrilineage

FIG. 11-4 Members of a contemporary Karo-Batak, Sumatra, Indonesia, composite unilineal family with their traditional joint-family house in the background. On the left may be seen the corner of a modern-type joint-family house built of commercial planks and corrugated iron roof. It is less beautiful and less symbolic of family solidarity than was the traditional house, but it is more sanitary, comfortable, and easier to build. (Photo courtesy of H. Slaats.)

(agnates) are called *senina*. Individuals who belong to the lineage from which a person's own lineage receives women in marriage are called *kalimbubu*. Individuals who belong to a lineage that gets women from a person's own lineage are called *anakberu*. Likewise, every Karo individual also fills each of these three statuses in reference to at least some other Karo; he is an agnate with those of his own clan, and in relationship to the other four clans his lineage is a woman-giver *(anakberu)* to some and a woman-taker from others *(kalimbubu)*.[28]

The Karo-Batak composite unilineal family is composed of individuals in the category *senina* who occupy, along with some of their *anakberu* and *kalimbubu*, a long house (Fig. 11-4) called the *ramah adat*. Ideally this house is built for eight conjugal families in separate screened sleeping areas arranged along four cooking areas. The four apartments on either side of the front and back entrances are considered to be the most important, and the positions of their occupants, as shown in Fig. 11-5, help to reveal the structure of the Karo joint family.

The highest ranking apartment is used by the head of the house; he is a patrilineal descendant of the village founder and thus he belongs to the ruling lineage in his village. The second apartment is that of the *anakberu*, that is a man from the lineage which "takes" its women from that of No. 1, so he necessarily belongs to a clan other than No. 1. The third apartment is that of the *senina*, who is an agnate of No. 1 and thus from the same clan. The fourth apartment is that of the *kalimbubu*, who is a man belonging to the lineage which "gives" its women to that of No. 1, so that No. 4 and No. 1 are also necessarily of different clans.[29]

The Karo joint family consists of the head of the house, his wife and unmarried children living in the most important room, and his agnates (brothers, married sons, patrilineal cousins, etc.) and their conjugal families; the latter are members of the status *senina*, and they occupy the third important apartment and other rooms in the house. Living in the house with them, but not as members of the composite unilineal family, are

[28]G. van den Steenhoven, "Musjawarah in Karo-land" (*Law and Society Review*, vol. 7, no. 4, 1973), pp. 694–697.

[29]*Ibid*, p. 695. By permission of the Law and Society Association.

the representatives of the traditional *anakberu* and *kalimbubu* of the household head's *senina*.

Because the joint family is the core of the patrilineage whose male ancestor founded the village, they are the owners of the village land and they rule on land allocation and use. More than that, the *senina*, *anakberu*, and *kalimbubu* each have very important roles as representative adversaries on behalf of the houseowner's lineage in all legal disputes involving claims against other clans—an important factor discussed in Chapter 17, pages 288–292.

THE MATRILATERAL GROUP

Some societies utilize the brother-sister relationship as a means of counterbalancing limitations of the conjugal-natal family. The result is a social unit that may be called the *matrilateral group*, which consists of a woman, her brother, and her offspring or a conjoint combination of lineal descendants of a female.[30]

Thus, among the Dobu of Melanesia, the conjugal-natal family is the household unit; i.e., its members live together. After a man marries, he never again enters his sister's house; consequently, the *susu*, as the matrilateral group is called in Dobu, has no household base. However, children cannot eat food grown in their father's fields; all fishing gear, including canoes, is used jointly and is inherited only by members of the *susu*. Consequently, the *susu* has an economic base, and the conjugal-natal family does not. Emotional security is found only in the *susu*, and not in the conjugal-natal family. All Dobuans believe that all other Dobuans except those of their own *susu* are their magical enemies. Husband and wife, coming as they do from different *susus*, are hostile at marriage and all their days thereafter. Each believes the other is trying to destroy him or her by foul magic. The *susu* inherits the corpses and skulls of its members. It bestows personal names and social status in relationship terms. Widows, widowers, and the children of a dead person may never enter the village of the deceased spouse or parent, but *susu*

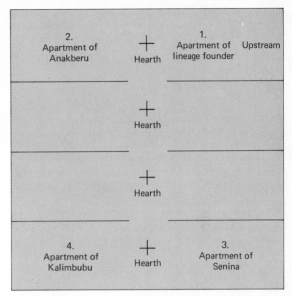

FIG. 11-5 Floor plan of Karo-Batak joint-family house, Sumatra, Indonesia. The unlabeled apartments are used by closely related members of the founder's lineage.

relatives of a dead person may enter the village of the surviving spouse or children.[31]

The Zuñi Household

The differentiation and interrelationship of conjugal-natal family and matrilateral group are also strikingly revealed by the Zuñis of New Mexico, of whom Benedict wrote:

To the women of the household, the grandmother and her sisters, her daughters and their daughters, belong the house and the corn that is stored in it. No matter what may happen to marriages, the women of the household remain with the house for life. They present a solid front. They care for and feed the sacred objects that belong to them. They keep their secrets together. Their husbands are outsiders, and it is their brothers, married now into houses of other clans, who are united with the household in all affairs of moment. It is they who return for all the retreats when the sacred objects of the house are set out before the altar. It is they, not

---

[30]It has also been called the *consanguineal family*.

[31]R. F. Fortune, *Sorcerers of Dobu*, pp. 5–30.

the women, who learn the word-perfect ritual of their sacred bundle and perpetuate it. A man goes always, for all important occasions, to his mother's house, which, when she dies, becomes his sister's house, and if his marriage breaks up, he returns to the same stronghold.

This blood-relationship group, rooted in the ownership of the house, united in the care of sacred objects, is the important group in Zuñi. It has permanence and important common concerns. But it is not the economically functioning group. Each married son, each married brother, spends his labour upon the corn which will fill his wife's storeroom. Only when his mother's or sister's house lacks male labour does he care for the cornfield of his blood-relationship group. The economic group is the household that lives together, the old grandmother and her husband, her daughters and their husbands. These husbands count in the economic groups, though in the ceremonial group they are outsiders.[32]

The Nayar Taravad

Of the matrilineal type of joint family household, that of the famous Nayar caste of Kerala, on the Malabar coast of southern India, has long held the interest of anthropologists.

The Nayar are supposed to have been the ruling class of the aboriginal society predating the Hindu influx. Today they form the third-ranking caste of a complex caste society. Above them is the erstwhile royal house of great wealth and power, which may have emerged long ago from the Nayars themselves. Beneath the royal house (but far above the Nayars in sublimity) is the caste of Nambudiri Brahmans, whose sacred families are patrilineally organized on a strict basis of primogeniture. The Nayars are a closed caste of landowners and professional soldiers, who in contrast to the Brahmans are strictly matrilineal and matrilocal. The household, or *taravad*, is a joint organization housed under one roof. The eldest woman is the titular head of the household, but the house, lands, and joint property are administered by the eldest brother for the benefit of the group. All the males (brothers, sons, and grandsons) contribute to the maintenance of the *taravad* and draw their support from it. The offspring of the women belong to the *taravad* and

are maintained within it. The men mate with women of other *taravad* without obligating themselves to any legal duties toward these "wives" or children, who live with their mothers.

Marriage by members of the *taravad* is often no more than a ritual bow to Hindu convention. If a ceremony is performed, it may soon be followed by legal divorce, even though the couple continues an enduring relation as mates. For unlike most joint-family practices elsewhere, the Nayar male may not live in the joint-family household of his mate. The couple merely visit together, and out of these visits come the children who people the *taravad* of the mother.

Both men and women may have several mates simultaneously, since mating involves no formal obligations. Younger sons of the Brahman class may enter into sexual alliances with Nayar women, but they still remain outside the *taravad*, and their children remain irrevocably fixed within it.

Under changing economic and social conditions, the Nayar matrilineal joint family has been gradually dissolving, and patrilineal tendencies have become increasingly strong.[33]

The matrilateral group exists because it offers certain advantages in which the conjugal-natal family is weak. Yet the conjugal-natal family is definitely preferred over the matrilateral group. The conjugal-natal family is universal; the matrilateral group is not.

What is defective or objectionable in the matrilateral group? The answer will be found in the incest tabu. The basis of the matrilateral group is the sibling bond of brotherhood and sisterhood. Yet all societies find it necessary to tabu sex relations between brother and sister, often manifesting extreme anxiety over the consequences of incestuous relationships. The matrilateral group encourages emotional and functional ties between a pair who must never become sexually involved with each other. This is dangerous business, so much so that many societies apparently prefer to make it impossible for such a situation to exist. In Dobu, for example, a man may not enter his sister's house. Another disadvantage of the

---

[32]R. F. Benedict, *Patterns of Culture*, pp. 75–76. By permission of Houghton Mifflin Co.

[33]K. Gough, in D. M. Schneider and K. Gough (eds.), *Matrilineal Kinship*, chaps. 6 and 7.

matrilateral group is that the splitting of loyalty between it and the conjugal-natal family may produce personal and cultural conflicts that are difficult to resolve. Meyer Fortes observed: "Ashanti discuss the subject interminably, stressing especially the inevitability of conflicting loyalties. For a woman the conflict turns on the difficulties of reconciling attachment to her mother with her duty to her husband."[34]

In a social system in which the matrilateral group is an important functioning unit, the woman who has few sisters and many brothers is certainly more apt to be better off than a woman who has several sisters and only one brother, for as Malinowski has written of the Trobrianders, ". . . the more brothers the merrier for each sister, the more sisters the less endowment for them."[35]

COMMUNES

The idealistic urge to break away from family exclusiveness is old in Western civilization. We have seen that family and kinship have predominated as the almost universal means of internally organizing human societies and of allocating status and accessibility of privilege, power, and con-

---

[34]M. Fortes, "Time and Social Structure: An Ashanti Case Study," in M. Fortes (ed.), *Social Structure*, p. 75.

[35]B. Malinowski, *Coral Gardens and Their Magic*, vol. 1, p. 189.

FIG. 11-6 The commune kitchen at The New Buffalo, a New Mexico "family" of three dozen members in 1970. (Dennis Stock, Magnum.)

sumable resources. With advancing civilization, kinship recedes in relative importance, while more universalistic modes of social identity come to the fore. Still, down to the nineteenth century in the West, and to the twentieth century in China, the family and the extended kinship group remained the virtually unchallenged vehicle of living, reproducing, and inheriting.

Until the Russian revolution of 1917, challenges to conventional family organization came from small prototype movements of limited success and duration, engendered by intellectual idealists, both religious and sectarian. The Shakers of Mt. Lebanon, New York, founded in 1787, lived in "family" units of fifty or sixty "brothers" and "sisters," housed by sex in two separate buildings and maintaining themselves by gardening, fruit preserving, and craftwork. The Shakers, however, suppressed sexuality and allowed for no matings among their members. New members were added through adult conversion and the adoption of children. Other notable family communes with a religious focus are the Amana, Hutterites, Harmonists, Zoarites, Perfectionists, and United Order.[36]

Current communes of the counterculture movement are more in the stream of the socialistic utopias of New Harmony, founded by Robert Owen in Indiana, Ohio, and New York between 1820 and 1828. They all represent withdrawal from urban industrialism to bucolic romanticism. The socialistic communes of the last century placed high value on work and common sharing. Contemporary youth communes seem more to emphasize common intimacy of feeling and being, with less value placed on work. It is too soon to

tell whether they foreshadow a new trend in organization of family life or whether they will be no more than a marginal fad of passing historical interest. In the last chapter of this book we shall return to this subject as we look beyond today's civilization.

SELECTED READINGS

Belo, J., "A Study of a Balinese Family" (*American Anthropologist*, vol. 38, 1936), pp. 12–31. An account based upon firsthand observation.

Bohannan, P. J., and J. Middleton (eds.), *Marriage, Family, and Residence* (1968). An excellently chosen collection of papers by a number of leading contemporary anthropologists. The most useful single supplementary source for the subject of this chapter.

Fortes, M., *The Web of Kinship among the Tallensi* (1949), chaps. 6 and 8, "Husband and Wife in the Structure of the Family" and "The Relationship of Parent and Child." An excellent study.

Geertz, H., *The Javanese Family* (1961). A modern descriptive account of life within the family circle, with an analysis of the family within the kinship structure.

Goody, J. (ed.), *The Developmental Cycle in Domestic Groups* (1958). The product of joint examination by a group of anthropologists of what happens in families and other domestic groups during the natural history of the family group. Covers a variety of societies.

LaBarre, W., *The Human Animal* (1954). Brilliantly written, this book presents a biosocial theory of the development and essential nature of family relationships.

Mead, M., *Male and Female* (1949). A provocative and interesting synthesis of the author's field studies and views on family relationships in seven primitive cultures and in the United States.

Schneider, D. M., and K. Gough (eds.), *Matrilineal Kinship* (1961). Although this book is focused on kinship rather than on the family per se, it contains a good deal on family structure in matrilineal societies.

---

[36]See D. W. Douglas and K. du P. Lumpkin, "Communistic Settlements" (*Encyclopaedia of the Social Sciences*, vol. 4, 1931), pp. 95–102.

12

THE EXTENSION OF KINSHIP

Lineages

I

A B

1 2 3 4

a b c d e f g h

LEARNING GOALS

Comment on the effects of the bilateral and unilateral modes as ways of organizing extended kinship groups in human societies. ¶ Show how an American kindred, such as the one you belong to, differs from a Samoan *ramage*. ¶ Describe the lineage, clan, moiety, and phratry as major forms of unilineal groups in social organization. ¶ Specify seven social functions of unilineal kinship groups. ¶ Trace the relative frequency of different types of descent groups according to levels of subsistence development in social evolution.

One of anthropology's most fascinating discoveries is that the seemingly simple matter of descent and kinship can be so variously perceived, so intricately defined, and assigned so central a role in the ordering of many total cultures. Yet, the contemporary Western cultural bias toward individually achieved identity seems to produce a general impatience with the anthropological stress on the many forms and complexities of kinship relations. It is a hard fact, however, that it is simply impossible to understand the workings of most past and present societies without grasping their approach to kinship—kinship systems, kinship functions, kinship terms. (Many unsuccessful economic, political, and developmental missions attest to this truth.) Therefore, we must look in detail at how kinship operates.

The family tie nowhere ends with parents and children, for parents have their parents, grandparents, uncles, aunts, brothers, sisters, and cousins to whom the bond of kinship extends. In all societies, the cementing effect of these bonds is strong enough to produce a network of special relations between relatives that makes the relationship group distinguishable as an entity within the larger society.

In primitive societies and most non-Western civilizations, the kinship bond is likely to override all others. Behavior toward relatives is not the same as behavior toward nonrelatives. Rich uncles win special deference. People always have certain obligations to their kinsmen. The status of a relative is unique, compared with that of the rest of mankind.

As a striking manifestation of this fundamental fact, E. E. Evans-Pritchard observed:

If you wish to live among the Nuer, you must do so on their terms, which means that you must treat them as a kind of kinsmen and they will treat you as a kind of kinsman. Rights, privileges and obligations are determined by kinship. Either a man is a kinsman, actually or by fiction, or he is a person to whom you have no reciprocal obligations and whom you treat as a potential enemy.[1]

Because we live in an industrialized society of great social mobility, in which we depend to a great degree upon our own efforts and those of mutual-aid associations (insurance and benevolent societies), unions, and philanthropic and governmental agencies to provide social security,

---

[1]E. E. Evans-Pritchard, *The Nuer*, p. 182. By permission of Oxford University Press.

rather than our relatives, it is hard for most of us to comprehend the importance of kinsmen in simpler societies. In primitive society, most of these responsibilities rest with the kinship group.

The contrast is philosophically stated by an old Pomo Indian of California, who soliloquized:

What is a man? A man is nothing. Without his family he is of less importance than that bug crossing the trail, of less importance than the sputum or exuviae. At least *they* can be used to help poison a man. A man must be with his family to amount to anything with us. If he had nobody else to help him, the first trouble he got into he would be killed by his enemies, because there would be no relatives to help him fight the poison of the other group. No woman would marry him. . . . He would be poorer than a new-born child, he would be poorer than a worm. . . . The family is important. If a man has a large family, . . . and upbringing by a family that is known to produce good children, then he is somebody and every family is willing to have him marry a woman of their group. In the White way of doing things the family is not so important. The police and soldiers take care of protecting you, the courts give you justice, the post office carries messages for you, the school teaches you. Everything is taken care of, even your children, if you die; but with us the family must do all of that.

Without the family we are nothing, and in the old days before the White people came, the family was given first consideration by anyone who was about to do anything at all. That is why we got along. . . .

With us the family was everything. Now it is nothing. We are getting like the White people and it is bad for the old people. We had no old people's home like you. The old people were important. They were wise. Your old people must be fools.[2]

In India a Hyderabad farmer repeats the refrain, "Without castemen and kinsmen to support him, a man is as good as dead. No one will marry him; no one will help him in times of trouble; no one will complete his karma when he dies."[3] And among the Mossi, a proverb-loving tribe on the Upper Volta River in West Africa, the folk saying runs, "A chicken isn't very big without his feath-ers," meaning "Always have some relatives with you in court."

Kinship provides a major category of building blocks as the foundation of all hitherto existing societies.

PRINCIPLES OF EXTENDED KINSHIP

The conjugal-natal family, although it is the seed-bed of society, is itself always embedded within a larger series of kinship groupings. These are the *kindred*, the *ramage*, the *lineage*, the *clan*, the *phratry*, and the *moiety*. Many societies, including those of Europe and their derivatives in North and South America, and such societies as the Eskimo, Ifugao, and Comanche, extend kinship only so far as the kindred. Many more build on the lineage and clan; a smaller number combine lineages and clans within moieties and phratries. What are these groups and how are they organized?

The basic division rests on the distinction between the *bilateral* and *unilineal* principles. A *bilateral* kinship group is one in which members receive their identity through the bond of descent reckoned from both parents. A *unilineal kinship group* is one in which members receive their identity through the bond of descent reckoned asymmetrically through lines of males or females. If descent is reckoned from father to sons to son's sons, etc., the system is patrilineal. If descent is reckoned from mother to daughter to daughter's daughter, the system is matrilineal. A *unilineal kinship system* is one in which all the kinship groups are either matrilineal *or* patrilineal. If patrilineal *and* matrilineal kinship groups exist side by side within the same society, the system is one of *dual* or *double descent*.

BILATERAL, OR COGNATIC, KINSHIP: THE KINDRED

The kindred expresses the bilateral principle in its most direct and undifferentiated form. In the largest sense, one's kindred includes every person to whom one can trace a genealogical bond. It includes all one's *cognates*, i.e., everyone who can be traced as related through a common relative, whether ancestral or contemporary, whether male or female. It spreads in all directions, and in a small tribe, pushing a bilateral

[2]B. W. Aginsky, "An Indian's Soliloquy" (*American Journal of Sociology*, vol. 46, 1940), pp. 43–44. By permission of University of Chicago Press.

[3]P. G. Hiebert, *Konduru*, p. 13. By permission of University of Minnesota Press, Minneapolis. Copyright © 1971, the University of Minnesota. *Karma* is a person's destiny or "fate" which has been determined by actions in a previous incarnation.

genealogy to its ultimate limits could result in the inclusion of every member of the tribe as a relative. Comanche Indians, for one people, explicitly recognized this and gave it as a reason for not identifying as members of their kindred those cognates who lay beyond the bilateral degree of second cousin.

A kindred as a functioning unit never organizes such a heterogeneous crowd as all potential relatives. Because cognate relationships ramify in all directions and multiply geometrically, their boundaries are too inclusive. They become so thin at the farthest edges that the definition of relationship is lost in the mists of uncertainty and vagueness. Consequently, anthropologists have found it very difficult to identify the actual, functioning kindreds in the societies where they are significant. The kindred is rather like a pool of personnel from which groups of individuals coalesce for specific cooperative activities, such as work parties, revenge groups, exchange groups, households, and transition rites. The composition of the actual kindred shifts and changes, dissolving and reappearing in altered form, depending on who among the kinsmen counts himself in for the occasion. Kindreds are flexible cells which are highly adaptable to fluid and relatively unstructured situations. They tend to be characteristic of simple hunting and gathering societies with limited resources, on the one hand, and of industrialized, free-market, urban civilizations, on the other.

Murdock describes the kindred very well for America:

In our own society, where its members are collectively called "kinfolk" or "relatives," it includes that group of near kinsmen who may be expected to be present and participant on important ceremonial occasions, such as weddings, christenings, funerals, Thanksgiving and Christmas dinners, and "family reunions." Members of a kindred visit and entertain one another freely, and between them marriage and pecuniary transactions for profit are ordinarily taboo. One turns to them first for aid when one finds oneself in difficulties. However much they may disagree or quarrel, they are expected to support one another against criticism or affronts from outsiders.[4]

While the bilateral kinship system appears to work satisfactorily in those societies which use it, it does have inherent limitations and disadvantages, which have been summed up by Murdock as follows:

A particular disadvantage of the kindred appears in the instances in which an individual belongs to the kindreds of two other persons and thereby becomes involved in conflicting or incompatible obligations. If they got into serious difficulties with one another, for example, he may be required to avenge the one and yet to defend the other. If they become estranged, both are likely to turn to him for support and to subject him to emotional conflict and strain. The reader can supply numerous examples from the rankling family quarrels in our own society.[5]

The Occurrence of Bilateral Kinship

Because we are so accustomed in Western society to reckoning our kinfolk or relatives bilaterally (we are equally "related" to our paternal and maternal families), it is easy to assume that this type of family pattern is universal and/or best. On the contrary, only about one-third of all human societies build their social structures on this foundation.

In Sub-Saharan Africa, where most tribes are gardeners or pastoralists, only one in twenty societies is based on the kindred. By contrast, two-thirds and three-fourths of the tribes of North and South America, respectively, were (or are) bilaterally structured. (See Fig. 12-1.)

Nonunilineal Kinship: The Ramage

The ramage is a blending of lineage organization in such a way that anthropologists have come to call the result *nonunilinear organization*. First, the ramage utilizes the lineage principle: a person claiming ramage membership must be able to trace unilineal descent from the putative founder of the ramage. This might seem to make the ramage a unilineal unit. But, second, a person may trace descent *either* patrilineally or matrilineally, according to convenience and the acceptability of the claim to existing members of the

---

[4]G. P. Murdock, *Social Structure*, pp. 56–57. Copyright © 1949, the Macmillan Co. Quoted with permission.

[5]*Ibid.*, p. 61. Copyright © 1949, the Macmillan Co. Quoted with permission.

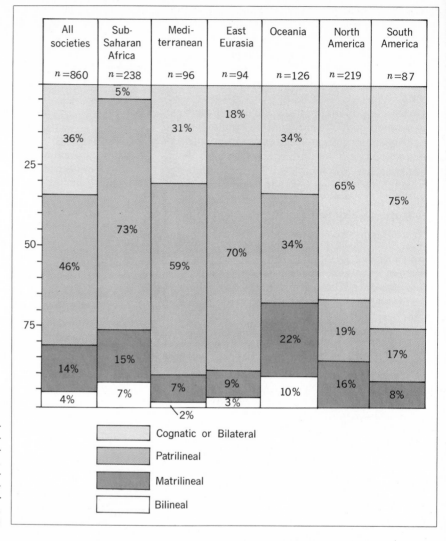

	All societies	Sub-Saharan Africa	Medi-terranean	East Eurasia	Oceania	North America	South America
	$n=860$	$n=238$	$n=96$	$n=94$	$n=126$	$n=219$	$n=87$

Cognatic or Bilateral: 36%, 5%, 31%, 18%, 34%, 65%, 75%

Patrilineal: 46%, 73%, 59%, 70%, 34%, 19%, 17%

Matrilineal: 14%, 15%, 7%, 9%, 22%, 16%, 8%

Bilineal: 4%, 7%, 2%, 3%, 10%

Legend:
- Cognatic or Bilateral
- Patrilineal
- Matrilineal
- Bilineal

FIG. 12-1 Relative frequency of forms of kinship organization according to geographic area. (Data from E. Bourguignon and L. Greenbaum, *Diversity and Homogeneity*, table 29, p. 51.)

ramage. Some members of the ramage get their identity as members through their mothers, others through their fathers. Hence the paradoxical lineal nonunilineality of the system. Murdock calls *ramages* "ancestor oriented *ambilineal* kingroups."[6]

Ramages have a stronger corporate quality than do most kindreds. They own land and other valued prerogatives. Hence, explicit ramage

membership can have more definite advantages for the individual. Conversely, the ramage is more inclined to be demanding on its membership and, at the same time, to be choosy about whom it acknowledges as rightful members.

To use the Samoan ramage as an example:

The Samoan *'aiga sa* [pronounced *ainga sa*] is a descent group controlling garden land, house sites, and certain ceremonials. It is exogamous, since the incest taboo is extended to all known relatives. Associated with each *'aiga sa* is one or more titles, from the senior of which

---

[6]G. P. Murdock, *Ethnographic Atlas*, p. 49.

the group takes its name. Title holders are selected from among the eligible males participating with the group. Affiliation with a descent group is through either father or mother, and a married couple may affiliate with the groups of either spouse. A person is mainly associated with one group—that with which he lives—but he may participate to some extent in several. Living with and using lands belonging to a particular 'aiga sa, as well as the right to speak at meetings of the group, are dependent upon the consent of its members, and this may be denied if there is doubt about a person's genealogical relationship to the group or if he has failed to fulfill his obligations to it. Here, too, indefinitely extended relationships through consanguinity become limited by the obligations of participation. Even though there is considerable overlapping membership, the number of potential affiliations is appreciably reduced by both remissness in obligations and failure to remember genealogical connections.[7]

The Samoan example is particularly apt, for half the societies in which ramages have been recognized are Oceanic. It could be that island ecology imposes limitation of available land for gardeners. Land is, therefore, highly valued. Thus, the exclusionary (yet flexible) membership qualifications, along with corporate land-holding, make the ramage a useful social response to the situation.

In spite of the great interest in nonunilineal descent stirred up among professional anthropologists since the late 1950's, the ramage is actually very rare. Only 31 of the 310 cognatic societies in the *Ethnographic Atlas* have ramages. And this is

---

[7]W. Davenport, "Nonunilinear Descent and Descent Groups" (*American Anthropologist*, vol. 61, 1959), p. 56. Quoted with permission.

but 3.6 per cent (31 in 860 societies) of all the societies in the sample.

THE UNILINEAL PRINCIPLE OF KINSHIP

The majority of human societies—two-thirds of those represented in the *World Ethnographic Sample*—are organized around the unilineal principle of kinship. One-third, including that of the United States, is bilateral (see Table 12-1). The popularity of the unilineal principle indicates that as an adaptive invention, it serves well in overcoming some of the difficulties inherent in the kindred (vagueness of membership, unwieldy ramification, and competing obligations at times of conflict) and in the ramage (exclusionary practices and possible conflict of identity and loyalty). By figuring descent through one parental line, kinship becomes more clearcut, and societies needing to rely on kinship groups to perform most of their basic functions are able to develop more predictable and reliable social patterns.

In a *patrilineal* system, the children of both sexes belong to the group of their father, which is, in turn, the group of his father's father, his father's father's father, and so on, as far back as genealogies are kept. The children of the man's sons and of the sons' sons, and so on, belong to the same group, as long as the line does not die out or break up.

In a *matrilineal* system, the children of both sexes belong to the group of their mother, which is, in turn, the group of her mother's mother, her mother's mother's mother, and so on, as far back as genealogies are kept. The relationship is *uter-*

TABLE 12-1   PER CENT OF OCCURRENCE OF TYPES OF DESCENT GROUPS IN A SAMPLE OF 505 SOCIETIES, CLASSIFIED BY DOMINANT TYPE OF SUBSISTENCE BASE

Type of Subsistence Base	Bilateral	Patrilineal	Matrilineal	Duolineal	Number of Tribes in Sample
Plow agriculture	32%	59%	8%	1%	117
Pastoralism	12%	77%	5%	6%	66
Developed agriculture	35%	35%	25%	5%	188
Incipient agriculture	45%	34%	15%	6%	33
Hunting and gathering	61%	19%	13%	7%	101

SOURCE: Data selected and converted to percentages from D.M. Schneider and K. Gough (eds.), *Matrilineal Kinship,* table 17-4, p. 677.

ine. The children of the woman's daughters and of the daughters' daughters, and so on, belong to the same group, as long as the line does not die out or break up.

Each unilineal kinship group is a collective body, a corporate entity, that endures through the ages. It may have a definite beginning, but it has the potential of unending endurance—unlike the conjugal-natal family. Unilineal kinship membership is therefore a matter of predetermined social heredity. One does not ordinarily join a unilineal group, for it is not a voluntary association. One is born into it perforce. The social fiction of adoption may make possible a change in unilineal affiliation, however. Unilineal group membership is discriminating and exclusive. It arbitrarily segments the population of a tribe; it separates genetic relatives into kinsmen and nonkinsmen. In compensation, it cements the genetic relatives who are included within the unilineal group into a firmer bond of kinship than is possible through bilateral extension of the family.

In a tribe segmented into lineages, sibs, or moieties . . . the individual knows exactly where he stands. . . . If both disputants are members of his own kin group, he is expected to remain neutral and to use his good offices to compose their differences. If neither is a member, the affair is none of his business. If one is a member but the other is not, he is expected to support his sibmate, regardless of the rights in the matter. In short, most conflict situations are simply and automatically resolved.[8]

In ceremony, economic activity, legal fracas and dispute, inheritance, and marriage, as these are related to kinship, the place and roles of members of unilineal groups are clear-cut.

A further consequence of the inclusive-exclusive character of unilineality is the sharp division it makes among cousins. Cross-cousins can never belong to the same unilineal group, although parallel-cousins may. This is what makes cross-cousin marriage possible.

Types of Unilineal Kinship Groups

The simplest type of unilineal group is known as the *lineage.* A lineage is an extended unilineal

kinship group descended from a known ancestor, or founder, who ordinarily lived not more than five or six generations back. He, in the case of the patrilineage, or she, in the case of the matrilineage, is a real person and not a mythological or legendary figure. On the next level, above the lineage, there is the *clan.* A clan is an enlarged unilineal kinship group that rests on the fiction of common descent from a founding ancestor who lived so far in the distant past as to be mythological. When a tribal society is divided into two unilineal halves, each half is called a *moiety* (Fr. *moitié,* half), and the structure is known as *dual division.* Finally, there are *phratries* (Gr. *phratria,* brother): linked groups of clans, where there are more than two such groups in the tribe. (If there were only two, they would be moieties.)

The possible extended unilineal groups are therefore (1) the lineage, (2) the clan, (3) the moiety, and (4) the phratry.

The lineage

The lineage is the simplest form of extended unilineal kinship group in that it normally is limited to closely related agnatic (male descent line) or uterine (female descent line) kin and is rarely more than six generations deep. The "begats" of Genesis chapters 5 and 10 reflect the ancient Hebrew method of counting descent within agnatic lineages.

Lineages may be divided and subdivided into smaller segments. In such cases, they are called *segmentary lineages.* In a common African form, such as described for the Nuer by Evans-Pritchard,[9] each lineage is divided into two secondary lineages, which bifurcate into four tertiary lineages, which bifurcate into eight quaternary (or minimal) lineages. (See Fig. 12-2). When a minimal lineage fights with its opposite lineage (e.g., *a* versus *b*), no one else is directly involved except a local Priest of the Earth, who will evoke a settlement if anyone is killed. But if *a* becomes involved in a fight with lineages of *c* or *d,* then *a* and *b* join as segments of *1* to fight with *2.* If *1* gets into a dispute with *3* or *4,* *2* will join it as a segment of *A* against *B.* But all will join together as a maximal lineage, *I,* against all other maximal lin-

---

[8]G. P. Murdock, *Social Structure,* p. 61. Copyright © 1949, the Macmillan Co. Quoted with permission.

[9]E. E. Evans-Pritchard, *The Nuer.*

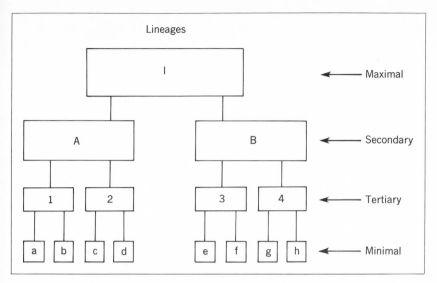

Lineages

I ← Maximal

A B ← Secondary

1 2 3 4 ← Tertiary

a b c d e f g h ← Minimal

FIG. 12-2 Bifurcating segmentary lineage relations. A and B are secondary segments of the maximal lineage, 1. These in turn are segmented into two tertiary lineages each, which in turn segment into two minimal lineages each.

eages. Such intensive lineage activity prevails in segmentary societies with weak central governments.

In general terms, the subdivisions of any lineage segment may quarrel with one another but unite against all other segments on the same level.

Lineages may or may not reside as territorially based units. Localized minimal lineages usually form joint-family households or compounds.

Modern recognition of the lineage as a key structure in many social systems is due largely to the influence of A. R. Radcliffe-Brown and the work done in the field by anthropologists who were trained by him.

The clan

Apart from size, the only essential difference between a lineage and a clan is that the members of a lineage can actually trace out their genealogies of common descent from a known ancestor, while clan members cannot. Nevertheless, if they belong to a given clan, people believe they have common descent, and their behavior is regulated accordingly.

Very often, however, the folklore of the clan includes a myth, as a part of its "charter," purporting to give a truthful account of how the clan came to be.

DAHOMEAN CLANS Thus among the patrilineal Dahomeans of West Africa, one clan was founded by the son of a horse "who, bounding from the water in a fury of passion, lay with a woman on the bank of the river." Another clan is said to have descended from the "offspring of a woman and a pig, another from that of a woman and a toad, one from that of a woman and a dog, and the royal family . . . originated from the mating of a female leopard with the King of Adja." Another clan is said to have been created when a peanut was magically transformed into a man, who then mated with a poor woman who lived on roots. Dahomeans believe that the members of the Peanut clan lack the fine, smooth skin of other Dahomeans: "It is rough like the shell of a peanut." Further, the members of the Peanut clan are said to be recognizable on sight.[10] How this can be genetically possible in view of clan exogamy is a little difficult to understand, but ideological stereotypes can dogmatically color perception.

The members of a Dahomean clan have a rather special set of attitudes toward the animal or plant creature who begat their clan founder. All clans revere their clan founder and his descendants, who are their ancestors. All Dahomean clans

[10]M. J. Herskovits and F. S. Herskovits, *An Outline of Dahomean Religious Belief* (American Anthropological Association, Memoir 41, 1933), pp. 24–27.

except one abjure the flesh of the animal species associated with the founder, and many of them bear the name of the founder. All these features give the clans a totemic tinge.

CROW CLANS The usages of the Crow Indians illustrate a different kind of clan-origin legend. The clan names are taken from certain alleged exploits of the founders, after the manner of a Plains Indian warrior who bestows names on children memorializing outstanding events in his life. It would be quite a mistake to jump to the conclusion that members of the Crow "Greasy-inside-of-their-mouths" clan are slippery-tongued, for the name is actually honorific. The clan founder was such a provident hunter that he was always surfeited with rich, fat meat. It is said that his mouth was so coated with fat that when he spat in the campfire, his saliva flared up in the flames. Other Crow clan names memorialize alleged historical incidents or clan characteristics. The Piegan clan was originally called "They-eat-their-own-mucus." When some members of this clan once abandoned a wounded comrade in battle, they were dubbed "Piegan," meaning that they acted like the Piegan enemies, *not* a complimentary epithet from the Crow point of view.[11]

In all these instances, and in similar ones which could be drawn from a multitude of tribes, the actual origin of the clan is lost in the hoary past; this is not the case with lineages. Lineages may exist with or without clans. Clans may also exist with or without institutionalized lineages within them. Iroquois clans are made up of related groups of maternal lineages; the lineages are localized for the most part in long-house groupings. Very often lineage heads constitute the clan council, if there is one. In most parts of Indonesia, lineages are the basic functional group, for lineages or subclans form the localized village, while the clans have a more regional character.

The moiety

Reciprocity is the basis of all social relationships, for there can be no social relations without interaction. Human beings are so constituted that the isolated person is not a complete human being.

They are also so constituted that dependence without interdependence is not readily or for long accepted by the giver of services. The individual who gives would also receive. The individual who receives is also expected to give in return. Through the building of a network of giving and receiving of services, a society expands its potentialities (see Reciprocal Gift Exchange, pages 256–260).

The principle of reciprocity is therefore operative in all societies. However, some societies are content to have it remain implicit in their cultures without placing much formal emphasis upon it. Others, such as the Trobriand Islanders and many other Melanesians, go to great lengths to institutionalize reciprocity and focus the spotlight of social awareness upon it.

One of the most effective ways of institutionalizing reciprocity is to organize the society on a moiety basis. Moieties are generally exogamous (except in the traditional Middle East, including North Africa); each moiety supplies the other with its marriage partners. Other reciprocal services are invariably linked to the moiety alignments. Moieties thus effectively control certain types of behavior and serve to give concrete form to the reciprocity principle.

In cases where there are only two clans in a tribe, such as the Water and Land groups of the Central Miwok in California, clan and moiety are automatically synonymous. Multiple clans are the more common order, however, and when clans are linked to moieties, the moiety is the larger unit, and the clans are subdivisions of the moieties. Most of the Iroquois tribes have this kind of arrangement. Among the Seneca, to take a typical example, the Bear, Wolf, Turtle, and Beaver clans constitute one moiety, and the Deer, Snipe, Heron, and Hawk constitute the other. Originally, the moieties were exogamous, but in recent centuries they have lost their control over marriage, and only the clans have retained the exogamous rule. Each moiety performs the important mourning rituals on behalf of the other; the moieties compete against each other in the old Indian game of lacrosse, which is as much a ceremonial ritual as it is a sport. On the other hand, they do not enter into the political structure, although clans and lineages do.

Many American tribes possessing moieties as-

---

[11]R. H. Lowie, *The Crow Indians*, pp. 15–16.

sociate them with the duality of the cosmos: sky and earth, water and land, winter and summer, red and white (war and peace). This may be seen as merely another way of objectifying the principle of reciprocity in the minds of the people.

The phratry

The clans in a phratry system retain their separate identities, but each clan in a phratry feels some sort of special identity to the others within its phratry. Moreover, they may have special obligations to fulfill toward one another.

The Hopi Indians have a large number of matrilineal clans, which are loosely linked into twelve exogamous phratries. The Aztecs, for their part, had four phratries embracing a number of clans among them. The Aztec phratries were important political and religious divisions in the structure of the empire, and they thus played a significant part in the social life of the people.

Nevertheless, it may be said that in general, phratry organization is a relatively rare and functionally insignificant phenomenon. It does not usually control marriage, although Crow Indians think that it is better if members of the same phratry do not intermarry. Still, they have no prohibition against such action. For the most part, the phratry sentiment seems to rest either on a tradition of common origin or on common interests in ceremonial activity.

The Universal Functions of Unilineal Groups

Unilineal groups, except for the phratry, have two universal functions: (1) to broaden the base of the security group founded on the kinship bond by providing mutual aid and collective protection and liability in legal action and disputes, and (2) to regulate and control marriage.

Mutual aid and security

The lineage, clan, or moiety provides a large mutual-aid-organization rooted in kinship. A human being never stands alone. In seeking a firmer base for personal security than the individual can find without organization of his or her efforts and those of fellow human beings, the individual casts about for some valid common interests that will serve to join with others in a social communion. There can be no doubt that the most generalized interest served by the clan is that of fulfilling the desire for security. The family, as we noted earlier, is the primary incubator of personal security. The clan expands this fundamental function of the family while at the same time tightening up the structure by reducing the diffusive effects of bilateral extension.

To meet the needs of security, lineages usually present a solid front to the rest of the world. In personal interrelations with all persons outside the lineage, every lineage member must ideally be aided, abetted, and protected by all other members. This is the source of feuding in many societies and the primary defect of so many tribal legal systems (see Chapter 17).

As a complement of its united protection of individual members, the lineage or clan frequently is collectively liable for the illegal acts of its own members against members of other clans or lineages. Thus, if a man commits murder, vengeance may commonly be taken on any member of the lineage, for even though he is innocent in fact, his person is legally merged with the persons of all his fellow kinsmen.

The regulation of marriage

The second universal function of the unilineal kinship group is to regulate marriage by means of exogamy, or, especially in the Middle East, through endogamy.[12] This, if we follow Malinowski's hypothesis, is a self-protective device that ensures solidarity by directing the sexual drive toward persons outside the essential kinship group.

We must not, however, overlook the fact that an additional security device is to be found in clan exogamy. Marriage imposes affinal obligations on the spouse's kin and clan. It tends to reduce overt aggression between the maritally allied groups; it also extends the base of support on which a human being may depend (see Chapter 10, pages 176–177).

---

[12]R. Patai, *Golden River to Golden Road: Society, Culture, and Change in the Middle East*, pp. 428–436.

Secondary Functions of Unilineal Groups

In addition to the broad and universal functions mentioned above, clans carry responsibilities in the maintenance of culture. Both the nature of these responsibilities and the means of carrying them out vary from culture to culture. However, in general, these secondary functions cover a broad range of legal, governmental, economic, religious, and symbolic purposes.

Legal functions

The lineage or clan commonly represents its individual members in lawsuits and is, conversely, responsible for their illegal acts. This function is discussed in detail in Chapter 17.

Governmental functions

A function that the clan may or may not take on is that of government or law. The Aztec clan heads, called *speakers*, made up the Aztec tribal council. This group controlled ordinary political decisions, made war and peace, and as a judicial body decided disputes between clans and members of different clans. These same clan speakers sat on the grand national council, whose jurisdiction covered the most important law cases and election of the king. Aztec clans were grouped in four phratries, each of which had a captain-general, who served as a high-ranking military officer and who, in addition to his military post, served on the grand national council.

Many tribes have raised one clan to the position of royalty, and the hereditary chief must come from this clan. In Melanesia, this is true of the Trobriand Islanders; in Africa, the Dahomeans and the Ashanti are two examples among many.

Among the American Indians, the Winnebago of Wisconsin assigned political functions to seven of their twelve clans. The tribal chief was selected from the Thunderbird clan. In addition, this clan performed important functions connected with the preservation of peace (its governmental functions were mainly civil). The Warrior clan, as its name implies, provided war leadership; the village and hunt policemen came from the Bear clan; and the camp crier and aide-de-camp for the chief was always selected from the Buffalo clan. The

Wolf, Water-spirit, and Elk clans had lesser political tasks. This was true not only of the Winnebago but also of the other highly organized Siouan tribes.[13]

Economic functions

Among clan-organized tribes practicing hoe culture, the garden lands are almost inevitably owned or administered by the clans. Each Aztec clan owned its specific segment of the land. Assignments for use were made by the clan headman, who kept a record of all holdings. Every family head had the right to a plot of land (unless he had forfeited his clan membership by refusing to marry or carry out his clan obligations, in which case he became a common proletarian laborer). As long as a clansman was in good standing, he could use his land or rent it to a fellow clansman (but not to an outsider). He could allot it to a clan descendant by testamentary disposition, but he could not alienate it (i.e., pass title to an outsider), for ownership of title was vested in the clan. He had what a lawyer would call a *possessory right of usufruct*, but not ownership. This same land-use system by clans prevails throughout Indonesia at this very time; it is also prevalent in Africa.

Clans may own other material goods in common, such as temples, meetinghouses, and sacred and ceremonial objects (see Chapter 15).

Religious and ceremonial functions

Clans or lineages may have their own supernatural beings and devices for controlling the supernatural world for their own ends, or they may possess certain ritual paraphernalia and ceremonies that they are expected to use for the well-being of the whole society.

Ancestor-worshiping Africans who have clan organization represent the first situation. The deceased clan ancestors are elevated to the status of clan deities. The clan head is usually the chief priest of the clan and the intermediary between his kinsmen and the ancestral spirits.

Among the Hopi and Zuñi, the all-important

---

[13]P. Radin, *The Winnebago Tribe* (Bureau of American Ethnology, Annual Report 37, 1923).

ceremonial organization is inextricably inter-twined with the clan system; each clan must perform its part of the ceremonial activities for the benefit of the whole pueblo. Winnebago clans possess sacred bundles of religious paraphernalia used in ceremonial activity. These are examples of the second kind of situation.

Totemic functions

Finally, clans may have totemic associations involving a feeling of identity with a plant, animal, or other natural object. This bond of emotional identity may extend from a mere feeling of kinship to actual reverence and worship. It may also lead to symbolic representation of the totemic object in clan fetishes.

DUAL (DOUBLE) DESCENT[14]

Prior to 1927, anthropologists thought that a society could embrace only one clan system, which had to be either matrilineal or patrilineal. Evidence to the contrary first came to the attention of English-reading anthropologists in R. S. Rattray's studies of the Ashanti, who were shown by this keen student of African tribes to have matrilineal clans called *abusua* and patrilineal groups called *ntoro*. The ntoro principle of inheritance is associated with the semen, and although the ntoro group is not organized, it, like the abusua, regulates marriage and sets certain incest prohibitions. It is totemic and imposes certain food tabus on its members.[15]

A subsequent report by Forde on another African tribe, the Umor, analyzes an even more precise system of dual descent.[16] The Umoran patrilineal, virilocal clan determines house and land affiliation and is called the *kepun*. There are twenty-two of these. At the same time, there are four *yajima* (plural form), which are matrilineal,

nonlocalized clans through which movable property—principally livestock and currency—is inherited and marriage exchanges (progeny price and dowry) are made. "A man eats in his kepun and inherits in his lejima [singular form]," is the native adage. Murdock has put the phenomenon into focus by showing that double descent has a widely scattered distribution in Africa, India, Australia, Melanesia, and Polynesia.[17]

Ten per cent of the Oceanic tribes use double-descent systems, as do 7 per cent of the African societies; it is totally absent from the New World, giving a worldwide frequency of only 4 per cent.[18]

That it took English-speaking anthropologists so long to discover double descent shows how difficult it is for even carefully trained scientists to formulate conceptions necessary to the perception of new facts when those facts are completely alien to their experience and cultural background.

LINEAGE AND CLAN IN SOCIAL EVOLUTION

In the evolutionary theories of the nineteenth century, a major issue was whether matrilineal or patrilineal clans came first in the evolution of human society. Morgan, followed by Marx and Engels, argued that matrilineal systems took priority in a kind of communistic elysium. Patriliny, according to Marx and Engels, followed after the introduction of paired marriages, whereupon men were no longer content to pass their property collaterally to their sisters' sons. They established patrilineal inheritance, initiated private property in their domesticated herds, introduced slavery, and subordinated women to patriarchal domination. These practices resulted in what Engels called the first great social revolution and "the world-historical defeat of the female sex"[19] against which today's Women's Liberation Movement is contending. Bachofen also argued for the priority of the maternal clan in his work *Das*

---

[14]Also called *duolineal descent* and *double unilineal descent*.

[15]R. S. Rattray, *Ashanti; Ashanti Law and Constitution*. Dual descent as found in a neighboring people is explicitly examined in detail in a monograph by J. B. Christensen, *Double Descent among the Fanti*.

[16]C. D. Forde, "Kinship in Umor: Double Unilateral Organization in a Semi-Bantu Society" (*American Anthropologist*, vol. 41, 1939), pp. 523–553.

[17]G. P. Murdock, "Double-Descent" (*American Anthropologist*, vol. 42, 1940), pp. 555–561. See also J. Goody, "The Classification of Double Descent Systems" (*Current Anthropology*, vol. 2, 1961), pp. 3–26.

[18]E. Bourguignon and L. Greenbaum, *Diversity and Homogeneity*, table 29, p. 51.

[19]F. Engels, *The Origin of the Family, Property and the State in the Light of the Researches of Lewis Henry Morgan*, p. 50.

Mutterrecht (The Motherright). Others, such as McLennan, claimed that the patrilineal clan with patriarchal rule came first. In the Western world, the battle has long since been stilled,[20] but Communist anthropologists in Russia still hold faithfully to Engels' interpretation of Morgan.

Of course, there is no way of knowing from direct observation just what prehistoric social organization was like. Archaeological data can tell us what the technological traditions of a given locale were; they can reveal the outlines of settlement patterns; and they can yield exciting treasures of art, as well as the bones of human beings and animals. But in the absence of historical records, they tell us little of certainty about beliefs, values, marriage practices, kinship, inheritance, economic exchange, mythology, religion, ceremonialism, government, or law.

As for descent groups, bilateral, patrilineal, matrilineal, and double-descent extensions of the kinship group appear on *all* levels of cultural development and in all the major geographic areas of the world.

Among the most primitive or culturally undeveloped tribes . . . the Andamanese pygmies, the Paiute of the Great Basin, and the Yahgan of Tierra del Fuego are bilateral in descent, the Vedda of Ceylon, the Ramkokamekra of east central Brazil, and the Kutchin of northern Canada are matrilineal, and the Witoto of Amazonia, the Gilyak of Siberia, the Miwok of California are patrilineal, while several native Australian tribes are characterized by double descent. All rules of descent are likewise well represented on the intermediate levels of culture, among agricultural and developed pastoral peoples. Even among literate peoples with relatively complex civilizations, our sample includes the bilateral Yankees and Syrian Christians, the patrilineal Chinese and Manchus, and the matrilineal Minangkabau Malays of Sumatra and Brahman Nayars of India.[21]

David Aberle has collated some very relevant data in which the societies represented in the *World Ethnographic Sample* are cross-classified by type (or level) of subsistence techniques and type of descent system.[22] Figure 12-3 shows the percentages of bilateral, matrilineal, patrilineal, and duolineal cultures that occur on each level of subsistence technology.

Descent Groups among Hunters and Gatherers

If hunting and gathering are taken as the most primitive food-getting techniques, such as were characteristic of the cultures of the Paleolithic era, we see that a majority (61 per cent) of such societies are bilateral and that there is no significant difference between the number that are patrilineal and the number that are matrilineal (19 and 13 per cent, respectively). Although 39 per cent of contemporary hunting and gathering cultures are unilineal or duolineal, it is not possible to say of any specific prehistoric culture whether it was organized bilaterally or not, except that the odds are 1.5 to 1 that it was.

Descent Groups among Intensive Foragers

Prehistoric intensive foragers marked the inception of the food revolution and the Era of Incipient Agriculture in the Neolithic Age. Among recent practitioners of hunting, fishing, and subsidiary gardening, there is a rise in the proportion of unilineal systems to 55 per cent. Patrilineality shows a marked increase. Thus, there is a slight trend toward lineages and clans, but it remains impossible to say whether any set of prehistoric foragers was unilineal or bilateral in a situation in which the odds are no greater than 5 to 4 in favor of unilineality over bilateralism.

Descent Groups among Developed Agriculturalists

On the level of developed agriculturalists, unilineality achieves a clear ascendancy: 65 per cent of the societies in the sample are unilineal, but there is no very great difference between matrilineal and patrilineal frequencies (25 per cent matri-

---

[20]R. H. Lowie finally laid the issue to rest in his great synthesis of cultural anthropology, *Primitive Society*, published in 1920. See especially chap. 6.

[21]G. P. Murdock, *Social Structure*, p. 186. Copyright © i949, the Macmillan Co. Quoted with permission.

[22]D. F. Aberle, "Matrilineal Descent in Cross-cultural Perspective," in D. M. Schneider and K. Gough (eds.), *Matrilineal Kinship*, table 17–4, p. 677.

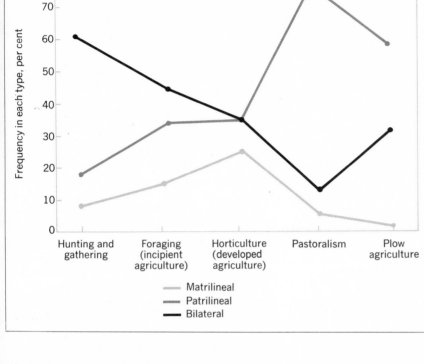

FIG. 12-3 Inferred evolutionary trends in the occurrence of types of descent groups are revealed by the percentage of frequencies of descent groups in societies classified according to subsistence base. Pastoralism is not to be read as a higher evolutionary form than horticulture.

lineal, 35 per cent patrilineal). Matrilineal descent as a principle of social organization reaches its highest peak of frequency among developed agriculturalists, but even so, it is less common than either bilateralism or patrilineality. Gardening obviously encourages the formation of uxorilocal residence, for although women rarely hunt, they are the root and seed gatherers and, quite often, the gardeners. This is all work that can be done while tending a baby. Mothers and daughters work together, and men come to live with their wives. Only in such situations are matrilineal and matrilateral socioeconomic interests sufficiently strong to coalesce into matrilineages and matriclans; "matrilocality is a necessary but not a sufficient condition for the development of matrilineal descent groups. . . .[23] Obviously, a rather unique and quite powerful combination of circumstances is required to overcome the more

usual and effective factors that favor bilateral or patrilineal organization.

Descent Groups among Pastoralists

The intimate relationship between males and livestock is dramatically reflected in the overwhelming patrilineality of pastoralism. Almost four-fifths (77 per cent) of all pastoral cultures are patrilineal.[24] ". . . [T]he cow is the enemy of matriliny, and the friend of patriliny."[25] This is the only safe

[23]Aberle, *op. cit.*, p. 659.

[24]This figure, as given in Figure 12-3, does not include Aberle's category of "New World pastoralists," which consists of societies that acquired domesticated livestock in post-Columbian times. There are 13 such tribes in the total sample of 565. Most of them are horse-herding hunters who were previously bilateral and who had acquired horses so recently that they did not have sufficient time to readjust their descent groups. Of the thirteen tribes, eleven (85 per cent) are bilateral, and two (15 per cent) are matrilineal. New World pastoralism is such an aberrant phenomenon that we have excluded it from the table.

[25]Aberle, *op. cit.*, p. 680.

generalization one could use in reconstructing the kinds of descent groups that were likely to have existed in any prehistoric stage of social evolution. And even this is of slight utility, since pastoralism is characteristic of a relatively minor proportion (12 per cent) of the cultures covered in the *World Ethnographic Sample.*

Descent Groups among Plow Agriculturalists

The hitching of the horse or oxen to the plow is the final step in precivilized evolution of subsistence techniques. It occurred in the Old World Late Neolithic Age. Plow agriculture subordinates the pastoralist's interest in animals to the horticulturalist's concern with farming. This is reflected in a reduction of the degree of frequency of patrilineality among pastoral societies as compared with societies with plow agriculture: from 77 per cent down to 59 per cent. There is a significant rise in bilaterality (12 to 32 per cent) as well as some increase in matrilineality and duolineal organization.

In Western civilization, the shift to bilateralism is a reflection of the influence of urbanization and the invention of the legal instrument of contract, whereby a person is able to stand as a self-determining, individual legal entity rather than as a unit in the corporate kinship group.

As Figure 12-3 graphically reveals, most hunters and gatherers are bilateral, and as one "moves up" the evolutionary scale to developed agriculture, bilateralism declines. The patrilineal curve is the obverse to the bilateral. Matrilineality realizes its highest potential among intensive agriculturalists, but at no level does it ever exceed other forms of descent groups. On the highest level of food production (plow agriculture), it all but disappears.

Looking to the future, as the scientific, industrialized technology of Western civilization is introduced all around the world, it is improbable that any unilineal systems of kinship organization will survive into the twenty-second century, except perhaps in a few peasant areas (see Chapter 24).

SELECTED READINGS

Bohannan, P. J., and J. Middleton (eds.), *Kinship and Social Organization* (1968). Parts II, III, and IV contain basic articles on unilineal, nonunilineal descent and bilateral systems by such authorities as Evans-Pritchard, Firth, Goodenough, Mead, Middleton, and Morgan.

Fortes, M., *The Web of Kinship among the Tallensi* (1949), chaps. 1, 5, and 11, "Kinship and the Lineage System," "Parents and Children in the Framework of the Lineage," and "The Web of Extra-clan Kinship." A masterful analysis of the complexities of kinship in an African tribe.

——, "Structure of Unilinear Descent Groups" (*American Anthropologist*, vol. 55, 1953), pp. 17–44. A most excellent exposition of the application of the unilineal principle in primitive cultures.

Fox, R., *Kinship and Marriage* (1967). Perhaps too advanced for the beginning student, but chapters 3, 4 and 5 will add much content to what has been outlined in the present book.

Goodenough, W. H., *Description and Comparison in Cultural Anthropology* (1970). Chapter 2, "Kindred and Clan," provides a clear-headed discussion of some current problems and thoughts in kinship analysis.

Lowie, R. H., *Primitive Society* (1920), chap. 6, "The Sib." Although this contains some discussions of problems that are no longer live issues in anthropology, the chapter is highly informative.

Murdock, G. P., *Social Structure* (1949), chaps. 3 and 4, "Consanguineal Kin Groups" and "The Clan."

Radcliffe-Brown, A. R., and M. Fortes (eds.), *African Systems of Kinship and Marriage* (1950). Descriptive analyses of a number of African examples of differing types of kinship organization.

Schneider, D. M., and K. Gough (eds.), *Matrilineal Kinship* (1961). An impressive work in which six anthropologists pool their efforts in ethnological examination of a series of matrilineal societies. Schneider proposes a set of hypothetical characteristics of matrilineal systems, Gough interprets the ethnographic data, and Aberle puts their propositions to the statistical test of cross-cultural validation on a broad scale.

13

KINSHIP SYSTEMS AND TERMINOLOGY

LEARNING GOALS

Account for the use of the classificatory principle in the classification of relatives by human beings. ¶ Illustrate the use of the classificatory principle in Comanche Indian kinship terminology. ¶ Explain Kroeber's eight principles of kinship distinctions. ¶ Identify the four types of kinship system based on the ways in which relatives are classified in the parental generation. ¶ Write a brief essay on the American kinship system as you have experienced it.

Kinship behavior is not instinctive. The genetic code says little or nothing about how a man should behave toward his brothers, his father, his cousins, and his aunts. It says little or nothing about how a woman should behave toward her father, her sisters, her mother-in-law, her mother's sister, or any other genealogical relative. Kinship, we have seen, is a matter of social organization, and social organization is an aspect of culture, reflecting ecology, subsistence, ideology, and a host of other things.

Kinship relations consist of the interacting roles customarily ascribed by a people to the different statuses of relationship. Every culture includes a set of words, or labels, symbolizing each of its kinship statuses. These labels are called *kinship terms*, and the whole is called the *system of kinship* (or *relationship*) *terminology*.

THE CLASSIFICATORY PRINCIPLE

The first important principle to grasp in the study of kinship systems is that *no system provides a separate and distinct term for every possible kind or position of genealogical relationship*. All systems equate, lump, or merge some relatives of different genealogical positions into one single category, which is identified by a specific term. For example, the Comanche Indians equate father, father's brother, and mother's sister's husband all under one term, *ap'*. Father's brother and mother's sister's husband (both of whom we call "uncle") are genealogically distinct from father, but to the Comanche they are merged or equated under the same identifying term of relationship.

Kinship terms that result from merging are called *classificatory terms*. The effect of classificatory terminology is to merge lineal relatives (as one's father) with collateral relatives (as one's father's brother).

A kinship term that applies to a particular genealogical status and no other is called *particularizing* or *descriptive*. Anglo-Americans, for instance, tend to apply the terms "father" and "mother" only to actual progenitors when referring to relatives. However, as no system is ever wholly particularizing or classificatory, we also have certain classificatory terms, such as "cousin," "uncle," "aunt," "niece," "nephew," "grandfather," "grandmother," "grandson," and "granddaughter."

Our insistence on particularizing "father" and "mother" is sociologically significant, for it will be noted that in addition to this particularization, we use the words "son" and "daughter" to mean only our own children and not those of our brothers or sisters. Likewise, we use the terms "brother" and "sister" to refer exclusively to the siblings of our own primary conjugal-natal family. Other relatives of our own generation level we call "cousins." Our terminology thus places strong emphasis upon the exclusiveness of our primary conjugal-natal family; it rigidly distinguishes more remote relatives. This reflects the great social significance of our close relatives in the conjugal-natal family as against the rest of our larger kindred. Lineal relatives are more important to us than collateral ones.

In most societies, as we have noted, extended kinship groups play larger roles than is the case with the civilizations of Europe and the Western Hemisphere. In such societies, merging or lumping of relatives on a collateral basis is therefore much more likely.

Since kinship terms designate social statuses, what you must call a person ideally determines how you should behave toward him. Further, all persons who are called by the same kinship term should (and again, ideally) receive the same sort of treatment, since they enjoy ideologically identical statuses in the system of social organization.

Comanche Kinship Terminology

It will help to get the feel of kinship if we briefly explore the way in which relatives are grouped and identified in a few systems other than our own. To do this, we shall begin with a look at the way the Comanche Indians classify relatives.

Comanche social structure is bilateral and bilocal. Polygynous marriages were permissible until forbidden by the federal law of the United States. The Comanche kindred is exogamous; no one may marry a relative within three degrees of recognized relationship.

In treating any system of kinship terminology, it is necessary to have a starting point in a particular individual. This person is called *ego* (L. *ego*, I). In this example, we start with ego as a male, for it makes a difference whether a man or woman is speaking.

A Comanche male calls his mother *pia*. But

there are also other female relatives called *pia*, namely, his mother's sisters, his mother's female cousins, and his father's brother's wife. *Pia* can thus be seen to mean not "mother" to a Comanche, but more exactly, "female relative of my mother's generation and kindred."

His father he calls *ap'*. But there are also other male relatives called *ap'*, namely, his father's brothers, his father's male cousins, and his mother's sister's husband. *Ap'* thus does not mean "father" for a Comanche, but "male relative of my father's generation and kindred."

The Comanche calls his mother's brother by a different term, *ara*. Thus, where we merge father's brother and mother's brother together as "uncle," the Comanche merges father and father's brother in one category, while distinguishing mother's brother in another.

The same thing is done with aunts. Mother and mother's sister are both classified as *pia*, but father's sister is distinguished as *paha*. This practice is called *forked merging or bifurcate merging.*

Father's brother   Mother's brother
merged with father   kept distinct

Ego (speaker)

Members of the agnatic and uterine kindreds are thus kept distinct.

Within ego's own generation, all relatives are "brother" and "sister" to a Comanche; cousins are not identified as such. But relative age is, so the Comanche distinguishes between *paβi* and *tami*, "older male relative of my own generation" and "younger male relative of my own generation." A *paβi* may be ego's elder brother, father's brother's son, father's sister's son, mother's brother's son, mother's sister's son, and wife's sister's husband (if ego is a male) or husband's sister's husband (if ego is a female). *Tami* applies to all these categories if the person referred to is younger than ego.

A "son" to ego includes not only his own boys but also the male offspring of all his *paβi* and *tami*, the sons of his wife's sisters, and his sister's daughter's husband. All these are called *tua*.

A "daughter" includes his own female offspring and the female offspring of all his *patsi* (elder female relatives of his own generation) and *nami* (younger female relatives of his own generation), his wife's sister's daughters, and his sister's son's wife. All these are called *pedi*.[1]

The kinship terms that have been described here cover the members of ego's primary and secondary conjugal-natal families. Whereas Anglo-Americans use exclusive, descriptive terms that isolate the two conjugal-natal families, it may readily be seen that the Comanches merge such individuals within the larger kindred. For them, the kindred is the socially more important group.

All in all, the Comanches recognize thirty-six different kinship categories, each of which has a different kinship term. None of them is identical to the groupings or distinctions drawn by us in our kinship system. *The way in which any society identifies relatives is dependent upon the nature of its kinship groups.* These, in turn, are predominantly determined by the rules of residence and subsistence practices that prevail in the culture.

PRINCIPLES OF KINSHIP IDENTIFICATION

In a classic paper, Kroeber identified the following eight principles of kinship distinctions that may be utilized in shaping a kinship system.[2]

1. Difference in generation levels (father, son; grandparent, grandchild; etc.)

2. Difference in age levels within the same generation (elder and younger brother; father's elder brother; etc.)

3. Difference between lineal and collateral relationship (father, uncle; brother, cousin; etc.)

4. Difference in sex of relatives (brother, sister; uncle, aunt; etc.)

5. Difference in sex of the speaker (males and

females may have two separate systems of terms)

6. Difference of sex of the person through whom the relationship is established (*father's* brother, *mother's* brother; *father's* father, *mother's* father; *father's* father's *sister's* daughter's daughter, etc.)

7. Difference between genetic relatives and those connected by marriage (mother; husband's mother, etc.)

8. Difference in status or life condition of the person *through whom* the relationship is established (living or dead, single or married, etc.).

Few systems make use of all eight distinctions, but many use the first seven.

If the reader will carefully examine the Comanche terms that we have given, he will be able to identify each of the first seven principles in them. The Anglo-American system, on the other hand, utilizes only four of the eight (1, 3, 4, 7).

TYPES OF KINSHIP SYSTEMS

It is a remarkable fact that although a very large number of differing kinship systems are theoretically possible, society after society classifies its kinsmen in essentially similar ways, so that the types of kinship systems that actually come into existence are few in number.

The classification (or typing) of kinship systems presents all of the usual problems of selection of criteria potential in any ordering scheme. A system of classification is merely a tool of the mind created by individuals in order to organize their knowledge. Scientific classification should be based upon a set of principles which define the criteria in accordance with which the phenomena in question are to be ordered. Inevitably the criteria have some ambiguity, confusion, contradiction, and lack of agreement resulting in battles in ink. With kinship, as is the case in the classification of human races, fewer or more types result according to the quality and number of criteria employed. The most significant criteria used by anthropologists for general classification of systems of kinship terminologies are of two orders: (1) the degree of merging and bifurcation of lineal and collateral kin in the parental generation, and

[1]For a full presentation of the Comanche system, see E. A. Hoebel, "Comanche and H3kandika Shoshone Relationship Systems" (*American Anthropologist*, vol. 41, 1939), pp. 440–457. For a highly sophisticated transformational analysis of the Comanche system, the tenacious and stouthearted student might try E. A. Hammel, "A transformational Analysis of Comanche Kinship Terminology" (*American Anthropologist*, vol. 67, part 2, 1965), pp. 65–105.

[2]A. L. Kroeber, "Classificatory Systems of Relationship" (*Journal of the Royal Anthropological Institute of Great Britain and Ireland*, vol. 39, 1909), pp. 77–84.

(2) the degree of merging and bifurcation of collateral kin in ego's own generation.[3]

Kinship Systems Based on Classification of Parental Generation

Use of the criterion of classification of lineal and collateral kin (see Fig. 13-1) on the parental level produces four types of kinship systems: (1) generational, (2) lineal, (3) bifurcate merging, and (4) bifurcate collateral. (See Table 13-1.)

Generational systems

The emphasis in this type of system is on merging of all relatives on a given generational level. Thus, mother, mother's sister, and father's sister are all lumped under a single kinship term. The same is true of father, father's brother, and mother's brother.

Lineal systems

A lineal system emphasizes the distinction between direct ascendant and descendant relatives as separate from collaterals. Therefore, mother is distinguished from mother's sister and father's

sister, who are merged, as in English "aunt." The same holds for father and his collaterals, who are merged, as in English "uncle." Lineal systems are also associated with bilateral systems of descent groups.

Bifurcate-merging systems

Lineage systems of descent groups tend to produce bifurcate-merging systems of terminology, as will be demonstrated in the analysis of Crow terminology given below. Father's brother is merged with father, while both are distinguished from mother's brother. Put in another way, father and paternal uncle are lumped, and maternal uncle is distinguished. Likewise, mother and maternal aunt are lumped, and paternal aunt is distinguished. Members of the two descent groups are rigorously kept separate from each other.

Bifurcate-collateral systems

In this type of system, all collaterals on the parental generation level are bifurcated, or distinguished. Father, father's brother, and mother's brother all are called by separate terms of designation, as are mother, mother's sister, and father's sister. There is no significant correlation between bifurcate-collateral terminology and any particular system of descent groups, nor is there any adequate theory to account for the preva-

---

[3]The first of these systems was formulated by R. H. Lowie and published in the fourteenth edition of the *Encyclopaedia Britannica*, in the article "Relationship Terms." The second system was formalized by G. P. Murdock, *Social Structure*, pp. 223–259.

FIG. 13-1 The distinction of collateral and lineal kinsmen.

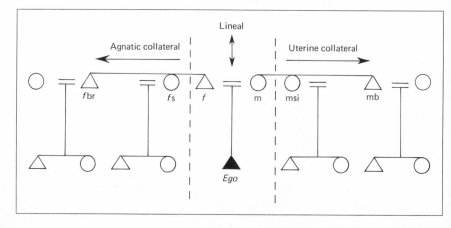

TABLE 13-1 TYPES OF KINSHIP SYSTEMS ACCORDING TO CLASSIFICATION OF RELATIVES IN THE PARENTAL AND IN EGO'S OWN GENERATIONS

Type of descent group	Classification of parental generation		Classification of ego's own generation	
	Type	Merging and bifurcation	Type	Merging and bifurcation
Bilateral	Generational	[Mo = MoSi = FaSi] [Fa = FaBr = MoBr]	Hawaiian (malayan)	[×Cos = ‖Cos = Sib]
Bilateral	Lineal	Mo ≠ [MoSi = FaSi] Fa ≠ [FaBr = MoBr]	Eskimo	[×Cos = ‖Cos] ≠ Sib
Matrilineal or patrilineal	Bifurcate merging	[Mo = MoSi] ≠ FaSi [Fa = FaBr] ≠ MoBr	Crow, Iroquois, Omaha	×Cos ≠ [‖Cos = Sib]
	Bifurcate collateral	Mo ≠ MoSi ≠ FaSi Fa ≠ FaBr ≠ MoBr	Sudanese	×Cos ≠ ‖Cos ≠ Sib

NOTE: The Hawaiian generational type merges all parents and all cousins; the Eskimo lineal type distinguishes parents and siblings from their collaterals; the three bifurcate-merging systems merge parents with collaterals of like sex and merge parallel-cousins with siblings, while distinguishing cross-cousins; the Sudanese bifurcate-collateral type distinguishes all parental kin and cousins.
KEY: [=] = merged categories; ≠ = distinguished or bifurcated categories; × Cos = cross-cousins; ‖ Cos = parallel-cousins; Sib = siblings.

lence of this highly particularizing method of classification.

RELATIVE FREQUENCY OF SYSTEMS BASED ON CLASSIFICATION OF PARENTAL GENERATION Approximately 44 per cent of the kinship systems in the *World Ethnographic Sample* are of the bifurcate-merging type. This happens because most descent systems are unilineal and automatically place mother's and father's brothers in different descent groups. Bifurcate-merging terminology reflects this simple fact.

Generational-type kinship systems go with bilateral descent systems and occur in 30 per cent of the cases. Bilateral systems do not separate mother's and father's kin, nor does generational terminology.

Lineal systems, which occur in approximately one-eighth of the cases, are strongly associated with the occurrence of bilateral descent systems.

Bifurcate-collateral types are fairly rare and do not correlate with any particular type of descent; they have not been adequately explained.

Kinship Systems Based on Classification of Cousins

Use of the criterion of merging and particularizing of siblings, cross-cousins, and parallel-cousins

produces more refined results than analysis of the parental generation terminology alone. Therefore, Murdock has developed a typology of kinship systems based upon these criteria.

Murdock's classification sets up six types of kinship systems with respect to distinctions or lack of distinctions made in their terminologies for cousins. They are (1) the Hawaiian, (2) the Eskimo, (3) the Iroquois, (4) the Crow, (5) the Omaha, and (6) the Sudanese. These are actually the same as the generational categories, as can be seen from Table 13-1, except that the category of bifurcate merging is refined into the Crow, Iroquois, and Omaha types.

The Hawaiian system

This is the same as the generational system. Because of its emphasis on generation equivalence, the Hawaiian system draws no distinction between cousins and siblings, all of whom belong to the same kindreds.

The Eskimo system

The Eskimo system draws no distinctions between cross- and parallel-cousins but does distinguish cousins from siblings. Its emphasis is on the immediate chain of conjugal-natal families. The Eskimo system is familiar to all speakers of the English language, for this is the system used in Anglo-American culture.

The Iroquois system

In the Iroquois system of terminology, siblings and parallel-cousins of the same sex are usually equated under one term, whereas cross-cousins are distinguished by different terms. Iroquois terminology is almost nonexistent among bilaterally organized tribes. It is weakly correlated (phi = 0.135)[4] with matrilineal and duolineal descent groups and appears to be the product of a weak matrilineal, uxorilocal system of social organization.

The Crow system

The Crow system usually reflects a social structure that contains strongly developed matrilineages and/or clans.

In cousin terminology, cross-cousins are distinguished from each other (i.e., there are separate terms for father's sister's son or daughter and mother's brother's son or daughter); these are also distinguished from parallel-cousins and from siblings. But paternal cross-cousins are merged with father and father's sister, according to sex.

It is in this last lumping of father's sister's daughter with her paternal aunt that the lineage emphasis is made clearest. Hocart has shown us how earlier anthropologists were trapped into false conceptions of kinship by thinking of such classificatory terms as "father" as meaning an extension of fatherhood.[5] Thus, Lowie translated the Crow Indian term *birupxe* as "father." *Birupxe* is the term applied to ego's father, father's brother, and father's sister's son (when ego is a male). Properly understood, it means not "father," but "male of my father's matrilineal lineage or clan." For the same reason, the term used in reference to ego's father's sister means "female of my

father's matrilineal lineage or clan." The term for "mother" means "woman married to a male of my own matrilineal lineage or clan."

Because father, father's brother, father's sister's son, and father's sister's daughter's son are all lumped together under one term as members of the same matrilineage, ego's mother is called "wife" by all of them. She may marry any one of them in secondary affinal marriage. Therefore, levirate and husband's-sister's-son marriages are preferential forms in systems of marriage related to strong matrilineal descent systems and Crow terminology. Conversely, a man may marry his mother's brother's wife. The effect of all this on cousin terminology is that patrilateral cross-cousins are called by the same term as that used for father, and matrilateral cross-cousins, as children of the woman ego calls "wife," are designated by the same term as that used for son and daughter. It should be noted, however, that although these secondary affinal marriages are permissible, they are not reported as preferred marriages in all cultures in which Crow-type terminology occurs.

The Omaha system

The Omaha system is the patrilineal obverse of the Crow system. Mother and female matrilateral cross-cousin (mother's brother's daughter) are merged under one term that means "female member of my mother's patrilineage or clan." Father's sister's daughter (patrilateral cross-cousin) is merged with sister's daughter under a term that means "daughter of a female of my father's patrilineage or clan." —

The Sudanese system

This type is at the opposite pole from the Hawaiian in that its terms are emphatically particularizing, or descriptive. Consequently, it has separate terms for each type of cousin, for siblings, and for aunts, nieces, uncles, and nephews.

The Anglo-American Kinship System

The Anglo-American kinship system is of the Eskimo type. It lumps all cousins, but distinguish-

[4]A. D. Coult and R. W. Habenstein, *Cross Tabulations of Murdock's World Ethnographic Sample*, p. 512.
[5]A. M. Hocart, "Kinship Systems" (*Anthropos*, vol. 32, 1937), pp. 345–351.

es them from brothers and sisters. In the absence of lineages and clans, it shows no lineal emphasis except within the primary and secondary conjugal-natal families. These are sharply set off from the kindred by the exclusive limitation of terms like "father," "mother," "brother," "sister," "son," and "daughter" to those who actually belong to the two conjugal-natal families.[6]

Monogamy is reflected in the fact that the words "father," "mother," "husband," and "wife" can apply to only one person within the kinship system. When these terms are used within the church system, they imply and evoke certain filial responses and behaviors that carry over from the kinship system, but no one makes the mistake of assuming that they imply genetic relationship. We see this also in the use of "brother" and "sister" terms among members of social and religious clubs and movements.

One thing that is genuinely distinctive about the Anglo-American kinship terminology is the abundance of alternative terms used in addition to "mother," "father," "husband," and "wife." For "father" these are "dad," "daddy," "pop," "pa," "old man," "boss," "pater," and "governor." None of these carries the respect connotations, however, of the word "father." Their use varies in accordance with the authority roles acknowledged to the father by his children within the particular family, and they reflect the flexible nature of American family patterns. By and large, the term "daddy," widely used by youngsters, is dropped by boys as they grow up, although it is often retained by daughters for many years. Father-son relations become more restrained and formal, whereas there is much evidence to support the inference that the persistence of the use of the word "daddy" by girls expresses a continuance of preadolescent affectivity between father and daughter.

A parallel series of terms exists for "mother": "mom," "mommy," "mummy," "ma," "mama," "mater," and "old woman." Very similar role qualities are ascribed to these terms as to the alternatives to "father." Both boys and girls tend to shift from use of informal mother terms to the more formal "mother" as they grow up. Boys, in other words, do not keep the familiar term for "mother" the way girls carry on with "daddy."[7]

Affinal relatives are all distinguished by means of the "in-law" suffix. However, a device of *teknonymy*, the practice of calling an adult by the name used by his child, is often used to soften the stiffness of the "in-law" term when addressing a mother-in-law or father-in-law. This is managed by identifying with the offspring and addressing spouses' parents as "grandmother" and "grandfather." They are lineal kin to the children, and so by this fictive device are drawn into the lineal family group.

Except for a slight linguistic emphasis given to the patrilineal line through patronymy, the consequences of which are more attitudinal than structural or behavioral, the system is symmetrically multilateral. All ramifications extending out from the immediate lineal line are treated with equal weight (or lack of it). Such distinctions in emphasis as do occur are the result of personal preferences or aversions and proximity of residence, not the consequences of any systematic emphasis.

Social effects of the American kinship system

The lack of structural cohesiveness outside the inner circle of families in lineal descent in the Anglo-American kinship system reflects the weak role kinship groups play in this society. This emphasizes the independence of separate conjugal-natal family units. Many problems concerning marriage and the family rise directly or indirectly from this fact. Parent-child conflict is generated because children must develop independence to be able to found their own economically independent families with separate households.

Much of the erratic behavior of adolescents, so baffling or frustrating to adults, may be traced in part to the insecurity of the emergent boy or girl, who is in transition from the bonds of the primary

---

[6]T. C. Parsons, "The Kinship System of the Contemporary United States" (*American Anthropologist*, vol. 45, 1943), p. 24.

[7]D. M. Schneider and G. C. Homans, "Kinship Terminology and the American Kinship System" (*American Anthropologist*, vol. 57, 1955), pp. 1195–1199; also, R. M. Burling, "American Kinship Terms Once More" (*Southwestern Journal of Anthropology*, vol. 26, 1970), pp. 15–24.

family of birth to the expectant secondary conjugal-natal family he or she must soon found. Insecurity in old age is the lot of many parents whose secondary conjugal-natal family has been pared down until only they are left. When one of them dies, the survivor is at sea, with no comfortable base in which to harbor. Old people's homes and old-age security legislation are the palliative social consequences.

Few of the social relations of children are predetermined by kinship status outside the immediate conjugal-natal family. Children are thrown into open competition for social status; some are rewarded with success and prestige, and others find only frustration and insecurity, or they choose to drop out.

Marriage in the United States rests heavily on the bond of love and affection, for there are no absolutely ascribed preferential matings to solve the problem of mating, nor is there much family control of mating, as in Asia and France. These are only some of the upsetting consequences of our open, weak kinship system.

The advantages of this system are those which derive from individual freedom of action in social and economic relations: freedom to choose one's friends within or without the relationship group, freedom to choose one's mate, freedom to find an occupation fairly untrammeled by kinship status, and freedom to live where one wills according to a self-chosen life style.

In America today, the individual couple is largely on its own, to stand or fall as a unit according to its ability to surmount the hazards of the loose, and weakening, kinship group, and to utilize the freedoms of a mobile and rapidly changing society. The divorce mills grind for those who fail, and rebellious youth share "pads" and seek a substitute for the rejected extended family in experimental communes of peers—creating new, fictive kin groups.

SELECTED READINGS

Bohannan, P. J. and J. Middleton (eds.), *Kinship and Social Organization* (1968). Part I, pages 1–148, presents eight landmark papers in the development of kinship theory and method. These are not really for the introductory student, but they are worth knowing about.

Eggan, F., *Social Organization of the Western Pueblos* (1950). This will not be easy reading for the beginner, but it is one of the finest comparative studies of kinship systems.

——(ed.), *Social Anthropology of North American Tribes* (2d ed., 1955). Contains highly informative articles on the kinship systems of six American Indian tribes.

——, "Kinship: Introduction" (*International Encyclopedia of the Social Sciences*, vol. 8, 1968), pp. 390–401. A useful supplement to the Lowie article, cited below. Contains an excellent, comprehensive bibliography on the anthropology of kinship.

Lowie, R. H., "Kinship," (*Encyclopaedia of the Social Sciences*, vol. 3, 1931), pp. 568–572. The elements of kinship systems clearly presented.

Murdock, G. P., *Social Structure* (1949), chaps. 6 and 7, "Analysis of Kinship" and "Determinants of Kinship Terminology." Requires hard thinking, but analysis of kinship systems is never easy.

Schusky, E. L., *Manual for Kinship Analysis* (1965). A helpful handbook for identification and analysis of kinship systems.

14

ASSOCIATIONS, CLUBS, AND AGE GROUPS

LEARNING GOALS

Distinguish associations from kinship groups and describe some of their functions in social organization. ¶ Account for the predominance of men's clubs in primitive societies. ¶ Compare tribal and nontribal secret fraternities and secular associations in terms of their structural form and social functions. ¶ Define age classes (or sets), and give some examples of how they operate. ¶ Explain why associations should tend to flourish in new or rapidly changing societies.

Although kinship regulates and controls a large part of the life of primitive peoples, it would be an error to assume that all areas of activity are confined to, or determined by, the kinship group, or by the class, caste, or geographical community. The urge to form voluntary associations, friendship groups, or clubs, is not exclusively a trait of contemporary, or even civilized, people. Most primitive societies, also, make some provision for voluntary, nonkinship groups, using them as a way to make life more intriguing, colorful, and meaningful, as well as to carry out certain functions not handled by other segments of the social system.

Such groups are frequently based on the common denominator of sex or age, or they may derive from shared experience or common skill. Although many of them have a recreational factor, with feasting, drinking, dancing, story telling, etc., incorporated into work or ceremonial activities, they usually serve important basic functions necessary to the welfare of the total society. Whether temporary and ad hoc, as in the case of a one-time job requiring a larger number of participants than a family can muster, or permanent and lifelong, as in the case of the tribal fraternities with responsibility for education and enculturation of the young, these associations transcend kinship groups and have the effect of creating bonds between nonrelatives.

THE NATURE OF ASSOCIATIONS

We may define an association as "a group organized for the pursuit of one interest or of several interests in common. Associations are usually contrasted with involuntary groupings serving a greater variety of ends, such as kin groups, castes, social classes and communities."[1]

Although "associations" are differentiated from "involuntary groupings," they are not, among tribal peoples, completely "voluntary." In few cases is membership a matter of wholly free choice. Some of the associations we shall examine embrace all the adults of a given sex in their membership; others include all males or females in a given age range; others invite only those with special characteristics, skills, or wealth. Kinship

---

[1]M. Banton, "Voluntary Associations: Anthropological Aspects" (*International Encyclopedia of the Social Sciences*, vol. 16, 1968), p. 357. Copyright © 1968, Crowell Collier and Macmillan, Inc. Quoted with permission.

and locality may also play some part in determining these affiliations.

In general, associations, clubs, or sodalities, as some anthropologists call them, may be characterized as follows: They are not based primarily on the kinship factor; they have an exclusive membership within the larger society; they possess a formal institutional structure; and they engender a discernible feeling of congeniality among the members along with *esprit de corps*, or the "we-feeling." Although many of these associations are traditionally known as "societies," (Plains Indian "military societies," Pueblo Indian "curing societies"), it may help to eliminate confusion if, in this chapter, we do not use the word "society" as a synonym for club or association, reserving it for its larger meaning. The term *fraternity* is traditional anthropological usage for a men's club in those instances where clubs promote the social fiction of brotherhood among their members. Those associations which include all the men or women of a given age range are known as *age grades*, *age classes*, or *age sets*. Even where membership is not based on age per se, a certain amount of age grouping is found in most associations. The latter fact is true, also, in our own culture.

Functions of Associations

As an illustration of how associations enhance tribal life, Banton cites the Blackfoot Indians of the North American Plains, whose primary subsistence pattern was based on buffalo hunting. During the winters when pastures were meager and the buffalo roamed in small, dispersed herds, small bands of Blackfoot kinfolk were adequate for the task of hunting, while larger encampments could not be fed from the small herds. However, with the lush grasses of springtime, the buffalo gathered in enormous herds. At that time:

The Blackfoot bands also combined, forming social and economic units that could most efficiently hunt the great herds. Most men were members of societies that included men of similar age. These societies organized the encampments, maintained order, and coordinated hunting operations during the summer migrations. The societies also performed dances and ceremonies. Quite apart from the explicit ends served by these associations, they brought men from different bands into rela-

tions of solidarity. Although a young man might choose which society he would join, it was hardly conceivable that he should belong to none.[2]

Whereas the Blackfoot organized their associations around economic need, the Tswana of Bechuanaland have utilized their highly structured associations to further the ends of political unity. Here, age and sex are the bases of membership, and the groupings are called "age-regiments." The regiments are formed every few years, and all the eligible boys and girls between about sixteen and twenty years of age are initiated at the same time; there are separate regiments for the men and women. Schapera notes:

Since every adult in the tribe must belong to one, a regiment consists of all tribesmen of the same sex and of about the same age. The initiation ceremonies they undergo simultaneously, the name given to their regiment and identifying it ever afterwards, their organization into a single body under the leadership of some member of the royal family, and the numerous activities they as a body are subsequently called upon to carry out, give them a strong feeling of group solidarity cutting across the parochial loyalties of family, ward, village, and tribal community. The regimental organization serves, therefore, as an effective means of binding together people on a tribal rather than a local basis. Next to the Chieftainship, it is perhaps the most conspicuous means of integrating the members of the tribe into a unified whole.[3]

A regiment may be called on at any time to work for the chief or for the tribe. Any kind of public work may be required: building roads, making dams, searching for lost children, rounding up criminals, etc. Women's regiments may be called upon to thatch a roof, gather wood, or weed the fields for the chief's wife. Women are called on less often and given lighter work. The lengthy and torturous initiation ceremonies which formerly were an important function of the regiments have been replaced by simpler and more benign rites. However, the regiments do have responsibility for inculcating their members with appropriate values and suitable behaviors, and it is the mates in

[2]M. Banton, "Voluntary Associations: Anthropological Aspects" *(International Encyclopedia of the Social Sciences*, vol. 16, 1968), p. 358. Copyright © 1968 Crowell Collier and Macmillan, Inc. Quoted with permission.
[3]I. Schapera, *A Handbook of Tswana Law and Custom*, p. 104. By permission of International African Institute.

one's own regiment who punish, by fines or thrashing, any member's transgressions in conduct or failure to work.

Explicitly or implicitly, many clubs and associations assume a variety of educational functions. "Bush schools," initiation ceremonies, and preparation for specialized leadership tasks are conducted by clubs or fraternities. These associations may also, either overtly or covertly, assume police, legal, or judicial functions. In recent years, as primitive societies have begun moving toward industrialization, associations have assumed increasing importance, taking on many of the roles carried in the United States by public welfare, labor unions, settlement houses, ethnic clubs, and credit unions. Opportunities for self-expression, fellowship, increased self-esteem, heightened status, and honor (frequently including elaborate ranking systems and honorific titles) often accrue from club membership, and these, too, serve a purpose—not only for the individual but also for his society.

Club Life and Sex Roles

Despite a long-held stereotype that women in American society are more active in club and organizational life than men are, and that, therefore, women are more "sociable" than men, there is considerable doubt as to which sex spends more time in social or civic associations. In the primitive world, however, there is no question but that men are the devotees of club life and women are not. The organizational woman of the modern civilized world is one of the revolutionary developments of recent times. There was nothing like her in earlier human history.

The vast majority of all nonkinship-based social groups operate exclusively for men. Associations such as the Tswana Women's Regiments are rare. Sometimes women enter into men's organizations as auxiliaries. When they do have clubs of their own, they are likely to be but weak counterparts of the vigorous organizations of the men. There are rarely all-embracing tribal associations of women, as there are of men.

Indeed, club life among primitive women was so undeveloped that Schurtz, who at the turn of the century gave anthropology its classic study of

men's societies and age grades, advanced the theory that females are innately unsociable. They are inhibited in the formation of clubs, wrote Schurtz, because by instinct their activities and interests concentrate on reproduction, hearth, and home.[4]

This, of course, must be dismissed as androcentric prejudice. In its stead, a cultural-functional explanation that is nearer the facts of human experience may be advanced. First, the demands of family nurture have tended to isolate women and leave them little time for club activities. American experience of the last few decades shows that given time and the opportunity, women can readily take to club and public life. Second, primitive women, in addition to having little time for club activities, are in most male-dominated societies definitely discouraged from entering into the club systems set up by men, and the men do not look with favor upon female imitations of their organizations. This is found to be true especially in tribes that link secret men's clubs with religious activities. Revelation of the secrets of ritual to women (and uninitiated boys) meant death in Australia and West Africa, and even among the matrilineal Pueblos of the Southwest. A woman who accidentally witnessed the secret rites of Central Australian men's groups might possibly still be speared on the spot, as she would have been before the days of Australian governmental police and courts. The men's secret clubs of the Banks Islanders and certain other Melanesian tribes terrorize and bully the non-initiates (including all women).

When so much ado is made about the necessity of protecting the sacred secrets from women and when the sanctions imposed upon women who happen to penetrate the secrets are so fatal, is it surprising that women do not expose themselves to such risks by undertaking the formation of clubs along the lines so jealously guarded by the men?

The demands of family and the discouragement of male attitudes notwithstanding, women have not been totally deprived of club-affiliation possibilities. The Plains Indians often had women's

[4]H. Schurtz, *Altersklassen and Männerbünde (Age Classes and Men's Associations).*

clubs. Indeed, numerous tribal systems included a few female functionaries within the men's clubs. Each Cheyenne unit had four unmarried virgins who had ritual responsibilities and were called "sisters" by the members. There were craft guilds for Cheyenne women who had demonstrated special skills, such as the highly esteemed robe quillers club open to those who had quilled thirty buffalo robes with porcupine-quill embroidery.[5] The Crow Indians had a "deep-rooted belief that husband and wife were intimately associated in ceremonial activity, certain feminine disabilities to the contrary notwithstanding." Thus, husband and wife were usually jointly initiated into the highly important and prestigious Tobacco organization.[6] The function of the Tobacco cult was the ceremonial planting of tobacco, believed necessary to the welfare of the tribe.

Similarly, in Africa, the subjugation and exclusion of women, so noticeable elsewhere, are much attenuated. Although the tribal associations may be for men, they often include women. And what is more notable, women frequently have powerful clubs of their own. In Sierra Leone and Liberia, although some men's associations admit females, no women's clubs admit men. In view of the greater social power and prestige of the men's organizations, when absolute exclusiveness breaks down, there is more pressure from the women to penetrate the men's clubs than vice versa. An egalitarian attitude between the sexes is most evident when associations take over the functions of social service and economic aid as tribal members move into unfamiliar roles as industrial workers in urban settings of developing countries. This we shall see in ensuing discussions.

TYPES OF ASSOCIATIONS

In primitive social systems, club groups and associations are organized as variously as in our own society: by one or both sexes, according to restricted or inclusive age standards, for a multiplicity of purposes, openly or secretly, and so on. Here we can only review a few of the major types

of associations most commonly found in primitive cultures. These include secret fraternities, both tribal and nontribal in membership, secular associations, and age classes.

Tribal Secret Fraternities

Secret fraternities that include all the adult men of a society are called *tribal fraternities*. The adjective "tribal" serves to distinguish them from the more limited type of associations that are open to only a privileged few. They are secret in that their meetings are not open to noninitiates and their lore and ritual may be revealed only to members (see Figure 14-1).

Tribal fraternities are a direct outgrowth of adolescence transition rites. Puberty rites, as we have seen (pages 159–165), serve to allay anxiety and reinforce societal values at the crisis period between childhood and maturity.Those who successfully complete the demands imposed by the puberty rituals do not necessarily organize into an association because of this fact. But because passage through puberty gives an exalted status of maturity and because puberty rites for boys and girls are almost always separate, all those men who have been made conscious of their newly achieved status by the rites are apt to crystallize their special status in an organized association. The puberty rite then becomes an initiatory rite. Not only is such an initiatory rite a transitional rite over a life crisis, but it also opens the door into the fraternity of men.

Such rites emphasize the destruction of the preinitiation personality of the neophyte. As Webster long ago noted:

Almost universally initiation rites include a mimic representation of the death and resurrection of the novice. The new life to which he awakes after initiation is one utterly forgetful of the old; a new name, a new language, and new privileges are its natural accompaniments.[7]

A new name and a new language are not in fact always forthcoming, but seclusion from the women and children followed by "rebirth" is a regular feature of primitive initiatory rites. In tribes where girls are initiated by the women, men

[5]G. B. Grinnell, *The Cheyenne Indians*, vol. 1, pp. 159–169.
[6]R. H. Lowie, *The Crow Indians*, p. 14.

[7]H. Webster, *Primitive Secret Societies*, p. 38.

FIG. 14-1 Interior of the house of a men's tribal secret fraternity on the Fly River, Papua, New Guinea. Ceremonial masks are stacked against the walls. (Photo courtesy of the American Museum of Natural History.)

and boys are rigidly excluded from their rites. Clearly, the process is one of intensification of sex-linked roles on either side.

The line to be drawn between puberty rites and tribal initiation ceremonies is not a sharp one. Whether we decide that a ritual falls into one class or the other depends on whether it leads merely to the status of adult or whether it brings adult status *plus* membership in a specific association of adults. Sometimes there is an intermediary borderline condition on which it would be most arbitrary to make a classificatory judgment.

Thus, in the case of the Andaman Islanders' puberty rites, we contemplate solemn and elaborate but nonsecret rituals that effect status shifts for boys and girls. Full-fledged men are distinctly separated from fledgling boys, and they enjoy many perquisities of adult status. They seem to be bound together by the bonds of consciousness of their common privileges and interests. Yet they do not seem to form a men's fraternity.

On the other hand, in the case of the Central Australian tribes, the initiated married men form a domineering, tightly knit group, possessed of much secret lore and enjoying many privileges, all of which indicates without doubt that here we have true tribal associations.

Aside from Central Australia and certain Melanesian areas, the great center for the development of tribal fraternities is Africa, particularly West Africa from Sierra Leone into Nigeria, Cameroon, and the jungle region of the Congo.[8]

In West Africa, the *porro* and *bondu* fraternities and sororities of such tribes as the Mendi and Temne of Sierra Leone are most famous. All boys, upon completion of their puberty rites, enter the *porro*; the girls usually find themselves members of the *bondu*. Among the Kpelle, the *porro* is a central integrating and controlling feature of tribal life—family, religious, and political.[9] The chief officer (grand master) of the *porro* wields effective political power and social prestige. Membership in the fraternity is a prerequisite for marriage and for admission to all other clubs and offices. The *porro* is internally graded according to the general social status and ages of the members. On the other hand, many women no longer go through initiation into the *sande*, as the women's sorority is called in Kpelle.

Nontribal Secret Fraternities

Nontribal secret fraternities are secret in the same sense as the tribal ones. They differ in that their membership is definitely more limited and selective. Not all the men or women in the tribe can belong—not even all those of a given age group.

By far the most notorious of the widespread African nontribal secret fraternities are the limited and exclusive secret orders of the Leopard, Crocodile, and Snake, or of other beasts, reptiles, or birds. Of these, the Leopards are the most feared. *Egbo*, *Ekkpe*, and *Ngbe* are but variant tribal names for the Leopard order. Human sacrifice and cannibalism gave a terroristic aura to the Leopards. They strike in the dark against their victims, who are selected because they have evoked the ire of the membership or merely because sacrifices are needed for fertility rites. The Leopard men wear leopard-skin cloaks. With wooden dies they make false leopard imprints in the earth to leave the impression that real leopards have seized the victims. With clawlike knives they mutilate and lacerate the flesh of their victims.

The terroristic activities of the Mau Mau among the Kikuyu tribesmen of Kenya in the 1950s was an aberrant development of the pattern of secret fraternities.

Functions of secret fraternities

The functions of African secret orders are by no means wholly homicidal. Their bloody activities are only incidental to deeper-lying interests. The associations are mutual-aid organizations that have taken on important social control responsibilities in addition to their magical, religious, and purely sociable aspects.

They counterbalanced the power of the tribal king and worked to keep royal power in check. Unquestionably, they served at times as the people's solution to the trying problems that result from the need to temper anarchy with monarchy, which in turn must be stopped short of despotism. Within the framework of the tribal constitution, the secret orders are often cited as assisting the king in the application of the sanctions that uphold the tribal laws.[10]

As mutual-aid protective associations, the secret orders of contemporary West Africa pay spe-

---

[8]W. D. Hambly, *Source Book for African Anthropology* (Field Museum of Natural History, Anthropological Series, vol. 26, part 2, 1937), p. 498.

[9]J. L. Gibbs, Jr. (ed.), *Peoples of Africa*, p. 223; also, K. L. Little, "The Social Cycle and Initiation among the Mende," in J. Middleton (ed.), *From Child to Adult*, pp. 207–225.

[10]See Webster, *op. cit.*, p. 115–120; and R. H. Lowie, *The Origin of the State*, pp. 91–94.

cial attention to the interests of their members as against those of the world at large. They collect private debts from delinquent creditors on behalf of their members, and they punish other transgressions against the brotherhood as well. In some sections of Sierra Leone, the overextension of these practices into exploitative terrorism has caused violent public reactions, resulting in the outlawing of such clubs as the Leopard.

Experience proves that secret orders are dangerous devices for use as instruments of government and social control. With the best intentions they may serve the public weal, but since the members are not publicly accountable for their acts, there can be no safe check on the inevitable temptation to use their heady power in their own selfish interests. Exclusive secret orders are inherently corruptible and corrupting in any society, be it *Egbo* in Liberia, *tamate* in the Banks Islands, or Ku Klux Klan in the United States.

Secret clubs of a purely congenial, ceremonial, or magico-religious nature are generally exempt from such strictures. Thus, in old Dahomey, where the power of the king appears to have become sultanistic in its strength, all secret orders were banned by royal edict. The king brooked no opposition or competition. There was, however, no objection to the banding together of men for mutual aid, as long as it was not done secretly. The Dahomean *gbe* was (and is) organized by a group of young men, not necessarily of the same age group. They socialize together, but the basic function of their organizations is to enable each member to make more impressive displays at weddings and funerals by calling upon the resources of all other members not in excess of a stipulated sum.[11] Women may belong to such clubs, or they may have separate clubs of their own. In effect, these secular nonsecret associations are exactly comparable to our own cooperative credit unions.

The various pueblos of the Southwest each have their several secret fraternities whose main functions are to perform masked dances impersonating the gods and to carry out complex rituals according to calendric cycles. The dances and rituals are performed for the benefit of all the people. Most of the ritual and accompanying liturgy is secret among the initiated members, but public dances are also presented. Thus, the village *cacique* (sacred chief) of Sia Pueblo calls upon the Flint fraternity to perform the stick-swallowing dance on behalf of the whole pueblo. The dancers shove sticks down their throats, imitating the poking of planters' dibbles into the ground, and the dance works to ensure a good spring sowing. Among the Hopi, secret fraternities join in a dramatic snake dance for rain-making, shown in Fig. 14-2.

The functions of such fraternities in the pueblos are largely religious, magical, and ceremonial. The high-ranking leaders of the secret orders form an ecclesiastical council which is even today the ultimate source of governing power in most pueblos.[12]

Secret ceremonial associations also played an important role in the lives of the Indians of the Northwest Coast.[13]

Secular Associations

Purely secular organizations, given to furthering nonmystic interests and not concerned with terrorizing women and children, have no compulsive need to surround themselves with secrecy.

Such were the military and dancing clubs of the Plains Indians. These associations of warriors were fellowships for conviviality among men, whose warlike flame was sustained and fanned by the stories, the rituals, and the songs and dances of their lodges. Their basic interests were two: warfare and congeniality. Their enjoyment was derived not from roistering but from the quieter glow that builds up in companionate smoking of a pipe, huddled singing about a thumping drum, parading two by two in all their finery upon their best horses, or dancing for all the tribe to see.

Plains Indian military associations

Although the Plains Indian men's clubs are commonly called "military societies," they were mili-

---

[11]M. J. Herskovits, *Dahomey*, vol. 1, pp. 250–253.

[12]See E. A. Hoebel, "Keresan Pueblo Law," in L. Nader (ed.), *Law in Culture and Society*, pp. 92–116.

[13]See F. Boas, *Social Organization and Secret Societies of the Kwakiutl Indians* (United States National Museum, Reports, 1895).

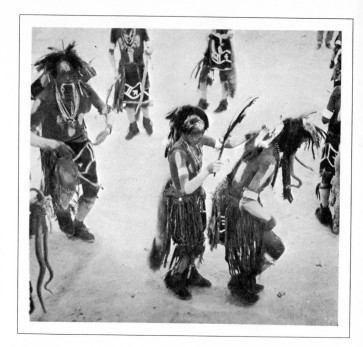

FIG. 14-2 Members of the Hopi Indian Snake and Antelope nontribal secret fraternities performing the rainmaking Snake Dance. Snake fraternity members dance with live rattlesnakes in their mouths and hands, while cooperating members of the Antelope fraternity control the snakes with eagle-feather fans. (Photo courtesy of the American Museum of Natural History.)

tary only in the sense that the American Legion is military—their members all were, or had been, fighting men. Rarely did these clubs go to war as units. They did not form regular segments of an army, for Plains Indian fighting was too individualistic for that, but they idealized and glorified war and labored to sustain the war ideal among their members.

Their officers were "chosen to die." In battle, they planted their insignia—a straight fur-wrapped staff, a crooked spear like a shepherd's crook, or a trailing shoulder sash that could be pegged to the ground—in the face of the enemy. They could not retreat from that spot unless a fellow member dashed into the melee to pull up the peg or staff. Nominees for such offices were supposed to be bashful toward acceptance of the honor. Witness what Lowie was told by the Crow Indian Young Jackrabbit:

"All declined to smoke, then they came towards me. Some one asked them, 'Whom are you looking for?' They answered, 'Young Jackrabbit.' I was seated in the rear and tried to hide. They brought the pipe to me, but I refused to accept it. One of the pipe-carriers was my own older brother. He seized me by the hair, struck my

chest, and said, 'You are brave, why don't you smoke the pipe?' He wished me to die, that is why he desired me to smoke the pipe. He said, 'You are of the right age to die, you are good-looking, and if you get killed your friends will cry. All your relatives will cut their hair, fast and mourn. Your bravery will be recognized; and your friends will feel gratified.' I took the pipe and began to smoke. They asked me whether I wished to have a straight or a hooked-staff. I chose the hooked-staff. My comrade also smoked the pipe."[14]

Thus were the chosen members recruited to these highly selective and exclusive positions.

Plains Indian men's clubs have been classified into ungraded and graded types. The ungraded, which occurred among the Crow, Cheyenne, Kiowa, Wind River Shoshone, and other tribes, were voluntary associations open to all men without regard to age. A man needed merely a sponsor within the club; he also gave "presents" to the club upon his entry. There was no initiation.

The number of such ungraded clubs varied in different tribes. The Crows, in 1833, had eight.

---

[14]R. H. Lowie, *The Crow Indians*, pp. 177–178. By permission of Holt, Rinehart and Winston, Inc.

Toward the end of the century, these had been reduced to only two active ones, the Foxes and the Lumpwoods (Knobby Sticks).[15] The Cheyennes had six clubs: the Fox, Elk, Shield, Bowstring, Dog, and Northern Crazy Dog.[16]

Age Classes, or Age Sets

We have defined age groupings as associations based on age and embracing within their membership all the men or women in a given age range. Usually, these age classes are defined and membership is determined when the individuals are at or near puberty. However, age classes are sometimes established at younger and also at older ages.

Plains Indian age clubs

Among the Plains Indians, age-graded associations occurred only among the Mandan, Hidatsa, Arapaho, Gros Ventre, and Blackfoot. Each of these tribes had a system of associations that were graded in a prestige hierarchy from young to old; age qualification was a prerequisite for membership in all cases. Normally, every member of a tribe, if he lived long enough, would pass through all grades. The higher grades naturally had progressively smaller membership, which, combined with the increasing age of the members, gave greater prestige.

Movement from one grade to another was by collective purchase of all the rights and paraphernalia of the club just above. Among the Hidatsa, for example, all the adolescent boys banded together and, aided by their families, made a great collection of hides, arrows, parfleches, etc. After indicating to the Kit Foxes, the lowest club, that they wanted to buy, arrangements would be made for ceremonial payment and transfer of the club to the upstarts. In addition, each neophyte chose a ceremonial father, or sponsor, who had to be a member of the neophyte's father's clan, from among the members of the Kit Foxes. To this man he offered gifts and entertainment—including the temporary favors of his wife if he had one. The ethics of ceremonial wife lending were mixed, however. The gesture had to be made, but most ceremonial fathers were "afraid" to use the privilege.

Thus, each candidate had to make individual payment to join an age society, but at the same time, it was absolutely necessary that his age group act collectively to acquire the rights to the club. Such clubs were therefore joint incorporeal property transferable only by sale (see pages 254–255). Northern Plains Indian age associations were not pure age grades or age classes, i.e., a series of groups each of which is automatically composed of all the persons of a given sex and approximate age. After an incumbent group of Hidatsa Kit Foxes sold their club to the next younger group, they were without any club organization until they succeeded in purchasing the Half-shaved Heads club from the group above them, who then had to purchase from the Dogs, who then had to purchase from the Lumpwoods. So it went up the line, until the oldest men entered the Bull club (see Fig. 14-3).

The element of age grading in the Plains is a piece of fancy embroidery added by the more sophisticated sedentary gardening tribes of the Upper Missouri Valley to the simpler ungraded complex as seen among the nomadic tribes. From the Mandan and Hidatsa, the pattern spread to the Arapaho, the Gros Ventre, and ultimately the Blackfoot. The breakdown of aboriginal Plains culture came before the complex could spread farther.[17]

African age sets

Age grades, or age sets (as they are called by English anthropologists), occur in their most highly developed form in Africa, and according to the *World Ethnographic Sample*, three-fourths of all societies containing age classes are African.[18]

---

[15]R. H. Lowie, *Societies of the Crow, Hidatsa, and Mandan Indians* (American Museum of Natural History, Anthropological Papers, vol. 11, 1913).

[16]K. N. Llewellyn and E. A. Hoebel, *The Cheyenne Way: Conflict and Case Law in Primitive Jurisprudence*, p. 99.

[17]Lowie worked out a classic age-area distribution study directed toward historical reconstruction of the development of such clubs. See his *Plains Indian Age Societies* (American Museum of Natural History, Anthropological Papers, vol. 11, 1916), pp. 877–984.

[18]A. D. Coult and R. W. Habenstein, *Cross Tabulations of Murdock's World Ethnographic Sample*, p. 27.

(a)

(b)

FIG. 14-3 (*a*) Plains Indian age grades in 1833; the Half-shaved Heads fraternity of the Mandans of the Missouri River earth-lodge villages; (*b*) The dance of the Bull fraternity, the senior age grade of the Mandans. Spectators are standing on the roofs of the village earth lodges. Paintings by Carl Bodmer. (Photo courtesy of the American Museum of Natural History.)

NANDI AGE SETS   Keeping in mind what has already been said about the Tswana, we may take the Nandi of Kenya as an additional example. There are a number of grades of males in this tribe. The first grade is that of the uninitiated boys. For the scion of a wealthy family, initiation may occur as early as at ten years of age, or a youth may be nearly twenty before he is put up by his family for initiation. Initiations, which occur every seven or eight years, are the highlight of tribal life and a rough time for the boys, who, as if circumcision were not enough, are beaten with stinging nettles and stung with hornets. The initiation includes military instruction, for, after initiation, the boys used to become warriors. The initiated group receives name emblems and ornaments. War formerly was their chief concern; they could play at love and enjoy sex, but they were not to be fretted with the responsibilities of marriage and children. After four years of experience, they were ready to "receive the country" from the elder grades. The age set above them, which was retiring from active warrior status, laid aside its warrior clothing, assumed the raiment of elders, and could then marry and settle down to connubial domesticity. This was not of an exclusive sort, however, since in formal custom each married man was expected to extend the hospitality of his home to any visiting classmate. Hospitality to a Nandi meant wife lending, a gratuity he would deny to all who were not members of his own age set. As a set advances in age, it ultimately enters the body of statesmen and tribal advisers.[19]

SWAZI AGE SETS   To the south, in Swaziland, the Swazi, a nation related to the better-known Zulus, reveal an age-set system remarkably similar to that just described. In the Swazi system, however, the whole organization was tightly controlled by the national king, who utilized the classes of fighting age as regiments in a standing army and as work corps in time of peace.

To this day, Swazi age sets, although shorn of their military reasons for existence, still carry on important tasks. In 1963, Hilda Kuper reported:

The age sets were more precisely organized in the days of intertribal warfare than at present, but much of the structure survives for other than military purposes, which they continue to fulfill. When the regiments were not fighting they served as labor battalions, particularly for the aristocrats, and this remains one of their major duties. Their most intensive work depends on the agricultural routine of plowing, weeding, guarding the corn against the birds, reaping, and threshing; they may also be summoned to gather wood, cut leaves and poles for building, move huts, drive locusts off the fields, skin animals, run messages, fetch and carry. No matter how arduous a task may be, work begins and ends with the *hlehla,* a dance song in the cattle pen. During the performance, which always attracts children and often the women of the homestead, individual workers dance out of the group and sing short songs of their own composition, boasting of some achievement or exhibiting their artistic virtuosity. . . .

The age classes are, however, still required for state ritual, and at the annual ceremony of kingship, designed to rejuvenate the king and strengthen the people, separate duties are allocated to the oldest regiments, to the regiment of men in full vigor of manhood, and to the youths who are considered sexually pure. Ritual is part of the educative process, a symbolic affirmation of certain social values, and in traditional Swazi society where specialized formal educational institutions are nonexistent, the age classes serve as the main channels for inculcating the values of loyalty and group morality. The emphasis is less on the content of a curriculum, and the acquisition of new knowldge than on traditional values. In the past, special "old people" were appointed as instructors; teaching was not a separate career and learning was a gradual and continuous process of consolidation. The warriors are expected to master the main skills associated with adult life—in the barracks they even perform tasks normally left to women—and to develop the qualities of "manhood," specifically those related to the code of sexual morality. When a girl accepts a lover, she and her friends are expected to visit his barracks in special courting dress, which is brief but elaborately decorated with beads, and to sing and dance to make the relationship public. Should she on a subsequent visit find him absent, it is the duty of his agemates to try to see that she remains faithful to their friend. They find her accommodations and provide her with food. Lovers of other regiments are considered fair game, but the man who steals a girl of his own agemate is beaten and ostracized. In some other societies, sharing of women is a right of group membership; among the Swazi the emphasis on sexual monopoly over a particular lover is related to the ritual obligations placed on each member of an age group. In the main annual

---

[19]A. C. Hollis, *The Nandi.* For an excellent detailed study of three variant systems of East African age sets, see A. H. J. Prins, *East African Age Class Systems.*

ceremony of the state, every individual of the unmarried regiment is responsible for contributing "pure strength" to kingship. At the present time, lover relationships are often not public and participation in state rituals is frequently evaded.[20]

NUER AGE SETS Age sets in Africa have been made to serve well as devices of social integration and efficiency. They cause greater internal segmentation, it is true, but it is a segmentation that promotes specialization of function along effective lines. It harnesses the energies of youth to the ends of the society and gives to each age group a strong awareness of its own status. In even so widely dispersed and scattered a population as the Nuer in the Nilotic Sudan, who have only the weakest of tribal structures in spite of the fact that they number over 100,000 persons, the age set system is one order of organization that runs through all divisions of the tribal society. Because of a generally undeveloped social and political structure, Nuer age sets are necessarily lacking in the qualities that distinguish their counter parts in Nandi and Swazi. As Evans-Pritchard reports:

The age sets have no corporate activities and cannot be said to have specific political functions. There are no grades of "warriors" and "elders" concerned with the administration of the country, and the sets are not regiments, for a man fights with the members of his local community, irrespective of age. In the rites of initiation there is no educative or moral training. There is no leadership in the sets.[21]

What then do they do? They fix and emphasize the status of all males in relation to other males as equals, juniors, and seniors. They are merely weak counterparts of the functionally more significant age sets to the south of them.

NYAKYUSA AGE SETS In sharp contrast to the weakly developed Nuer age sets are those of the Nyakyusa, who live on the northwest shores of Lake Nyasa. Little Nyakyusa boys of six to eleven years of age band together to herd their fathers' cattle, and for several years, they spend their waking hours together on the range. When they reach twelve or so, they leave off herding to take up the hoe in the gardens of their fathers; they then move into a village of older boys, no more to sleep at home. They return to the parental homestead for meals, but only when accompanied by a group of their age-mates. Boys should associate with boys even when visiting their parents. They live as members of a tightly knit juvenile gang, but without the element of gangsterism. They have no need to express hostility to the adult world. Their culture moves them steadily and early into the shouldering of the responsibilities of men through the concerted activities of youth.

When the young men approach the age of twenty-five, one by one they marry. Each brings his wife into the age village of his peers, and what was once Boys' Town is gradually transformed into a family village of husbands and wives and their children. It is unique in that all the men of the village are of an age. Now each youth receives his own fields from his father, and he ceases to return to his parents' house for meals, eating instead, under his own roof, his food prepared by his wife rather than his mother.

In another ten years, when all the villages of a given age level within a district have matured, the formal government of the territory is ritually handed over to them, and they rule the land while their generation of sons begins anew the process, breaking off to start the formation of their own age villages-to-be.

In Nyasaland, the age set is more than an auxiliary to the kinship group or a segment of village life. While closely linked to his primary conjugal-natal family in many ways, the Nyakyusa boy begins the severance of the primary family strands long before he is ready to start a family of his own, and his age set becomes the core of the social structure of his entire society.[22]

Incidence of age sets

The use of age as a basis of status identification is, as was pointed out in Chapter 8, a universal cultural phenomenon. The institutionalization of

[20]H. Kuper, *The Swazi: A South African Kingdom*, pp. 55–56. By permission of Holt, Rinehart and Winston, Inc.

[21]E. E. Evans-Pritchard, "The Nuer of the Southern Sudan," in *African Political Systems*, p. 289. By permission of International African Institute.

[22]M. Wilson, *Good Company: A Study of Nyakyusa Age-villages*.

age groups into definite age sets is, on the contrary, exceedingly rare; it occurs in only 23 out of 547 cultures included in the *World Ethnographic Sample*, or 4 per cent of the sample. Sixteen of the twenty-three are located in Africa,[23] where the frequency of age grading (which even there equals only 15 per cent of the tribes) is clearly a result of diffusion, as it is among the Plains tribes of North America. But the sporadic distribution of age grades around the world is good evidence of its independent invention in the several continental areas.

Eisenstadt's theory of age groupings

In a comparative study of age groupings, S. N. Eisenstadt developed the hypothesis that: "Age-homogeneous groups tend to arise in those societies in which the allocation of roles, facilities and rewards is not based on membership in kinship— or otherwise particularistically defined—units and criteria."[24]

This hypothesis is plausible, for it does seem reasonable to suppose that where desirable statuses do not flow from kinship ties, alternatives will be seized upon. Age groups would seem to be easily developed substitutes in view of the universality of age as a biological fact. However, the data of the *World Ethnographic Sample* raise serious doubts as to the significance of the hypothesis. There are too many societies that allocate roles outside the kinship system and do not develop age grades. Unidentified negative forces neutralize whatever tendency there might logically seem to be at work. Age grades are, it is true, very interesting to contemplate in themselves, but surprisingly they are not of as much significance in human affairs as anthropologists once thought.

ASSOCIATIONS AND SOCIAL DYNAMICS

No clear-cut relation of club occurrence and distribution shows up through such cross-cultural comparison as has been done to date. Obviously, however, one would expect these associations to occur more frequently in societies with larger, rather than smaller, populations, and with more complex cultures which provide for a greater differentiation of functions and interests. Urbanization and any other tendency which works to weaken the strength of the kinship bond will concomitantly contribute to a compensatory tendency to form clubs.

It is quite clear that associations flourish in rapidly changing, nontraditional social situations. Early in the nineteenth century de Tocqueville observed, "In no country of the world has the principle of association been more successfully used or applied to a greater number of objects than in America."[25] It will be remembered that Americans of that era, many of them migrants from either Europe or rural communities, were struggling to adjust to alien urban situations, separated from their kin, bewildered by new work and social roles, and frequently helpless in time of trouble. The multiplicity of voluntary associations of which de Tocqueville spoke was an adaptive response to new cultural circumstances. Just so, in a number of new African nations, voluntary credit unions among village and urban dwellers abound, and cooperative work groups and trade unions vie for members' loyalties, while helping to organize energy and resources for mutual improvement of their lot in life.

Professor A. L. Epstein, who pioneered the study of urbanization of mineworkers in Rhodesia, has penned an eloquently phrased summary of the process:

But as the urban communities themselves took root, new problems arose for which the traditional wisdom of the Elders provided no solution, and of which they were sometimes unaware. The need for new roads in the town, the need to seek avenues of employment for African women, the need in the towns for hostels for old people, the problem of discharged mine employees— these were some of the problems facing the new urban communities. They were drawing the attention of the younger and better-educated men in the Advisory Councils: they aroused little response among the 'Elders.'

The Africans who were led to join the Welfare Societies were of a younger generation, and were better educated. They were more conscious of the problems of urban life, and of the rapidly developing pattern of

[23]Coult and Habenstein, *loc. cit.*
[24]S. N. Eisenstadt, *From Generation to Generation*, p. 54.

[25]A. de Tocqueville, *Democracy in America* (1945), vol. 1, p. 198.

relations between the races. Significantly, the discussions of the Welfare Societies were conducted, and the minutes of their meetings recorded, in English. A District Commissioner had once sneered at the Welfare Societies as debating societies where the educated native had the opportunity to get up before his fellows and air his English. The District Commissioner did not appreciate that in using English at their meetings, the Africans were learning to handle one of the most important tools of the new culture. When Africans conversed together in English, they showed that they had interests in common which cut across tribal divisions. Furthermore, in the handling of novel concepts they were broadening their intellectual horizons, and making possible closer contact and acquaintance with the world outside. But more than this, in their professions of schoolteacher, of Christian minister of religion, and of clerk, they were actively engaged in pushing forward into a new form of society where clan affiliation or attachment to village headman and chief were no longer mechanisms of primary significance in ordering social relations. Through such organizations as the Welfare Societies, these people were beginning to stake out their claim to full membership in the new industrial society that was growing up around the mines.[26]

SELECTED READINGS

Banton, M., "Voluntary Associations: Anthropological Aspects" (*International Encyclopedia of the Social Sciences,* vol. 16, 1968), pp. 357-362. A helpful, brief summary of the subject.

---

[26]A. L. Epstein, *Politics in an Urban African Community*, p. 84. By permission of Humanties Press, Inc., New Jersey.

Bradfield, R. M., *A Natural History of Associations: A Study in the Meaning of Community* (1973). This two-volume work constructs a carefully documented argument about the function, content, meaning, and development of associations as a kind of social organization contrasted to kin-based organization. Detailed ethnographic analyses of several African, Melanesian, and North American Indian tribes are used to illustrate and validate the presentation.

Eisenstadt, S. N., *From Generation to Generation* (1956). Particularly interesting in its comparative analysis of youth movements in Germany and Israel in relation to primitive age grading.

Epstein, A. L., *Politics in an Urban African Community* (1958), chap. 4, "Trade Unionism and Social Cohesion," pp. 86–156. Presents a rich account of this modern form of voluntary association as adopted by African workers in the copperbelt of Rhodesia.

Little, K. L., *West African Urbanization: A Study of Voluntary Associations in Social Change* (1965). An intensive study of associations in the shift from tribal to city life in new African nations.

Llewellyn, K. N., and E. A. Hoebel, *The Cheyenne Way: Conflict and Case Law in Primitive Jurisprudence* (1941), chap. 5, "The Military Societies." A case study of Cheyenne Indian men's clubs in operation.

Lowie, R. H., *Primitive Society* (1920), chaps. 10 and 11, "Associations" and "Theory of Associations." An excellent comparative discussion of clubs and age groups in several primitive societies.

Webster, H., *Primitive Secret Societies* (1908). An old but valuable work.

Wilson, M., *Good Company: A Study of Nyakyusa Age-villages* (1951). A truly fascinating account of a unique development of the age-grading principle.

15

ECONOMIC ORGANIZATION

LEARNING GOALS

Show that property is a social creation. ¶ Summarize the general features of property rights in game, garden produce, and livestock in primitive cultures. ¶ Describe the main patterns of property rights in tools and weapons among primitives. ¶ Discuss the concept of incorporeal property and the patterns for its use. ¶ Distinguish and exemplify primary and secondary consumption of goods. ¶ Illustrate reciprocal exchange with examples from the Andamans, Melanesia, and Africa. ¶ Show the relation of redistributive exchange to the rise of civilizations. ¶ Briefly describe the different modes of inheritance of property.

The anthropological study of economic organization is a focal point for discovering the relationship between the material and nonmaterial aspects of the environment and human behavior, called property, and the social system within which property is exchanged and redistributed as cultural goods and services. We treat economic organization as a link between the material base to culture and social structure because it is concerned on one hand with the products of technology, and on the other, with their differential distribution through the social structure—the modes of exchange. In no society is everything up for grabs. Economic order, in one form or another, is a functional prerequisite to societal survival and continuity (page 30). As such, it is a universal aspect of culture, for if there have been societies which failed to adequately motivate men and women to work and production, and which failed to develop effective systems of distribution of the products of work input, then such societies have failed to adapt to the circumstances of life. They have not survived for our study!

PROPERTY

Property is a universal feature of human culture. However, from the anthropological point of view, the concept of property embraces a far larger inventory of possessions, both tangible and intangible, than the twentieth-century Western individual is likely to realize. The land upon which the social group is located and from which it draws its sustenance, the beasts that rove upon it wild, the animals that graze upon it tame, the trees and the crops, the houses that people erect, the clothes they wear, the songs they sing, the dances they execute, the charms they incant, these and many more are objects of property. Human beings tend to bring within the scope of property whatever they rely upon for the maintenance of life or value for other reasons. So it is that property is as ubiquitous as mankind, a part of the basic fabric of all society.

THE NATURE OF PROPERTY

People may relate to property in various ways: individually (to personal property), by groups (to joint property), or by the society at large (to communal property). Property may be fixed and immovable (real estate), or it may be movable (chattel). It may be material and concrete, or it may be an idea or a way of acting (incorporeal). It may be transferable by gift, barter, sale, inheritance, or confiscation, or it may be inalienable. It may or may not be protected by law. It may be reinforced by ritual or protected by magic. Or it may be sustained as customary usage sanctioned without the aid of either law or the supernatural. Many people habitually think of property only as a thing or as things. Yet the thing itself is but one aspect of property, for the essential nature of property is found in its qualities as a social institution. Property lends formal expression to social structure. It specifies and allocates access not only to concrete necessities such as land and food supplies, but to items of symbolic value such as a feathered headdress, house decoration, and honorific titles.

Property: A Social Creation

Property in its full sense is *a web of social relations with respect to the utilization of some object (material or nonmaterial) in which a person or group is tacitly or explicitly recognized to hold quasi-exclusive and limiting connections.*

As an illustration, a stone conveniently shaped for use as an axhead lies unnoticed and unused for years on the surface of the ground. It is not property. It is, in legal terminology, a *res nullius*: a nothing. A wandering tribesman finds it, takes it, and uses it as a hand ax. This in itself makes the stone merely an object of possession. If the social practices of the possessor's tribe are such that any other person could appropriate this tool at will, it would still be a mere matter of possession. But if the custom is such that his fellow tribesmen recognize that he has special *rights* in possessing that piece of rock and that all others have a *duty* to desist from using or taking it, then it is an object of property. The stone has not changed, but the social pattern with respect to it has. It is the special and peculiar set of social relations which has transformed the rock into an object of property. Thus, we have two irreducible aspects of property: (1) the object, and (2) the web of social relations that establishes a limiting and defined status relationship between persons and the object.

This limiting relationship is often referred to by lawyers and economists as an *exclusive right of use*. It is exclusive insofar as it excludes nonowners from legitimate use without the express or tacit approval of the owner. However, the right is rarely, if ever, so absolutely exclusive that the owner may utilize the object in any way his whim may dictate. The individual's rights of use are always limited to some extent by the demands of society. After all, society, not the individual, creates and maintains the institution of property. This is not to say that society created the *object*. The point of emphasis is that an object does not become property until the members of the society at large agree to bestow the property attribute upon it by regulating their behavior in a self-limiting manner. This is done because social experience has led to the conclusion that social benefits are derived from granting "exclusive" rights to individuals and groups with respect to certain classes of objects that they have created or acquired. By the same token, individuals always limit the extent of that exclusiveness in accordance with their conception of the needs of social good. Property—a social creation—is consequently always subject to social limitations, even in the most individualistic societies. Thus it is that as social concepts change from time to time, the specific content of property concepts undergoes alterations. The form and content of property notions are not the expression of immutable instinct or of any imagined laws of nature. Property in the United States today is not what it was in the mid-nineteenth century, nor what it will be at the dawn of the twenty-first.

Yurok canoe ownership

As an example of the way in which property is constituted, we may briefly analyze canoe ownership among the Yuroks of California—a highly individualistic people. A Yurok boat owner nominally possessed his canoe as private property. It was his. He had a series of demand rights against all other persons not to molest or damage his boat. He had the privilege right to use it upon the public waters. He did not have to sell it or give it away. These are all marks of exclusive rights. Yet he was also subject to a series of well-recognized duties which limited his exclusive prerogatives.

For one thing, he was obligated to ferry any traveler over the river when called upon to do so. Failure to perform this duty gave the traveler a demand right for legal damages equal to one dentalium shell.[1] On the other hand, if the owner suffered injury because of the service he had to render, the traveler was subject to damages. Thus, when one canoeman's house burned down while he was in midstream, his passenger had to pay for it.

This is what Cook meant when he said, ". . . ownership . . . is found to consist not only of an indefinite number of rights in the strict sense of claims available against an indefinite number of persons, each of whom is under a corresponding duty, but also a large and indefinite number of privileges, powers and immunities. . . ."[2]

Property and law

Finally, we should take note of the relation of property to law. In the modern world, it is a fact that a vast proportion of the law of the state is devoted to the definition of the relationships between owners of property. Much of the activity of our courts and police is concerned with maintaining and enforcing these relationships. Government feeds and grows on the complexity of property in a heterogeneous industrial civilization.

But to state that property rights "exist only because government recognizes and protects them"[3] is an expression of an amazingly myopic point of view. Property rights are tacitly and explicitly recognized and upheld by all forms of social sanction, legal and nonlegal alike. And in the case of primitive society, the recognition and support of property institutions are in fact more frequently nonlegal than legal. Even when legal in nature, primitive property law falls predominantly within the area of private law, which operates independently of the formal governmental machinery.

LAND AS PROPERTY IN PRIMITIVE CULTURES

Land is a *sine qua non* of human existence. It is therefore the most important single object of property. All societies are territorially based,[4] and most sustenance is drawn from the soil, either directly or indirectly. The analysis of specific land-property patterns has already been presented in Chapter 7, where land ownership was related to differing techniques of food exploitation as they are associated with the environmental complexes of the world. There can be derived from the study of these food technologies and land-use patterns some general principles of land tenure among primitive peoples. Primitive gardeners assign the rights of use to individuals or families. In some instances title is vested in the clan, but usually ultimate ownership is vested in the community. In parts of Africa, this communism is traditionally transformed into a type of feudal monarchy, where the king symbolizes community entity. Unused land is public domain from which enterprising individuals may carve their plots, with or without official approval, depending on tribal practice.

On the whole, primitive peoples overwhelmingly treat their land resources as a communal asset. In this sense, they are preponderantly communistic. Pastoralists are, for the most part, land communists because the necessity to rove makes individual ownership impractical. In the case of the hunters and gatherers, there is also little impulse to private ownership of land, since so far as the hunters are concerned, most animals are free-ranging, and it is more advantageous to rove at will when on the chase. When the habits of prized animals made it feasible, such peoples as the Algonkians and Northwest Coast Indians were quite ready to abandon land communism for

[1]A narrow, tubelike seashell, harvested by the Nootka tribe, traded and used as shell money among other tribes of the Northwest Coast of North America. See P. Drucker, *Cultures of the North Pacific Coast*, pp. 151–152, 177–178.

[2]W. W. Cook, "Ownership and Possession" (*Encyclopaedia of the Social Sciences*, vol. 11, 1933), p. 521. Copyright © 1933 by the Macmillan Company. Quoted with permission.

[3]R. M. MacIver, "Government and Property" (*Journal of Political and Legal Sociology*, vol. 4, 1946), p. 5. For an opposite point of view refer to A. I. Hallowell, "The Nature and Function of Property as a Social Institution" (*Journal of Legal and Political Sociology*, vol. 1, 1943), pp. 115–138, especially pp. 130ff. See also the article by W. H. Hamilton and I. Till, "Property" (*Encyclopaedia of the Social Sciences*, vol. 12, 1934), pp. 528–538.

[4]One notable, possibly the only, exception to this is the case of the Orang Laut, the Malayan sea gypsies of the Java and Flores Seas. These tribes are autonomous units, living a roving existence entirely in boats.

vested rights. Primeval human beings were not "by nature" communists. But they responded to ecological and economic factors which usually made communal land ownership the most feasible means of allocating access to basic food resources.

Theories of social evolution which assume "primitive communism" as the first mile on humanity's rough road thus have some foundation, as far as use of the land resources goes.

Those who take the institutions of private property for granted are prone to point to the widespread communism of primitive humanity as proof of the "advanced" quality of private-property institutions. Communism, they hold, is representative of a primitive state, and the spread of modern Communism is a reversion to a condition of savagery.

With equal lack of balance, Marxists see the land communism of the primitives as proof that communism is the "natural" and therefore the proper and manifest condition for all human society.

The anthropologist notes that the real estate practices of primitive peoples are not properly to be conceived as a justification for any particular economic forms in modern civilization. These varying property practices merely demonstrate that human beings can, and usually do, adjust their social institutions to the special needs of their subsistence technologies and natural resources.

PROPERTY RIGHTS IN CONSUMABLES

Food is undoubtedly one of the most basic property interests of omnivorous mankind. Land may seem important, but that is largely because it is the chief original source of the food supply. We have already seen that some foodstuffs are in some societies free goods, as is the air we breathe. But elsewhere and oftentimes access to food is limited; the ethics of food use fluctuate. The sense of the necessity of mutual aid and a realization of the inescapable interdependence of individuals struggle eternally with the self-assertive urges of barebones survival (when resources give but slim pickings) and selfish gratification of desires. Selfishness corrupts altruistic

ideals; mutual aid tempers the harshest self-interest. Property rights in food are the formal crystallization of each society's struggle to regulate the distribution and use of this essential commodity.

Property Rights in Game

Wild plants and animals on communal lands are communal property, but the slaying of game and the collection of plant stuffs alter the economic condition of these goods, subjecting them to altered property statuses. So it is that, while the general principle of collective ownership of free-running game and unharvested plants holds good, we find that in most instances the expenditure of work in reducing the game and plants into consumable food stocks converts them into private property. All peoples recognize private ownership of food. Yet inasmuch as private ownership never entails absolute exclusiveness, and since among hunters and gatherers food is derived from communally owned resources, the communal claim upon privately owned foodstuffs is insistent.

Among the Comanches, anyone coming upon a hunter who had just made a kill could claim the choicest quarter of the animal merely by placing a hand upon it. If four different people happened on the unfortunate hunter, they took everything except the hide. This, custom decreed, the hunter could retain by hanging onto the tail of the beast. Far to the north, Boas recorded, the following was typical for the Baffin Land Eskimos: "Who first strikes a walrus receives the tusks and one of the forequarters; the next man, the neck and head; the following, the belly; and each of the next two, one of the hindquarters."[5]

Again, in the practice of the Comanches, any hunter returning to the camp with game was obliged to come in openly and share the spoils with all who came to his lodge for a portion of it. "If a man won't give it away, they camp on him until he does."[6] To frustrate this social lien on the products of their individual efforts, some families camped alone during hard times.

[5] F. Boas, *The Eskimo of Baffinland and Hudson Bay* (American Museum of Natural History, Bulletin No. 15, 1907), p. 116.

[6] E. A. Hoebel, *The Political Organization and Law-ways of the Comanche Indians*, p. 119.

After the communal antelope hunts of the Plains Indians, the meat was equally divided among all participating families, for the whole project was a gigantic cooperative undertaking. In communal bison hunts, after the acquisition of horses, all Plains tribes allowed each man whose marked arrow had killed a bison to keep the meat. But even so, the old and infirm who could not hunt and the wives of luckless hunters received their shares from those who had made a kill, and it was the usual thing to teach a boy to give away all his first kill of any large game animal.

Food sharing

Sharing of food, even though the food is privately owned, is the basic virtue of almost all American Indian tribes and of most of the primitive hunters of the world. To be generous with food—that is the ideal. But as Lowie pointed out, etiquette which demands that all comers be fed from a person's private larder is something quite different from actual communal ownership of a common hoard by all the members of the group.[7] The psychological and social response to private beneficence results in a different order of social prestige ranking from that which is produced by common ownership.

The successful hunter reaps prestige from his beneficence as a public provider. In return for food, which does not come easily, the hunter is accorded a leadership position among his people. His rewards, beyond what he may eat himself, are sociopsychological. He is motivated to extend himself as a hunter not only that he may eat but also that he may enjoy the pleasures of socially recognized achievement. There is real survival value for a marginal subsistence society in this arrangement. The African Bushman headman known to Elizabeth Thomas is a perfect example of this common pattern among hunting peoples:

Toma flourished as a young man and became an excellent hunter with tireless legs, tireless eyes, and a deadly aim, and it was said of him that he never returned from a hunt without having killed at least a wildebeast, if not something larger. Hence, the people connected with him ate a great deal of meat and his popularity grew.[8]

Outright pooling of food occurs less commonly among the hunting and collecting peoples than among the gardeners. In the South Pacific, it is associated with prestige competition between local groups and tribes. Great quantities of produce are offered to the chief to be used in feasting rival tribes. The chief's storehouses among the Maori, for example, were the people's storehouses, for the people identified his needs as their needs. They were regularly fed from the great storehouses, but above all, their great concern was that the chief should be able to entertain visitors munificently. Should he fail in this, their outraged pride would make them ashamed before the world. Eating was to the Maori the supreme pleasure, and only by the joint efforts of all could it reach the great heights they so cherished.

Communal pooling of certain foods is also characteristic of American Pueblo Indians. Annual rabbit hunts are held every fall, and all men must participate as a religious duty. The dried rabbits are offered to the head priest-chief of the pueblo, who stores them in his house to be used in ceremonial meals and to be doled out by him to the poor and hungry families of his pueblo in time of need.

Individual property rights in game

At the opposite extreme, certain Algonkian hunters of North America, such as the Ojibwa, demonstrate the ideological lengths to which rugged individualism in food procured from wild game can go. Says Landes:

The game and fish that a man catches in the winter are his private property. When he returns with them to his lodge . . . he decides what to do with them. . . . When he gives game to his wife . . . he has lost all claim to it. It is never said that he gives game to his wife for her use in making food and clothing for the family; but they phrase it that a man gives game to his wife and therefore the game belongs to her to do with as she pleases. . . . The wife now employs "her" property in the manufacture of food and clothing. She gives the finished product to her husband, immature children, and herself. When these

---

1958, 1959, Elizabeth Marshall Thomas. Published by Alfred Knopf. Quoted with permission. See also J. H. Dowling, "Individual Ownership and the Sharing of Game in Hunting Societies" (*American Anthropologist*, vol. 70, 1968), pp. 502–507.

[7] R. H. Lowie, *Primitive Society*, pp. 207–210.
[8] E. M. Thomas, *The Harmless People*, p. 182. Copyright ©

gifts have been given, they become the property of the recipients.[9]

Among many hunting tribes, animals having a fixed abode, such as a hibernating bear, a bee, or an eagle, are often seized upon as objects of private ownership, even where all other claims to animals are communal. The Nama Hottentot places a few broken twigs before a wild beehive, and a Sia Indian publicly announces the location of bee trees which he has discovered—not to invite others to find the way to the delicacy, but to warn them off. Eagle nests are privately owned among all the Pueblo Indians, so that eagles born in the nest belong to the owner of it. A Pueblo hunter who finds a bear's den marks it, and the bear is his to take in the spring.

Similarly, wild fruit trees in Indonesia and among many peoples of the South Pacific may be blazed or otherwise marked by an individual so that he alone may harvest the tree's yield. In the Melanesian area, the tree is guarded by a magic charm that brings foul diseases to any violator of the property right of the owner. Ownership of such trees is usually divorced from the land upon which the tree stands. In some places, it is even possible to own a tree that stands on another man's land.

Property Rights in Garden Produce

Ownership of foodstuffs produced by gardening tends generally to be vested in individuals or family households, but the lines are not drawn with universal consistency. Since most garden plots are worked under individual rights of use or outright ownership, and since most of the expended effort is individual effort, harvests are commonly individually owned. Polynesian practices in contravention of this usage have already been noted, however. Among the Keresan-speaking Pueblos, just as rabbit hunts are communal duties, so are the planting and cultivating of the cacique's, or chief's, garden. The harvest is stored in the cacique's house for communal use.

Matrilateral practices in Melanesia require that a man raise his crops on his sister's behalf. Since his sister's household is not his own household, he must in effect transfer the yams from his garden to the storehouses of her husband. His storehouses in turn are filled in part by his wife's brother. What a man produces does not necessarily remain his own property.

Property Rights in Livestock

The word "chattel," which means any object of personal ownership, is derived from the Old French word *chatel*. The modern Anglo-American word "cattle" has the same origin. *Chatel* has its ultimate etymology in the Latin word *caput*, meaning "head." *Chatel* in ancient France referred to property of the greatest value, head property. Cattle were so much the chief form of property among our pastoral ancestors that our specialized word for personal property grew from the same root. And the word "pecuniary" (pertaining to money) derives directly from the class of movable property known as *pecunia* in Roman law, where the term was itself derived directly from the Latin word *pecus*, meaning "herd."

This small fragment of word history formulates the universal principle of stock ownership among all primitive peoples. Cattle are chattels (see Fig. 15-1). They are privately owned. The one great known exception occurred in that remarkable precursor of the totalitarian socialist state, the Inca Empire. Among the Incas, private citizens could own up to ten llamas, but the vast majority of the beasts were state property. The wool collected from the state herds was stored in government warehouses, to be distributed annually in equal allotments to each family head.[10]

Grazing land among migratory primitive pastoralists does not economically lend itself to subdivision. Hence, as has been noted, it is usually communally held and used. But livestock comes in individual units to which individuals may readily attach themselves. Undoubtedly, there is a deep emotional impulse underlying this tendency.

---

[9]R. Landes, "The Ojibwa of Canada," in M. Mead (ed.), *Cooperation and Competition among Primitive Peoples*, pp. 90–91. By permission of M. Mead.

[10]J. H. Rowe, "Inca Culture at the Time of the Spanish Conquest," in J. H. Steward (ed.), *Handbook of South American Indians*, vol. 2, pp. 219, 267.

FIG. 15-1 Livestock are chattel. Karamojong pastoralists of Uganda, in East Africa, placing their property mark on one of their animals. (Photo courtesy of Rada and Neville Dyson-Hudson, *Natural History*.)

Domestication begins in a symbiotic relationship between man and animal which is fundamentally personal. It is most clearly seen in the affectionate relation between man and his dog, the first of the domesticated beasts. It runs through all herders in greater or lesser degree. Nuer men, when they have nothing more pressing to do, spend hours in sensuous contemplation of their cattle.[11]

"Some men," said Post Oak Jim, of the Comanche herders of 1850, "loved their horses more than their wives." Favorite horses among most Plains Indians were treated almost as family members. Among the Solomon Islanders and other Melanesians, pigs are the chief objects of value.

In the history of mankind, the domestication of animals has undoubtedly been a great stimulus to the development of private-property institutions. Thus the *World Ethnographic Sample* shows wealth to be a significant factor in the social differentiation of freemen only among pastoralists (phi = 0.157).[12]

PROPERTY RIGHTS IN ARTIFACTS

Weapons and implements for individual use are ordinarily owned either by their creator or by their user. Primitive women ordinarily own the pottery

[11]E. E. Evans-Pritchard, *The Nuer*. pp. 16–50.

[12]A. D. Coult and R. W. Habenstein, *Cross Tabulations of Murdock's Ethnographic Sample*, p. 518.

they have modeled. A man owns the spear or ax he has shaped himself. There is to some extent an identity between the artisan and his creation, as though it were an extension of his personality. Most of mankind has recognized this identity and respected it by establishing protective devices in the form of personal-property institutions. The stimulus to individual effort which is activated as a result contributes to the adaptive success of the society in self-maintenance.

Trobriand Canoe Ownership

Joint and mixed ownership of artifacts is also common. Thus, among the Trobriand Islanders, each canoe is nominally "owned" by one man; yet others, who make up its crew, have proprietary rights in the use of the vessel.

All these men, who as a rule belong to the same sub-clan, are bound to each other . . . by mutual obligations; when the whole community go out fishing, the owner cannot refuse his canoe. He must go out himself or let someone else do it instead. The crew are equally under an obligation to him . . . each man must fill his place and stand by his task. Each man also receives his fair share in the distribution of the catch as an equivalent of his service. Thus the ownership and use of the canoe consist of a series of definite obligations and duties uniting a group of people into a working team.[13]

INCORPOREAL PROPERTY

It no longer surprises anthropologists that non-material things of value are objects of property in primitive society.[14] It never would have surprised us at all if our grandfather's generation and its predecessors had not been so smugly self-assured that uncivilized peoples were of childlike mentality and that Europeans alone were capable of mental abstraction.

However, the better to understand the nature of incorporeal property, consider the case of a Plains Indian visionary who has fasted and sought supernatural power. A bear has appeared to him

in a dream; it spoke to him and taught him four new songs, and it also instructed him in the preparation of a rawhide shield to be painted with a bear symbol and other devices. The bear in the vision also instructed his tutelary that a shield made in accordance with the instructions would provide immunity in battle if the four songs were sung before an engagement began. The visionary has made a shield as instructed; he has sung the songs; his comrades have heard the words; and he has deliberately exposed himself to the missiles of the enemy, coming through unscathed. The value of the shield and the songs has been publicly demonstrated. The shield, as Lowie has made clear, is a material object that is clearly personal property.

But the shield as such, in the culture of the Plains Indians, is of little value. What is of value in conjunction with the shield are the songs and the mystic power which the two engender together. The incorporeal property is the thing of worth. The complex of shield, song, and power may be transferred as a gift to son, nephew, brother, or friend. (In at least one Comanche case, which the senior author has recorded, the transfer had to be followed by the recipient's having a vision before the mystic power would become operative, however, and this may frequently be the case among other tribes.) Or this same complex may be sold in a commercial transaction having the qualities of a contractual sale. In either case, the recipient may use the complex if he has properly acquired the rights through regularized transfer, but not otherwise. The consequence of unauthorized use of the shield and songs is that the usurper will most certainly be killed by enemy missiles because of the punitive action of the supernatural power. But there is no reason to believe that the true owner may not recover the shield if it is stolen, and with it his enjoyment of the songs.

Certainly we have here a sufficiently large aggregate of rights denoted by ownership so that we may properly speak of them as incorporeal property. Thus, we find again and again that magic rites and charms, songs, dances, and names are the property of persons and groups of persons. Myths and legends may belong to lineages, as among the Indians of the Northwest Coast. These are objects of property in exactly the same sense

---

[13]B. Malinowski, *Crime and Custom in Savage Society*, p. 18. By permission of Humanities Press, Inc.

[14]See R. H. Lowie, "Incorporeal Property in Primitive Society" (*Yale Law Journal*, vol. 38, 1928), p. 551; and *Primitive Society*, pp. 235–243. See also E. A. Hoebel, *The Law of Primitive Man*.

as are our copyrights, patents, and "goodwill." After all, if a people is capable of creating intangible patterns for behavior, such as magic and songs, it is not a great step into the abstruse to attach protective social rules to these abstractions when and if they become objects of value.

Likewise, the hereditary right to work is a traditional incorporeal property right for certain groups in India, and the available work is distributed accordingly. N. S. Reddy writes of the Madiga caste of leatherworkers in Madras: "The right to work is inherited as any other piece of property, and the quantum of employment that accrues to the individual holder is upheld by the community at large."[15]

ECONOMIC ORGANIZATION FOR CONSUMPTION AND EXCHANGE

Many items of property produced and owned within a society are exchanged and consumed in a patterned manner. Food property is consumed and disappears from the economic realm as a material item even though it might remain economically as a reciprocal obligation or a money debt. Other items, such as tools, containers, clothing, transportation devices, etc., may be exchanged many times but eventually they wear out and are discarded, to be replaced by the production of a new item by the last owner or through exchange with someone else who possesses or produces the item. Some property, such as land, housing, or incorporeal property, may not be exchanged often or not at all except through the process of inheritance when one owner dies and the property rights are passed on to others who stand in some special social structural relationship to the deceased. The anthropological study of social processes whereby property items and property rights move from individual to individual reveal that, especially in primitive societies, the same social structures that are used to organize marriage, child-rearing responsibilities, social control, and other social processes also function to coordinate economic exchange and redistribution. Cross-cultural studies further reveal that

regardless of the differences between societies in specific social structures, there are a few basic patterns of consumption and modes of exchange and inheritance which can be used to characterize economic organization in all cultures.

PRIMARY AND SECONDARY CONSUMPTION

A notable difference between primitive and civilized economic systems is that in simple primitive societies a high proportion of food and goods is consumed by the producer and the members of his own family or household. The consumption is *primary* and no exchange outside the primary group is necessary. A man literally "brings home the bacon"—and not from the market, or from some other farmer's enterprise, but from the bush. A man not only does his own hunting, his wife her own gathering, but he makes his own spear, his own bow and arrows, his own house, etc. But as soon as it becomes customary to share food with members of other primary groups, as soon as it is recognized that another man can make better arrows and specialized division of labor sets in—then a system of exchange is created. Exchange systems involve *secondary* consumption: food and goods are used by persons who are not members of a primary group of the original producer. Secondary consumption, as shall soon be demonstrated, occurs in primitive societies and sometimes to a high degree. However, in civilizations (particularly those of urban dwellers), primary consumption is very low. Just consider what, if anything, of the food, clothing, shelter, and other goods which you are using this day, you have produced any part of! Primary production may be the woof of the fabric of civilization, but exchange to effect secondary consumption is its economic web.

How do exchange systems work?

THREE MODES OF EXCHANGE

The economist Karl Polanyi (1893–1964) brought into focus three contrasting modes of cultural channeling of ultimate access to valued goods in human societies. These are: (1) reciprocal ex-

[15]N. S. Reddy, *Transition in Caste Structure in Andrah Desh with Particular Reference to Depressed Castes*, p. 61.

change, (2) redistributive exchange, and (3) market exchange.[16]

Reciprocal exchange consists of obligatory gift giving and countergiving of goods and services between persons (and groups) of specific statuses (see pages 142–144) within a social system. A Trobriand Islander, for example, raises yams on land which is assigned to him in his own village. All but the poorest of these he carries to another village where his married sister lives with her husband. There they are shown in ceremonial display, and then carefully packed in thatched-roof storehouses made of horizontally laid logs through which the yams may be seen and continually admired until they are consumed. No man sells best-quality yams to another. Nor does he trade them to just anybody. Lesser-quality yams and melons he may trade for fish with an exchange partner, but he cannot walk up and down the beach looking for any random fisherman with whom he may strike a good bargain. *This is not a market economy.*

From his sister's husband, a Trobriander receives return gifts, but most important of all, he gets his sister's sons, who leave their father to live with a maternal uncle, well before the onset of puberty. They become the uncle's helpers, are trained and educated by him; they also become his heirs and successors to his rights of use in land, his magical formulas, his wealth and prerogatives—as well as membership in his matrilineal clan. The prime yams, which a man laboriously produces and ostentatiously gives to his sister's husband, are well repaid by services received from the latter.[17]

Redistributive exchange occurs when a holder of economic or political office—a hereditary chief or monarch, or a priest, for instance—is vested with the power to exact goods or services as tribute. These are first funneled into the "royal" or cult holding centers. After the governing elite has creamed off what custom or its power enables it

to use for its own consumption, a portion is redistributed to the populace. Redistribution may or may not be equitable. The basic handicraft producers are apt to get less in return than they put out. Yet, over all, they and other members of the society may collectively benefit from the higher levels of production which result from their combined, élite-directed efforts. Such systems are characteristic of a number of state-organized, preliterate horticultural societies (see Maya, below) and early civilizations.

Market exchange is based on direct barter (the more primitive manifestation) or on sale and purchase through use of a commercial medium of exchange: money. Where markets exist within the economic systems of tribal societies, they are usually peripheral; i.e., the goods available for exchange or sale through the market do not include "everything" available through the production system—especially land and labor. In other words, the bulk of exchange is reciprocal or redistributive, although markets do exist.

In cultures in which *most* exchange of goods and services is effected through transfer of symbolic tokens of unitary value (money), *market exchange* dominates. In a market economy all money uses are related to "free exchange"—free of kinship requirements, fealty to overlords, personal friendship, and other status limitations. In the free market, there are but two questions: do you "own" what you have to offer? and do you have the money (or the money credit) to make the payment? The market is impersonal. You can buy from anyone. You can sell to anyone. In reciprocal and redistributive exchange the relations are absolutely a matter of personal status.

Reciprocal Gift Exchange

Within many primitive societies gift giving which builds into gift exchange marks every important crisis period in the individual life cycle or any other change of personal status. Birth, puberty, marriage, death, entrance into a club, or assumption of an office is called to public attention by the bestowal of gifts. The famous potlatches of the Northwest Coast Indians, with all their lavish expenditure of gifts, center around such occasions. Contractual arrangements such as marriage call

---

[16]K. Polanyi, *The Great Transformation.*

[17]B. Malinowski, *Coral Gardens and Their Magic,* vol. 1, "The Customary Law of Harvest Gifts," pp. 188–217.

In 1967, the yam gardens, storage houses, and exchange system in the Trobriand Islands were virtually unchanged from Malinowski's descriptions of 1914–1917. In the case of this society it is, therefore, quite proper to use the present, rather than the past, tense.

for immediate two-way exchanges, often extending over months.

Gift exchange of economic significance may border on trade. Yet it may be merely symbolic in nature when the rule of equivalence is strong. The person who views our ceremonial gift exchanges on the occasion of the Christmas festival only in terms of the usableness of the gifts measured against cost and effort naturally thinks the whole business is silly. But this poor soul misses the point. Quite true, we all end up with a number of things we neither need nor want. Quite true, it would be more rational to offer gift certificates or even money to one's friends or family so that they could buy what they want and need. But how flat are such gifts! Their donors confuse the social function of gift giving with utility. They forget that the gifts are symbolic of a social bond between giver and receiver. Gifts represent a state of social relations and a set of emotions, not only business.

The Andaman Islands

On the lowest level of culture, the Andaman Islanders, in the Indian Ocean, nicely exemplify gift exchange. Movables were all privately owned by these people, and yet no one could possess a particular article for long.

When two friends meet who have not seen each other for some time, one of the first things they do is to exchange presents with one another. Even in the ordinary everyday life of the village there is a constant giving and receiving of presents. A younger man or woman may give some article to an older one without expecting or receiving any return, but between equals a person who gives a present always expects that he will receive something of equal value in exchange. At the meetings that take place between neighbouring local groups the exchange of presents is of great importance. . . .

Almost every object that the Andamanese possess is thus constantly changing hands.[18]

Pig exchange in Melanesia

In like manner, the elaborate extremes to which Melanesian "Big Men" go to operate exchange networks of pig-growing and pig-giving indicate

clearly that there is more than just the utilitarian production and distribution of pork involved (Fig. 15-2). In it one sees the very weaving of the fabric of societal interdependence. Margaret Mead's account of the Arapesh of New Guinea will help give some feel for the meaning of pig exchange in Melanesia:

We must now turn from the organization of everyday economic life to the organization of large-scale feasts. Here again, no matter how large the undertaking, it is phrased as one individual acting for a hamlet, or even sometimes for a cluster of hamlets, taking the responsibility of organization, while the others merely help him. It is a chain organization grouped around a leader who is called the *trunk* or *base* of the enterprise. The organization of feasts makes a man a "big man," but the Arapesh conceive this as an onerous duty which is forced upon him by community recognition of his ability to organize and lead, a duty which he fulfills without real enthusiasm and from which one retires as soon as one's first child reaches adolescence. In addition to organizing specific feasts centering about initiation, the exhumation of the bones of the dead, or the importation of some ceremonial dance complex from the Beach, the "big men" stand in a continuous exchange relationship with exchange partners, theoretically members of the opposite moiety, and always members of a different clan. These exchange partners call each other *buanyin*, are hereditary, usually in the male line, but not necessarily in the direct line. Old buanyin partnerships which have been unsatisfactory, that is, unequally matched, may be abandoned and new ones founded at any time. Such new ones again become hereditary. The buanyin relationship is modeled upon the relationship of brothers-in-law and the relationship which continues from it in the next generation, the cross-cousin relationship. Buanyins are conceived as members of autonomous groups, and engage in exchanges one with the other. But whereas between relatives and between trade friends, cost accounting, dunning, reproaching in economic terms are regarded as disgraceful, between buanyins there is a frank accounting system. Each one is expected to initiate exchanges with the other, and they are expected to insult one another publicly and to goad one another on to economic activity. The major exchanges between buanyins are of meat, and an exchange is initiated usually by the present to one of the buanyins of big game—wild pig or cassowary—or a domestic pig which has been trussed to a pole ready to be killed. If the man who now has become the temporary owner of the meat does not wish to use it, he gives it to his buanyin. He cannot refuse it, and will owe a return of

---

[18]A. R. Radcliffe-Brown, *The Andaman Islanders*, pp. 42–43. By permission of Cambridge University Press.

FIG. 15-2 Slaughtered and roasted boars being distributed by a Chimbu "Big Man" in a ceremonial exchange of sixty-seven pigs in settlement of a dispute over land. Near Goroka, East Central Highlands, New Guinea, 1967. (Photo by E. A. Hoebel.)

the same amount to his buanyin in the future. If he has no pig or game with which to repay, he will have to rear domestic pigs in order to return the gift. Giving meat to a buanyin is therefore a way of banking. When a man receives this large present of meat from his buanyin, he in turn distributes it to his relatives, who are thus obligated to help him make returns to his buanyin when necessary. Buanyins give each other feasts, at which neither buanyin eats, but each distributes food to his helping friends and relatives. . . . When the time for the final feast is set, each dog [cooperating pig partner] gives back a whole pig, representing the three-quarters of a pig which he has received, plus the other food. The trunk thus has all his negotiable wealth in his hands at once, and exchanges it either for dance ceremonial or for other pigs, or arranges for a return feast in another community which has similarly been organized around a trunk.[19]

Exchange of cattle in Africa

The joining of families by marriage affords a major means of reciprocal distribution in most primitive societies. Since in much of Africa the cow is the

principal unit of value—indeed, it has been written that the transfer of cows "has had the function of making concrete certain already existent social relationships"[20]—it is not surprising that weddings involve complicated transactions in cattle.

DISTRIBUTION OF MARRIAGE CATTLE AMONG THE NUER To illustrate the complex and highly ritualized socioeconomic aspects of progeny price, we may turn to the Nuer, a tribe of cattle raisers living on the upper reaches of the White Nile. Here, each marriage ideally calls for the transfer of forty head of cattle. Of these, twenty go to members of the bride's primary composite family, ten to her father's primary composite family, and ten to that of her mother. The distribution is as follows (see Fig. 15-3):

1. *Primary family of the bride:* To the bride's father *(a)*, eight head, specified as three cows and their calves and two oxen; to her brother born of another mother *(b)*, two cows; to her brother born

---

[19]M. Mead, *Cooperation and Competition among Primitive Peoples*, pp. 32–34. By permission of M. Mead.

[20]P. G. Gravel, "The Transfer of Cows in Gisaka (Rwanda): A Mechanism for Recording Social Relationships" (*American Anthropologist*, vol. 69, 1967), p. 322.

of the same mother *(c)*, two oxen, three cows, and a cow and its calf (seven head); to her mother *(d)*, a cow and its calf and a heifer.

2. Siblings of the bride's father: To the bride's father's elder brother by the same mother *(e)*, a cow and its calf, a calf, and an ox (four head); to the bride's father's younger brother by the same mother *(f)*, a cow and an ox; to the bride's father's sister *(g)*, one heifer; to the bride's father's brother by a different mother *(h)*, a cow and its calf and an ox.

3. Siblings of the bride's mother: To the bride's mother's elder brother by the same mother *(i)*, a cow and its calf, a cow, and an ox; to the bride's mother's younger brother by the same mother *(j)*, a cow and its calf; to the bride's mother's sister *(k)*, one heifer; to a brother of the bride's mother through a different mother *(l)*, a cow and its calf and an ox.[21]

In addition to these specific rights to cattle,

[21]These figures represent the ideal norm among the Eastern Nuer as reported by Evans-Pritchard, "Nuer Bride-wealth" (*Africa*, vol. 16, 1946), p. 4. In the real culture, they vary by circumstance and district within the tribe. See P. P. Howell, *A Manual of Nuer Law*, pp. 101–124.

every patrilineal relative of the bride, even though the relationship be so remote as that of descent from a common ancestor six or seven generations back, may claim a small gift from the groom's kinsmen. Special symbolic gifts of cattle may be called for in the name of ancestral spirits of the bride, of her "father's best friend, of an age classmate of her father, of her father's fireplace, and to the priest who performs magic rituals for enhancement of the bride's fecundity."

All this should make it very clear how much more than just a commercial transaction is the transfer of bride wealth, or progeny price.

The Kula

Without doubt, the most elaborate and exciting system of reciprocal exchange yet noted for the primitive world is the *kula* of northwestern Melanesia. Malinowski's thorough description of the *kula*, published in 1922, will continue to stand as a classic of anthropological economics for many years to come. The *kula* enterprise is a vast complex of trade, magic, ceremonial exchange, overseas travel, and pleasure seeking that in-

FIG. 15-3 Identification of relatives in Nuer progeny price distribution.

Paternal siblings   Primary conjugal-natal family of the bride   Maternal siblings volves the enterprisers of tribes many miles apart. The framework through which the whole organization is expressed is the exchange of white shell armbands, called *mwali,* and long necklaces of red shell, called *soulava.* Exchange is intertribal and interisland. *Soulava* are always traded in a clockwise direction. *Mwali* go counterclockwise (Fig. 15-4). There is no exception to this rule.

Each of these articles . . . meets on its way articles of the other class, and is constantly being exchanged for them. Every movement of the Kula articles, every detail of the transactions is fixed and regulated by a set of traditional rules and conventions, and some acts of the Kula are accompanied by an elaborate magical ritual and public ceremonies.

On every island and in every village, a more or less limited number of men take part in the Kula—that is to say, receive the goods, hold them for a short time, and then pass them on. . . . Thus no man ever keeps any of the articles for any length of time in his possession. One transaction does not finish the Kula relationship, the rule being "once in the Kula, always in the Kula," and a partnership between two men is a permanent and lifelong affair. . . .

The ceremonial exchange of the two articles is the main, the fundamental aspect of the Kula. But associat-ed with it, and done under its cover, we find a great number of secondary activities and features. Thus, side by side with the ritual exchange of armshells and necklaces, the natives carry on ordinary trade, bartering from one island to another a great number of utilities, often unprocurable in the district to which they are imported, and indispensable there.[22]

Although the nonutilitarian nature of the *kula* exchange has been much emphasized, the *kula* expeditions are also seized upon as opportunities to engage in free barter for various artifacts. Such activity, which takes on the character of market exchange, is recognized as being different in quality and function; hence, the Trobriander knows it as *gimwali.*

Redistributive Exchange

In redistributive exchange, "surplus" goods and labor are channeled as gifts, tribute, or corvée into the hands of a ruling or managerial class which usually keeps some for its personal use, but

[22]B. Malinowski, *Argonauts of the Western Pacific,* pp. 81–83. By permission of E. P. Dutton and Co., Inc.

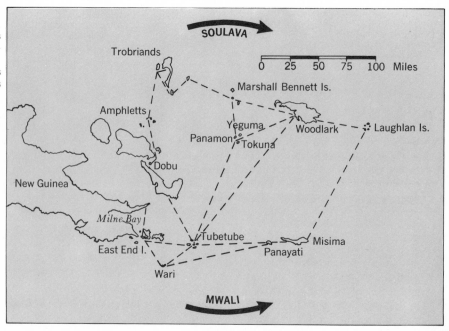

FIG. 15-4 The kula ring of the southwest Pacific. Lines show overseas trade routes. Arrows indicate directions in which necklaces (soulava) and armbands (mwali) are traded. (Adapted from Malinowski.)

which also redirects a portion (often large) to "general" social goals.

Redistributive exchange as the foundation of complex states

The archaeological record reveals that during the dawn of civilization in the evolution of culture there developed some interesting aspects of redistributive exchange. As agricultural efficiency increased so that not all working time went into food production, specialized labor developed, and assignments of both the tasks and the necessities of life were directed by strong governmental leaders.

Sumerian civilization

In Mesopotamia during the early dynastic period (3200–2800 B.C.), at the site of Sumer, there is evidence illustrating the significance of the development of this mode of exchange.

Allotments of land, work assignments, and raw materials were designated by the head priest administrator of each temple district. Each worker had to deliver a specified amount of produce; anything beyond this was the worker's own. Some goods went to maintain the priest, and much was redistributed among the producing populace. Thus, the division of labor and the economic exchange necessary for effective civilization were achieved—in this case without an internal market system.

Mayan civilization

Far to the west, in Mesoamerica, two thousand years after Sumer, the same type of redistributive exchange developed quite independently. Of the Maya civilization of 1000 B.C., Eric Wolf has written:

A man is buried at Kaminaljuyú in a mound 20 feet high, and set to rest surrounded by 400 pots, jade, marble greenstone vessels, jade-incrusted masks, pyrite mirrors, and ornaments of shell and bone. . . . This man is the priest, set off from common humanity by dress, deportment, and skills, as well as by his vision of the universe and his dedication to the realization of this vision. . . .

The dominant figure of this new social order was the

religious specialist. . . . These specialists . . . were not only devotees of the supernatural; they were also devotees of power, power over men. In them, society had developed a body not only of full-time religious practitioners but also of specialists in organization, capable of exacting labor and tribute as well as worship from the mass of men. . . . As servitors of their gods they also administered the many goods made as offerings to the deities. The temple centers became veritable storehouses of the gods, where costly produce accumulated in the service of the supernatural.[23]

Redistributive exchange in tribal societies

Lest one get the impression that redistributive exchange is characteristic only of civilizations and class-exploitative societies of more modern times, let us note that it also exists on the tribal level.

THE PUEBLOS As cultural outposts of the great Mesoamerican cultural tradition, the southwestern Pueblos thinly reflect its qualities, even today. Apart from the universal obligation to participate in ceremonial dances, every able-bodied man in the Rio Grande Pueblos of New Mexico is required: (1) to help cultivate and harvest the field set aside for the head priest-chief, or cacique; (2) to join in the communal rabbit and deer hunts to fill the cacique's storeroom; (3) to join in the labor of cleaning and repairing the irrigation ditches; (4) to sweep the pueblo plaza in preparation for ceremonies; and (5) to help replaster the Catholic mission church once a year.

The cacique drains off very little of the economic goods for his own use. His house is as undistinguishably modest as any man's in appearance. He wears the same clothes and eats no more, nor any less, than others. He is freed, however, from tilling the gardens, herding, and hunting. He concentrates all his efforts on "thinking good thoughts" and on ritual activity. He is freed to serve as the symbolic vessel of the pueblo's "collective soul," its full-time intercessor between his "children" and the manageable forces of the universe. In addition, he feeds ceremonial partici-

---

[23]E. R. Wolf, *Sons of the Shaking Earth*, pp. 70, 78–79, 81. Copyright © 1959, the University of Chicago Press. Quoted with permission.

pants and redistributes meat and vegetables to widows, orphans, and the aged poor.

Trade and Market Exchange

The essential difference between trade and gift exchange is in their relative functions. In trade, the emphasis is on economic redistribution. In gift exchange, the emphasis is on social relationships. Trade rests on and fosters social interaction, but its main concern is with the distribution of goods. Gift exchange distributes goods, but its main concern is with personal relations.

Within small tribes, there is little trade. Gift exchange suffices for the most part. The level of culture is also a factor of some influence. Simple cultures with little specialization of labor do not call forth much intratribal trade. It is primarily the high cultures with large populations that are capable of considerable specialization of effort among their members. Services and products are then available for exchange and trade.

However, virtually all societies, large and small, engage in intertribal or international trade. Every society has its unique goods or possesses natural resources from which to supply materials not available elsewhere. Salt-water shells find their way hundreds of miles inland in New Guinea and North America. In the Bronze Age, copper from Cyprus followed trade routes all over Europe. Beeswax flint from Grand-Pressigny, France, found wide use over all western Europe in Neolithic times. Melanesian inlanders trade vegetables for fish with the coastal dwellers.

Specialization based on custom rather than limitation of resources induces a good deal of trade. In New Mexico, Sia Indian women make excellent pottery. The pueblo of Jemez, less than ten miles away, made none for many centuries, although the same clays are available to both. Jemez exchanged corn for Sia pots in the old days. Hopis trade maize with the nearby Havasupai for buckskins and paint, and maize for wood and wool with the surrounding Navaho. But within the Hopi tribe, only the women of the pueblos on Second Mesa make coiled baskets; those who live on Third Mesa make them of wicker, and painted pottery is produced only on First Mesa.

The Crow Indians of the Plains were capable of growing tobacco. Indeed, they had a ceremonial organization, the Tobacco Society, whose interest centered around the growing of tobacco as a sacred ritual. Nevertheless, the nicotine plant was not grown for use, and common tobacco had to be obtained by trade with other tribes.[24]

In western Melanesia, the Southern Massim own large seagoing canoes. They do not manufacture these boats themselves, although they could. Instead, they obtain them in trade from the tribes of the Northern Massim district.

Within the small group of Trobriand Islands, local specialization is very marked. Two towns alone produce the red shell disks so valued in the *kula* exchange. The people of the island of Kayleula make canoes and trade with the inhabitants of the western D'Entrecasteaux Islands for betel nuts, sago, pottery, and turtle shell.

To the east of the Trobriands, the natives of Woodlark Island produce homogeneous greenstone for tools and the best carved ebony of the area; both products are valued objects of trade.[25]

Dumb barter

It shocks many people to discover that business people carry on trade with enemy nations. A high command will deliberately spare certain enemy plants because by means of trade through neutrals, it is possible to secure products of those plants. Enemies not infrequently find it advantageous to let economic interests override their antagonisms.

This is the basis of the dumb barter, or silent trade, among certain primitives. The pygmy Semang of Malaya, for example, exchange forest products for goods offered by their enemies, the Sakai. Neither group sees the other party during the transaction. The Semang place their goods in a customary place and retire. When the Sakai find the offering, they appropriate it and replace it with whatever they wish to exchange. Later, the little Semangs come back to pick up the goods before retiring to their jungle fastness. In like manner, the Mountain Vedda of Ceylon trade game for iron arrowheads with the Singhalese smiths. They lay

---

[24]R. H. Lowie, *The Crow Indians*, pp. 274ff.
[25]B. Malinowski, *Argonauts of the Western Pacific*, chap. 1.

their game in front of the smiths' huts at night, to come back the next night to gather the returns.

Herodotus describes how Carthaginian merchants carried on dumb barter with the natives of the northwest coast of Africa. The Carthaginians placed their goods on shore and retired to their ships, sending up a smoke signal. The natives came and replaced the goods with gold. They got what they deemed necessary, for the natives knew that if the mariners were shortchanged they would not return.[26]

A modernized version of dumb barter was practiced in the Ozark Mountain country of Arkansas into the 1930s, where "moonshine" corn whiskey could be bought as "stump liquor." As a means of avoiding revenue officers, it was the practice to leave one dollar on a known tree stump. During the night, a gallon of corn whiskey would replace it, to be picked up by the purchaser in the morning. The moonshiner did not have to expose himself to possible arrest.

Markets

Open trade is naturally much more convenient, and primitive peoples have often developed elaborate machinery for this purpose. In Nigeria, huge market towns of great antiquity are in existence. Native artisans bring their brasswork, pottery, mats, baskets, leatherwork, and foodstuffs many miles to these trading centers (Fig. 15-5). The Kede tribe of northern Nigeria act as river transporters of trade goods, for the Kede are the consummate canoemen of the Niger. They carry kola nuts and palm oil north from Nigeria, bringing back gowns, mats, fish, rice, horses, and potash from the Hausa and Nupe tribes.[27]

AFRICAN MARKETS In Africa, the marketplace is often under the magical protection of some great native chief, whose supernatural authority evokes the "peace of the market" so that enemy tribes may trade in safety. Chiefs frequently provide police and courts for markets in their districts, as well.

Bohannan points out that African markets in tribal subsistence economies are "peripheral"; that is, the markets are not essential to the economic livelihood of the societies because the number of people who actually derive their living from the markets is small. The economic function of African markets is but one part of the whole picture. Markets are public meeting places and communication centers for dispersal of gossip, news, and official pronouncements. Entertainers use markets as fairs are used in the United States—as places where audiences are gathered without effort. And markets, like fairs, are ready-made festivals. "The market day," observes Bohannan, "usually falls off into a beer drink."[28]

AMERICAN INDIAN MARKETS European traders found a strong trade network already in existence among the Indians of the northern Plains of North America when they first arrived at the Mandan, Hidatsa, and Arikara villages on the Missouri River, in the middle of the eighteenth century. The village tribes grew surpluses of corn and squash which they traded to the nomadic tribes. They also tanned fur robes and painted hides and ornamental clothing. These they traded with the Assineboin, Cheyenne, and Crow for meat and skins. Spanish trade goods also found their way to the Middle Missouri along the intertribal trade routes from the Southwest by way of the Cheyenne, who in turn got them from the Kiowas, who got them from the Comanches and Mexicans.

When French and British traders introduced the gun and metal utensils, after 1738, and horses were acquired from the Southwest, the flow of new materials along the old trade networks drastically altered the cultures of the nomadic tribes. The great flowering of the buffalo-hunting cultures suddenly occurred. Within a hundred years, the same forces which had created them— European trade, the horse, and the gun— destroyed them in an epic tragedy.

Primitive money

Not all trade among primitive peoples is by means of direct barter. Various media of exchange are known in several parts of the world. Shells serve

---

[26]W. D. Hambly, *Source Book for African Anthropology* (Field Museum of Natural History, Anthropological Series, vol. 26, part 2), p. 650.

[27]S. F. Nadel, "The Kede," in E. E. Evans-Pritchard and M. Fortes (eds.), *African Political Systems*, p. 169.

[28]P. J. Bohannan, *Social Anthropology*, p. 242.

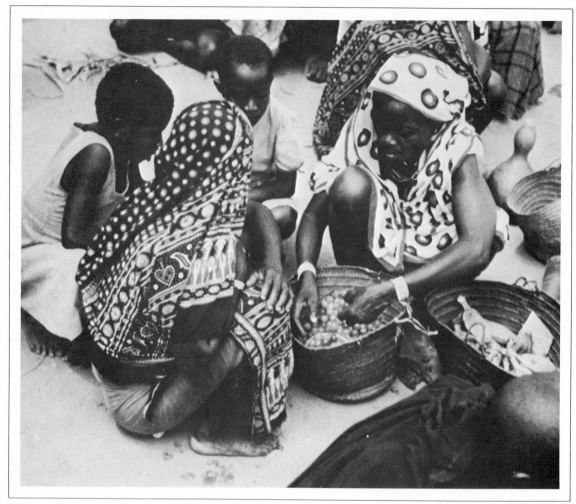

FIG. 15-5 Women traders in a Digo market, Kenya, East Africa. (Courtesy of Luther P. Gerlach.)

most commonly as a species of money: cowrie shells in the Pacific area and in Africa, and dentalium shells among the Indians of California. Wampum beads were used in exchange among the eastern Indians, and the early Dutch in New York treated wampum as good cash. Importation of poor counterfeits caused the city council of New Amsterdam in 1650 to pass an ordinance pegging the exchange value of good-quality beads at six white and three black per *stiver* (a Dutch coin). Poor wampum was pegged at eight and four, respectively.

Iron hoes have served as a medium of exchange in parts of Africa, but perhaps the strangest of all primitive moneys were the huge limestone wheels of the Island of Yap in Micronesia.

INHERITANCE

The transfers of goods which have been discussed thus far are "across the board," so to speak. They consist of lateral exchanges between the living. The continuity of society, however, requires that there be an orderly flow of property statuses in goods and incorporeals from one generation to the next. This constitutes inheritance.

Inheritance, in the words of G. D. H. Cole, "is the entrance of living persons into the possession of dead persons' property."[29] That is one way of putting it. This, however, leaves much unsaid. Earlier in this chapter, property was identified as consisting of (1) an object (material or incorporeal), and (2) a web of social relations that establishes and maintains a limiting and defined relationship between persons and that object. This web of relationships consists of the roles or patterns of behavior that are associated with certain statuses, which are in turn related to the object of property. Ownership, therefore, is a complex of statuses and roles that allows certain persons the socially recognized privilege-right of limited control of the use or disposition of objects. These rights of control, though limited, establish the owners' active and positive relations to the object. Nonowners are under a duty to refrain from use of the object, or they are at least subject to much more restrictive access to its use. In other words, the statuses and roles of A with respect to property are distinct and special as against those of X, Y, or Z.

Analyzed in terms of culture theory, inheritance is not transfer of possession; it is the transference of statuses. And although much inheritance involves transfer after death, many statuses may be transferred *inter vivos*, during life. Nyakyusa sons of chiefs "inherit the country"; i.e., they assume the chieftainship, while their fathers still live. Ifugao children inherit the parental rice fields on marriage. But obviously not all transfers of status are what we recognize as inheritance. Cheyenne peace chiefs on the Council of Forty-four were replaced every ten years by selection, not inheritance. The Presidency of the United States involves a transfer of status every time we change administration, but the office is noninheritable.

Inheritance, therefore, means a transference of status based upon a preexisting relationship between the predecessor and the successor. The relationship is personal, usually traditional, and usually based on kinship.

Radcliffe-Brown, in his survey of patrilineal and matrilineal succession in primitive societies, came very close to realization of this when he concluded: "In general, though there are a few exceptions, transmission of property follows the same line as transmission of status."[30] The reason is that transmission of property *is* transmission of status. It follows that if most kinds of status are transmitted down one line or another, property statuses will follow along the same line. Therefore, a close correlation of type of social organization and devolution of property will naturally occur.

Effect of Unilineal Descent

In the event that a death is followed by a sororal or levirate marriage (see pages 182–184), the movable property of the deceased spouse stays right in the household of the surviving spouse, and the landed property remains in the relation to the survivor that it exhibited before the death of the spouse. But this is only because of the coincidence of identity of status between the deceased spouse and the one who replaces her (or him) in the household. The inheritance runs from deceased wife to her sister who replaces her, not from deceased wife to husband to his second wife.

Inheritance of rights of use in land follows fairly clear lines. Among matrilineal gardeners, where women till the soil, inheritance runs from mother to daughters. If the picture is complicated with matrilineal organization coupled with virilocal residence (see pages 198–200) and male gardening (as in the Trobriand Islands), inheritance runs from mother's brother to sister's son. In parts of Melanesia, although land is inherited matrilineally, fruit trees privately owned by males are inherited patrilineally.

Whether matrilineal or patrilineal organization prevails also strongly influences the lines of inheritance of movable and incorporeal property. Patrilineal societies favor filial inheritance. Matrilineal societies favor inheritance from maternal uncle to sister's son. It is quite possible for a tribe

---

[29]G. D. H. Cole, "Inheritance" (*Encyclopaedia of the Social Sciences*, vol. 20, 1935), p. 286.

[30]A. R. Radcliffe-Brown, "Patrilineal and Matrilineal Succession" (*Iowa Law Review*, vol. 20, 1935), p. 297; also in his *Structure and Function in Primitive Society*, pp. 32–47.

to subject some forms of property to the avunculate and other forms to paternal succession. It is not necessary that the inheritance system be absolutely consistent with one principle or the other.

The sexual equivalence of brothers in marriage arrangements is reflected in their equivalence in relation to property. Thus *collateral inheritance*, or inheritance by brothers or sisters from brother or sister in preference to the children, indicates that the members of a fraternity have a solidarity that supersedes that of the conjugal-natal family. Plains Indians applied this rule to the inheritance of horses especially. The generation tie outweighs the filial or avuncular. This may well be reinforced in political inheritance of chiefship, where it is advantageous to avoid letting the mantle of leadership fall on a callow youth.

Incorporeal properties, especially magic formulas and medical powers, must be partially transferred before death if they involve secret knowledge. A man may transfer his charms or songs to son or nephew as a gift, without anticipation of his departure from life. This would be a gift *inter vivos*, not properly a matter of inheritance. Or it may be that the necessary knowledge is taught to the beneficiary without transfer of the right of use until after the death of the donor, which would be a true case of a gift *causa mortis*, a gift made in the prospect of death and properly an aspect of inheritance.

Distinctions by Sexes

In general, it may be said that husband and wife do not inherit from each other in the primitive world. This is an easily understood consequence of the nature of marriage as an alliance of two kinship groups.[31] What is left by either spouse is more than likely to revert to the family or lineage from which he or she came. Men's goods are inherited by men, and women's by women. Two factors that are present on the primitive level are responsible for these conditions. The first is the absence or undeveloped state of a free market

and money economy. Goods cannot be divorced from use with any appreciable degree of ease. They are not readily convertible into fluid capital. Therefore, they must be possessed by a competent user; the sexual division of labor bars inheritance of sex-linked property across sex lines. Second, in all primitive societies a person is more closely tied to his or her kinship group than to the marriage partner. The claims of surviving kinsmen outweigh the claims of the surviving spouse.[32]

Testamentary Disposition

In instances in which an individual wishes to transfer property status to another person who is not specifically defined as an heir in custom or law, *testamentary disposition* may be allowed for. This is what we know as "making a will." The power of testamentary disposition probably exists in most primitive societies, although this matter has not been subjected to systematic investigation. In those societies in which it does exist, it does not apply evenly to all forms of property. The disposition of garden plots, for example, is usually governed by strict rules of inheritance not subject to individual meddling. At the same time, a man or woman may be quite free to alter the normal lines of inheritance of personal property in movables by use of the will. In some instances, the spoken will is inviolable; in others, it may be set aside by the living as contrary to law and custom. What is proper and what is improper at this point may often be as troublesome a question for primitive peoples as it is for us.

A case occurring among the Ashanti of Ghana in 1942 is a good example. Inheritance of land among the Ashanti runs down the maternal line; it should go from a man to his brother (who belongs to the same maternal clan) and then to a sister's son, but not to a son of either man, for this person belongs to a different clan.

A man when on his death-bed made a dying declaration giving one of his cocoa-farms to his son, and swore an oath enjoining his brother, who was his successor, to

[31]See R. F. Barton, *Ifugao Law* (University of California Publications in American Archaeology and Ethnology, vol. 15, 1919), p. 26, for the Ifugao exemplification of this rule.

[32]See R. F. Benedict, "Marital Property Rights in Bilateral Society" (*American Anthropologist*, vol. 38, 1936), pp. 368–373.

see that the gift was honoured. "If you do not give it to him," said the dying man, "I shall call you before the ancestors for our case to be judged."

... The man died and his brother succeeded to the property, but refused, with the concurrence of the other members of the family, to give the cocoa-farm to his deceased brother's son. Three months later a fire broke out in the village. The surviving brother fell from a roof while helping to put out one of the fires, and sustained an injury to his leg from which he subsequently died. Before he died, he told his family that he believed his deceased brother was summoning him to the spirit world to answer for his conduct in not honouring his brother's death-bed declaration. The general belief was that his death was due to his failure to carry out his deceased brother's instructions. The next successor to the property duly gave the cocoa-farm to the son to whom it had been left.[33]

Contrary to the sophisticated Ashanti, in the simplest societies inheritance is poorly developed. Nomadic hunters and collectors have few goods, and most of these are personal working equipment. Because of the universality of belief in an afterlife, many primitives assume that the deceased want and need their goods. The result is, as Radcliffe-Brown has noted:

With us one of the most important aspects of succession is the transmission of property by inheritance. Yet in some of the simplest societies this is a matter of almost no significance at all. In an Australian tribe, for example, a man possesses a few weapons, tools, utensils, and personal ornaments, things of little value or permanence. On his death some of them may be destroyed, others may be distributed among his relatives or friends. But their disposal is of so little importance, unless in relation to ritual, that it is often difficult to find any rules of customary procedure.[34]

The same may be said of the African Bushmen, the Andaman Islanders, the Semangs, the Eskimos, and the Shoshones.

Primogeniture

In societies of growing populations given to gardening or agriculture on limited land resources, there is always the problem of dispersal of the

family holdings through inheritance by too many heirs. Primogeniture is the solution hit upon by some peoples. All property devolves upon the eldest son, who then has the duty to support the other members of the family in exchange for their labor. "A family must have a strong center," say the Ifugaos. Primogeniture more often applies to inheritance of chiefship and office, however, than to landed property. The mana of the Polynesian chief passes to the first-born son in an unending line. So strong is the primogeniture rule among the Maoris of New Zealand that on occasion a first-born woman may take a man's name and acquire the status of a first-born son.

Primogeniture can be a force in an expansionistic movement. Power and glory are available to second-born sons who sally forth to gain new land, wealth, and rank and who found new lineages by leading a group of colonists to unsettled territory.

The evidence is clear for the Maori, and we may infer that primogeniture was a force in Polynesia that worked to drive younger sons out on overseas expeditions of exploration and colonization.[35]

How much of the brunt of empire building was borne by the younger sons of Britain who were shut out at home by the laws of primogeniture? In the classical laissez-faire economics of nineteenth-century England, primogeniture was hailed as a double-acting social device: it avoided inefficient division of the family inheritance, and it forced the younger members to fend for themselves, thus enriching society by their efforts. Those primitives who practice primogeniture recognize the first of these benefits, but it is unlikely that the second ever entered their conscious thoughts. Primogeniture is not much favored in the Western world today. Feudalism is gone, and enterprise capitalism is not favorable to primogeniture.

Ultimogeniture

There are a few tribes that turn the tables completely about. By means of *ultimogeniture*, the

---

[33]K. A. Busia, *The Position of the Chief in the Modern Political System of Ashanti*, p. 43. By permission of Frank Cass and Co., Ltd.

[34]A. R. Radcliffe-Brown, "Patrilineal and Matrilineal Succession" (*Iowa Law Review*, vol. 20, 1935), p. 286.

[35]B. W. Aginsky and P. H. Buck, "Interacting Forces in the Maori Family" (*American Anthropologist*, vol. 42, 1940), pp. 195ff.

youngest son inherits the greater portion of the family estate. Among certain peoples of India, Asia, and Africa, the elder brothers are set up with herds or households in part by family resources used in progeny price. What is left over at the father's death tends in cases of ultimogeniture to go to the youngest of them all on the grounds that he is the least likely to be well set up in life.

In concluding a discussion of primogeniture and ultimogeniture, a note of caution should be sounded. The vast majority of societies adhere to neither of the set rules.

Destruction of Property
In the instance of the Comanches:

In the disposal of a deceased's property there is but one rule which stood out with constancy: *upon the death of a person all effects of his (or her) personal usage were destroyed.* This included clothing, weapons, saddles, tools, paraphernalia, and horses customarily ridden by the deceased. . . . Further, even the tipi in which the dead person, man or woman, lived was totally destroyed; also for a child, but not for a baby. Articles of intimate personal usage were buried with the corpse. Other less important articles were burned. Possessions with medicine powers were either destroyed by throwing them into the river, or by placing them in an unfrequented tree where they could rot.[36]

All Plains Indians had similar rules. Surpluses were variously handled. The Comanches passed the residual estate to the widow, who in turn was obliged to pass some of it on to her husband's friends and relatives, and especially to nonrelatives, who hung around as enthusiastic mourners; they mourned and mourned until they were given sufficient gifts to stop them. Inheritance by nonrelatives was, in point of fact, characteristic in the Plains area. A family that went the whole way in mourning made itself destitute, until in due time friends and relatives reoutfitted them with gifts.

On the lower levels of culture, it is difficult to generalize inheritance rules with accuracy. Often

there is no single rule of inheritance controlling all situations, or any single line of practice under any of the legal rules. Our canny Cheyenne informant, Calf Woman, cautioned: "Some families did differently than others."

SELECTED READINGS

Bohannan, P. J. and G. Dalton, *Markets in Africa* (1962). A modern analysis based on good anthropological accounts of indigenous trading centers.

Bunzel, R., "The Economic Organization of Primitive Peoples," in F. Boas, et al., *General Anthropology* (1938), chap. 8. A useful general summary.

Codere, H., "Exchange and Display" (*International Encyclopedia of the Social Sciences*, vol. 5, 1968), pp. 239–245. A brief and concise discussion of primitive exchange systems.

Dalton, G. (ed.), *Tribal and Peasant Economies: Readings in Economic Anthropology* (1967). A rich selection of materials representing modern research and thought.

Goody, J., *Death, Property, and the Ancestors* (1962). Part III (pp. 273–327) is an excellent conceptual analysis of property in primitive and civilized cultures. The entire book is a masterful study of mortuary ceremonies and property transmission and of their functional relation to social structure in two African tribes.

Hallowell, A. I., "The Nature and Function of Property as a Social Institution" (*Journal of Legal and Political Sociology*, vol. 1, 1943), pp. 115–138. The most thorough anthropological treatment of the subject currently available.

Herskovits, M. J., *Economic Anthropology* (1952), part III, "Exchange and Distribution." Provides an extensive descriptive and theoretical analysis. Part IV, "Property," provides an extensive treatment of the subject.

Mauss, M., *The Gift: Forms and Functions of Exchange in Archaic Societies* (1954). The classic study of the social functions of organized gift exchanges in primitive societies and classical civilizations.

Sahlins, M., *Stone Age Economics* (1972). A collection of Sahlins' essays from the anthropological perspective of "substantivist" economics. This work not only illustrates the substantivist categories of production, distribution, and consumption exchange, but also takes issue with the formalist notion that economy is a category of behavior rather than simply a category of culture.

Schneider, H. K., *Economic Man: The Anthropology of Economics* (1974). An argument from a social anthro-

---

[36]E. A. Hoebel, *The Political Organization and Law-ways of the Comanche Indians* (American Anthropological Association, Memoir 54: Contributions from the Laboratory of Anthropology, 4, 1940), pp. 120–121.

pologist for an anthropological "formalist" approach to comparative economics. The position defended is that economics is a type of behavior and a motivation for activity rather than the study of types of social structures used in production, distribution, and con-sumption of material and nonmaterial goods and services.

Thurnwald, R., *Economics in Primitive Communities* (1932), chaps. 5–9, "Barter," "Trade," "The Market," "Purchase," and "Distribution of Goods and Wealth."

16

SOCIAL CLASSES AND CASTES

LEARNING GOALS

Give a working definition of *social class* as a concept. ¶ List Murdock's two *categories* of social class systems and his three *types* of class societies. ¶ Outline five examples of variation in the organization of class systems among American Indians and in the South Pacific. ¶ Describe Ankola social organization as an example of a simple ethnic caste system. ¶ Discuss the Hindu concept of *varna* as the ideological rationalization of the complex caste system of India. ¶ Comment on the concept of *social race*. ¶ Examine the social conditions which give rise to slavery.

Wherever there exists an unequal allocation of goods and power throughout a society, there exists the possibility of social classes. Classes express social differences. However, the mere existence of differences does not necessarily give rise to a clear-cut class structure on the one hand, or to a "class mentality," or a class consciousness, on the other. Nor does the existence of class self-awareness necessarily produce class conflict or war. It may, or it may not.

The procedures and problems of classification, which were discussed in dealing with the analysis of kinship systems (Chapter 13, pages 227–228), come to the fore once more when dealing with "social class." The question of whether a phenomenon is a concept (a classificatory idea) or a thing (a reality that exists as a discrete entity) plagues us in our consideration of social class. Even more than the controversial topic of human race, class has become freighted with overtones of social politics. Class consciousness and revolutionary class movements did not begin with the thought and writings of Karl Marx (1818–1883), but through Marx and his associates, especially Friedrich Engels (1820–1895), they received their modern ideological charter. This, in one form or another, has been developed into dogmatic Marxism as a sociopolitical creed, commonly called Communism.

The Communist doctrine asserting class exploitation of the landless by landowners, and of industrial workers by capitalists, and the accompanying dogma of class struggle leading to the ultimate establishment of a classless, socialistic society, pose one of the great challenges to contemporary humanity. The drawing of the Iron Curtain and the polarization of East and West Europe across the Berlin Wall in the cold war of 1946 to the present are but one manifestation of it. Under current conditions, to separate fact from dogma is especially difficult. Yet, a clear understanding of what social classes are and how they act in different types of societies is absolutely essential to a rational response to the Marxist challenge. To deal with the whole problem is more than we can assay in this introduction to anthropology. Nonetheless, we can bring the comparative findings of anthropology to bear on such questions as the following: Are there any societies that are classless? Is class differentiation the unique development of civilizations? Is exploitation an inherent feature of classism? Are classes in primitive society usually at war with one another? What of castes? And how does slavery fit into the history of human societies?

THE CONCEPT OF SOCIAL CLASS

"The concept of class is concerned with the differentiation of social groups."[1] So far, so good. But that does not take us very far. Kinship groups are differentiated, often with refined, far-reaching, and arbitrary precision, as we have already seen. Associations are differentiated social groups. So are political parties and nations, religious sects and cults. Therefore, we must understand at the outset that "social class" as a concept actually has narrower denotations than the term literally suggests.

Marx defined class in terms of relation to the means of production, i.e., power over the use of productive resources and control over the disposition of products and access to consumable goods, both being backed up by the coercive power of the state.

The German sociologist Max Weber (1864–1920) accepted this economic criterion as a starting point. To this base he added two more factors: (1) standard of living, or subcultural life styles, and (2) prestige ratings of differing economic groups within the society. Virtually all non-Marxist social scientists have followed Weber's lead, although there is no agreement on the relative importance of the three criteria.[2]

To conclude these introductory remarks, let us recapitulate by quoting A. L. Stinchcombe on social stratification systems (higher and lower social classes):

The study of stratification systems involves three main topics: *the degree of inequality of rewards and privileges* (in wealth, power, and fame) in different societies and the causes and effects of different amounts and kinds of inequality; *the relation between the distribution of the good things of life and the solidarity of categories of people with different levels of reward* (such as social classes, ethnic groups, and regions within societies) and the causes and effects of different patternings of solidary groupings in relation to the distribution of privileges; and the *patterning of social relations between people of different levels of reward (conflict, domination, ritual equality, and so forth) and its causes and effects.* The pattern of a stratification system can be fairly well outlined if we know the amount of inequality in the distribution of rewards, the amount and patterning of solidarity among people at approximately the same level in the distribution, and the relations between "the rich, the wise, and the well-born" and the poor, the ignorant, and the lowly [italics added].[3]

R. M. MacIver (1882–1961) put it more directly and simply, with heavier emphasis on class attitudes:

We shall then mean by a social class any portion of a community which is marked off from the rest . . . primarily by a sense of social distance. Such a subjective character involves also as a rule objective differences, income levels, occupational distinctions and so forth, within the society. But these differences, apart from a recognized order of superiority and inferiority, would not establish cohesive groups. It is the sense of status, sustained by economic, political, or ecclesiastical power and by distinctive modes of life and cultural expressions corresponding to them, which draws class apart from class, gives cohesion to each, and stratifies a whole society.[4]

Social Class Defined

We may now specify a working definition of social class.

A social class is a category of persons within a society, who hold a number of distinctive statuses in common and who, through the operation of the roles associated with these statuses, receive differential rewards and privileges, and who, through a common life style, develop an awareness of their like interests in contrast to those of other such groups.

A social class can exist only with reference to other social classes. A one-class society is necessarily a classless society. Furthermore, if there is

---

[1]P. Mombert, "Class" (*Encyclopaedia of the Social Sciences*, vol. 3, 1930), p. 531.

[2]For a general overview of theories of social class, see the articles on "Stratification, Social," by B. Barber, S. M. Lipset, A. L. Stinchcombe, and H. Rodman in the *International Encyclopedia of the Social Sciences*, vol. 15, 1968, pp. 287–315, 325–337.

[3]A. L. Stinchcombe, "Stratification, Social" (*International Encyclopedia of the Social Sciences,* vol. 15, 1968), pp. 325–326. Copyright © 1968, Crowell Collier and Macmillan, Inc. Quoted with permission.

[4]R. M. MacIver and C. H. Page, *Society*, pp. 78–79. By permission of Holt, Rinehart and Winston, Inc.

no consciousness of class, there can be no dynamics of class action. People must act in terms of class, if the *class concept* is to be functionally significant.

Finally, there are a number of things that a social class is not. It is not organized. Classes are not in themselves associations. But there may be, of course, associations that represent the interests of specific classes, as the AFL-CIO does for certain segments of the industrial workers in the United States or as the National Association of Manufacturers does for a portion of the industrial owners and manufacturers. Yet even in Russia, only a small part of the population of workers is organized within the Communist party and its affiliate associations.

TYPES OF CLASS SYSTEMS

Inasmuch as social classes express themselves in attitudes associated with differences in status and role, which in turn mean differences in authority, power, and access to goods, the characteristics of class systems exhibit marked qualitative differences from one type of culture to another. Obviously, simple hunters and gatherers who have no food surpluses to manipulate and who allocate food and other goods through balanced reciprocal exchange are not likely to develop social classes. On the other hand, post-Neolithic peoples who have a system of redistributive exchange with ultimate title to the land vested in a paramount chief or a king, with royal lineage or clan, will almost certainly have a highly institutionalized class system.

Yet it does not necessarily follow that sedentary horticulturalists will develop social classes, either. Title to Pueblo Indian land, for example, is vested in the pueblo, in perpetuity, and plots are equably assigned to clans and households in universal succession (page 125) with enduring rights of use. Everyone has equal access to the available economic goods of the society. There is no possibility of differentiation based on wealth. There are no social classes. Or are there?

In the pueblos, power is very unequally distributed. The priests who head the religious secret fraternities form a totalitarian oligarchy with power of life and death over all members of the pueblo. Their prestige is often awesome; and a

good part of their life style, devoted as it is to the management of the esoteric ritual through which the universe is kept operating (see Chapter 19, pages 326–329), is different from that of ordinary commoners. In terms of religious and political power, they certainly form a class. In terms of food, clothing, and shelter, not at all. Therefore, Murdock codes the twelve Pueblos which are a part of the world sample in the *Ethnographic Atlas* as classless.

Cross-Cultural Categories

Murdock's cross-cultural categories of social class systems are as follows:

1. *Classless societies*, which lack significant class distinctions among freemen (slavery is treated as outside the class system), ignoring variations in individual repute that have been achieved through skill, valor, piety, or wisdom.

2. *Wealth distinctions*, based on the possession or distribution of property, which are present and socially important but not crystallized into distinct and hereditary social classes.

3. *Dual stratification* (a two-class system) in a hereditary aristocracy and a lower class of ordinary commoners or freemen, where traditionally ascribed noble status (high prestige) is at least as important as control of economic resources.

4. *Elite stratification*, in which an elite class derives and maintains its superior status by control over resources, especially land, in contrast to a propertyless proletariat or serf class.

5. *Complex stratification*, in which social classes are related to extensive differentiation of occupational status.

In sum, Murdock's classification presents two *categories* of classless societies (1 and 2, above), and three *types* of class systems (3, 4, and 5, above).[5]

Frequency of Social Classes

Taking the world at large, the majority (68 per cent) of the societies in the *Ethnographic Atlas* are classless. A third of these recognize socially

---

[5] G. P. Murdock, *Ethnographic Atlas*, pp. 57–58.

important wealth distinctions (prestige) but have no hereditary social classes (2, above). One-fourth (24 per cent) of all societies have a ruling class which controls access to goods (types 3 and 4), and only one-twelfth (8 per cent) have multiple class systems (type 5). As shown in Fig. 16-1, complex class systems are limited almost exclusively to the civilizations of the Mediterranean area and Asia. In the New World, only such pre-Columbian societies as the Aztec, Maya, and Inca qualified as complex. Eighty-seven per cent of all New World societies were classless! In Sub-

Saharan Africa and the Pacific, approximately two-thirds had no classes.[6]

The class phenomenon is Old World and civilizational—at least to this point in time.

THE ORGANIZATION OF CLASS SYSTEMS

Having looked at the types of class systems and their relative frequency around the world, let us

[6]Data from E. Bourguignon and L. Greenbaum, *Diversity and Homogeneity*, table 19, p. 41.

FIG. 16-1 Relative frequency (in percentages) of social classes according to major geographic areas. (Data from E. Bourguignon and L. Greenbaum, *Diversity and Homogeneity*, table 18, p. 40.)

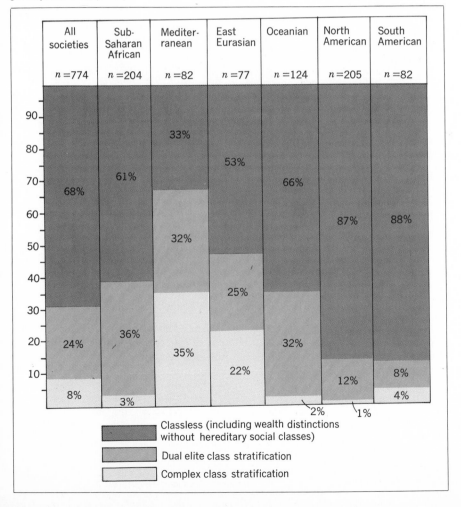

now examine just what is implied in various kinds of class or no-class societies. Some of the difficulties in assigning arbitrary labels will be readily noted as we observe that the lines between types 1, 2, 3, etc., are often blurred rather than completely clear-cut.

Plains Indians

Among the nomadic Plains Indians, whose cultures encouraged competitive status achievement, a nascent sense of class was noticeable. Grinnell wrote:

Family rank, which existed among the Cheyennes as among other Indians, depended on the estimation in which the family was held by the best people. A good family was one that produced brave men and good sensible women, and that possessed more or less property. A brave and successful man has raised his family from low to very high rank; or a generation of inefficient men might cause a family to retrograde.[7]

But there was no real social gap between good and not-so-good families, and the Cheyennes are considered classless. The poor, instead of being driven into servitude to the more prosperous by means of debt, wage dependence, or clientage, seem, rather, to have sponged upon the chief and the successful hunter.

Similar attitudes existed among the western Apache, who distinguished sharply between poor people and the rich. "Those who had little or no property, lacked the ability or desire and energy to accumulate it, and had no social prestige were termed poor; the people with opposite traits were called rich." Poverty was pitied, and the wealthy person was expected to be generous with largess. For this he received public approval and attracted hangers-on among the poor who were then called *bidigisihi*, meaning "his incompetents" or "weaklings."[8] The Apaches, however, also qualify as classless. In each of these instances, it is the fact of equal access to basic resources which leads us to so categorize them.

Yet out of such elemental recognition of class differences, the Kiowa Indians of the Plains developed a strong sense of prestige ranking based on wealth and behavior.

Four classes were recognized by name: *onde*, *ondegupa*, *kɔɔn*, and *dapom*. The *onde*, who constituted about one-tenth of the population, were those whose family heads were "handsome on a horse," wealthy and generous, proud in bearing, courteous in demeanor, and, above all, possessed of an outstanding war record. The *ondegupa* were the able artisans, hunters, herders, and medicine men, who had wealth, were generous, and were "noble" in character and behavior, but who lacked sufficient war credits. They made up one-third of the tribe. The *kɔɔn* were the common stuff, undistinguished in war or other accomplishments. They lived with their more illustrious kinsmen as poor relatives. Half the tribe was of this lower class. The *dapom* were simply *déclassé*. Shiftless and lazy, they filched and stole within the camp. Practically disowned by their own relatives, they were virtual outcasts. They imposed upon the generosity of the good people; theft was not looked upon or treated as a legal infraction. The *dapom* were not punished or extruded from the group. They were merely scorned and suffered to be borne.[9]

In general, all Plains Indian social systems were open and competitive, although there was a tendency, as in the Kiowa, toward wealth distinctions. Buffalo and antelope were there for all. In the nineteenth century, enemy horses were for the taking, and war was chronic. It was necessary only to have the "strong medicine" bestowed by "guardian spirits" (see pages 353–357) and the will, spirit, and skills—plus a little bit of luck—to move right up the social scale.

Northwest Coast Indians

Class was more marked on the Northwest Coast of North America, where in every tribe a sharp division existed between freemen and slaves—unfortunates captured from other tribes. In the early nineteenth century, slaves constituted from 10 to 30 per cent of the total populations of

---

[7]G. B. Grinnell, *The Cheyenne Indians*, vol. 1, p. 129. By permission of Yale University Press.

[8]G. Goodwin, *The Social Organization of the Western Apache*, pp. 541–543.

[9]J. Richardson, *Law and Status among the Kiowa Indians* (American Ethnological Society, Monograph 1, 1940); and B. Mishkin, *Rank and Warfare among the Plains Indians* (American Ethnological Society, Monograph 3, 1940).

various Northwest Coast tribes. They were in effect a depressed social group whose functions were to produce food for their masters by hunting and fishing, to do the menial work around the village, and to paddle the seagoing canoes. Whatever their rank in their own tribe, all slaves were reduced to the level of productive capital in the tribe of their masters. Just as any valuable good, such as a canoe or copper, could be destroyed at a potlatch, slaves too could be killed to show their master's unconcern for wealth.

Most authorities have described the body of freemen in Northwest Coast society as consisting of two classes (type 3): nobles and commoners. Nobles were those men (and their wives) who had attained the rank of chieftain through the inheritance of chiefly titles, which they had validated by potlatching. Since most tribes held to primogeniture, the nobility consisted of the first-born, while subsequent offspring and nephews (in matrilineal societies) became commoners. Among the Tsimshian, according to Jenness, even finer distinctions were drawn. Intermarriage among the first-born children of the highest-ranking families of the nobility was reputedly obligatory, so that there was even an endogamous "royalty" within the nobility.[10]

Drucker, who has studied Northwest Coast culture at firsthand, takes issue with the orthodox view of Northwest Coast social classes. He flatly maintains that there was no class of nobility set off from a class of commoners, with slaves standing outside the class order, much less a threefold or fourfold class system. What actually occurred, as he sees it, was "that each society consisted not of two or more social classes, but of a complete series of statuses graded relatively, one for each individual of the group."[11] He argues that between high and low there were differences in degree but not in kind.

This particular conflict of interpretations is not resolvable; it merely points up the ambiguity of the concept of class in certain settings. It precisely parallels the situation that existed in the United States, when most Americans argued that we had no social classes at the same time that Warner and his coworkers were assiduously dividing us into upper upper, lower upper, upper middle, lower middle, upper lower, and lower lower (than which there are no lower) classes.[12]

Murdock, however, classifies the Tsimshian, Haida, Bellacoola, and Kwakiutl tribes, all of the Northwest Coast, as having dual stratification (type 3) rather than as classless with wealth distinctions.[13]

The Aztecs

Among the peoples of high culture in Central America and the Andean region of South America, class differentiation was strongly fixed as a classical system of complex stratification (type 5).

The Aztecs, in their meteoric rise and fall, developed from an apparently classless, unsegmented society with a rude material culture, prior to A.D. 1300, to an organized, sophisticated protocivilization in the fourteenth century. At the time of the arrival of the Spaniards in 1518, they were rapidly evolving a feudal aristocracy at the expense of the earlier clan socialism. The society then consisted of royalty, nobility, common freemen, propertyless proletariat, and slaves.

The core and largest part of the Aztec population was the body of free commoners, members of one or another of twenty localized "clans" *(calpulli)*. Every married man enjoyed the right to cultivate a plot of clan garden land and to have a flat-roofed, one-room hut of adobe or clay-plastered wattle. He might become a craftsman, specializing in one of the many productive arts and trades. He had security and continuous employment and an obligation to perform military service. But he was hedged in by a code of sumptuary laws that reserved to the rich and to distinguished warriors and officials the rights of wearing fine cotton, jewelry, and particular hairdos. Presumption above one's rank was summarily and severely punished.

Class distinctions cut across kinship groups,

[10]D. Jenness, *The Indians of Canada* (National Museum of Canada, Bulletin 68, Anthropological Series, no. 15, 2d ed., 1934), p. 337.

[11]P. Drucker, "Rank, Wealth, and Kinship in Northwest Coast Society" (*American Anthropologist*, vol. 41, 1939), p. 57.

[12]W. L. Warner and P. S. Lund, *The Social Life of a Modern Community*.

[13]G. P. Murdock, *op. cit.*, column 67, p. 105.

for the class of honorary lords was recruited from all clans. They formed a nonhereditary order of merit with various grades conferred by the government as a lifetime reward for outstanding military accomplishment, service in civil office, service to the state as a traveling merchant-spy, or exceptional religiosity. They wore the beautiful and elaborate costumery depicted in Aztec art. They lived in the mansions of Tenochtitlan. They received homage and led a rich life apart from their common fellow clansmen. In theory, the huge parcels of conquered lands that they received as rewards for their services could not be inherited as family estates. All such rewards were to be redistributed to a new worthy after the death of the holder. This was always done, but, by a process not difficult to understand, a system of preference was crystallizing whereby sons of nobles were appointed to their fathers' positions of nobility. Inheritance of rank and landed estates was thus leading rapidly to the freezing of a hereditary aristocracy.

Above the nobles, in luxuriant splendor, stood the royal lineage, from among whose members the *tlacatecuhtli*, or king, was elected by the great council of lords.

Far below the royalty and nobles was the hapless proletariat. Aliens whose goods and lands had been expropriated by the state and Aztecs who had lost their clan privileges for failure to fulfill clan obligations eked out a meager and sweaty existence as burden-bearing laborers on the streets of the city and roads of the country, or they grubbed for their livelihood upon the estates of the lords. Taxes and feudal services left little to them.

Slavery was the lot of impecunious Aztecs who could not meet their bills. In like manner, criminals who could not make restitution for their thefts became the slaves of the freemen they had victimized. Children were sold into slavery by impoverished parents, and even adults among the proletariat might voluntarily sell themselves into servitude. Many slaves were alien boys and girls taken as tribute from conquered neighbors.

The society of the Aztec Indians was on the road to becoming the same type of pyramidal, exploitative society that existed in the flourishing days of the archaic Mediterranean civilizations. The Aztecs, however, had not hardened the inequalities

of their society. Children of slaves were born free (into the proletariat). Slaves could not be killed or abused by their masters; they could even acquire property in their own right (although it is not likely that this opportunity meant much to many slaves); they could not be sold to another master except by self-consent; and if married by master or mistress, they became freemen.[14]

Melanesia

In the western and interior parts of New Guinea inhabited by the more primitive Papuans, social classes as such are practically nonexistent. In the eastern islands, where the Melanesian-speaking people predominate, differentiation into dual social classes is characteristic, even though there are many classless tribes, such as the Dobu. The actual governing of men throughout Melanesia is usually in the hands of a council of village elders, but there is frequently a class of wealthy "Big Men" who enjoy much social prestige by reason of their economic, ceremonial, and religious powers related to inherited prestige and a redistributional economic system (type 2).

Melanesian chiefs are often descendants of an immigrant group which has tricked the local populace into believing that its members have superior magical powers and control valuable rituals that will benefit the community. For this reason, it is considered only right that the chiefly class enjoy exalted sanctity and privileged superiority. The chiefs are also universally regarded by the people and themselves as a class of feast givers and ceremonialists who reflect glory upon their people.

Polynesia

Traditional Hawaiian society (at and before the time of Captain Cook's arrival in 1778) was divided into a rigidly stratified, hereditary social class system composed of nobles *(ali'i)*, commoners *(maka'āinana)*, and polluted inferiors *(kauwā)*.

The great majority of the society were commoners with specific occupational tasks: agriculture, fishing, crafts, etc. What they did not produce for

---

[14]G. C. Vaillant, *Aztecs of Mexico*; but especially see *The Florentine Codex* (A. J. O. Anderson and C. E. Dibble, trans. and eds.), book 8, *Kings and Lords*, and book 10, *The People*.

themselves they traded for, or were given as recompense for their labors by the ruling chiefs. There were some variations in wealth and, therefore, in standards of living, and occasionally a paramount chief rewarded a commoner for special services by conferring "quasi-aristocratic" status on him.

Above the commoners were the *ali'i*, and from this aristocracy came the military forces as well as all important political officials. Their magnificent, feather-covered cloaks and helmets gave visible evidence of their social rank. This nobility was subdivided into a high, sacred group and a lower, nonsacred group, and there were rigid prescribed forms of deference which the lower order was obliged to follow in relation to the sacred group. Death followed any infraction of the rules, as when a commoner or a nonsacred *ali'i* failed to remain prostrate in the presence of the sacred, godlike *ali'i*.

Below the commoners was a small group of hereditary, segregated inferiors, similar to a pariah caste (discussed below). Marriage within each class was endogamous, and miscegenation with the pariah class was especially abhorrent because of the fear of polluting family lines. Too little is known about this group to feel secure in calling them slaves, but there was an element of servitude and they were attached to masters.

In summary, Davenport writes:

. . . Hawaiian society was internally differentiated by hereditary ranked social classes. Because the classes tended to be endogamous, had occupational as well as ritual specialties, and were partially set apart by ideas of defilement, the society had some features of a true caste system.[15]

CASTE

Caste is class hypertrophied. It represents hereditary freezing of the principles upon which class is based: differential and unequal distribution of goods and power; formation of social groups, each with its own life style, based on such distribution; and differential patterns of relation between caste groups.

Castes are always higher and lower in a hierarchical order. Castes are rigid: a person is born into a caste and can rarely escape from it; this person must (usually) marry within his (or her) caste, and the offspring will remain in it. Castes usually have traditionally prescribed occupations within the productive and service system of the society. Caste behavior toward members of other castes is rigidly prescribed. In India, for instance, each caste refuses to drink water or food which has been handled by anyone belonging to a lower caste; to do so would be "polluting" and would acknowledge the equality or superiority of the handler. Although social intercourse between members of different castes may be highly circumscribed and severely limited, the intercaste relations form a functional social and economic network of interdependence in which even the lowliest and most economically deprived caste has its own autonomy and degree of independence. Caste members are not personal property; slaves are. Therefore, slavery and caste are separate social categories and are treated as such in all social science analyses.

TYPES OF CASTE SYSTEMS

Caste systems tend to be *simple* or *complex*, without much gradation between the two types. A *simple* system has two or three castes. A *complex* system encompasses a multitude of castes.

Simple systems break down into two types:

1. *Pariah* castes: In which one or more hereditary occupational groups such as blacksmiths or leatherworkers are treated as pariahs (low, despised, outcast) by the general population, and are strictly endogamous. The Japanese butchers *(eta)*, described on page 149, are a very good example of this type. Another example would be that of the Northern Somali of the East African Horn, of whom I. M. Lewis writes, with reference to all metalworkers: "Traditionally they are excluded from marriage with other Somali and have their own separate social organization modeled on and attached in subservience to that of their patrons."[16]

---

[15]W. Davenport, "The 'Hawaiian Cultural Revolution': Some Political and Economic Considerations" (*American Anthropologist*, vol. 71, 1969), p. 4.

[16]I. M. Lewis, "The Northern Pastoral Somali of the Horn," in J. L. Gibbs, Jr. (ed.), *Peoples of Africa*, p. 338.

2. *Ethnic castes:* In which a socially superior endogamous caste (usually composed of conquerors) subordinates and holds down a socially inferior caste of conquered people or of foreign immigrants of different race and/or culture, barring them from equal privileges. The white/black ethnic populations of the United States still show residues of ethnic caste distinctions in spite of great strides toward equalization of economic, political, and social opportunities in recent decades.

The Simple Ethnic Caste System of Ankole

The African kingdom of Ankole as it existed in the late nineteenth century is a good example of a simple ethnic caste system combined with social classes.

The basic caste division in Ankole was between pastoralists, who called themselves *Bahima*, and gardeners, who were known as *Bairu*.[17] The Bahima were Hamitic or Hamiticized Negro cattle people, who came down the grassland corridor between Lake Victoria on the east and the mountain and lake chain on the west. Their original home was probably southern Abyssinia. Racially and culturally, they were and are distinct from the Bantu horticulturalists, who had preceded them in occupation of the country. As they moved southward, the Bahima proved themselves as fighters to be superior to the Bantu-speaking Bairu and capable of effective enlargement of their social groups for politico-military ends. They conquered the Bairu and proceeded successfully to subjugate them without apparent difficulty, although the Bairu outnumbered them ten to one. The Bahima formed a dominant conquest-based caste; the Bairu were socially incorporated as a subjugated, inferior caste.

Unbreachable disabilities were imposed upon the Bairu:

1. All Bairu were forbidden to own fecund cattle. It is true that they were sometimes given barren cows or bull calves for services rendered a

Muhima, but any Muhima could arbitrarily expropriate any productive cows found in the possession of a Mwiru.

2. While all Bahima males were liable to be called for military service, the Bairu were barred from bearing arms. They were kept militarily ineffective, and the chances of successful revolution kept at a low level.

3. There could be no intermarriage between Bahima and Bairu. Aside from the customary prohibition of intermarriage, the injunction against Bairu cattle holding was an effective bar. No marriage could be valid without progeny price in cattle, and the Bairu could receive no reproductive cows, nor did they have any to give.

4. Bahima men (especially chiefs) could take Bairu girls as concubines, but Bairu men had no equal right to Bahima girls.

5. No Bairu could hold high political office. At best, he might serve as district tax collector under a Muhima.

6. All Bairu had to work for, and pay tribute to, the Bahima chieftains, who in turn distributed the garden products and derivatives to their fellows. The Bahima had no desire to kill the goose that laid the golden egg, however, and therefore the individual Muhima was barred from abuse of the Bairu, who was privileged to plead before a Bahima chief for compensation when ill-treated or exploited by an unauthorized Muhima.

7. When a Mwiru killed a Mwiru, that was a matter for retaliatory revenge among their own group. But if a Muhima killed a Mwiru, the law denied the right of direct action to the Bairu kinship group. The most its members could hope for was to be able to plead with the Bahima king that he obtain compensation on their behalf, and they were lucky if they got anything at all. But if a lowly Mwiru dared to kill a Muhima, the Bahima dispatched him forthwith.

Domination and exploitation in the Banyankole state was a direct, unabashed, and efficient process. It was an example par excellence of the oft-repeated story of the parasitic mastery of a sedentary people by nomadic herdsmen.

However, the caste structure was not the simple dichotomous arrangement we have thus far described. The Banyankole kingdom did not exist in a vacuum, and there were other Bahima king-

---

[17]In Bantu speech, the prefix "Mu" refers to a particular person; "Ba," to the tribe collectively; "Bu" to the tribal territory; and "Lu," to the language. Thus we have Bahima, Muhima, Buhima, and Luhima, and also Bairu and Mwiru.

doms and tribelets in the area. Although racially self-conscious, the predatory Muhima was not averse to raiding alien Bahima. To put a stop to this, the kingdom of Ankole undertook the subjugation of various Bahima neighbors, who were then incorporated into the Banyankole tribal society as a separate tribute-paying class, known as *Abatoro*. They could intermarry with their conquerors, and they suffered no serious legal disabilities.

Yet a fourth class was the *Abambari*. Prohibition of intermarriage never prevents miscegenation. Out of the Bahima-Bairu concubine relations came half-caste offspring. Legally, the *Abambari* were classed as Bairu in the same way that mulattoes used to be classed as Negroes by American laws. But the personal interest of a Muhima father often mitigated the strict working of this rule. Those who had no legitimate heirs often raised the son of a concubine to the status of heir. Thus the exclusive separatism of the ruling caste was self-defeated and, ironically enough, to the greatest degree among the chiefly families and lineages. For it is just in this group that today a definitely larger percentage of dark Bantu Negroid physical types is found than occurs among the ordinary Bahima herdsmen in the more remote rural districts.

Lastly, there were the *Abahuku*, or slaves. Because of the convenience and effectiveness of the system of exploiting the Bairu and the limited economic possibilities in slavery when Bairu tools and gardening methods were used, slavery was never extensive. The slaves were Bairu taken in raids upon neighboring kingdoms. Ankole Bairu were never enslaved. Slaves were used as menials in the households of the very rich. They neither gardened nor tended the herds. They were chattels of their individual masters, and their ears were cut off to keep them from passing as Bairu if they succeeded in running away.[18]

The Complex Caste System of India

Identifiable castes in India number in the hundreds and the web of caste forms a richly detailed tapestry. Caste is ubiquitous in all matters of daily life, and the system is so refined in its ramifications, that some anthropologists propose that the term "caste" should be restricted solely to the Indian phenomenon. Most view the Indian system as the utmost, rather than the only, manifestation of complex caste organization. It is presented as such in this book.

The idea of varna

According to ancient Hindu belief, still very much alive, four so-called *varna* castes emerged from the body of primordial man. This was the beginning and the ideological justification of the whole Indian caste system for more than 2,000 years.

From his mouth issued the Brahmins, who became priests and scholars. From his arms came the Kshatriyas, warriors and rulers; from his thighs came the Vaishyas, tradesmen, and from his feet rose the Shudras, cultivators. Traditionally, those in the Brahmin category are supposed to manage the culture through their control of religion, Kshatriyas to manage the society through their control of armed might, Vaishyas to manage the distributive economy through their control of trade, and Shudras to produce the economic wherewithal for the whole society.[19]

The four *varna* castes are all ritually clean and unpolluted, but the first three have superior purity and prestigious privileges because their male members are "twice-born." The "twice-born" go through a transition rite which symbolizes a second birth; hence, "twice-born." Each "twice-born" wears a sacred thread, called *dvija*, over his left or right shoulder, depending on his caste's rank. Shudras, who are *varna*-caste farmers, are but once-born; their rank is middling.

Harijan castes: the untouchables

The *Harijan* castes are (were)[20] the untouchables. By the nature of their work, which puts them in close contact with "unclean" materials, they are considered polluted. As a result, great symbolic

---

[18]K. Oberg, "The Kingdom of Ankole in Uganda," in E. E. Evans-Pritchard and M. Fortes (eds.), *African Political Systems*, pp. 121–162.

[19]D. G. Mandelbaum, *Society in India*, vol. 1, pp. 22–23. By permission of University of California Press.

[20]The constitution and law of India, since 1949, have abolished the social disabilities of the *harijans*, making their observance illegal. Old caste attitudes, though weakening, still persist, however.

and actual social distance is maintained between the *varna* and *harijan* castes.

Jatis

Over all India the four *varna* castes and the *harijan* categories are divided into a thousand or more *jatis*, or specific castes. "A jati is an endogamous, hereditary social group that has a name and a combination of attributes."[21] The latter refers to the kinds of food which may be eaten or are prohibited, to pollution versus purity and the relative degrees thereof, to sacred thread or no thread, and to learning and occupation, plus multitudes of lesser privileges and disabilities. *Jatis* are specified subsections of the *varna* and *harijan* categories.

Yet not every *jati*, nor even every *varna*, is present in every community. Thus, in Konduru, a South Indian village studied by Professor Paul Hiebert, thirty *varna* castes are found—but none of them is *Kshatriya* (warrior). Among the thirty are clerk, priest, merchant and moneylender, temple lamplighter, goldsmith, blacksmith, carpenter, brassworker, farmer, braceletmaker, tailor, weaver, potter, bodyguard, fisherman, courtesan, herdsman, winetapper, bodyservant, barber-surgeon, and washerman *jati*. Among the *harijans* are five *jatis* of priests, musicians, weavers, sweepers, and leatherworkers.[22] Special services are provided by itinerant members of other *jatis* who wander through the country as peddlers or entertainers.

The jajmani system

Each *jati* has traditional relations to various other *jatis* in the rendering of their special occupational services. At the center of a web of such relations stands a hereditary landlord. At harvest time all of a landlord's, or *jajman's*, harvest of grain is piled in a heap on the threshing floor. The *jajman's* dependent field workers gather around, as do his "contracted" washerman, leatherworker, carpenter, barber, etc. The *jajman* presides like a lord, but the share each shall take is fixed, according to

custom and service rendered. Each man comes forward to claim his share in order of caste rank—Shudras first. When the barber's turn arrives, for example:

The Barber measures out a gift share, four to six fans of grain, for shaving the household males and a *poli cherta* for ritual performances. He pulls aside his bonus *(addam dōsili)* "for showing the mirror" to his prosperous masters so they can have the privilege of observing their tonsure while it is taking place. Since the poor do not give a bonus at harvesttime, they are shaved without the benefits of soap or a mirror. The Barber does more than shaving, however; his knive is used at births to sever the umbilical cord while his wife assists in the delivery of the child. After funerals he shaves his clients at the time of their purification. But it is at weddings that he is most needed. He prepares the groom and is given small gifts of grain, liquor, coins, and the clothes that the young man had been wearing. He pares the nails of the couple during the ceremonies and claims the unhusked rice used in making the ritual designs. He arranges for a Barber band to play for the ceremony and also for the many processions that welcome the bridal party, that fetch the ceremonial pots and sacred earth, that accompany the wedding party to the temple, and that parade the newlyweds through town. Finally, on an auspicious day fixed by the family *purohit*, the Barber performs the ritual tonsure and receives the groom's turban as a symbol of his assumption of the jajmani rights over the new home.

When the Shudras have taken their share, the Leatherworker approaches for his: a gift share of a half pot of grain for repairing shoes and harnesses and a share for repairing the irrigation bucket at the well. He also claims the meat and one-half of the skins of the jajman's cattle that die throughout the year. The other half of the skins he must tan and return for the jajman's use. After the grain is cleared from the threshing floor, the Leatherworker sweeps up the tailings as his bonus *(danda kaṭṭu)*. The biggest reward of the harvest often goes to the Leatherworker who has been a faithful worker during the past year. Such a man helps in the field work by drawing water before dawn to irrigate the rice, by sleeping in the fields to protect the harvest from wild pigs from the surrounding forest, and by guarding the cut grain from thieves. He beats the large leather-covered drum in his master's processions and sleeps before his door at night. The jajman rewards such a servant with a generous portion which can amount to ten pots of grain.[23]

[21]D. G. Mandelbaum, *op.cit.*, p. 14.
[22]P. G. Hiebert, *Konduru*, pp. 17–28.

[23]P. G. Hiebert, *Konduru*, pp. 87–88. Copyright © 1971, the University of Minnesota. Quoted with permission.

A service caste worker may serve one or several *jajmans*, as the case may be.

In spite of the teeming millions in India's great cities, about 90 per cent of India's half-billion population live in rural villages in *jajmani* caste ordering. It may be a unique social system, but it embraces about one-twelfth of all mankind alive today!

The Frequency and Distribution of Caste Systems

Caste systems of social organization are relatively rare numerically. Of 819 societies in the *Ethnographic Atlas* on which there is sufficient information to make a judgment, only 103, or about 12.5 per cent, have castes of any type. Of these, simple pariah caste systems are most common (65, or 8 per cent of the whole), while simple ethnic caste systems are found in only 24 (less than 2 per cent) of the whole. Complex caste systems occurred in 14 societies.

In ethnographic distribution within the sample, caste organization is wholly an Old World phenomenon. The egalitarian societies of the American Indians were casteless.

Simple pariah caste systems occurred in half (48 per cent) of the 77 Mediterranean societies in the sample, and in one-twelfth of the 216 Sub-Saharan African societies.

Simple ethnic caste systems are found exclu-

sively (with one exception) in the Mediterranean and African samples, but with relative frequencies of less than one in twenty.

Complex caste systems, conversely, are exclusively Asian creations. Thirteen of the 81 Asian societies in the sample (16 per cent) have complex caste systems. One Oceanic society in 128 (the Belu, on Timor, in Indonesia) had a complex caste system.[24]

The data on the comparative distribution of caste systems are summarized in Table 16-1.

"SOCIAL RACE," CLASS, AND CASTE

Both class and caste systems use some characteristic or behavior of a society's subgroups, either real or socially defined, to differentiate between the various classes or castes. One common criterion for marking social subgroups is that of race. In the section of Chapter 2 entitled "The Relation of Race to Culture"(pages 30–35), we have pointed out that anthropologists and geneticists have no evidence to demonstrate that the differences in behavior between the racial subgroups of mankind are caused by biological or genetic differences; rather, because cultural behavior is learned and not genetically determined, differences in behavior between apparently physi-

---

[24]These data are compiled from column 67 of the *Ethnographic Atlas.*

TABLE 16-1   THE DISTRIBUTION OF CASTE SYSTEMS BY TOTAL FREQUENCY AND BY RELATIVE FREQUENCY IN MAJOR GEOGRAPHIC AREAS

Type of Caste System	All Societies *n* = 819	Sub-Saharan Africa *n* = 216	Mediter-ranean *n* = 77	East Eurasia *n* = 81	Oceania *n* = 128	North America *n* = 219	South America *n* = 88
Castes absent	86% (706)	82% (178)	48% (37)	73% (59)	98% (125)	100% (219)	100% (88)
Simple caste system: Pariah	8% (65)	12% (27)	48% (37)	— (0)	.08% (1)	— (0)	— (0)
Simple caste system: Ethnic	3% (24)	5% (11)	4% (3)	11% (9)	.08% (1)	— (0)	— (0)
Complex caste system	1.7% (14)	— (0)	— (0)	16% (13)	.08% (1)	— (0)	— (0)

SOURCE: Data compiled from G. P. Murdock, *Ethnographic Atlas,* column 69.
NOTE: Percentages above the figure "2" have been rounded off; totals do not equal 100% in all cases.

cally different groups of human beings can be attributed to variation in the enculturation and acculturation experiences. Regardless of whether a society's understanding of the nature and causes of the physical and behavioral differences between human subgroups is scientifically valid, some societies use these differences to either mark or justify class or caste differences.

In a study of social classification among various societies in the American continents, anthropologist Charles Wagley analyzed class and caste differences based on apparent physical differences, and he proposed the term *social races* to refer to these groupings. Wagley argues that these groups are not biologically defined but rather are socially based on cultural concepts of differences that may have little to do with real biological variation. Because this subgroup definition does not have a genetic basis, ". . . they may in one society be classifications based on real or imaginary physical characteristics; in another they may refer more to criteria of social status such as education, wealth, language and even custom; while in still another they may indicate near or distant ancestry."[25]

To illustrate the complexity of social race systems, reference can be made to the region of Mexico and Guatemala where physical appearance is not a useful criterion for distinguishing social race. The three categories of the population (the first two of which originally had separate ancestry) include: the *indigenas*, or Indian population; the white population; and a third population, intermediate between the other two, the *mestizos*. Because a great deal of miscegenation (interbreeding) has gone on between the originally separate and later mixed populations, there is currently no way (either by physical appearance or ancestry) to perceive the category to which an individual belongs. Instead, it is necessary to rely on behavioral criteria, such as language, wearing apparel, community membership (see Fig. 16-2), or simply by asking individuals to state to which group they belong.[26]

The importance of the cross-cultural anthropological study of race has been the discovery of this kind of pattern of racial classification, demonstrating that human concepts of racial groups are based on differences that can be attributed to nongenetic cultural behavior rather than physiologically determined behavior patterns or limitations. The anthropologist thus perceives the subdivision of a society into classes or castes as the result of the various subgroups' perceptions of the differences between themselves and others and not as the result of any natural, inherent, or scientifically based genetic division of the people. This conception of the source of human differences focuses the study of class and caste on the kinds of criteria proposed by Max Weber (page 271), and accepts that presently there is no scientifically acceptable evidence demonstrating that behavioral differences between racial classes and castes are genetically produced. In other words, race as an aspect of social structure is *social race*; that is, the racial division of people on the basis of socially rather than genetically defined differences.

SLAVERY IN PRIMITIVE SOCIETIES

Slavery has entered several times into our discussion of class systems. Slavery has been one of the most important of human social institutions; it occurred in half the world's societies in the eighteenth and nineteenth centuries.

The Nature of Slavery

Contemporary democratic morality in industrial civilizations condemns slavery in such strong terms that we recoil from the idea of it in horror. It is now hard for us to conceive of involuntary servitude as an implicit aspect of any society, and yet slavery has been an important part of human cultures for a far longer period of time than that during which contemporary civilizations have extirpated it from the social body.

Slavery is not in itself an absolute concept. In operation, it ranges from the complete degradation of a whole class of people by means of dogmatic denial of their humanity (slaves as chattels) to the inclusion of slaves as adopted mem-

[25]C. Wagley, "On the Concept of Social Race in the Americas," in D. B. Heath and R. N. Adams (eds.), *Contemporary Cultures and Societies of Latin America*, pp. 531–545.
[26]*Ibid.*, pp. 538–540.

FIG. 16-2 Caste and class (social race) in the land of the Incas to-day. An elite-caste political spokesman with Indian leaders in a public meeting in Callejon, Peru. Observe the marked differences in the status symbolism of clothes and posture. (John Collier, Jr., for the Cornell-Peru Project at Vicos.)

bers of the master's family and kinship group. Slavery, we are safe in saying, is a condition rarely welcomed by the slaves. There are few social advantages in being a slave and usually a good many disadvantages. The lot of the slave depends to a large degree on whether the tribe customarily utilizes its slaves as household servants or as laborers. In the former case, the relation of slave to master is unavoidably intimate, and slaves reap the benefit. If slaves are used as laborers, the owner's chief interest becomes one of economic exploitation, and, especially where there are great

numbers of slaves, relationships become impersonal and harsh.

Slaves are derived both from within and from without a society. Internal slavery occurs only in the more advanced primitive societies with quasi-capitalistic practices of borrowing and lending. A borrower might pledge himself or a son or daughter as security on a loan. Default meant servitude. Or, as in the case of the Ashanti of Ghana, a man could pawn his brother's son to raise a sum. The boy then worked for the creditor until the loan was repaid; the labor he performed

TABLE 16-2 FREQUENCY AND PERCENTAGE DISTRIBUTIONS OF SLAVERY IN 565 CULTURES, ACCORDING TO LEVEL OF SUBSISTENCE BASE

Subsistence Base	Number of Cultures with Slavery	Percent of Cultures with Slavery
Plow agriculture	59	53
Pastoral	27	55
Intensive gardening	103	47
Foraging	6	20
Hunting and gathering	27	27

SOURCE: Data from A. D. Coult and R. W. Habenstein, *Cross Tabulations of Murdock's World Ethnographic Sample,* p. 522.

constituted the interest on the loan. Debt slavery did not ordinarily produce huge masses of slaves, nor were their positions inordinately harsh. A second internal source of slaves was the condemnation of criminals to servitude. This, too, is found only in the more highly advanced cultures, since a strongly centralized law system is a necessity.

The great source of slaves, however, was war and the exploitation of war captives, but war may or may not be waged to take captives. Slaves are in the tribe, but not of it. Without citizenship, slaves are outside the realm of jural personality, and their debased status does not contradict the slaveholders' notions of social equality—for themselves, exclusive of the slaves.

Frequency and Distribution of Slavery

Slavery is clearly associated with the evolution of culture; its origins appear to be very ancient. Table 16-2 shows the distribution of slavery according to the subsistence patterns of 565 cultures. Slightly more than one-fourth of the simple hunters and gatherers of recent times practiced slavery. The ratio drops to one-fifth among intensive foragers, rises to nearly half among horticulturalists and to more than half among societies predominantly based on plow agriculture or pastoralism. Slavery flourished in most preindustrial civilizations. After the industrial revolution, its economic usefulness disappeared, slavery was viewed as immoral, and it was legally rooted out

TABLE 16-3 DISTRIBUTION OF CULTURES WITH SLAVERY, BY MAJOR GEOGRAPHIC AREAS

Geographic Areas	Number of Cultures by Area $n = 774$	Number of Cultures with Slavery $n = 363$	Percentage of Occurrence of Slavery in Each area
Africa	204	160	78
Circum-Mediterranean	82	50	61
Eurasia	77	43	56
Pacific Islands	124	26	21
North America	205	62	30
South America	82	22	27

SOURCE: Data from E. Bourguignon and L. Greenbaum, *op. cit.,* table 19, p. 41.

as a social institution—but not until well into the nineteenth century.

Prior to the expansion of European cultures, slavery was unevenly distributed around the world (see Table 16-3). It was most rare in Oceania, where one-fifth of the societies practiced it. The Indians of North and South America had worked it into 30 and 27 per cent of their societies, respectively. The Old World was by all odds the home of slavery. More than half the societies of Asia and two-thirds of those around the Mediterranean took slavery for granted. But Africa was the true indigenous home of slavery. There, four-fifths of the societies included in the *Ethnographic Atlas* held slaves. The high incidence of pastoralism and developed agriculture might have contributed to the spread of slavery in Africa. Yet the presence of both these types of subsistence economies in high frequency in Eurasia and the Mediterranean regions did not produce nearly so much slavery in those parts of the world. Future research into the structural-functional aspects of slavery may provide an answer to the African problem; little is available now.

SELECTED READINGS

Berreman, G. D., "Caste: the Concept of Caste" (*International Encyclopedia of the Social Sciences*, vol. 2, 1968), pp. 333–338. An expanded discussion of ways of looking at caste.

Hiebert, P. G., *Konduru: Structure and Integration in a South Indian Village* (1971). Presents a clear and understandable description and analysis of the dynamics of caste in relation to other forms of social organization in a specific village community of India today.

Kroeber, A. L., "Caste" (*Encyclopaedia of the Social Sciences*, vol. 3, 1930), pp. 254–256. A summary of the phenomenon.

Lipset, S. M., "Stratification, Social: Social Class" (*International Encyclopedia of the Social Sciences*, vol. 15, 1968), pp. 296–316. A very helpful survey of the different theories of social class.

Mandelbaum, D. G., *Society in India*, vol. 1 (1970), parts 1, 3, and 4. A complete overview of the *jati* system in India set in the theory of modern social anthropology.

Mishkin, B., *Rank and Warfare among Plains Indians* (American Ethnological Society, Monograph 3, 1940). The basis of class differentiation among some American Indians.

Oberg, K., "The Kingdom of Ankole in Uganda," in E. E. Evans-Pritchard and M. Fortes (eds.), *African Political Systems* (1940), pp. 121–164. For greater detail on the system described in this chapter.

Polanyi, K., and A. Rotstein, *Dahomey and the Slave Trade*. A historical, economic, and anthropological treatment of one of the great ports of trade in slaves.

Tuden, A., and L. Plotnicov (eds.), *Social Stratification in Africa* (1970). Contains eleven chapters on class, caste, or slavery as they have existed, or do exist, in African societies.

17

SOCIAL CONTROL AND LAW

LEARNING GOALS

Identify the three basic features of law. ¶ Formulate a working definition of law and its major variations. ¶ Enumerate the functions of law in human societies. ¶ Characterize the nature of case law and the settlement of disputes. ¶ Compare four primitive legal systems to indicate how they work. ¶ Cite the major similarities and differences between primitive and civilized legal systems. ¶ Write a summary of the major trends in the development of law in relation to cultural evolution.

We have learned in earlier chapters that a culture is the integrated sum total of the learned behavior traits characteristic of the members of a society, embracing their total way of life—technological and ideological. Law is one aspect of culture, just as are kinship, subsistence patterns, language, and art.

Specifically, it has been stressed that, in every society, human behavior must be narrowed down from its full range of potential variety to a moderately limited body of norms, so that people can manage their lives with a reasonable degree of certainty that their own activities will evoke anticipated responses and results from their fellows. Social control is exerted to guide the learning process of all members of the society in the development of the appropriate behavioral customs.

Custom consists of social norms (Chapter 2, pages 25–27), and all social norms are sanctioned. Behavior in accord with norms is usually rewarded. Behavior which departs too far from the norms is penalized. Social control consists of the entire gamut of rewards and dissuasions. All child training, all education, all the unending responses of peers and associates throughout life, as discussed under "Enculturation and Personality" (Chapter 4), are involved. Their positive responses range from the smile, the giving of food, the friendly pat, through consent to do something strongly desired, to bestowal of privileges, honors, and wealth. These are the positive sanctions that are constantly at work. On the other hand, there are negative sanctions which punish with a frown, a hateful word, a scornful curl of the lip, or a slap in the face (or elsewhere); by ostracism (social isolation); by deprivation of food, of clothing, or of other wanted things; by humiliation—all of these in everyday intercourse. They may be very effective, indeed. Yet their simple effectiveness does not make law of them.

So, too, the supernatural enters into social control. Ghosts, spirits, and gods may be believed to reward the moral and the just, just as they may punish the wrongdoer. Sin is the violation of a social norm which is negatively sanctioned by the supernatural.

Law consists of social norms, *plus*. Not all enculturation is effective for all individuals. Some ignore the norms now and then, or go beyond the limits of permissible leeway. Ordinary day-to-day social control has not worked in their cases. As reflectively stated by an old-time Cheyenne leader: "The Indian on the prairie, before there was the White man to put him in the guardhouse, had to have something to keep him from doing wrong." Not only the Indian on the prairie, but every society has to struggle to maintain its social order, for society is a human creation. As such it is fallible and fragile. There is no instinct of social morality or law observance. Individuals must be induced to act within socially prescribed limits of behavior because they believe in the values of their society, or they must be constrained because some behaviors are ruled out.

Most societies include law within their systems of social control designed to achieve this end: "Anthropologically considered, law is merely one aspect of . . . culture—the aspect which employs the force of organized society to prevent, redress or punish deviations from prescribed norms."[1]

In law, the pressure of the sanctions is stepped up and the penalties are no longer only psychological. The wrongdoer's goods may be confiscated: he or she is assessed damages or must pay a fine. Something valued is taken. Or the offender is physically injured or constrained: whipped, mutilated, incarcerated (a form of ostracism), exiled, or killed (the absolute form of ostracism, an irrevocable removal from the social scene). Such is the force of the law.

THREE BASIC FEATURES OF LAW

Within the broad area of social control, then, we may say that law is set off from the general social norms by three characteristics:

1. The legitimate use of economic deprivation or physical coercion.
2. The allocation of official authority.
3. The element of regularity (consistency).

The Legitimate Use of Physical Coercion

The real *sine qua non* of law in any society is the legitimate use of physical coercion. The law has teeth, and teeth that can bite, although they need

not be bared, for, as Holmes put it: "The foundation of jurisdiction is physical power, although in civilized times it is not necessary to maintain that power throughout proceedings properly begun."[2] We would merely add to that declaration that it was not necessary to limit the latency of power to civilized times; primitive human beings often found that it was not necessary to display the power behind the law when the defendant acceded to proceedings carried through properly. Jhering has emphasized the factor of force in law: "Law without force is an empty name." Again, more poetically, we find: "A legal rule without coercion is a fire that does not burn, a light that does not shine."[3] In this we agree.

However, it is true that not all writers on law, especially primitive law, accept the criterion of force as an essential attribute of law. Professor Leo Pospisil, for example, holds that *how* a social obligation is enforced is less important than that it *is* enforced. "Is not the effect (social control, conformity) of a sanction more important than its form?" he asks. "Some psychological sanctions, although of nonphysical nature, perform as strong a control as do physical sanctions." In this age of familiarity with brain-washing, no one will deny that. Nor will we deny the effective importance of "ostracism, ridicule, avoidance, or a denial of favors—sanctions that are sometimes very subtle and informal."[4] These, however, are (we believe) better viewed as other-than-legal forms of control.

The threat of the law is more often than not a sufficient deterrent; people wish to avoid the public exposure, the embarrassment, inconvenience, and ultimate risk of economic loss or physical coercion. Law has its effect of psychological deterrence. For law exists primarily not to punish but to channel behavior toward socially acceptable goals, thus preventing the breach of social norms. But in the last resort, law deals in physical realities—the sanctions of forceful confiscation of property, if need be, or the use of direct physical compulsion.

---

[1]S. P. Simpson and R. Field, "Law and the Social Sciences" (*Virginia Law Review*, vol. 32, 1946), p. 858.

[2]O. W. Holmes, Jr., *McDonald v. Maybee* (*Supreme Court Reporter*, vol. 37, 1917), p. 343.

[3]R. von Jhering, *Law as Means to an End*, p. 190.

[4]L. Pospisil, *Kapauku Papuans and Their Law* (Yale University Publications in Anthropology, No. 59, 1958), p. 267.

The Official Element

But force in law has a special meaning. Force means coercion, which in its absolute form is physical compulsion. There are, of course, as many forms of coercion as there are forms of power, and only certain methods and forms are legal. Coercion by gangsters is not legal, unless it is "accepted" as a regular part of the social system. Even physical coercion by a parent is not legal if it is extreme in form. The essentials of legal coercion are general acceptance of the application of physical power, in threat or in fact, by a privileged party, for a legitimate cause, in a legitimate way, and at a legitimate time. This distinguishes the sanction of law from other social rules.

Private law

The privilege of applying force constitutes the official element in law. In most primitive societies, this privilege is vested in the wronged individual or kinship groups. They must prosecute on their own behalf and exact the proper legal penalty. This is known as *private law*. If a public official is responsible for penalizing a breach of law, it is *public*, or *criminal law*. One who is generally or specifically recognized as rightly exerting the element of physical coercion is a fragment of social authority. It is not necessary that one be an official with legal office or a constable's badge. In any primitive society, the so-called private prosecutor of a private injury is implicitly a public official *pro tempore, pro eo solo delicto*. This individual is not, and cannot be, acting solely on behalf of personal, familial, or clan interests and still enjoy the approval or tacit support of the disinterested remainder of society. If the rest of the tribal population supports the prosecutor in opinion, even though not in overt action, it can mean only that the society feels that the behavior of the defendant was wrong in its broadest implications, i.e., contrary to the standards of the society as a whole. Thus the behavior is in itself an injury to the society, although the group feeling may not be strong enough to generate overt and specific action by the group as a group and on its own initiative.

However, the private prosecutor remains the representative of the general social interest as well as of that which is specifically his own. This fundamental fact is ordinarily ignored in discussions of primitive law, and it is in this sense that we may say that the difference between criminal law and private law is a difference in degree rather than in kind, though there can be no doubt that some matters touch the general interest in fact and evoke group feeling much more vigorously than others in primitive law, e.g., sacrilege, homicidal tendencies, and, frequently, treason.

Public law

When responsibility for initiating legal action against a wrongdoer rests not with the person wronged or his kinsmen, but rather is in the hands of a public officer—a headman, a chief, a bailiff, or a member of the chief's staff or royal household, or perhaps a shaman or a priest—then the offense is a *public wrong*. Public wrongs are traditionally called *crimes* in Anglo-American usage. Public law is the concern of government; private law operates apart from government, although it is one aspect of the political organization of any society. But it must be reemphasized that the actions of the private prosecutor have legitimacy (if the prosecutor is acting in accordance with the provisions of the tribal system of private law) because the public at large supports the rightfulness of action against the socially defined wrongness of the transgressor.

Regularity

Regularity is what law shares at the core with social norms. Regularity is what law in the legal sense has in common with law in the scientific sense. Regularity means predictability. Yet, regularity, it must be warned, does not mean absolute certainty. There can be no true certainty where human beings are involved; and yet there is much regularity, for all society is based on it. In law, the doctrine of precedent (*L. stare decisis*, to adhere to decisions) is not the unique possession of the Anglo-American common law jurist. Primitive law also builds on precedents, for new decisions rest on old rules of law or norms of custom. Regularity removes the threat of personal whim and caprice from law. Regularity lends to law its attribute of certainty. The norms of law make prediction of legal outcomes reasonably certain.

The characteristics of law are therefore *the right to apply economic sanctions or force (legitimate coercion), official authority*, and *regularity*. It is these qualities which distinguish law from custom or morals in any culture.

LAW DEFINED

Thus we may form a working definition of law that fits primitive as well as civilized law in the following terms: *A law is a social norm of which it can be predicted with reasonable probability that its violation beyond the limits of permissible leeway will evoke a formal procedural response initiated by an individual or a group possessing the socially recognized privilege-right of determining guilt and of imposing economic or physical sanctions upon the wrongdoer.*

We may further define *civilized law* as the law of societies whose cultures include writing; *archaic law* as the law of early civilizations; and *primitive law* as the law of nonliterate peoples.

Two other kinds of distinctions in law should be mentioned. These are the distinctions between *substantive* and *adjective* law, and between *organic* and *tyrannic* law.

Substantive Law and Adjective Law

Legal norms are social norms that are reinforced by legal sanctions, as identified above. They are selected in accordance with their consistency in relation to jural postulates: the cultural assumptions that undergird the legal system.

FIG. 17-1 Law in contemporary Ibo art. An Ibo couple of Nigeria publicly punished.

Substantive law

Substantive law identifies the norms that are to be sanctioned by legal action. In most instances, substantive law undertakes to translate basic cultural postulates into social action by decision as to what particular behavior in a given instance may best be interpreted as conforming to the basic assumptions underlying the culture. Law implements the imperative of selection by saying implicitly: "In this society, this is permitted and that is not."

Adjective law

Procedural or *adjective law* designates the person, or persons, who may rightly punish a breach of substantive law; it also lays down the rules for prosecuting a case and fixes the customary penalties to be applied to each type of offense. In one form or another, the idea of "due process of law" exists in every society. Due process consists of the socially recognized right ways of carrying through a legal action once a plaintiff moves to act against an infringement of the substantive law. The "right ways" limit and channel the time and place of prosecution; the finding of evidence; the relevance of evidence; and the kinds and degree of coercion that may be used; what goods may be confiscated, or what physical sanctions are appropriate and allowable. The norms of *adjective law* institutionalize the sanctioning procedures. They separate right from sheer might. They are mankind's bulwark against the anarchy of strife and the terror of tyranny.

Organic versus Tyrannic Law

Because of its element of coercion, law has its peculiar dangers. Out of control or in the hands of a vested minority, it can become a tyranny of terror directed not to the realization of the basic values of the society at large but to the subjugation of those who are not a part of the ruling clique, class, or caste.

When a law system is imposed on a people through conquest or by a minority which dominates through raw power not consensually allocated as a socially recognized privilege-right, that law system is *tyrannic*.

When a law system is self-developed by a people, when its rules and practices are generally accepted as in accord with commonly held ideas as to the nature of their society, its goals, and the legitimacy of its leaders and rulers—in sum, when the law system is in accord with the total social value system—we can call it *organic law*: a vital system rooted in healthy soil. Most, but not all, primitive, tribal law systems have been of this order. And in the ensuing discussion, it will be of organic law that we speak, unless otherwise noted.

THE FUNCTIONS OF LAW

Law performs four fundamental functions essential to the maintenance of societies and their cultures. They are substantive, adjective, mediative, and readaptive in quality. These functions are:

1. The definition of obligatory relationships between the members of a society, so as to assert which activities are permitted and which are ruled

out and to maintain at least minimal integration between the activities of individuals and groups within the society. This involves the culture-building process in response to the imperative of selection (the substantive).

2. The allocation of authority and the designation of the person who has the socially recognized privilege-right to initiate and carry through legitimate corrective actions leading to economic or physical sanctions when substantive norms are violated, so that force is controlled and directed toward social goals (the adjective).

3. The disposition of trouble cases as they arise; to clean up social messes (tangled claims, squabbles and fights, killings and woundings) so that people may get on about their business of everyday living with reasonable certainty and security (the mediative).

4. The continuing redefinition of relations between individuals and groups as the conditions of life change, to maintain adaptability and flexibility in both substantive and procedural law in response to shifting values and new technologies (the readaptive).

A society may manage these functions with more or less skill; its legal system may function with sure effectiveness, achieving justice and order with a minimum of bungling and harshness; or it may be rigid and brutal, with order imposed by tyranny, and justice a fugitive in the land.

CASE LAW AND THE SETTLEMENT OF DISPUTES

In their search for understanding of primitive legal systems and how they came into being, anthropologists have benefited greatly from modern jurisprudence, which points up the fact that breach and disputes in conflicts of claims are the most constant source of the law. "Breach," says Seagle, "is the mother of law as necessity is the mother of invention."[5] On the authority of Holmes, we have it that ". . . a law embodies beliefs that have triumphed in the battle of ideas and then translated themselves into action." In the same vein, Pound has written: "The law is an

---

[5]W. Seagle, *The Quest for Law*, p. 35.

attempt to reconcile, to harmonize, to compromise . . . overlapping or conflicting interests."[6] Law exists to channel behavior so that conflicts of interest do not result in an overt clash. It moves into action when interests do clash. New decisions are ideally so shaped as to determine which interests best accord with the accepted standards of what is good for the society. Of course, it is unfortunately true that tyrants, usurpers, and pettifoggers can and do pervert the ends of law to their own designs without regard to social interests or prevailing standards of what is right.

As a canon of realistic law, we may say that, regardless of the law that exists concerning a particular situation, an actual dispute may arise before the principles of the law can be tested; a law that is never broken may exist as nothing more than a custom, for one will never know the full implications of it until it is tested in a legal action.

The role of the claimant is the most important single factor in the development of law in primitive societies. Numerous writers have commented upon the relative absence of legislative enactment by primitive government. Lowie, who is distinguished among American anthropologists for his early contributions to the study of legal phenomena, has offered a general statement that is fairly typical of the prevailing opinion: ". . . it should be noted that the legislative function in most primitive communities seems strangely curtailed when compared with that exercised in the more complex civilizations."[7] Salmond parallels this with the statement that ". . . the function of the State in its earlier conception is to *enforce* the law, not to *make* it."[8] Lowie continued: "All the exigencies of normal social intercourse are covered by customary law, and the business of such governmental machinery as exists is rather to exact obedience to traditional usage than to create new precedents."[9]

Now this would be true for wholly static societies, but, as Lowie would have been among the

first to acknowledge, no society is wholly static. New exigencies always arise. One permanent thing about human society is its impermanence. Especially when unlike cultures come into contact do new materials, new ways of behaving, and new ideas enter into the cultural picture.

These new elements are not usually adopted simultaneously by all members of the society. The consequence is that when some members get new goods and new ideas, they have new interests for which the old lines of the culture have made no provision. Their use of their new acquisitions comes into conflict with the old standards held by others. New custom and new law must then be generated.

However or by whomever the judgment may be rendered in any dispute, it is the claimant and the defendant who lay the grounds of the claim and counterclaim or denial. If one or the other does it skillfully, soundly, and wisely, the basis of decision is likely to be found in the statement of claim. No matter how selfish the motivation of a disputant may be, unless it be that of a fool, a claim is posed against the background of "right" social principles, general rightness, and the well-being of the entire social group. How else can the disputant gain enduring social acceptance of his or her position? Naturally, also, the more skillfully the case is argued, in terms of the consonance of the disputant's claim with the well-established principles of social order, the greater the probability that the disputant will shape the law as he or she wishes it to be determined.

Legal action and the pressing of claims may take place in the direct confrontation of the parties concerned, in an entirely informal situation. This is commonly the case among the simpler of primitive peoples. On the other hand, among many advanced gardening peoples, especially those who have centralized government with powerful chiefs and kings, the legal institutions may provide for formal courts and refined legal rituals. The essential feature is the accepted intervention of third parties endowed with the recognized privilege-right of decision and enforcement. On the intermediate level of development, an obscure type of court may be found in the Cheyenne Indian military fraternity. Consider the case of Wolf Lies Down, whose horse was "borrowed"

---

[6]R. Pound, "A Theory of Legal Interests" (*American Sociological Society, Publications*, vol. 16, 1920), p. 44.

[7]R. H. Lowie, *Primitive Society*, p. 358.

[8]J. W. Salmond, *Jurisprudence*, p. 49.

[9]Lowie, *op. cit.*, p. 358. (By "customary law" is meant "unwritten law.")

by a friend in the absence of the owner. When the friend did not return from the warpath with the horse, Wolf Lies Down put the matter before his fraternity, the Elk Soldiers. "Now I want to know what to do," he said. "I want you to tell me the right thing." The fraternity chiefs sent a messenger to bring the friend in from the camp of a remote band. The friend gave an adequate and acceptable explanation of his conduct and offered handsome restitution to the complainant in addition to making him his blood brother. Then said the chiefs: "Now we have settled this thing." But they went on, half as a legislature: "Now we shall make a new rule. There shall be no more borrowing of horses without asking. If any man takes another's goods without asking, we will go over and get them back for him. More than that, if the taker tries to keep them, we will give him a whipping."

Can anyone deny that the Elk Soldiers were in effect sitting as a court for the entire tribe? The test is, first, one of responsibility. That they knew. Second, it is one of effective authority. That they achieved. Third, it is one of method. Unhampered by a system of formal precedent that required them to judge according to the past, they recognized that the rule according to which they were settling this case was new, and so they announced it.[10]

Among the Yurok Indians of California, as typical of a less specifically organized people, the court was less definite, but it was nevertheless there. An aggrieved Yurok who felt he had a legitimate claim engaged the services of two nonrelatives from a community other than his own. The defendant did likewise. These persons were called *crossers* because they crossed back and forth between the litigants. The litigants did not face each other in the dispute. After hearing all that each side offered in evidence and argument, the crossers rendered a judgment on the facts. If the judgment was for the plaintiff, they rendered a decision for damages according to a well-established scale that was known to all. For their footwork and efforts, each received a piece

of shell currency called a *moccasin*. Here again we have a court.[11]

On an even more primitive level, if an aggrieved party or his kinsmen must institute and carry through the prosecution without the intervention of a third party, there will still be a court, if the proceedings follow the lines of recognized and established order. There will be, then, at least the compulsion of recognized legal procedure, although the ultimate court may be the bar of public opinion. When vigorous public opinion recognizes and accepts the procedure of the plaintiff as correct and the settlement or punishment meted out as sound, and the wrongdoer in consequence accedes to the settlement because he feels he must yield, then the plaintiff and his supporting public opinion constitute a rudimentary sort of court, and the procedure is inescapably legal.

Consider the Eskimo dealing with recidivist homicide. Killing on a single occasion led merely to feud, inasmuch as the avenger enjoyed no recognized privilege of imposing the death penalty on the murderer of his kinsman with immunity against a counterkilling. A feud, of course, represents an absence of law, since blood revenge is more a sociological law than a legal one. But to kill again on a second occasion made the culprit a public enemy in the Eskimo view. It then became incumbent upon some public-spirited individual of initiative to interview all the adult males of the community to determine whether they agreed that he should be executed. If unanimous consent were given, the leader then undertook to execute the criminal, and no revenge could be taken on him by the murderer's relatives. Cases show that, in fact, no revenge was taken.[12] A community court had spoken.

Judicial Hearings

Any lawsuit or criminal trial involves at least two questions: "Is the alleged offense an illegal act?"

---

[10]For a full account of this case, see K. N. Llewellyn and E. A. Hoebel, *The Cheyenne Way: Conflict and Case Law in Primitive Jurisprudence*, p. 127.

[11]See A. L. Kroeber, "Yurok Law" (*Proceedings of the 22d International Congress of Americanists*, 1922), pp. 511ff. A dramatic presentation of a Yurok case-in-action is given in *The Ways of Mankind*, Series I, No. 5, "The Sea Lion Flippers: A Study in Ethics."

[12]For a report of such a case, see F. Boas, *The Central Eskimo* (Bureau of American Ethnology, Annual Report 6, 1888), p. 668.

"If so, is the defendant guilty of the offense?" The first is a question of law. The second is a question of fact. If the first can be brought to a negative answer, then there is no need to seek an answer to the second. The case must be dropped.

Assuming that there is a legal rule covering the alleged act, how are the facts then determined? On the lower levels of legal development, the question of evidence is not of great importance. In a small community, not much behavior is secret. As a Shoshone once commented: "They just wait around. Sooner or later the facts will come out."

In systems in which the administration of law is centralized in the hands of regular judges, the eliciting of evidence may be skillfully conducted. As an example, Max Gluckman's penetrating analysis of the judicial process among the Barotse of Rhodesia, in Africa, reveals in rich detail the institutional structure of the Lozi courts *(kuta)*, made up of three sets of councilors: headmen or nonroyal chiefs, royal officers or stewards, and princes and prince consorts. Because the Lozi have no lawyers, ". . . the whole onus of eliciting and analyzing the evidence falls on the judges." Standards of judicial impartiality are explicitly strong: "A marked feature in all the judgments is the emphasis that the kuta decides by evidence and reasoning, and without favour."[13] Kinship allegiance should not enter.

The key concept here . . . is trial by due process of law *(tatubo kamulao)*. The process is based on hearing evidence *(bupaki)* which establishes proof (also *bupaki*) on the facts (*litaba* = also things). Evidence itself is reduced by concepts of relevance *(bupaki bobuswanela*, appropriate or right evidence; *bupaki bobukena*, evidence which enters); of cogency *(bupaki bobutiile*, strong evidence); of credibility *(bupaki bobusepehala)*; and of corroboration *(bupaki bobuyemela)*. These types of evidence are tested as direct, circumstantial, or hearsay.[14]

When, through direct examination, the judges have elicited evidence sufficient to their needs, they enter a process of explicit formulation of a judgment. One after another, from the most junior judge up, in reversed order of seniority, the members of the *kuta* render their individual opinions, until the holding of the case is stated in the opinion of the senior chief:

Large parts of the judgments read like sermons, for they are all lectures on the theme "your station and its duties." The standards publicly stated for the parties are the norms involved in their social positions and relationships. . . . The essence of the judicial process is to state these norms to the world and to assess against them the behaviour of the parties in a specific series of situations.[15]

Lozi judges are shrewdly appraised by the people, who express the reputations of individual judges in the following terms:

kutalungusha—to be able to classify affairs;
kunyanyama—to be clever and of prompt decision;
sishongololi—a judge who relates matters lengthily and correctly;
muswanikisi—a judge who has good reasoning power and is able to ask searching questions.
Other words scorn poor reasoning:
kuyungula—to speak on matters without coming to the point;
kunjongoloka—to wander away from the subject when speaking;
kubulela siweko—to talk without understanding;
muyauluki—a judge who speaks without touching on the important points at issue;
siswasiwa—a person who gets entangled in words;
siyambutuki—a talker at random.[16]

Obviously, judges are themselves judged by severe standards of performance.

Supernatural Legal Devices

Generally speaking, however, the role of judges is much less significant in primitive legal systems than it is in the more developed legal orders of civilizations. Other devices used by primitive societies include resort to supernatural devices such as *divination, conditional curse,* and *ordeal.*

Extortion of confessions by third-degree methods occurs in a few tribes; for example, a Comanche husband could choke his wife or hold her over a fire until she named her lover. But more commonly the primitive human being, when the

---

[13]M. Gluckman, *The Judicial Process among the Barotse of Northern Rhodesia*, pp. 82 and 61.
[14]*Ibid.*, p. 316. By permission of The Humanities Press, Inc.

[15]*Ibid.*, p. 49. By permission of The Humanities Press, Inc.
[16]*Ibid.*, p. 277. By permission of The Humanities Press, Inc.

facts could not be gotten by direct means, had recourse to the supernatural.

Divination

Divination is the most common device. It is the process of evoking knowledge of some secret or hidden thing by mechanical or manipulative techniques. Thus an Eskimo shaman searches out answers by tying a thong to some reclining object such as a person, a bundle, or even his own foot. After inducing a spirit into the object, he asks it questions to which "yes" or "no" answers may be given. Then he tries to lift the object with the thong. If it is hard to lift, the answer is "no." If it raises easily, the answer is "yes."

Among many North American Indians, the still surface of water that has been put into the abdominal cavity of an animal reveals the image of the culprit. "Just as easy as reading a newspaper," said Post Oak Jim, the Comanche informant. Trobriand Islanders dug up a newly buried corpse to see what signs it might reveal. Maggots meant the lamented one was killed by the chief's sorcerer for having been too successful with women. If the lips were pursed, the same conclusion was indicated. Blotches of color on the skin meant he painted his house too ostentatiously for one of his social station, and so was done in by a jealous chief.

The Azande of Africa fed poison to a chicken, declaring repeatedly: "If this charge be true, let the chicken die. If this charge be false, spare its life." After the first chicken had responded, a second was given the test, but with the invocation reversed ("If the charge be true, let the chicken live; if it be false, let it die"). Thus, if the first chicken died and the second lived, the allegation was confirmed.[17]

Conditional curse

Conditional curse enters into trial procedure among almost all peoples. It is the assertion that always includes or implies the sentence: "If what I say is not true, *then* may the supernatural destroy

me." "You [Sun] saw me. May the one who lies die before winter."[18]

Even our own courts do not rely wholly upon our laws against perjury, since every witness must first swear a conditional curse: "So help me God." ("May God smite me if I lie.") Or is it, since the laws of criminal perjury are more recent than the conditional curse, that the courts do not have full faith in the efficacy of the curse?

Ordeal

Ordeal is peculiarly rare in the New World, which was to the good fortune of the Indians, to say the least. But most of the hideous forms known to medieval Europe were practiced with variations throughout Asia, Indonesia, and Africa. The ordeal by hot iron, with which Ibsen opens his historical play *The Pretenders*, had its counterpart in Ifugao. Various Philippine tribes used the old technique of tying up the two litigants and throwing them in a river. The one who rose to the surface first was guilty. Ordeal by poison was popular in Africa. In Ashanti, the defendant in a trial could drink a poison brew. If the defendant vomited, the verdict was innocent; if the defendant did not vomit, death was the result. And that is proof enough for any person!

Oath

Oath is merely a formal declaration that the testimony given is true. It may or may not imply the sanction of a supernatural power against falsehood. Often it is accompanied by a ritual act, such as touching the pipe to the lips among Indians, touching an arrow laid across the horns of a buffalo skull, or—as in American courts—placing one's hand upon the Bible.

CULTURAL CORRELATES OF CONDITIONAL CURSE AND ORDEAL   The virtual absence of appeal to the supernatural in legal disputes among American Indian tribes and its common occurrence in the Old World, especially Africa, shows how much it is an artificial, cultural invention. American Indians never thought up the idea of ordeal; a few of them

---

[17]E. E. Evans-Pritchard, *Witchcraft, Oracles and Magic among the Azande*, pp. 258–351.

[18]R. H. Lowie, *The Crow Indians*, p. 217.

FIG. 17-2 An Ifugao, northern Luzon, ordeal by boiling water. (Lowie Museum of Anthropology, University of California, Berkeley.)

knew and used the conditional curse. Somewhere in the Old World both ideas were hit upon, proved their social utility, and spread widely throughout the hemisphere.

A cross-cultural statistical survey undertaken by John M. Roberts indicates that the use of conditional curse and/or ordeal as the means of settling issues of fact and simultaneously invoking supernatural punishment is rare among hunters and gatherers, important among pastoralists, but most frequent among peoples who rely on agriculture for subsistence. Also, the more highly stratified the society, the more likely the use of conditional curse and ordeals. Finally, the same holds with respect to political systems: the more centralized the government and the larger the community governed, the more likely the appeal

to the supernatural in the legal settlement of disputes.[19]

What this means is this: in small tribal communities in which there is little differentiation in access to goods and resources, there tend to be fewer conflicts of property interests to generate disputes, and when disputes do occur, it is harder to hide the facts. Contrariwise, as populations become larger and more heterogeneous, as there are more goods to quarrel about, the task of the law becomes greater and more difficult. Direct and rational juridical devices fall short of meeting the demands of the law jobs in societal mainte-

---

[19]J. M. Roberts, "Oaths, Autonomic Ordeals, and Power," in L. Nader (ed.), *The Ethnography of Law* (*American Anthropologist*, vol. 67, no. 6, part 2, Special Publication, 1965), pp. 186–212.

nance. Recourse is then had to the convenience of the supernatural, until in modern, rationalistic, and secularized civilizations the ritual oath loses its efficacy.

REPRESENTATIVE LEGAL SYSTEMS

In order better to understand the nature of primitive law systems, it will be useful to sketch several thoroughly studied legal cultures, ranging from very simple types to highly developed ones that employ centralized governmental control. For this purpose we shall use the Eskimo, Comanche, Ifugao, Nuer, and Ashanti.

Eskimo Law

The Eskimos provide a good example of law on the lowest levels of social organization. The small Eskimo local group rarely numbers more than 100 members. Its organization is based on the bilateral family, beyond which there is nothing. There is no lineage, no clan, no clubs of either men or women, and no government. Each group has its headman: he who is "tacitly, half-unconsciously, recognized as first among equals"; he who is variously called *ihumatak*, "he who thinks (for others)"; *anaiyuhok*, "the one to whom all listen"; or *pimain*, "he who knows everything best." The headman leads, but he does not govern. He lends direction to his people's activity, but he does not direct. No Eskimo will give an order to another; therefore, the headman exercises no legal or judicial authority.

Prior to the imposition of Danish law in Greenland, of Canadian law in Canada, and federal and state law in Alaska, many acts prohibited under these legal systems were accepted as necessary by the Eskimos. Thus, certain forms of homicide were socially justified and legally permitted. Infanticide, invalidicide, suicide, and senilicide fell in this category. They are all responses to the basic Eskimo postulate that only those may survive who are able, or potentially able, to contribute to the subsistence economy of the community. Life is precarious in the arctic.

There were few legal offenses against property among the Eskimos because there was no property in land and free borrowing of goods made stealing pointless.

Eskimo law grew out of the aggressive status struggle that bedeviled the men. The society was wholly democratic, but prestige rivalry among the men was strong. Status could be gained through superior hunting skill and by stealing the wives of other men. The better the reputation of a man, the more likely he was to have his wife stolen. Wife stealing was not done primarily for sexual reasons. An Eskimo could enjoy sex without running the risks involved in home breaking. The motive lay in an attempt to outrank the man whose wife he took, if he could get away with it.

Wife stealing was not a crime, but most litigation arose from it. The challenge resulted either in murder or in wager of song, wrestling, or buffeting. Rasmussen found in the 1920s that all the adult males in a Musk Ox Eskimo group had been involved in murder, either as principals or as accessories; ". . . the motive was invariably some quarrel about a woman."[20] The fact that Eskimo husbands would lend their wives did not mean that they were free of jealousy. If a man lent his wife, he enjoyed the prestige of a giver of gifts. But if another man assumed sexual rights without permission, that was adultery and an assault on the husband's ego that could not go unchallenged. He would try to kill the wife stealer. But if he himself were killed, his murder had to be avenged, sooner or later. Since it was the usual Eskimo custom for the killer to marry his victim's widow and to adopt his children, a man might raise the boy who, when coming of age, would slay him in revenge for the murder of his father.

The alternative to killing an aggressor (and thus becoming involved in feud) was to challenge him to a juridical song contest. In the manner of Provençal troubadours of the thirteenth century, the two litigants scurrilously abused each other with songs composed for the occasion:

Now I shall split off words—little sharp words
Like the splinters which I hack off with my ax.
A song from ancient times—a breath of the ancestors
A song of longing—for my wife.
An impudent, black-skinned oaf has stolen her,
Has tried to belittle her.
A miserable wretch who loves human flesh.
A cannibal from famine days.[21]

---

[20]K. Rasmussen, *Across Arctic America*, p. 250.
[21]K. Rasmussen, *Grønlandsagen*, p. 235.

He who received the most applause won. Thus was the issue settled without reference to the right or wrong of the case. But what was more important, the dispute was laid to rest.

Recidivist homicide, excessive sorcery (which is *de facto* recidivist homicide), and chronic lying were crimes punishable by death. Such was the nature of rudimentary law in the Eskimo anarchy.[22]

Comanche Law

Comanche Indian law-ways represented a somewhat higher development on the same general plane as Eskimo law.

The Comanches had chiefs, both civil and military. The band was larger than the Eskimo local group, and the Comanches had considerable property, especially in horses. They shared with the Eskimos a fierce drive toward male dominance and competitive rivalry among males for status by means of wife stealing. To this they also added the road of military glory. The Comanches recognized nine common legal offenses against the individual: adultery, wife absconding, violation of levirate privileges, homicide, killing a favorite horse, sorcery, causing another person to commit suicide (a form of homicide), failure to fulfill a contract, and theft.

Homicide called for the killing of the offender by the aggrieved kin of the dead person. This was a true legal penalty, for custom prevented the kin of the executed murderer from retaliating.

Adultery and wife stealing were handled variously, but in every case the aggrieved person was forced by public opinion to act. He could, and often did, proceed directly against the erring wife, killing her, cutting off her nose, or otherwise mutilating her hapless body. This was a husband's legal privilege. Or, if he preferred, he could collect damages from the male offender. This would be done by a direct demand. Whether or not he got what he first went after depended on how courageous the defendant was. If the aggrieved husband was not strong or fearless

enough, he could call in his friends or kinsmen to prosecute for him. But then "the lawyers got the a' of it," for his helpers kept all the damages for themselves. Or, lacking kin and friends, he could call upon any brave warrior to prosecute for him. Great braves were willing, for prestige reasons, to do this without any material recompense whatever.[23]

Ifugao Law

The Ifugaos provide another example of law on the primitive level of organization. These mountain-dwelling head-hunters of Luzon possessed no government worthy of being called such. Over 100,000 tribesmen live scattered throughout the deep valleys that crease their rugged homeland. Although there are clusters of houses in the more favorable spots, the Ifugaos have no true villages, nor do they have a clan organization. The bilateral group of kinsmen is tightly knit, however. In the course of centuries, the Ifugaos have carved the steep walls of their mountains into stupendous rice terraces fed by intricate irrigation systems. Their paddies are privately owned and protected by a complex body of substantive law. Ifugaos are capitalists who have many legal rules controlling credit and debt. In addition, they are litigious in the extreme, for each man is sensitive about his "face" and quick to take offense. Their list of possible legal wrongs was long indeed.

How did they handle a legal case prior to the establishment of American control around 1905, and, subsequently, of Philippine national law? A man with a grievance or a claim tried first to exact a satisfactory settlement from the opposite party. Failing this, he went to a *monkalun*, or "go-between," who was a member of the highest social class and who had a reputation as a man of affairs and a number of enemy heads to his credit. The *monkalun* heard his story and accosted the defendant with the charges. The defendant in turn pleaded his cause. Meanwhile, both plaintiff and defendant marshaled their fighting relatives—just in case. The *monkalun* shuttled back and forth

[22]E. A. Hoebel, "Law-ways of the Primitive Eskimos" (*Journal of Criminal Law and Criminology*, vol. 13, 1941), pp. 663–683, or *The Law of Primitive Man*, chap. 5. An Eskimo song contest is vividly dramatized in "The Case of the Borrowed Wife," in *The Ways of Mankind*, Series II, No. 1.

[23]E. A. Hoebel, *The Political Organization and Law-ways of the Comanche Indians* (American Anthropological Association, Memoir 54: Contributions from the Laboratory of Anthropology, 4, 1940), or *The Law of Primitive Man*, pp. 127–142.

between the two parties, wheedling, arguing, threatening, cajoling—attempting to induce them to give ground so that they might meet on terms acceptable to each. Customary law made the penalties and obligations of both parties quite explicit for every conceivable offense, but first there had to be agreement on the exact nature and degree of the offense. Claim was balanced against counterclaim. Each side weighed the fighting strength and inclination of the other. But at long last, if the patience of the *monkalun* and the litigants endured, a settlement was reached and damages were paid (if it was an assault case), or the debt was satisfied (if it was an economic dispute). But if no settlement satisfactory to each disputant could be reached, the *monkalun* finally withdrew from the case. Then the plaintiff or his kinsmen undertook to kill the defendant—or any convenient kinsman of his. Feud was forthcoming. The legal machinery had broken down.[24]

The *monkalun* represented the public interest by his intervention. Yet he was only incipiently a public officer. He made no decision and enforced no judgment, but he provided the means, through his good offices, of bringing disputants to a resolution of their conflict. All Ifugao legal offenses were wrongs to be prosecuted by the aggrieved individual. There were no recognized crimes against society at large and, therefore, no public law.[25]

Nuer Law

The legal system of the Nuer of the African Sudan was similar to that of the Ifugaos in many respects. The Nuer, like the Ifugaos, had no state. Unlike the Ifugaos, they were organized into segmented lineages (see page 216). The lineages represented the legal units that stood in opposition to one another. Evans-Pritchard saw them as a people who had no law because ". . . there is no constituted and impartial authority who decides on the rights and wrongs of a dispute and there is

no external power to enforce such a decision were it given."[26]

According to Evans-Pritchard's analysis, feud and the threat of feud were the legal mechanisms by means of which adherence to norms was maintained. Violation of a norm could set off a feud between lineages. But among the Nuer, "A feud cannot be tolerated within a village and it is impossible to maintain one for a long period between nearby villages."[27]

We have already indicated that formal judges are not a necessary attribute of law. The Nuer, like the Ifugaos, employed the services of a mediator, the Priest of the Earth, to settle serious disputes. This is the priest who is especially related to the sanctity of the earth and who is also called the Leopard Skin Chief because he wears a leopard skin as an emblem of his office. Most Nuer offenses are legally settled by direct negotiation between the lineages without intervention of the Priest of the Earth. Bodily injuries gave rise to damages paid in cattle according to a definite and detailed scale commensurate with the degree of injury done the victim. Adultery and seduction of unmarried girls were also private wrongs for which compensation in cattle could be demanded and received. There were also suits over the return of progeny price after a divorce had taken place.

According to P. P. Howell, who knew them well, ". . . the Nuer are, and always have been, acutely conscious of the need for unity and are always seeking someone by whom and through whom social disharmony can be averted."[28] Nuer traditions, he tells us, are full of references to great leaders:

Their principal characteristics are to be seen in the Nuer ideals: the desire and the ability to bind the people together; to mediate and to settle internal quarrels and disputes; to negotiate agreement with other tribes and peoples if they are to the advantage of the Nuer; to maintain good relations between neighbours; in fact, to check the process of fission which to the Nuer is highly

[24]Ifugao procedure is dramatized in "The Case of the Bamboo-sized Pigs: Ifugao," in *The Ways of Mankind*, Series II, No. 2.

[25]R. F. Barton, *Ifugao Law*; also Hoebel, *The Law of Primitive Man*, chap. 6.

[26]E. E. Evans-Pritchard, "The Nuer of the Southern Sudan," in M. Fortes and E. E. Evans-Pritchard (eds.), *African Politica. Systems*, p. 293.

[27]E. E. Evans-Pritchard, *The Nuer*, p. 159.

[28]P. P. Howell, *A Manual of Nuer Land*, p. 33.

undesirable. These qualities are stressed in Nuer tradition far more frequently than ability to lead the warriors into battle against the Dinka, and are more important than their sagas of great exploits and daring.[29]

Such men are called *ruic naadk*, "spokesmen of the people"; the Nuer have headmen of essentially the same quality as many other simple primitive people.

The killing of a Nuer by a Nuer resulted in the spiritual contamination of the murderer and all his household. The contamination, called *nueer*, was believed to bring disease and death unless it was ritually removed by the Priest of the Earth.

A killing, therefore, could entail the inconvenience of a feud, and it certainly entails (even today) the dangers and costs of *nueer*. A murderer would therefore seek asylum in the homestead of the Priest of the Earth. There he was secure against revenge while the priest arranged the payment of blood money by the killer's lineage to the lineage of his victim. If one or the other lineage held out unreasonably in agreeing to an

acceptable settlement, the priest could threaten to curse them. If the curse were uttered, their cattle would sicken, their crops wither, and their people die—not a happy prospect! The ultimate sanction in Nuer law, therefore, was physical, albeit by supernatural means. When the blood money had finally been paid, the homestead, cattle, and body of the murderer were ritually purified in elaborate ceremony. Social relations between the two kinship groups were thus restored, and life could resume its course. The "social mess" had been cleaned up.

Ashanti Law

Finally, the Ashanti of West Africa may be cited as a highly advanced people who were well on the road toward civilized law by the middle of the last century. Today they are part of the nation of Ghana.

The Ashanti were a powerful nation who developed their own constitutional monarchy. Clan feuding was checked, and all private law was brought within the potential jurisdiction of the

---

[29]*Ibid.* By permission of International African Institute.

FIG. 17-3 A defendant, head shaven, charged with possessing stolen goods, stands before the outdoors court of village chief and elders in Sierra Leone, Africa. (United Nations.)

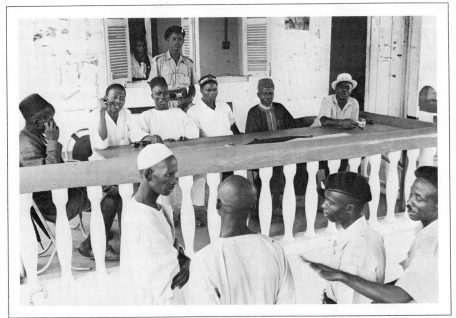

royal criminal courts. Any private dispute ordinarily settled between the household heads of the two disputants could be thrown into royal hands by the simple device of one of the quarreling persons swearing an oath on the Great Forbidden Name of a god that the other was guilty of an offense. In rebuttal, his adversary would swear on the same forbidden name that he did not commit the wrong. One or the other was then guilty of a false oath, perjury, which was a capital crime for which the liar lost his head.

Whoever heard the swearing had to arrest the two, for every citizen was the king's agent in such an event. He led them to a log kept for the purpose and chained them to it, after which he trotted off to the king's bailiff with the news. A day was then set for the trial. When hauled before the king and his council of elders, each litigant was called upon to tell his story. The stories were then repeated verbatim by the king's speaker, and each affirmed the accuracy of the repetition. So was the issue joined. Next, one or the other of the prisoners before the bar named a witness, who was brought forth to swear a deadly conditional curse that what he was about to say was the truth of the matter. In this the Ashanti placed implicit faith, for the whole trial hinged on what was now said. On the testimony of the single witness, one party was freed and the other condemned to be beheaded—unless the king in deference to the needs of his treasury allowed the luckless one "to buy his head," i.e., pay a fine.[30]

Aside from this crude but remarkable device for extending the king's peace, there was also a great body of criminal regulations; the violation of any one of these would be punished by death. These ranged from homicide—"only the king may wield the knife"—to carrying a chicken on top of a load. Even suicide was a capital offense, for it constituted a usurpation of the king's exclusive right to kill. The corpse of the suicide was hauled into court, tried, and ostentatiously decapitated. As a more practical gesture, his properties were also confiscated on behalf of the king's treasury.

Ashanti criminal law overreached the mark in much the same way as did the law of eighteenth-century England, with its 200 capital crimes. It is significant as an example of the way in which monarchy becomes the means of expressing the social interest in the maintenance of order by replacing of private law by criminal law. This is a genuine social advance over the chaos of societies that allow feuding.[31]

THE TREND OF THE LAW

It is a seeming paradox, on first thought, that the more civilized a society becomes, the greater is the need for law, and the wider the reach of law becomes. But it is no paradox, if the functions of law are kept in mind. Simple societies have little need of law, and on the earliest levels of human culture there were probably no legal institutions. In such groups as the Shoshones, Eskimos, Andaman Islanders, and African Bushmen, there is only a little of what we would call law. Almost all relations in the tribe are face to face and intimate. The demands imposed by culture are relatively few; child training is direct and comprehensive. Ridicule is keenly felt, for there is no escape in anonymity. Tabu and the fear of supernatural sanctions cover a large area of behavior. Special interests are few, for there is little accumulated wealth. Conflict arises mostly in interpersonal relations. Hence, homicide and adultery are the most common legal focuses. Sorcery as a form of homicide always looms large as an illegal possibility, but among the simpler peoples, sorcery, which uses supernatural techniques, is usually met with supernatural countermeasures rather than with legal action.

Among the higher hunters, the pastoralists, and the ruder gardening peoples, the size of the group and the increased complexity of the culture make possible greater divergence of interests between the members of the tribe. Conflict of interests

---

[30]This description applied a century ago, R. S. Rattray, *Ashanti Law and Constitution*; K. A. Busia, *The Position of the Chief in the Modern Political System of Ashanti*; and E. A. Hoebel, *The Law of Primitive Man*, chap. 9. Ashanti legal procedure is dramatized in "The Forbidden Name of Wednesday," in *The Ways of Mankind*, Series II, No. 6.

[31]The present status of the Ashanti chiefs, which is much reduced in the law of Ghana, is thoroughly discussed in W. B. Harvey, *Law and Social Change in Ghana*; see especially chap. 2, "Status of the Traditional Authorities," pp. 66–122.

grows, and the need for legal devices for settlement and control of the internal clash of interests begins to be felt. Private law emerges and spreads. It exerts a restraining influence, but, like the clan, it has inherent limitations that prevent it from completely satisfying the need it must meet. As no person is competent to judge one's own cause, procedure under private law leads too often not to a just settlement but to internecine fighting—to feud.

Feud and Law

Feud is a state of conflict between two kinship groups within a society, manifest by a series of unprivileged killings and counterkillings between the kinship groups, usually initiated in response to an original homicide or other grievous injury. Legal historians traditionally have seen primitive society as marked by a horrid and constant state of feud, rent by violent retaliation and blood revenge, and, in general, an arena of violence ruled by the law of the jungle and the retaliative *lex talionis* ("an eye for an eye, a tooth for a tooth, a life for a life"). It appeared that feud was the curse of primitive society from which individuals could escape only through law.

The fact is that there is very limited evidence for the actual occurrence of feud in primitive societies. Legal procedures or ritual devices such as regulated combat as a means of avoiding or terminating feud have been universally found to exist in such cultures. The idea that feud is called for is widespread among primitives, but they actually prefer to accept damages rather than take blood revenge. An example would be the case of the Trobriand Islanders for whom Malinowski reported that although honor made "vendetta" obligatory in cases of homicide, it was evaded by the substitution of blood-money (compensation). There was much Trobriand talk of feud, but Malinowski found not one specific case. In all anthropological reports, this is the rule rather than the exception.

But if there are strong grounds for doubting that feud occurs with anything like the frequency we have been led to believe, there is no question but that the folk belief in feud as a cultural

expectancy, as both ideal and presumed behavior, is widespread. It is a folk phenomenon in its own right. The idea of feud, if not its reality, assumes importance.

Real feud is socially destructive and dangerous. When it does occur, it does represent a breakdown of peaceful resolution of conflict. As Drucker has written of the Northwest Coast Indians of North America, ". . . the threat of violence was always present if the claims of the aggrieved were disregarded. . . . Settlements of these conflicts were usually reached, but never easily. . . . And at times negotiations did break down and were followed by a period of bloody feuding."[32]

Law exists everywhere to preclude the recourse to bloody battles within societies. Law consists of procedures designed to obviate feud. Folk belief in the expected requirements of honor to engage in feud is customarily blown up to feed the fear of the effects of feud. It seems quite likely that this very fear of feud is one of the factors that nourishes and sustains primitive legal systems.

As the scope of commonality expands, as community of interest reaches out beyond the kindred and clan, beyond the local group and tribe, men gradually create the means to check internecine strife within the bounds of the larger society through the expansion of the scope of law.

Experience in the development of other branches of culture is also accompanied by experience in the manipulation of the social-control phases of culture. Instruments and devices of government are created. To a greater and greater extent, private law is replaced by public law.

World Law

The next development in law that may be foreseen on the basis of past trends and growing need is the freeing of the individual from the limitations of nationality and, concomitantly, the expansion of the scope of law to embrace a worldwide system framed and administered by a world commonwealth. Ultimately, it will be this or regression. Today, primitive law prevails between nations. What passes as international law consists of no

---

[32]P. Drucker, *Indians of the Northwest Coast*, pp. 73–74.

more than normative rules for the conduct of affairs between nations as they have been enunciated and agreed upon from time to time by means of treaties, pacts, and covenants. In addition, a body of prevailing custom in international intercourse, recognized by tacit consensus or verbalized in arbitration, World Court awards, and United Nations decisions, provides the other main source of its substance. But this body of social norms for international intercourse is as yet no more than the bylaws of the subgroups we call nations. International law now consists of substantive rules without imperative legal sanctions.

The United Nations today, like the League of Nations of yesterday, because the power of universal coercive, absolute force is withheld from it, cannot make law of the international norms upon which it determines. Whatever the idealist may desire or the nationalist fear, force and the threat of force remain the ultimate powers in the implementation of law between nations, as they do in law within the nation or tribe. But until the use of force and the threat of force as now exercised by nation against nation are brought under the socialized control of a world community, by and for world society, they remain not the sanctions of world law but the instruments of social anarchy and the constant threat to the survival of present societies.

The metamorphosis from primitive law to modern law on the plane of international intercourse awaits the emergence of the consciousness of world community by all humanity. If the fulfillment comes in our time it will be our happy destiny to participate in the greatest event in the legal history of mankind.

SELECTED READINGS

Barton, R. F., *Ifugao Law* (1969). The classic monograph on the Ifugao, now readily available in book form, is to be highly recommended.

Bohannan, P. J., *Justice and Judgment among the Tiv* (1957). An inside view of how a "stateless" West African society operates its law.

Gluckman, M., *The Judicial Process among the Barotse of Northern Rhodesia* (1955). How trouble cases are settled in an African tribe. Also, *The Ideas in Barotse Jurisprudence* (1965). A brilliant comparative analysis of Barotse legal concepts.

Hoebel, E. A., *The Law of Primitive Man* (1954). Presents a theory of law and society. Describes and analyzes the legal culture of seven selected primitive societies, followed by a functional interpretation of law in culture.

Llewellyn, K. N., and E. A. Hoebel, *The Cheyenne Way: Conflict and Case Law in Primitive Jurisprudence* (1941). Contains a number of case records of Cheyenne legal disputes and a systematic analysis of the law-ways of this remarkable Indian tribe.

Pospisil, L., *The Kapauku Papuans and Their Law* (1958). Particularly useful for its analysis of what this New Guinea people think their legal norms are and what they actually are according to the outcome of specific cases.

——*Anthropology of Law: A Comparative Theory* (1971). A theoretical and empirical treatment of law and society from an anthropological point of view which is both sound and informative.

Schapera, I., *A Handbook of Tswana Law and Custom* (1938). A very competent and thorough treatment of the social system and formal law of an African tribe.

18

POLITICS

LEARNING GOALS

Explain the nature and function of political organization. ¶ Summarize the concept of the state in political theory, and discuss the relation between three principles: kinship, territorialization, and associations. ¶ Outline six patterns of political organization under the headings of stateless, state, kingdom, and council-type organizations. ¶ Identify the attributes of the political process, and exemplify their functions in the tribal societies of the Cheyenne Indians and the Tswana of Africa.

Politics is more than government and government is less than law. The political process performs much the same functions as have just been specified for law: (1) the definition of behavioral norms for acceptable conduct, (2) the allocation of force and authority, (3) the settlement of disputes, and (4) the redefinition of norms for conduct.

Political organization, and especially government, may well go beyond this, however. In addition, (1) it may organize group efforts for public works, such as tribal hunts, tending the chief's gardens, digging and repairing irrigation ditches, and building roads, temples, and pyramids; (2) it may carry ritual and ceremonial responsibility for religious control of the supernatural world and human conduct (see Sacerdotal Chiefs and Kings, pages 309–310); (3) it may organize and maintain markets and trading networks; and (4) it usually carries responsibility for defense of the home territory and the waging of war against enemy societies.

Law can exist without government in the form of private law. Much political activity does not express itself as law. Yet the very existence of law is itself an expression of political organization, for the legitimacy of the legal acts of a private prosecutor is an expression of public interest and public consensus.

Political organization is more than government as such, and it is not synonymous with the state, for the state is a specialized social phenomenon, while political organization is generalized. Government exists when there are specialized functionaries, or officers, designated and empowered to make and execute political decisions.

THE NATURE OF POLITICAL ORGANIZATION

The only kind of society that could be said to be without political organization would be one consisting of a single bilateral extended family within which there were no organized subdivisions. Sex and age differences would be present, to be sure, and there would be one or two religious specialists. But the society would be organized as a single large family operating under familial controls. All problems would be settled as family problems, and there would be no other divisive groupings within the community. Family and community would be one.

This kind of society was approximated among some of the simpler primitive peoples, such as the

Shoshones, but it exists nowhere among human beings today, nor has it been observed to have existed since written records have been kept.[1]

Political organization comes into being wherever societies are segmented on the basis of kinship, economics, religion, sex, fraternities, or community. Where there are subgroups that are discrete entities within the social entirety, there is political organization—a system of regulation of relations between groups or members of different groups within the society at large and between one society and another.

Our earlier discussions of subsistence techniques and land tenure have indicated the importance of ecological relations, the patterns of adjustments of human populations to the territory in which they live. Because skillful exploitation of the immediate environment is absolutely essential to survival, humanity, like all other living creatures, develops an intimate relation to the soil and to its plants, to its lakes, rivers, and springs, and to its denizens. In cooperation with day-to-day fellows, the individual works it for all that the particular technology enables to be won from it. The group molds its culture to the offerings of its territory, and although migrations are common, the general pattern is for a people to hold fast to the land they know—and have come to love.

Because the members of a community live together under a common culture, they share their patterns of living and ideas in common to a large extent. Community means commonality, in which diversity exists but unity prevails. Community means that the feeling of oneness—a sense of entity, an *esprit de corps*—extends to the whole territorial society. It means that the culture sets values that orient behavior in the direction of common as well as individual or subgroup interests. The common interests are what constitute political interests. The community is the polity. Political organization, therefore, is *that part of the culture which functions explicitly to direct the activities of the members of the society toward community goals.*

THE STATE

It is quite possible to analyze political organization without any recourse to the concept of the state whatsoever. Indeed, the failure of political scientists to realize this until quite recently seriously handicapped the development of viable political theory beyond the realm of European types of government.[2] For a long time, thinking in terms of the state did more harm than good because it diverted attention from the broader, institutional aspects of political processes as they are woven through the entire weft of social life. This type of thinking kept both political scientists and anthropologists from paying attention to the political process in simply organized societies. Yet the state is so overpoweringly important in modern civilization, and is growing so steadily more so, that it cannot be ignored. Anthropologists now distinguish between stateless and state-organized societies.

The idea of a state embodies three elements: (1) a territory, (2) a culturally organized population, and (3) a centrally organized government with strong coercive powers.

The state is an institution among other institutions within a given community's culture. It is not the society or the community; it is a complex of behaviors characteristic of the members of the community in one part of their lives—the political. Thus, as Linton observed, the tribe is a social entity marked by a sentiment of community due to common culture; the state is a subentity marked by common political organization with a well-developed government.[3]

Government is to be thought of as an executive instrument of political organization. The personnel of government are the specialists and functionaries who perform the state's business. They are the headmen, chiefs, kings, and council members, and their various aides.

Three Bases of Organization

A political system may use one or more of three major units of social organization as the basis for its structure: (1) genealogical, or kinship, units;

---

[1]"Among all known people—the autonomous, land-owning socio-political group is greater than the bilateral family." J. H. Steward, "The Economic and Social Basis of Primitive Bands," in *Essays in Anthropology in Honor of Alfred Louis Kroeber*, p. 333. A contrary view is advanced, however, by L. Sharp, "People without Politics," in V. Ray (ed.), *Systems of Political Control and Bureaucracy*, pp. 1–8.

[2]G. A. Almond and J. S. Coleman (eds.), *The Politics of Developing Areas*.

[3]R. Linton, *The Study of Man*, p. 240.

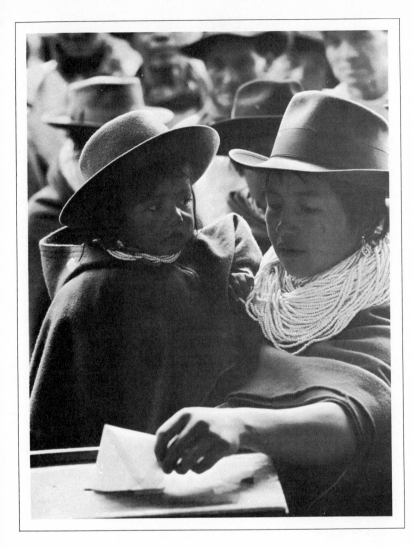

FIG. 18-1 Andean woman voting in a township election in the Bolivian highlands. (United Nations.)

(2) geographical, or territorial, units; or (3) associational units.

Kinship

Primitive societies, as has already been shown in previous chapters, generally rest most heavily on the kinship principle. Lineages, clans, phratries, and moieties may each have their headmen who not only are responsible for the regulation and guidance of affairs within their respective kinship groups but who also formally represent their groups vis-à-vis other kinship groups. Collective-

ly, they may form the several levels of councils that act within or for the tribe in public affairs. How much of the structure and functioning of primitive legal systems is built upon kinship groups has already been made clear.

But note, on the other hand, that so far has the kinship principle fallen into desuetude in many modern states, and especially in the United States, that favoritism on behalf of relatives, called nepotism, is often forbidden by law, although a new trend in equal employment opportunity for women is waiving the prohibition in favor of wives.

Territorialism

On the other hand, since every community is a distinguishable territorial entity, every political system, both primitive and civilized, uses the geographical unit as a basis of organization as well. The smallest such unit is the *household*. The next largest is the *camp* (among nomadic hunters and gatherers) or the *village* (among sedentary peoples). The next largest is the *band*, comprising a number of camps (among the nomads) or the *district*, comprising several villages (among settled peoples). Above these is the *tribe* or *nation*, the largest group with a common language and culture. (Actually, a tribe may incorporate alien groups.)

Tribes may ally on a more or less permanent basis with other tribes to form a *confederacy*. This is usually done on a voluntary basis for mutual defense or aggression, and in confederacy each tribe remains self-determining in political matters to a greater extent than it yields decisive power to the confederacy. The only real difference between an alliance and a confederacy is in the development of more enduring and explicit institutions for determination of questions of mutual concern between the tribes.

When a tribe or confederacy incorporates the victims of its conquest into a permanent state system on a subordinate basis, the political system has expanded to become an *empire*.

All these forms of territorial organization were achieved by one or another primitive society.

Associations

The use of special associations as a principle of political organization is, on the whole, relatively weak in primitive cultures, but nevertheless quite widespread. The heads of the secret religious fraternities form the tribal council in a number of pueblos. The military fraternities of the Plains Indians performed major governmental functions, as do many of the secret societies of Africa and Melanesia. The age sets of other parts of Africa do likewise. In India, castes still operate as units of politics, although the modern constitution of India proscribes them.

The constitutional structure of the United States ignores the associational principle, but churches, labor unions, manufacturers' associations, and a host of other special-interest organizations have secondary political functions, of which lobbying is but one form of expression. One need only stroll the streets of Washington, taking note of the many stately headquarters maintained by a legion of organizations, to become aware of how true this is.[4]

TYPES OF POLITICAL ORGANIZATION

As a society emphasizes one or another principle of organization, or a combination of principles, it produces political organizations of different types. Some of these are structurally identifiable among primitive cultures as follows.

Stateless Systems

Stateless systems have no formal government embracing the entire society. Political functions are performed by subgroups and by functionaries whose political jobs are secondary to other interests and responsibilities. There is no person or group of persons with centralized authority applicable to the society as a whole.

Undifferentiated

In such cultures as those of the South African Bushmen, the Eskimos, and the Shoshones, kinship and political relations are one and the same entity. Small, local groups live as isolated, self-governing units, subject to no higher political power. Tensions between members of individual families are settled directly without intervention of a band headman.

Segmentary lineage

This is the uncentralized political system in which lineages rather than villages or bands form the significant units of organization. There is little or no common decision making for the tribe, nor is there much in the way of broadly integrative ceremony or ritual. The Nuer of the African Sudan

---

[4]Even the American Anthropological Association maintains its headquarters in Washington, D.C.

are the classic example.[5] The segmentary lineage organization provides the structural framework. Such systems of political organization are very common in East Africa and in Melanesia, where the Kapauku and the Kuma are good examples.[6]

Age set
Under this system, political matters are largely in the hands of age sets and their officers. The age sets cut across village and district boundaries and form the framework of political integration, as among the Nyakyusa. By virtue of the relatively limited distribution of age sets, this system is quite rare.

Village council and associations
In this type, there is no tribal government as such, nor do corporate lineages function in government, but authority is vested in village councils and men's fraternities. The Pueblos of the southwestern United States and such tribes as the Ibo of West Africa are representative.

Village or band with headman
Here, the tribe lacks overall government; each band or village, as the case may be, has a headman or chief endowed with mild political authority. Kinship may be important in many aspects of life, but it is not a major factor in political organization. Territorial identity and personal qualities of leadership on the part of a headman are the determining factors. For example: "The headman of a Chiricahua [Apache] local group can be thought of as a natural-born leader, one who earns the confidence and support of his neighbors. His influence is considerable, but it is of an informal nature."[7]

The leader is expected to speak on all important occasions. Among the Yavapai of Arizona, the headman was moderate in speech, stopped quarrels, and knew the best campsites. People fol-lowed him because his personality won their confidence. Of the Comanche headmen, That's It sagely observed: "I hardly know how to tell about them; they never had much to do except to hold the band together."[8] That's It put his finger on it. The headman in the primitive world rarely has explicit authority; his functions are so subtle that they defy easy description. Yet he is the focal point of the local group.

As Harrasser notes, among the Central Australians, the "chief is at most *prima inter pares* with few exceptions among the Dieri and in West Victoria."[9] Similar evidence comes from the Shoshones and the Eskimos. The Shoshone headman is called *tegwoni*, which in its fullest sense means "good talk thrown out to the people." In western Alaska, the headmen are those who "by their extended acquaintance with the traditions, customs and rites connected with the festivals, as well as being possessed of an unusual degree of common sense, are deferred to and act as chief advisers of the community."[10]

The simplest primitive societies are always democracies; rarely are they subject to dictatorial political leadership (see Fig. 18-1).

State Systems
State systems have chiefs, kings, or councils with authority over certain spheres of social activity covering the entire society.

Chiefdoms
Complexity of social life sharpens the need for leadership and the delegation of responsibility. Societies that are developed enough to have a tribal state always possess chiefs. A chief is differentiated from the headman by degree of authority and social distinction. His position may or may not be inherited. His functions and powers are variable among different peoples.

---

[5]E. E. Evans-Pritchard's *The Nuer* became the model for a number of penetrating studies of this type of organization.

[6]L. Pospisil, *The Kapauku Papuans of New Guinea*, pp. 32–63; and M. Reay, *The Kuma*.

[7]M. E. Opler, *An Apache Life-way*, pp. 233–234.

[8]E. A. Hoebel, *The Political Organization and Law-ways of the Comanche Indians* (American Anthropological Association, Memoir 54: Contributions from the Laboratory of Anthropology, 4, 1940), p. 18.

[9]A. Harrasser, *Die Rechtsverletzung bei den australischen Eingeborenen* (Beilageheft zur vergleichende Rechtswissenschaft, vol. 50, 1936).

[10]E. W. Nelson, *The Eskimos about Bering Strait* (Bureau of American Ethnology, Annual Report 18, 1899), p. 304.

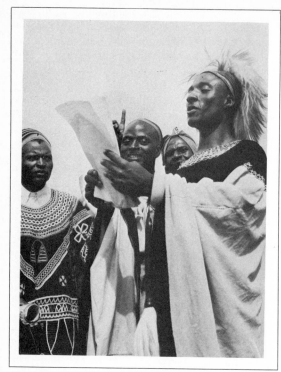

FIG. 18-2 West African chieftains, the Cameroons. (United Nations.)

In North America, it was unusual for a chief to have strong power. Great care was taken in many tribes to separate the offices of peace chiefs and war chiefs. Peace chiefs were the civil governors. Usually they were band or clan headmen elevated to the status of membership in the tribal council. They supervised internal tribal relations and had judicial powers over a few classes of crime. Most legal offenses, however, remained in the area of private wrongs to be settled by the parties concerned. Sometimes, as in the case of the Cheyennes (see pages 313–315), Omahas, and Iroquois, the civil chiefs were explicitly chosen for limited tenure. War chiefs were the heads of military fraternities, or a war chief could be any man who had an outstanding war record. Naturally, such war chiefs could make their opinions felt in the tribe, but they had very limited constitutional powers in the operation of the camp in peacetime. The most militaristic American Indians were

astute enough to realize that military dictatorship is the greatest of all threats to the democratic way of life.

BANTU CHIEFS The functional significance of chiefs in the Bantu tribes of South Africa may be sensed from Schapera's listing of their activities:

1. He attends habitually at his council-place where he listens to news, petitions, and complaints, from all over the tribe, and gives orders for whatever action is required.
2. Legislation has always been a recognized function of the chief.
3. He periodically creates a new age-regiment, and thus formally admits youths into the social category of adults.
4. He controls the distribution and use of land.
5. He also regulates the calendar of agricultural and certain other activities.
6. He organizes large collective hunts.
7. He mobilizes his people for defense and aggression.
8. He organizes religious ceremonies upon the due performance of which his tribe's security and prosperity are held to depend and which ensure that the rainfall is adequate.[11]

Small wonder that Tsonga proverbs say: "A tribe without a chief has lost its reason; it is dead. It is like a woman without a husband"; and "In a country without chiefs, the people devour one another."[12]

CEREMONIAL CHIEFS In some systems, the primary responsibilities of chiefs are not necessarily concerned with governing. If we consider the Queen of England, her political functions have atrophied, but her symbolic and ceremonial functions evoke a stir of emotion in British hearts the world over.

In the primitive world, the Trobriand chief enjoys high status and many privileges. Tribute must be paid him, but he utilizes it mostly to put on ceremonial feasts on behalf of his people and his own renown, as well as to organize gardening and magically to control fertility and rainfall. This is

[11]From I. Schapera, *Government and Politics in Tribal Societies*, pp. 68–75. Copyright 1956, 1957 by C. A. Watts and Co., Ltd. Reprinted by permission of Schocken Books, Inc.
[12]*Ibid.*, p. 105.

true in greater or lesser degree for all Oceania (even in tribes where chiefs stem from conquerors), for as Forde observes:

The origin and development of chieftainship in Melanesia is by no means clear, but everywhere the chiefs claim the same essential rights and powers. They are nearly always real or alleged immigrants who make similar claims to sanctity, superiority and to the control of valuable ritual.

[The chiefs of the Sa'a people on the island of Mala, Solomon Islands, are aliens who] established and maintained their position by arrogance and determination. They are regarded, and regard themselves, as feast givers and the controllers of certain ceremonies. By the splendour of their feasts they enhance the prestige of their district and win the approval of the commoners who make gifts of food for yet more feasts.[13]

Exactly the same could be said of the Indians of the Northwest Coast of North America, with their potlatching chiefs.

Kingdoms

Kingship results from the development of the hereditary tendency into a hereditary principle. Its main function is to introduce stability into the administration of government. Strong clans make for intratribal strife. Lineages and central government are inherently incompatible. Lineage autonomy must be superseded by a stronger law of the whole society. This can conveniently be the king's law and the king's peace. But the power of paramount chieftains is in itself a luscious prize for power-hungry individuals. With bloody intrigue and with turmoil in their struggles to project themselves into chieftainship, they can rend the peace of the tribe. Clearly defined hereditary succession puts a check on such social abscesses. Yet the oftentimes fatal defect of the hereditary principle is that the heir to succession may have no aptitude for the job. The king may be an indecisive weakling or, worse still, a dangerous egomaniac. In the one event, the state may fail to function effectively in times of crisis. In the other,

tyranny supplants social justice, and men suffer under corruption.

Kingship is so common among advanced primitive societies that we must conclude that the need for centralized control outweighs the urge for democratic freedom at this level of social development. The resurgence of democracy comes later. But where democracy fails, the need for centralization produces dictatorship or fitful moves for the restoration of monarchy.

The hereditary principle is no thought-out device. It develops quite naturally and without conscious awareness. We can see this among those American Indian tribes which explicitly deny hereditary succession to chieftainship. In spite of the fact that any good man may become a chief, records show again and again that a chief is succeeded by one of his sons or maternal nephews. Chiefship runs in family or lineage lines. This arises from the fact that the training and high example set by the senior relatives engender chiefly qualities in the boys. People come to expect leadership from such lines. The boys assume that people will respond to their superior leadership—and they do. Eventually, the tendency may become a prescription.

In Polynesia and Africa, primogeniture often fixes succession upon the eldest son. Yet most tribes maintain functional flexibility by leaving succession open to selection from among the chief's heirs by the royal council or the matriarch (in Ashanti, the Queen Mother; among the Iroquois, the oldest woman in the lineage). This is a sound device except as it leads to palace feuds between the parties of the heirs who rely on the *coup d'état* to circumvent council deliberations. Civil war and temporary anarchy are the usual concomitants of the death of a monarch in many a Bantu kingdom. Indeed, as a precaution against this sort of thing, the death of the king is often kept secret until his successor is chosen and everything is ready for the coronation.

SACERDOTAL CHIEFS AND KINGS The skeins of religion and politics are composed of separate threads. Yet they are woven into the tapestry that is society, sometimes carefully separated, each forming its own design, and sometimes intertwined, joining church and state in one pattern.

---

[13]C. D. Forde, *Habitat, Economy, and Society*, pp. 182 and 183. By permission of E. P. Dutton and Co., Inc. See also C. S. Ford, "The Role of a Fijian Chief" (*American Sociological Review*, vol. 3, 1938), pp. 542–550.

The warrior's sword and the magician's wand are different artifacts. A man may wield one or the other, but if he is skilled enough and if his culture permits, he may seize the sword in his right hand and the wand in his left. Then, indeed, he becomes an awesome power to cope with. The essential doctrine of separation of church and state in American democratic tradition is a defensive reaction to that power.

Shamans and priests are specialists in controlling the action of the supernatural; headmen, chiefs, and kings are specialists in controlling the actions of individuals. But the actions of individuals must be controlled in their relations to the supernatural as well as to their fellow human beings; the priest always has temporal influence. The politician uses religious means for political purposes when he is able to control religious power; the priest in turn is apt to use political means to attain religious ends when he has the techniques to do so. When either one has specialized peculiar techniques to a high degree and religious and political instruments are clearly developed, it sometimes occurs in the primitive world, as it so often does in the modern world, that rivalry and hostility between church and state are sharp. Among primitive human beings, however, a working agreement between the two often exists; for example, the Trobriand chief employs his hereditary sorcerer to destroy upstarts,[14] and the Yokuts-Mono chiefs in California connived with medicine men to mulct the guileless public.[15] On the other hand, use of supernatural power for self-advantage through black magic is almost universally treated as a deadly crime if carried too far.

In general, supernaturalism is so ubiquitous in the primitive world that it colors all government to a greater or lesser degree. Political officers almost invariably possess some magic power or religious sanctity. War making, legislation, and judicial procedure inevitably involve religious ritual.

In highly organized gardening societies of sedentary peoples dependent on fixed crops, the chief is usually the high priest of the rain, fertility, and garden cults. As he is the supervisor of politico-legal relations, so is he also responsible for the economic well-being and religious security of his folk. If his society is one of ancestor worshipers, as is usually the case in Africa and Oceania, he is also the ancestral viceroy on earth—his people's highest link to the ancestral spirits. He is himself a direct descendant of the gods and has godhood in him. In Africa, again and again, he symbolizes the tribal soul: a soul that must be hale and vigorous, or else the tribe wanes and dies. Hence, the fate of the king who became feeble or sickly was to be poisoned or strangled by his chief councilors.[16] It is no unalloyed privilege to be a ruler. Eminence entails responsibility.

The extreme sacredness of the god-king limits his activities. In Tonga (Polynesia), the *tuithonga* may not walk abroad, for where he places his foot, the earth becomes tabu.

THE TALKING CHIEF "A White House spokesman announced today. . . ." The device of presidents is a possession of primitive chiefs and kings the world over. The Ashanti king or the paramount chief of a district rarely speaks in public. To do so is bad etiquette and policy on his part. He has his *okeyame* to serve as his mouthpiece. Most African kings have a court spokesman. In Samoa, each chief has his Talking Chief, who recites his chief's genealogy before every meeting of the native council. He speaks his chief's mind in debate. Kwakiutl and other Northwest Coast chieftains have their speakers at potlatches to extol the ancestry and virtues of their masters. Every Plains Indian peace chief had his crier, who announced decisions to the camp at large; his "loudspeaker," our Cheyenne interpreter, High Forehead, always called him.

The reason for these spokesmen is subtle but sound. When chieftains rise above the level of headmen, their power increases. He who wields powers of decision and enforcement must not be too familiar to the multitude. Some good men can maintain influence and fraternity simultaneously, but they are rare. It is a safer and surer technique

---

[14]B. Malinowski, *Crime and Custom in Savage Society*, pp. 85–86 and 92–93.

[15]A. H. Gayton, *Yokuts-Mono Chiefs and Shamans* (University of California Publications in American Archaeology and Ethnology, vol. 24, 1930), pp. 361–420.

[16]See J. G. Frazer, *The Golden Bough*, chap. 24, "The Killing of the Divine King."

to let a minion undertake the vulgar task of shouting to the masses.

The Council
The one universal instrument of government is the council. No tribe or nation does without it. No man can govern alone, nor is he permitted to. Monarchy, if taken literally, is a misnomer. Every king or chief operates within the network of his advisers and cronies. Some are helplessly enmeshed in it.

In small primitive bands and tribes, the council is a democratic gathering of adult males. In gerontocratic Australia, participation is limited to the elders. Elsewhere, it is mostly open to all males. Among American Indians, decision of the council had to be unanimous; one stubborn holdout could block action. Still there were neat devices for attaining unanimity. Tribal councils commonly consisted of all the band headmen. Among the Aztecs, for a special example, every family sent its headman to a clan council. Each clan council had a clan headman, a war chief, and a speaker. The speakers of the twenty clans formed the tribal, or national, council, which worked with the king and his executive officer, the Snake Woman (who was not a woman, but a man).

Among the great African monarchies, the king has the superficial appearance of an absolute autocrat. Yet he can rarely act without full approval of the council, and this is not forthcoming until the royal elders have sounded out tribal public opinion. Kings who abuse their power can generally be deposed; in the old days, they could be destroyed.

Monarchy, like every other social relation, rests on reciprocity. If the exalted ruler receives great social privilege, he must give service to the people in return. Some kings and dictators may ignore this precept, but it is difficult for them successfully to ignore for long the principle voiced in the Balinese proverb: "The ruler owes his might to the people."

Nonpolitical Associations in Government
It is an error to think of government solely in terms of the organs explicitly designed for gov-

ernmental purposes. All government is pluralistic, and various extrastate organizations play their parts in determining and executing political policy.

Take, for example, a small-town volunteer fire company in the State of New York today. It is a closed fraternity, which elects its members by secret vote. It has all the trappings of a lodge: sworn secrecy, uniforms with gold buttons, rituals, dances, and ceremonial feasting. It also puts out fires as the occasion demands. This firemanic fraternity is a private association, a true men's club. Yet it is an official branch of government under the laws of the State of New York. The costs of its fire-fighting equipment and meeting rooms are met by public taxation. It is regulated by public law and is controlled by publicly elected fire commissioners. It remains a club and yet is an organ of government, just as the Plains Indian military fraternities were, the social aspects of which have already been discussed in Chapter 14. Fraternity, feasting, dancing, and social enjoyment were the primary activites of such men's clubs, but they also took on police, judicial, and legislative powers when the need arose.[17] The tribal councils constitutionally possessed all judicial and legislative powers covering criminal activity. However, the council chiefs were peace chiefs not given to coercive action. When coercive restraint or punishment was needed, they were not suited to the task. They were "fathers" to all the tribe, and Indian fathers do not punish their children. What was more natural than that the extragovernmental societies of warriors should take over policing the hunt, the rice harvest, and the great tribal ceremonials of the sun dance? This they did with vigor and dispatch. In later years, as the Plains tribes began to crumble before the onslaught of the white men, the Cheyenne military societies assumed more and more governmental power as crisis piled on crisis. But to no avail; they were overwhelmed.

In Africa, as we have already seen, various secret societies among certain West Sudanese tribes imposed peace, collected debts on behalf

---

[17]R. H. Lowie, *Primitive Society*, p. 415; *The Origin of the State*, pp. 94–107; "Property Rights and Coercive Powers of the Plains Indian Military Societies" (*Journal of Legal and Political Sociology*, vol. 1, 1943), pp. 59–71.

of their members, and, in the case of the Egbo society, punished wrongs.

In Melanesia, the numerous men's secret societies also directly and indirectly determine policy and operate as law-enforcing agencies.

Plains Indian military societies were not secret, and as a result their role in government was essentially democratic. It is quite otherwise with the exclusive secret orders of Africa and Melanesia. They are more akin to the Ku Klux Klan and other such cryptic groups that spring up in our midst to usurp the functions of the state and to corrupt democracy. That these extralegal bodies can sporadically attain a measure of success is testimony to the Hydra-headed nature of government in society.

THE POLITICAL PROCESS

Having briefly examined the major ways in which societies are politically organized, or structured, let us turn to the more intricate matter of how these structures work. According to the famous aphorism, "Politics is the art of who gets what, when, and how." Like all good aphorisms, this packs a good deal of truth in a few pithy words. But, again, like all aphorisms, it leaves out as much as it says. All role definition, which runs through every aspect of culture, defines activities and duties, expectancies and obligations. All norms of social organization spell out who does what, who gets what—when, where, and how. And politics is but one aspect of the cultural patterning and behavioral processes which are involved.

As we attempt to examine political processes in the anthropological context, it is important to keep in mind what has already been said on social structure in the preceding chapters, especially those on economic organization, the extension of kinship, clubs and associations, social classes and castes, and law. Every one of these facets of society has its political implications, and politics sinks its roots into each.

Politics, it must always be remembered, is not something discrete, an arena of life absolute unto itself. Politics is social behavior with an orientation, a slant, that gives it a coloring sufficiently different to warrant its own identity. But it is many-hued, and its colors, taken separately, are shared with other fields.

THE ATTRIBUTES OF POLITICS

In the "Introduction" to *Political Anthropology*, the editors, Marc Swartz, Victor Turner, and Arthur Tuden, specify several qualities which identify the political process:

1. It is public rather than private: it is not an individual matter, nor familial. "An activity that affects a neighborhood, a whole community, a whole society, or a group of societies is unquestionably a public activity; whether it is *also* a political activity depends upon other characteristics—in addition to its being public." One of the important activities implied in this is achieving settlements that are of a public, rather than merely a private, concern. Such settlements, to be public, "must concern a group as a whole, in a rather direct and immediate way."[18]

2. Politics is goal-oriented; it is concerned with ends and means—"What is it we want?" and "How do we go about doing it?" The political process always involves decision making—the selection of specified aims from among possible alternatives and the choice of administrative procedures. Politics is, like law, deeply involved in culture building, by defining social norms which it is believed will result in conversion of values (normative postulates) into social reality.

Politics involves public goals. However much vested groups within the society may strive and quarrel in pressing each its own interests as against those of others, the political decision relates to what goal shall be sought by the action of the community *as* community on the question at issue.

3. A third feature of the political process is that it allocates and focuses power. It assigns and specializes authority, either in decision making (as in the case of the law enforcers) or in directing activities (as in the case of the task-force leaders, whether in hunting, war, temple building, ritual, or whatever). Malinowski, in *Freedom and Civilization*, put it succinctly:

The principle of authority comes into being from the beginnings of mankind. . . . Political authority as we know it is indispensable even at primitive levels; we have defined it as the legally vested power to establish

---

[18]M. J. Swartz, V. W. Turner, and A. Tuden (eds.), *Political Anthropology*, p. 4.

norms, to take decisions and to enforce them through the use of sanction by coercion.[19]

In small face-to-face hunting and gathering societies the power allocation aspect poses few problems. With his usual astuteness, That's It (the Comanche informant previously quoted) stated the reason for this: "We were not like you white men. We didn't have to have an election every four years to see who would sit in the White House. A *paraivo* [band headman] just got that way. Everybody knew who he was." So clear and consensual were cultural goals and leadership requirements that leaders "emerged." When people no longer heeded a headman's ideas, he simply was no longer a headman.

On the other hand, in larger, more complex societies in which the decision-making powers of a chief, king, or president are far-reaching, control of the office assumes the utmost importance, and legitimation of the political administration is a matter of critical concern if tyranny is to be avoided.

Government: Law, Political Organization, and Politics

It will be clear by now that there is a good deal of overlapping in the attributes of law, political structures, and political processes, and also in the manner in which each relates to government. Definitions are not easily arrived at, nor is there unanimous agreement on such definitions as are most commonly used. Implied in all of these concepts are the organization of activities for the general welfare, the establishment of norms, the use of coercion and the assignment of authority for the maintenance of these norms, and the acknowledgment of legitimacy of all these ends.

For our purposes, it is sufficient to say that the political sphere of social organization here means ". . . everything that is at once public, goal-oriented, and that involves a differential of power (in the sense of control) among the individuals of the group in question."[20]

The study of the formal designation of public offices with their established norms of statuses and roles is the study of *political organization*, or *structure*, a subdivision of social structure.

Government consists of the men and women who hold designated statuses of authoritative leadership as decision makers and exercisers of power in the public sphere. It is expressed in the ways in which they exercise their powers and in the ways in which the governed respond to (and sometimes limit) their power.

The study of the ongoing maneuvering—pushing and hauling, wheedling, cajoling, arguing, threatening, punishing, and rewarding—by which the goals are agreed upon or set, and by which the people are led or shoved in the desired direction (or by which they resist and obstruct the "official" intent) is the study of *political processes*, or *politics*.

Modern (since World War II) anthropology, like modern political science, has become much more interested in the study of political *processes* than of political *structure*. And well it might, for this tells us much more of what is going on than does a formal comparison of the organization of different kinds of "chiefdoms" and "states."[21]

To demonstrate the operation of the political processes in their varied functional manifestations, let us look first at the Cheyennes, who represent the chiefdom type of political organization as integrated with both a tribal council and politically active military associations. Then, we shall summarize the structure and functioning of an African monarchistic state, using the Tswana of Bechuanaland in southern Africa.

Cheyenne Government and Politics

Professor John Roberts has recently extolled the old Cheyenne system for its outstanding quality in cultural self-management. Specifically, he comments on their excellence in respect to (1) "the storage and retrieval" of traditional knowledge and information, (2) their skill at problem solving on the tribal level, and (3) their effective imple-

---

[19]B. Malinowski, *Freedom and Civilization*, pp. 187–188 and 248.
[20]M. J. Swartz, V. W. Turner, and A. Tuden, *op. cit.*, p. 7.

[21]For an excellent exemplification of this trend, see H. A. Powell, "Competitive Leadership in Trobriand Political Organization" (*Journal of the Royal Anthropological Institute*, vol. 90, 1960), pp. 118–45; reprinted in R. Cohen and J. Middleton (eds.), *Comparative Political Systems*, pp. 155–192.

mentation of decisions through "staff work" and "command responsibility."[22]

Tribal organization

The Cheyennes had a bilateral family system with no lineages or clans. Beyond the family, there were uxorilocal kindreds, each headed by an active senior male. Related kindreds tended to camp together, thus forming the band, of which there were ten major ones. During the fall and winter months, when the buffalo herds were dispersed, the Cheyennes accommodated by scattering the band camps miles apart in protected river bottoms. Bands were then politically autonomous. In late spring, when the grasses were green, the Cheyennes all drew together for one of the great tribal ceremonies—the Sacred Arrow Renewal, the Sun Dance, or the Animal Dance. Throughout the summer the Council of Forty-four Tribal Peace Chiefs ruled supreme, assisted by the military associations.

Allocation of leadership

Membership in the Council of Forty-four was for a term of ten years. Nominally, each band had four representatives on the council—and these chiefs were headmen in their own bands. They were chosen for their even tempers, energy, wisdom, courage, kindliness, generosity, and altruism. They were the "fathers" of everyone in the tribe and addressed as such. Although on page 274 we indicated that the Cheyennes recognized wealth distinctions, there was no class exploitation in the distribution of power. "Whatever you ask of a chief, he gives it to you. If someone wants to borrow something of a chief, he gives it to that person outright," old-time Cheyennes said over and over.

By combining the dual roles of band headman and tribal chieftain in the same person, the Cheyennes effected an efficient link between the kinship and local segmentary interests of the tribe

and the tribal entirety. This is an absolute essential for maintenance of the tribe as an integrated whole.

The role of the chiefs

Within the Council of Forty-four there were five sacred chiefs who represented the great spirits of the five directions. One of them held a supreme ritual position as the Sweet Medicine Chief—the personification of the culture hero who gave the Cheyennes their way of life. The legitimacy of the chiefs was chartered by the deepest of Cheyenne beliefs.

The role of the associations

Alongside of, but subordinate to, the supreme and sacred Council of Forty-four, stood the ungraded military associations. They enforced the Cheyenne law against intratribal killing and violation of the rules of the communal buffalo hunt. They sometimes made new law (see page 292, above). They also interacted with the Council when important tribal decisions had to be faced, as the Comanche Peace Agreement of 1840 reveals.

Tribal decision making

The customary way of making tribal decisions followed a pattern for the use of political power.

A war party of eight Cheyennes, on its way south to take horses from the Kiowas, Comanches, or Apaches, was stopping at a large [friendly] Arapaho camp. At the same time some Apaches came to visit Bull, an Arapaho leader. The Apaches told their host that the Kiowas and Comanches were seeking peace with the Arapahoes and Cheyennes. Bull took the opportunity to bring the eight Cheyennes together with the Apaches in his tipi; he filled his pipe and offered the smoke. The Cheyennes declined, Seven Bulls, the leader of the war party saying, "Friend, you know that we are not chiefs. We cannot smoke with these men, nor make peace with them. We have no authority; we can only carry the message. I have listened to what you say and tomorrow with my party I will start back [he has authority to call off his own raid,] to our Cheyenne village, and I will carry this word to the chiefs. It is for them to decide what must be done. We are young men and cannot say anything, but we will take your message back to the chiefs."

[22]J. M. Roberts, "The Self-management of Cultures," in W. H. Goodenough (ed.), *Explorations in Cultural Anthropology*, p. 452.

When Seven Bulls reached the Cheyenne camp with his companions, he told of the Kiowa-Comanche proposition. That night a crier went about the camp calling for the chiefs to convene the next day. The big double-sized chiefs' lodge was pitched and early the next morning the chiefs all gathered there. Seven Bulls and his companions were sent for to deliver their message officially. The proposal was then on the floor.

After the first speakers had sat down, it was evident that there was no ready agreement at hand within the Council, so the proposition was made and accepted that the Dog Soldier Society should be asked to render a decision to the Council on the question.

High Backed Wolf, who was the directing head chief of the Council, sent one of the door-servants to bring in White Antelope and Little Old Man, the bravest chiefs of the Dog Soldier Society. When these two had been greeted in the chiefs' lodge, High Backed Wolf told them about the order of business, describing to them the state of opinion in the Council. "Now, my friends," he concluded, "you go and assemble your Dog Soldiers. Tell them about this matter and talk it over among them. Let us know what you think of it. Tell us what you think is best to be done."

When the Dog Soldiers had assembled, White Antelope laid the problem before them. "The chiefs are leaving this matter to us," he told his followers, "because we are the strongest of the military groups. It is my own thought that our chiefs are in favor of making peace. What do you all think about it?"

Said another of the Dog Soldier chiefs, "I think it best to leave the decision to you two, White Antelope and Little Old Man. Whatever you say will please us all." All the Dogs agreed to this with one assent.

The two men accepted it and declared for peace. Leaving their troop, they went back to where the Council was waiting for them, to tell the Council that they would make peace with the enemies. The chiefs all stood up at this and gladly said, "Thank you, thank you, Dog Soldiers."[23]

The political process, we have said, is public, is goal-oriented, and allocates and focuses power. There can be no question of the public nature of this case. It was "official" and concerned the well-being of the entire Cheyenne tribe. It was also clearly goal-oriented: peace with the Comanches from whom the Cheyennes could obtain horses and a useful ally. Allocation of authority?

Authority was designated clearly. The war-party leader said he could not speak for his people. He conveyed the message to a proper authority who convened the Council of Forty-four. The tribal chiefs knew they had the formal power to make a decision by themselves. But they also knew that without public support they could not make it stick. So *all* the military lodges were convened. Opinion was divided. So the Dog Soldier Society—the most powerful and prestigious of all the fighting associations—was delegated to "decide" the issue. The Dogs, in turn, knew that unending filibuster could prevent achievement of unanimous consent which was always required for action on a proposal. So they put it to their two bravest chiefs, the Door Keepers. The decision was for peace. Back up the line it went, as the military fraternities' recommendation to the Council of Forty-four who accepted the "decision" with thanks—and relief. Finally, the Sweet Medicine Chief announced it to the entire tribe *as the decision of the Tribal Council*, so giving the decision the seal of the highest authority. The soldiers had been co-opted, and no hothead would dare to lift a hand against the Comanche again. None ever did—from that day to this.

Such is the political process at its effective best.

Political Organization among the Tswana

The Cheyenne represented a simple form of state organization in a small tribe. The Tswana of Bechuanaland in southern Africa represent state organization on the level of monarchy in "large" tribal nations. Professor Schapera's lucid report on the Tswana provides us with one of the finest examples of how this is done.[24] It forms the basis for this summary.

The Tswana, or Bechuana, constitute an ethnologically identifiable group of tribes. Each tribe is a politically independent unit, although the more newly formed tribes recognize the seniority of the tribes from which they broke off. The population of the Tswana exceeds 100,000.

---

[23]From *The Cheyenne Way*, pp. 91–93, by K. W. Llewellyn and E. A. Hoebel. Copyright 1941 by the University of Oklahoma Press.

[24]I. Schapera, *A Handbook of Tswana Law and Custom*, pp. 1–34 and 53–124.

Tribal organization

The integrating focus of the tribe is in the person and office of the chief, who is not only the supreme ruler but also "the visible symbol of its cohesion and solidarity." People may leave the tribe of their birth, and tribal citizenship is expressed by allegiance to a particular chief. Each Tswana tribe has a capital town (ranging in population from 600 to 25,000) and a number of smaller outlying villages.

Within the village or town, the households (which consist of one or more conjugal-natal families) are clustered to form the spatially distinguished family group. Closely related family groups live in a well-defined administrative unit, called a *ward*. All the wards together make up the tribe, except that in two of the larger tribes, the wards are grouped in sections.

A small hamlet may contain no more than one household. A small village may consist of a single family group. A larger village may have only one ward. A village, if large enough, may, however, embrace several family groups and wards. Each of these groups is a kinship-territorial-governmental unit of social structure.

Local leaders

The leader of the household is the husband and father; for the family group, the leader is the senior male descendant of the common paternal grandfather whose name the group bears. His position is hereditary and ascribed. He directs the group's activities and keeps the peace within his flock. In important matters, he acts in consultation with a family-group council of all adult males.

The headman of a ward holds his position by right of hereditary descent as the senior son of the preceding headman. He is not appointed by the chief except upon formation of a new ward. He does, however, act as his ward's representative to the chief, and he is responsible for the orderly conduct of his people and the execution of the chief's commands. He collects tribute for the chief and holds judicial authority in minor cases involving two family groups within his jurisdiction. He is also the leader of the men of his ward in their common age set.

The council

A headman must act in consultation with a ward council made up of the senior members of his own family group and the leaders of the other family groups in his ward. If guilty of malfeasance in office, his own council will reprimand him or complain to the chief, who may then try to punish him through the Royal Court. Occasionally, the ward headman convenes all the adult males of the ward in a general folk moot for review of problems of wide concern. The headman carries many burdens of responsibility for which he receives little material compensation but great prestige and respect—providing he does his job well.

Each village, in turn, has its headman. If the village and ward are one, the ward headman and village headman are one and the same. Should there be two or more wards, the headman of the senior ward is the village head. His duties are similar to those of the ward headman, except that they are townwide in scope.

In those tribes which have districts, village organization remains the same as that described above, but the district will have, as a special representative to the capital, the headman of one of its more important indigenous villages (some outlying villages will consist of immigrant aliens).

The king

This brings us to the central tribal government organized around the hereditary chief, or monarch. He is chief of state (king) through primogeniture. *Kgosi ke kgosi ka a tsetswe*, a chief is chief because he is born to it. In succession, the direct line precedes all collateral lines; i.e., the sons of the king succeed, but his brothers and their sons cannot, although a brother of a dead king may serve as regent during the minority of the heir. If a monarch dies with no male issue, the chieftainship passes to his next senior brother.

Functionally, the Tswana chief "is at once ruler, judge, maker and guardian of the law, repository of wealth, dispenser of gifts, leader in war, priest and magician of the people."[25] He and his family take precedence in all things and receive high honors. Failure to obey his orders or to show him

---

[25]*Ibid.*, p. 62.

respect is a criminal offense. He is sustained by a royal coterie and with tribute.

In return, much is expected of him. His time is his people's. "Every man thinks he is the king's only subject" is a common folk saying. He must keep himself well informed of tribal affairs, be accessible to all who have complaints, organize and direct the army, sit as chief justice, preside over the tribal council, perform the major religious rituals, and above all be generous, redistributing most of the tribute that comes to him.

Other functionaries
The male relatives of the chief form a nobility, a kind of privy council, with whom he must remain in close consultation. To maintain effective democratic control, the chief has an informally constituted body of confidential advisers (a "cabinet") drawn from among the important men of the tribe on whom he feels he can rely; they are usually, but by no means always, paternal relatives.

The government also includes a formal tribal council of all the ward headmen, who meet in secret executive session whenever convened by the chief.

Schapera has published a translation of the condensed record of the promulgation of a Tswana enactment of partial prohibition in 1924. After discussing the problem of rowdy nighttime beer drinking with his council of senior uncles and getting their approval, Isang, king of the Kagatla tribe of the Tswana, convened the council of headmen. The "Congressional Record" reads as follows:

Chief Isang: "I do not say that beer should be prohibited, but that a law should be made about it."

Segale Pilane (chief's uncle and principal adviser): "We seek a plan for dealing with beer-drinking. Beer has ruined us; we have no children; we tried to educate them, but beer has spoiled them."

Komane Pilane (another senior uncle): "Let there be a law about beer-drinking, and let whoever violates it be punished."

Abel Madisa: "Let the sale of beer be prohibited." (Supported by Nasone Pilane, Montswe Rapalai, Mokalane Makgale, Pilane B. Pilane, Ramodisa, Klaas Segogwane, Antipas Sello, Masilo Ntsole.)

Chief Isang: "I endorse the suggestion that beer

should no longer be sold. But now I ask, is there not some one who can suggest a law whereby beer may continue to be sold, but in such a way as not to cause trouble among the people?"

Maretele Mangole: "Let beer be sold, but the purchaser should go home to drink it."

Pule Mogomotsi: "Let it be sold, but on condition that it is no longer drunk at night."

Motshwane Pilane: "Let beer-drinking at night be prohibited, and also let beer be sold only for consumption at home."

Kgari Pilane: "Beer-drinking goes together with sexual immorality. You should not find fault with the boys alone, and ignore the girls. As long as beer continues to be brewed, immorality will be associated with it."

Mabuse Letsebe: "I say, let beer continue to be sold."

Segale Pilane: "Headmen, you have helped us; it is you who are the chief's policemen, and whoever breaks the law must be dealt with by you."

Chief Isang: "Let those who say that beer should not be sold raise their hands."

(85 men raised their hands; only two said that beer should still be sold.)

Chief Isang: "You are not of two opinions, you are unanimous. And what I say to you is that when you go astray and are turned back you should listen. To err is human, but to find fault with oneself is often lacking. Therefore I say: Beer must no longer be drunk at night. See to it that beer is brewed not by the girls but by their mothers. I shall allow the brewing and sale of beer from the beginning of June until December, and if there is no improvement I shall call you together again to kill the sale of beer. Women of the Maatlametlo age-regiment and downwards must not any one of them drink beer. Headmen, help to support the law."[26]

In this situation, the chief and his principal adviser put their problem to the headmen. Some of the latter advance a suggestion that does not immediately satisfy the chief, and he asks them to consider a more specific issue. After further discussion, during which several different views are expressed, a vote is taken on the original and more drastic suggestion. Despite almost unanimous agreement, the chief finally decides not to prohibit the sale of beer, but to try out a compromise for an experimental period. The two points that seem most important in the whole procedure are the method of consultation and the fact that

---

[26]I. Schapera, *Tribal Legislation among the Tswana of the Bechuanaland Protectorate*, pp. 14–15. By permission of The Humanities Press, Inc.

the chief is guided but not bound by the views of the headmen; he actually follows the course that seems best to himself—in this particular instance, one less far-reaching than was generally agreed upon.

Affairs of great tribal import, although they are first taken up by the two preceding groups of advisers, cannot become official policy until they have been discussed and approved in open tribal assembly. To this all the headmen come and all adult men who want to make it their business.

Thus, although a chief is king because he is born to it, the Tswana have an even more fundamental proverb: *Kgosi ke kgosi ka morafe*, a chief is chief by grace of his tribe. The constitution of the state is such that he is subject to representative checks and balances. A self-willed chief does not last long.

Age sets

There is yet another arm of the Tswana state to be mentioned. All Tswana men and women are initiated into sex-segregated age sets at puberty. These have important congeniality functions to perform, but they are equally important as units of political organization. An age set cuts right across the local segments of the tribe and counteracts the parochialism that inherently exerts a neutralizing effect on national integration. Each age set (which numbers from fifty to several hundred boys or men, depending on the size of the tribe) is headed by a commander, who is always a member of the royal family. In war, the age sets constitute regiments in the tribal army. The men of a given ward form "companies" within the regiment under the leadership of a son or close relative of their ward headman. In times of peace, the age sets serve as work brigades to perform any public service or job of construction that the king deems necessary.

Women's age sets also exist and are organized along the same lines as the men's. In the sphere of women's work, they also perform public services, though of a lighter nature.

A system of checks and balances

The Tswana system exemplifies how the state, as a political system in an advanced primitive socie-

ty, weaves and balances kinship, territorial, and associational groupings into a harmonious whole. It shows how the functional prerequisite of allocation of authority to responsible leaders is checked and balanced with concomitant reliance on organized group consultation, through the provision of councils on each level of administrative structure, with a final check imposed through general assemblies at each level for consideration of all major or crucial decisions. Tswana political organization has the essential elements of monarchy, democracy, oligarchy, theocracy, and gerontocracy. It is each of these and all. It has no need for elective procedures and spares itself a good deal of trouble and uncertainty thereby, for internal social mobility is limited and in this type of society the hereditary principle works well enough.

SELECTED READINGS

Banton, M. (ed.), *Political Systems and the Distribution of Power* (1965). Especially good for the article by Ralph Nicholas on factions in the political process in India and elsewhere, and for the analysis of differing types of African kingdoms by Peter Lloyd.

Cohen, R., and J. Middleton (eds.), *Comparative Political Systems* (1967). A reader which contains twenty long selections on a number of aspects of political organization and process in a wide range of tribes.

Evans-Pritchard, E. E., and M. Fortes (eds.), *African Political Systems* (1940). A symposium of excellent studies of political structure in a number of African tribes.

Fried, M. H., "State: the Institution" (*International Encyclopedia of the Social Sciences*, vol. 15, 1968), pp. 143–150. A succinct overall discussion of the state, anthropologically viewed.

Gluckman, M., *Politics, Law, and Ritual in Tribal Society* (1965). Especially for chapters 3 and 4, on stateless societies and on the state and civil strife.

Lowie, R. H., *The Origin of the State* (1927). A stimulating pioneer study of the processes of state development among primitive peoples.

Mair, L., *Primitive Government* (1964). A general, non-theoretical description of the major types of government in African tribal societies. Contains an informative final chapter entitled "Primitive Government and Modern Times."

Rattray, R. S., *Ashanti Law and Constitution* (1927). A most valuable study of the historical development of the great federated monarchy of the Ashanti of the Gold Coast of Africa, now Ghana.

Schapera, I., *Government and Politics in Tribal Society* (1956). A comparative study of three South African tribal systems.

Southall, A., "Stateless Society" (*International Encyclopedia of the Social Sciences*, vol. 15, 1968), pp. 157–168. The concept, structure, and functioning of stateless systems of political organization, briefly discussed.

———, *Alur Society* (1956). Subtitled *A Study in the Processes and Types of Domination*, this book analyzes the structure of a primitive political state embracing a multiple number of tribes.

SYMBOLIC EXPRESSION

19

CULTURE AND WORLD VIEW

LEARNING GOALS

Clarify the concept of world view, and demonstrate its importance in understanding cultural behavior. ¶ Distinguish between the emic and etic perspectives on cultural behavior and their relation to the ethos of a people. ¶ Discuss the relation between the Aztecs' "feeling of pessimism," the stylistic forms of Aztec art and poetry, and the Aztec drive to imperialist conquests. ¶ Compare the Cheyenne world view with that of the Hopi, showing similarities and differences. ¶ Write a brief essay on the question as to whether there is, or is not, an American world view today.

Humanity faces the bewildering chaos of experience armed with mental artifacts of its own invention with which it organizes the natural phantasmagoria into a manageable and meaningful unity. Mankind takes the inchoate mass of formless clay that is the experiential world and works it into a meaningful form according to its cultural preconceptions. Humanity thereby assures itself of a reasonable amount of certainty and builds a base of understanding upon which to organize its life in comprehensible terms; absolute chaos is inconceivable, and if this is indeed a disorderly universe, humanity will impose order on it. Man is ". . . endlessly simplifying and generalizing his own view of his environment; he constantly imposes on this environment his own constructions and meanings; these constructions and meanings are characteristic of one culture as opposed to another."[1]

Again, as Kluckhohn has written:

Cultures or group life-ways do not manifest themselves solely in observable customs and artifacts. There is much more to social and cultural phenomena than immediately meets the ear and eye. If the behavioral facts are to be correctly understood, certain presuppositions constituting what might be termed a philosophy or ideology must also be known. The "strain towards consistency". . .in the folkways and mores of all groups cannot be accounted for unless one postulates a more or less systematic pattern of reaction to experience as a characteristic property of all integrated cultures. . . . Each different way of life makes its own assumptions about the ends and purposes of human existence, about ways by which knowledge may be obtained, about the organization of the pigeonholes in which each sense datum is filed, about what human beings have a right to expect from each other and the gods, about what constitutes fulfillment or frustration. Some of these assumptions are made explicit in the lore of the folk; others are tacit premises which the observer must infer by finding consistent trends in word and deed.[2]

THE NATURE OF WORLD VIEW

The cognitive view of life and the total environment which an individual holds or which is characteristic of the members of a society is frequently referred to as *Weltanschauung*, or world view. World view carries the suggestion "of the struc-

---

[1]G. Bateson, quoted in C. Kluckhohn, "The Philosophy of the Navaho Indians," in F. S. C. Northrop (ed.), *Ideological Differences and World Order*, p. 356. By permission of Yale University Press.
[2]*Ibid.*, pp. 357–359.

ture of things as man is aware of them,''[3] and it is thus the life scene as people look out upon it. It is the human being's inside view of the way things are colored, shaped, and arranged according to personal cultural preconceptions. The planet we live on, a world of physical objects and living things, is by no means the same world to all peoples. Indeed, a simple description of the most basic observable components of this world (the sky, the land, water, trees) by a member of one culture might prove totally unintelligible to a member of another. This was well understood by a Sia Pueblo Indian, who said to his anthropologist friend, ''You see this bush,'' pointing to a desert plant called chamiso. ''You may not understand this, but that plant is I. I am it, and it is me and all my ancestors. We call it *'wawshap.'* ''

Juan was a member of the *wawshap* clan. He was saying that in his eyes and in his deepest feelings, as he looked on that bush or any other one of its kind, he was embodied in it—he and all his clan ancestors. An anthropologist would easily have an intellectual understanding of what Juan was saying, but the anthropologist's own world view would forever prevent him from the same kind of emotional identification with the plant. The anthropologist could see the chamiso in botanical terms, and could think of its function as a symbolic representation of *wawshap* clan unity in the maintenance of what Durkheim referred to as the organic solidarity of the social group.[4] The anthropologist could analyze Juan's perception of the plant in terms of its moral effect in maintaining a vital sense of ''the meaning of life.'' But the anthropologist could not *be wawshap*, as his Sian friend is. For his world view is that of a Sian; the anthropologist's is that of a rational, scientific, mechanistic Westerner. Both live in the same world, but each views it differently.[5] (Or, do

our differing views make it really a different world?)

Institutions, relationships, arts, and technologies vary throughout the world in manifestly observable forms, but underlying them are the existential postulates that orient a people's particular slant on life and the ways in which they organize their culture.

Etic, Emic, and Ethos

When seen from the outside and reported by an observer who is not, by training and living, thoroughly enculturated with the culture observed and written of, the view is called ''etic.'' The inside view is labeled ''emic.'' Regarding the chamiso, Juan's view was emic; the anthropologist's could be only etic.

World view, as a concept, focuses on the ways of knowing and identifying the component elements of the world—the existential and cognitive. Ethos expresses a people's qualitative feeling, their emotional and moral sensing of the way things are and ought to be—their ethical system.

Not all peoples or persons can by any means articulate systematically what their world view is. It is improbable that any Comanche could. At the same time, it is probable that many of the more reflective Aztec priests could have spelled out an Aztec world view quite clearly and consistently. This difference is in itself a cultural characteristic in its presence or absence. Usually it is up to the anthropologists or philosophers descriptively to analyze and formulate a people's world view from what they learn of their thinking, feelings, and actions. World view and ethos are found expressed in technology, personal relations, myth, song, dance, art, and religious and magical ritual in a multitude of gross and subtle ways. They are the reflected essence of a people's inner feelings and their ways of knowing ''the way things are.''

No world view is a given, in spite of the numerous peoples who believe that their way of life was bestowed upon them by culture heroes (such as Sweet Medicine and Erect Horns of the Cheyennes) or the divine revelation of prophets (such as the early Hebrews, Christians, and Muslims). World views grow with cultures. Generations of anonymous human beings contribute to the un-

---

[3]R. Redfield, *The Primitive World and Its Transformations*, p. 86.

[4]*Organic solidarity* is characterized by structural differentiation of status and roles (division of labor) within the society imposing the need for linking subgroup systems of norms in effective functional relationships. Organic solidarity is contrasted to *mechanical solidarity*, which is held to be characteristic of small homogenous types of societies—namely, the simpler primitive tribes and peasant groups. Such societies are bonded by an undifferentiated commonness of beliefs and sentiments. (E. Durkheim, *Division of Labor in Society*, pp. 70–122.)

[5]E. A. Hoebel, Keresan Pueblo Field Notes, 1945, unpublished.

ending quest to make the unknown knowable, to transform meaningless bafflement into meaningful understanding.

We do agree with Andrew Lang and Paul Radin, however, that there are individuals in every society who are thinkers and systematizers, the idealists who crystallize the myths, shape the ceremonies, express the concepts in art—symbolic creators. But even they must work within the cultural framework.

To exemplify the nature of world view let us first listen to Alphonso Caso, the distinguished Mexican anthropologist, writing of the Aztecs. Then we shall explore the phenomenon more deeply by considering the Hopi, Cheyenne, and American versions.

THE WORLD VIEW OF THE AZTECS

In Aztec belief, the human being was created by the sacrifice of the gods and in turn was reciprocally bound to sustain them with the magical sustenance of life itself—the blood of human sacrifice (Fig. 19-1).

The Aztec's Burden

Hence the pride of the Aztec, who looked upon himself as a collaborator of the gods, for he knew that his life was dedicated to maintaining cosmic order and struggling against the powers of darkness.

In a sense the universe depended upon him for its continued existence; upon him depended the food for the gods, upon him depended the beneficence of the gifts which they showered on mankind. Likewise, the light of the sun, the rain that formed in the mountains and watered the corn, the wind that blew through the reeds, bringing clouds or turning into a hurricane, all depended upon him. . . .

In addition to this cosmological ideal, the Aztecs also believed that they had an ethical ideal to attain. The struggle of the sun against the powers of darkness was not only a struggle of the gods, but it was also, above all, the struggle of good against evil. . . .

Opposed to this imperialistic and religious ideal there was always a feeling of pessimism in the depths of the Aztec soul. The Aztecs knew that in the end their leader, the sun, would be defeated . . . and then the powers of evil would prevail . . . and would destroy mankind.

Therefore, this life, for the Aztecs, was only transitory, and a feeling of pessimism and anguish appeared in

FIG. 19-1 Aztec sacrifice of a human heart to the sun. (From Bernardo de Sahagun, *General History of the Things of New Spain: The Florentine Codex*, Arthur J. O. Anderson and Charles E. Dibble (trans.), The School of American Research and The University of Utah, illustration from Book II. Copyright © 1957, The University of Utah.)

their vigorous and terrible sculpture and a tinge of profound sadness in their poetry.[6]

Poetic Sadness

The Aztecs countered gloom with profusions of flowers and the beauty of songs as means of lifting the heart. Yet, their writers say that the surcease was fleeting and happiness elusive. The lord Xayacamach lamented that the pleasures to be found in flowers and song are as ephemeral as the psychedelic glories experienced by the Aztec eaters of the hallucinogenic mushroom in group religious rites. Indeed, they saw "marvelous vi-

[6]From *The Aztecs: People of the Sun*, pp. 93–95, by A. Caso. Copyright 1958 by The University of Oklahoma Press.

sions, ephemeral forms of many colors, more real than reality itself. But afterwards this fantastic world fades like a dream, leaving man weary and empty.''[7] Their despair appears in such songs as this:

Given over to sadness
we remain here on earth.
Where is the road
that leads to the Region of the Dead,
the place of our downfall,
the country of the fleshless?

Is it true that perhaps one lives
there, where we all go?
Does your heart believe this?
He hides us
in a chest, in a coffer,
the Giver of Life,
He who shrouds people in the grave.

Will I be able to look upon,
able to see perhaps, the face
of my mother, of my father?
Will they loan me
a few songs, a few words?
I will have to go down there;
nothing do I expect.
They leave us,
given over to sadness.[8]

Cultural Motivation

Driven by their sense of divine destiny, the Aztecs built monumental pyramids to elevate their temples of sacrifice; their armies reached out for many leagues to sweep up victims to be fed to the gods; their vast symbolic dramas reenacted the cyclical struggles to maintain life and the universe. Their compulsive and gloomy outlook on life was not the sole cause of their institutions and social organization, but it colored all they did. Without awareness of their world view there is no comprehension of their character or their society.

THE HOPI WAY AND THE PUEBLO WORLD VIEW

The Hopis are the westernmost of the living Pueblos of the United States today. They are as typical

of the different Pueblos of the Southwest as any Pueblo can be, although all Pueblos differ from others in some respects.

The Hopis are intensive gardeners living in compact, permanently settled villages built of plastered stone houses set wall to wall around a central ceremonial plaza. Fields and houses are owned by women; the matrilineage is the bridge between household and strong matriclans. Kinship and economic life are female-centered, although men may own sheep. Ceremonial life and political life are male-centered and are organized around a complex system of secret religious fraternities (Fig. 19-2).[9]

An Intricate Balance of Parts

Laura Thompson summarizes the Hopi world view in these words:

Here we recognize an organic view of the universe. The cosmos is formulated as a living whole in which the subtly balanced relationships of the various parts to one another and to the multidimensional totality are similar to those which characterize living organisms. The parts and the whole are believed to transact for the good of all, according to a single, harmonious, immanent law. Man is a psychophysiological whole, differentiated from the rest of nature by his power of volition, which is an integral part of the scheme and is to be used for the commonweal. He cooperates with other men and with his nonhuman partners in fulfilling the law, through kinship and ceremonial groups. And the main mechanisms through which he expresses symbolically the cosmic process are ritual and art, reinforced by concentrated will-prayer.[10]

Expressing it more simply, a Sia Indian put it this way, ''Yes, it's like the Hopi. If I would refuse the request to drum in the Fiesta, it would delay the answers to the people's prayers. There would be no rain. Or else too much rain would come and flood everything. It wouldn't come just right. It is a hard world that requires correct treatment.''

Among all the Pueblos, as a matter of fact, this orientation of viewpoint is general. The late Professor Edward Dozier, born and raised in Santa Clara pueblo, said:

---

[7]M. León-Portilla, *Pre-Columbian Literatures of Mexico*, pp. 82–83.

[8]From *Pre-Columbian Literature of Mexico*, p. 85, by M. León-Portilla. Copyright 1969 by The University of Oklahoma Press.

[9]The best general summary of the Hopi social system is found in F. Eggan, *Social Organization of the Western Pueblos*, chap. 2, pp. 17–138.

[10]L. Thompson, *Toward a Science of Mankind*, p. 189. By permission of McGraw-Hill Book Co.

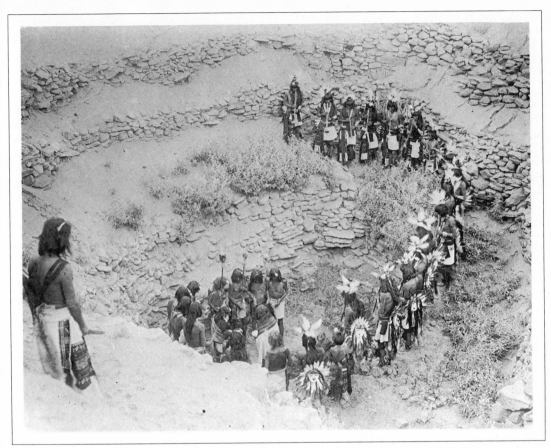

FIG. 19-2 A Flute Fraternity ceremony of the Hopi pueblo of Oraibi in which the members position themselves in a symbolic spiral pattern. (Photo courtesy of the Peabody Museum, Harvard University.)

The dominant integrating factor of Rio Grande Pueblo culture is the view of the universe as an orderly phenomenon. People or things are not merely "good" or "bad." "Evil" is a disturbance in the equilibrium that exists between man and the universe, while "good" is a positive frame of mind or action that maintains harmonious balance.

To keep man and the universe in harmonious balance, all must work together and with "good" thoughts. Unanimous effort of body and mind is not only a key value, but it is also enforced. . . . Any action, whether physical or verbal, which is construed by Pueblo authorities to be contrary to group concerns and unanimous will of the village is promptly and severely punished. Rio Grande Pueblo culture thus makes rigorous demands on the individual and fills him with deep anxiety

and suspicion toward his fellow men. Not only is his personal behavior and social interaction strictly circumscribed, but his thoughts as well are rigidly harnessed. He is constantly plagued by an apprehension that he or his fellow man may break the harmonious balance of the universe and bring illness, famine, or some other form of dreaded disaster.[11]

Thus, for other Puebloans as well as for the Hopis, the most fundamental postulate premises the world as a complex, ordered system in which all parts are intimately interdependent on an es-

[11]E. P. Dozier, "Rio Grande Pueblos," in E. H. Spicer (ed.), *Perspectives in American Indian Culture Change*, p. 122. By permission of The University of Chicago Press.

sentially equivalent footing, each with its role to play in the maintenance of the harmonious working of the whole. Humanity is on the same footing as all other orders of phenomena—the birds, the beasts, the plants, the insects, the clouds, the mythic beings, the ancestors—all these and many more, each with its ordained function. The world in the Hopi view is tightly integrated and complexly organized, a delicately balanced mechanism.

The Human Role in the Universe

The Hopis view the world as beneficent and predictable—except where human irresponsibility disrupts it. The nonhuman part of the universe is automatically controlled by the "correlativity principle." But individuals have a measure of willful self-determinism. They have a margin of choice. They may or may not carry out their functions according to the Great Scheme. If they do, the universe continues its orderly unfolding of events—healthily, happily, productively, satisfyingly. If they do not, crops fail, babies die, and famine, pestilence, and disaster sweep over the little community. Chaos and disorder reign.

The Hopis, in the Hopi view, must *want* things to go right. They must want this with all their being, which means that they must work industriously in their fields, at weaving, and at pottery or basket making, and that they must participate faithfully in all the ceremonies in which they have an assigned part by virtue of their statuses. In addition, they must concentrate all their psychic energy on "willing" or "praying for" (synonymous terms in Hopi) the result. They must think "happy" thoughts.

In other words, the Hopis must self-consciously keep themselves committed to a positive minding of their role in the universe. Less than this constitutes failure as human beings and such failure is heresy and treason. There is no room for indifferent or uncommitted individuals in the Hopi scheme of things, nor is there room for individualistic innovators who think they can improve on the Great Scheme. Such persons are dangerous deviationists, even more immediately dangerous than slovenly slackers. Both in their way are saboteurs of the order, the one because he or she does not make the effort to will enough, the other because he or she wills the wrong things. Each is

ka-hopi, un-Hopi; each runs a great risk not only of being called a "two-heart" (a witch who stays alive by taking the lives of relatives), but also of being condemned and killed as a witch by the Kwan secret society. Hopi society is theocratic, collectivistic, and totalitarian.

To the Hopi (as to other Pueblo Indians), knowledge is not only power but also an obligation. Knowledge is a requisite to maintaining the balance of the universe; one must strain to know what is expected and needed, and one must will to make it work. But what one is privileged to know is ordained in the pattern. Roles for all persons and things are ideologically blueprinted, and to presume to roles that have not been assigned to one is *ka-hopi*. To know a ceremony for which one is not properly a priest means only that one will misuse it. Possession of unauthorized knowledge is feared by men and women throughout the pueblos, for to say of a person, "He knows something," is to mean that he is a witch.[12]

As an ideological adaptation to a harsh environment in which the Hopis have achieved a highly effective survival capacity, their world view unquestionably represents a high level of consistent integration that permeates their social structure, their art and ritual, and their personalities. Its demands upon the individual are severe, for each person is an Atlas, supporting the weight of the world upon the shoulders. There is little room for individualism, and there is no tolerance for the wayward. The Hopi socializes—or else. The world view of his society demands it.

The Mechanistic-Vitalistic Character of the Hopi World View

Although the Hopi posit the existence of spirit beings, and in this sense their world view is colored with animism, they are also fundamental-

---

[12]Thus Bandalier wrote of the New Mexican Pueblos: "[A cacique, the priest-chief,] can also be removed if the tribe so directs in general council, or if the war captain or the leading shamans so dispose. A degraded cacique seldom, if ever, lives long. There is too much danger in suffering him who is in possession of the most precious arts and knowledge to live while under a cloud. It is the war captain who, officially at least, attends to such executions." A. F. Bandalier, "Final Report" (*Papers of the Archaeological Institute of America*, vol. 3, 1890), p. 284.

ly mechanistic in their outlook. This mechanistic viewpoint is displayed in their concept of the universe as an intricately meshed set of systems, delicately interrelated in a total order that individuals must help to maintain by positive willing and correct role performance.

THE CHEYENNE WAY AS WORLD VIEW

Among another American Indian tribe a mechanistic view of the universe predominated, but in essentially a different way from that of the Hopi. Cheyennes talked about the Spirit Who Rules the Universe, the Spirit Who Gives Good Health, the Big Holy People Who Know Everything. They believed in Heammawihio, the all-knowing high god who lives above. *Wihio* means a high order of intelligence, like that of the spider who spins a web, seemingly walking on nothing. He knows more about how to do things than all other creatures. Heammawihio once lived on earth as a being, but ages ago retired to the sky where, symbolically represented by the sun, he lives remote from all things, now more an abstract principle of "knowing" than a being. All first offerings of the pipe or smoked cigarette were made to him. There were other big spirits such as Aktunowihio, the Wise One Below (in the earth), and the Thunder, Heammawihio's great bird who brings the summer rains. There were the innumerable animal and bird spirits who were sought on the vision quest, who appeared in visions and bestowed medicine power for curing, divination, or war on lucky individuals. Maiyunahu'ta, Spirits Who Told Me in Sleep, they were called. All these were animistic beings, not in themselves mechanical forces. Yet they behaved mechanically. One offered them food, cloth, an enemy scalp, a piece of one's flesh, perhaps a chopped-off joint of a finger. "In a narrow sense," observes Robert Anderson, "it was giving; in a wider sense, simply doing, that which was valued by the supernaturals. . . . [T]he goal or response was a concrete return—health for oneself or kin, a wealth of horses, many coups on a raid, success in the hunt, or a shaman's powers."[13]

In Cheyenne ceremonies, the rites, not the words, were most important. The spirits, great and small, were like puppets who responded to the strings that were manipulated by compulsive ceremony and ritual.

The Theory of Limited Energy

Cheyenne wise men did not speak of an energy theory of the universe. Nonetheless, they subscribed to one; it was implicit rather than explicit in the tribal world view.

All Cheyennes knew that if a man wanted his son to mature as an outstanding person, he, the father, had to vow not to have sexual relations for seven, or fourteen, years after the boy's birth. All the father's "growth energy" had to be concentrated in that one child until he was mature.

If he had a colt which he wanted to become a fast, long-winded war pony, he asked a shaman with "horse medicine" to bless it with symbols of male sexual energy, while he himself vowed not to ride it at all for a given number of months. Then he rode it only in battle. Its energy had to be generated and stored for the special occasion.

Man and ritual in regeneration

Every year, the world had to be regenerated through the tribal Sun Dance or the Sacred Arrow Renewal ceremony, for each year the world runs down, its limited amount of energy dissipated. But in the ceremonies, replete with imagery and symbolism of rebirth and growth of man, beast, and plant life, the energy quotient of the universe was renewed.

The Cheyenne myths tell that eons ago there was famine. "Vegetation withered, the animals starved, the land became barren and dry, and the ancient Cheyenne were on the verge of starvation, for they had no food but dried vegetation and their dogs of burden."[14] One of the two Cheyenne culture heroes, Erect Horns, went into the Sacred Mountain, where the spirits taught him the Sun Dance, which he in turn taught to the Cheyennes. In this ceremony:

At the time of the Lone-tipi, though everything is barren,

---

[13]R. Anderson, "The Buffalo Men, A Cheyenne Ceremony of Petition Deriving from the Sutaio" (*Southwestern Journal of Anthropology*, vol. 12, 1956), p. 102. Quoted with permission.

[14]G. A. Dorsey, *The Cheyenne* I, *Ceremonial Organization*, p. 46. By permission of Field Museum of Natural History.

the earth is beginning to grow. Now it has grown. Thus they make the earth, buffalo wallow, grease, wool, and sinew to make growth. By the time of the end of the lodge, things have grown, people have become happy; the world has reached its full growth, and people rejoice.[15]

By not wasting energy and by ritual knowledge of how mechanically to recharge it, the Cheyenne, in his view, could keep things going. The power of mechanical manipulation was learned from an instructor who was a priest, who had learned from a priest, who had learned from a priest, in an unbroken chain back to Sweet Medicine and Erect Horns, the mythical heroes who had been given the secrets of the universe by the Big Spirits themselves (Fig. 19-3).

The Cheyennes, like the Aztecs, believed that they bore a special burden of maintaining the universe for all mankind.[16] Unlike the Aztecs, they did not believe they had to feed the gods with human blood to renew their energy. They performed no human sacrifices.

Cheyenne Personality

Not all Cheyennes incorporated the Cheyenne world view with equal intensity. But many did, and these acted in accordance with moral and personal norms of behavior which clearly stamped the Cheyenne among other tribes of the Plains in the nineteenth century.

Reserved and dignified, the adult Cheyenne male moves with a quiet sense of self-assurance. He speaks fluently, but never carelessly. He is careful of the sensibilities of others and is kindly and generous. He is slow to anger and strives to suppress his feelings, if aggravated. Vigorous on the hunt and in war, he prizes the active life. Towards enemies he feels no merciful compunctions, and the more aggressive he is, the better. He is well versed in ritual knowledge. He is neither flighty nor dour. Usually quiet, he has a lightly displayed sense of humor. He is sexually repressed and masochistic, but that masochism is expressed in culturally approved rites. He does not show much creative imagination in artistic expression, but he has a firm grip on reality. He

deals with the problems of life in set ways while at the same time showing a notable capacity to readjust to new circumstances. His thinking is rationalistic to a high degree and yet colored with mysticism. His ego is strong and not easily threatened. His superego, as manifest in his strong social conscience and mastery of his basic

FIG. 19-3 Cheyenne Sun Dance pledgers wearing the yellow paint of the First Day. Body paint changes with each day of the ceremony, as the symbolic focus progresses. (Photo courtesy of the American Museum of Natural History.)

---

[15]*Ibid.*, II, *The Sun Dance*, p. 57.

[16]This is still true; The Sun Dance of the northern Cheyenne, in Montana, is performed every year, culminating on the Fourth of July. The Sacred Arrows are renewed whenever there has been a murder in the tribe.

impulses, is powerful and dominating. He is "mature" —serene and composed, secure in his social position, capable of warm social relations. He has powerful anxieties, but these are channeled into institutionalized modes of collective expression with satisfactory results. He exhibits few neurotic tendencies.[17]

THE AMERICAN WORLD VIEW

It may seem that the formulation of a descriptive analysis of *a* world view for the people of the United States is too great an undertaking. There are so many, and such diverse, cultural backgrounds represented in their recent immigrant origins; there is such a wide range in manifest belief, from atheism to devout religiosity; there is such a broad spectrum of interests in terms of occupation, recreation, and learning; and there are such vast differences between life in a tiny crossroads hamlet and life in New York's megalopolis, between the black separatist and white segregationist, between the middle-aged Kiwanis and the hippie countercultural revolutionist, that one may well wonder where lies the common denominator, or if one exists at all.

Yet outsiders generally agree that Americans are, by and large, highly standardized in outlook and manner. Relatively speaking, this is true. American society is marked by a very high degree of consensus and general agreement. There is little of the dogmatic in American ideology— certainly nothing that can be stated so succinctly as a Communist credo, for example. Nonetheless, a distinctive American world view does exist and may be stated in its bolder outlines as the anthropologist sees them. This, then, is how it appears— allowing for subgroup and individual variations, which are screened out in order that the major themes can be brought into clearer focus.

Rationalism and the Mechanistic View

Historically, the American world view is a derivative of the Hellenistic–Judeo-Christian traditions as they were blended and modified through the Renaissance, the Reformation, and the industrial

revolution in Europe. In the American setting, these traditions have taken on their own intensifications and selective qualities.

However much the Judeo-Christian traditions may survive and influence the American life-way, American thought patterns are rational rather than mystic; the operative conception of the universe is mechanistic. The bedrock proposition upon which the whole world view stands is that the universe is a physical system operating in a determinate manner according to discoverable scientific laws. Thus, Americans use religion for purposes of social organization, but they rely relatively little upon prayer, ritual, or sacrifice to achieve their ends. Instead, they depend primarily upon basic scientific research and the technical application of the findings of science. Because they view the universe as a mechanism, Americans implicitly believe that individuals can manipulate it. Human beings need not accept it as it is; they may work on it, and as they gain in knowledge and improve their techniques, they may even redesign it so that it will be more to their liking.

From this springs the conviction that the conditions of living are improvable: materially, biologically, and socially. Improvement means betterment; betterment means progress. Americans are progressive: neither revolutionary nor conservative, but progressive. Humanity can itself, in the American view, eliminate hunger and poverty, disease, and social injustice—if it sets itself to the task. This fundamental motivating postulate of contemporary American culture expresses itself in a focal value orientation of "effort-optimism." Because the world view is rational-mechanistic rather than mystic-vitalistic, it leads to action rather than contemplation, and to aggressive engagement rather than passive renunciation. Americans "make war" on poverty, "stamp out" disease, "wipe out" illiteracy, and embark on the "conquest" of space, as their forebears "conquered" the wilderness. Such an action orientation makes for emphasis upon technology and science rather than upon philosophy and the arts. It has produced a mechanized agricultural, industrial, business-centered civilization rather than an ecclesiastical, scholarly, militaristic, or feudalistic one.

---

[17]E. A. Hoebel, *The Cheyennes*, p. 90. By permission of Holt, Rinehart and Winston, Inc.

Pragmatic empiricism

Concomitantly, the American cultural emphasis is pragmatic-empirical rather than theoretical-dogmatic. Americans are concerned more with "know-how" and "can-do" than with abstract wisdom or ancient knowledge, even, to a considerable degree, in science. In our universities and colleges, and in government grants-in-aid for research, this emphasis may be seen in the lopsided support for medicine, technology, and agriculture as against the humanities and social sciences.

The test of the validity of the American premise is, in the American view of things, continued expansion of the gross national product, ever-new medical breakthroughs, and continuous expansions of social well-being and opportunity. As long as the standard of living, expressed in wide distribution of consumers' goods, keeps rising, it is felt that things are going well. When the system temporarily collapsed in the Great Depression of the 1930s, Americans panicked and had to be reassured that "all they had to fear was fear itself." What unnerved them, however, was not unreasoning fear but the logical anxiety that the most basic premise of the American world view was an unworkable illusion.

Individual-centeredness

When the Americans look away from the universe and inward toward themselves and their society, focus of view is individual-centered, rather than kin-centered, class-centered, or collectivistically oriented, even though Americans are widely given to group organization. In the religious belief that has permeated much of the morality of the culture, it is premised that a person's moral responsibility rests in one's private conscience. In the view of human nature held by Christianity, which is the dominant religion, humanity is inherently corrupt and sin-ridden by nature, and personal salvation (that is, purification from the moral stain of sin) is possible only in an emotional act of identification with God through Jesus (or his mother, Mary). Americans are therefore generally internally plagued with inner conflict and anxiety. Believing in the improvability of the self as an individual responsibility, and yet also holding (to a certain extent) that the individual is a sorry being, they set out the proposition that inner psychic conflict is the very essence of human existence. Pastors are expected to be half counselor and half priest. To control the extreme consequences of inner conflict, there is less reliance upon religious or philosophic solutions than upon psychiatry and mental hygiene programs.

Rites of passage are weak or lacking, and the individual is left to wrestle with his own "identity crises." External values are weakly anchored in the America of today, and in the wildly swirling cultural revolution of the age many find it hard to get a grasp on meaningful standards.

Two-thirds of the American population are nominally religious in that they belong to some church. One-third are sufficiently uninterested in religion as to identify with no church. In contrast to the primitive world view, God, gods, spirits, ghosts, witches, and ancestors in the American world view are more residual than dominant.

Status and Social Mobility

The individual-centeredness of the American world view, combined with its pragmatic action orientation, gives emphasis to status achievement and social mobility. Achievement-in-being is what counts, not so much an illustrious background. American egalitarianism and its proposition that all persons are created equal derive from this combination of qualities. Americans have to prove their worth to themselves first and to their fellows second—to succeed in manifest ways. They see themselves in a fluid social organization that necessitates fluid status symbols whereby achievement can be tangibly expressed. In a business-based culture, money serves this function. Money is the measure of success; it validates one's efforts, and therefore oneself, by providing the means to purchase such external symbols of success as a college education, a discreetly selected foreign car, or a large house at a good address.

The world view of older, but contemporary, status-structured societies in Europe deprecates the materialism of Americanism. At the same time, a major feature of the revolutionary innovations of the postcolonial world since World War II has been the avid desire of the so-called underdeveloped nations to learn the mechanical-material techniques that have followed from the kind of world view that has had its most intensive development in the United States.[18]

The Counterculture Revolution

The countercultural revolution of the current younger generation rejects the traditional American world view as false-valued. It inverts the status symbolism of clothing—dressing in rags, Hollywood Indian style, romanticized workingmen's garb, gypsy and peasant dress, all in variations which ebb and flow in favor. It abhors regular time-clock-punching work and hopes to get along with little or no money.

It does not completely reject automobiles, but prefers beat-up cars to the latest models, and in housing it chooses a simply furnished pad rather than a "good address." It seeks social bonding in marriageless habitation, and searches for new substitutes for the rejected values in psychedelia, communes, mystical experiences (including the occult), mind expansion, and back-to-nature experiments. Personal guilt, ambition, and "success" are devalued, and emphasis is placed on honesty, intimacy, and sharing. The permanence of the movement and its impact on the ideological mainstream of American culture remain to be seen.

SELECTED READINGS

Forde, D. (ed.), *African Worlds: Studies in the Cosmological Ideas and Social Values of African Peoples* (1954). Nine studies of the world views of a selected group of African societies. Includes a very remarkable formulation of world view by a native informant from the Dogon of the French Sudan (pp. 83–110).

Geertz, C., *The Religion of Java* (1960). The world view of Javanese analyzed in terms of Hindu tradition, Islamic precepts, and indigenous beliefs.

Hamilton, E., *The Greek Way to Western Civilization* (1930). A sympathetic approach to Greek thought and action by way of Greek literature.

Hoebel, E. A., *The Cheyennes* (1960). Part I, "Ritual and Tribal Integration," and Part IV, "World View and the Cheyenne Personality," show how the Cheyenne view of the need to husband and renew the limited energy quotient of the universe is culturally expressed.

Hsu, F. L. K., *Americans and Chinese: Purpose and Fulfillment in Great Civilizations* (1970). An updated presentation of comparative contrasts of American and Chinese cultural orientations and their related behaviors. The account presents rich data and penetrating insights by an objectively knowledgeable American anthropologist of Chinese origin.

——, *The Study of Literate Civilizations* (1969). A handbook on the application of anthropological methods in the study of complex societies. Chapter 8, "Postulates as a Solution," succinctly states the underlying assumptions of the world views of China and the United States.

Leslie, C. M., *Now We Are Civilized: A Study of the World View of the Zapotec Indians of Mitla, Oaxaca* (1960). A penetrating and gracefully written expression of the world view of a Mexican people in transition from the old to the new.

Radin, P., *Primitive Man as Philosopher* (1927; rev. ed., 1955). This is the classic work that opened the door to the inside view of primitive thinking. It disposed of the condescending clichés that had prevailed about primitive simple-mindedness.

Redfield, R., *The Primitive World and Its Transformations* (1953). Chapter 4, "Primitive World View and Civilization," explores some implications of the concept of world view for modern life.

——, *The Little Community* (1956). Chapter 6, "The Little Community as an Outlook on Life," emphasizes the differences between the outside and inside views of cultures and the problems of investigation of the latter, plus the theoretical significance of world view.

---

[18]It will undoubtedly have been noted in the foregoing description that, allowing for certain variations in the conception of the individual in relation to the state and in various degrees of coloration, the "world view" of the Russians is not so dissimilar from the American as is commonly thought.

20

RELIGION AND MYTH: SYMBOLIC IDEOLOGY

LEARNING GOALS

Discuss Emile Durkheim's theory of the social functions of religion, with particular attention to the role of ritual experience. ¶ Contrast the concepts of the sacred and the profane. ¶ Show how myths are an essential part of religion and how they contribute to personal ends and social purposes. ¶ List and explain five components of a comprehensive definition of religion. ¶ Write a summary of the Mandan Okipa ceremony as an example of sacred symbolic transformation of beliefs and social structure.

Throughout the history of mankind, world view and religion have been intimately intertwined, for both are expressions of ideational systems—products of human intelligence and emotional concern: expressions of the culture-creating ferment of the human mind.

World view, as we have just explored it, provides each people with its "set" toward the universe. Religion defines a part of that experience through the spirits and gods it creates; it clothes them with their own peculiar attributes of behavior, and provides individuals with guidelines for their own behavior in response to the presence and demands of the spirit beings with whom they must interact. Religion does more than this, however. Through ritual and myth, religion provides symbolic expression which subtly and pervasively impresses on participants and watching members of the society an emotional and intellectual commitment to the ordered belief system on which their lives rest.

In Chapter 2, "Man, Culture, and Society," we cited the sixth and most difficult functional prerequisite of society as defining the meaning of life and maintaining the motivation to survive and engage in the activities necessary to survival (page 30). This is the task of cultures at large, world views in general, and religions in particular. Atheistic cultures, such as those in modern Russia and China, deal with similar problems but without the use of religion. "The Thoughts of Chairman Mao" are specifically directed to this end, and judging from reports emerging from China, apparently quite successfully, for the present at least.

ANTHROPOLOGICAL THEORIES OF RELIGION

Over a period of a hundred years, anthropology has worked to develop an objective understanding of religion in human cultures, an understanding that is free of dogma and separate from the value judgments that the religions of the East and West may have imposed on the intellectual climate of our times.

The earliest theories, those of the late nineteenth century, such as Sir Edward Tylor's, were primarily psychological; they undertook to explain the origins of religion in terms of mental responses to the puzzling aspects of life—dream experience and death in particular. They were directly and simply concerned with overt belief in spirit beings. The theory of animism, as it was called, dominated anthropological thought until challenged by the sociological theory of Emile Durkheim. Animism and related ideas will be examined in the next chapter. At this point it will be useful to take a brief look at Durkheim's contribution.

The Sacred and the Profane: Durkheim's Theory of Religion

Much religion is, indeed, a matter of individual experience, such as that of the North American Indian who must seek a vision in which a spirit bestows the power of medicine (supernatural power) upon him. Yet all religions build on the participation of the public, if only as spectators, in acts that not only affect the workings of extra-human forces but also express the solidarity of the group and at the same time internalize group loyalty and commitment to unified social purposes. This was the thesis of Emile Durkheim, Mali-nowski, and the functionalists. For Durkheim, to whom society was the supreme reality, to explain religion on the basis of dreams, as did Tylor, was to explain a reality by recourse to a fantasy.

Durkheim saw ritual participation as the true essence of religion. The individual rises above the humdrum monotony of eking out a living and shares in the ecstasy of sacred experience obtain-able only through periodic group dances and ceremonies, such as the *corroborees* of the Aus-tralian aborigines. Religion, for Durkheim, is an expression of social solidarity and collective be-liefs. Human beings alone are as nothing. They realize their significance and worth only as a member of a social group. Sacred rituals and beliefs symbolize society. Out of the ritual experi-ence arises the difference between the sacred and the profane.

As phrased by Professor Lowie, the religious emotion expresses "a sense of something tran-scending the expected or natural, a sense of the Extraordinary, Mysterious, or Supernatural."[1] Re-ligious belief is essentially mystical and subjec-tive, whereas naturalistic belief emphasizes ob-jective and rational determination of the facts.

[1] R. H. Lowie, *Primitive Religion*, p. xvi.

This becomes clearer when put in terms of *profane* and *sacred*, as polarized by Durkheim.

The Profane	The Sacred
The sphere of the routine, mundane, taken-for-granted, workaday world.	The sphere of the un-usual, extraordinary, not-to-be-taken-casually, "out-of-this-world."
Attitudes: blasé accept-ance on a basis of com-mon familiarity.	Attitudes: awe, sense of mystery, circumspection in dealing with something special.

The terms "profane" and "sacred," so used, have meanings somewhat broader than ordinarily accorded them in common English usage, and care should be taken to keep this constantly in mind. The profane, then, is that which is viewed as natural; the sacred, that which is viewed as super-natural. The natural works in ways that are ac-cepted as ordinary, as in accord with daily experi-ence. The supernatural works in ways that are looked upon as unusual and special. The emo-tional connotations are consequently different. They are the product of human mental states.

Religion and magic therefore rest upon a belief in the supernatural, and they are basically matters of ideology and the kinds of feeling that accompa-ny them. They require thought. Animals, although they certainly feel, do not engage in symbolic thought, as we have seen. Human beings alone symbolize, and their ideas about the supernatural are always symbolically expressed. So it is that on the subhuman level there is no religion or mag-ic—no supernaturalism.

Today, anthropologists combine both the soci-ological and psychological approaches to religion in a kind of master theory which, while it embrac-es Tylor's simple animism, goes far beyond it in sophistication. In this and the following chapters, we shall present the essence of the modern view and then relate to it what is still relevant in the earlier theories of religion.

ANTHROPOLOGICAL THEORIES OF MYTHOLOGY

The questing human mind has always asked the eternal "Why?" The creative minds of artists have always spun a literary web of answers in words and ideas. The human animal does not submit supinely either to the harsh demands of the physical world or to the ever-pressing demands of the society and its culture-bound limitations of individual freedom. Reasons are demanded. Reasons are given.

Myths, as distinct from folklore and legends, deal with sacred and semidivine beings in a time when the world was different and they tell how, through the activity of such beings, things came to be as they are. They instruct human beings in what must be done to avoid chaos—the state that humanity, individually and collectively, fears most.

In Malinowski's functional theory of myth, myth is more than idle speculation about the origins of things.

It justifies by precedent the existing order and it supplies a retrospective pattern of moral values, of sociological discriminations and burdens and of magical belief. . . . the [Myth] of magic [of religion, or of any other body of customs or single custom] is definitely a warrant of its truth, a pedigree of its filiation, a charter of its claims to validity.[2]

Myth believing is more than infantile self-deception; it is social reassurance—a device of education and learning, of culture maintenance.

Today, however, anthropological interests, while not ignoring function, relate myths more to symbolic transformations in which change and establishment of a new order of things is of more interest than origins. Victor Turner writes:

Myths relate how one state of affairs became another: how an unpeopled world became populated; how chaos became cosmos; how immortals became mortal; how the seasons came to replace a climate without seasons; how the original unity of mankind became a plurality of tribes or nations; how androgynous beings became men and women; and so on. Myths are *liminal* phenomena: they are frequently told at a time or in a site that is "betwixt and between."[3]

Myths are an important component of transition rites (see Chapter 9). They restate the first principles or basic postulates upon which a people's belief system and social structure rest. Myths phrase the nature of the personality a person must seek to transcribe in himself. Myths assist to "re-create or transform those to whom they are . . . told and alter the capacity of the initiand's being so that he becomes capable of performing the tasks of the new status ahead of him."[4] Because they are told in a sacred context and deal with sacred beings, myths are the timeless handmaiden of religion. They are the fertile seedbeds from which grew the sacred books of the great religions of later civilizations.[5]

A Comprehensive Definition of Religion

The anthropologist Clifford Geertz, a foremost contributor in this field, has recently defined religion as:

1. A system of symbols which acts to
2. establish powerful, persuasive and long-lasting moods and motivations in men by
3. formulating conceptions of a general order of existence and
4. clothing these conceptions with such an aura of factuality that
5. the moods and motivations seem uniquely realistic.[6]

What Geertz is saying is that religion is a system of transformation in which conceptions of order and the denial of chaos, along with a belief in justice and morality in the face of injustice and evil, are passionately affirmed as dominating reality in the face of contrary evidence. Through symbolic transformations, the inchoate human sense of order and moral rightness becomes convincingly affirmed for the believer who bears the imprint of the symbols.

We shall now try to make this clearer with a single interpretive example: the drama of the Okipa ceremony of the Mandan Indians of the upper Plains region in what is now South Dakota. Although the Okipa ceremony and its accompanying myths made up but one part of a fabulously

---

[2]B. Malinowski, "Culture" (*Encyclopaedia of the Social Sciences*, vol. 4, 1937), p. 640. Copyright © 1934, The Macmillan Co. Quoted with permission.

[3]V. W. Turner, "Myth and Symbol" (*International Encyclopedia of the Social Sciences*, vol. 10, 1968), p. 576. Copyright © 1968, Crowell Collier and Macmillan, Inc.

[4]*Ibid.*, p. 577.

[5]For example, see J. G. Frazer, *Folklore in the Old Testament*.

[6]C. Geetz, "Religion as a Cultural System," in W. A. Lessa and E. Z. Vogt (eds.), *Reader in Comparative Religion* (2d ed.), p. 206. By permission of Harper and Row, Inc.

rich myth-ceremonial system of the Mandans and explained only a part of their world and life to them, we believe it will serve our purposes, for it was indeed the greatest and most spectacular of all Plains Indian religious rites. It is necessary to present an extended account in this case, for only so is it possible to convey the sense of emic feel and etic analysis of the complex.

MANDAN CULTURE

One may think of the Mandans as the Parisians of the Plains. Their villages were centers of cultural sophistication and intertribal trade for all the northern Plains area. Their archaeological tradition goes back a thousand years to the Initial Middle Missouri (River) version of the prehistoric Plains Village Tradition.[7]

The subsistence base of Mandan culture was, equally, intensive horticulture (maize, squash, and tobacco growing in the bottoms of the Missouri River and its tributaries) and buffalo hunting (without the aid of the horse). The climax of Mandan culture was reached between 1738, when the Assineboines led LaVerendrye's party of French traders to the Mandan villages, and 1782, when a decimating series of smallpox epidemics began the destruction which Sioux attacks completed by 1860. Even before the arrival of the French with their European trade goods, the Mandans were prosperous producers and traders, exchanging surplus maize and beautifully dressed and ornamented hide robes for meat and furs brought in by foot nomads from farther south and west.

Nonetheless, theirs was a precarious existence. Their fixed villages of large earth lodges were well fortified against marauding attackers. Equally important, maize raising in North Dakota has always been unpredictable. The Mandan had much to cope with, and in the course of a thousand years of experience developed the ideology and ritual to manage it.

Finally, we should note that Mandan social organization was based on matrilocal households, matrilineal clans, and a dual organization of a Sky and an Earth moiety, symbolizing the twofold nature of the subsistence base upon which their survival depended.

The Moiety Symbolism

The Earth People, also called Those-Below (or People-Below) and also Corn People, were believed to have once lived under the ground, later emerging from a hole in the earth, bringing the corn plant with them. Whenever an Okipa ceremonial lodge was built, the Earth People placed yellow corn under the postholes on their side of the Okipa lodge. They owned all the corn medicine bundles, which had power over growing plants, and also the priesthoods which carried secret knowledge of the origin myths and how to perform the elaborate corn ceremonies. The corn bundles and their accompanying priesthoods were inherited from priest to sister's son (matrilaterally) within the clans which were within the Corn, or Earth People, moiety. Without their intervention no corn would grow.

The Sky People, Those-Above, belonged to six clans named after birds and animals. They were symbolically related to the creatures of the animal world, and they planted mats of buffalo hair under the posts of their side of the Okipa lodge.

They owned all the animal medicine bundles, which had power over buffaloes, antelope, birds, etc. They owned the priesthoods which carried secret knowledge of the origin myths and how to perform the ceremonies which controlled the animal world. Thus the double-dual nature (above/below and animal/plant) of their mythically based concept of the universe and of their livelihood was fundamentally built into the social structure and the medicine bundles which controlled their tribal well-being.

The Mandan Theory of Power

The Mandan image of a human being was one of inherent lack of any personal aptitudes. "I claim no power for myself," a Mandan would say, "I have no power except what my sacred objects have promised me."[8]

---

[7]See D. J. Lehmer, *Introduction to Middle Missouri Archeology*.

[8]A. W. Bowers, *Mandan Social and Ceremonial Organization*, p. 336.

Power could primarily be acquired from three sources: (1) inheritance and purchase of clan-owned medicine bundles and the priestly knowledge which went with them; this was the main road to prestige status; (2) the personal vision quest in which one fasted, chopped off segments of fingers, and cut out strips of one's own flesh as offerings to the spirit beings; and (3) "walking with the buffalo," an act in which a young man asked an older power holder to have ritual sex relations with the young man's wife. The woman, wearing a buffalo shirt, played the role of a female bison: a vessel of power from which a man could draw strength, ability, and success.

Like the Cheyennes (who surely got the idea from the Mandans), the Mandans believed that the energy available to any individual was limited and was steadily used up. A man went on only four war parties and went "walking" no more than four times—his powers were then exhausted.

Psychological factors in the power concept

A few fortunate individuals received power through adoption by a supernatural being without being aware of it. This accounted for the rare successful achievers who had no important medicine bundles, inherited or individual. Thus the general power theory was not invalidated by their successes.

A Mandan was born empty. He had to strive and struggle hard to establish himself. His need for achievement exceeded that of *all* other tribal populations rated by David McClelland in his comparative analysis of achievement motivation.[9] For the Mandan male, the absolute test of his worthiness to succeed came in his performance in the torture rites of the Okipa.

THE MALE SYNDROME   The Mandan was born into a mother-dominated, semi-subterranean earth lodge in which his father was an outsider. His inherited bundles came from his mother's brother, and were paid for not by himself, but by his wife's brothers and sisters (lineage siblings). They owned his medicine bundles. He, in turn, had to pay them for his rights to the bundles. For every-

thing he learned, every song, every technique, every ritual act, he had to pay in goods. Women did, too. Nothing came for nothing, either from parents or friends. With no striving to win the help of relatives and friends, with no uncanny trading and skillful hunting on his own part to get the goods to buy power, a Mandan remained— nothing. The Mandan male became the manipulator of goods, external things, and of medicine power which was usually not his own.

In actual purchases he had to surrender his wife to a ceremonial "father." Only so could he help his wife maintain a good home, keep his family in good health, and be himself successful in war and hunt. "The sexual act was tantamount to intercourse with the buffaloes. . . ."[10] So even when acting as a ceremonial father, the sexually giving male was nothing in his own right.

In the myths, the great supernaturals of Mandan society were born of virgins who conceived by supernatural means. A mate was not required in their procreation.

In psychodynamic terms, the Mandan male had to deal with a culturally engendered sense of worthlessness and self-hatred. Hostility to the father, who possessed his mother, is indicated. The ceremonial "fathers" who substituted for him as potent buffaloes with his wives, would be included; so also, his mother's brother, who had sexual rights in a maternal nephew's wife and from whom the younger man had to buy the hereditary medicine bundles on which his ultimate standing in the society would depend. Internalization of tribal values led to repression of sexual and aggressive aims in favor of manipulatory striving for externals—goods, medicine bundles, and priestly office. Repressed hostility and sense of self-worth found orgiastic outlet in the extreme sadism and masochism of the Okipa, to be described below.

For the male there were delayed rewards in fraternity membership in the graded societies, but not in war. Remember, after being used on four war parties his fighting power was normally depleted. He could become a village chief, but in this there was little political authority. Unlike the Comanche, he could find no rewards in the conquest

---

[9] D. C. McClelland, *The Achieving Society*, p. 66.

[10] Bowers, *op. cit*, p. 336.

of women. That avenue was not available to him. The greatest ultimate rewards were in the ritual and ceremonial roles that would come with bundle priesthoods, but these rewards were long deferred. And first there was the Okipa rite to be surmounted.

THE FEMALE SYNDROME   Woman's personal worth in Mandan society was clear. She was the generator of life and the transmitter of vital power upon whom her husband had to depend. A woman's kin bought a man's bundles for her husband—bundles, the rights to which he inherited through his mother's clan. Women were the owners of the houses in which men lived all their lives. The psychosymbolic implications of the lodge as earthwomb are strong and clear. Women were not only the corn growers; they were also the symbolic bison from whom men drew their war and hunting powers. The Mandan woman had little cause for self-doubt.

How, then, did these deep-lying factors project themselves into world view and religion? How was the religious system of myth, ritual, and action which support Mandan society translated into ". . . the ability of its symbols to formulate a world in which those values, as well as the forces opposing their realization, are fundamental ingredients"?[11] How did this complex system impel men to a manageable and effective adulthood?

THE OKIPA MYTH

The essence of the sacred Okipa myth (distilled to its minimum) is as follows:

Lone Man wandered for a long time in an unconscious state. When he became conscious, his first thoughts were, "Who am I? Where did I come from?"

He retraced his steps until he came to a plant on which was a bug. Was the plant or the bug his mother? No answer. Later he came upon Coyote, the First Creator, who had made the world. They argued over their relative ages (Coyote won) and then they decided to fix up the earth, which was too sandy and wet. They made it as it is today and went their separate ways.

Lone Man met the first buffalo, from whom he received tobacco (the sacred herb).

After he had traveled all over the land, he decided it should have people on it. He created a man and a woman from the ends of his own ribs. In time, through intermarriage of their offspring, their number increased to form a large village, of which Lone Man was the protector-adviser. However, the people kept calling him back from his wanderings so much for advice that he said he would only send the South Wind to them instead of appearing himself.

Next, the Sky People arrived—and the Corn People (each event accounted for in separate myths)—until there were five separate villages.

Lone Man returned and liked what he saw, so he decided he should be reborn as one of the people. He picked a virgin to be his mother but failed to get into her womb as a seed of corn. Later, he made himself into the kidney fat of a buffalo, which she ate and so conceived. Lone Man grew up to be the Buffalo Spirit.

Another spirit man was born of a virgin in another village. This was Hoita, the Spotted Eagle. He grew up to be the Eagle Spirit and a rival of Lone Man. In anger at Lone Man, Hoita enclosed all the living animals and birds inside Dog Den Butte, which lies east of the Missouri River and north of Bismarck, North Dakota. The Mandans starved.

Lone Man got into the cave by various stratagems and learned the Animal (Buffalo) Dance, or Okipa, by means of which Hoita had called all the animals into the cave. He had a young Mandan, acting as his son, impersonate Hoita in the dance. Hoita released the buffalo and said that thereafter he would work with Lone Man for the good of the people.

Later, Lone Man got three turtle-effigy drums made of hide for the Okipa ceremony from the Great Turtle Spirit. To save the Mandan from the flood that would be sent by Maniga, a mythological chief of another tribe, Lone Man put a cedar post, symbolizing himself, in the center of the village in which he lived. He put a cedar plank palisade around it, like a fortification. The planks were tied with willow withes above which water could never rise. The post and palisade protected the village from floods.

[11]C. Geertz, "Ethos, World View and the Analysis of Social Symbols" in A. Dundes (ed.), *Every Man His Way*, p. 309.

Origin Myth of Oxinhede, the Foolish (Evil) One

A virgin Mandan girl was impregnated by a shadow (the Sun). She gave birth to a hyperactive black baby, called Oxinhede (see Fig. 20-1). Nobody could do anything with him. He was always jumping and running about. When he got to be a little older, he was given a bow and arrows. With these he killed the sacred snakes and many other holy things. He would not stay away from sacred things, always molesting them. He was known as the Foolish, or Evil, One. Although the people liked him, the Spirits of Sacred Things decided he had to be killed. And this was done.

THE OKIPA: A RITUAL DRAMA IN THREE ACTS AND AN EPILOGUE

The Okipa was first observed in 1832 by George Catlin, who painted his visual impressions and published his written observations in 1833, 1841, and 1867.[12]

The description of the Okipa which follows here is presented as a synoptic scenario, so to speak, of the great "Passion Play" of the Mandans, which took five days and nights to perform. It was put on every summer in each of the villages, if possible. The producer of each Okipa performance was a man of a wealthy family who had managed to accumulate large amounts of food and fine goods to be given away in connection with the rite. He was called the Okipa Maker. Primary roles were played by chosen impersonators of Lone Man, Hoita, and the Foolish One. Owners of appropriate bundles performed as Buffalo Bulls, Beavers, Wolves, Bears, etc. (all the creatures who controlled the animal powers on which the Mandan depended). Other officiants beat the three turtle drums. Two masked priests performed as surgeons. A score or more of young men played the roles of sacrificial initiates. Major bundle holders painted the actors.

---

[12]The 1867 account, George Catlin's *O-kee-pa: A Religious Ceremony and Other Customs of the Mandans*, is now available in a 1967 reprint by Yale University Press. In this summary description, we rely mostly on Catlin and A. W. Bowers, *Mandan Social and Ceremonial Organization*.

Act I. The Father Figure: First Day

At dawn of the first day, the chiefs and medicine priests were called to the Okipa ceremonial lodge. At sunrise, the figure of Lone Man approached from the south. The Blackmouth fraternity met him at the village gate and reverentially led him to the lodge where he was solemnly received by the chiefs and priests. In an archaic tongue Lone Man retold them all the myths of his life when he was alive among the Mandan. That done, throughout the day he walked about the village, collecting bone knives with which the skin of the initiates would be pierced and their finger joints severed. In return he gave them buffalo meat. Women, children, and dogs were confined in their lodges, for this was the time of the male, the father figure. At various places around the village, Lone Man gave orations on the origins of the people, their struggles against floods and starvation, reminding them of how he had given them all the things to make life better.

At dusk, he retired to the Okipa lodge. Soon after, the sacrificial initiates (boys from eight years of age to men of thirty-five) entered to begin their fasting, while Lone Man ate buffalo meat.

The meal ended, Lone Man transferred his pipe, the symbol of his power, to the Okipa Maker. Hoita was next called forward by Lone Man, who exhorted him to supervise the Animal Dance and see that it was performed exactly as it had been when Hoita kept the animals captive in Dog Den Butte. Lone Man's work was done; he quietly left to return to his home in the south. Immediately, the dancing began—in the lodge as it had in the cave in Dog Den Butte.

Interpretive comment

Lone Man returned to the Mandan as an asexual, benign father figure, the designer of the Mandan life style, the bestower of buffalo, the bringer of all animal spirits from whom vital medicine power was derived. He brought the turtle drums on which the world rests. He reasserted the authenticity of all the symbolic acts which legitimated the Mandan view and way of life. With the transfer of his pipe, he bestowed his active power on the Okipa Maker, called upon Hoita to do his part, and

FIG. 20-1 The Foolish One, the being who symbolized untamed male sexuality in Mandan mythology as he was dramatized in the Okipa ceremony of 1832. (George Catlin, *O-kee-pa, A Religious Ceremony and Other Customs of the Mandans*, John C. Ewers (ed.). Copyright © 1967, Yale University Press.)

so retired from the immediate affairs of men. He became an otiose deity who might be appealed to from afar, but who left the management of the affairs of the universe to lesser executive gods (Hoita and the Okipa Maker) and to human beings who were now on their own.

Act II. The Male Principle Conquered: Second, Third, and Fourth Days

Throughout the second day, the eight Buffalo Bull dancers emerged eight times from the lodge to dance in the plaza (see Fig. 20-2). The Okipa Maker took a position at the plank wall around the Lone Man cedar post in the center of the plaza. There he wept and beseeched Lone Man to help the people. The presence of Lone Man was now an ungraven image—a faceless idol.

Throughout the morning the animal impersonators and sacrificiants were being painted. Each was first prepared by an old man who tightly tied the prepuce over the head of each initiate's sex organ with sinew. Then he obliterated the whole

FIG. 20-2 The scene in the village plaza during the Okipa ceremony. At the extreme left is the Foolish One in spotted paint, with bald-headed staff. Bull dancers are performing in the foreground. At the center of the scene, the Okipa Maker may be seen leaning against the plank wall which surrounds the sacred cedar post. (Photo courtesy of the American Museum of Natural History.)

genital area with clay plaster. The impersonators were then meticulously painted with symbolic designs over their entire bodies.[13]

The third day was called "Everything Comes Back Day." All the creatures who inhabited the earth with Lone Man and Hoita emerged from the lodge to do their mimetic dances along with the Bull dancers. "They all had some peculiar and appropriate songs, which they constantly chanted and sang during the dances."[14] Day and Night, as they were in Lone Man's time, danced, too.

In the meantime, in the lodge, the initiates were

being prepared. Each one had selected a man from his father's clan to perform the operation. With a serrated knife to make a jagged wound, the clan father cut four holes over the shoulder blades or breasts and pushed two wooden skewers through the flesh. These were for the thongs by which the initiate would be suspended. More skewers were put into the legs; buffalo skulls would be suspended from them.

On the fourth day, the Bulls and other animal dancers "came out" to dance twelve times. The Okipa Maker was again at the Lone Man post, crying and praying to Lone Man.

In the course of one dance, a crazy figure appeared, leaping and running zigzag across the prairie from the west. He rushed in among the

---

[13]See Bowers, *op. cit.*, pp. 131–132, for a detailed list of the impersonators.
[14]Catlin, *op. cit.*, p. 57.

spectators as women and children scattered in shrieking alarm. It was the Foolish (Evil) One (Fig. 20-1). His body was painted black with white circles. He had a grotesque phallus. He jumped over sacred paraphernalia. He burlesqued a buffalo bull in intercourse with a man masquerading as a woman. He advanced threateningly toward other women. They screamed in terror. The Okipa Maker left the Lone Man post, advancing deliberately, Lone Man's pipe in hand. Thrusting it in the Foolish One's face, he paralyzed him, while the crowd of spectators hissed and groaned at the sacrilegious one as the Animal Dance proceeded unheedingly. The Foolish One controlled, the Okipa Maker returned to his prayers and supplications at the cedar post.

Three times the Foolish One recovered and assaulted the women. Three more times he was subdued by the Okipa Maker. Each time the women became less terrified and began closing in on the Foolish One. After the fourth time, he turned his attention to the Buffalo dancers, simulating mating with four of them. His energy expended, one woman threw yellow ocher in his face. Others smothered him from all sides. The leader of the women took his mock phallus from him. He collapsed within himself, whimpered, and bolted for the prairie, pursued by hissing, screaming women, who pelted him with filth.

In triumph the women returned, escorting the woman who had deprived the Foolish One of his power. She mounted the entrance to the Okipa lodge and took command. In a long declamation she let it be known that *she* held the power of creation, the power of life and death over the people, and all control over the buffalo. They would come or stay away at her command, as *she* pleased.

She ordered the animal dancers to stop dancing. She directed the chiefs to go back in the lodge and witness the sacrifices of the young men which should now begin. She also demanded the most beautiful dress in the village, and this was dutifully given to her by the Okipa Maker.

Interpretive comment
The turtle drums symbolized the eternal and deathless continuity of life. The dancing animals reaffirmed the constructive power of Lone Man and all associated with him. The lamentations of the Okipa Maker in his prayers to Lone Man reiterated the theme of dependency on the far-removed father figure.

Into this scene of variegated order came Chaos—the Black One, the Male Principle Uncontrolled. It is Foolish One, the sacrilegious scoffer at Mandan ethos. In his phallic grotesqueries, the unbridled male id, he terrified both women and children. Only the calm, controlled male power of Lone Man could master him.

Finally, the Female Principle boldly took over. With yellow clay signifying corn pollen and the People Below, women subdued Chaos and mocked him. In smashing the symbol of his exaggerated sexuality, they destroyed all his power and banished him from Mandan life, even as the spirit beings had killed him in the long ago.

The Female Principle was now dominant; even Lone Man (in the form of the Okipa Maker) was subordinate to the imperious control of the symbolic Mother of All.

Act III. In Limbo: Fifth Day
With all the initiates painted and ready, two of them were led to a position beneath the smoke-hole in the roof of the Okipa lodge. A war shield and four buffalo skulls were tied to the skewers in the skin of each one. By means of rawhide ropes fastened to the skewers in his chest or back, each man was drawn upward three or four feet off the floor—suspended in limbo betwixt heaven and earth, while his body was spun crazily around until he fainted (Fig. 20-3). Onlookers cried out, "Dead! Dead!" Lowered to the floor, the two initiates lay lifeless. On recovering consciousness, each made his way to a buffalo skull to offer his little finger in thanks. Others then went through the same process.

Thereafter, in groups of six, the revived initiates came out to run around the Lone Man post until the buffalo skulls, skewered to their legs and dragging on the ground, tore loose (Fig. 20-4). Then, and only then, could they make their ways unassisted to their homes.

FIG. 20-3 In the Okipa lodge. Suspended initiates are whirled with sticks while turtle drums are beaten at the right foregound. At the left, a performer is offering a finger joint for sacrifice. (George Catlin, *O-kee-pa, A Religious Ceremony and Other Customs of the Mandans*, John C. Ewers [ed.]. Copyright © 1967 by Yale University Press.)

Interpretive comment

The initiates had been in limbo since first they entered the lodge. Their sex had been neutralized with sinew and clay. They neither ate nor drank. They had retired from normalcy. Suspension betwixt heaven and earth is limbo. The rites of torture were clear in their intent—the ultimate proof of worth and self-esteem. For the sacrificer, the masochism meant, "I surmount everything and achieve pleasure [goals]." For the priests and onlookers, the sadism of the act meant, "I triumph." With symbolic death the initiate's suffering was ended. The insufferability of life was made sufferable. He returned from limbo to creep back to the symbolic womb of his maternal earth lodge for recovery and reconstitution as a matured male, ready for marriage and the manipulation of the bundles he might now acquire.

Epilogue. Woman Triumphant: Fifth Night

The O-kee-pa having ended, and night having approached, several old men . . . perambulated the village . . . announcing that "the whole government of the Mandans was in the hands of one woman—she who had disarmed the Evil Spirit, and to whom they were to look during the coming year for buffaloes to supply them with food; . . . that the chiefs on that night were old women; that they had nothing to say. . . ."[15]

The Bull dancers and the priests of the Okipa were invited by the Chieftess to a Feast of the Buffalo before the Lone Man pole. Ten young women came with her. All other people had to remain secluded in their lodges. One by one, the women led the men onto the prairie to mate as

---

[15]Catlin, *op. cit.*, p. 69. By permission of Yale University Press.

FIG. 20-4 The finale of the Okipa ceremony. Initiates are running and being dragged about the Lone Man Post until their shields and the buffalo skulls tear loose. (George Catlin, *O-kee-pa, A Religious Ceremony and Other Customs of the Mandans*, John C. Ewers [ed.]. Copyright © 1967 by Yale University Press.)

buffaloes, until each man bought his release with a small payment. So ended the Okipa.

Interpretive comment

It was driven home to all Mandans that this was indeed a matrilocal, matrilineal, matrifocal, matri-dominated society. Men were an integral but subordinate part, while the Female Principle was the locus of power. Buffalo hunting was important to Mandan survival, but it was the female bison who was acknowledged as the major factor in the reproduction of the herds. Nonetheless, for the Mandans it was horticulture which most uniquely marked their character in the northern Plains. Anybody could hunt buffalo but only very special people could grow corn. And horticulture was associated with women and the Female Principle of life and social structure. This, all Mandans had to learn and accept. This was the central focus of

Mandan religion. This was the message of the Okipa. From this there could be no departure.

As Victor Turner states for the closing of all mythological cycles, "The interstructural transition stage is over. Creative chaos has become created cosmos."[16]

SELECTED READINGS

Bascom, W. R., *The Sociological Role of the Yoruba Cult-group* (American Anthropological Association, Memoir 63, 1944). An excellent study of a West African manifestation of religious organization.

Bowers, A. W., *Mandan Social and Ceremonial Organization* (1950). Pages 111–163 present a somewhat disorganized, and therefore difficult-to-read, account

---

[16]V. W. Turner, "Myth and Symbol" (*International Encyclopedia of the Social Sciences*, vol. 10, 1968), p. 581.

of the Okipa ceremony. Nonetheless, it is an essential source.

Bunzel, R., *Introduction to Zuni Ceremonialism* (Bureau of American Ethnology, Annual Report 47, 1932). Gives an idea of how pervasive and complex a highly developed primitive religious system can be.

Catlin, G., *O-kee-pa: A Religious Ceremony and Other Customs of the Mandans* (1867; Yale University Press, 1967). The first eye-witness account of the Okipa, it also contains color prints of Catlin's original paintings. Should be perused in connection with this chapter.

Geertz, C., "Religion: Anthropological Study" (*International Encyclopedia of the Social Sciences*, vol. 13, 1968), pp. 398–406. A brief summary.

Lessa, W. A., and E. Z. Vogt, *Reader in Comparative Religion* (2d ed., 1965). Parts 3, "Myth and Ritual," 4, "Symbolism," and 12, "New Methods of Analysis" contain very valuable papers by Geertz, Kluckhohn, Lévi-Strauss, and others.

Turner, V. W., "Myth and Symbol" (*International Encyclopedia of the Social Sciences*, vol. 10, 1968), pp. 576–582. Offers a lucid analysis of myths and structural transformations.

21

SUPERNATURAL BELIEFS AND PRACTICES

LEARNING GOALS

Write a summary of Tylor's theory of animism, the soul concept, and nature worship as elements in the development of religion. ¶ State how mana differs from animism, and identify its characteristics as a supernatural force. ¶ Define magic and sorcery, and specify the contrast between religious and magical concepts of supernatural power. ¶ Explain the functional nature of tabu and the belief in the danger of supernatural power. ¶ Distinguish between shamans and priests, and analyze their contrasting roles. ¶ Distinguish between ancestor worship, nature worship, and the High God concept as dominant patterns of supernatural belief.

Religion is manifest not only through symbolism and tribal ceremony. It also permeates the thought and feeling of individuals as individuals; it expresses itself through spells and incantations; it blends into magic and sorcery: it is managed by specialists—the shaman and the priest; and it may be organized into cults. Each of these will now be treated in turn.

ANIMISM

Although the overall purpose of religion is, as presented in the last chapter, symbolic transformation of humanity's perception of the universe, thus creating a conviction of order and purpose to society and individual alike, all religions encompass manifestations of *animism* and *mana*.

Animism (L. *anima*, soul, spirit), as defined by the nineteenth-century English anthropologist Sir Edward Burnett Tylor, is the belief in spirit beings.[1] They are known in many forms: plant and animal spirits, souls, ghosts, goblins, poltergeists, genies, trolls, sprites, elves, pixies, leprechauns, fairies, witches, demons, devils, angels, and gods. Their essential quality is their ethereal embodiment; they are beings without real flesh and blood—nonmaterial, but real enough for those who believe in them.

As spirits, they are uninhibited by the limitations of physical matter, by the weaknesses of human or animal flesh. They transcend matter, time, and space. They are supernatural. It is this that makes them wonderful, mysterious.

Tylor's Theory

In his remarkable study (1871), Tylor examined many manifestations of animism among primitives, but he was interested in more than just describing its forms. Tylor was essentially an evolutionist. For him the ultimate question was: "How and why did human beings create the concept of spirit beings?" Somewhere along the line in prehistoric times, the human mind peopled the universe with spirits. What led it to do so?

Tylor saw the origin of animism in the phenomena of dreams, of life and of death. Dreams are a form of hallucination, an illusory experience. But that individuals dream is an empirical fact. In dreams we transcend reality. We soar to great heights of attainment and pleasure; we experi-

---

[1]E. B. Tylor, *Primitive Culture*, vol. 1, p. 424.

ence horrible happenings; we relive the past and anticipate the future; we visit places once visited and those where our feet have never yet been; we commune with the dead and with the living who are far distant. Time, space, and limitations of the body do not hinder us—in our dreams.

Yet, in sleep or in coma, the body does not leave its resting place. We wake where we lie down to rest—except in the case of the unfortunate somnambulist. The body has not performed the miracles dreamed, but it is hard, even for the sophisticate, not to take dream experiences as real. To primitive and, indeed, to many civilized human beings, the dream experience *is* reality.

The soul concept

Primitive human beings reflected and concluded that there were two parts to a person: the bodily self of mortal flesh and the spiritual *alter ego*, the soul. The soul concept is the root of animism. It is a universal concept.

The soul is, in itself, quite intangible. In the language of many peoples, the word "soul" is synonymous with "shadow" or "shade." Intangible though it is, it is oftentimes perceptible in the image of the body it normally inhabits.

The soul is the vital force. Its presence animates the body; its departure stills it. It is in the stillness of sleep that the soul goes wandering. Humanity's restlessness is of the spirit, not the body.

The long sleep that is death comes when the sojourning soul does not return. The body that is the vessel for the soul has no further function once its soul has abandoned it. Disintegration follows. Illness is due to intrusive corruption of the soul or to soul loss.

This, according to Tylor, is the logic of the soul concept—in part.

Human beings do not live alone. The beasts of wood and field, the fowl of the air, and the fishes of the waters are also endowed with vitality. So too are the plants. By means of analogical reasoning, primitive human beings attributed souls to them also, as the cause of their vitality. Yet they do not do this completely by false analogy, for animals appear in dreams, even as do people. Thus, in most primitive belief, not only humanity but all living beings possess souls.

Souls after death may become ghosts or free spirits wholly disembodied. They live on in the world of human beings, within their very community or in a special realm, which the spirits of the living may on occasion visit or from which souls may come to visit the living.

Whether or not the concept of free spirits could arise only from the soul concept, as Tylor thought, or whether early human beings were imaginatively capable of creating the spirit concept out of mere nothingness, we shall never know. It is enough that pure spirits inhabit the believing minds of people in all societies and that these imaginary beings are thought to be beyond the laws of nature. They and souls are living elements in all religions.

Nature worship

The attribution of spirit qualities to plants and objects then produced, according to Tylor, what we call *nature worship*. From this came totemism and the creation of species deities, i.e., the deification not of persons (ancestor worship) but of animals and plants (Fig. 21-1). From these practices, Tylor derived the higher polytheism of the later barbarians, with its sky, earth, rain, thunder, lightning, fire, wind, water, sun, and moon gods, as well as gods of agriculture, hunting, birth, war, and death.

What ethnography has to teach of that great element of the religion of mankind, the worship of well and lake, brook and river, is simply this—that what is poetry to us was philosophy to early man; that to his mind water acted not by laws of force, but by life and will. . . . [2]

Tylor's notions on the origins of monotheism and the Supreme Deity will be noted in the discussion of High Gods at the close of this chapter (pages 360–361).

Of Tylor's anthropological theory of religion, it may be said that it suffers some inadequacies, but in the main we can concur with Lowie's judgment:

His theory is avowedly a psychological interpretation pure and simple, but inasmuch as it not only explains the empirical observations, but operates exclusively

---

[2]E. B. Tylor, *Primitive Culture*, vol. 2, p. 209. By permission of Harper and Row, Inc.

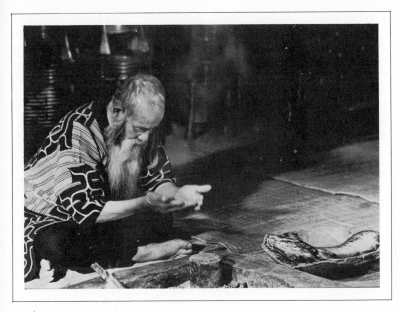

FIG. 21-1 Nature worship in an Ainu village on the island of Hokkaido, Japan. A family headman offers a prayer of thanks to the god of fishing for the first salmon of the autumn season. (Ruiko Y. Ante.)

with facts like death, dreams and visions, all of which demonstrably exercise a strong influence on the minds of primitive men, it must be conceded to have a high degree of probability. I, for one, certainly have never encountered any rival hypothesis that could be considered a serious competitor.[3]

Like all evolutionary theories that try to formulate the details of nonmaterial culture in prehistoric times, Tylor's theory is speculative and unverifiable. But, stripped of its evolutionary ordering of the data, it stands, as Lowie has said, as a valuable general analysis of a large part of the religious attitudes and behavior of human beings. Animism, however, is not the whole story. There is also *mana*, which calls for theoretical explanation.

MANA

Supernaturalism does not find its only expression in beliefs in spirit beings; there are also beliefs in the existence of supernatural forces that do not emanate from any kind of being. Such forces are expressed as special attributes of things, much as

the force of gravity is related to objects that have mass. Following the suggestion of another early student of primitive religion, R. R. Marett (1866–1943), anthropologists call it *mana*, a word derived from the languages of Melanesia where the concept of mana is strong and clear in native life.

Mana is a force, but not a vitalistic force. It exists as a supernatural attribute of persons and things. Above all, it is the exceptional power to do things that are unusual. Mana is therefore manifest in the unusual, when the unusual is not the work of spirits.

Extraordinary aptitudes of individuals are explained in terms of mana. The master craftsman in Polynesia excels in his skill because he possesses mana. The learned pundit excels in lore and knowledge because he possesses mana. The mighty warrior excels in the killing of men because he possesses mana. The outstanding healer, the expert canoeman, and any others who stand above their fellow men do so because of personal possession or control of mana. Mana, though it is an impersonal force, can be manifest in and through persons, as well as in stock and stone. The queerly shaped or unusually marked stone may be believed to possess miracle-working power. This is its mana. The canoe that

---

[3]R. H. Lowie, *Primitive Religion*, p. 108. By permission of Liveright Publishing Co.

can outdistance all others, the song that heals, the war club that smashes more than a normal quota of skulls, the talisman that in itself brings good luck—all these have power, power that is mana.

The power that is extraordinary is not mundane force. It does not follow the regular laws of ordinary technologies or skills. Like the power of spirits, it transcends the natural. Mana is supernatural.

RELIGION AND MAGIC

Human beings act on the basis of their beliefs. Animism and mana are attributes of the subjective aspects of supernaturalism. Religion and magic are concepts based upon the ways in which an individual behaves in relation to the supernatural forces in which he or she believes. They constitute two forms of the external objectification of beliefs. The distinction rests on the individual's assessment of the motivating forces behind the supernatural. Is the individual subordinate to the caprice and will of the supernatural beings to whom psychological characteristics are attributed? If the answer is "yes," the individual's dealings with these beings, and vice versa, will be religious in nature. Can the individual under certain conditions dominate and control the supernatural forces, be they animistic or manaistic? If the answer is "yes," the individual's dealings with the supernatural will be magical in nature.

Prayer and magic are the two basic techniques of dealing with the supernatural. The first is a means of seeking spiritual rapport on a basis of subordination to animistic beings. The second is a technique of gaining external control over supernatural powers, animistic and manaistic. Between these poles, every possible form of interpersonal behavior may find its religious counterpart. As Benedict observed: "There is probably no customary behavior towards one's fellows that is not to be found somewhere as a religious technique."

The only limits on religion are the limits set by imagination and the human physical system. Both allow tremendous scope for variation and elaboration. Hunting is limited by ecology, animal habits, and the physical laws of mechanics in the development of weapons. There are few variants among hunting techniques the world over; not so the varieties of religious experience and practice.

The Religious Attitude

That which distinguishes religion from magic is neither the goodness of one nor the evil of the other, but the state of mind of the believer and his consequent modes of behavior. This is the distinction that was originally pointed out by Sir James G. Frazer.[4] In the religious state of mind, the individual acknowledges the superiority of the supernatural powers upon whose action his or her well-being depends. The believer's attitudes are preponderantly those of submission and reverence. The Okipa Maker was a supplicant to Lone Man throughout the ceremony, while the initiates, according to Catlin, ". . . began crying in the most heartrending tones to the Great Spirit; imploring him to enable them to bear and survive the painful ordeal they were entering on."[5] The objective behavior put forth is manifestly that of beseeching, petition, and appeasement in prayer, offerings, and sacrifice.

> Father have pity on me,
> Father have pity on me,
> I am crying for thirst,
> I am crying for thirst,
> All is gone—I have nothing to eat,
> All is gone—I have nothing to eat.

Such is the tenor of an Arapaho ghost-dance song, "sung to a plaintive tune, sometimes with tears rolling down the cheeks of the dancers."[6] It epitomizes the religious attitude, as does the Lord's Prayer, with its "Hallowed be thy name" (reverence); "Give us this day our daily bread" (petition); "Thine is the Kingdom, the Power and the Glory, forever" (subordination and awe).

"Oh spirits, here, humble in heart, I stand beseeching you" is the opening plaint of the Winnebago on a vision quest.

---

[4]See J. G. Frazer, *The Golden Bough*, chap. 4. Frazer argued a theoretical priority of magic over religion in prehistoric origins. This is a futile and irrelevant problem for which there are no empirical data upon which to base a conclusion.

[5]G. Catlin, *O-kee-pa* (1967 edition), p. 64.

[6]J. Mooney, *The Ghost Dance Religion and the Sioux Outbreak of 1890* (Bureau of American Ethnology, Annual Report 14, 1896), p. 977.

The Magical Attitude

The magician, on the other hand, believes that he *controls* supernatural power under certain conditions. He has power over power. He feels confirmed in his belief that if he possesses a tested formula and if he executes the formula perfectly, barring outside interference, he will get the results which that formula is specified to give. The supernatural power has no volition or choice of its own. It must respond. The magician works with a confidence similar to that of the student in the laboratory who knows that if the manual instructions are followed correctly, a predictable result will be attained. The religious attitude and behavior are devout; the magician works with a kind of arrogance—or, at least, self-assurance.

Magic often does appear to produce the expected results. It seems to meet the pragmatic test. What works is so. At least, it must work in its initial applications, or the magical formula is usually rejected as false or worthless. When magic works, it does so for two reasons: (1) coincidence—if sufficient time is allowed, the desired event may well come to pass—and (2) psychological suggestion—when magic is directed against persons who suspect or fear that they are its objects, hysteria or compulsion grips them; they sicken and often die. Psychologists call this *somatic compliance* and *thanatomania* (the depression of the will to live to the point of extinction). The records of travelers and anthropologists abound with cases from the primitive world. Clinical records reveal many authentic cases among civilized people. Doctors well know the importance of the psychological state of the patient in crucial illness or injury.

Magic also serves its ends by giving the magician and his clients a needed psychological boost. As Malinowski reiterated, magic begins where mechanical technology ends. A Melanesian knows that magic cannot dig the soil in which he must plant his yams, so he does his own digging. He knows that he must hoe to keep down weeds, so he hoes. But he also knows that, no matter how great his skill, pests, foraging animals, and climate are beyond his technological ability to control. Yet these and unknown factors affect his crop for better or worse. He desperately needs a good crop. It is the object of his most ardent wish,

so he endeavors to control the unknown element by magic or religion, and the confidence they give him quite definitely helps him to outdo himself in achievement of his wished for goal.[7]

The warrior who believes he has magic invulnerability can surmount fear and leap to heroism far more easily than the man who confronts danger without such support.

Not only does magic actually help the magician to attain his end in reality, but it also fosters the illusion of attainment. When the dogma of magic is strong, the practitioner often thinks the magical result has come to pass when nothing of the sort has occurred at all. Magic has much in common with daydreaming as a form of wish fulfillment.

Thus, magic, in some of its aspects, is similar to science. When the magician proceeds on the mechanistic assumption that the magical formula is a cause that must produce a given effect, his thinking parallels that of the scientist. His method, however, rests on fantasies. But it may be well to remind ourselves that much scientific belief, formerly useful but now discarded, also rested on similar unrealistic belief. It would, perhaps, be more accurate to call magic a technique based upon different premises.

Finally, it should be noted that magic often appears to work because the primitive magician is a canny prestidigitator. He simply deceives the credulous with skilled stage settings and sleight-of-hand artistry, some of which is really convincing.

It is thus possible analytically to distinguish magic from religion. The difference between the two methods of approach to the supernatural has tremendous social consequences. Religious emphasis on supernaturalism leads to subordination of mankind to gods and to the power of cult functionaries—the shaman and the priest. Religion is much more readily centralized and organized than magic, which is inherently more individualistic. Although organized religions always use a certain amount of magic in their rituals, churches are implicitly antagonistic to magic, since the magical attitude is incompatible with the religious attitude of submission. The conflict endures through the ages.

---

[7]*Cf.* B. Malinowski, *Coral Gardens and their Magic*, vol. 1.

Because of its elemental kinship to science, magic is more susceptible to displacement by technological advances than religion is, and conversely, religion, with its element of personal dependence, is not so readily displaced by an advance in knowledge as magic is. Modern scientists may still hold to their religious faiths, but all will renounce magic.

Sorcery

Sorcery is magic used for antisocial purposes. Magic is in itself amoral, neither good nor bad. It is the uses to which magic is put that determine its moral qualities. Thus, a medicine man or witch doctor, as one who has control over magic, may be thoroughly good in the eyes of his people, or he may be evil, or both. A Shoshone medicine man is called *pohagant*, meaning "one who has power." A sorcerer is called *tidjipohagant*, or "one who uses power evilly."

Sorcery is a form of aggression against fellow beings or their possessions that is not socially approved. Magic may also be used aggressively, but it is not sorcery if its use is a socially recognized privilege-right. This is clearly shown in the attitudes of the Azande.

Azande sorcery

Among the Azande of Africa, described by Evans-Pritchard, good magic is *wene ngua* and bad magic is *gbigbita*. Vengeance magic *(bagbuduma)* may be legitimately used to kill a person if the poison oracles used by the sorcerer's kin and those used by their chief both say the alleged sorcerer is guilty. *Pe zunga* magic, which may be used when the perpetrator of homicidal sorcery is not known, is also good. "It is regarded as a judge which seeks out the person who is responsible for the death, and as an executioner which slays him." In the words of the Azande, "it decides cases" and "settles cases as judiciously as princes." Even though its effect is to kill, it is socially approved because it will work only on behalf of a just cause. If there is no just cause, it will return to kill the person who evoked it. The Zande who wants to kill another without just cause can use a

number of forms of *gbigbita* magic, but if he is discovered, he will be executed.[8]

TABU

Tabu is the inevitable negative element in religion. Supernatural power is implicitly dangerous. It is like fire or a heavy charge of electricity. When under control and directed toward desirable ends, it is beneficent. When out of control, it may well be disastrous. Humanity cannot get along without fire, and yet it must fight a constant battle against it. Modern civilization cannot function without electricity, but electricity must be handled with insulated tools and gloves.

Spirits and mana are deemed by most people to be absolutely essential forces in the human conception of the universe. They must be manipulated for human ends, but if improperly approached or used, they can react most dangerously. Running Water, the Bannock Indian, was nearly killed by his own pack-rat medicine because he became careless.

Supernatural power, it must be remembered, is above the realm of the ordinary. Because of this, it may not be approached or dealt with casually. It, too, must be handled with rubber gloves. Figuratively, tabus are great "Caution! Handle with Care!" signs. Tabu does not mean *verboten*, in the German sense. Rather, it carries the overtones of the French *défense de toucher*. The sense of awe that Professor Lowie saw as the important component of religion is intimately linked to the psychology that is responsible for the development of tabus.

In content, tabu consists of a series of negative rules, each of which states a form of behavior that will cause a supernatural power to backfire and injure the user. In reality, very few tabued acts are physically or socially dangerous in themselves. This is why rationalistic attempts to explain the Hebraic or Islamic tabus on the eating of pork in terms of hygiene are really beside the point.

Typical of the irrelevance of most tabus was the injunction that went with the war bonnet of the famous Cheyenne chieftain, Roman Nose. His

---

[8]E. E. Evans-Pritchard, *Witchcraft, Oracles and Magic among the Azande*, pp. 388–389.

bonnet had the power to give invulnerability in battle. With it Roman Nose rose, unscathed, to fame on the western Plains. One of the rules of the bonnet was that its wearer must not eat any food taken from a dish with an iron utensil. If he did, a bullet or iron-tipped arrow could pierce him, just as the sharp metal pierced the meat, and the protective power of the hat would be nullified until restored through a long and elaborate ceremony of purification and atonement.

Just before the famous Beecher's Island fight with Colonel Forsyth's men on the Republican River of western Nebraska, in 1868, Roman Nose ate as a guest in the camp of the Sioux Indians. When it was pointed out to him that the wife of his host was using a fork in her cooking, he said, "That breaks my medicine." The battle began before Roman Nose could make atonement, so, like Achilles, he sulked in his tent. But under pressure, like Achilles, he donned his war gear, saying, "My food was lifted with an iron tool, I know that I shall be killed today." Roman Nose was killed by a bullet before he had a chance to strike a single blow in the battle.[9]

Violation of a tabu not only nullifies the positive power of medicine but may also bring disaster as a consequence.

The Functions of Tabu

The first function of tabu, as just indicated, is to sustain the awesomeness of the supernatural by reinforcing attitudes of care and mystery and by punishing attitudes of carelessness and profanity in dealing with the supernatural. It helps keep the sacred, sacred.

The second function of tabu is to set off the members of one social group from those of another and to strengthen their sense of solidarity. Just as a traditional hairdo may indicate that the social status of a married woman is different from that of an unmarried girl who has only reached puberty, or as men's hairdos used to set them apart from women, so adherence to special tabus may help set off the medicine man from the ordinary person. Thus the Hebraic and Islamic

tabus on pork help to identify membership in these religious groups, as did abstinence from meat on Friday by Catholics and as does the Mormon tabu on the use of tobacco and the drinking of coffee, tea, or alcoholic beverages.

Third, tabu is an essential ingredient of social control. In Polynesia, whence comes the word "tabu," high-ranking nobles possess mana because of their direct descent from the gods. So potent is their charge of mana that their very persons are surrounded with tabus, as is everything they touch. Sin, in Polynesia as elsewhere, is the violation of a tabu—an act punishable by supernatural sanction.

Not only is tabu applied to the requirements of care in handling supernatural objects, but it also can be, and is, applied to social standards of behavior which are not directly associated with the supernatural but in which, it is held, the supernatural takes an interest.[10] Incest, for example, is commonly subject to supernatural punishment as well as to mundane social sanctions, in most societies.

RELIGIOUS SPECIALISTS

In every primitive society, all the people participate in some aspects of religious observances. Yet, because every society is internally segmented by sex, age, kinship, and marital groupings, access to religious power and the privileges of religious participation are not equally distributed. In the first place, years of experience and learning are necessary before an individual can know enough about basic religious beliefs to be in a position to master religious activities. Children always participate on a lower level.

Religion and magic are sources of power; they are means of influencing or controlling supernatural power, the greatest of all powers. Authority vested in adults is implicitly necessary to the perpetuation of culture. This is a special reason for keeping the heart of religious power in the hands of grownups.

Although women are not uncommonly shamans

---

[9]A full account of the episode is given in G. B. Grinnell, *The Fighting Cheyennes*, pp. 267–282.

[10]For an excellent example, see A. I. Hallowell, "The Social Function of Anxiety among the Salteaux Indians," in D. G. Haring (ed.), *Personal Character and Cultural Milieu* (3d rev. ed.), pp. 389–403.

and priestesses, the centers of religious power are usually vested in men. Male-dominance tendencies lead men to keep access to the supernatural as a vested interest of their own sex. The matrifocal emphasis of Mandan religion was, as we saw, an expression of their matrilineal system and as such would represent a minority of human societies.[11] In more advanced, class-stratified societies, official religious power is almost inevitably an upper-class monopoly, while folk practitioners may operate on a lower level.

Shamans

Within the group of those who qualify for religious power, there are those who achieve an even more intimate access to the supernatural. They become religious specialists. Religion and magic are always so complex and, by their very nature, so extraordinary that the lay person who is wrapped up in the day-to-day activities of making a living cannot penetrate very far into the realm of the sacred. To do this, a person must spend time away from the basic tasks of food production and must have an unusual personality and special aptitudes and skills. The men who have the time and the skills may become religious functionaries: shamans or priests. The shaman is the more primitive type of specialist. He exists in systems in which religion has not developed a church. *The shaman derives his presumptive power directly from a supernatural source*, either through mystic experience or through his ability to perform rites and his possession of paraphernalia as an individual. *The power of priests is derived from their office in a cult or church.*

Siberian shamanism

A center of the most intensive development of shamanism in the primitive world is aboriginal Siberia. The very word "shaman" comes from a native Siberian tongue. Synonyms also meaning "shaman" are "medicine man" (usually applied to American Indians), "witch doctor" (usually applied to shamans of Africa and Melanesia), and *angakok*, in Eskimo.

The Siberian shaman is more definitely set off from his fellow individuals than his North American counterpart is. For one thing, his personality is more clearly marked. For another, his "call" and training are more definite. Bogoras, the famous Siberianist, wrote of the Chukchi:

For men, the preparatory stage of shamanistic inspiration is in most cases very painful, and extends over a long time. The call comes in an abrupt and obscure manner, leaving the young novice in much uncertainty regarding it. He feels "bashful" and frightened. . . . The young novice, the "newly inspired," loses all interest in the ordinary affairs of life. He ceases to work, takes little food and without relishing it, ceases to talk to people, does not even answer their questions. The greater part of his time he spends in sleep.[12]

Bogoras observed that shamans were as a rule excitable and hysterical. He even opined that not a few of them were "half crazy." Psychiatry was not the vogue in Bogoras's day or he might have labeled the personality of the Siberian shaman "schizophrenic."

Becoming a shaman

The personal experience of a Northern Paiute Indian, who lived in western Nevada, is more or less typical of the way in which an American medicine man received power. As recorded by Willard Park, it runs as follows:

When I was a young man I had dreams in which I doctored people. I did not take those dreams seriously. My uncle was an Indian doctor. He knew what was coming to me. He told me to be careful in talking, not to speak harshly [in order not to offend the supernatural spirits]. I did not become a doctor from these dreams. Finally, I decided to go to the cave near Dayton. I was about fifty then. My uncle did not tell me to go there. I just decided to do this myself.

I went into the cave in the evening. As soon as I got inside, I prayed and asked for power to doctor sickness. I said, "My people are sick. I want to save them. I want to keep them well. You can help me make them well. I want you to help me to save them. When they have died give me power to bring them back [return the lost soul]." I said this to the spirit in the cave. It is not a person. It

---

[11]See page 214.

[12]W. Bogoras, "The Chukchee: I. Religion" (*Jesup North Pacific Expedition*, vol. 7), p. 420. By permission of the American Museum of Natural History.

comes along with the darkness. This is a prayer to the night.

Then I tried to go to sleep. It was hard to sleep there. I heard all kinds of noises. I could hear all the animals. There were bears, mountain lions, deer, and other animals. They were all in caves in the mountain. After I went to sleep I could hear people at a doctoring. They were down at the foot of the mountain. I could hear their voices and the songs. Then I heard the patient groan. A doctor was singing and doctoring for him. A woman with a sage-brush shoot in her hand danced. She moved around the fire jumping at every step. Each time she jumped she said, "hə,' hə,' hə'." Then the shaman sprinkled water on the patient with sage-brush. The singing and dancing went on for a long time. Then the singing stopped. The patient had died and the people began to cry.

After a while the rock where I was sleeping began to crack like breaking ice. A man appeared in the crack. He was tall and thin. He had the tail-feather of an eagle in his hand. He said to me, "You are here. You have said the right words. You must do as I tell you. Do that or you will have a hard time. When you doctor, you must follow the instructions that the animals give you. They will tell you how to cure the sickness. I have this feather in my hand. You must get feathers like it. You are also to find the things that go with it. Get dark beads. Put them on the quills of the feathers and tie a strip of buckskin to the quills. Also get a hoof of a deer, and down from the eagle. With these you can go to people to cure them. These are your weapons against sickness. You must get three rolls of tobacco. You can use them to tell your patients what made them sick and then you can cure them. The tobacco will also help you if you are choked with clots of saliva when you suck out the disease. With this you are beginning to be a doctor. You will get your songs when you doctor. The songs are now in a straight line [ready for use]. Bathe in the water at the foot of the cliff and paint yourself with *i · bi* [white paint]."

Then I woke up. It was daylight. I looked around but I could not see anyone. The man was gone and there was no sign of the animals or the people who had been singing and doctoring. Then I did as the spirit had ordered and waited to become a doctor. In about six years I had received enough instructions to begin to cure.[13]

Suggestibility and a greater or lesser degree of emotional instability are essential traits of the shaman who obtains power by mystic experience. He or she must be capable of hallucinations. The person who cannot respond with visions and hallucinations to the pervading cultural suggestion that these form the road to power is out of luck if he would be a shaman. Crashing Thunder, a Winnebago Indian, was one of these. Even when he faked a vision and luck seemed to confirm his power, he knew in his inner self that his power was false. An extrovert whose aggressive personality demanded social prestige and the opportunity to amount to something, he was frustrated by his intellectual hardheadedness. Not finding the social means (supernatural power) to greatness open to him, he took the antisocial road—drunkenness, rowdyism, debauchery, murder, and fraud. Then when peyote at last reached the Winnebagos, the vision-stimulating drug brought visions and power to the tortured man. With power came the reorientation of his personality. He became a pillar of society, a moral leader, and a decent citizen—much to the relief of his fellow tribesmen.[14]

The evidence is clear that as far as becoming a spirit-endowed shaman is concerned, the odds favor those who belong to what might unkindly be called the "lunatic fringe." But the cultures of these people turn their peculiarities to account and make honored medicine men and women of them.

Shamanistic magic

The shaman, as inheritor of magical power, is a different matter. True, the magician is the dupe of his own beliefs, but it is possible for him to work with cold calculation. Highly developed magic often involves sheer fraud, skill in prestidigitation, and the creation of optical illusions (see Fig. 21-2). Siberian and Eskimo shamans are skilled ventriloquists, using their tambourines so to deflect their voices that the listeners "after a few minutes . . . begin to lose the power to locate the source of the sound. . . . The song and drum seem to shift from corner to corner, or even to move about without having any definite place at all."[15]

---

[13]W. Z. Park, *Shamanism in Western North America*, pp. 27–28. By permission of Cooper Square Publications, Inc.

[14]P. Radin (ed.), *Crashing Thunder*. This book should not be missed by any student of anthropology.

[15]Bogoras, *op. cit.*, p. 430.

FIG. 21-2 Shamanistic curing by a Zulu doctor of South Africa. The illness is caused by an intrusve element in the head which is sucked out through the ear with the aid of the horn. Herbs and other materials used in the ritual cure lie ready-to-hand on the blanket. (Photo by Ewing Galloway.)

The Algonkian Indian medicine man holds impressive séances in which the tent rocks and pitches violently upon the arrival of his "spirit." The tent is cleverly constructed to be manipulated mechanically with ropes and thongs.[16]

Pueblo Indian priests put on miracle dramas in which corn grows and ripens overnight and deer and bears materialize before the astounded eyes of uninitiated spectators. Some *kivas* are equipped with secret tunnels through which the props and actors are brought upon the scene.[17]

However, the deceit practiced by shamans may not always be such crass charlatanism as it at first appears. Eskimo shamans often disclaim their own skill, as did one of the best of them to Peter

Freuchen: "This is nothing for a man like you to look at. I am only a big liar, and even if these idiots are stupid enough to believe me, I never expected you to stand for it. I am a foolish old man, and what happens here has nothing to do with the truth."[18] But the effect of his performance on the people in the igloo was ecstasy. People are not averse to being fooled if it gives pleasure. Beyond that, of course, credulous ones are duped without their being the wiser.

It is difficult to draw an accurate balance between the exploitative and the social-service activities of the primitive shamans. It is a false gesture to dismiss them solely as a class of exploiters. Yet it is true they often turn their position and power to self-advantage. Eskimo shamans can impose almost any tabus they wish on individuals. They can sexually exploit women, married and unmarried, to gratify themselves in the name of spirits. Shamans can use their power

---

[16]F. Densmore, "An Explanation of a Trick Performed by Indian Jugglers" (*American Anthropologist*, vol. 34, 1932), pp. 310–314.

[17]E. A. Hoebel, "Underground Kiva Passages" (*American Antiquity*, vol. 19, 1953), p. 76; and F. M. Hawley, "Jemez Kiva Magic and Its Relation to Features of Prehistoric Kivas" (*Southwestern Journal of Anthropology*, vol. 8, 1952), pp. 147–163.

[18]P. Freuchen, *Arctic Adventure*, p. 113.

particularly to consolidate the position of the elders as against the younger generation. But for this they must pay a price in self-denial of many things, for their work is dangerous in its own terms, and the burden of shamanism is often hard.

PRIESTS

Priesthood is a manifestation of developed religion. It occurs in the more ordered primitive societies whose cultures are rich and complex. On the whole, it calls for an economic base of sufficient richness to support fairly large populations, plus some food and wealth surpluses. It is necessary to be able to organize and sustain permanent cults. The priest may have mana, but his power is less his own than the power resident in the office he holds. Unlike the shaman, he does not acquire his sacredness personally. He is vested in his succession to the *office* of priest. He becomes part of a religious corporation.

There are basically three kinds of priests: (1) those who serve inherited or enduring medicine bundles; (2) the family heads in ancestor-worshiping religions who serve as priestly intermediaries between the kinship group and the deceased ancestors; and (3) the priests who serve cult groups whose interests are directed toward special spirits or deities.

Incipient priesthood is revealed in Gulliver's account of a Jie rainmaking ceremony:

At a ritual assembly, supplications are made by a leader, supported by the chorus of the other men present. The seniormost man present, holding a ritual wand, stands in the open space inside the cluster of seated men; he addresses *Akuj* [the High God] directly, explaining the reason for the assembly and seeking benevolent assistance. Interspersed in the monologue are communal supplications led by the standing man, in which his specific pleas . . . are echoed by the others' chorus. After the seniormost man, other seniors in turn take up the leadership. When a man begins to assume this role with the approval of his more senior associates he has achieved notable seniority [which includes the priestly role].[19]

It should be added that to achieve seniority and

priesthood, he must have power from the High God, too.

Although in many primitive cultures there is a recognized division of function between priests and shamans, in the more highly developed cultures in which cults have become strongly organized churches, the priesthood fights an unrelenting war against shamans. Priests work in a rigorously structured hierarchy fixed in a firm set of traditions. Their power comes from, and is vested in, the organization itself. They constitute a religious bureaucracy. Shamans, on the other hand, are arrant individualists. Each is on his own, undisciplined by bureaucratic control; hence, a shaman is always a threat to the order of the organized church. In the view of the priests, they are presumptive pretenders. Joan of Arc was a shaman, for she communed directly with the angels of God. She steadfastly refused to recant and admit delusion, and her martyrdom was ordained by the functionaries of the Church. The struggle between shaman and priest may well be a death struggle.

Priestesses are much less common than female shamans, probably because the organization of associations tends to be correlated almost exclusively with the male sex in primitive societies.

ANCESTOR WORSHIP AND CULTS OF THE DEAD

Ancestor worship is by no means a universal form of religious expression, although belief in the spiritual immortality of the dead is. All cultures call for cognizance of ghosts, and all provide some means of dealing with them. The intensity of ghost awareness, however, and the amount of concern over the activity and feelings of ghosts are variable. In North America, the Pueblo Indians pay little attention to ghosts; the Plains Indians fear them, but their ghosts are not too prevalent; and the Navahos and Eskimos are bedeviled by ghost anxiety. They possess definite ghost cults, a body of practices and ritual observances associated with the propitiation or avoidance of ghosts.

Most traditional Plains Indians and the Navahos even today abandon any house in which a person has died. The ghost haunts the house and disturbs the inhabitants. Navahos, therefore, take a seriously ill patient who is about to die outdoors

---

[19]P. H. Gulliver, "The Jie of Uganda," in J. L. Gibbs, Jr. (ed.), *Peoples of Africa*, p. 188. Copyright © Holt, Rinehart and Winston, Inc. Used by permission.

in order to save the house, or they rush him to the Indian Service Hospital, which is already heavily inhabited by ghosts: a house of the dead, not of healing. The Arizona desert is dotted with hogans abandoned because a death has occurred within. In recent times, one Shoshone Indian dismantled a log house that he had inherited from his brother, moved it a few hundred feet, and then reassembled it, after mixing up the logs to fool the ghost of his brother, who was then unable to recognize the new house. Ghost fear has been a hindrance to Indian Service efforts to provide modern housing on some reservations. In the northern Plains, a workable expedient acceptable to the Indians in some places has been the fumigation of the house as an effective antidote to ghosts.

Eskimos believe that ghosts are harmful and relentlessly malicious as long as they remain in the memory of the living. On death, the corpse is not removed from the igloo by way of the door; this would make it too easy for the lingering ghost to reenter. Rather, a hole is chopped in the back, later to be refilled after removal of the body. This baffles the ghost. Then, in case the ghost does find the entrance, knives are set in the snow floor of the doorway for three nights after burial. Such booby traps discourage ghosts. Among Eskimos, as with many other people, the name of the dead is tabued, lest it summon the reappearance of the ghost. Later, the name is given to a newborn child, reincarnating the name soul of the deceased ancestor.

Comanches also tabu names of the dead, but when they want to mention a defunct friend named Pork, for example, they call him Bacon. Ghosts are literal-minded, but people can get the idea.

Eskimos, like many other people, bury the dead with grave offerings—the personal equipment and gifts of friends and relatives to serve the ghost in the other world. These are "killed." They are broken to release the animate soul of the object. For it is the spiritual counterpart of the goods that obviously is used in the spirit world.

Plains Indians also sacrificed a warrior's favorite horse on his grave, as did medieval Europeans at times. This is no longer Occidental practice, but the officer's horse led behind the casket-bearing caisson with reversed saddle and upturned stirrups still follows the hero to his grave, only to be spared the final sacrifice.

Grave sacrifices were stepped up to extravagant heights for the royalty of Africa and India. Into the nineteenth century, Hindu wives were immolated on the funeral pyres of their princely husbands. In Dahomey in West Africa, whole corps of wives and retainers were slain to provide an adequate retinue for the deceased king. Shoshone and Comanche tradition has it that in ancient times, wives were killed to accompany their husbands' spirits, but in more recent days, the wives followed the general Plains Indian practice of self-mutilation and abnegation.

Ghost cults usually emphasize the malevolence of ghosts. The people of Manus in Melanesia are an exception. The ghost of the last deceased household head is the preceptor and protector of his family. He is addressed as "Sir." He punishes their moral derelictions, but above all he is busy thwarting the malignant efforts of other ghosts. All ghosts are malicious toward people not of their own kinship group. The social and economic rivalry that is characteristic of everyday Manus life continues in the afterworld through the jealousy and rivalry of the ghosts. Each ghost enjoys a brief span of immortal existence while his skull adorns the doorway of his family hut. But the death of an adult male in the household is an indication that the family ghost has not been on the job. He has been negligent enough to permit a rival ghost to kill his descendant. He is no good. Therefore his skull is thrown out and replaced by that of his successor, who then rules as the Honored Ghost of the household until he, too, fails in his duty.[20]

Ancestor Cults

Ancestor worship is both an elaboration and an abstraction of the ghost cult. As an elaboration, it is best seen among the Bantu tribes of Africa. Every lineage and clan has its distinct ancestral deities, who are gods to their descendants but

---

[20]R. F. Fortune, *Manus Religion* (Proceedings of the American Philosophical Society, 1935); and M. Mead, "The Manus of the Admiralty Islands," in *Cooperation and Competition among Primitive Peoples*, pp. 210–239. But see M. Mead, *New Lives for Old*, for post-World War II changes in Manus religion.

who are ignored by the members of other kinship groups. The gods of royal clans, because the heads of such clans must be honored by all the kingdom, are worshiped not only by the royal clan itself but also by all the subjects of the king. In ancestor-worshiping cults of this order, the eldest ranking member of the kinship group is not only its headman but also its priest. He stands nearest to the ancestral gods. He is the intercessor on behalf of his kinsmen. On the gods' behalf, he is the intermediary who is responsible for controlling the acts of his family or clan members. As in modern Japan, he has to keep the ancestral gods informed of the state of affairs within his domain. The Mikado had merely to make a ceremonial report at the ancestral shrine, but in Dahomey in West Africa, it was customary to execute a couple of victims to carry the royal message to the ancestors whenever the king had anything of moment to report.

Periodic elaborate feasts and sacrifices on behalf of the ancestral gods are characteristic of the western Sudan. In Dahomey, such ceremonies are held by each clan every year, with litanies, dancing, offerings of food and libations of liquors, and sacrifice of animals. In the annual ceremonies of the royal clan, human victims used to be offered.

Voodoo

Vodun,[21] among West Indies Negroes, is a syncretism of Dahomean ancestral rites and Catholicism.[22] The clan founders of Dahomey are known as *tovodun,* from whom the *vodun* cult is named. Vodun rites are fundamentally family rituals with offerings and sacrifices accompanied by chants and dances, in which various gods are impersonated and called upon to visit the ceremony. Dancers representative of specific gods are possessed in turn as each god is called with his drum *salute* (greeting). The trance behavior of the votaries and the ecstasy of the worshipers lend the eerie wild-

FIG. 21-3 An ancestral cult figure from the Sepik River of New Guinea. (Private collection. Photo by Don Breneman.)

---

[21] *Vodun* is the phonetically correct name for the cult complex popularly called *voodoo.*

[22] See M. J. Herskovits, "African Gods and Catholic Saints in New World Negro Belief" (*American Anthropologist,* vol. 39, 1937), pp. 635–643; and G. E. Simpson, "The Vodun Service in Northern Haiti" (*American Anthropologist,* vol. 42, 1940), pp. 236–254.

ness to the performance that has given *vodun* its exotic reputation.

Ancestor worship as an abstraction of ghost worship occurs where gods are thought once to have been human beings but where the more recently deceased are not believed to be potent deities. This may be said to be true of Polynesian and Pueblo Indian religions. Maori chieftains are lineal descendants of gods through primogeniture. Honor is due these gods, but there is no cult of the dead. The masked gods, *kachinas*, of the Pueblos are vaguely thought of as ancestral beings, but dead ancestors are not worshiped as such.

Social conservatism is a characteristic feature of ancestor-worshiping religions. The ancestors as moral preceptors do not favor change from the social practices they knew while alive. Since they punish moral lapses with death and illness and their standards are the old ones, the religious sanctions toward conformity are powerful.

NATURE WORSHIP

Cults deifying various features of nature abound in the primitive world. Among agricultural and gardening peoples, sun, rain, and fertility deities are outstanding. Solstitial rites marked the annual crisis of the sun in the religion of the megalith builders of Neolithic Europe. Mysterious Stonehenge and Avebury in England and the cromlechs of Carnac in Brittany are aligned to the rising sun at the time of the spring solstice, as is the sun stone in the famous Sun Temple of Mesa Verde National Park in Colorado, built by prehistoric Pueblo Indians 700 years ago. In ancient Rome, the solstice rites of the Mithraic cult gave way to the Christian Christmas celebration of the birth of Christ as the new light of the world. Each pueblo in the Southwest today has its priestly sunwatcher, who controls the ceremonial cycle with the movements of the sun. Pious people greet the sun with prayer each day.

All the religions in the great Central American culture complex made much of the sun. The Pyramid of the Sun near Mexico City is one of the truly great monuments of all the world. The Natchez of Mississippi and the Incas of Peru built theocratic states around the principle of sun divinity. The Natchez high chief was also high priest, called the Sun, or Brother of the Sun. The Inca of Peru was the personification of the divine sun. And until the disaster of 1945 induced the Emperor of Japan to deny it by imperial edict, he was supposed to be a divinity directly descended from the mythical sun goddess Amaterasu.

The sun figured greatly in Plains Indian religion. All tipis opened east, and tribal camp circles likewise. By the nineteenth century, the midsummer Sun Dance had come to be one of the most spectacular of Plains ceremonials.[23]

Although the sun looms large in the mythologies of the peoples of the Pacific area, it does not assume importance as an actual deity. This is true also of Africa and most of North America. Ancient Europe, the countries of the Mediterranean basin, and India were the great seats of sun worship.

In Africa and Polynesia, although the sun is not glorified, nature worship is not neglected. The entire universe is departmentalized among gods of the skies, earth, waters, trees, and thunder, with myriads of subdivisions among the specialized deities. On the less-than-god levels, all primitive religions include multitudes of nature spirits associated with particular spots, trees, volcanoes, mountains, rivers, lakes, and rocks.

To primitive human beings, the whole world lives. Souls, animate things, and whatsoever embodies the soul are spirit beings to be treated with religion or magic—or both.

THE HIGH GOD CONCEPT

The time has passed when informed civilized people could think the primitive mind incapable of conceiving of a Supreme Being or High God. Tylor's greatest error was to infer that the High God concept could be only the end product of a long intellectual evolution, beginning with the soul concept and leading through ghost and ancestor worship to polytheistic nature worship and monotheism.[24]

The actual occurrence and distribution of the High God concept is now clearly delineated in the *Ethnographic Atlas.* It is rarest in Pacific Island religious systems, where only one-fourth manifest

---

[23]See G. A. Dorsey, "The Cheyenne, II, The Sun Dance" (*Field Columbian Museum, Publication 103, Anthropological Series*, vol. 9, no. 2, 1905) for a good description of a typical sun dance with many illustrations. Volume 16 of the *Anthropological Papers of the American Museum of Natural History* contains descriptions of other tribal sun dances.

[24]E. B. Tylor, *Primitive Culture.*

it. In East Eurasia and North and South America, somewhat less than half the cultures include the idea of a High God.

Among the Oceanic and American Indian tribes which did have the High God concept, he was usually otiose, on the whole unapproachable and disinterested.

Clearly, however, the center of the idea is the Mediterranean area, where 97 per cent of all cultures center around it. Judaism, Christianity, and Islam are its most evident manifestations, but the idea goes much deeper than that. In Sub-Saharan Africa 86 per cent of the tribal religions include the High God. There is a marked difference in the relation of the High God to societal ethos in the Mediterranean and Sub-Saharan areas, however. In Negro Africa the High God figures in the cosmology but he is not involved with human affairs or morality. What human beings do is their concern and that of their ancestral gods, but none of his. In Mediterranean religions, on the other hand, the High God is very much concerned with human affairs and morality (in 86 per cent of the cultures). He is a moral censor, rewarding and punishing according to strict behavioral codes. He is the apex of the system of social control.[25]

Outside of the strongly monotheistic Mediterranean religions, the acts of creation by the High God are only vaguely conceived in cosmological lore. Myths tell how he created departmental, executive subdeities charged with the responsibility for filling in the details of creation and running the universe. These are the gods individuals must appease and pray to. They are the ones who deliver or withhold the goods. Evil in life is due to their perversity or maliciousness. A common counterpart of the High God is a Trickster or Transformer, like Coyote among the western American Indians, who spoils or modifies the good work of the creator to burden man with death, sin, and travail. The Trickster is the equivalent of the serpent in the Garden of Eden.[26]

Radin's Theory

Paul Radin (1885–1963) posited two contrasting types of human mentality, idealist and realist.[27] Idealists are individuals of intellectual and reflective temperament, individuals whom anthropological experience has shown to be present in small numbers among all peoples. They philosophize on the conundrum of life and the universe. Their thought seeks a direct, unified, orderly cause in explanation of the universe. The product of their thought is the Supreme Being. As idealists, they are little concerned with crass, material desires. Their god is free from the petty demands of men.

Pospisil's description of Kapauku religious ideology states Radin's case exactly:

Most of the Kapauku people do not ponder the nature of life and the universe around them. They are empiricists who are not inclined to speculate and philosophize. The topics that interest them do not concern the supernatural or metaphysics; indeed, they usually talk about such unphilosophical subjects as contemporary power relations, concrete monetary transactions, love affairs, or news concerning pig feasts and dancing. Philosophizing they leave to the few especially gifted individuals who make it their hobby to try to penetrate the nature of things beyond the barrier imposed by the human senses. Accordingly, the systematic and logically consistent philosophy that is described next is by no means the property of the Kapauku tribe as a whole; it belongs to a few very intelligent individuals from the southern part of the Kamu Valley who have elaborated their views of the universe into a logical systematic whole.[28]

The bulk of individuals, alas, are materialists. Their bellies, their health, wealth, and social power mean much to them. They develop religion in terms of gods and spirits, who control the means to satisfy these needs. When prayer, appeasement, and magic suffice to win the desired results, all goes well. But hunger, illness, failure, and death stalk the earth, for which the lesser gods and the forces of evil are responsible. Toward them human emotions are ambivalent. The gods and spirits are both loved and feared. The emotional overtones of religion are mixed indeed. But taken in the main, the anthropologist cannot,

---

[25]Data from E. Bourguignon and L. Greenbaum, *Diversity and Homogeneity*, table 23, p. 45.

[26]Compare here the Mandan Okipa myth in its handling of Coyote as Creator, Lone Man as beneficent transformer, and the Foolish One as would-be destructive transformer.

[27]P. Radin, *Monotheism in Primitive Religion*; see also *Primitive Man as Philosopher*.

[28]L. Pospisil, *The Kapauku Papuans of West New Guinea*, p. 83. By permission of Holt, Rinehart and Winston, Inc.

on the basis of the facts, concur in the idealistic belief that religion in all its history represents solely humanity's striving for the highest values of life. Nor is it possible to derive religion from any single mainspring of motivation. Belief in souls, fear of ghosts, fear of fear, worship of ancestors, traffic with hosts of spirits, nature worship, and philosophical reflection all play their parts. Emphasis shifts from culture to culture, but religion is a growth with many roots and many fruits.

SELECTED READINGS

Evans-Pritchard, E. E., *Nuer Religion* (1956). A penetrating field study of the concept and role of supernatural forces in a culture that lacks dogma, liturgy, sacraments (in a strict sense), and a developed religious cult and mythology.

Goode, W. J., *Religion among the Primitives* (1951). This book undertakes to scrutinize the interrelations of religion with other aspects of culture.

Howells, W. W., *The Heathens* (1948). A lively overview of primitive religious practices.

Hsu, F. L. K., *Religion, Science and Human Crisis* (1952). A case study of the uses of magic, religion, and scientific medicine in the folk response to a cholera epidemic in a Chinese village.

LaBarre, W., *The Ghost Dance* (1970). The origins of religions brilliantly analyzed and presented as a crisis phenomenon. The approach combines anthropology, psychoanalysis, and classical scholarship with great erudition, insight, and readability.

Lessa, W. A., and E. Z. Vogt, *Reader in Comparative Religion* (2d ed., 1965). Pages 253–559 contain a wealth of original articles and selections on the subjects of the present chapter.

Lowie, R. H., *Primitive Religion* (1924). Vignettes of several primitive religions, followed by a critical discussion of a number of anthropological theories of religion.

Norbeck, E., *Religion in Primitive Society* (1961). A concise and well-balanced general introduction to the subject of religion as a social phenomenon.

22

LANGUAGE*

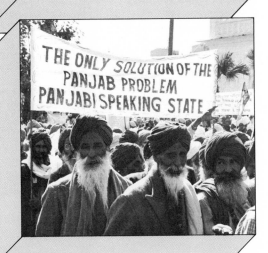

LEARNING GOALS

Briefly account for the origins of language. ¶ Discuss some types of nonverbal communication. ¶ Demonstrate that language is a cultural phenomenon. ¶ Identify phonology, morphology, syntax, and transformational grammar. ¶ Characterize the study of semantics and its relation to the structure of language and individual speech patterns. ¶ Explain the relation between language and culture according to the Sapir-Whorf hypothesis. ¶ Identify ethnosemantics and componential analysis. ¶ Summarize the comparative method, glottochronology, and lexicostatistics as tools for studying the growth of languages.

Without language, human culture would be wholly impossible. All sentient animals communicate, and some, like bees and porpoises, apparently do so extremely well. But it is only human beings who are able to generalize, to create explanations, and thus to build up the body of traditions which can be identified as human culture. What is not clear about animals other than human beings is the extent to which their patterns of communication are learned. Human beings learn a language just as they learn a culture; they are not born with a language. Thus language is "a distinctly human system of behavior based on oral symbols" which is "used to describe, classify and catalogue experiences, concepts, and objects."[1] Language, therefore, is a special system of communication that is specifically *oral* and *symbolic*. And it is learned.

ANTHROPOLOGICAL LINGUISTICS

Anthropologists, whether social or cultural, interested in penetrating the modes of life of different peoples around the world, are confronted with the problems of communicating with those peoples. They may observe what goes on, noting the patterns which arise in the day-to-day activities among the people whose culture concerns them. But they also need to know the meaning of what goes on and how the people feel about it. Researchers must rely on interpreters or learn the language themselves. Ideally, to comprehend the lifeways of a people requires more than the simple sentence or even the hints which may come from the use of a bilingual person who serves as an interpreter. Therefore, conscientious field workers will probably undertake to use the language spoken by the group under study. But quite apart from the need to communicate in an alien speech, to learn it and achieve some degree of mastery over it, anthropologists quickly become aware that through a study of language new avenues of perception are opened, with unsuspected perspectives on human behavior reflecting special kinds of insights. Language, in other terms, not only underlies culture but offers a series of ways of penetrating culture and cultures.

Linguistics is a field of study in its own right. Here the specialists are not necessarily anthropol-

---

*This chapter was written with the collaboration of Robert F. Spencer.

[1]R. F. Spencer, "Language," in J. Gould and W. L. Kolb (eds.), *Dictionary of the Social Sciences*, p. 377.

ogists, although they may be. The interests of linguists lie in the many and varied forms of language of which the human being is capable. Linguists may be concerned, for example, with differing grammatical structures or with the fact that one language may have very different modes of expression from another. They may be interested in the history of languages or in learning how one language is related to another. To conventional linguists, the study of language and languages is often an end in itself. Anthropological linguists tend to add a somewhat different dimension. They are more interested in language as a phenomenon within cultures, and in understanding the intricate ways in which language and culture relate to each other.

Anthropological linguistics grew out of the need of anthropologists to learn unwritten, exotic languages which are very different from anything that Europeans had previously known. Out of necessity, anthropological linguists like Franz Boas, Edward Sapir, and Leonard Bloomfield were in the forefront in developing ways of learning strange languages quickly and of reducing unwritten languages to writing by means of phonetic alphabets. In recent years, however, the techniques and problems associated with language have been so refined that a virtually new discipline has emerged. As this book is being written, anthropological linguists are engaged in opening some suggestive and sometimes startling frontiers (see pages 375–376).

The Origins of Language

Prehistoric archaeology, as we now know, provides some evidence on the origins of culture, but we can find no artifacts that suggest when or how language might have come into being. Does the making of fire or a stone ax require language? Who knows? But the development of technological traditions over time implies that some sophisticated means of communication proved necessary. Around the turn of this century, scholars devoted considerable time to speculation about the origins of language. Then the question was abandoned as a fruitless pursuit, only to be revived in the present day as better knowledge of the ecological, social, and physiological factors underlying the existence of language has been developed.[2]

It is an interesting fact that the human being has no organs which have evolved especially to produce speech. Most mammals can make sounds, and they have tongues, lips, teeth, larynx, and lungs, none of which has sound-making as a primary function. Yet human beings have these body parts so combined that they can produce the sounds of language. Apes, which are like humans in their general facial and mouth structure, are capable of producing all the sounds that human beings make. Yet none of mankind's closest primate relatives has developed patterns of speech. How is it then that human beings can talk? The answer is that rather than any special adaptiveness to speech as such, the human being possesses a brain which makes speech possible. It is a matter of cortical control over the speech organs.

Perhaps it is here where language bridges the gap between the biological and the cultural. Any language is a learned system, it is true; but there is every indication that humanity's capacity for language is genetic, related to the growth of the forebrain and reflecting a neurophysiological breakthrough, or "tipover," toward true speech. It is known that mammals and primates other than human beings possess calls in which meaning, a semantic element, may be present. But sounds or even meaning alone do not make language. What mankind has achieved is to be able to give structure to its utterances, giving them significant form and clothing them with an "aura of displacement," i.e., a quality of metaphorical allusion and abstraction. To some extent, animals other than human beings can do this, and there is the laboratory evidence in the recent studies of the chimpanzee Washoe, who learned to use some eighty signs from the American Sign Language, the language used by deaf people in North America.[3] Yet Washoe could not do what a human infant

---

[2]For a full and well-informed discussion of this matter, see C. D. Hockett and R. Ascher, "The Human Revolution" (*Current Anthropology*, vol. 5, 1964), pp. 135–168.

[3]J. Bronowski and U. Bellugi, "Language, Name, and Concept" (*Science*, vol. 168, 1970), pp. 669–673. See also R. A. Gardner and B. T. Gardner, "Early Signs of Language in Child and Chimpanzee" (*Science*, vol. 187, 1975), p. 752.

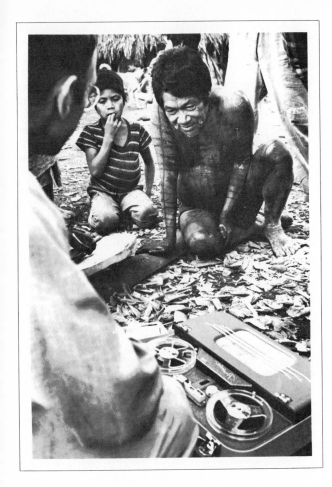

FIG. 22-1 Playback. An Amarakaeri tribesman listens to his tape-recorded speech. (Cornell Capa, Magnum; from Matthew Huxley and Cornell Capa, *Farewell to Eden*, Harper and Row, New York.)

does; she could not attach meaning to specific sounds, form them by analogy, and so develop a series of speech patterns.

The ability to achieve this sense of "grammar," or patterned structure, must have been slow in developing. A modern human being gets it early in life, and relatively quickly, receiving a neural "imprint." The human brain, like the man-made computer, has developed to the point where information can be stored and retrieved, patterned and reproduced at will.

Assuming that a genetic breakthrough to true language as a result of mankind's biological evolution took place in Lower Pleistocene times, it no longer becomes necessary to ask why the languages of human beings are so diverse. It is rather that the preconditions of human behavior which evoked language, social life, and the use of tools appeared at various places wherever clusters of human populations arose. By the same token, wherever human beings appeared they quickly produced and still produce languages as finished systems. This is why there is no such thing as a "primitive" language today. All languages (however much they differ) are matured speech systems.

Cues and Communication

Many ways of communicating exist that do not utilize language. Cries of warning and aggression and "purrs" of contentment and affection are forms of communication not limited to people. Much progress has been made since the early 1960s by *ethologists*, the students of the comparative behavior of all living beings, toward the understanding of the circumstances under which various living species effect communication between themselves. The mating dances of various birds, the grooming and licking in which some species engage, and the establishment and defense of space by other species are all points suggestive of aspects of communication. Nor can mankind be excluded from ethological studies either. Human beings do use their bodies to communicate virtually as much as they employ formal language. What indeed can be more universal than the friendly expression of a smile? And yet such facial expressions, in themselves modes of communication, are also learned. There are happy smiles and sad smiles, different smiles for different occasions. Even the smiling baby becomes aware that its expression may bring a reward.[4] Yet the use of the smile is by no means universal. There are cultures where babies do not smile. Moreover, in such a facial gesture as the smile, muscles and movements are brought into play and controlled according to understandings which lie in learned behavior, i.e., in culture.

Kinesics and proxemics

We all know that languages may call for the use of the hands or the body as a means of conveying what the verbal sentence does not say. Gestures, in short, may become an adjunct of language and a vital factor in various kinds of social communication. The study of gestures *(kinesics)* is still in its infancy. By examining the nature of the message expressed through the use of gestures, one can perceive a good deal of the emotive, the psychological, direction of communication. Such gestures may be seen to relate to culturally defined habits. To an American, the nod of the head means "yes," but in the Middle East, a single nod of the head is a clear "no."

Some students of the communication problem have been concerned with *proxemics*, an area which may be defined as reflecting nearness or distance in human communication. The use of space in communication is also a culturally learned thing. North American business persons in a conference may choose to sit or stand at a prescribed distance from each other, usually keeping a table between them; they may well be taken aback by a Latin American colleague who inclines to move in much closer in a conversation. To a Westerner, it is sometimes surprising to see two Arab boys walking hand in hand. Yet this is expected behavior in the Arab world and carries with it no sexual implication. American men usually walk closely side by side, while they permit women to precede them as a form of politeness. But among Shoshone Indians it is different; the clincher in an argument over the senior author's presence at a sun dance was, "He is one of us. He is not like those whites who hold hands with their wives. Haven't you seen how he always walks in front of his wife?" (An anthropological adage: When in Shoshone, do as the Shoshones do.)

These are only some of a vast range of cues (events or things that have a conventional meaning) in which human beings may engage. It is clear, however, that all social behavior depends on the understanding of cues. The responder who "reads" a cue is in a position to act in a predictable manner within a given situation. The understanding of cues is absolutely essential to effective participation in any social setting, be it animal or human. In order to have the inside view of a culture, one must know its cues like a native.[5] Language cues are *spoken* cues. They are able to rise to high levels of complexity—far beyond anything achievable in animal communication—because of mankind's capacity to generalize and abstract.

Parallels and Process in Language and Culture

Culture and language, both learned, are the distinctive attributes of mankind. All human beings live in accordance with a culture, but the culture of the modern Englishman is not the same as the culture of a Zulu. This we already realize. Similarly, all people have language, but English is not the

---

[4]R. L. Birdwhistell, *Kinesics and Context*, pp. 29–39.

[5]This fact is demonstrated in a fascinating way in a popular book by E. T. Hall. He makes a point when he calls his book *The Silent Language*, but confuses the issue by so doing, because language is spoken. Communication may be silent.

same as Zulu, Chinese, or Twi. As cultures vary, so also do languages.

But language and culture do not necessarily go hand in hand. There are peoples who speak mutually unintelligible languages but who share in the same cultural traditions. In the American Southwest, for example, the town-dwelling Pueblo Indians, basically much alike in culture, speak languages related to four quite separate groupings. Unless a man from Zuñi learns Hopi, he cannot communicate with a Hopi, unless they both speak Spanish or English! Or, on the other hand, peoples with very different cultures may be able to communicate through language across the barriers of cultural difference. Again, in the native American Southwest, the populous Navaho can converse quite readily with his Apache neighbor, even though the two have essentially different cultures. What is still more interesting is that both Navaho and Apache can make themselves understood in interior Alaska, thousands of miles away. The Athabascan speech family, to which both the Navaho-Apache and the interior Alaskan Indians belong, has apparently been spread fairly recently, so that some degree of mutual intelligibility remains. Clearly, too, the cultures of the southwestern desert dwellers differ from those of the peoples of the subarctic coniferous forest.

Culture and language may relate in special and subtle ways. The reason a people speaks the language that it does depends largely on the accidents of history, on such factors as isolation, contact, migration, or conquest. It does not follow that because a people has a certain kind of culture, it will speak a certain type of language. What appears to occur is that, as distinctly human phenomena, language and culture parallel each other processually, i.e., in the ways in which they *operate*. Thus, just as one may conceptualize a culture as an integrated system, a "whole" that is more than the sum of its parts, so also does a language assume a holistic character. It is, in fact, easier to delimit linguistic boundaries than it is to draw cultural ones. Where one language leaves off to be replaced by another, even though there may be blurring or bilingualism at the borders, is still easily seen. Great Russian, for example, a dominant language of the U.S.S.R., shades off in the western part of the country and is displaced by Ukrainian and Polish. Closely related to Russian though these languages may be, they are still quite distinct; there is no doubt in the mind of anyone familiar with them that a linguistic boundary has been crossed.

A culture, as we know, may incorporate borrowed elements; it may have inventions added to it; it changes gradually and organically through time. Language operates in the same way. Speakers of one language may borrow and incorporate, not only words, but also elements of grammatical structure from other languages. In English, for example, there is a vast number of *lexemes* (words, dictionary entries) drawn from languages all across the world. From Japanese come "typhoon" and "kimono," and from Carib, an American Indian language of the West Indies, there are "cigar," "hammock," and "hurricane." English can invent as well, admitting new concepts to both the language and the culture. "Hifi," "generation gap," or "pot" would have been pure nonsense words to Shakespeare. But just as some cultures accept change readily, others may resist change. The same is true of language where there can be striking conservatism. Unlike English, there are languages whose very structure is incapable of accommodating new terms or words. Chinese, to name one such, with its basic vocabulary made up of words of essentially a single syllable, cannot adapt to polysyllables. The result is the Chinese "loan translate" of a new item of technology; for example, the telephone is called "lightning speak." Yet the Chinese people clearly understand this to mean the same thing as "telephone." Chinese evolves a whole series of single-syllable combinations which handle adequately the complexities not only of technology from the West, but philosophical ideology as well. The Navaho in the American Southwest, to cite another example, becomes quite anatomical in referring to the parts of an automobile; an engine is the car's "stomach," the fenders its "wings." And the Germans, when tanks first appeared in World War I, named them *Grabenübergehendenkraffwaggonen* "trench/over/going/power/vehicles."

Some languages borrow not only words from others, but elements of grammar as well. In the Far East, there are the many languages classed with the Sinitic or Chinese grouping. To be sure, there are the different languages, sometimes erroneously called dialects, of China itself. But there are also Burmese, Thai, Vietnamese, Laotian, and many others that seem to share with Chinese the tonalities, the pitch of the voice necessary to communication. Although there may be a genetic relationship between these languages, it appears that they resemble each other primarily in the tonal pitch of the voice. And on the Northwest Coast of North America, the use of numerical classifiers, i.e., the categorizing of elements to be counted, reflects a concept which crosses the boundary of several apparently unrelated languages.

Language fits cultural needs

What becomes clear from the foregoing is that each language is a completed system of symbols and abstractions. It once seemed quite reasonable to assume that one or another existing language might be more archaic or more primitive than another. Yet, as we have already said, this does not appear to be the case. Every language represents a finished product, a perfect system in the sense that each tongue is wholly adequate to all human situations. The ideas that a language can express are in some measure dependent on the interests and preoccupations of the society which develops it. It would be surprising to hear a discussion of logical positivism or cultural anthropology in Eskimo, but this does not mean that ideas of this kind cannot be expressed in Eskimo. English, similarly, must resort to circumlocutions to convey with exactness the subtleties of which Eskimo is eminently capable. Neither of these languages, nor any of the other 6,000 languages of the world, can thus be regarded as more archaic or primitive than another.

It has sometimes been contended that a language has evolved further than others if it possesses a larger vocabulary. But one of the knottiest problems confronting the science of linguistics is to define the "word." Even in English, is "the" a word? Is "the man" one word or two? The verb "do" might be regarded as a word, but what of "does" and "did"? The latter case, to be sure, involves changing forms of the same element, but the very fact that the form changes raises some further questions about language and its nature. The speaker of English uses only a small fraction of the dictionary, or more properly, of the language lexicon. Many unwritten languages are far more elaborate in terms of the number of words employed by a speaker in normal converse. By such a standard, English might be regarded as more primitive. If Arabic has over 1,000 words for "sword," something cultural and stylistic is implied; the culture stresses poetry, and thus it is no surprise to discover an amazing array of synonyms and figures of speech.

Anthropologists are fond of pointing out that Eskimos have a large number of words for "snow," each denoting snow of a particular state of being, such as softly-falling-snow, dry-wind-driven-snow, drifting-snow, powder-snow, wet-packed-snow, dry-packed-snow-suitable-for-cutting-into-blocks (for igloo building,) ice-crust-surface-snow, and so on. It is perfectly true that we can linguistically express different conditions of snow through the use of modifiers, but the point is that Eskimos, whose very survival depends upon snow conditions, do not view snow as "crystallized water vapor" or "that beautiful white fluffy stuff that falls from the sky on some cold days," but rather as a series of *different* substances.

The American city dweller does recognize snow, sleet, slush, and ice as four distinctly different linguistic categories for crystallized water in different states of being—because this much, and no more, is culturally significant to his comfort and well-being. Since the birth of wide popular enthusiasm for skiing in the United States, however, a skier's vocabulary for snow, similar in its distinctions to that of the Eskimo, has been borrowed from the Austrian Tyrol because the state of snow is important to ski culture. Hence we hear the terms *Pappschnee* (wet, heavy snow), *Kornschnee* (barley snow that has melted under spring sunshine and frozen at night), *Pulverschnee* (powder snow), *Fernschnee* (broad expanse of breakable crust), and so forth.

In our own equestrian subculture of cowboys a comparable example exists. To most Eastern city dwellers a horse is a horse. Not so to the cowpoke. It is a mare, stallion, or gelding in denotation of its sex; a gray, sorrel, piebald, strawberry roan, palomino, or white face, in denotation of its color.

The basic principle illustrated by these examples is that every language is adequate to express the needs of its culture. As the culture expands, the language expands. If the belief or knowledge system embodied in the culture requires the expression of abstract ideas, the language will provide the means of getting those ideas across, regardless of what syntax is involved. If a culture stresses rhetorical style, oratory, folktale, or poetry, these cultural interests will find their linguistic expression. No existing language is so primary as to contain half-formulated grunted thoughts or so limited in expressions as to suggest that it exemplifies the dawn of human speech. English, it is true, like other European languages, accompanies a culture in which there is great diversity of occupation and activity. Since each specialty has its specialized vocabulary, no one person can command the whole lexicon of the language. But every culture has its specialties, occupational or otherwise. If anyone still has the notion, which was so common in the nineteenth century, that primitive languages are childlike and inherently incapable of expressing complex thoughts and ideas, this error should be dispelled.

The Universal and the Specific in Language

If language and its use represent a genetic "tip-over" passed sometime in the evolution of human beings as human beings, it follows that the resulting diversity in language is not unexpected. Moreover, it can be suggested that each language becomes a structured system in its own right. True, language changes in time and it is possible to trace language history, as where, for example, Latin of some 1,500 years ago swung toward a French, a Spanish, or an Italian variant. Similarly, English arose historically out of an Anglo-Saxon beginning, accepted a heavy overlay of Norman-French vocabulary after 1066, and so became fixed as a distinct and separate language as time passed. But these historic processes raise other questions than those connected with the comparison of languages as they exist today. It is important to look at each language as a structured whole, a functional system in its own right. The implication of such a statement is that languages are relative entities; each one has to be seen in its own terms.

Cultural and linguistic relativism

The problem of cultural and linguistic relativism is a difficult one. What one culture may consider right, elegant, and beautiful, another may view as wrong, debased, and ugly. Similarly, in language, one tongue, such as Hopi, may be much involved with statements about *action* and *movement*, emphasizing verbs and stressing activity. Conversely, another language may be involved in discussing *things*, giving attributes to them, and thus be emphatically concerned with descriptive categories. The implication is that languages, by virtue of the kind of structure which they have brought out of the past, may be focused toward certain kinds and modes of expression.

Anyone who has studied a language other than one's own becomes aware of the problem. One begins to see elements of structure which do not wholly dovetail with what is brought from one's own language and may find difficulty in making the full transfer. Certainly, one of the first and most obvious suggestions of difference is seen when one attempts to catch the meaning of a word in another language. The dictionary gives the equivalence, but somehow there is never a direct association. To look up the word for "hand" in an English-language dictionary, and in one for some other language, seems simple on the face of it. Yet where does the word begin and end? Does the language classify the hand as inclusive of the fingers? Does it include the wrist? Does the word refer to the back of the hand, the palm, or the whole hand with wrist and elbow? In other words, there are implicit classifications of experience and phenomena even in the use of apparently simple words. One might think that all human beings would agree on such seemingly basic issues, but the reverse is true.

But the relativistic suggestion may be carried further. Do all languages have verbs? The answer is a guarded "yes," assuming that one can agree on what constitutes a verb, a noun, an adjective, or any other part of speech. It is sometimes said that relational words are the most difficult for an outsider. If a language lacks prepositions, with which English expresses such relations as "on," "above," "in," and so on, how does one express these basic ideas? "The on-ness of the flat object related to a suspended plane discerns itself me," sounds to an English-language speaker like a weird way for saying, "The book is on the table" or "I see the book on the table." Yet this kind of existential statement is demanded by the structure of some languages outside the English-speaker's experience. The result is that what to the speaker of one language may seem wholly logical is chaotic illogic to the speaker of another.

The common denominator of all languages

But if languages are relative systems, is there any common denominator among the languages of the world? Anthropological linguists have paid some attention to this question in recent years in the same way as cultural anthropologists have looked for universals in culture patterns. Languages in themselves are isolable, unique, idiosyncratic, but at the same time language is language—in itself a common human phenomenon. Thus a wholly relativistic perception of languages may be off the mark. Languages may differ markedly from each other but the difference is one of degree rather than of kind. All languages employ sounds, all accord meaning to symbolic utterances. Sound and symbol, it is true, may differ markedly from group to group and area to area. Individuals speak, however, and this is universally true.[6]

Writing and Language

Some languages are written, some are not. Indeed, the term "primitive" is usually held to be synonymous with "nonliterate." But when anthropological linguists give their attention to the components of a language, they are concerned only with the oral system, or more accurately, with the oral-aural, the spoken and the heard. Writing is not a part of language in any vital sense. English could be written equally well with Chinese characters. As it happens, it uses a Latin alphabet. Systems of writing are inventions going back to the Bronze and Iron Ages. Language had been in existence long before. Nor should we think that because a language lacks writing it is crude. On the contrary, it is more frequently the unwritten language which preserves oral tradition with fi-

delity, and stresses correctness and precision of speech.

Some languages, such as Latin (in the past) and English, French, German, Chinese, and Russian, by virtue of writing and the accompanying transmission of elaborated traditions, have assumed greater importance than others in world affairs. While it is doubtful that the world will ultimately move toward universal use of English, Russian, Chinese, and Spanish because of their being fully dominant in certain world areas, languages with writing tend to be more encompassing. There are also "great" traditional languages. Such languages are usually found in association with one or another of the great religious systems. There is Latin, for example, which, although "dead" in the sense that it has no living day-to-day native speakers, still retains importance in the total world of Roman Catholicism. Similarly, Hebrew, with its link to Judaism and its modern renaissance in Israel, Arabic in the world of Islam, Sanskrit in the religious traditions of India, and Chinese and its tie to Confucianism and Taoism, are all examples of the cultural effects of the written tradition in the functioning of "universalistic" religious ideology and practice.

To reiterate, when a language is not written, there is an unfortunate tendency on the part of literate people to think of it as possessing limited worth. From the broad perspective of human history, this may be in a sense true, but from another standpoint, considering that any language serves the cultural needs of the people who speak it, all languages appear to have equal value and function.

THE STRUCTURE OF LANGUAGE

Whether English is spoken by Americans in the Midwest or in the Deep South, by the Englishman at Oxford, or the cockney cab driver in London, English still remains English. There are the dialects, to be sure, local turns of expression and sound variations which sometimes make it difficult for the speaker of one dialect to understand another, but the *structure* of the *language* remains consistent. A speaker of any language follows, and must follow, a definite structure in his speech. He has learned the basic structure of his language, and thus knows how to generate

---

[6]J. H. Greenberg, *Anthropological Linguistics*, pp. 137–154.

new utterances to suit the occasion and to transform mere words into *sentences* and *phrases of meaning* framed according to strict, "unconscious" rules.

The Time Element in Linguistic Analysis

In regard to both culture and language *the major concern is with the predictable*, with the elicitation of *pattern*. Language, in fact, appears to offer a more convincing example of this than does culture for the reason that language, by its very nature, cannot admit so many variables. One can readily supply—or predict—the missing words in such a sentence as *John and Mary are____to the* movies. Here, whether one chooses the verbs *go*, *walk*, *drive*, *come*, or another among the host of choices, one can predict from the nature of the sentence that the verb will contain an *ing* ending. The precise structure of each language permits variations, but they differ according to the linguistic system.

In thinking about language, as in thinking about culture, one may ask initially how the system works. In doing so, we place language at a point in time with no concern for its origin or for its historical relationships. Children learn the language of their group as it is spoken by those around them. The structure of English today is different from what it was in Chaucer's time, but the speaker of English need not know the history of the language. To see language (or culture) as a temporal end product and to ask how the system operates at a given time is to look at structure, at the parts which interrelate to make up the whole. This approach is structural, or *synchronic*. In synchronic studies, languages are analyzed as each exists at a given moment in history.

The historical, or *diachronic*, approach poses a very different kind of question. Rather than "How does it work?" we ask, "How did it get that way?" If the history of English as a language is the issue, then clearly, Chaucer's English and Shakespeare's English, as well as the earliest discernible forms of English, must be taken into account. Further, one wishes to see the parts of English which relate to the Germanic ancestor, to Latin, to Norman French, or to the great Indo-European family of which English, German, French, Latin, Russian, and the languages of modern India are also descendants.

Both approaches, the synchronic and the diachronic, have relevance for the understanding of language processes. The historical relationships of language may provide a clue to cultural relations. Similarly, to comprehend a language as it is spoken—not only to speak and understand it but also to see it as a structured entity—may provide some leads to a greater awareness of how cultures, too, are organized, the nature of their concerns, and their world views.

Synchronic, or Structural, Linguistics

Although any language contains a distinctive series of patterns, because language is spoken and heard, the initial approach to a language is through its sound system by means of phonology (Gr. *phono*, sound + logy).

Phonology

Every language has its own distinctive and characteristic total series of sounds. A single sound in one language, or even a series of them, can appear in another. Taken as a total system, however, the sounds of a language offer a remarkable uniqueness. Linguistic science employs the term *phoneme* (Gr. *phonema*, a sound) to refer to these characteristic sound units in a given language. Some languages, such as Hawaiian, possess only a few basic sounds; others, such as Kwakiutl, may have considerably more. Rarely are there more than 45 to 50 basic sounds in any language.

A phoneme is thus the smallest sound unit of a language. But the sound alone, in isolation, is only a starting point. In the human speech mechanism, sounds, usually conventionally divided into vowels and consonants, not only appear in combination with each other, but in a given language, a sound is articulated or pronounced in a way peculiar to that language. The sound usually designated /t/ is pronounced by most speakers of English by placing the tip of the tongue on the gum just back of the front teeth (postdental). The sound is *stopped*, meaning that /t/, unlike /s/, cannot be continued, even though /s/ is pronounced in much the same position as /t/ in English. There are thus classes of sounds—those that are *stopped*, *continued*, *nasalized*, or *trilled*, along with possible combinations of these—as well as points of articulation—the use of the tongue, lips, teeth, vibration and resonance, and the various hard and soft parts of the oral chamber—to produce particular types of sounds. /t/ in English is not the same as /t/ in some other languages. In Tagalog, a Philippine language, for example, /t/ is pronounced with the tongue directly against the teeth. As between English and Tagalog this makes little immediate difference. But it could happen, and often does, that a language differentiates between a postdental and a dental /t/, /s/, or /n/, and the result can be most confusing, at least to an English-speaker. Because he is used to a single postdental /t/, the English-speaker actually fails to hear the difference in the points of articulation. His own phonemes have not made him receptive to two, three, or four different tongue locations of /t/.

Sounds in a language also follow a pattern of arrangement, English /sk/ is wholly compatible with the sound structure of the language. But the same sound is impossible to pronounce in Spanish, where an initial vowel must enter before /s/ followed by any consonant, as Spanish *escuela* (eskwéla). Bantu languages in Africa build many words beginning with /ng/ (for instance, *ngbatu*). Not a single word in English starts so; it is against the English rule which requires that /ng/ may be used only at the end of a phonemic series. Similarly, no language incorporates all the phonemes that are in use among all the tongues of mankind. Strongly fixed motor habits in one's own speech make it extremely difficult to pronounce a foreign language like a native when it involves different habits. The difference between the English /z/ and /th/ is only a matter of a few millimeters in the placement of the tongue. In /z/, the tip of the tongue rests against the lower edge of the gums of the upper dental arch. In /th/, it is between the teeth themselves. But how many English-speaking Frenchmen and Germans never succeed in mastering that little shift!

It should be clear that even so apparently simple a system as the sounds of language is fraught with difficulties. True, the number of sounds a human being can make is limited, and one learns to follow the linguistic patterns of one's group. But when secondary phonemes, such as stress or accent, tone or pitch, length of vowel, presence or absence of resonance, throating, nasalizing, and many other possible factors, are added to the basic patterns, we can readily see that no language is a simple, phonetic system.

The sounds of a language, being adequate for that language, are thus relative to that particular language as a system. Languages are culturally determined systems not only in their sounds but in the ways in which they put these basic elements together in structured order.

PHONEMIC ANALYSIS   How is a phoneme recognized? Trained linguists bring their own judgments to bear, based on their knowledge of *phonetics*, the general science of sounds. Equipped with a good ear, training, and practice, linguists have acquired a sense of the general range of sounds which human speech has produced. In respect to a single language, linguists look for contrasts, for the differentiation of minimal pairs, /t/, for example, as against /d/. Both, as in English, may be aspirated; one is unvoiced, the other voiced. Both sounds thus stand out in English as distinctive phonemic elements. But in a language other than their own, even trained linguists, unless they are exceptional mimics, may do something wrong, failing to get the hang of a particular unit of articulation and making their utterances—often to the amusement of native speakers—with an atrocious accent. Linguists can generally tell what they are doing wrong; they can locate the uttered sound in its proper place and can describe it scientifically. But neither with mouth nor mind can they replicate the action of the native speaker. Told that he has articulated an unaspirated, unvoiced dental stop, the native speaker's reaction may be, "So what?" All he knows is that this is the way one speaks in his language. For him that is usually enough.

But a kind of impasse is reached. There is nothing abstruse about a phonetic-phonemic distinction. One returns again in fact to the problem of the universal as against the specific. Yet it is this issue which has come to have some implications for the study of culture and which again suggests some analogies in process between language and culture.

ETICS AND EMICS   Some anthropologists, examining both language and culture, have found the concepts *etic* and *emic* useful and suggestive of modes of analysis.[7] *Etic* analysis expresses an objective, descriptive, outside view. It presents statements about a people's behavior based on a broad comparative knowledge, but does not emphasize what the people themselves think or feel. A formal analysis of kinship, for example, can give us a sense of the structure of social units. Thus, when the father's brother is called by the same term as the progenitor, a specific type of kinship organization comes to light. But of itself this does not tell what the user of this "father" term thinks or feels in regard to the persons to whom the term is customarily applied. The *emic* approach takes this into account. How, in fact, does the native participant in a cultural system think of himself, other members of the society, and the universe? With language, one knows the "correct" grammar from linguistic experience. With culture, one knows "correct" behavior from cultural experience. As in language, phon*etics* and phon*emics* are two sides of the same coin; the same is true of cultural behavior viewed in terms of the etic-emic distinction.

Morphology and syntax

A language is a whole system. It has a structure, or morphology. Its parts are assembled in a particular way and reflect a special kind of adaptation. So it is that some languages build their meaningful concepts out of verbs, forming names for things and concepts, i.e., nouns, from stems that reflect action. Arabic and Hebrew are good examples of such a process. Others, such as many of the European languages, appear to stress things rather than actions. In English, any verb may be made into a noun. In fact, the tendency in English is to teach children the names of things first—"mouth," "kitty," "doggie," and so on—and to introduce the child to verbs only later. Conversely, in Navaho, the child first becomes familiar with actions—"sitting," "running," "moving," and so forth. In Chinese, we can say that there are no nouns or verbs. Whether the concept expressed refers to a thing or an action (a noun or a verb) depends on its relations to other conceptual units expressed in an utterance.

MORPHEMES The basic element in any language is the phoneme, but phonemic units are put together in various ways to form the elements of *structure*, or the *morphology*. If phonemes are basic units of sound, *morphemes* (Gr. *morphe*, form) are basic units of structure. Synchronic linguists, interested in determining the facts of the structure of a language, reduce the language first to its bedrock of sounds. They then note that sound arrangements follow a pattern, that a clustering of certain kinds of discernible elements occurs. These may be actual words. More often, these clusters are parts that form units which are set off by the secondary phonemic element of *juncture*. Junctures are simply the breaks between words. The sentence *The man is eating* suggests these junctures. Almost no break occurs between /the/ and /man/, indicating that when the definite article is used in English, it is almost a prefix, that is, something bound to the element following. Between /man/ and /is/ and between /is/ and /eating/ there is a slight rest, a tiny hesitation that sets each element off. In French, for instance, the junctures are less apparent; words flow together; other languages stress them more. The point here is that any language may have "free" morphemes (in this instance they equal words) or "bound" morphemes, that is, those which are in some way modified.

To illustrate what a morpheme is, let us take a closer look at the sentence given: *The man is eating*. /man/ is a primary morpheme with the bound /the/; /is/ refers to the state occupied by some singular person or object; /eating/ consists of two morphemes—the root form /eat/ and a suffixed bound form /-ing/ which in English refers to an action going on, continuing, proceeding. Again, a sentence such as *Birds fly* consists of several morphemes. /bird/ is made plural by a bound suffixed /z/.[8] /fly/ is a single morpheme, but since it is preceded by the plural noun /birds/ it is not the same as /fly/ in /to fly/; a third-person

---

[7]K. L. Pike, *Language in Relation to a Unified Theory of the Structure of Human Behavior*, parts 1–3.

[8]This also illustrates the problem of the change of a sound because of morphological factors. The rule in English is that if a noun ends in a vowel or a voiced consonant, i.e., a consonant which is accompanied with resonance, the suffixed /-s/ becomes itself voiced, i.e., /z/. A word such as *bee* /bij/ takes its plural as /bijz/; *dog* /dawg/ becomes /dawgz/; but *cat* /kaet/ becomes /kaets/. This is true of any suffixed /-s/ in English, however variable the function of /-s/ may be. Its functions include: inflection of the third-person singular verb, present tense; possession; and designation of number, i.e., the plural.

plural, present tense is understood. Linguists can treat this as a "zero" morpheme, one in which there is no inflection but in which a distinct environment, in this instance, agreement between noun and verb, is held to prevail.

Is such a way of looking at language really any different from the way in which many of us have studied and learned languages—the method of the paradigm, where one encounters such patterns as *I hit, you hit, he hits*? Indeed it is, since by listing and categorizing the morphemes of a language, one obtains a total perspective on the potential range of variations in the whole system. Because languages differ so markedly from each other in the ways they put their concepts together, it is necessary to "get the feel" of the system by means of the morphology. It is here that the understanding of language cues begins. Since languages do differ it is also necessary to obtain some sense of the meaning of the morphemes and the contexts in which they are used. Translation from one language to another is always difficult. Can one get all of the nuances, can one understand all that is conveyed in the oral-aural situation in a language that is not one's own? Morphemic analysis, which takes account of the language in its structural totality, offers a lead.

MORPHEMES AND MEANING   So far, little has been said about meaning in language. A morpheme, however, is a meangingful unit, not only in the sense that it may be a word with the psychological and emotive reactions that words evoke, but because it appears in environments with other morphemes to create meaningful forms.

A few examples chosen from selected languages may illustrate the point.

To an English speaker, the sentence *When I was going to the store, I saw a dog* seems infinitely logical and simple. In Turkish, a Ural-Altaic language that originated in Central Asia, the same thought possesses a rather different structuring, which uses Turkish morphemes and is not in any way suggestive of English. The Turkish sentence is: *Dükkâne gittiğim zaman bir köpek gördüm.*

English uses eleven word units, with several more morphemes, while Turkish employs only five. The Turkish morphemes are: /dükkân/ which means "store," with a suffixed /e/ "place to which

action is directed"; /gittiğim/ consists of a root morpheme /git/ "go," with a suffixed /*d(t)ik/ which is marked with an asterisk because it can never appear without some pronoun modification, but which refers to a continuous action in the past, and /-im/ referring to action by a first person "I," "my"; /zaman/ "time"; /bir/ "one," an indefinite single something; /köpek/ "dog," an indefinite noun (if the noun were definite, i.e., "the dog," the Turkish would be /köpeği/, the /-i/ morpheme being used only where there is a definite direct object of a verb); /gördüm/ from a root morpheme /gör/ "see," plus /d(t)/ indicator of any part action, plus /-um/ action by a first person, again "I," "my."

In this case, what is the literal meaning of the Turkish sentence? One might render it into English, although meaninglessly: *To* (definite) *store my wenting time* (indefinite) *dog I saw.* Such a contrived rendition is scarcely necessary, since the Turkish sentence has much the same meaning as the English. We are simply attempting to convey the difference in the way in which concepts are put together.

SYNTAX   A language, however, is much more than a series of morphemes clustered haphazardly. Generally, morphemes, bound or free, follow some kind of ordered pattern. The pattern may be quite strict or fairly free. *Syntax* refers to *the arrangement of elements in phrases and sentences.* English, which has shed many of its inflections, or morphemic modifications, depends on a fairly rigid syntax. In the sentence *John and Mary to the movies went*, the hearer is at once aware of something wrong. But *John went the movies to Mary and* violates the rules of all English syntax and meaning.

When a language is more dependent on morphology, syntax may relax. In Latin, for example, the sentences *Canis ursum videt*, *Videt ursum canis*, *Videt canis ursum*, and so on through any other possible variations, all make good sense, "*The dog sees the bear.*" The morphemic arrangement of /canis/ and /ursum/ make it completely clear that it is the dog which is doing the seeing and the bear which is being seen. Mandarin Chinese, and the Chinese languages generally, even more than English, have shed their morphology almost completely. For them, syntax has become a wholly necessary feature.

Languages thus vary tremendously in their structures, whether in sounds, in morphology, or in syntax. Some linguists have attempted to type languages according to the kind of morphology and syntax they possess, a process that is useful in showing the great potential range of human speech patterns. It also becomes eminently clear that one cannot read the structure of one's own language into another. What holds for English will not hold for even a closely related language.

Every language is bound by its own firm rules of grammar, and each speaker who wants to be understood must master the rules and abide by them. Language is a tyrant that does not permit much individual liberty, although there will always be great differences in individual skill in the use of a language.

One really intriguing point, however, is that although firm grammatical, that is, morphological and syntactic, rules control the use of language, the rules are not made by grammarians. They have been arrived at naïvely by generations of speakers who had no consciousness of what they were doing. Once certain elemental ways of shaping and combining morphemes were established, the mold for the future growth of the language was pretty well set. Rules of grammar give consistency to the tongue; they integrate the use of vocal symbols. Yet, the tyranny of grammatical rules notwithstanding, no primitive individual can state the rules of his grammar. He can only tell you that a certain thing must be said this way and not that way. It is only the sophisticated linguist who can analyze a language into expressly stated rules. A bright informant working with a field worker may discover some elemental rules for himself, however. This happened when a Shoshone Indian was asked how to say: *my house, his house, her house, our house, their house.* /gani/ is the morpheme for "house." In the informant's responses each word contained *ngani* preceded by a different personal pronoun prefix. As the list was written down by the anthropologist, a great light dawned upon the Shoshone-speaker and he excitedly exclaimed, "Say! That /n/ in there must mean that something belongs to someone." On being assured that this was so (he had discovered the possessive infix), he marveled, "Well, what do you think of that? Here I've been talking Shoshone all my life and I never knew that /n/ in the middle of a word means it belongs to someone."

The rules of a language are unconsciously obeyed by its speakers. The normal way to learn any language is to become habituated to its unformulated rules through using the language, not by learning the rules. It has taken American language teachers a long time to learn this simple fact.

Transformational Grammars

Grammatical transformations are the ways in which speakers combine and recombine strings of morphemes to form phrases and sentences.

There is considerably more to the concept of language as a total system than the mere rules of sound and structure. These are no more than the bare bones of a linguistic system. There is, in addition, an ordering that description alone cannot cope with. In English, for example, one can say, "three big round red balloons," and there is no quarrel with the ordering of the adjectives. But suppose you modify this to, "three red big round balloons." The sense is changed, the adjectives are given a slightly different emphasis and the listener is clearly bothered. Go a step further and say, "red big three round balloons," and the listener will think you are nutty. On the other hand, the famous illustrative sentence coined by the linguist Noam Chomsky, "colorless green ideas sleep furiously," makes perfect structural sense, even though it lacks meaning; it "feels" all right—even good. But what gibberish to utter, "furiously sleep ideas green colorless!" This transformation of the word order is chaotic. It was awareness of problems of this kind that led Chomsky to a reformulation of some of the concepts of linguistics.[9]

The "transformational" model conceived by Chomsky stresses the element of syntactic structure. The model seeks to account for all the variations in a language system. These include not only the patterning of sound, but also the element of meaning. What Chomsky's transforma-

---

[9]N. Chomsky, *Language and Mind.*

tional system does is to suggest that all elements in a total system should be specified, even if the totality of relationships in a given language system can be discerned only with difficulty. The point is stressed, however, that the goal of a transformational description is to elicit a formal statement (virtually mathematical) about the "competence" of a speaker and hearer of a language. As a speaker, one generates concepts in language by putting elements together in structured ways. Transformationalists are concerned with the "deep structures" of a language, not only the surface structures of sound and morpheme, but with the phrase and the ways in which a speaker of a language rearranges the parts to form sets of meanings. The semantic quality relates to the deeper structure of the language. The result is that in transformational grammars the way is opened for a much fuller understanding of language as a total structure. More than this, however, the transformational approach seeks to arrive at a uniform theory of language in terms of description and as a communicative device.

The theories of syntactic structure as put forth by Chomsky have drawn increasing attention from both anthropologists and linguists and may well be a highway to a broader and more comprehensive theory of the components of language.

SEMANTICS: THE MEANING OF MEANING

Because the primary function of language is communication, the question of meaning is central. A linguist can, to be sure, look only at the structure of a language, noting the kinds and variety of verb forms or what constitutes a noun under varying sets of circumstances. But this is linguistics without meaning, an approach to language aimed solely at an analysis of the interaction of parts. It is not a treatment of the whole language. It is precisely this sense of the whole which the transformationalists are seeking, and they suggest that meaning lies in the "deep structure," vitally related to all other facets. The study of semantics is to some extent still in its infancy. As new modes of analysis are developing and as greater awareness of the symbolic nature of human behavior arises, some startling new insights are coming to light.

Initially, one may think of semantics when

crossing from one language to another and from one culture to another.

Between languages, meaning is constantly a problem. This is true not only on the level of words alone but in terms of the basic definitions that are resident in the structure of language. It has been contended that because Russian and English employ different built-in concepts of time—that is, time is differently expressed in the structure of the two languages—there is a basis for much misunderstanding on the international level. Whether or not this is so in this particular case, it is probable that the varying structures of languages do inhibit cross-cultural understanding. A case in point is provided by the Keresan-speaking Pueblo Indians of New Mexico. Suppose a missionary were to bring to these peoples his particular brand of religion. In Keresan, no idea can be expressed without containing the morphemes indicating whether the action described depends on experience undergone by the speaker or whether the speaker has his information from hearsay. If the missionary tells his listeners in Keresan that in the beginning God created heaven and earth, he cannot use the experienced mode—*he* was not there. His remarks can only imply, "So I've been told."

But does one really need "meaning" in a study of language? While it is possible to be concerned solely with structure, with phonology, morphology, and syntax, no one who takes the study of language seriously (unless the goal is a puristic structuralism) will wish to ignore the semantic issues. It is this kind of point which the transformationalists stress. Each of a pair of utterances, "occasionally it rains in May" and "it rains occasionally in May," generates a very different set of meanings. A perspective on a whole language seeks to answer both the question of structure and that of meaning as well.

Emotional Quality in Meaning

But what of meaning within a language? Every person, in any language, has one's own *ideolect*, a particular style of speech, favorite words and expressions, a particular set of images and thoughts which are evoked by words. Everyone can agree on the definition of "table"; what each hearer sees in the mind's eye may reflect a host of differing images, all of which, however, are acceptable tables. The field of *psycholinguistics*, which relates to the psychology of language, is as yet only in its infancy. Some breakthroughs have been made, to be sure, especially in the area of language learning. A speaker encodes an utterance, delivers it, and the hearer decodes it and responds. The linguistic system is internalized; the cues relate intimately to individual personality. It is clear from the experience of our own culture that some words are holy, some are obscene, some are proper for certain social occasions and improper for others. These distinctions indicate the continuing presence of the emotive quality of language. An expressed thought may be purely neutral, but it serves to relate the speaker to his cultural environment.

Meaning in a language poses some further problems. Just what does an utterance mean? The answer to this question depends in part on the social setting of the conversation, who is present, whether those present are men or women of superior or inferior statuses. The manner in which this problem is resolved depends on the demands of the cultural setting.

Getting away from the emotive element in meaning, we should mention the purely academic issue of just what words do mean. Does one really express his primary thoughts with any exactness? Actually not, since the word is accompanied by a host of other culturally determined nonlinguistic cues. I do not have to say precisely what I think. Indeed, in our own culture and in most others, care is necessary to avoid creating problems in social interaction. Some Americans prefer to say that a person has "passed away" rather than that he is "dead." And clearly, to say that he has "kicked the bucket" is in very bad taste. Meanings thus have social as well as psychological dimensions. Nowhere, perhaps, is the question of meaning so vital as in the specialized language of the law. Here exactness becomes imperative, a matter recognized by every society that has codified and verbalized its legal codes.

CULTURE AND LANGUAGE

Several ways in which language and culture may interact have been suggested. It seems clear that every language is in itself a cultural phenomenon.

Language has absolutely nothing to do with biological inheritance; therefore, there is no inherent relationship between race and language. If, as is sometimes the case, a certain language is spoken solely by the members of a given race, it is only because the racial population, having been isolated from other populations, developed its own mode of speech. Once the isolation breaks down, this need no longer be so. Twenty million Afro-Americans speak only English, but their ancestors of two centuries ago spoke only one or another of the African languages.

The fact that it is difficult for English-speakers to master some of the phonemes of other languages—ones that are used with ease by native speakers—does not mean that the native speakers have a natural ability to produce such sounds. It merely means, providing the adage is not taken too seriously, that "you can't teach old dogs new tricks." Once vocal habits are set, they become so firm that to break them is quite a task. There is nothing in the physical structure of the members of any race, however, that makes certain populations genetically suited to the pronunciation of some phonemes and not others.

Therefore, if the question "What is the relation between race and language?" is asked, the answer is, "None." On the other hand, if the question "What is the relation between culture and language?" is put, the answer is, "A great deal" (Fig. 22-2).

Subgroup Dialects

Most languages, although they are systems consistent within themselves, do have spoken variations that are used by different groups. Such groups may be localized, and in such instances the variety is recognized as a dialect or subdialect. Or such groups may be status groups within a society. Men employ certain speech usages that differ from those of women. In the same way, usages of adults differ from those of infants; those of professors from those of laborers; those of politicians from those of preachers. In Javanese, for example, socially inferior people address their superiors with one form of speech and are answered in another. Superiors use yet a third speech among themselves, while inferiors have still another.

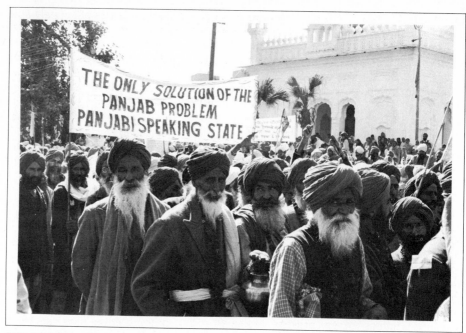

FIG. 22-2 A mother tongue can easily become a symbol of social and personal identity. Panjabi speakers demonstrate for a separate Indian state. (Marc Riboud, Magnum.)

The Sapir-Whorf Hypothesis: Language and Thought Habits

Every language is adequate to the needs of its culture insofar as the speakers of the language can communicate to each other the ideas and feelings that their culture makes it possible for them to have. But the very structure of a language subtly molds the way in which people conceive of the nature of the world in which they find themselves. Philosophically, we know that mankind's idea systems are the screens through which it perceives reality. We saw in Chapter 2 how the basic postulates of each culture provide the assumptions about the general nature of things with which the members of each society view nature and themselves. Taken together, culture at large and language in particular grind the multiple lenses through which human beings view the world that surrounds them. Indeed, as Edward Sapir (1884–1939) was one of the first to perceive, in a real sense "language and our thought-grooves are inextricably interwoven, are, in a sense, one and the same."[10]

We say we have mastered a language, but only recently have we begun to realize that the primary language we learn to speak in turn masters us.

How does this identity of language and thought-grooves become manifest? Perhaps two illustrations will suffice.

English- and Indo-European-language speakers confront time as a divisible entity that falls "naturally" into a past, the present, and a future. Until Einstein pushed the special language of mathematics and physics into a new sphere that could not be described by any of these conventional Indo-European distinctions, time could not be thought of by any of us in any other terms.

Benjamin Lee Whorf (1897–1941), a chemical engineer and fire insurance executive, became concerned with the problem of how English

[10]E. Sapir, *Language*, p. 232.

words betray people into burning down buildings. One example from Whorf's argument will do:

In a wood distillation plant the metal stills were insulated with a composition prepared from limestone and called at the plant "spun limestone." . . . After a period of use, the fire below one of the stills spread to the "limestone," which to everyone's great surprise burned vigorously. Exposure to acetic acid fumes from the stills had converted part of the limestone (calcium carbonate) to calcium acetate. This, when heated in a fire decomposes, forming inflammable acetone. Behavior that tolerated fire close to the covering was induced by use of the name "limestone," which because it ends in "stone" implies noncombustibility.[11]

Shawnee syntax and conceptualization

The principles put forth by Whorf can be demonstrated by Shawnee, a language of American Indians in what is now the southeastern United States.

Whorf confronts us with two English sentences:

1. I push his head back.
2. I drop it in the water and it floats.

The acts performed according to these two statements are quite unlike. In (1), the physical act is presented as the exertion of a force: subject $\longrightarrow$ force $\longrightarrow$ object. In (2), the emphasis is on an attribute of the object (it floats).

Shawnee language is so structured that in describing these same two events the Shawnee Indian sees and thinks of them in terms of similarity. How? To tell what happens in the first situation he says:

1. *ni*	*kwaškwi*	*tepē*	*n*	*a*
I	push back	on the head	by action of the hand	cause to a person

To tell what happens in the second situation, the Shawnee says:

2. *ni*	*kwašk*	*ho*	*to*

I	push back	at the surface of water	cause to an inanimate thing

Literally translated, (1) means, "I cause the head of a human being to be pushed back by action of my hand." Similarly translated, (2) means, "I cause an inanimate thing to be pushed back at the surface of water." Pushing against, a reverse force, is what Shawnee grammar induces the Shawnee speaker to *see* in *both* situations; not pushing and floating as separate phenomena. The Shawnee grammatical approach to what takes place is closer to the reality of the situation than is the action-idea of "floating," as any student who learned Archimedes' principle in high school physics knows.

In other words, it is not always that "sentences are unlike because they tell about unlike facts" (although, of course, in some situations other than those just mentioned, they may be unlike in fact). In some cases, it may be that: "Facts are unlike to speakers whose language background provides for unlike formulation of them."[12]

COGNITIVE ANTHROPOLOGY: EMIC CLASSIFICATION AND FOLK CATEGORIES

The emic approach, noted above, suggests that it is possible to free data from the categories which pure objectivity might seem to impose. In other words, can anthropologists shed their own biases, those derived from their culture, and see the world through the eyes of the people with whom they are concerned? Perhaps they can; the question is, how can they do it?

Ethnosemantics

An initial answer lies in the development of *ethnosemantics*, a study of meaning and meanings resident in the system being analyzed. What, for example, does the speaker of a language perceive about the surrounding world? The speaker pos-

[11]B. L. Whorf, *Language, Thought, and Reality*, pp. 135–136. By permission of M.I.T. Press.

[12]*Ibid.*, p. 235.

sesses a *cognitive system*, that is, a built-in system of classifications. An example of such a human tendency to classify can be seen in the use of color words in various languages. English is very perceptive of color and there are perhaps 3,000 words dealing with all the possible shades of color—"red," "crimson," "scarlet," "cerise," "rust," etc. Another language, however, may limit the categories of color and be unable to express the subtle differences in color tones. A recent study has shown that all languages have terms for black and white. If there is a further distinction, it will predictably be red. Does this mean that the native speakers of a language fail to perceive the variations in color? Hardly; it is simply that the language limits the kind of classifications available to them, with the result that there are categorical limitations.[13]

Color terms represent a semantic domain for all languages. Any culture has a great variety of different domains which reflect the native taxonomy of the things as they exist in both nature and culture. All that is suggested here is that different peoples have different ways of dividing up the spectrum. When Navaho says "green," the language also means "blue" and "purple." The Zuñi language embraces both "yellow" and "orange" in a single term. Other semantic domains may encompass the terms used for the animal world, for plants, for foods, and so on through the categories which a culture perceives as significant. In English, for example, a "chair" describes a vast array of things on which people sit, from camp stools to reclining armchairs. Yet hassocks and sofas are not chairs, even if made to be sat on, while the difference between "chair" and "table" is certainly categorically and taxonomically marked.

A formal analysis, one which simply notes the classifications which are made, can thus be applied to the domains which any group of people establishes in language and culture. In language, an investigator seeks paradigms, the formal patternings of linguistic elements. Verbs may pattern out differently from nouns. So also in culture and

meaning, there are always elements which go together (associate)—"tire" and "automobile" are related components; "automobile" and "ocean" are clearly not.

Componential Analysis

Componential analysis is a conceptual tool for the ordering of taxonomy and classificatory principles within a culture; it seeks to elicit the cognitive realms of the bearers of the culture in question.[14] These are essentially difficult concepts to get at, especially since the kinds of ordering and the classifications employed by the group may be on an unconscious level.

One important aspect of the contemporary concerns with componential analysis and ethnosemantics lies in studies of kinship and kinship terminologies as employed in different cultures. These are related not so much to the actual behavioral or structural implications of such a system as they are to the domains of semantic contrast resident in a kinship pattern. Floyd G. Lounsbury, for example, by applying principles of category and meaning to the sets of kinship terms in both the Crow and Omaha systems, is able to demonstrate the inherent classificatory relatedness of terms for relatives, suggesting that one system is a mirror image of the other and that there are semantic issues in generational designation which relate to the bases of kinship classification.[15] The effect is to avoid the errors in categorization which arise when an outsider imposes his own formulation based on his own categories. In other words, the meaning of a structured system of kinship is one generated by the group employing it.

Ethnoscience

The upshot of these concerns with meaning lies in the development of an essentially newly conceived disciplinary focus—that of *ethnoscience*.

[13]B. Berlin, "A Universalist-Evolutionary Approach in Ethnographic Semantics," in A. Fischer (ed.), *Current Directions in Anthropology*, vol. 3, no. 2, part 2 (1970), p. 8.

[14]See W. C. Sturtevant, "Studies in Ethnoscience," in A. K. Romney and A. G. d'Andrade (eds.), "Transcultural Studies in Cognition" (*American Anthropologist*, vol. 66, no. 3, part 2, Special Publication, 1964), pp. 99–131.

[15]F. G. Lounsbury, "A Formal Account of the Crow and Omaha-type Kinship Terminologies," in W. H. Goodenough (ed.), *Explorations in Cultural Anthropology*, pp. 351–387.

In ethnoscience the purpose is to lay bare the semantic element, the kinds of taxonomies with which various linguistic, and, by extension, cultural systems are concerned. Just as in a grammar there is an elicitation of a series of paradigms and the formulation of a set of rules applicable to the specific language, so also in an ethnoscientific approach there is the concern with the paradigms of cultural behavior. The approach of Lounsbury and others working in this field stresses an economy of description. A grammar allows a tightly focused prediction of form and structure. An ethnoscience allows the same for a statement about culture. And by the same token, a grammar has its own sets of categories; the ethnoscientist does not impose categories on the cultural situation but allows the cultural system to generate its own. The anthropologist as ethnoscientist is a neutral vehicle for the expression of the system in English or whatever other language is being used.

THE GROWTH AND DIVERGENCE OF LANGUAGES

The origins of languages are lost in the distant past. There simply is no way today to learn how it happened that the original developers of a given language happened to hit upon the grammatical principles that they began with. Nonetheless, it is possible to observe and study how living languages change through time.

Diachronic (Historical) Linguistics

The scientific study of the patterns of change in given languages may be done in two ways. Once a language is committed to writing, the changes that occur may be followed through a sequence of documents. The other approach is to push the history of related languages back into prehistoric times through internal analysis of homologous languages. The major principle underlying this second method is similar to that used in reconstruction of organic phylogenies; namely, that forms which have in common a number of functionally similar qualities that is greater than the level of chance occurrence are genetically related.

The comparative method

The criteria used in historical linguistics are morphemic and syntactic identities. The quickest way to get an indication as to whether two languages are related is to compare their vocabularies, or word forms. (Thomas Jefferson, even while President of the United States, prepared word lists to be sent out to explorers and traders living among the Indians so as to answer the questions of American Indian origins and relationships.)[16] By sheer chance, under the law of limited possibilities, they will possibly have some words in common. It is surely puerile to argue that two tribes are related because they share a handful of words. There must be a concurrence in a significant number of words and their associated meanings.

What constitutes significance? Two languages that are clearly unrelated and also phonemically unlike in structure will ordinarily share only 4 per cent of their total terms in like form and meaning. If it happens that the phonemic structure of morphemes in the two languages is similar, then the concurrences may be double. It is therefore safe to hold that vocabulary identities of less than these percentages may be the product of nothing but chance, and the identities may not be taken as evidence of historical relationship. Conversely, it is the considered and well-supported judgment of linguists, as expressed by the American expert Professor Joseph Greenberg, that:

It can be safely asserted that a resemblance of 20 per cent in vocabulary always requires a historical explanation and that, unless similarity of phonetic structure leads to the expectation of a high degree of chance similarity, even 8 per cent is well beyond what can be expected without the intervention of historical factors.[17]

By means of mathematical comparisons among three or more languages, it is possible to work out even sharper determinations of possible genetic relations along the lines just indicated.

Languages are apt to include a large number of words borrowed from other languages (e.g., in

---

[16]Long vocabulary lists prepared by Jefferson are in the manuscript collections of the Library of the American Philosophical Society, Philadelphia.

[17]J. H. Greenberg, "Historical Linguistics and Unwritten Languages," in A. L. Kroeber (ed.), *Anthropology Today*, p. 270. By permission of University of Chicago Press.

English, *totem*, *canoe*, *tobacco*, *tabu*, *automobile*, and so forth). Fundamental words such as pronouns and those representing parts of the body are most likely to retain their identity with the morphemes of their ancestry. Free borrowing from unrelated languages occurs more commonly in what are called the *cultural* (nonpersonal) *items*. Therefore, when linguists are confronted by a group of languages that exhibit similarities greater than chance probability would account for in their *fundamental vocabularies*, while at the same time lacking similarities in their *cultural vocabularies*, they are certain that these languages were remotely derived from a common ancestor. If these languages had only recently come into contact with each other, the one would have borrowed words from the cultural vocabulary of the other before it would displace its own fundamental words with those from an alien source. Thus another device for establishing historical relations between languages is available.

Sounds change over time. This means that the phonemic system of a given language does not remain constant. In seeking relationships among languages, linguists with historical interests again may return to the bedrock of the language in question, its phonology. In comparing sounds between one language and another that they assume to be related to it, they may observe a distinct pattern, a systematic change through the phonology of both. This principle was first elicited in the nineteenth century by Jacob Grimm, the same scholar who along with his brother, Wilhelm, collected the famous fairy tales—not for purposes of entertainment, although that was a happy by-product of their efforts, but to see historical relationships in the distributions of the stories. Grimm's *law of phonetic change*, set forth in 1822, made possible the designation of the great Indo-European speech family. Taking Sanskrit, the language of ancient India, as a kind of prototype of Indo-European, the brothers Grimm observed that systematic changes took place from one language to another as time went on. For example, the Sanskrit word *pitar* became *patēr* in Greek, *pater* in Latin, *vater* in Germanic (*v* is pronounced *f*), and *father* in English. Similarly, Sanskrit *bhrata* becomes Latin *frater*, Germanic, *bruder*, English, *brother*, and Russian, *brat*. It can

be seen that earlier Indo-European *p* may become *f*, that a weak *b* (bh) may also move to *f*, and the *f* may move back to *b*. Other regular modifications are demonstrable among the the numerous Indo-European tongues, and similar relationships have been established for many other language groups.

This means that in comparing vocabularies for identities, exact phonemic similarity is not to be expected. The linguist, however, comes to recognize phonemic correlates that should be treated as identical. In cases where written documents extending over a number of centuries are available for related languages, it is possible to validate directly the specific functioning of Grimm's law and its derivatives.

Languages may also be related by comparison of their morphological and syntactic features. Thus an isolating language, such as Chinese, which sets up its words as simple monosyllables, is hardly likely to be related to such an extremely polysynthetic language as Eskimo, which builds up single words with as many as a dozen or more morphemes. More refined criteria, such as the presence or absence of gender, or inflection, and so forth, are also relied on.

Looking thus at Indo-European, it becomes possible to suggest some ultimate relationships. The speech phylum (family) has grown over a period of thousands of years, presumably from a single geographic center. Dialect changed to language as mutual intelligibility ceased; groups moved, forming their own variations on themes of the original language. Once a parent language broke off from the main stem, it, too, was subject to further changes, giving rise to a kind of family language tree, with lesser branches off the main branches of the trunk. This comparative method has been applied to all the world's languages so that in a general way, it is possible to see wide relationships. In Africa, among the American Indian, in Asia and the South Seas, classifications suggesting historical relationships have been made.

Thus, although the Cheyenne Indians live far out on the western Plains, because their language is Algonkian, we know that they are an offshoot of the great Algonkian group of tribes that dominated the northeastern part of North America. The linguistic fact confirms Cheyenne legend that they came from the vicinity of a great body of water in a wooded land to the east. The fact that the Navahos and Apaches speak Athabascan dialects leads us to look for their original homeland far to the north in the woodlands of the MacKenzie-Yukon basin of western Canada, where all the tribes speak Athabascan.

Glottochronology

The use of radioactive carbon counting as a means of reading the built-in "time clock" for the dating of archaeological sites is one of the really exciting techniques developed since 1947. Equally exciting is glottochronology, the recently developed method for calculating the approximate time of the divergence of two dialects or languages from a common mother tongue. Thus the date at which the speakers of the dialects separated from each other can be established.

The fundamental premise of the method is that the basic vocabularies of a language change at a given rate. A basic, or fundamental, vocabulary is one which consists of words referring to universal "culture-free" phenomena, such as air, cloud, sun, rain, hand, foot, and so forth. Standard word lists of 100, 200 or more terms are used for comparison and analysis. Judgments are made according to established principles of linguistic analysis as to whether the two forms of a given word are cognate (i.e., of the same stock or origin) or noncognate. The relative number of noncognates to cognates is calculated. This provides a statement of the relative amount of change that has occurred since the two languages began to be separated from the original parent stock.

The rate of language change was first calculated on the basis of documented changes (noncognates) in a number of historic (written) languages. The replacement of terms in the fundamental vocabulary was measured at the rate of 19 per cent in a thousand years. The residue of cognates represents the rate of retention. The rate of retention actually varies among Indo-European languages from 86.4 per cent to 74.4 per cent per thousand years. This means that fundamental vocabularies may in fact change at rates of from 13.6 per cent to 25.6 per cent per thousand years.

The average figure is 19.5 per cent, but, for convenience, 19 per cent is still used.

By use of a standard algebraic formula for computation of time depth, the number of years which have elapsed since the languages became separated can be calculated within a limited range of probability.[18]

In a number of applications of the principle, the dates derived through glottochronology coincide nicely with historically known dates from the archeological sites of the presumed ancestral populations. Glottochronology has useful possibilities in giving a measure of time precision to historical reconstructions. It is not reliable where no other supporting evidence is at hand, however. Its validity decreases outside the range of 500 to 2,000 years.

While glottochronology has been much criticized, it appears that where data can be carefully controlled, as when there are closely related languages or dialects, it has some validity. The studies of Shoshone dialects in the Great Basin of the United States, for example, show fairly conclusively a series of changes occurring within a time span of roughly a millennium.[19]

Lexicostatistics

The statistical summations that reside in the glottochronological word lists may have yet another utility. Lexicostatistics begin to suggest hitherto unsuspected relationships between languages. To be sure, such relationships may be very ancient and one may be interested in the actual dating process. However, the problem of whether or not one language relates to another, easily resolved for Indo-European and other languages with a long written history, is less readily apparent among unwritten languages where historical depth must be inferred. Lexicostatistic similarities (cognate words) shed some light on the matter.

We said that a treelike scheme can be used in formulating linguistic relationships. However, this

[18]See S. C. Gudschinsky, "The ABC's of Lexicostatistics (Glottochronology)," in D. Hymes (ed.), *Language in Culture and Society*, pp. 612–623, for a succinct discussion of the assumptions and procedures to be followed.

[19]Wick R. Miller, James L. Tanner, and Lawrence P. Foley, "A Lexicostatistic Study of Shoshoni Dialects" (*Anthropological Linguistics*, vol. 13, 1971), pp. 142–164.

is an older way of viewing language history, and, in the light of lexicostatistical formulations, such a pattern seems in some measure subject to rethinking. Morphological features, syntactic elements, as well as cultural items of the lexicon may spread by a process of diffusion. The suggestion that there is a parallel between diffusion of language and diffusion of culture has some further application. A language can assimilate new elements from without, whether these are in lexicon, element of sound, or element of structure. It is known that this happens to such an extent that some languages appear to take on the apparent structure of neighboring but unrelated languages. The linguist Morris Swadesh has formulated the concept of a "mesh principle," showing that diffused or convergent patterns may be operative among unrelated languages over wide areas. The reverse may also be true. Languages may remain apparently distinct from each other. Yet when compared lexicostatistically, using the basic word lists, relationships are beginning to be found between languages where previously none were thought to exist.

SELECTED READINGS

Birdwhistell, R. L., *Kinesics and Context: Essays on Body Motion Communication* (1970). Body signals as language adjuncts.

Bloomfield, L., H. Hoijer (ed.), *Language History* (1965). The modern classic, first published in 1933 as a part of Bloomfield's *Language*, now reprinted. Covers the basic principles by which historical derivation of languages is worked out.

Burling, R., *Man's Many Voices: Language in Its Cultural Context* (1970). The effect of the cultural setting on the whole process of communication. The emphasis is on the nonlinguistic factors which affect the use of language; linguistics with a strong cultural anthropological slant.

Carroll, J. B. (ed.), *Language, Thought, and Reality: Selected Writings of Benjamin Lee Whorf* (1956). Whorf's original essays in metalinguistics in a readily available form.

Chomsky, N., *Language and Mind* (1968). By the formulator of modern transformational grammatic methods.

Hall, E. T., *The Silent Language* (1959). A popular and intriguing account of extralinguistic cues as they operate in cultural communications. Holds up for understanding what everyone acts upon but rarely is conscious of. Particularly helpful in its analysis of failure in cross-cultural communication because of unsophisticated awareness of meaning of cues on the part of business and public officials.

Hall, R. A., Jr., *Linguistics and Your Language* (2d rev. ed. of *Leave Your Language Alone!* 1960). A penetrating, easily understandable exploration of process and function in languages.

Hockett, C. F., *A Course in Modern Linguistics* (1958). A clear-headed introduction to the subject.

——, and R. Ascher, "The Human Revolution" (*Current Anthropology*, vol. 5, no. 3, 1964), pp. 135–168. A highly imaginative, hypothetical reconstruction of the origin of language during the transition from ape to man. Highly inferential and speculative, it is stimulating reading, but the thesis has not been discussed in this chapter because of its extreme tentativeness.

Smith, A. G. (ed.), *Communication and Culture: Readings in the Codes of Human Interaction* (1966). Covering more than linguistics, this collection contains a number of interesting articles on communication in its broadest sense as written by outstanding thinkers.

Tyler, S. A. (ed.), *Cognitive Anthropology* (1969). Essays on method and results in the study of how different people define and classify the world and experience and ideas.

23
ART

LEARNING GOALS

Define art and discuss the relationship between art, handicrafts, and "primitive art." ¶ Discuss the psychological significance of art for the individual, and explain its functional significance for primitive and civilized societies. ¶ Contrast naturalistic and abstract art as culturally patterned art forms. ¶ Account for the close relationship between art and religion in most cultures. ¶ Show how some forms of writing began as conventionalization of symbolic art.

WHAT IS PRIMITIVE ART?

Before answering the question, "What is primitive art?" one must, of course, ask first, "What is art?" Definitions proffered by artists, art historians, aestheticians, philosophers, politicians, semanticists, and others are legion. Not surprisingly, all these definitions "vary with the purposes of the definers,"[1] the artist stressing the creative impulse, the art lover emphasizing the emotional response, the Marxist stressing the opinion-molding purpose of the art, etc. All definitions, by whomever given, cast valuable illumination on the fascinating, complicated behaviors involved in the creation of, and response to, the artistic process. Since we have already stated that art is to be perceived in the total cultural context, we shall concentrate on a few definitions offered by anthropologists.

Art Defined

One working definition of art for anthropological purposes is given by E. G. Burrows in his work *Flower in My Ear: Arts and Ethos in Ifaluk Atoll*:

... art is any human activity or product (artifact) that emphasizes form beyond all requirements except those of a distinctive pleasure that the manufacture and contemplation of form can give. By form is meant a perceptible relation of parts to a whole. The distinctive pleasure it gives is here called "aesthetic experience."[2]

More simply, Herskovits states:

In the widest sense ... art is to be thought of *as any embellishment of ordinary living that is achieved with competence and has describable form....* [T]he student of culture must regard as art whatever a people recognizes as manifestations of the impulse to make more beautiful and thus to heighten the pleasure of any phase of living.[3]

R. Sieber feels that it is necessary to add that

[T]his embellishment of life ... its beautification or adornment, can and, indeed, usually does sustain a level of meaning. In short, there are two basic aspects of art: its esthetic or presentational context comprised of form and skill and embodying style, and its meaning context comprised of subject and symbolic associations.[4]

---

[1]G. Mills, "Art: An Introduction to Qualitative Anthropology," in C. M. Otten (ed.), *Anthropology and Art*, p. 77.

[2]E. G. Burrows, *Flower in My Ear: Arts and Ethos in Ifaluk Atoll*, p. 11. By permission of University of Washington Press.

[3]M. J. Herskovits, *Cultural Anthropology*, p. 235. By permission of Alfred A. Knopf, Inc.

[4]R. Sieber, "The Arts and Their Changing Social Function" (*Annals of the New York Academy of Sciences*, vol. 96, 1962), p. 653. Quoted with permission.

Regardless of differences in wording, certain basic elements are stated or implied in most definitions of art: there is a creator(s), a process, a medium, a product presented for public (sometimes limited) view, a content and meaning, and a response on the part of the beholder(s).

Art is a transformation. The beauty of nature may be aesthetically overwhelming—as a gorgeous sunset—but it is not art. Its transformation to a painting, a dance, a song, a poem is. However, some natural objects may become *art by metamorphosis*; that is, something that was not created with the intention of its being art is accepted as art. In most art, however, the human artisan intervenes more actively in the transformation process. This is *art by intention*, the outcome of a human creative process.

Art and handicrafts

Many handicraft works may or may not be viewed as art. Jacques Maquet, in a penetrating analysis of problems in the anthropology of art, has clearly spelled out the distinction between the concepts of *instrumental form* in relation to *noninstrumental* features. He suggests:

Let us take an example: a wooden bowl with some engraved marks. Its context is everyday life; it is used to serve food. Its shape is circular, its rim rounded, its bottom flat. These formal characteristics are instrumental; circular shape and rounded edge make cleaning easier; flat bottom prevents the vessel from being overturned. Some of the engraved marks are magical signs that keep the evil spirits away and prevent them from spoiling the food; they are instrumental too. But we notice also that the rim of the bowl is a perfect circle, which is not easy for a carver working with only adze and knife to achieve. The magical symbols are well balanced and elegant; and beside them there is an engraved pattern, which is just ornamental. These noninstrumental characteristics pertain also to the form. By revealing noninstrumental features, the bowl's form discloses its aesthetic quality.[5]

Noninstrumental expression is the embellishment of an artifact. Plains Indian moccasins were embroidered with dyed porcupine quills. Later,

[5]J. Maquet, "Introduction to Aesthetic Anthropology" (*McCaleb Module in Anthropology*, 1971), p. 8. Quoted with permission of Addison-Wesley Publishing Company, Inc.

when traders made colored beads available, beadwork replaced quillwork. Basket makers found that variations in twilling produced interesting and pleasing designs within the structure of the basket. They discovered that the use of varicolored fibers made possible tasteful coil and twill work. Potters discovered that slips, painting, and sculptural detail made infinite variety a possibility in ceramic production. Clay vessels can be mere household articles, or, by attention to line and form, they can be transformed into objects of aesthetic contemplation. Rawhide boxes could have been left as crude and undecorated as our corrugated shipping cartons. But Plains Indians preferred to decorate them with geometric designs in color. A lime spatula could be a simple stick, but the natives of eastern New Guinea prefer to carve out a handle with painstaking skill. Northern Shoshones were content with roughed-out spoons of mountain-sheep horn, whereas Northwest Coast Indians worked intricate totemic designs into their handles.

These are all examples of noninstrumental embellishment—modification in line, form, or color of useful articles—which is superfluous in the sense that such modifications do not contribute to the utilitarian effectiveness of the article. But they please their owner, impress guests, and whet the acquisitive appetites of museum collectors.

A valid principle seems to be that as soon as a people solves the fundamental technical problems in the production of an artifact or tool, the artistic inpulse begins to assert itself. The more aesthetically endowed individuals begin to play with the surface in an effort to increase the interest potentials of the object.

As a rule, instrumental technique must be mastered before art develops. Beyond mastery of technique, the more leisure the subsistence techniques and resources of a people's culture allow, the greater the likelihood of decorative embellishment. This must not, however, be taken as a bald assertion that leisure produces art. It may, or it may not. Surplus energies and time may be directed into other channels to satisfy other interests, such as war, trading, or games.

To take one more step with Maquet, the quality that makes the noninstrumental significant rather than just "useless" is *aesthetic contemplation*. If the added elements arrest the attention of a public for their own sake, if one sets aside other concerns for the sake of beholding the object for the interest evoked by its form (not its symbolic content), then that is aesthetic experience—good or bad.

Anthropologists agree that aesthetic sensibility is a universal human feature: "one of the few fundamental ways man relates himself to the world."[6] The human being is, indeed, an aesthetic animal.

Primitive art

What, then, is primitive art? Primitive art is simply the art of primitive peoples. It includes music, dance, myths and oral literature, religious ceremonies such as the sun dance (pages 42–44) and the Okipa (pages 340–345), decorative arts and crafts, religious icons, weaving, pottery, statuary, carvings, and painting. (The place of architecture and tools in both the "fine arts" and the "primitive arts" is somewhat in dispute.) Ideally, our discussion of art should perhaps give equal attention to all these media, but because of both the superabundance of graphic and plastic art objects and the greater ease of reproducing them on the printed page, we shall deal primarily with these permanent and visible products. It must be kept in mind, however, that any comment on their role and function in the particular societies from which they come is likely to pertain in one respect or another to all the other art forms as well.

An unfortunate semantic confusion arises over the term "primitive" in art discussions. The so-called primitivists in recent Occidental art stripped down their art forms to an essential simplicity but were not necessarily emulating primitive art, even though they may have been consciously influenced by the art of certain primitive peoples, especially African sculpture. On the other hand, the "American Primitive" school of art consisted of the untutored representatives of an American offshoot of the European cultural and artistic tradition. These painters, working in the early nineteenth century (and some, like Grandma Moses, more recently), had access to

only a very limited history and knowledge of technique. Their paintings and sculptures were simplistic and naïve.

The inclination in art criticism to equate "primitive" with "crude" or "childish" is in part due to the fact that, when primitive art objects were first presented to European artists and connoisseurs (a presentation beginning several centuries ago, but accelerating rapidly in the nineteenth century), these objects were evaluated in terms of classical and traditional standards. "Everything was reckoned according to the degree it approached Judeo-Christian and Classical Western concepts. Thus, art (meaning idealized nature) was beyond the achievements of primitive man. . . ."[7]

The art of primitive peoples runs a wide gamut from technical clumsiness to high skill, from childlike simplicity to impressive complexity, from naturalism and realism to conventionalized abstraction. Even when we eliminate the more florid forms of primitive art from our consideration and concentrate on the arts of the most primitive of known peoples, this is still true. Bushman art is naturalistic and full of vitality (Fig. 23-1). Australian art is highly stylized and in certain forms is abstract and symbolic (Fig. 23-2). Eskimo art is naturalistic and technically quite sophisticated. Shoshone art was almost nonexistent.

No qualities that universally characterize primitive art forms can be adduced from the art of primitive peoples, unless it is that no primitives

[7]D. Fraser, "The Discovery of Primitive Art," in C. M. Otten (ed.), *Anthropology and Art*, p. 26.

FIG. 23-1 Bushman rock painting. The dancers.

[6]*Ibid.*, p. 9.

FIG. 23-2 Australian aboriginal bark painting: a kangaroo hunt. The style combines naturalism with a special focus of interest on the interior anatomy of the kangaroo, producing the so-called x-ray effect. (From the New York Graphic Society, *Australia, Aboriginal Paintings—Arnhem Land.* (Photo courtesy of UNESCO.)

ever solved the problem of perspective—with which most of them never dealt.

THE FUNCTIONS OF ART

The very universality of art, its presence in all times and places where human societies are known, indicates a significant role and several profound functions in human life. This we can say with some certainty. Exactly what these functions may be is more difficult to state.

Psychological Functions

It has been commonly assumed that one function of art is to release tensions by enabling the artist to externalize some of his emotions and ideas in an objective way. In the classical and Western view, the artist experiences "divine discontent" or "creative tension," which he expends or "sublimates" in a specialized "artistic process," which culminates in the production of a "work of art"—be it drama, music, dance, or a graphic art form. The release of the tensions brings satisfaction and pleasure to the artist. In their turn, the viewers of the art object, if it has meaning for

them, are stimulated to sensuous perceptions that likewise produce emotional responses ultimately resolving into pleasurable feelings of euphoria and balance. This is not to deny, however, that the artistic experience may be highly disturbing and may even cause both the artist and the audience great discomfiture while it runs its course. The expression of art begins in a state of tension, and the process of translating these feelings of tension into high artistic form is not an easy one.

Thus, even from the individualistic point of view, art never exists literally for art's sake alone. It exists for psychophysiologic reasons—at least in Western cultures. And because our scientific knowledge of the physiology of emotion is still crude, we understand little of the workings of the artistic impulses. Aesthetics, the study of beauty, remains almost entirely a branch of philosophy, for beauty is still subjective, as far as our understanding of it goes.

Societal Functions

But art may not be seen in its entirety if analyzed only from the individualistic point of view. Art is also a social expression, and inevitably exists as a part of culture. Since the individual is always a creature of society and the child of culture, art *ipso facto* serves social as well as individual interests and needs. Art is inextricably tied to religion and magic—and to politics. It cannot help expressing and reflecting social relations and systems. It can serve to sustain them, as Renaissance art so notably served medieval Christianity or as art in Russia is expected to evoke Socialist sentiments in Soviet citizens. It can also aim at their destruction, as has protest art at various times in recent history, and as does the contemporary anarchist art of those who hold modern civilization to be so false and meaningless that the artist can only ridicule it in the hope of bringing about its downfall.

In the words of Alan P. Merriam,

Through the humanistic elements of his culture, man seems to be making pointed commentary on how he lives; he seems in the humanities to sum up what he thinks of life . . . commenting upon himself and enunciating and interpreting his actions, his aspirations, and his values.[8]

In most primitive societies, art is an expression of world view and a handmaiden of religion.

The Functions of Art in Primitive Society

In the present age of individualistic romantic idealism in the West, the functions of art appear to be more antisocietal and countercultural than otherwise. The old world view is dissolving and the avant-garde is hurrying the process on its way.

Whereas the modern artist consciously creates or invents a personal style in defiance of convention, "the primitive artist is . . . making works of art within a highly formalized, intensely local and very long established style, . . . he is probably largely unaware of the qualities of the style he follows; he uses it as he does his language, rightly, and without self-consciousness."[9]

In primitive societies the artist-creator, therefore, works from a clear set of social expectations, with traditional media, from agreed-upon values toward known and approved social ends. The personal satisfactions and achievements of the artist are incidental. What is important is that the artist's product must satisfy the social needs of the occasion, must evoke the appropriate response, must fulfill the given social function. These social functions may be specific as with the Navaho artist who makes dry paintings for both religious and medical functions "because art for the Navahos is intimately bound up with the maintenace of health and cosmic organization."[10] Or they may be generalized. The Okipa Maker must plan, cast, choreograph, rehearse, and present, with each part being played out correctly, the great Mandan myth in such a way as to reaffirm societal goals and reinspire moral and proper behavior.

The transcendent function, then, of primitive art is to communicate symbolically the value scheme of the culture.

[T]he arts . . . are symptomatic of cultural values and . . . they are for the most part oriented positively, that is, toward man's search for a secure and ordered existence . . . [T]hey can be considered positive, integrated cultural manifestations, reflecting and reinforcing the basic values of the cultures that gave rise to them. . . . The arts at any time or place . . . evolve what might be called the "value image" that culture has of itself.[11]

In this regard, art in primitive societies is inextricably intertwined with politics, religion, world view—the entire complex of social insitutions which seeks to bind each community.

The vital importance of art as social communication in primitive societies cannot be emphasized too strongly. The heterogeneous populations of complex civilized societies, with their plurality of backgrounds, values, and identifications; their geographic and social mobility; and their multiplicity of communications media (books, newspapers, periodicals, radio and television, movies, tapes, satellites) are dramatically different from the small, isolated, homogeneous, closely knit, stable (slow-changing) primitive societies. The function of art in the two types of societies, while sharing certain attributes, thus assumes an important quantitative difference. In

---

[8]A. P. Merriam, *A Prologue to the Study of African Arts*, p. 14.
[9]R. Redfield, "Art and Icon" in C. M. Otten (ed.), *op. cit.*, p. 48.
[10]G. Mills, "Art: An Introduction to Qualitative Anthropology," in C. M. Otten (ed.), *op. cit.*, p. 68.
[11]R. Sieber, "The Arts and Their Changing Social Function," *op. cit.*, p. 655. By permission of New York Academy of Sciences.

primitive societies, art must carry a far greater symbolic burden in maintaining the society's cohesiveness than does modern art outside of Communist countries. Indeed, according to Charlotte Otten,

Here . . . lies the heart of the matter, and a crucial reason why we *cannot* validly equate the arts of nonliterate peoples with those of late civilizations in which writing has permeated the culture as the ordinary medium of communication and information storage. . . . In pre-literate or proto-literate culture, the art symbol *becomes* the fact; that is it simultaneously represents, defines, and manifests its referent. In such cultures, art objects and events serve as media for information storage, rather than books. . . .

Western . . . art only partially and sporadically carries this freight of prescribed symbolic meaning functioning simultaneously on many levels, reinforcing cultural values and at once enlarging, sensitizing, and unifying our perceptions.[12]

---

[12]Excerpts from C. M. Otten (ed.), *Anthropology and Art*, pp. xiv-xv. Copyright © 1971, Charlotte M. Otten. Reprinted by permission of Doubleday and Company, Inc.

FIG. 23-3 Naturalistic representation portrayed in an effigy jar from Mochica, Peru. (Photo courtesy of the American Museum of Natural History.)

For the very same reasons, when a primitive society comes into contact with a civilization and starts to acculturate to it, one of the first things to go is its traditional art. It is not production for the tourist trade that destroys primitive art. It is the disintegration of the value system which the art had been originally produced to sustain.

Art as communication has an additional importance in our consideration in that artistic symbols provided the bridge to written language, and we have thus included art as transition to writing in this chapter (see pages 395–399).

FORMS OF GRAPHIC ART: STYLE

Art forms may be *naturalistic* or *abstract*, with all degrees of transition between the extremes. A form is naturalistic if the transformation of the object results in a faithful representation of the original model (as in the Peruvian effigy jar shown in Fig. 23-3). The form is abstract if the identifying attributes of the original object have been transformed by means of a symbolic identity which does not closely resemble the original form. The face and body of the ancestral figure painted on the facade of a Sepik River men's spirit house in New Guinea, as shown in Fig. 23-4, is more abstract than naturalistic. The ideographic wall paintings from prehistoric Portugal are wholly abstract.

Style

The term "style" means a departure from absolute naturalism. Artists always compose their creations to some degree. Documentary photography, as well as the snapshots of most amateurs, is not art. But by selective lighting, screening, and retouching, photography can be made to approach art. A textbook line illustration of an anatomical specimen is a scientific representation, but hardly ever art. Style denotes a standardized selective modification of the image in a way that produces an aesthetically effective and distinctive representation (Fig. 23-5).

Style in Northwest Coast art

One of the most distinctive of all primitive art styles is that which originates on the Northwest

FIG. 23-4 Abstract of a human face and body, painted on the facade of a men's spirit house (Haus Tambaran), Maprik District, Sepik River, New Guinea. (Photograph by E. A. Hoebel.)

Coast of North America and is exemplified in the carving and painting of masks, totem poles, boxes, rattles, dishes, spoons, canoes, houses, and other objects. Exaggerations in representative art have led not to geometric design but a unique stylization in which a body form can still be distinguished, in spite of the fact that it is greatly distorted in size and arrangement. All Northwest Coast art objects are utilitarian in intent, and therefore the decorative element is more or less subordinated to the object. This is definitely not free art.

The effects of this subordination of the art to the object are most interesting. The artist is given, so to speak, a decorative field that must be covered. Blank spaces are abhorrent. The artist also wants all the decorative elements to represent some aspect of animal life. Hence, the artist is impelled to dissect, dismember, distort, and remold creatures to fill the space whether it is the surface of a box, bowl, wooden hat, or rattle. Distortion becomes such that the representation is in the end a caricature.

TOTEMIC SYMBOLISM   Design does not annihilate representation wholly, however, because the im-

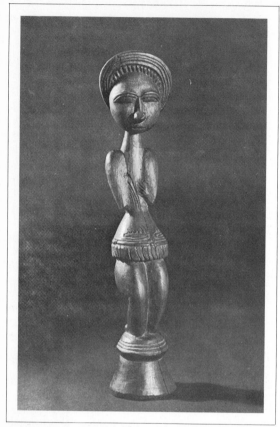

FIG. 23-5 A contemporary Trobriand Island statue combining naturalism and abstraction in its style. (Private collection. Photo by Don Breneman.)

pulses of the Northwest Coast artist are not unalloyedly aesthetic. Totemic heraldry, with its rich mythology of clan and lineage origins from heroic animal ancestors, pervades most Northwest Coast art. The representative art portrays not just an animal but an animal that symbolizes some mythical or historic event in the social background of the artist. This interest in the art counterbalances the tendency for caricature to get out of hand. The device by means of which this purpose is made effective is the standardization of certain immutable symbols based on one or a few outstanding anatomical traits of the natural creature portrayed. Thus, no matter how weird the distortion in the interests of design or in the flight of

imaginative fancy, the message to be conveyed by the representation cannot be lost in meaningless form and line.

RELIGION AND ART

Religion and art are by no means inseparable, but for deep-rooted reasons they have a strong affinity. In essence, religion is subjective—a matter of belief. Yet the covert concepts of religious belief need objectifying, and art is an outstandingly effective medium. By artistic embellishment, the paraphernalia of religion and magic may be lifted out of the realm of ordinary artifacts or activities to become endowed with qualities of the unusual that should be associated with the supernatural—the sacred.

Yet even more important than the elaboration of religious paraphernalia is the representation of the spirits and gods. Gods are imaginative conceptions who exist in belief. If the belief can be translated into concrete form, it becomes more real and convincing. Paintings and statues objectify the subjective concepts of the divinities (Fig. 23-6). The presence of a god at a ceremony is more directly felt by the majority of people if he is there in solid stone or wood looking out on the believers. The visual religious art of any primitive people communicates eloquently. Edmund Leach has stated it well:

It is intended to be understood. And in the ordinary way it will be understood by the audience for whom it is designed. For the audience for which a primitive artist works is composed of members of his own community steeped in the same mythological tradition as himself and familiar with the same environment of material fact and ritual activity; the primitive artist can therefore afford to communicate in shorthand; symbols have the same basic significance and the same range of ambiguity for artist and audience alike.[13]

Leach goes on to observe that the European art critic who tries to understand primitive art is forced to concentrate on its form alone, without reference to its meaning; the critic is ignorant of

[13]E. R. Leach, "Aesthetics," in E. E. Evans-Pritchard, *The Institutions of Primitive Society*, p. 32. By permission of Basil Blackwell and Mott, Ltd.

primitive peoples in many parts of the world. Only Polynesia and Micronesia, in the Pacific, and the Plains and Basin areas, in the United States, are conspicuous in that masking is absent, or nearly so. In the religion of the Plains Indians, deities are of little importance; there is nothing much to mask. In Polynesia, although the pantheon is elaborate and deities are portrayed as statues, masking is abjured for reasons that are obscure.

In North America, the masks of the Northwest Coast attain a richness of variety and form that is rivaled only in parts of Melanesia. Many Northwest Coast masks, by means of hinges and strings, have movable parts that may be manipulated by the actor to heighten the dramatic effect. Some have an inner and an outer face to portray the dual character (animal and human) of the early mythological progenitors. The most important of the factors that have combined to produce the exotic elaborateness of Northwest Coast masks are (1) a social organization emphasizing hereditary status based in part on descent from mythological ancestral lineage founders, (2) elaboration of dance drama depicting the deeds of the mythical heroes, (3) technical mastery of the skills of carving, and (4) a vigorous creative drive to translate ideas and mental imagery into objective representations.

At the eastern end of North America, Iroquois masks as made and used by the False Face Society of curers are not so rich in variety or so elaborate as those of the Northwest Coast, but they bear the stamp of a grotesquely humorous realism designed to frighten away evil spirits (Fig. 23-7). While the intent of the masks is serious, one cannot help feeling that the artist carves with tongue in cheek.

FIG. 23-6 A Sepik River, New Guinea, statue portraying a mythic human head in which the pendant nose, so characteristic of Sepik art, becomes the tail of the spirit bird which clings to the back of the statue. (Private collection. Photo by Don Breneman.)

the religious and mythic content of the object of analysis.

Masks and Rituals

Primitive religious sculpture is in the form of masks or statues—that is to say, idols. Without artists there can be no idolatry. The use of masks to portray supernatural beings is prevalent among

African Sculpture

Statuary as a medium of primitive religious art is common in Africa and Melanesia, and also in Polynesia and Central America. African statuary has had considerable influence upon modern European artists, beginning with Picasso. It possesses a living quality eagerly sought after by modernists. It embodies the people's hopes and fears; it terrorizes or delights them as it portrays the nature of the gods on whom they lean or

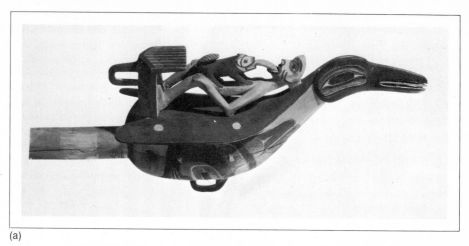

(a)

FIG. 23-7 (*a*) A Tsimshian (Northwest Coast of North America) shaman's rattle. The raven, which forms the body of the rattle, is believed to possess the secret of life, while the tongue contains the spirit of life. The beaver, which stands on the stomach of a man who has just died, is receiving the supernatural power of the shaman. (Courtesy of the American Museum of Natural History.) (*b*) A masked shaman of the Iroquois False Face Curing Society, with turtle shell rattle in hand, performing in a sacred tobacco patch.

(b)

before whom they prostrate themselves, not only in African sculpture, but also in Polynesian and Melanesian. The artist is close to the work, and the work is close to the interests and well-being of the people.

Mass, solidity, and plainness of surface are the impressive features of African sculpture, even though the figures are not usually very large. These qualities are induced partly by the nature of the material in which the artist works, and partly by a personal inimitable style. The material is hardwood—mahogany, the aristocrat of timbers, and ironwood—tough, challenging material. No light-minded whittler can work the sculptor's transformation on such a block. The wood is close-grained and invites a high polish with dark lustrous tones. The glistening highlights of the smooth African skin are beautifully reflected in the finished statues. The wedding of subject matter and materials is perfect.

African sculpture is characteristically disproportionate. The head is always large in relation to the torso; the legs are squat and sturdy. All the work is subject to the limitations of the mass of the block with which the artist works, which is to say that the African woodworker is no joiner.

Since the woodworker cannot attach projecting pieces to the mass, the arms must be formed close to the body. The legs must be confined within the area of the original block. Such limitations contribute to the feeling of compactness that emerges from the art (Fig. 23-8). Concentration of attention on the head of the statue, lineal elongation of the body, and dwarfing of the lower limbs are matters of stylistic choice in the African tradition.

Most African statues represent dead ancestors; they are created to house their spirits. The statue, when the spirit has taken up its abode, is in the true sense a fetish, an object possessing a supernatural quality. It is not just a work of art to be viewed objectively in a museum. It is a personage, alive with all the pulsating powers of the personality it represents—powers that are superhumanly potent because the personality it represents is no longer that of mere man but is godlike. As Maquet notes, contemporary Africans often protest with vehemence against the inclusion of their religious and political symbolic objects in European and American art museums. "They point out that these objects were not art for their forefathers."[14] They have become art by metamorphosis.

ART AS SEMANTICS

Throughout this entire book, but particularly in this section, we have emphasized the symbolic attributes of culture in the definition of world view, the infusion of meaning into life, and the generation of states of emotional commitment of the individual members of society to the groups of which they are members and to the society to which they are bonded. In addition to ritual and myth as aspects of religion, art, too, speaks a symbolic message. The message may be clear and explicit, as when a Tlingit totem pole presents the actors in a household mythic "history." Or it may be diffuse and ambiguous but nonetheless heard and sensed, as it is in contemporary junk art and the works of the counterculture abstractionists, which give vent to the emotional instability, anxieties, irritation, free-floating anger, and

[14]J. Maquet, "Introduction to Aesthetic Anthropology" (*McCaleb Module in Anthropology*, 1971), p. 13.

FIG. 23-8 Bakongo wood statue of mother and child. The large head and small legs, along with cicatrization on the upper torso, reveal common stylistic features of West African art. (Photo courtesy of the Museum of Primitive Art.)

frustrations so widely experienced throughout the modern world. What art communicates is not explicit but, rather, implicit.

The messages in Northwest Coast totemic art, for example, are clear and explicit only to the members of the tribe and clan who know the meanings of the "signs" in the art through knowing the myths, the specific forms (like the beaver's tail), and the symbolic referents of the different colors. Art as language speaks only to those who understand the language. It is particularistic and ethnocentric. Symbolic content is more important than the form. The form is conventionalized. The more the art is intended to convey a narrow and specific message rather than to evoke a generalized social effect, the greater will be the tendency toward economy of effort in the production of visible artistic signs and symbols. The movement in the development of visual language may be expected to be from naturalistic representation to simplified abstract representation. From such a process writing has developed. Hence, it will be treated here as the most specialized outgrowth of art.

Capsian and Azilian Picture Writing

In the rock shelter of Cogul, in Spain, is a painted wall upon which prehistoric man of the Capsian culture left many paintings (Fig. 23-9). One shows a man confronting a stag. On another part of the wall is a crudely conventionalized picture of a hunter who has just shot a large arrow at a stag. In yet another spot is a very queer figure. We know, however, that the Capsian hunters were very much interested in dead deer, and with the more naturalistic examples before us, we can compare the number of prongs in the forklike projections on this figure with the prongs of the antlers in the naturalistic pictures. That a deer is meant is certain. Furthermore, since the four feet of the object are sticking straight up in the air, we may feel reasonably sure that this is the symbol for a dead deer, presumably a magic hunting symbol to help the deerslayer.

What took place at Cogul occurred elsewhere on the Iberian Peninsula. Obermaier, in arguing for a genetic relationship between the Azilian painted pebbles and the painted petroglyphs of the Spanish caves and rock shelters, prepared the comparative chart shown in Fig. 23-10. Clearly, the Azilian ⋀ symbolizes a squatting female, and the ⋀ is a male. Azilian man had apparently progressed from picture writing to the use of ideographs—drawn or written symbols that stand directly for things or notions instead of the sounds of words in the language of the users. Such is the first step in the evolution and origin of all systems of writing. The scribe is the intellectual offspring of the artist.

Chinese Ideographs

On a much more elaborate level, the Chinese system of characters is fundamentally an ideographic picture writing which has become reduced to a set of timesaving brushstrokes and which is in some aspects also phonetic. Its ideographic quality may be readily discerned in the manner of writing such words as "prisoner," and "happiness." In the character for "prisoner," we see a man, 人, in an enclosure, 囚. "Happiness" is a woman (wife), 女, with a son, 好 子. The earlier pictographic derivation of a number of Chinese characters may be seen in Fig. 23-11.

The occurrence in all languages of words that are identically pronounced but have different meanings (homophones)[15] makes possible a ready extension of ideographic writing as soon as a people is able to make the mental leap of partially disassociating the picture from the idea and linking it to sounds as such. Thus the Chinese word for "horse," which is "mar," is represented by 馬. The Chinese term for "mother" used within the intimate confines of the family is sometimes "mama." Phonetically, then, it would be possible for the Chinese to write "mama" as 馬馬. This, however, would be ambiguous, for unless the context made it clear, the reader would not be certain whether the symbol represented two horses or one mother. The Chinese get around this difficulty by first writing the symbol for woman, 女, followed by the homophone symbol for "mar." Thus they have produced a way of writing

---

[15]For example, *saw*: (1) past tense of *to see*; (2) a cutting tool with a serrated edge; (3) to cut with a sawlike tool; (4) to cut as if with a sawlike tool; (5) a sententious saying or proverb.

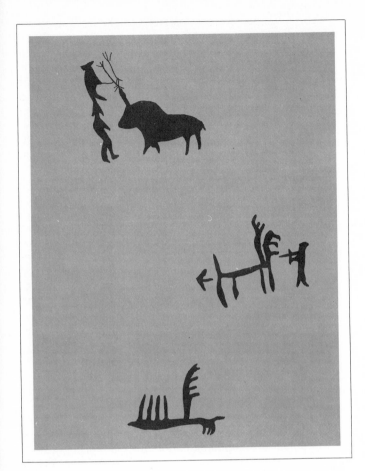

FIG. 23-9 Three degrees of conventionalization in the representation of the stag in the Capsian art from Cogul.

FIG. 23-10 Probable female and male symbols on painted pebbles from Le Mas d'Azil (right) compared with female and male pictographs from Late Upper Paleolithic cave art in eastern Spain (left). (After Obermaier.)

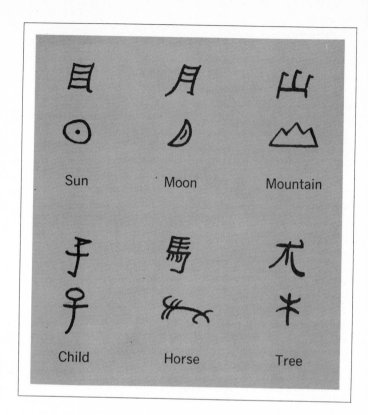

FIG. 23-11 Pictographic derivation of some seventeenth-century Chinese characters. (After Brouner and Fung.)

''mama'' that is half ideogram and half phonogram. Because of its way of mixing ideograms and phonograms, Chinese writing is classed as a *transitional system*, a means of written communication which has gone beyond the more primitive forms of pictography but which still falls short of pure phonetic representation.

The ancient Egyptian, Hittite, Cretan, and cuneiform (Sumerian, Babylonian, Assyrian) script systems also developed out of picture writing by use of similar basic principles, although each evolved its own special forms. These and the Chinese, plus the Indic and Mayan-Aztec systems, are the only definitely known independent basic scripts invented by man. The transformation of art to writing is a supreme human achievement, so difficult that few peoples have done it on their own. Most individuals have achieved literacy through borrowing.

Alphabetic Origins

Our own alphabet had its beginnings in Egyptian pictography. Its development from early Greek inscriptions is well known and, indeed, testified to by the very word by which we identify it: a compound of the first two words of the Grecian system, the *alpha* and *beta*. Beyond the Grecian alphabet, however, lies the Semitic from which it in turn is clearly derived: Hebrew, *aleph*, *beth*, *gimel*. Some Semitic symbols have clear derivation from Egyptian hieroglyphs; many do not. Known archaic Semitic inscriptions are few and far between, far too few to enable paleographers to advance well-founded reconstructions of the full history of the emergence of the alphabet. Although there are indications that parallel attempts at developing alphabetic systems were more or less simultaneously under way among several different Semitic peoples around the second millennium B.C., only one system (that of the Phoenicians) was finally perfected. From this, and this alone, all the extant alphabets of the world have descended. Here was a cultural triumph so difficult to conceive, and so perfect in form and function, that with minor modifications it could be adapted to any and all languages. It has superseded all other alphabetic systems; mankind has never again had either the need or the capacity to evolve a new system.

Of the Semitic symbols derived from Egyptian hieroglyphic ideograms, the first letter of the alphabet will suffice for illustrative purposes. *Aleph*, in Semitic, means "ox." The Egyptian hieroglyph is ◖. On the Moabite stone, which presents a Semitic inscription of Mesha, king of Moab, in the ninth century B.C., the symbol is formed with three straight lines, ◁. In later Greek it was inverted on its horns, and became A. Similar transitions may be seen for *beta*, *gamma*, *delta*, and other letters. The Egyptian word sounds for "ox," "house," and so on were ignored by the Semitic scribes; what they succeeded in doing was to make pictorially derived symbols from Egyptian prototypes, which were subsequently associated with the separate consonants that went to make up their speech. The Semites never included vowels in their script, but wrote each word with only its consonantal sounds. The *aleph* symbol stood for the glottal stop, which is exceedingly important in Semitic speech. The Greeks had no use for the glottal stop, but they were able to represent the vowels of their speech in a way the Semites could not, and they completed the basic modern alphabet with the invention of vowel symbols. They converted the A to represent the first vowel and made other adjustments to take care of the rest.

The capstone was thus put on the transition from art to writing. The communication of generalized states of emotion and ideas through the aesthetic medium had at long last been transmuted to the communication of precise linguistic expression through phonetically representative symbols.

SELECTED READINGS

Boas, F., *Primitive Art* (1929). The classic work on the subject.

Breuil, H., *Four Hundred Centuries of Cave Art* (1950). The most comprehensive summary of Paleolithic art.

Buehler, A., T. Barrow, and C. P. Mountford, *The Art of the South Seas, Including Australia and New Zealand* (1962). Many beautiful color plates and numerous line drawings together with a very competent ethnography of Oceanic art.

Deringer, D., *The Alphabet* (1948). A detailed, but not too technical, discussion.

Dunn, Dorothy, *American Indian Painting of the Southwest and Plains Area* (1968). Illustrated with many handsome color plates. Especially interesting in its accounts of the development of modern Indian painting—a wedding of contemporary techniques and Indian cultural interests.

Herskovits, M. J., *Backgrounds of African Art* (1945). A useful survey of the major art styles of Africa.

Holm, B., *Northwest Coast Indian Art: An Analysis of Form* (1965). A study of the basic principles underlying the decorative art of the Northwest Coast.

Krieger, H. W., "Design Areas in Oceania" (*United States National Museum, Proceedings*, vol. 79, 1932), pp. 1–53. A good example of an ethnological study of stylistic distributions.

Kroeber, A. L., "Art," in J. H. Steward (ed.), *Handbook of South American Indians*, vol. 5, *The Comparative Ethnology of South American Indians* (1946), pp. 411–492. A comprehensive survey of aboriginal, including prehistoric, art in South American cultures.

Maquet, J., "Introduction to Aesthetic Anthropology" (*McCaleb Module in Anthropology*, 1971). A penetrating and beautifully reasoned formulation of a general anthropological theory of art.

Otten, C. M. (ed.), *Anthropology and Art: Readings in Cross-cultural Aesthetics* (1971). Contains twenty-four well-chosen articles on theory and method in the study of primitive art, primitive artists, and art forms in relation to culture areas.

Smith, M. W. (ed.), *The Artist in Tribal Society* (1961). An anthropological exploration of the roles and functions of the primitive artist by a symposium of experts convened by The Royal Anthropological Institute in London. The verbatim record of the discussions is particularly interesting.

ANTHROPOLOGY TODAY
AND TOMORROW

24

BEYOND CIVILIZATION: WHAT OF THE FUTURE?

LEARNING GOALS

Expound the concepts of moral order and technical order, and show how they relate to the social changes in primitive societies when they come into contact with civilizations. ¶ Specify the ways in which peasant society is a transition between tribal and civilized societies. ¶ Evaluate the image of limited good and the nature of kinship structure as factors influencing peasant behavior. ¶ State the relationships between the control of energy and the development of culture. ¶ Formulate the concept of surbanization and the characteristics of future society as predicted from the imperatives of the six functional prerequisites of society.

The study of mankind as it has been presented in this introduction to cultural anthropology has focused on the ways of life which have dominated the human scene for more than a million years. Tribal life characterized the entire Pleistocene period. It evolved slowly and steadily into ever larger units of social organization, with more variations on the common themes of obtaining a living and of distributing goods, of organizing the family and kinship groups, of political determination of social goals, of ways of viewing the surrounding environment and the forces of the universe, and of giving symbolic expression to all these factors in language, art, myth, and religious ritual.

Then came the domestication of plants and animals followed by civilization with its explosion of culture linked to the life of cities. This was the first of humanity's great revolutions. Civilization, as we know, means "the culture of cities," the urban way of life. Like tribal culture before it, civilization has unfolded in a number of variations, with subsistence, kinship, government, and world view always present although manifested variously. Perhaps the most radical changes it produced, however, were a quantum leap in the amount of usable energy made possible by the domestication of plants and animals; a vast increase in the numbers of people freed from subsistence farming for other specialized roles; the addition of writing, monumental architecture and public buildings, to art, myth, and religion as forms of symbolic expression; the decline of the kinship group in social importance; and the increasing dominance of controlling elites over the economic and political orders.

The task of studying and interpreting the course of civilizations has (except for New World archaeology) been largely the responsibility of historians, rather than anthropologists. Hence, it has been touched on only peripherally in this book. Nonetheless, anthropologists have been much concerned with what has happened to mankind in the transformation from primitive to civilized life. Civilization has been the great triumph of human achievement during the past six millennia. Now it is giving way to a new kind and level of culture. The task for anthropology is not only to complete the story of mankind's prehistoric past and to reveal the nature of all known and knowable social systems of yesterday and today, but also to clarify the transformations that so confuse our times and to help build a decent and rational life-way for all humanity in the future.

403

THE TRANSFORMATION OF THE PRIMITIVE WORLD

The process of revolutionary culture change that is now overtaking civilization has recurred repeatedly in the world of primitive man as civilization overtook it. It involves great technological innovations, to be followed by far-reaching changes in ideology and social structure. The effects of the change are manifest in crises in what Redfield called the "moral order" within cultures.[1]

The Moral Order

The moral order is what generates the sense of social commitment in a people—the emotional sense of being a significant part of a community of human beings to whom one has obligations and duties and from whom one receives support, emotionally and socially. The moral order consists of shared understandings about individual and collective goals and their meanings. It becomes manifest as patterns of kinship, neighborhood, club, and work groups, and of recreational, artistic, religious, and community roles in social contexts in which the roles are performed with an accompanying sentiment of "rightness" and gratification. Obviously, the moral order may be closely related to the world view.

The moral order of primitive societies

The cultures of most preliterate societies have been governed by their moral orders. Few primitive peoples have doubted the validity of their social systems. Their moral orders have sustained them from their early period of enculturation until death. Most primitive cultures are what Edward Sapir called "harmonious, or genuine," cultures:

The genuine culture is not of necessity either high or low; it is merely inherently harmonious, balanced, self-satisfactory. It is the expression of a richly varied and yet somehow unified and consistent attitude toward life, an attitude which sees the significance of any one element of civilization in its relation to all others. . . . The major activities of the individual must directly satisfy his own creative and emotional impulses, must always be some-

thing more than means to an end. . . . A culture that does not build itself out of the central interests and desires of its bearers, that works from general ends to the individual is an external culture. . . . The genuine culture is internal, it works from the individual to ends.[2]

Through selective adaptation in which symbolic integration and close personal relations are effectively developed, long-enduring cultures have always possessed effective and "genuine" (in Sapir's sense) moral orders.

We may follow Redfield further in his characterization of primitive societies as possessing certain general characteristics: (1) the community is usually quite small; (2) kinship relations and close, personal bonds extend throughout the community; (3) economic and social interests are homogeneous, and there are few specialists; (4) attitudes and behavior are dominated by religious-mystical assumptions about the nature of humanity and the outer world; and (5) suspicion of outsiders (nonkinsmen) commonly leads to a chronic state of warfare with some other groups.

As we know full well by now, the qualitative expression of these traits varies among primitive cultures, but they characterize all small, primitive societies held together by the moral bond.

The Technical Order

A complement to the moral order within cultures is what Redfield called the *technical order*:

The bonds that co-ordinate the activities of men in the technical order do not rest on convictions as to the good life; they are not characterized by a foundation in human sentiments; they can exist even without the knowledge of those bound together that they are bound together. The technical order is that order which results from mutual usefulness, from deliberate coercion, or from the mere utilization of the same means. In the technical order men are bound by things, or are themselves things.[3]

---

[1]R. Redfield, *The Primitive World and Its Transformations*, pp. 20–25.

[2]E. Sapir, "Culture, Genuine and Spurious" (*American Journal of Sociology*, vol. 29, 1924), p. 410. Of course Sapir uses the words "genuine" and "spurious" in specific senses. All cultures are genuine in the sense that they exist. By permission of The University of Chicago Press.

[3]R. Redfield, *The Primitive World and Its Transformations*, p. 21. By permission of Cornell University Press. Copyright 1953.

The technical order of civilizations

The rise of cities has repeatedly shattered the moral orders of the people who have been drawn into them. A city is rarely, if ever, the product of a local population that has stayed put and "just growed." As far back as the time of Çatal Hüyük, trade was the lifeblood of the city, although it relied, too, on the food products of the surrounding country. All cities incorporate strangers, and in the initial phases of a city's life, the separate little moral orders, according to which the strangers have previously been organized in tribal lifeways, dissolve. New urban civilizations are held together mainly by reliance on technical order. Regulations, prescripts, and edicts set the formal patterns to be observed. Magisterial and priestly exactments drive or exhort men to obey. Religious spectaculars and civil carnivals are designed by the priests and rulers to substitute as symbolic integrators for the old tribal rituals. Soldiers, jailers, and executioners coerce the recalcitrants into behavior which they feel insufficiently committed to adopt for themselves. The dungeon and the prison are inventions of early civilizations.

This is the period in which the moral order becomes managed by an elite, or functional class, and in which the reflection and systematization accomplished by the literati have added a new dimension to the ethical and intellectual life. The moral order now has a public phase connected with deliberate policy. . . . Religion is now, in short, a way of making citizens.[4]

Civilization, the city way of life, is always marked by a new kind of social bonding. At the outset, the moral order of each urban culture in civilization is *managed* in contrast to the *self-maintaining* moral order of primitive societies. For the great civilizations of the past, such orders sufficed for long periods of time. Eventually, they declined in effectiveness as disintegrating forces dissolved their influence. Urban populations of antiquity acquired *proletarii*, which in Rome meant the lowest class of the city, who were regarded as contributing nothing to the state but children. Some urban populations became caught in a welter of conflicting beliefs that tended to nullify one another's influence. The reform

religions of Christianity, Islam, and Buddhism each arose to provide foundations for new moral orders upon which new civilizations could be built.

In antiquity, the urban revolution churned up the old tribal world into a condition that was, apparently, both frightening and exhilarating. The Egyptians and the Aztecs, as we have seen, built on fear; the Greeks, on exhilaration. Medieval civilization in Europe was reconstituted on a feudalistic Christian moral order, and ultimately on an industrial Christian moral system that has proved to be tremendously effective down to the twentieth century.

ANOMY AND CIVILIZATION Anomy[5] occurs when drastic change causes moral orders to lose their bonding and motivating effect, or when segments of the population are alienated because no satisfying place exists for them in the changing social structure. The resulting anomy is marked by

. . . the retreat of the individual into his own ego, the skeptical rejection of all social bonds. . . . It signifies the state of mind of one who has been pulled up from his moral roots, who no longer has any standards but only disconnected urges, who no longer has any sense of continuity, of folk, of obligations.[6]

Anomy is the disease of the disintegrating or reconstituting civilization—or of the shattered primitive society. Apathy and demoralization characterize many American Indian populations that have not become extinct or been absorbed into the civilization that has engulfed them. A contemporary journalist's description of anomy embraces much of Western society:

The sense of belonging, of place, of a shared heritage of memories, has disappeared in an anonymous urban sprawl, and each of us forages orphan-like in alien streets where all the dreams have died, armed with plastic credit cards that vainly protest our identity.[7]

---

[4]*Ibid.*, p. 65. By permission of Cornell University Press.

[5]The French spelling, *anomie*, is also used by some American sociologists under the influence of Émile Durkheim, but the English word has been well-established for at least four hundred years.

[6]R. M. MacIver, *The Ramparts We Guard*, p. 77. By permission of Macmillan Publishing Co., Inc. Copyright 1950.

[7]S. Hempstone, "Leaving Grandpa to Die by a Dry Waterhole" (*Minneapolis Tribune*, Dec. 5, 1971), p. 37A.

A major task of applied anthropology today is to assist national planners and international development agencies in finding ways to promote modernization without causing the paralyzing disruption of ongoing moral orders before new and effective orders can replace them. This requires, in the first place, a genuine understanding of the moral orders by which people who are to be "modernized" now live. Even in city slums, the anthropological approach provides the understanding, in ways that otherwise seem to be overlooked. The work of Oscar Lewis in Mexico City, San Juan, Puerto Rico, and New York City is the prototype of what the new anthropology can offer to this end.

In Lewis's words:

One of the major obstacles to more rapid and significant progress in the current war against poverty is the great gulf that exists between the values and way of life of the very poor and those of the middle-class personnel—teachers, social workers, health workers, and others—who bear the major responsibility in carrying out these programs. We know a great deal about the statistics and economics of poverty, but we are only beginning to understand the psychology and inner life of some of the very poor. In the case of the Puerto Ricans, many of whom have come from rural areas or urban slums, the obstacles to understanding are even greater because of the barrier of language and the differences between cultures. And while Puerto Ricans have been one of the most surveyed and studied groups, most of the studies have been of a questionnaire type and have told us too little about the intimate details of their lives and the conditions which have formed their character.[8]

PEASANT SOCIETIES

Before we look to the next stage of cultural evolution, an overview of the place of peasant society in the scheme of things is in order.

Peasant societies are the tribal communities of the primitive world transformed into a special and long-enduring type of little community within the structure of civilizations.

A peasant society may be defined as a subsociety of a large stratified society which is either preindustrial or only partly industrialized. It is further characterized by most or all of the following traits: rural residence; familial agriculture on self-owned small land holdings or other simple rural occupations providing a modest or subsistence livelihood; the family as the centrally important social unit; low social status; economic interdependence in varying degree with urban centers; simple culture; and attachment to the soil, the local community and tradition.[9]

The peasant community is like the tribe in certain aspects of the quality of its moral order; it differs in its lack of autonomy and independence and in other respects mentioned below. It is part of a larger social system in which it is related to and dominated by the cities of the civilization of which it is a part. "It required the city to bring it into existence. There were no peasants before the first cities. And those surviving primitive peoples who do not live in terms of the city are not peasants."[10]

Historically, the original peasants were Neolithic agriculturalists who were not sucked into the cities and retained a subcultural identity of their own. They lived in marginal and partial isolation upon the land they tilled. Their food and craft surpluses were taken through taxation, or traded or bartered in open markets located in the towns and cities, and fed into the exchange and consumption systems of the local states and empires of which they were part. Peasants adapted to the existence of cities but steadfastly remained apart from the cities. Usually illiterate, they could not master the arts and learning essential to knowing the mysteries of civilized life. Or if, as individuals, they did do so, they entered at first into the lower bureaucracy of the state and church systems, cutting off their peasant ties. Or they disappeared in time into the urban proletariat. Cities have always replenished themselves and nourished their own growth with migrants from tribal and peasant populations. The reservoir of peasants has been vast, for as observed by Daniel Thorner, ". . . [T]he peasantry has constituted the most numerous social group in all organized states,

---

[8]O. Lewis, "Mother and Son in a Puerto Rican Slum; Part 1: Felicita" (*Harper's Magazine*, December, 1965), p. 72. Copyright © 1974, The Minneapolis Star and Tribune Co., Inc. Quoted with permission.

[9]E. Norbeck, "Peasant Society," in J. Gould and W. L. Kolb (eds.), *A Dictionary of the Social Sciences*, p. 490. By permission of Macmillan Publishing Co., Inc., Copyright 1964.
[10]Redfield, *op. cit.*, p. 31.

from ancient to modern times, that have rested on traditional forms of agriculture."[11]

During the eighteenth and nineteenth centuries, extinction was the fate of many tribes. In the twentieth and twenty-first centuries, except in the case of such marginal peoples as the African Bushmen, incorporation into post-civilizations, rather than extinction, will undoubtedly be achieved by most tribal groups. As populations, either they will be pulled into the industrial-surban complex, or they may retain a measure of group identity for a while through a transformation from a tribal to a peasant existence.

Yet, strangely, except as a source of anachronistic beliefs, looked upon as survivals in the writings of Tylor and Frazer, there was little study of peasant communities and social structure until after World War II. Then with a newly ignited interest in India and other Asiatic countries, along with the rapid acculturation of the remaining tribal populations in all parts of the world, anthropologists began to give attention to European, African, and Middle and South American peasantry, as well as Asiatic. Just when anthropologists have begun paying attention to peasantry as a special cultural manifestation, peasantry, like the civilization of which it is a part, is disappearing.

Qualities of Peasant Culture

Peasants have their own integrity and a clear sense of their own identity, but they are usually backward, unsophisticated, and underprivileged relative to city dwellers—and they know it. They may resent their lowly and powerless position, but historically they have rarely revolted. Peasants must pay tribute or taxes to landlords, middlemen, and the state; they and their wives go to market and touch upon the life of the city, but they are not of or in it.

The home village is the peasant's base of security; yet it is not a whole society, because of the presence of the city beyond the horizon. The peasant community has its own cycle of folk rituals and festivals, usually marking the high points of the annual cycle of crops and move-

ments of the sun. Folk beliefs are thinly watered versions of the great religions which characterize each major civilization. The peasants' folk ceremonies may be colorful and boisterous enough, but they rarely seem to exhibit anything like the rich symbolic tapestry of many of the great primitive tribal rituals. For the peasant, world view expresses a limited segment of culture and society—and therefore a limited conception of the universe.

The image of the limited good

In their limited and constricted corner of the great world upon which their experience impinges but rarely penetrates, peasants adjust to their marginal status with the "image of the limited good,"[12] as George M. Foster has labeled it. "Self-improvement," family advancement, and community betterment are not accepted as social goals. Peasants see not an expandable universe but a fixed and limited, closely bounded source of available resources. It is a "zero-sum" situation in which it is believed that if one gets more, another must get less. As expressed by Foster:

By "Image of Limited Good" I mean that broad areas of peasant behavior are patterned in such a fashion as to suggest that peasants view their social, economic, and natural universes—their total environment—as one in which all of the desired things in life such as land, wealth, health, friendship and love, manliness and honor, respect and status, power and influence, security and safety, *exist in finite quantity* and *are always in short supply*, as far as the peasant is concerned. Not only do these and all other "good things" exist in finite and limited quantities, but in addition *there is no way directly within peasant power to increase the available quantities.*[13]

The result, according to the reports of most anthropological field workers, is that peasants struggle desperately for survival with sweat, hard work, and resignation. A stroke of good luck may bring a windfall to a villager, but in the tight little village community this commonly brings with it

---

[11]D. Thorner, "Peasantry" (*International Encyclopedia of the Social Sciences*, vol. 11, 1968), p. 504.

[12]G. M. Foster, "Peasant Society and the Image of the Limited Good" (*American Anthropologist*, vol. 67, 1965), pp. 293–315.
[13]*Ibid.*, p. 304. By permission of the American Anthropological Association.

"envy, gossip, criticism, and calumny."[14] Such cutting down of the fellow villager is a functionally effective way of choking off competition for closely limited goods and minimizes the possibilities of disruption of the conservative, face-to-face social order. It also makes life niggardly.

Kinship structure

An interesting feature of peasant social structure is that although peasant societies are strongly male-centered they do not develop patrilineages or patri-clans. The most common residential unit of peasant societies has been found to be the patrilineal composite family. Of forty-six peasant societies analyzed by Walter Goldschmidt and Evalyn Kunkel, ten have virilocal "stem" families and eighteen are organized around virilocal joint families. In the stem families, one son continues to reside in his parents' household after marriage. Others move out when they marry. The stay-at-home son inherits the family farm as a unit. The estate is indivisible.

In peasant societies which are built around virilocal joint families, all (or most) sons stay on in the homestead when they marry, working the land jointly for a time but eventually each taking his separate share of the land. The estate in these instances is partible (divisible).

The stem family and indivisible estate exist where land is scarce, while the joint family and divisible estate occur where new farm land is, or has recently been, available.

In thirteen of the forty-six peasant societies studied, newly married couples establish independent households of their own with neolocal residence, and all sons and daughters inherit equally from their parents.

Finally, "peasant societies never show a preference for matrilineal land inheritance, and none consistently forms joint households on the basis of matrilocal residence."[15]

One may ask: "Why the male-centeredness of peasant society? And why have lineage and clan, which are so important to primitive social systems, disappeared so completely in the peasant complex?" The answers seem to lie in the facts that peasant subsistence is agricultural, not horticultural (and agriculture is a predominantly male activity); that war is no longer an activity for kinship groups among peasants (it is the prerogative of the national state); that hunting lands are not open to exploitation by peasants; and that major legal crises with respect to land and homicide must be settled within the legal framework of the larger civilization in which the peasant segment is embedded. In other words, neither ecology nor the overall social structure provided the conditions which would give lineages or clans anything functionally significant to do. Therefore, they died out.

The Passing of Peasant Society

The advent of industrialization first sounded the death knell of the peasant way of life. The swelling factories of Europe and North America in the nineteenth and twentieth centuries were urban generators of a new form of life into which millions of European peasants were fed. Today, for a few brief decades, the same flight to the cities is occurring all around the world as industrial development takes root in South America, Asia, and Africa, while simultaneously, peasant society dissolves. For:

In the modern world peasant societies are anachronisms, and it is inevitable that they disappear. Peasants themselves have demonstrated time and time again that they prefer a different, and what they believe to be a better life. Poverty, illiteracy, oppression, disease and early death, and a backbreaking life of sweating over a piece of land, have little nostalgic value to peasants, a great many of whom will take every reasonable opportunity to escape to the new life of the city. Modern technology as well as human desires have conspired to hasten the end of traditional peasantry.[16]

Peasant societies are the little communities of

---

[14]G. M. Foster, "Peasant Character and Personality," in J. M. Potter, M. N. Diaz, and G. M. Foster (eds.), *Peasant Society: A Reader*, p. 297.

[15]W. Goldschmidt and E. J. Kunkel, "The Structure of the Peasant Family" (*American Anthropologist*, vol. 73, 1971), p. 1061.

[16]J. M. Potter, "Peasants in the Modern World," in Potter, Diaz, and Foster (eds.), *op. cit.*, p. 378. Quoted with permission of Little, Brown and Company.

the primitive world transformed into culturally marginal units of civilizations. They occupy a developmental position between tribal society and industrial urban society.

But urban society itself is now in the process of a great transformation. For today we are witnessing not only the passing of the primitive world and the demise of peasant society, but also the dissolution of civilization itself—"civilization" meaning the culture of cities.

THE ATOMIC SPACE AGE AND SURBANIZATION

Professor Leslie White has emphasized the close correlation between technology, the amount of controlled energy at the disposal of a society, and the evolutionary development of the nontechnological aspects of culture.[17] This theme, which has run throughout this book, is called the Energy Theory of Cultural Evolution.

Energy and culture

The difference between the simple hunting society at the Paleolithic beginning of human social evolution and the vastly complex technological society of the twentieth century is a good deal more than the difference between a population of 100 persons as against 220 million for the United States or 700 million for China.

We have already touched on the qualitative differences in the moral and technical orders which characterize the two extremes in size and social structure. But underlying it all is the great difference in the amounts of energy directed to human use—a difference made possible by the technological aspects of evolving culture.

At the Stone Age end of the evolutionary continuum the potential daily average energy output of a healthy man is estimated to have equalled approximately 50 pounds lifted 1 foot in 1 second, or roughly 1/600 horsepower-hour. Taking into account infants, the sick, and aged or feeble adults who could do little or no work, the daily amount of

energy available in the earliest societies was approximately 1/1,200 horsepower-hour per person. For a very primitive local group, this would amount to an energy utilization of no more than 1/24 horsepower-hour a day for the entire society. Not much could be accomplished with that. As long as the individual was restricted to such a level, the development of culture was destined to be limited regardless of other factors. This condition prevailed throughout the Old Stone Age and was characteristic of all societies before the development of hoe culture and the domestication of animals.

The great revolution of the Neolithic Age was wrought by the domestication of plants and animals. Domestication of plants increased man's control over solar energy, which is stored in plants. Domestication of animals made him an exploiter of animal energy. More efficient tools reduced energy waste, and new tools made possible new applications of energy. All culture expanded rapidly; the mode of life changed from that of hunters to that of gardeners and pastoralists. Old institutions and customs went down, and new ways had to be worked out. The savages became barbarians.

The Bronze and Iron Ages are but extensions of the Neolithic Age, which fulfilled its potential in the urban revolution. Metal was substituted for stone. Increased efficiency of tools, leading to stepped-up productiveness in handicraft industries and gardening, gradually expanded the cultures of the Old World.

The next cultural revolution awaited the harnessing of steam, the invention of the internal combustion engine, and the artificial production of electricity. With the industrial revolution, feudalism gave way to modern capitalism. The reorganization of society and culture shook the modern world through and through.

To sense the significance of the energy increase brought about by the industrial revolution (prior to the atomic revolution), consider that the total horsepower capacity of all prime movers (work animals, automobiles, factories, mines, railroads, ships, aircraft, windmills, electric power generators, and farms exclusive of work animals) in the United States of America was 8,495 in 1850. At the beginning of the second half of the twenti-

[17]L. A. White, "Energy and the Evolution of Culture" (*American Anthropologist*, vol. 45, 1943), pp. 335–356. See also W. F. Cottrell, *Energy and Society*.

eth century (in 1955), it was 7,143,723.[18] Yet in 1955, the horsepower capacity of animals in use had dropped for the first time to a level below that of 1850.

In 1965, the actual electrical energy output and consumption of the United States was 1.5 billion horsepower-hours.[19] This is nearly ten billion times the total from all sources which is estimated for the typical Stone Age society—and the figure does not include automotive energy or fossil fuel energy used in steam and internal combustion engines in factories, ships, or airplanes.

Thermonuclear energy

In 1945, the most stupendous energy conquest of all time was accomplished. Einstein's theory of the equivalence of mass and energy $(E = mc^2)$ indicates that 1 kilogram (2.2 pounds) of matter, if it could be converted entirely into energy, would release 25 billion kilowatt-hours of energy, or approximately 33 billion horsepower-hours. Splitting the uranium atom, as was first done in 1945, converted 0.1 of 1 per cent of the uranium mass

---

into energy. Thirty-three million horsepower-hours of energy could then be released from one kilogram of uranium.[20] And this was but the beginning, for not only has the efficiency of techniques for splitting the atom been improved, but also we have learned since then how to release energy through fusion of the hydrogen atom.

By 1971 the efficiency of energy conversion by fission had been increased tenfold. In November, 1971, the U.S. Atomic Energy Commission tested a nuclear warhead deep in an underground shaft in Amchitka Island in the Aleutian Island chain off the coast of Alaska. It was described as a 5-megaton bomb, meaning that it had an explosive power equal to that of 5,000 tons of TNT. But what does this mean in terms of energy conversion? One way to illustrate the meaning is this: that single instantaneous conversion released 10^{10} (10 billion) horsepower-hours of energy, or nearly 500 million times as much as an entire Paleolithic society could put to work in an entire day. Nuclear bombs capable of releasing 2,000 × 10 billion horsepower-hours of energy stood ready for war use by Russia and the United States at the beginning of 1972.

---

[18]U. S. Bureau of the Census, *Historical Statistics of the United States, Colonial Times to 1957*, p. 506.

[19]*Britannica Book of the Year: 1968*, p. 364.

[20]H. D. Smyth, *Atomic Energy for Military Purposes*, pp. 2 and 224.

FIG. 24-1 A modern high-capacity nuclear power electric-generating plant on the banks of the Mississippi River, Montecello, Minnesota. (Courtesy of The Northern States Power Company.)

FIG. 24-2 Man on the moon. Astronaut Charles M. Duke, Jr., drills a lunar core sample, with his moon buggy (Lunar Roving Vehicle) parked in the background. Photo by astronaut John W. Young. (Courtesy of the National Aeronautics and Space Administration.)

In 1957, there were no atomic-powered electric plants at work in the United States. In 1970, thermoelectricity was just beginning to become a significant factor in the productive energy output, but still accounted for less than 1 per cent of the total productive energy used in the United States. What fabulous amounts of energy will be harnessed for human use in the next era of biocultural evolution is only beginning to be realized.

Space exploration and travel

On July 20, 1969, Astronaut Neil Armstrong, placing the first imprint of a human foot on the moon, uttered the prophetic words, "That's one small step for a man, one giant leap for mankind." Meanwhile, several hundred space satellites were continuously orbiting the earth, some scanning the weather, others collecting atmospheric data, some serving as radio and television relays, some simply following their endless orbits, their recording and transmitting instruments played out.

At the end of 1971, after a ten-month flight through space, the U.S. Mariner IX was in continuous orbit around the planet Mars, nearly 49 million miles from the earth, and was sending back photographs. At the same time a Soviet spacecraft arrived to land the first human artifact on that far-off planet. Plans for the Mariner X project were already far advanced. On July 4, 1976, a space laboratory is scheduled to land on Mars, containing mass spectographs and other necessary equipment to do automatic chemical-physical analyses of the atmosphere of Mars, the mineral surface of the planet, and possible life forms. All data are to be radioed and televised back to Earth. Mars landings by human beings may be expected before the century is out, and other planets will also be probed.

Surbanization

The Atomic Space Age is already here. The greatest cultural revolution of five million years of hominid experience is under way. Civilization is fast being relegated to obsolescence. By the end of this century, you will very likely have witnessed the passing of the last primitive tribe, the disappearance of most remaining peasant societies, and the dissolution of cities into residual nuclei within vast settlement sprawls covering hundreds of square miles (Fig. 24-1). The Atlantic seaboard of the United States has already become one continuous residential, factory, and commercial complex from Virginia to Maine. From eastern Wisconsin, across southern Michigan and northern Ohio, and into western Pennsylvania, more than a quarter of what was farm land in 1900 has already been converted into "urban" land. The same process is well-advanced in England, where hopefully planned garden cities have been swallowed up and engulfed in the compact settlement pattern which is stretching out across the midlands to link Manchester to London. Indeed, the great planner Constantinos Doxiadis finds it impossible to form any idea of the sizes of cities of the future because, "all cities will be interconnected in major urban complexes where no distinction between large and small will be possible; they will all have become one."[21] The terrestrial environment of the future is becoming noncity and noncountry.

[21]C. A. Doxiadis, "Ecumenopolis: Tomorrow's City" *(Britannica Book of the Year: 1968),* p. 26.

FIG. 24-3 Suburbanization. Continuous settlement sprawl marks the pattern of the near future. (Wide World Photos.)

Increasingly, social scientists and other future-oriented scholars have recognized that humanity's future way of life will be so vastly different from the past as to require a new nomenclature.

Kenneth Boulding was one of the first writers to coin a new term for the social system ahead, offering "post-civilization" as the appellation of the future.[22] Sociologist Daniel Bell suggested "post-industrial,"[23] while Doxiadis refers to the huge urban complexes of tomorrow as "ecumenopolis."[24] Toffler's choice is "super-industrial," a term "intended to mean a complex, fast-paced society dependent upon extremely advanced technology and a post-materialist value system."[25]

Other writers put forth other names, each endowed with special meanings and attributes by its creator.[26] As Toffler comments, "There is, as yet, no widely accepted or wholly satisfactory term

[22]K. E. Boulding, "The Death of the City: A Frightened Look at Post-civilization" (1961, mimeographed); also, *The Meaning of the 20th Century: The Great Transition.*
[23]D. Bell (ed.), *Toward the Year 2000.*
[24]C. A. Doxiadis, *op. cit.*
[25]A. Toffler, *Future Shock,* p. 491. See his discussion, pp. 490–491, of other terminology to describe the social system of the future.
[26]Michael Marien has listed eighty-eight names which have been proposed by various writers for the new phase of human culture which we are discussing. See "Who Coined 'Post-Industrial' Society?" (*The Futurist,* vol. 7, 1973), pp. 268–269.

FIG. 24-4 Suburbanization. Superhighways provide mobile arteries through the industrial and settlement sprawl.

to describe the new stage of social development toward which we seem to be racing."[27] It is interesting to note, however, the frequency of the prefixes "post-," "beyond-," and "super-" in the various tentative labels. Interesting, also, is the common agreement that "civilization" (with its implication of "cities" surrounded by settled communities whether "suburban," or "rural," and "wilderness") will no longer be a satisfactory rubric. The sheer mass and concentration of people in the noncity, noncountry, nonanything-ever-before-known, plus the immediacy of the electronic-connectedness of all populations, makes the era ahead different not only in quantity, but in kind. This author's choice of a term to describe the new social setting of mankind is *surbanization*. "Post-civilization," "post-industrial," "super-industrial," etc., attempt to define the future in terms of the admittedly outmoded past. The social setting that is to come (and that is already well on its way) must be recognized as that which has evolved *above and beyond the*

cities. Why not, then, call it *surbanization*, a convenient contraction of sur-urbanization, and meaning "above and beyond the culture of cities"?[28] For the remainder of this book, the term will be so used. (If the reader has an alternate preference, well and good, so long as we keep in mind that we are speculating on the next stage in social development.)

The Transformation of Society

Surbanization, the society of the future, is not yet a historical fact. Nonetheless, without even suggesting that *future studies* is a discipline, to say nothing of its being an empirical science, let us read the outlines of future society insofar as past experience and current trends tell us what we may expect.

How long will it take mankind to work out the great transformation? How long before surban-

[27]Toffler, *op. cit.*, p. 490.

[28]Sur-urbanization was first proposed in E. A. Hoebel, *Anthropology: The Study of Mankind*, third edition, but even in the author's mind, the word proved to be phonetically too clumsy.

ization will be a reality? Whether the great transformation will be achieved in one hundred or five hundred years, no one can predict. A Third World War, with hydrogen bombs directed from outer space, could initiate a new Dark Age of retrogression around the globe in which cultural recovery could be held back for several centuries. Even without global war, there is serious danger that as the rejected values and societal structures of civilization progressively lose their hold on individuals, more and more human beings will lose their holds on themselves, lapsing into apathy or raging in violent social destructiveness. If mankind lapses into apathy, the human energy to carry on the transformation will be lacking. If rage takes hold, the problem will be to survive in a world of anarchy. However it goes, the immediate future is bound to be beset with dissension, uncertainty, and swirling tides of controversy and disorder as new life styles vie for acceptance. Such turmoil is an inevitable part of the new cultural revolution into which we have been thrust with hurricane force. The scientific postulates which engendered the Atomic Space Age are not compatible with many of the assumptions of traditional world views. Religion, government, and science will be under continuous pressure to redefine, reformulate, and reshape new and viable postulates, values, and institutions. One cannot expect such a gigantic task to be easily or smoothly accomplished. Yet if five million years of human endeavor mean anything, we are probably safe in prophesying that most human populations will hold together, will retain their integrity. Enough realistic innovators and enough creators of culture will continue to work to achieve the breakthrough into the next higher order of human living experience. Many social ideas will be stillborn. Others will not meet the test of survival, even though they may prevail for some little time.

In the future, as in the past, men will require a social system. In the future, as in the past, we may expect that such social systems must fulfill certain basic functions if they are to prevail. Early in this book (page 30) six functional prerequisites for societal survival were introduced into our discussion. Let us restate them here and see how they relate to future possibilities. Each society must (1) maintain the biologic functioning of the group members; (2) reproduce new members for the group; (3) socialize new members into functioning adults; (4) produce and distribute goods and services necessary to life; (5) maintain order within the group, and between the group and outsiders; and (6) define the "meaning of life" and maintain the motivation to survive and engage in the activities necessary for survival.

Maintenance of the biological functioning of the group

Despite the great scientific advances of recent times, this will be a more complex problem than ever before in the past of mankind. While technology has made possible, as evidenced in Chapter 5, humanity's adaptation to an ever-widening range of habitats (even including the environment of the moon), it has also brought grave problems of pollution, overexploitation of vast quantities of nonrenewable resources, and conditions that have prompted population growth beyond that which even advanced scientific agricultural and food production techniques can successfully feed. The population explosion of the twentieth century could have serious carry-over effects for a long time to come. As of this moment, there is little hope of slowing down the current rate of population increase before the turn of the century. The year 2000 will see six billion people crowding the earth, and demographers do not expect to see the total stabilize there. They project a probable maximum global population of twenty billion and a possible saturation of the earth's surface with fifty billion people. How well such numbers may be fed remains a dubious question. Certainly they are not likely to be meat eaters, for animal raising will probably be too inefficient a method of energy conversion. Fish, synthetic foodstuffs, and distilled seawater will be the primary human-energy-producing inputs.

The need for a greatly expanded production of food is not the only significant problem of overpopulation. The 1974 World Food Conference in Rome clearly demonstrates that the *distribution* of food from "have" to "have not" nations is perhaps going to be an even more difficult problem. Here the knowledge of social scientists, in the past not often sought by politicians to solve

FIG. 24-5 Meat for the future. Processed soybean protein forms synthetic fibers which may be artificially flavored and so constituted that it tastes and looks like poultry, beef, or pork. (Courtesy of Ralston Purina Company.)

social problems, will be needed to assist in making the social structural and ideological changes necessary to establish a balance in the access to food around the world. The World Food Conference has made clear the complexity of the problems of distribution. The "have" countries, beginning to feel population pressures themselves and having already expended much of their former food reserves, are understandably reluctant to commit their food production to the "have-nots" when their own futures are unsure. Even more difficult to comprehend is the economic impact felt by the exporting country when major international food transfers take place. The complexities of international and national economies and problems of supply and demand force politicians and business people to make decisions about food distribution not only on the basis of need or the market but also with a consideration of how such transfers will affect the national economic situation. Obviously, future people, if they are to solve these problems, must place as much effort

into the scientific study and resolution of the social structural problems as they will with the technological problems.

A second significant threat to the biological functioning of future groups is pollution. It almost seems as if each new technological development carries with it a new environmental impact. We feel almost a contradictory relationship with our environment. Each development that seems to make better or more pleasant our relationship with the environment also apparently changes our environment, thus presenting us with new problems to solve and new restrictions on old, often habitual and preferred forms of behavior. For the people of the future, as with overpopulation, the problem will be both technological and social. Many things that Western cultures especially have sought as socially desirable technological developments now seem to have serious environmental impacts. The future solutions to problems of pollution seem to require the analysis not only of the technological changes but also of the basic sociocultural motivations and needs for these developments so that the social value of innovations can be weighed against their environmental costs before they are widely adopted.

The third, and certainly not the least challenge to the biological functioning of the group, is the problem of the rapidly disappearing supplies of nonrenewable resources. The energy specialists seem most concerned about the scarcity of oil, which is not only basic to the generation of electricity, heat, and to fuel motor vehicles, but which is also basic to the production of plastics, some fertilizers, and other products. The oil supply crisis has suddenly made many small and politically weak nations of the world (especially in the Middle East) political giants, as they control significant deposits of oil, one of the life-giving fluids desperately needed by industrialized nations. To maintain the biological functioning of future peoples will require the discovery of more efficient ways to use present resources and the development of wholly new energy sources. Just as important will be the resolution of the issue of determining who does and should control the earth's resources and their manner of distribution.

The future of the biological functioning of man-

FIG. 24-6 The ocean floor and the deep waters covering it hold new resource possibilities for the future. Launching the self-propelled underwater explorer *Deepstar*. (Courtesy of Westinghouse Electric Corporation.)

kind is not all dim and frought with problems though, especially in the area of health. Mankind in the era of surbanization may be expected to live in a golden age of good health. Health, a basic concern of both primitive and civilized individuals, will no longer be a source of serious worry. Debilitating and death-producing diseases as we now know them will long since have been conquered, as have polio, tuberculosis, smallpox, and others in the present era. Hereditary defects in biological constitution will have been wholly eradicated through genetic engineering. Prenatal diagnosis of such serious genetic defects as may occur will almost certainly lead to selective aborting of fetuses. This, however, will be an outmoded negative action which will rarely be called upon. Far more likely will be the actual restructuring of the genetic codes of individual gametes so as to tailor living human beings for healthy functioning in the kinds of environments—physical and social—which will then exist. With tissue and organ transplants, it is predicted that life expectancy will rise to 100 or more years and that adults will look

and feel young and vital for most of that long life span.

Reproduction of new members for the group

This, we may be sure, will be the least serious of all the societal maintenance problems for the surbanizations of the future. In the first place, when once the global population has been stabilized, the need for reproductive replacements will be minimal. A newborn replacement for each living person will be needed only at the rate of one a century or thereabouts. Babies will be relatively rare, children and young people small minorities. Adults will form the great majority, but they will remain "young" in body. And in spirit?

Sexual activity will be wholly obsolete—imagine that! Will it be retained for erotic amusement and an antidote to boredom? Or will it be eradicated as a bothersome nuisance? This much is certain, the actual sexual relation of male and female will be biologically unnecessary.

Bisexual reproduction, wholly or partly carried

through in population-replenishment laboratories—with or without a female host—could well continue for purposes of experimental development of new variations of human types designed for new functions (such as life in space) or for specific characteristics (reduced sexuality, increased range of visual or auditory acuity) or for particular social niches (managerial, artistic, physical sports, or drone). But if the reproduction of new individuals directly from single body cells is accomplished as sober biologists predict, then previously existing individuals could be reproduced over and over in genetically exact replications at will. Bisexual reproduction would be wholly passé, except for experimental purposes. Cloning would take care of most of the reproductive needs of surbanization. However, who is to decide who gets to be reproduced, when, in what type, in what numbers, for what purposes? This could be the major issue in political contests in the society to be. Would races be maintained? If so, in what proportions? Or would functional "specialist populations," different from others in intelligence, physical skills, and emotional affect, be produced according to plan? The latter is a good possibility.

Socialization of new members

With the population replacement input at a low level, infant care and child training will be easily handled. Even though socialization will continue to be extremely important, it will be a relatively simple task which will take but a small part of the time of grownups. The specific techniques which may be utilized cannot be foreseen, but that they will be akin to operant psychology as advocated by Professor B. F. Skinner today seems wholly feasible.[29]

The tantalizing question is: What will happen to the family and kinship? As anthropological evidence has so overwhelmingly demonstrated, the family has been the seedbed of socialization in all heretofore known cultures (except Nayar). The extended kinship group has been the supportive socializer of the young, the vehicle of physical and economic security, and the means of inheri-

tance of property and statuses. Through marriage and the family, sex has been regularized so as to establish jural parents who are socially responsible for the nurture and enculturation of the young, thus preparing them to fulfill the statuses that will come to them through their kinsmen. The family has provided for complementary division of labor between the sexes in mutual maintenance of the unit and its members.

The signs are now clear that the family is atrophying. Hair and clothing styles, women's liberation, equality in jobs and pay—i.e., the trend to unisex—plus the growing social acceptance of homosexuality, all bespeak the shrinking significance of the conjugal base of family structure. A continuing spread of governmental underwriting of economic needs (aid to dependent children, free and universal education, guaranteed basic income, Medicare, and old age security) with little private wealth left over for inheritance presages the disappearance of the economic functions of family and kinship. As for legal protection, kinship has long since been stripped of this one-time important function by the later civilizations. It will not be revived in surbanization.

But what of intimacy and the emotional support of close personal ties? Is interpersonal dependency a universal human requirement that will persist into the next stage of human living? Surely it is at the present time. The countercultural experiments of the 1960s and 1970s all bespeak it. Hippie communes extoll love and sharing, calling themselves "families"; they speak the kinship ideology without the fact of kinship. Yet they may well be one variant of the residential groups of the future, once the generation gap has closed, as it certainly will when surbanization is achieved. Group life in innumerable variations will abound. Clubs, associations, and other manifold interest groups, including a revival of ethnocentric movements, will be the antidote to separateness, providing rich variety to the social fabric in co-residential "cells" of fictive brotherhood and enduring comradeship.

Production of goods and services

Subsistence needs will be no less important to individuals of the future than they have been to

---

[29]B. F. Skinner, *Beyond Freedom and Dignity.*

primitive and civilized peoples. The earth and its atmosphere are not infinite; natural resources are not unlimited. Whether food production can be expanded to meet the survival needs of expanding populations is a moot issue. Whether the balance between world population and world subsistence resources is achieved at a level which provides enriched living for all or marginal subsistence for most will depend on the degree of success in population control and management. One thing is clear: very few workers will be engaged in basic food production. In precivilized societies, all able-bodied adults, even kings, were engaged in food production. In early civilizations, probably not more than 10, or at most 20, percent of a population could be freed from food production to serve as administrators, artisans, and soldiers. In the United States today, not more than 10 per cent of the population is directly engaged in agriculture. At the end of this century, it will be 3 per cent or less. The farmer is nearly as extinct as the dodo. In surbanization the family farm will be only a historical memory, and farming will be a large-scale industry. Most food production, however, will be synthetic.

It is not unreasonable to expect that the great free market economies of the world today will be displaced by managed systems of rationed distribution according to controlled allocation plans. The economy would then not be reciprocal, redistributive, or market, but would be distributive-managed and would operate without the use of money.

Power-generating, construction, communication, transportation, entertainment, health, and other personal service activities bid fair to be the central productive concerns of surbanization. Of these, only construction (for there may be much building and rebuilding), entertainment, health, and personal services may give occupation to many people.

In the view of G. S. Stent:

The will to power will not have vanished entirely, but the distribution of its intensity among individuals will have been drastically altered. At one end of this distribution will be a minority of the people whose work will keep intact the technology that sustains the multitude at a high standard of living. In the middle of the distribution will be found a type, largely unemployed, for whom the distinction between the real and the illusory will still be meaningful and whose prototype is the beatnik. He will retain an interest in the world and seek satisfaction from sensual pleasures. At the other end of the spectrum will be a type largely unemployable for whom the boundary of the real and the imagined will have been largely dissolved, at least to the extent compatible with his physical survival. His prototype is the hippie. His interest in the world will be rather small, and he will derive his satisfaction mainly from drugs or, once this has become technologically practicable, from direct electrical inputs into his nervous system. This spectral distribution, it will be noted, bears some considerable resemblance to the Alphas, Betas, and Gammas in Aldous Huxley's *Brave New World*.[30]

Stent's view of the nonproducing, sensate, consuming majority in the image of the hippie must not be narrowly construed. What he means to say is that the bulk of humanity in surbanization will be consumers with lots of time and little work. And what will they do for fun, for satisfaction, for fulfillment?

Maintenance of order

Law, as we have found, has been a nearly universal feature of human cultures. Will it so continue in the new social order of surbanization? Presumably. The functions of law in society, as they were stated on page 290 above, are:

1. The definition of obligatory relationships between the members of a society, so as to assert which activities are permitted and which are ruled out and to maintain at least minimal integration between the activities of individuals and groups within the society. This involves the culture-building process in response to the imperative of selection.

2. The allocation of authority and the designation of the person who has the socially recognized privilege-right to initiate and carry through legitimate corrective actions leading to economic or physical sanctions when substantive norms are violated, so that force is controlled and directed toward social goals.

3. The disposition of trouble cases as they arise; that is, to clean up social messes (tangled

---

[30]G. S. Stent, *The Coming of the Golden Age*, pp. 137–138. By permission of Natural History Press.

claims, squabbles and fights, killings and woundings) so that people may get on about their
business of everyday living with reasonable certainty and security.

4. The continuing redefinition of relations between individuals and groups as the conditions of
life change, to maintain adaptability and flexibility
in both substantive and procedural law in response to shifting values and new technologies.

The imperative of selection in culture building
will be intensified in its effects. Two factors, at
least, will be responsible. Crowding and the heter-
ogeneity of the masses of humanity which will
have to be organized will require insistence on
standard and predictable behavior in crucial
areas of public interaction. A great increase in the
intensity and scope of communications will enhance the frequency of personal and intergroup
contacts. They will require increased regulation.

The instruments of power and social control
will be so sophisticated in their effects that the
allocation of legitimate power (the second function of law) will be of critical importance. Will this
be determined through mass public participation
(democracy) or by a self-perpetuating managerial
elite? There is no answer at the present time. One
thing is certain, however: throughout the transition decades (or centuries) which lie immediately
ahead, the power struggles for legal and governmental control of the reshaping of social machinery will be waged with the greatest intensity.

Dispute settlement may shift from person
against person, business against business, to the
hearing and disposition of grievances against the
great bureaucracy itself. This would certainly be
the case if there were no longer much in the way
of private property or free economic enterprise.

When once surbanization is achieved, society
will be stabilized for a long future, as discussed
below. The fourth function of law will then become less weighty. But between now and then,
law will be put to such strains as it has rarely
experienced in the past. Can the legal systems of
mankind change and adapt rapidly and skillfully
enough to contain criminal disorder, preventing
destructive anarchy, while at the same time re-
sponding to shifting values and new technologies?

The legal order of surbanization must solve the
"barebones" issue for all mankind. This means at
least a minimal world law and a multiplex global
government. Failure in achieving these goals will
mean that there will be no surbanization, no next
higher level of human culture achievement. If they
are achieved, then it is not too much to expect
that the central concerns and creative energies of
mankind will no longer focus on technology but
will shift to the questing aspect of law and society:
finer justice directed toward fuller, richer life for
all.

Definition of the meaning of life

Just as the breakdown of tribal moral orders in the
rise of early civilizations was ultimately met by
the emergence of universalistic religions—
Zoroastrianism, Buddhism, Christianity, Islam—
expressing enlarged views of the nature of humanity and the universe, and fixing mankind's
relation to a "civilized" conception of the supernatural and social life—so new philosophies of
life and life-ways will certainly emerge. Many
competing attempts and movements, secular and
religious, will vie for acceptance in efforts to
provide viable moral orders in a society dominated by a supertechnical order.

What will be the world view of surbanized man?
No one can yet tell. It may be quite matter of
fact—profane, in the Durkheimian sense. Almost
certainly this may be expected to be true of the
managerial and technocratic specialists who will
organize, maintain, and operate the automated
production and computerized memory and
problem-solving systems. Their world will of necessity be ordered and mechanistic. And since it
will be central to the very lives and livelihood of
the leisured masses, their outlook will most likely
be dominant, if not universal.

The concern of the vast majority will not be with
the mechanics of subsistence and the ordering of
society, however. It will be with the finding of
meaning in life in a planetary system in which
there is little biological turnover (death rarely
occurs), little child raising, and no work for the
vast majority. Will men culturize masochism in
order to sustain a contrast to endless horizons of
hedonism? What prophets will speak to humani-

ty? In what words? What symbolic drama, what forms of ritual, will vitalize a mechanical existence? Philosophers, artists, and playwrights will have their work cut out for them.

Social Equilibrium or Endless Innovation?

The final questions to be considered are: "What of evolution? Will it go on forever?" Many alarms have been raised over the potential unmanageability of rapidly increasing new knowledge. How can knowledge and technology—which together mean culture—keep on expanding indefinitely? Many scientists now hold that an inevitable slowdown in the expansion of the scope of science is near at hand. The era of exciting discovery is drawing to a close with the climax of civilization.

Bentley Glass, speaking as president of the American Association for the Advancement of Science on December 28, 1970, observed:

The great conceptions, the fundamental mechanisms, and the basic laws are now known. For all time to come, these have been discovered, here and now, in our lifetime. They can never be discovered again unless man loses his scientific heritage; and even so, they cannot be discovered again for the first time. They can only be reexhumed, refined, or modified.

The uniformity of nature and the general applicability of natural laws set limits to knowledge. If there are just 100, or 105, or 110 ways in which atoms may form, then when one has identified the full range of properties of these, singly and in combination, chemical knowledge will be complete. There is a finite number of species of plants and animals—even of insects—upon the earth. We are as yet far from knowing all about the genetics, structure and physiology, or behavior of even a single one of them. Nevertheless, a total knowledge of all life forms is only about 2×10^6 times the potential knowledge about any one of them. Moreover, the universality of the genetic code, the common character of proteins in different species, the generality of cellular structure and cellular reproduction, the basic similarity of energy metabolism in all species and of photosynthesis in green plants and bacteria, and the universal evolution of living forms through mutation and natural selection all lead inescapably to a conclusion that, although diversity may be great, the laws of life, based on similarities, are finite in number and comprehensible to us in the main even now. We are like the explorers of a great continent who have penetrated to its margins in most points of the compass and have mapped the major mountain chains and rivers. There are still innumerable details to fill in, but the endless horizons no longer exist.[31]

Certain it is that scientific progress cannot and therefore will not proceed indefinitely. Concomitantly, although technical refinements may continue, technology may be foreseen as reaching a condition of relative stability.

Whether the mineral resources of the earth and other planets will be adequate to meet the material needs of surbanized society indefinitely, only the future can tell. If they are inadequate, then there will be no ultimate stability. If they are adequate, however, then a state of homeostasis in environment and technology may be realized. And if technical evolution slows to a halt, so too will social and biological evolution. Equilibrium theory will be the order of the day; progress will be a historical memory, rather than an expression of human aspiration. Mankind could live long generation after long generation on a "golden plateau," working toward an ultimate refinement of social life.

ANTHROPOLOGY AND THE FUTURE

Anthropology's great contribution is to the understanding of mankind by individuals. It has a vast task ahead. How great it would have been if anthropologists had been present to record and analyze the urban revolution as civilization was being born! How infinitely richer and more certain our understanding of the human enterprise would be, had that been possible. Today we are more fortunate; we can observe, record, interpret—and help guide—the greatest cultural revolution of all time, the dawn of the Atomic Space Age of Surbanization.

SELECTED READINGS

Boulding, K. E., *The Meaning of the 20th Century: The Great Transition* (1965). One of the most imaginative contemporary social thinkers examines the barriers that are to be surmounted in reaching the new society

---

[31]B. Glass, "Science: Endless Horizon or Golden Age?" (*Science*, vol. 171, no. 3966, 1971), p. 24. Copyright 1971 by the American Association for the Advancement of Science.

of the era that is just opening. A brief and stimulating book that looks beyond civilization into the culture of the twenty-first century.

Glass, B., "Science: Endless Horizons or Golden Age?" (*Science*, vol. 171, 1971), pp. 23–29. A sober evaluation of where scientific technology may be taking us, presented as the presidential address to the American Association for the Advancement of Science in 1970.

Potter, J. M., M. N. Diaz, and G. M. Foster, *Peasant Society: A Reader* (1967). A compendium of articles by various authors presenting recent anthropological thought and studies concerning peasant society, economics, personality, and contemporary problems.

Redfield, R., *The Primitive World and Its Transformations* (1953). Primitive, peasant, and urban life-ways are reviewed to provide an overview of how urbanization has transformed humanity from the primitive to the civilized state.

Rosenfeld, A., *The Second Genesis: The Coming Control of Life* (1969). The potential of biological engineering presented and rationally explained.

Scientific American, "Energy and Power" (*Scientific American*, vol. 224, 1971). The entire issue is devoted to eleven articles, well illustrated, on all aspects of the physical, industrial, and social components of energy, earth, and mankind. A very valuable discussion.

Seidenberg, R., *Posthistoric Man* (1950). This author expects that the end of scientific advances will lead to the end of human striving. Society will settle down to a Golden Age of endless cycles of Elysial existence devoid of emotional feeling.

Stent, G. S., *The Coming of the Golden Age* (1969). Like Seidenberg, Stent predicts a static future for mankind but with more emphasis on the possibility of blissful freedom from the "divine discontent."

Toffler, A., *Future Shock* (1970). Discusses the social and individual disorientations of today which are the consequences of too much change coming upon us too rapidly; this best seller also suggests strategies for surviving into the future.

NORTH AMERICA

Scale at 40° N

500   0   500
Miles

CULTURE AREAS:

I. **Arctic Coast**
II. **Northwest Coast**
III. **Intermontane (California Basin—Plateau)**
IV. **Southwest**
V. **Northern Subarctic**
    A. Yukon-McKenzie Area
    B. Eastern Subarctic Area
VI. **Plains**
VII. **Eastern Areas**
    A. Eastern Maize Area
    B. Southeastern Area
VIII. **Mexico and Central America**
IX. **Antillean**

TRIBAL GROUPS:

1. Eskimo
    A. Chugach Eskimo
    B. Nunivak Eskimo
    C. Bering Strait Eskĭmo
    D. North Alaska Eskimo
    E. McKenzie Eskimo
    F. Copper Eskimo
    G. Caribou Eskimo
    H. Iglulik Eskimo
    J. Labrador Eskimo
    K. West Greenland Eskimo
    L. East Greenland Eskimo
    M. Polar (Smith Sound) Eskimo
2. Tlingit
3. Haida
4. Tsimshian
5. Kwakiutl
6. Yurok, Karok, Hupa
7. Pomo
8. Shoshone

9. Cheyenne
10. Crow
11. Hidatsa
12. Mandan
13. Dakota
    A. Yankton-Yanktonai
    B. Santee
    C. Teton
14. Pawnee
15. Kiowa
16. Comanche
17. Osage
18. Ojibwa
19. Winnebago
20. Iroquois
    A. Mohawk
    B. Oneida
    C. Onondaga
    D. Cayuga
    E. Seneca

21. Cherokee
22. Creek
23. Natchez
24. Havasupai
25. Papago
26. Navaho
27. Hopi
28. Zuni
29. Keresan Pueblos
    (Acoma, Laguna, Zia, Sant'ana,
    San Felipe, Santo Domingo,
    Cochiti)
30. Jicarilla Apache
31. Tarahumare
32. Aztec (Nahua)
33. Zapotec
34. Maya

CULTURE AREAS:

    I. Chibcha
    II. Andean
    III. Antillean
    IVA. Amazon
    IVB. Eastern Brazilian Highlands
    V. Chaco
    VI. Patagonian
    VII. Araucanian
    VIII. Fuegian

TRIBAL GROUPS:

    1. Carib
    2. Arawak
    3. Jivaro
    4. Mundurucú
    5. Apinayé
    6. Inca
    7. Aymara
    8. Sirionó
    9. Botocudo
    10. Tupinamba
    11. Araucanians
    12. Ona
    13. Yahgan

Scale at equator

500   0   500

Miles

SOUTH AMERICA

CULTURE AREAS:

I. North Africa
    A. Mediterranean Coast
    B. Egypt
II. Sahara
III. Sudan
    A. Western Sudan
    B. Eastern Sudan
IV. Guinea Coast
V. East Horn

VI. Cattle Area
    A. Eastern Cattle Area
    B. Western Cattle Area
VII. Congo
VIII. Khoisan
    A. Bushman
    B. Hottentot
IX. Madagascar

TRIBAL GROUPS:

1. Dogon
2. Wolof
3. Mano
4. Hausa
5. Kpelle
6. Tallensi
7. Nupe
8. Ashanti
9. Dahomeans (Fon)
10. Yoruba
11. Ibo (incl. Ibibio)
12. Tiv
13. Azande (Zande)
14. Pygmy Tribes—Twa (Batwa)
15. Herero
16. Bushman
17. Hottentot (incl. Nama, Bergdama)
18. Lozi (Barotse)

19. Ba-lla (Ila)
20. Zulu
21. Tswana
22. Swazi
23. Bemba (Babemba)
24. Nyakyusa
25. Chaga (Tschagga)
26. Ankole (Banyankole, incl. Bahima and Bairu)
27. Sukuma
28. Watussi (Tussi)
29. Nyoro (Banyoro or Bakitara)
30. Alur
31. Masai
32. Nuer
33. Dinka
34. Tanala-Betsileo
35. Sakalava

Scale at equator

500   0   500

Miles

AFRICA

OCEANIA

CULTURE AREAS:

    I. Polynesia
   II. Micronesia
  III. Melanesia
  IV. New Guinea
   V. Indonesia
  VI. Australia

TRIBAL GROUPS:

1.	Hawaiians	16.	Igorot (Bontoc, etc.)
2.	Marquesans	17.	Ifugao
3.	Samoans	18.	Siang Dyak
4.	Maori	19.	Menangkabau
5.	Solomon Islanders (and Buin)	20.	Balinese
6.	Admiralty Islanders (and Manus)	21.	Alorese
7.	Tikopia (Polynesian)	22.	Murngin
8.	Kaoka	23.	Arunta (Aranda)
9.	Kapauku	24.	Tiwi
10.	Trobriands (and Dobu)	25.	Trukese
11.	Arapesh (Iatmul, Mundugumor)	26.	Nayar
12.	Banaro	27.	Toda
13.	Kwoma	28.	Ainu
14.	Palau	29.	Koryak
15.	Ponape	30.	Chuckchee

GLOSSARY

ab·u'sua The matrilineal clan in Ashanti society.

ac·cul'tur·a'tion The process of inter-action between two societies in which the culture of the society in the subordinate position is drastically modified to conform to the culture of the dominant society.

A·cheu'le·an A culture of the Lower Paleolithic Age.

af·fi'nal Related by marriage.

age class, age grade, age set An organized association that includes all the members of a tribe who are of a given age and sex.

ag'nate A kinsman related in the male line of descent, i.e., patrilineally.

am·bi·lin'eal Affiliation with either the father's or the mother's descent group, at the option of the individual.

am·bi·lo'cal See bilocal.

am'i·tate The complex of special behavior patterns governing relations between a child and its father's sister.

a·mok' (to run amok) A form of psychotic behavior prevalent among Malayan peoples. It is characterized by inattention followed by a violent outbreak, often directed toward homicidal assault.

An"a·sa'zi The prehistoric and contemporary culture of the Pueblo Indians of the Southwest.

an"dro·cen'tric Centered about the male.

an"dro·crat'ic Ruled by males.

an'ga·kok" An Eskimo shaman.

an'i·mat·ism The attribution of life to inanimate objects.

an'i·mism The belief in the existence of spiritual beings. (Tylor's minimum definition of religion.)

an'thro·poid Having the characteris-tics of the highest family (that of man and the tailless apes) within the primate order.

an"thro·pom'e·try The division of physical anthropology concerned with the measurement of man's bodily characteristics.

an"thro·po·morph'ism The attribution of human form to any object.

an"thro·poph'a·gy Cannibalism.

Ap"ol·lo'ni·an A configuration of culture that emphasizes restraint, moderation, and "middle-of-the-road" behavior in human conduct.

ar'ti·fact Any material object that has been "worked" or has been used as a tool. Also, an imaginery concept used in logical analysis.

as·so"ci·a'tion A social group specifically organized for the pursuit of special interests.

aus·tra"lo·pith'e·cine One of any of the varieties of fossil hominids of the genus *Australopithecus*.

Aus·tra"lo·pi·the'cus af"ri·can'us A genus of fossil hominid first found at Taung, South Africa; Lower Pleistocene epoch.

Aus·tra"lo·pi·the'cus ro·bus'tus A heavy-bodied genus of fossil hominid found in Africa; Lower Pleistocene epoch.

a·void'ance The inhibition of social interaction, especially between affinal relatives.

a·vun'cu·late The complex of special relations between a mother's brother and his sister's child.

band A territorially based social group that is less inclusive than the tribe.

bar'ba·rism A classification of cultures possessing gardening, agriculture, or domesticated herds but devoid of written language.

bar'ter, dumb Exchange of goods between hostile people without face-to-face contact and without the use of middlemen.

Bas'ket Mak'er A prehistoric culture (or the people who produced it) widely spread throughout the southwestern parts of the United States and antecedent to the Pueblo cultures.

bast The fibrous inner bark of certain trees.

ber·dache' (ber-dash') An American Indian transvestite who assumes the social roles ascribed to women.

bi"fur·ca'tion Separation into two branches or sections.

bi·lat'er·al de·scent' The system of kinship structure in which an individual belongs equally to the kindred of both parents.

bi·loc'al The practice in which a newly married pair establishes residence with or near the parents of either spouse. (*Also called* ambilocal.)

Bon'du The women's tribal secret society among the tribes of Sierra Leone and Liberia in West Africa.

brach"i·a'tion Use of the arms; in a special sense, movement through the trees by swinging from the branches.

broth'er e·quiv'a·lence The classifying of brothers within a single kinship status.

broth'er·hood, blood A pact of reciprocal assistance sealed by a ritual act of intermingling or drinking each other's blood.

bull'-roar'er A flat board that, when whirled at the end of a string, makes a whirring noise.

bu'rin An Upper Paleolithic flint blade, one end of which has a sharp-pointed, chisel edge.

ca·cique' The Carib word for "chief"; often used for the sacerdotal head of a Pueblo Indian tribe or any Central or South American tribe.

car'bon 14 A radioactive isotope that provides the basis for a method of archaeological dating.

car'go cult A reactive social movement intended to bring the material goods of civilization to an acculturating society.

caste An endogamous social group, usually linked with a specific occupation.

Chel'le·an The Lower Paleolithic "hand ax" culture.

chief, peace A chief whose functions are concerned largely with the direction of civil affairs.

chief, talking In many societies the chief does not publicly address the people. A "speaker," or talking chief, does this for him.

cic"a·tri·za'tion Scar tissue produced by making incisions in the skin. Often done in patterns for ornamentation.

civ"i·li·za'tion A classification of cultures possessing gardening, agriculture, or domesticated herds, and a written language.

clan A unilineal kinship group that maintains the fiction of common genetic descent from a remote ancestor, usually legendary or mythological.

cli·to·ri·dec'to·my Surgical removal of the clitoris. A rare mutalation performed as a part of female puberty rites in certain cultures.

clon'ing The reproduction of plants or animals by propagation of individual body cells.

cog'nate A kinsman related through either the father (male filiation) or the mother (female filiation).

col·lat'er·al Kinship relations which are identified across a generation level rather than by lineal descent.

com·po·nen'tial analysis A method of determining the units of classification used in a cultural system.

con·cu'bi·tant A male who has the status of marriageability to a person without necessarily being married to that person.

con·di'tion·al curse A ritual declaration that if the facts are not as stated, or if certain conditions come to pass, ill fortune may strike the person cursed.

con·fig"u·ra'tion of cul'ture The distinctive and characteristic quality of a culture that derives from the special relationship of its parts to one another.

con·san'guine Kinsmen who are related by descent rather than marriage. Literally, "blood relatives."

con·ver'gence A process of cultural dynamics in which two or more cultures contain similar institutions or behavior patterns independently arrived at, i.e., without historical connection.

cos'mic time All time prior to the formation of the earth.

coup An attested deed of valor among the Plains Indians.

coup counting The social practice of publicly reciting coups.

coup de poing A flint hand ax characteristic of the Chellean, Acheulean, and Mousterian cultures.

cou·vade' The practice whereby a husband retires to bed upon the birth of his offspring and acts as though he had just gone through childbirth.

cow'rie shell A small glossy marine shell of the genus *Cypraea*, highly valued for decoration and use as a medium

of exchange in the Pacific area and Africa.

cra'ni·al ca·pac'i·ty The interior volume of the cranium measured in cubic centimeters.

cross-cous'ins Cousins whose related parents are siblings of unlike sex. Offspring of a person's mother's brother or father's sister.

cult An organized system or a group, characterized by performance of supernatural rituals and ceremonies and possessing an underlying body of dogmatic belief.

cul'tur·al or"tho·gen'e·sis The relative overdevelopment of one aspect of a culture.

cultural relativism The view that culture elements and institutions should be evaluated in terms of their own cultural setting. (*See also* postulates, cultural.)

culture The integrated sum total of learned behavior traits characteristic of the members of a society.

culture area A geographical territory within which the cultures tend to be similar in some significant aspects.

culture complex An integrated system of culture traits organized about some focal interest.

culture construct A selective and descriptive formulation of the modal or normal behavior characteristic of the members of a society.

culture, ideal A verbalized formulation of normative patterns for behavior as stated by the members of a given society.

culture pattern A normative form of behavior laid down by the consensus of the members of a society.

culture trait or **element** A reputedly irreducible unit of learned behavior pattern or material product thereof.

cus'tom A traditional norm of social behavior.

de·mand'-right An individual's legally supported expectancy that another person behave in a certain way with respect to him.

deme (1) An endogamous community consisting of a single kindred. (2) A territorial political unit in Attica after the reorganization by Cleisthenes in 509 B.C.

den·ta'li·um shell An elongated, tubelike sea shell used as money and

treasure among the Northwest Coast Indians of North America.

di·a·chron'ic Through time.

dib'ble A pointed digging stick.

dif·fu'sion A process in cultural dynamics wherein culture elements or complexes spread from one society to another.

di·mor'phism, sexual A difference in bodily characteristics between the two sexes.

Di'o·nys'i·an A categorical label attached to cultures that emphasize sensate experience.

DNA Deoxyribonucleic acid, the molecular structure of which constitutes the hereditary determinants in genes.

dou'ble de·scent' The existence of a maternal and a paternal descent system side by side within the same culture.

drive A state of neurophysiological tension that motivates an organism toward action.

drive, acquired or **secondary** A learned drive.

drive, basic A drive that is innate in the organism, the satisfaction of which is ultimately necessary to survival of the organism or the species.

Dry"o·pi·the'cus A genus of Miocene fossil ape from which man and the great anthropoids evolved.

earth lodge A house built wholly or partially of sod or made of a framework covered with dirt.

e·col'o·gy The study of the relationships between organisms and their total environments.

ec·u·men·op'o·lis The settlement pattern of surbanization which with interspersed parks will cover the earth as a continuous system forming a universal settlement. (Coined by Doxiadis.)

Eg'bo A secret fraternity identified with the leopard in certain West African tribes.

e'go (1) In kinship analysis, the person who is used as the reference point for identification of kinship relations and terms. (2) in psychoanalysis, the individual's concept of himself.

E'le·men·tar'·ge·dank·en- Elementary ideas. Cultural concepts that, according to Adolf Bastian, are universal because they are psychic responses to universal human experiences.

em'ic The perception of a phenomenon as seen and felt by an inside participant.

en·cul·tu·ra'tion The process by which the individual learns and assimilates the patterns of a culture.

en·dog'a·my The rule that requires a person to marry within a given social group of which he is a member.

E'o·cene The first period of the Cenozoic era.

eth·no·cen'trism The view of things in which the values and ways of one's own group are the center of everything, and all others are scaled and judged with reference to it.

eth·nog'ra·phy The division of anthropology devoted to the descriptive recording of cultures.

eth·nol'o·gy The division of anthropology devoted to the analysis and systematic interpretation of cultural data.

eth·no·sci'ence The systematic study of the cognitive systems, or ways of classifying the experienced world, which are implicit in cultures.

eth"no·se·man'tics The study of meaning from the point of view of speakers raised in differing societies and speaking different languages.

e·thol'o·gy The biological study of behavior.

et'ic The perception of a phenomenon by an outside observer.

ev"o·lu'tion, biological or organic- The continuous modification of Mendelian populations through modifications in genetic composition.

evolution, cultural Modification of culture patterns in a given direction through persistent social change. *General evolution* purports to express modifications characteristic of all cultures at specific stages in their development. *Multilineal evolution* purports to express modifications characteristic only of like cultures. *Specific evolution* purports to express changes characteristic of specific cultures.

evolution, divergent or **radiating-** The process of evolutionary development that results in several lines of progressive modification from an original common form.

evolution, unilinear The evolution of social forms in a universal and ordered sequence; a theoretical process.

ex·og'a·my Marriage outside a specific social group of which a person is a member, as required by custom or law.

fam'i·ly A bilateral kinship group.

family, conjugal-natal A social group consisting of spouses and their offspring.

family, extended A social group consisting of near relatives in addition to the mated pair and their offspring.

fa'ther·hood, sociological The institution whereby the adult male who is the husband of a child's mother is functionally the father to the child, regardless of his biological relationship.

fet'ish An object that is revered because it is believed to house a supernatural power.

fil·i·a'tion The culturally determined tie between parent and offspring.

fos'sil An organic object that has been transformed into stone or has left an imprint in stone.

fra·ter'ni·ty (1) An association of men. A men's society. (2) The children of a woman. *See* sibling.

func'tion·al·ism A theoretical and methodological approach to anthropology that emphasizes concern with the part each unit within a culture plays in the total existence of the culture.

gen"er·a'tion e·quiv'a·lence The classifying of relatives of different genetic relation, but within the same generation level, into a single kinship status.

gen'i·tor A biological parent.

gens A patrilineal clan.

ge'o·log'ic time All time since the formation of the earth.

ger"on·toc'ra·cy A society dominated by the old (usually men in primitive societies).

Ghost' Dance A nativistic reactive movement among western American Indians in 1890. The dance was intended to revive the dead and restore the old way of life.

glot'tal stop A phoneme produced by closing the glottis.

glot"to·chro·nol'o·gy A method of calculating the time elapsed since the speakers of two related languages separated from each other.

God, High The supreme deity in a polytheistic system.

gram·i·niv·o·rous A subsistence diet consisting largely of seeds.

G-string A string or band of material worn between the legs and fastened around the waist.

half-life The amount of time required for a radioactive substance to lose one-half of its radioactivity.

har·i'jan caste The impure, therefore "untouchable," castes of India.

head'man A leader of a kinship or territorial unit who is not endowed with specific and determinative authority; less than a chief.

hi'er·o·glyph" A highly conventionalized symbol developed from pictorial representation and used as an element in certain archaic writing systems.

ho'gan The Navaho dwelling.

Ho'ho·kam Pertaining to a prehistoric culture localized in the desert areas of south-central Arizona.

hom'i·nid (1) A primate who belongs to the family of Hominidae, or human beings. (2) Having the characteristics of a human being.

hom'i·noid A primate who belongs to the super family Hominidae, apes and man.

Ho'mo e·rec'tus e·rec'tus A Lower Pleistocene fossil species of man found in Java and Africa. Formerly called *Pithecanthropus erectus*.

Ho'mo e·rec'tus hei'del·berg·en'sis Middle Pleistocene fossil variety of man found in Europe.

Ho'mo e·rec'tus lea·key·i A Lower or Middle Pleistocene fossil species of man found in East Africa.

Ho'mo e·rec'tus mau"ri·tan'i·cus Middle Pleistocene fossil variety of man found in North Africa.

Ho'mo e·rec'tus pe"ki·nen'sis A Middle Pleistocene fossil species of man found in China. Formerly called *Sinanthropus pekinensis*.

Ho'mo ha·bi'lis A fossil hominid found in Bed 1 at Olduvai Gorge. It may be either an advanced form of australopithecine or the earliest known member of the genus *Homo*.

Ho'mo sa'pi·ens sa'pi·ens Modern man. The sole existing species of the genus *Homo*.

hy·per'ga·my Marriage upward from a lower social class or caste into a higher one.

id The Freudian term for all the innate, unmodified biological impulses of the human being.

id′e·o·graph″ A drawn, carved, or painted symbol which stands directly for an object or idea and which is nonphonetic in the language of its user.

id′e·o·lect The uniquely individual choice of words and other language usages of a particular person.

id″i·o·syn′cra·sy An aspect of behavior uniquely characteristic of an individual.

in′cest Sexual contact between persons who are members of the same culturally defined kinship group.

in′dus·try (archaeological) All the known objects, artificially produced or not, used by a group of prehistoric people in one area over a span of time.

in·fan′ti·cide The killing of infants.

in″sti·tu′tion, social A complex of behavior patterns organized about some dominant central interest.

in″va·lid′i·cide The killing of invalids.

in·ven′tion, independent *See* parallelism.

jaj·mani′ The system of customary services between the members of a Hindu jati and a landlord.

ja′ti A localized subcaste in India which is endogamous, named, and possesses a distinctive combination of culture traits.

jok′ing re·la′tion·ship″ An institutionalized pattern of privileged familiarity or joking between persons of specific social statuses.

jur′al parent The culturally defined adult from, or through, whom a child receives its kinship identity. The jural parent may or may not be a genitor.

K-A dat′ing The long-range method of archaeological dating by measuring the degree of disintegration of potassium 40 into argon 40 that has occurred in geological materials.

ka·chi′na The gods in certain Pueblo cultures, who are represented in ceremonials by masked dancers.

kay·la′si Adultery among the Trobriand Islanders.

kin′dred A local group that is constituted of bilateral relatives.

ki·nes′ics The study of gestures.

kin′ship, classificatory The lumping, merging, or equating of relatives of differing genetic relationship into the same kinship status.

kinship system The customary complex of statuses and roles governing the behavior of relatives.

kinship terminology The set of names applied to the various statuses in a kinship system.

ki′va A semi-subterranean ceremonial chamber, usually round, in the Southwest Indian pueblos.

ku′la ring The system of intertribal ceremonial exchange of shell armbands and necklaces in southeastern Melanesia.

Kul·tur′kreis A conception of large culture complexes that, in the theory of the culture historical school (*Kulturkreislehre*) of ethnology, diffuse en bloc over large areas of the globe.

ku′tu The judicial body among the Barotse of Zambia.

la′bret A plug worn through an incision in the lip.

lau′rel-leaf point A flint blade shaped like a laurel leaf and characteristic of the Solutrean culture.

law A social norm whose violation beyond permissible leeway evokes a formal procedural response initiated by an individual or group that possesses the socially recognized privilege-right of determining guilt and of imposing economic or physical sanctions upon the wrongdoer.

law, adjective The part of the law that governs legal procedure and the application of legal sanctions.

law, private Law that is normally enforced by the wronged party rather than by a public officer.

law, public Criminal law; that which is enforced by a public officer.

law, substantive The norms that define illegal activity.

le·ji′ma The nonlocalized maternal clan in Umor society.

Le·val·loi′si·an A Lower Paleolithic culture characterized by a flint flake tool with a prepared striking platform.

lev′i·rate Brother-in-law marriage. The marriage of a woman to her deceased husband's brother.

levirate, anticipatory The practice in which a husband extends limited sexual privileges with his wife to his younger brother

lex″i·co·sta·tis′tics A method of counting the frequency of cognate

(related) words in basic vocabulary lists for dialects or languages in order to calculate how long ago the languages may have been one. (*See also* glottochronology.)

li·bi′do The Freudian term for the id energies.

lig′a A pile of heated stones used for baking taro in New Ireland, Melanesia.

lin′e·age A unilineal kinship group that traces descent from a known common ancestor, who lived not more than five or six generations back.

lo′bo·la Progeny price among the Bantu-speaking tribes of South Africa.

mag′ic The control of supernatural forces by means of compulsive formulas.

magic, contagious A form of sympathetic magic. It operates on the principle that things once in contact with each other can exert a continuing influence upon each other.

magic, imitative A form of sympathetic magic. It operates on the principle that like influences like.

magic, sympathetic Magic that operates on the principle of homeopathic association, i.e., that one object can exert an influence upon others that have an identity with it.

ma′ka·ra′ta A formal, regulated combat among the Murngin of Australia.

ma·lang′gan A complex of memorial festivals in New Ireland, Melanesia.

ma′na Supernatural power that does not occur in the form of a spirit being.

man′i·oc A tropical plant of the genus *Manihot*, whose roots yield a nutritious starch; also called *cassava*.

ma′no A grinding stone that is held in the hand.

mar′riage The social institution that regulates the special relations of a mated pair to each other, their offspring, their kinsmen, and society at large.

marriage, affinal Marriage to a spouse's relative. In-law marriage.

marriage, cross-cousin, asymmetrical A preferred marriage form that is restricted to one type of crosscousin only. Marriage of a man to his mother's brother's daughter is permitted, while marriage to his father's sister's daughter is prohibited or vice versa.

marriage, cross-cousin, symmetri-

riage to an affinal relative of a higher or lower generation. Marriage based upon an extension of the levirate or sororate principles.

ma·tai′ The titular head of a Samoan household.

ma″tri·arch″ate A society distinguished by uxorilocal residence and matrilineal descent.

ma″tri·lat′er·al Pertaining to descent that is reckoned through one's mother's brother or sister.

ma″tri·lin′e·al Of or pertaining to descent through the mother; descended through the mother.

ma″tri·lo′cal *See* uxorilocal.

mean, arithmetical The average. That point in the range of variabiity of a phenomenon at which exactly equal quantities fall on either side.

me′di·an The midpoint. That point in the range of variability of a phenomenon which falls exactly at the middle of the two extremes.

Mel″a·ne′si·a Black Island The area of the Southwest Pacific inhabited by darkskinned natives.

Men·de′li·an pop·u·la′tion A localized group of members of a species who interbreed mostly among themselves but occasionally with members of sister populations.

merg′ing (in kinship systems) *See* kinship, classificatory.

Mes″o·lith′ic The Middle Stone Age; characterized by intensive seed gathering and foraging.

me·ta′te A flat or grooved grinding stone that functions as a mortar.

mi′cro·lith A minute stone artifact made from fine flint flakes.

Mi″cro·ne′si·a Small islands. The island area of the West Central Pacific.

mil·le′nar·ism A reactive social movement based on the belief that the gap between the cultural ideal and the social reality will be closed (and will last for a thousand years).

mil′pa The Maya Indian method of gardening, involving the slash and burn technique of clearing garden plots in the forest.

Mi′o·cene The middle, or third, period of the Cenozoic era.

mis″ce·ge·na′tion Interbreeding between two Mendelian populations.

Mith·ra′ic cult The religious system devoted to the worship of Mithras, the

Persian god of light, upholder of the truth and the foe of evil.

mode The high point. That point in the range of variability of a phenomenon which occurs with the greatest frequency.

moi·e·ty Half. The social unit based upon kinship that occurs when the tribe is divided into two recognized units.

mo·nog′a·my Marriage of one man to one woman.

mon′o·lith A structure consisting of a single stone.

mon′o·the·ism The worship of one god.

mor′pheme A minimal unit of language that has meaning.

mor·phol′o·gy The study of the form and structure of an organism or social manifestation.

Mous·te′ri·an The culture associated with Neandertal man during the third interglacial and fourth glacial epochs in Europe.

mu·ta′tion An abrupt modification of the genetic composition of an organism.

na·tiv·ist′ic movement A reactive movement which would restore a bygone culture.

Ne·an′der·tal A variety of hominid fossil found in Europe and Southwest Asia from the second interglacial to the end of the fourth glaciation; *Homo sapiens neandertalensis*.

Ne″o·lith′ic The New Stone Age.

ne′o·lo·cal The practice in which a newly married pair establish a new household in a locality other than the households of their parents.

neu·ro′sis A mild form of behavior disorder.

Ngbe *See* Egbo.

Ni·lot′ic Pertaining to or designating a people who live in the Nile Basin.

no·bil′i·ty A class or caste with hereditary status of high prestige and ceremonial or political power.

nor′ma·tive Relating to or inducing conformity to a norm.

nto′ro The patrilineal clan in Ashanti society.

oath A formal declaration that the facts are as stated.

Oed′i·pus com′plex A psychological state of a male characterized by sexual

desire for the mother and antagonism toward the father.

o·ke·ya′me The talking chief in Ashanti society.

Old′u·wan cul′ture A Villefranchian and Early Pleistocene African pebble-tool culture.

ol′i·gar′chy A state whose government is controlled by a small group within the larger society.

or·deal′ A ritual method of verification of testimony in which the litigants are subjected to a physical test designed to injure or kill the falsifier.

os·te·o·don″to·ker·a′tic An assemblage of bone, tooth, and horn artifacts.

Pa′le·o·lith′ic The Old Stone Age.

Pa′le·o·zo′ic The third era of geological time.

pal″y·nol′o·gy The branch of science concerned with the study of pollen and spores.

pa·py′rus The Egyptian paper made from the pith of *Cyperus papyrus*, an Egyptian sedge.

par′al·lel-cous′ins Cousins whose related parents are of like sex. The offspring of a person's mother's sister or father's brother.

par′al·lel·ism The development of similar cultural forms through identical steps without historical interaction or contact.

par′fleche An oblong rawhide box made by Plains Indians.

pas′to·ral·ism A culture marked by a subsistence technique centered about the herding and husbandry of domesticated animals.

pa″ter·fa·mil′i·as The authoritarian father in the Roman family.

pa·tol′li The Aztec form of pachisi, a game played with dice.

pa′tri·arch″ate A society dominated by the father as head of the kinship group, characterized by patrilineal descent and virilocal residence.

pat″ri·lin′e·al Pertaining to descent through the father. Children belong to the kinship group of their father.

pat″ri·lo′cal *See* virilocal.

pa·tron′y·my The custom of giving children the name of their father's kinship group.

peas′ant A social type of rural farmer associated with preindustrial civilization, dominated by the city and its culture but marginal to both.

pem′mi·can A preserved cake of shredded dried meat and berry pulp.

per·cus′sion flak′ing The technique of shaping flint artifacts by removing flakes with blows of a hammerstone.

per″son·al′i·ty The sum total of behavior traits, overt and covert, characteristic of a person.

personality, basic structure The constellation of behavior traits and attitudes established in the members of a given society by their childhood reactions to the methods of child training characteristic of their culture.

personality, ideal type The construct of the personality configuration most highly emphasized in a culture.

personality, modal The personality configuration most commonly manifested by the members of a society or group.

pe·yo′te A variety of cactus *(Lophophora williamsii)* ingested by Indians (notably Plains Indians) to stimulate visions as a form of religious experience.

pho′neme The smallest sound unit used in a language.

pho·net′ics The general study of spoken sounds.

phra′try A social unit consisting of two or more linked clans between which exists a special bond of unity as against clans joined in other phratries within the society.

phy·log′e·ny The natural history of a species or variety.

phys′i·cal an″thro·pol′o·gy The branch of anthropology concerned with the bodily characteristics of mankind.

pic′to·graph A simple picture, or series of pictures, intended to describe a situation or record an event.

pile dwell·ing A house raised from the ground or built over water on piling.

pit dwell·ing An earth lodge built over an excavated pit.

Pleis′to·cene The fifth period of the Cenozoic era. The glacial age during which man rose to dominance among life forms.

Pli′o·cene The fourth period of the Cenozoic era; a warm period during which early human types became differentiated from apes.

pol′y·an″dry The marriage of a woman to two or more men simultaneously.

polyandry, attenuated The marriage relationship in which a married brother extends limited sexual privileges with his wife to his unmarried younger brothers. Also called *anticipatory levirate*.

polyandry, fraternal A polyandrous marriage in which the husbands are brothers.

po·lyg′a·my Any multiple marriage.

po·lyg′y·ny The marriage of a man to two or more women simultaneously.

Pol″y·ne′si·a Many islands. The area of the Central Pacific that falls within a triangle formed with Hawaii, Easter Island, and New Zealand as the apexes.

pol′y·the·ism Worship of many gods. A system of religion recognizing multiple gods.

pop·u·la′tion A group of individuals or of possible observations united by some common principle or principles.

population ge·net′ics The study of gene frequencies and changes in Mendelian populations.

Por′ro The men's secret fraternity in Sierra Leone and Liberia, West Africa.

pos′tu·late, cultural A basic proposition as to the nature of things (existential) or the desirability or undesirability of things (normative) which underlies a cultural system.

pot′latch The Northwest Coast Indian institution of ceremonial feasting accompanied by lavish distribution of gifts.

pref′er·en′tial mar′riage A form of marriage that is enjoined or preferred between two persons of specifically defined statuses.

priest A religious functionary whose supernatural authority is bestowed upon him by a cult or organized church, in contrast to the shaman, who derives power directly from supernatural sources.

pri′mate An order within the mammalian class.

prim′i·tive Pertaining to a culture or an aspect of a culture that is not characterized by the inclusion of a written language; also pertaining to an individual whose culture includes no written language. Therefore, nonliterate or preliterate.

pri″mo·gen′i·ture Inheritance by the first-born son or child.

pri′vi·lege-right The legal relation in which a person is free to behave in a certain way to another without legal prohibition or consequence.

priv′i·leged fa·mil″i·ar′i·ty A culturally permissive relation of free joking between individuals of certain statuses.

prog′e·ny price The wealth transferred by the kin of a groom to the kin of his bride in compensation for their release of claim to the children that are produced in the marriage; also known as *bride price* and *bride wealth*.

prom″is·cu′i·ty The absence of any social restraints limiting or regulating sexual behavior.

prop′er·ty The special and socially sanctioned relation of a person or group to the utilization of some object.

property, communal Property that is owned by the entire community.

property, incorporeal Property that involves a nonmaterial object.

property, joint Property that is owned by a group smaller than the entire community.

prox·e′mics The study of the use of space (nearness and distance) in communication and social relations.

psy″cho·lin·guis′tics The study of psychological processes in relation to the formation and use of speech.

psy·cho′sis An extreme form of behavior disorder marked by relatively fixed patterns of maladaptive attitudes and responses.

pueb′lo A village constructed of clay bricks (adobe) or stones, characteristic of the Indians of the southwestern United States and northern Mexico.

race A human population that is sufficiently inbred to reveal a distinctive genetic composition manifest in a distinctive combination of physical traits.

race, geographical A human population that has inhabited a land mass or an island chain sufficiently long to have developed its own distinctive genetic composition, as contrasted to that of other continental populations.

race, local A distinctive Mendelian population located within a continental land mass or island chain.

race, microgeographic An extremely isolated, tightly inbreeding small Mendelian population.

rac′ism A doctrine that assumes the

cal Marriage in which either type of

cross-cousin is permissible or preferred as a spouse.

marriage, extended affinal Marinherent superiority of one or another race over others.

ram·age' A nonexogamous, extended corporate kinship group in which members get their identity by descent from a common ancestor traced either patrilineally or matrilineally, according to individual preference and convenience. It is thus ambilineal.

rel'a·tives, affinal Persons related through marriage.

relatives, genetic Biologically related persons.

re·li'gion A belief in supernatural beings and the attendant ways of behaving in consequence of such a belief.

rite de pas·sage' *See* transition rites.

rite, fertility A ritual complex designed to promote genetic reproduction.

role The customary complex of behavior associated with a particular status.

sac"er·do'tal Of a priestly nature.

sanc'tion Any social reaction operating to induce conformity to a normative standard of behavior.

sav'age·ry A state of cultural development marked by the absence of gardening or agriculture and written language.

scar'i·fi·ca'tion The process of mutilation of the body through the artificial raising of scar tissue. *See also* cicatrization.

schiz"o·phre'ni·a A behavior disorder marked by a replacement of the learned behavior systems with desocialized behavior dominated by private fantasy.

se·nil'i·cide The killing of the aged.

set·tle·ment pat·tern The spatial arrangement of the subgroups of a society in relation to each other, to their environmental resources, and to other societies.

sha'man A religious specialist who has received his power directly from supernatural sources; synonymous with *medicine man*, *witch doctor*, *angakok* (Eskimo).

sib A unilateral kinship group; synonymous with *clan*.

sib'ling Brother or sister; a member of a sib or clan.

si'lent trade *See* barter, dumb.

slav'er·y The institution whereby persons are subjected to involuntary servitude, are denied the right of freedom of movement or action, and must place their productive efforts at the disposal of the master.

so'cial class A category of persons within a society who (1) hold a number of distinctive statuses in common, (2) receive differential rewards and privileges, and (3) have an awareness of their like interests and life-style in contradistinction to other social classes.

social dis'tance A term covering the relative "spatial positions" of two statuses; generally used to emphasize limitations on social intercourse.

social struc'ture The ways in which groups and individuals are organized and relate to one another.

so·ci'e·ty, human A spatially identifiable population, centripetally-oriented, acting in accordance with a distinctive culture, and emotionally bound through common language and symbolic experiences.

society, military An association of warriors.

society, secret A fraternity or association whose membership and activities are shrouded in secrecy. A tribal secret society embraces all adult males in its membership.

sor'cer·y The use of supernatural power as an aggressive instrument to further the interests of the sorcerer. *Magic* is a more neutral term.

so·ro'ral po·lyg'y·ny The simultaneous marriage of two or more sisters to one husband.

so·ro·rate The practice whereby a younger sister marries the widowed husband of her deceased elder sister.

sou·la'va The red shell necklaces exchanged in the Melanesian kula.

spe"ci·a'tion The genetic divergence of a species to produce two new populations that are no longer capable of gene exchange (interbreeding) with each other.

state The association within a society that undertakes to direct and organize social policy on behalf of and in the name of the entire society.

sta'tus The social position of an individual with reference to the other members of his society.

Stein'heim A Middle Pleistocene fossil precursor of modern man found in Germany and often classified with the Swanscombe and Fontechevade fossils as *Homo sapiens steinheimensis*.

stim'u·lus dif·fu'sion The process of cultural dynamics in which one people receive the idea of a cultural invention from another but give a new and unique form to the idea.

stra·tig'ra·phy Analysis of geological deposits in terms of discernible layers. Derivative time sequences are inferred from the relative positions of the strata or layers.

sub"in·ci'sion A surgical operation in which the urethra of the male sex organ is slit open; a mutilation performed as part of the male puberty rites in certain Australian tribes.

suit'or ser'vice A substitute for, or equivalent of, progeny price, in which the potential groom works for his intended bride's kin.

su"per·or·gan'ic Pertaining to the phenomena, known as *cultural*, that occur on a level over and above the organic; i.e., they are not preset in the organic structure.

sur·ban·i·za'tion The culture which is beyond civilization. The mode of life-to-be in the Atomic Space Age.

sur·viv'al In evolutionary methodology, a culture trait that is purported to have lost its original function. A conceptual equivalent to vestigial remains in biological evolution.

su'su The kinship group formed of a woman, her children, and her brothers.

su·va·so'va Breach of exogamy among the Trobriand Islanders.

Swans'combe man A fossil hominid found in Middle Pleistocene deposits in southern England; classified as *Homo sapiens steinheimensis*.

sym·bi·o'sis The living together of two or more species of organisms in which the relationship is not destructive of either and is necessary to the existence of at least one of them.

syn·chron'ic Existing at the same time.

syn'cre·tism The fusion of two distinct systems of belief and practice.

ta·bu' Prohibition of an act, violation of which is punishable by supernatural sanctions.

ta'pa Polynesian bark cloth.

tar'a·vad The joint-family household consisting of the members of a matrilineage among the Nyar caste in Kerala on the Malabar Coast of India.

ta′ro A staple food plant of the Pacific area.

tax·on′o·my The systematic classification of things according to scientific principles.

tek·non′y·my The practice of addressing an adult after the name of its child, and vice versa.

tell In the Middle East, a mound built up by prolonged human occupation of a site.

than″a·to·ma′ni·a The depression of the will to exist to the point of death.

thau′ma·tur″gy Magic.

the·oc′ra·cy A social order controlled by religious specialists.

ti′pi A conical skin tent.

tort See wrong, private.

to′tem An object, often an animal or plant, held in special regard by an individual or social group.

to′tem·ism The institutional complex centering about a totem.

to·vo·dun′ The deified ancestors in Dahomean religion. (See also vodun.)

trans·hu′mance A mixed food-producing economy involving nomadism and gardening according to the season of the year.

tran·si′tion rites Ritual complexes associated with important changes in personal status, such as birth, adolescence, marriage, and death.

trans·ves′tite An individual who effects a transfer of sex roles, such as occurs when a male takes on the dress and roles of a female, or vice versa.

trau′ma A bodily or psychologic injury, or its effect.

tra·vois′ A carrying device that has two poles, like the tongues of a buggy, hitched to a draft animal. The free ends of the travois drag along the ground.

tribe A social group speaking a distinctive language or dialect and possessing a distinctive culture that marks it off from other tribes. It is not necessarily organized politically.

Trick′ster A character in mythology who alters the order of things by tricking human beings or animals into choices or circumstances that they do not expect or desire.

ul″ti·mo·gen′i·ture Inheritance by the youngest son or daughter.

u″ni·lin′e·al Pertaining to descent through one parent only.

u″ni·lo′cal Relating to or designating the practice whereby a married couple regularly settles with, or close to, the parents of one of the spouses. See also uxorilocal; virilocal.

u″ni·ver′sal A behavior pattern characteristic of all the members of a society.

u′su·fruct The right to use an object of property without possessing title of ownership.

ux·or″i·lo′cal Pertaining to the practice whereby a married couple settles in the domicile of the wife's family; synonymous with matrilocal residence.

var′na The four mythically founded castes of India which emerged from the body of primordial man.

Vertesszollos A Middle Pleistocene site in Hungary which contained skull fragments probably belonging to the European Homo erectus group.

Vil·la·fran′chi·an The early part of the Pleistocene, prior to the first glaciation, in which modern genera of animals appear for the first time.

vir″i·lo′cal Pertaining to the practice whereby a married couple settles in the domicile of the husband's family; synonymous with patrilocal residence.

vo·dun′ A system of religious belief and practice developed by Caribbean Negroes and combining elements of Catholicism and African, particularly Dahomean, religions. Magic is only a minor element in the entire complex. It is called voodoo in the American vernacular.

wam′pum Elongated beads drilled out of clamshells, used by Indians of the northeast woodlands.

warp The parallel-lying foundation threads of a fabric.

weft The threads woven at right angles through the warp; also called the woof, or filler.

wer′gild The money payment made by the kin of a murderer to the kin of a murdered man.

wick′i·up″ A beehive-shaped grass hut.

wife lend′ing The custom whereby a husband extends to a household guest the sexual favors of his wife as a symbolic gesture of brotherhood.

wig′wam A domed bark hut of the Algonkian Indians of the northeast woodlands.

win·di′go A type of homicidal psychosis involving cannibalism in Ojibwa and other Algonkian Indian cultures.

woof See weft.

wrong, private An offense against an individual that is customarily punished by legal action instituted by the injured person or his kinsmen. Private wrongs make up the body of private law.

wrong, public An offense against the social entity punished by the legal action of the group at large or by its official representatives.

wur′ley A lean-to shelter built by Australian aborigines.

ye·pun′ The virilocal, patrilineal clan in Umor society.

yuc′ca A plant belonging to the lily family and possessing long fibrous leaves. The sap of its roots produces suds in water.

INDEX

Bibliographic note: To find the full title of any book or article referred to in the text, first look up the name of the author in the index. Next note the page references which are printed in boldface type. These indicate the pages in the text on which titles of publications by the author are first cited. If more than three citations for an author occur, they are listed with subheadings to indicate the subject matter of the specific reference. Titles of books and full bibliographic information on articles and monographs will be found on the pages indicated.

If you want more information on books, such as place and date of publication, consult your instructor. A comprehensive bibliography of all references is included in the Instructor's Manual that accompanies this text.